Human Relations in

School Administration

DANIEL E. GRIFFITHS

School of Education, New York University

Human Relations in
School Administration

New York

APPLETON-CENTURY-CROFTS, INC.

FOREWORD

Nowhere in our culture is the social revolution more marked and more evident than in the changes which are taking place in the theory and concept of educational administration.

Since the appearance of Jesse H. Newlon's *Educational Administration as Social Policy* * in 1934, there has been a growing emphasis on process and the personal aspects of school administration. Since the close of World War II and especially following the historic contributions of the W. K. Kellogg Foundation to the improvement of theory and practice of school administration through its grants to the Cooperative Program in Educational Administration under the aegis of the American Association of School Administrators, newer and more dynamic concepts of public school administration have been slowly but persistently taking shape.

Running through the evolving concepts of educational administration one finds a continuous thread—human relations—in the job, the man, and the social setting; respect for human personality, know-how in dealing with people, and appreciation of the human factor in the whole process of educational planning and improvement. It is refreshing and stimulating to some of us who have spent our lives in public school administration struggling for the establishment of some of these principles to see the national trend toward emphasis on direction and process rather than description of job assignment.

Many familiar with the pressures, tensions, conflicts, and demands upon the public schools would agree that the basic need is general application of the principle of the golden rule to school and community. This is the meaning that the author gives to "human relations" as employed in this book—simply the acceptance and application by the school administration of the spirit of good will of one toward another in all human relations. He is less concerned with the techniques than the spirit of good will, less with the form than the dynamics. Good human relations in the concept of this textbook for school administrators includes effective communication, responding to social situations in ways to assure positive results, capitalizing for the common good upon the unity of interacting individual personalities.

The author has enlivened the book and added measurably to its interest-arousing aspects by the employment of fresh research from the labo-

* Jesse H. Newlon, *Educational Administration as Social Policy* (New York, Scribners, 1934).

v

ratories of education, business, industry, and the military. With great deftness, he has related this research to human relations as applied to public school administration in a series of chapters which stress motives of men, communication, perception, power structure, authority, morale, group dynamics, decision-making, and leadership.

The profession has been made richer because of the scholarly production of Professor Daniel Griffiths and those associated with him in CDPSA (Cooperative Development of Public School Administration). His imaginative and lucid narrative will inspire bright young men and women to lift their eyes toward this fertile field of educational leadership.

Professors of educational administration will have a new and useful tool for their courses in administration, and classroom teachers and laymen as well as students of public administration will find in this volume much that will be helpful.

Virgil M. Rogers
Dean, School of Education
Syracuse University

PREFACE

For many years there has been a demand for a new content in the teaching of school administration. The vast amount of interest and research stimulated by the Cooperative Program in Educational Administration (CPEA) has demonstrated clearly that the new content is *people*. This book is concerned with the behavior of people in the social institution known as the public school. It is written from the frame of reference of the administrator, but it carries concepts of importance to teachers, students, parents, and that undefinable person, the lay citizen. If one is to know about behavior, one cannot stay within the confines of any single discipline and expect to gain real insights. This book draws upon psychology, with its many branches and subdivisions, sociology, perception, group dynamics, political science, anthropology, business and industrial administration, and educational administration. All of these have much to offer. Educational administration is not a pure science in itself, and so it must draw upon all areas of investigation. The relevant findings must be synthesized and focused upon the problems and issues of school administration in such a way that a theory will some day be constructed.

Many people in school administration may be discouraged with this book because it does not contain lists of human relations rules or techniques of behavior. This is not a cookbook; it is a textbook. As such, theory will be discussed and evaluated and brought to bear on the important problems in school administration. The basic purpose of this book is to bring together in one volume what is known about human relations and relate it to school administration.

The basic assumption of the text is that human behavior can be changed. Through the use of substantive knowledge, actual situations (cases), meaningful exercises, and the case method of discussion in the classroom, the administrator can gain new insights into the people with whom he works. He will have no need for a list of techniques; in fact, he will grow to be quite suspicious of this approach to human relations.

It is hoped that the student, as he proceeds through this text, will begin to develop a theory of how people behave in the social institution which is the American public school. It is hoped that he will begin to formulate answers to such questions as: Why do I, as a principal, feel the way I do toward the teachers in my building? Why is it that I accept decisions made by my superintendent when I know I have a better decision? Why are certain members of the board of education re-elected continually

vii

when others are defeated? How can I better understand the behavior of all of my associates in the public schools?

The book is organized into three parts. Part 1 deals with the basic concepts of human relations and might be termed the theoretical background for the next two. Part 2 is built around several major problems, and Part 3 is composed of thirty cases, all of which are "true." In each case, the situation remains essentially as reported by teachers, students, administrators, or case writers, but the *names have been changed in every case*. There is no intentional reference to the name of any person living or dead.

The use of this section on cases is thoroughly discussed in the Appendix. Suffice it to say here that the cases depict real life situations which involve administrators in human problems with students, teachers, parents, board members, members of the community, and other administrators. There is no attempt made in writing these cases to present "all sides of the situation" or to be "objective." These cases present the emotions, feelings, actions, and words of people who are involved in the situations as recorded by observers. A few of the cases are written by one of the characters in the case. The student might try to determine which of the cases are of this type.

I have discovered that many people are willing and anxious to help in the preparation of a book. I am most grateful to all of these for comments and criticism. Early discussions with Dr. Joseph Leese, State University, New York State College for Teachers, Albany, stimulated some of the first ideas on this book. Criticism of Chapter 2 and general constructive help throughout came from Dr. Morris Eson, as did much help from Dr. Donald Van Cleve, both of the same institution. Dr. David Clark, Garden City, New York, Public Schools read and commented on the entire manuscript. Mr. Howard Goff, Superintendent of Schools, East Greenbush, New York read and commented on much of the manuscript. Dr. Richard Wynn, Teachers College, Columbia University, Dr. Lloyd Elliot, Cornell University, Dr. Franklyn Barry, Superintendent of Schools, Cortland, New York, Dr. Richard Lonsdale, Syracuse University, and Dr. David Clark all contributed to the research on organization and staffing referred to in the book. My thanks also to Dr. Daniel Davies, Teachers College, Columbia University, for many discussions of topics later developed in this book.

I wish to express my thanks to the many people who aided in the preparation of the case part. Dean Harry Benz of the Department of Education, Ohio University, Dean Francis Keppel of the School of Education, Harvard University, Dr. Wendell Bash of Colgate University, Dr. Marston M. McCluggage and Dr. Charles K. Warringer of the University of Kansas very graciously allowed the use of cases prepared at their institutions. I should like also to thank the following who aided in the preparation of one or more cases: Dr. Katherine Black, Charles Smith, Willard Ossont, Norman Stewart, Herbert Bothamley, Herbert Walsh, George Maybury, Armen Jermakian, Frank Mullet, Paul Waterman, James Beaverson, Alexander Barras, Morgan Chester, Robert Reno, Robert Hunter, Raymond Royal, Joseph Rich, Alexander Sabo, and Malvin Guralnik. I also thank those students who have discussed these cases, commented upon them, and so screened them for your use.

Mrs. Jeanette Andresen, Miss Elsie Barth, and Mrs. Ruth Mills typed the manuscript and its revisions.

Mrs. Marion Blake and Joseph Colpoys were research assistants.

To Dr. Virgil Rogers, Dean of the School of Education, Syracuse University, my sincere thanks for writing the foreword.

The constant encouragement and help of my wife, Tommie, has made possible this book. I am grateful to her not only for help on the book itself but for the creation of a home atmosphere which enables our family to be happy and productive.

Daniel E. Griffiths

CONTENTS

Part One

BASIC CONCEPTS OF HUMAN RELATIONS

CHAPTER

the Art of (Proven) of Planning. Medium Emphasize this.

Part Two

SOME PROBLEM AREAS

Part Three
CASE STUDIES

Basic Concepts of Human Relations

CHAPTER 1

Human Relations: Concepts and Content

ADMINISTRATION IS THE CAPACITY of coordinating many, often conflicting, social energies in a single organism so adroitly that they shall operate as a unity. This presupposes the power of recognizing a series of relations between numerous special social interests, with all of which no single man can be intimately acquainted. Probably no very highly specialized class can be strong in this intellectual quality because of the intellectual isolation incident to specialization; and yet administration or generalization is not only the faculty upon which social stability rests, but is, possibly, the highest faculty of the human mind.[1]

We are now in the midst of the greatest period of change in school administration since its origin in American education. Through the energizing role of the Cooperative Program in Educational Administration, the whole profession has undergone the most penetrating examination and revision of practice. The underlying concepts of the functions and process of administration have also been critically examined. As a result, school administration now is quite different from what it was ten years ago. In all probability, it will be much, much different fifty years from now.

It is our purpose, in this book, to discuss school administration in relation to the findings of this critical examination and revised practice. The approach will not be very familiar to those who are acquainted with the traditional texts on the subject. It is, however, the normal outgrowth of some of the newer books that have put increasing emphasis on the process [2] and the personnel aspects of administration.[3] This emphasis accomplishes a dual service: (1) it presents the changing and improved practices in the field, and (2) it gives impetus to the swing toward the newer concepts of administration.

---

[1] Brooks Adams, *The Theory of Social Revolutions* (New York, Macmillan, 1914), pp. 207-208.

[2] Of these, Harlan Hagman and Alfred Schwartz, *Administration in Profile for School Executives* (New York, Harper, 1955), is the most outstanding. An earlier book by Jesse B. Sears, *The Nature of the Administrative Process* (New York, McGraw-Hill, 1950), treats the subject from a slightly different point of view.

[3] In 1954-1955 alone, five books in personnel administration appeared.

A COMMON FRAME OF REFERENCE

School administration has generally lacked a unifying theory around which to solidify. It has lacked a way of looking at itself. Likewise, both practitioners and students have lacked a procedure or method by which they could examine school administration. In order that we have a common frame of reference for the discussion of school administration, a concept of administration and method of examining the way in which an administrator functions will be presented. Neither of these is original with the author. The first, an emerging concept of the superintendency of education, was developed largely through the leadership of Daniel Davies, co-ordinator of the Cooperative Program in Educational Administration (CPEA) in the Middle Atlantic region,[4] and was tested in the field under the supervision of Ernest Weinrich, director of the Cooperative Development of Public School Administration (CDPSA) in the state of New York.[5] The method of examination was developed by Robert L. Katz of The Amos Tuck School of Business Administration, Dartmouth College.

The Tridimensional Concept

The concept of school administration, particularly of the role of the chief school administrator, advanced by Davies, deals with three components: the administrator's *job*, the *man* he is, and the *social setting* in which he functions. Defined very briefly, the job includes the administrator's tasks and responsibilities, which vary in importance and emphasis as time passes, and encompasses all that is relevant to the administration of today's schools. The man brings to the job certain capacities of body, mind, emotion, and spirit. He has beliefs, values, expectations, behavior patterns, energy reserves, and skills. While the job shapes him, he also shapes the job. The social setting encompasses the pressures and compulsions of society. These not only establish and set limits for the job but influence the thinking of the man and set values by which he adjusts himself and is judged.

Probably the chief contributions of this concept of the job, the man, and the social setting are the convenience in categorizing and the ease of locating other important concepts. In examining this concept further, we will find that each of these three major components is subdivided into three dimensions: *content, process,* and *sequence.* Taken together, these

---

[4] The CPEA was a nationwide effort to improve the quality of school administration. It was established under a grant of the Kellogg Foundation and was administered through eight university centers. A description of the objectives of CPEA can be found in A. H. Rice, "AASA-Kellogg Project Promises a Better Life for the Superintendent," *Nation's Schools,* Vol. 46 (November, 1950), pp. 31-35.

[5] The central ideas of this section are taken from *A Developing Concept of the Superintendency of Education,* rev. ed. (Albany, N. Y., Cooperative Development of Public School Administration, 1955).

constitute what is known as the tridimensional concept of educational administration.

The Job. In looking at the content of the job of the school administrator we find that it can be conveniently divided into four areas: [6]

1. Maintaining effective interrelationships with the community.
2. Improving educational opportunity.
3. Obtaining and developing personnel.
4. Providing and maintaining funds and facilities.

These areas of content are not arranged in order of importance; in fact, it is claimed that each has equal importance in the job of the administrator. From one point of view this is probably correct; that is, the chief school administrator is the only person who can see the educational enterprise as a whole. All others have responsibility for small segments and do not view their segment in relation to the whole enterprise. On the other hand, it does seem that in relation to the purposes of education the second area should receive prime consideration, and the other areas should function to improve educational opportunity.

In discharging the responsibilities outlined above, the administrator must work through a problem-solving process. A brief analysis of this process is suggested as follows: [7]

1. Sensing the problem and surveying its aspects.
2. Relating the problem to people.
3. Making decisions.
4. Implementing and reviewing.

It can be seen that discharging any of the areas of responsibility will give rise to numerous problems. The administrator may try to solve these problems "off the top of his head" or use a more reasoned approach. The reasoned approach, of course, is recommended and is outlined above. Later chapters will go into much more detail on this subject.

The process of problem-solving takes place in a time *sequence.* Although the administrator always works in the present, he needs to look back into the past to determine the circumstances which produced the problem, and he also must look to the future in order to predict the consequences of the solutions to the problem. [8]

The Man. The man in the job may be viewed in much the same manner as above. In this case, however, content is considered to be the *capacity* of the man. Capacity may be thought of as having four aspects: physical, intellectual, emotional, and spiritual. The process, which in the job is the solving of problems, now becomes the *behavior* of the man and is categorized as follows:

[6] *Ibid.,* p. 8.
[7] *Ibid.*
[8] For a more comprehensive discussion of this concept, together with illustrations of each point, consult *A Developing Concept of the Superintendency of Education.*

1. Sensing the problems and collecting relevant data.
2. Making inferences.
3. Relating to people.
4. Predicting and deciding.
5. Implementing and reviewing.

The time sequence remains the same as that of the job.

Thus we have the framework for discussion of the man as he performs the job of superintendent of education. As each person enters the position, he brings to it certain capacities. These capacities are made operational through his behavior patterns. It can be seen that no one factor is predominant in this discussion. It would be incorrect, for instance, to assume that high intelligence alone will make a successful administrator. It is also incorrect to assume that high intelligence is not necessary.[9] What is necessary is to have an individual's capacities operating through his behavior patterns at the highest possible potential. It is unfortunate that we cannot as yet specify in detail the degree to which each capacity should be developed or the behavior patterns that will unquestionably be most acceptable; but this book will develop several leads which now seem promising.

The Social Setting. The school administrator is an important part of the total social setting. The school as a social institution has long been recognized as a vital part of the culture. Whether it leads in social change or maintains the *status in quo,* it is, nevertheless, the way by which society prepares its youth for citizenship. It would be unreasonable then, to consider the man and the job without discussing the way in which they are both modified by the social setting in which they are placed. We also need to investigate the ways in which the social setting can be modified by the man in his job.

We first look at the content of the social setting. This content may be divided into four categories which are interrelated to a large degree:

1. Physical, technological, and human resources.
2. Relational systems in the community.[10]
3. The network of organization.
4. Patterns of thought, belief, and value.

This content is studied in reference to the process by which society changes and operates. Any aspect of the content may be at any of the different phases of process at any particular time. The process consists of:

[9] Studies seem to indicate that school administrators as a group are well above average in IQ. There seems to be little or no correlation between IQ and success in school administration, however. Bills studied the IQ of certain Kentucky school administrators and found a range of from 109 to 133 with a median of 127. It was concluded that the intelligence of school administrators is high but not significantly correlated with success. See Robert E. Bills, "Attributes of Successful Educational Leaders," *Interdisciplinary Research in Educational Administration,* Bulletin of the Bureau of School Service, University of Kentucky, Vol. 26, No. 2 (December, 1953), pp. 16-38.

[10] Such as family, age, sex, occupation, and class, and whether the community is urban or rural.

1. Continuity and stability: in this phase of process things are going along smoothly and regularly.
2. The new and different: into the stable situation *something* new is injected. This may be most anything from a new type screwdriver to the H-bomb. At any rate, reaction to the new will be mixed, and a social change is underway.
3. Stresses and strains: unless the new can be absorbed easily, a period of stress and strain results, which, if serious, can bring about a period of crisis. We have been in a period of crisis since about 1930.
4. Resolution and readjustment: as society seeks a way out of its dilemmas it seeks readjustment of the culture and resolution of its problems. Educational leadership is a very important aspect of this process.

Thus we have seen how the content of the social setting influences the process or the way in which society reacts to changes in the content. These changes take place in reference to a time sequence of four phases:

1. Deeply rooted traditions.
2. The recent past.
3. The present and near future.
4. Long-range future.

As the man in the job works in relation to the social setting, he must be constantly aware of the content, the process, and the sequence of the social setting. The school is not something apart or separate from the rest of the society. The removal of a large industry from a community, for example, can have more of an impact on the schools than can the invention of a new method of teaching reading.

The Tridimensional Concept of Educational Administration

THE JOB	THE MAN	THE SOCIAL SETTING
Content	*Capacity*	*Content*
1. maintaining 2. improving 3. obtaining 4. providing	1. physical 2. intellectual 3. emotional 4. spiritual	1. physical, technological, human resources 2. relational systems 3. network of organization 4. patterns of thought, belief, value
Process	*Behavior*	*Process*
1. sensing the problem 2. relating the problem to people 3. making decisions 4. implementing and reviewing	1. sensing the problem 2. making inferences 3. relating to people 4. predicting and deciding 5. implementing and reviewing	1. continuity and stability 2. the new and different 3. stresses and strains 4. resolution and readjustment
Sequence	*Sequence*	*Sequence*
1. past 2. present 3. future	1. past 2. present 3. future	1. deeply rooted traditions 2. recent past 3. present and near future 4. long-range future

The foregoing outline of the tridimensional concept has been introduced, not because it will be constantly referred to throughout this book
but because it is the frame of reference in which our thinking about school
administration now is taking place. It should be considered in much the
same way as one would consider a magnetic field of force. One cannot see
the field itself, but one can always see its results. Just as iron filings are
shaped by the magnetic field, so our thinking about school administration
has been shaped by this concept.

The Three-skill Method of Examination

School administration will be considered from many points of view,
from many disciplines, and from many practical considerations. School
administration has long since passed the day when it could be considered
as technical skill in budget making or plant maintenance. It is not merely
assigning teachers to classrooms or accounting for pupils or managing the
school cafeteria. Neither should it be construed in terms of maintaining
records or providing supplies. Although all these are necessary attributes
of a school system, they are not the *sine qua non* of school administration.
Therefore, over and above what we have already discussed, we need a
method of examining the job performance of the administrator. We turn
to Katz, who has devised a three-skill approach to the consideration of
administration.[11] Some may object to the use of the term skill in discussing administration; here it will be used in its broadest and most comprehensive meaning. It does not refer to skill in the sense that a carpenter
has skill in driving a nail or a plumber has skill in wiping a joint. Rather,
it refers to an understanding or judgment or the reason for doing or saying or, in its broadest sense, the ability to use one's knowledge effectively.
We are using the three-skill approach in our further analysis of school
administration in that we are asking the questions: What is a good administrator? How does he function?

The three-skill approach to administration does not have its basis in the
traits or qualities which may or may not be prerequisite to executive success but is based upon "what a man can accomplish." [12] The search for an
answer to what constitutes a good administrator in this direction rather
than along the more traditional lines was given impetus by a number of
studies made in the past few years. These are summarized by Stogdill,
who analyzed 124 studies of such traits as appearance, intelligence, personality, and the like. He concluded:

---

[11] Robert L. Katz, "Skills of an Effective Administrator," *Harvard Business Review,*
Vol. 33, No. 1 (January-February, 1955), pp. 33-42.
[12] *Ibid.,* p. 33.

The findings suggest that leadership is not a matter of passive status, or of the mere possession of some combination of traits. It appears rather to be a working relationship among members of a group, in which the leader acquires status through active participation in and demonstration of his capacity for carrying cooperative tasks through to completion.[13]

Stryker also came to the same conclusion in discussing industrial executives: [14]

The literature of executive development is loaded with efforts to define the qualities needed by executives, and by themselves these sound quite rational. Few, for instance, would dispute the fact that a top manager needs good judgment, the ability to make decisions, the ability to win respect of others, and all the other well worn phrases any management man could mention. But one has only to look at the successful managers in any company to see how enormously their particular qualities vary from any ideal list of executive virtues.

With this backlog of research it is necessary to move in a different direction to determine how well the administrator is doing. The emphasis in Katz's three-skill approach is all in *what the man does*. The three skills are:

1. Technical skill.
2. Human skill.
3. Conceptual skill.

Let us now take a look at these skills and see what they mean in relation to school administration.

Technical Skill. This particular skill is defined as follows: [15]

... an understanding of, and proficiency in, a specific kind of activity, particularly one involving methods, processes, procedures, or techniques. Technical skill involves specialized knowledge, analytical ability within that specialty, and facility in the use of the tools and techniques of the specific discipline.

This is the kind of skill most commonly acquired by school administrators during their training period. Courses in school finance, pupil accounting, school-building planning, construction and maintenance, schedule making, purchasing, and similar skills insure a certain level of competence in the embryo administrator. Technical skills are those most easily taught and most easily learned and in which the highest degree of proficiency is achieved. They are also the most certain of learning, since achievement in technical skills carries a built-in evaluator. For instance, taking the school census is a technical skill. An administrator devises a method by which he can obtain the names of all children of legal school age (and whatever

---

[13] Ralph M. Stogdill, "Personal Factors Associated with Leadership: A Survey of the Literature," *Journal of Psychology*, Vol. 25 (1948), p. 66.

[14] Perrin Stryker, "The Growing Pains of Executive Development," *Advanced Management* (August, 1954), p. 15.

[15] Katz, *loc. cit.*, p. 34.

other age in which he is interested, that is, from birth to the age of twenty-one). He makes a map with census tracts, devises a census card, assigns census takers, tabulates the results, and projects them in terms of grade levels. He can then check his figures each year as the children come to school and so evaluate the accuracy of the census figures.

Human Skill. This second skill may be defined as "the executive's ability to work effectively as a group member and to build cooperative effort within the team he leads." [16] Essentially, human skill is contrasted with technical skill: working with people versus working with things.

What is an administrator like when he has a highly developed set of human skills? First of all, he knows himself—his strengths and weaknesses. He is aware of his own attitudes and assumptions. He has an inner security which enables him to consider new ideas and can work to bring about orderly changes in both the system and the people in the system. He is skillful in understanding others' words and behavior because he accepts viewpoints, perceptions, and beliefs which differ from his own. He works to create an atmosphere of approval and security for all in his organization. He knows that all that he does or fails to do has an effect on his associates. Human skills have become an integral part of his whole being. They are not easily attained, and the graduate schools are now seeking better methods of teaching them.

Conceptual Skill. The last of the three skills under consideration is defined as: [17]

the ability to see the enterprise as a whole; it includes recognizing how the various functions of the organization depend on one another, and how changes in any one part affect all the others. Recognizing those relationships and perceiving the significant elements in any situation, the administrator should then be able to act in a way which advances the over-all welfare of the total organization.

Some one has said that we need administrators so that we can have a person around to make decisions. There is more truth in this than we sometimes wish to recognize. *The success of any decision depends in large part upon the conceptual skill of the administrator.*

Let us examine this skill, which is the most difficult to acquire, in a little more detail and in relation to the other skills. Working out the budget each year is a well-known administrative task. Like many administrative duties, it requires all three skills. There are many *technical* aspects of the job: surveying the staff for needed materials, projecting salaries to determine amount of money needed, computing fuel costs, and so forth. *Human skills* also are required: in compromising with each of those who request alloca-

---

[16] *Ibid.*
[17] *Ibid.*, pp. 35-36.

tions which cannot be granted, or in presenting the budget at the hearing or annual meeting. And, finally, *conceptual skill* is required: in providing funds for those things which will be of greatest value to the school system, in fitting the budget into a scheme of long-range planning, in recognizing those departments which need funds in order to develop most rapidly or in withholding funds from those departments which should be curtailed.

We also note that the attitudes of the superintendent color the attitudes of the entire school staff. These attitudes reflect his perception of, and response to, school policies and objectives and the way in which the school develops, even so far as to indicate how the school personnel will respond to visitors.

This conceptual skill was summed up by Chester Barnard, former president of the New Jersey Bell Telephone Company, when he said that "the essential aspect of the [executive] process is the sensing of the organization as a whole and the total situation relevant to it." [18]

Relative Value of Each Skill. The chief value of the three-skill approach is its use in analyzing school administrators. It is obvious that there is some degree of overlap; conceptual skill, for example, carries with it some technical as well as human skill. However, the three-skill approach is used in two additional ways: (1) in discussing administrators at various levels of responsibility and (2) in discussing the "successful" or "good" administrator.

Technical skill has its greatest value at the level of administration where the administrator is more concerned with things than with people. This includes the group of school administrators known as business managers, clerks of the board, purchasing agents, and the like. The chief school administrator may be almost entirely lacking in technical skill, but administrators on lower levels cannot be. We should note, too, that in most schools as *they are now staffed,* the chief school administrator acts more as a business manager than he does as chief school officer.

Human skill has its greatest value to building principals and to supervisors—those administrators whose responsibility is in the area of person-to-person contacts with the school staff. One study made in this area showed that several top-quality superintendents in large schools (more than 100 teachers) had relatively low scores when rated by their teachers on a 22-item scale of administrative behavior traits.[19] When the ratings of their administrative staffs were used, each of their scores increased. This could be interpreted as meaning that human skill with teachers was less necessary for these superintendents than was skill in working with the central administrative staff. Since the great majority of school districts in

[18] Chester I. Barnard, *Functions of the Executive* (Cambridge, Mass., Harvard University Press, 1938), p. 235.
[19] See above, Ch. 11.

the country are small districts of less than 100 teachers, human skills are of great importance to the majority of chief school administrators and to all other administrators.

Conceptual skill is most important to the chief school administrator. If he has subordinates who have strong capabilities in technical and human skills, the chief school administrator may lack these and still be successful. In small schools, where the administrative staff is correspondingly small, he must have all three skills, but his conceptual skills must be highly developed so that he can relate all of his tasks to that which is the most important at a given time.

A recent study of the differences between successful and unsuccessful superintendents demonstrated that there was very little difference between the two groups of superintendents in those practices called *technical*. The difference between the two groups in those practices called *human* was very great. The difference between the two groups in those practices called *conceptual* was even greater. It is evident that success in administration is related to the degree of human and conceptual skill the individual brings to the job.[20]

Recent Studies of School Administration

The frame of reference which we have sketched is significant because it emphasizes certain aspects of school administration and minimizes the importance of others. The validation of this way of viewing administration has its basis in a large number of studies which have recently been completed. An early study by Rast indicated that at least in one section of the country, the metropolitan New York area, the concept of the character of the superintendent's job was changing to one of leadership of education on a broad scale.[21] In following up this study, Ovsiew demonstrated, through a study of "emerging practices," that top school administrators were more concerned with human and conceptual aspects of the job than with the more traditional and technical aspects. In analyzing the 97 practices selected by 70 superintendents as most promising, he found that only 9 were connected with the technical classification and that 88 concerned relations with the public, the staff, and the board of education.[22] Other studies have given insights into the difference between suc-

---

[20] Daniel E. Griffiths, "An Evaluation of the Leadership of the School Superintendent" (Unpublished Ph.D. dissertation, Yale University, 1952). A digest of this work was published by the CPEA-MAR Center of Teachers College, Columbia University.

[21] G. E. Rast, "The Study of the Changing Character of the Superintendent's Job" Unpublished doctoral project (New York, Teachers College, Columbia University, 1951).

[22] Leon Ovsiew, *Emerging Practices in School Administration* (New York, Metropolitan School Study Council, 1953).

cessful and unsuccessful superintendents,[23] interpersonal relationships,[24] and traits and abilities of school superintendents.[25]

The New England CPEA Center investigated the problems which school superintendents indicated were the most bothersome to them. They used a 5 per cent sample of New England superintendents, and their conclusion after analyzing the problems is most pertinent to our discussion: [26]

> There are no easy answers to the 350 problems raised by the New England superintendents, but perhaps some helpful clues can be uncovered if problems of administration are approached as questions of relationships and of motivation and co-ordination, rather than merely questions of plant, curriculum, or finance.

In reviewing the changes in the concept of the job of the chief school administrator over the past years, Ross presents an argument for a more professional type of training with strong implications for increased emphasis on working with people and for a better conceptualization of the tasks of education.[27]

In January, 1954, *The Nation's Schools* published a portfolio of articles which presented what is becoming an accepted point of view with regard to the importance of human relations in school administration. These studies clearly demonstrate the relationship between human and technical skills. McLaughlin, investigating the amount of *time* spent on human problems by progressive administrators, reported the following conclusions: [28]

> Reliable estimates indicate that 90 per cent of the time of forward looking school administrators is spent in working with people, and only 10 per cent in working with things. Studies of reasons for failure in school administration clearly show that it usually results from the inability of the administrator to work with people and not from incompetence in technical skills.

Chandler indicated the relationship between *human* and *technical* skills that should prevail: [29]

> In effect, the superintendent must be expert in human relations. He can employ persons with technical skills required in the construction of buildings, in budget making, and in school business areas, but no staff member can relieve the superintendent of his human relations function.

[23] Griffiths, *op. cit.*

[24] Richard Wynn, "Interpersonal Relations of School Administrators" (Unpublished Ed.D. project, Teachers College, Columbia University, 1952).

[25] Bills, *op. cit.*

[26] George E. Flower, "Relationships with People Is the Key," *American School Board Journal*, Vol. 124 (June, 1952), p. 27.

[27] Donald Ross, *Some Arguments for Requiring a More Rigorous Professional Preparation for Chief School Administrators* (Albany, N. Y., Cooperative Development of Public School Administration, 1954).

[28] Frederick C. McLaughlin, "New Kind of Statesmanship," *Nation's Schools*, Vol. 53, No. 1 (1954), p. 44.

[29] B. J. Chandler, "Working Relationships," *Nation's Schools*, Vol. 53, No. 1 (1954), p. 47.

The consensus of present-day studies in all areas of school administration appears to be that although technical skill cannot be disregarded, the human and conceptual skills are of far more importance. It would seem, that administrators must acquire much more skill in dealing with human problems than they have ever had in the past.

THE STUDY OF HUMAN RELATIONS

If human relations is such an important facet of school administration as has been indicated above, we must be definitive about the term. When we speak of *human relations,* does everyone understand our meaning? Just what are human relations? The term is one which has come into common usage in the past ten or fifteen years. We have available a large number of books, articles, and speeches on the subject, all of which offer advice and guidance. In examining some of this material, however, one is confused by the vast range of topics it covers. It is alarming to note that several books entitled "Human Relations in This or That" do not define the term at all. It seems to be an expression that is largely taken for granted, and there is likelihood that this approach will shortly render it useless. This term should not be so treated, for like many others, such as democracy, it carries many desirable connotations. Certainly, as it relates to school administration, there can be little doubt of its value, and in order that the term be clearly understood and narrowed in its scope, we shall specify what we mean when we say that a school administrator should be skillful in human relations.

Basic Attitude

Prerequisite to the administrator's skill in human relations is his basic attitude. He must have a strong and overwhelming belief in the supreme worth of all individuals. This belief must be manifest in all his behavior. It is not enough for him to profess his belief in democracy each year at the preschool meeting or to constantly tell others how democratic he is in his every day dealings. This regard for others, this spirit of good will must be habitual and readily evident to each member of his staff. If an administrator feels that he must tell his staff of his regard for them he is certainly on very weak ground! In its review of the growth of human relations in business *Time* magazine concluded: "Actually, far from being an occult science, human relations is nothing more than good will and applied common sense." [30] In summarizing several case studies of administrators, Wynn used much the same language: "The foregoing accounts illustrate the simple truth that good human relations are applied good will. The

[30] "Human Relations," *Time* (April 14, 1952), pp. 96-97.

humanistic spirit, lucidly expressed in the Golden Rule, thus becomes the basic test of human relations in school administration as in life itself." [31]

For the administrator, then, the basic imperative of good human relations is good will. A successful school system must be permeated with a spirit of good will. All of the techniques of human relations will be wasted, in fact will be dangerous, to all involved if a feeling of mutual good will does not exist. This feeling must stem from the board of education, the chief school administrator, and his administrative staff. Without good will, human relations techniques are manipulatory in nature. There are many in both education and industry who believe they are practicing good human relations when they provide such employee benefits as lounges, good salaries, recreational facilities, picnics, and music on the job. Too often, however, these are provided out of a spirit of paternalism, with the idea that the employees will be more compliant. Needless to say, this technique-without-good-will approach does not bring about the desired results.

We find, therefore, that it is not enough for an administrator merely to say what his interest is; it is imperative that he behave in such a way as to create a feeling of good will and mutual respect at all times. A person in a status position communicates through words it is true; but he also communicates through such actions as facial expressions, hand and arm motions, walk, and, of course, behavior patterns. The administrator whose behavior patterns belie his statements will invariably find it difficult to maintain good human relations with his staff. There is the case, for example, of a superintendent of schools who had his office in the high school building of his district. One morning he was more rushed than usual and finding he could not get some written work done with all of the interruptions, he left his office in search of a quieter spot. He entered the back of the first classroom he saw, smiled at the teacher, and said, "Good morning, please don't let me interrupt, go right ahead as though I was not here at all." He sat down and wrote furiously for the rest of the period and then got up and left the room much the same way as he entered. The teacher couldn't imagine what was going on. She thought his writing concerned her, and she reached a state of utter distraction, especially when the superintendent never did explain fully what he had been doing.

Here, the superintendent was saying what he meant but acting in such a way as to have the teacher misunderstand completely what he was doing. He was unintentionally *using* the teacher to further his own purposes. The teacher and her room was the convenient spot for him, and he used it without considering that *any* action on his part would be interpreted in terms of the teacher's frame of reference. It is difficult, if not impossible, for people to be present in a situation and not be

[31] Richard Wynn, "The Application of Good Human Relations," *Nation's Schools*, Vol. 53, No. 1 (January, 1954), p. 54.

involved. Being told, "Don't mind me," does not remove an individual from involvement.

The job of building good will and mutual respect is continuous and never ending. An administrator may be trying as hard as possible to develop this feeling, and a single small incident can undo most of what he has built. The only way in which he can avoid failure is to have the staff believe in him and he in them so sincerely that occasional slips will be overlooked.

Another illustration of destructive behavior is the case of a high school principal who called an all-day meeting of his staff to consider ways of solving a problem which was extremely important to the school. The meeting was held in pleasant surroundings, coffee breaks were provided, the principal was pleasant and informal, the atmosphere relaxed and permissive. The meeting extended through the day, and the staff came to a decision which all agreed was the best possible. The principal then took from his folder a typewritten sheet. He read from the sheet precisely the decision to which the staff had just agreed. He then stated that this had been written the night before.

We might wonder what the principal was trying to accomplish. We might also wonder what the effect of this behavior was on the faculty. The principal said later that he was trying to demonstrate the disadvantages of the democratic process. Here the faculty needed all day to make a decision which he had made by himself in a short period of time. Needless to say, the dangers which an administrator runs when taking a course of this sort are enormous. The faculty could well wonder whether or not they had been manipulated into the decision and also how often this would happen in the future. They would wonder each time they met whether or not they were just working to "prove something" or whether their efforts were to be taken seriously. If good will and mutual respect are to be built, the faculty must be certain that the administrator is *always* being fair and honest, that all of his actions which impinge upon them both as a group and as individuals are aboveboard.

Definition of Good Human Relations

It would be a mistake to think that there is nothing more to human relations than good will and mutual respect. Although these two form the imperative, they cannot stand alone.

Let us now consider three definitions of human relations to see what, in addition to good will and mutual respect, is necessary for good human relations in administration. In discussing the way in which the supervisor should look at human relations, Wiles states: [32]

[32] Kimball Wiles, *Supervision for Better Schools,* 2d ed. (New York, Prentice-Hall, 1955), p. 106.

A supervisor should exhibit a belief in the worth of all individuals, respect for the wishes and feelings of others, the will to see that all live and work in harmony, plus skill in working with individuals and groups in such a way that these ends are promoted.

Roethlisberger stresses a different point in his definition: [33]

"Human relations" is thus at its present stage of development the practice of a skill by which one learns to relate himself to his social surroundings. It is the way Tom, Dick, and Harry learn about themselves and their relations to each other in the first instance and how they improve this understanding in the second instance.

"Human relations skill" in particular is the capacity of a person to communicate his feelings and ideas to others, to receive such communications from others, and to respond to their feelings and ideas in such a fashion as to promote congenial participation in a common task.

A third point of view is presented by Boykin: [34]

"Human relations" is a way of behaving, of acting or not acting toward human beings in terms of the ideals and value patterns of our democratic society; a way of responding to social situations, and to the individuals and groups which produce these situations; the unity of interacting personalities bound together in an organized relationship in which the characteristic mode of social interaction is determined not by racial or ethnic differences, interfaith conflicts, socio-economic disparities, and cultural and educational factors, but by respect for individual personality, and the dignity and worth of human beings.

These three definitions cover much of the area commonly covered by those working in the field. These writers represent the various concepts very closely. Our view of human relations differs somewhat from all three of the writers. We say that good human relations in administration are built upon a firm foundation of mutual respect, good will, and faith in the dignity and worth of human beings as individual personalities. It is further necessary for the administrator to develop skills in relating himself and others to the social situation in which they are placed. These skills are integral parts of the behavior of the administrator and may be developed and improved by an understanding of the content of human relations and by constant practice.

Content of Human Relations

In order to achieve the skill necessary for successful human relations, the school administrator must understand the content of human relations as it applies to his job. The following topics, which will be discussed in detail in subsequent chapters, are those which constitute the content of

[33] F. J. Roethlisberger and others, *Training for Human Relations* (Boston, Harvard University, Graduate School of Business Administration, 1954), p. 172.

[34] Leander L. Boykin, "Let's Get It Straight: What Are Human Relations?" *The Social Studies*, Vol. 46, No. 2 (1955), p. 59.

human relations most pertinent to school administration. In establishing this content, use has been made of educational, business, industrial, military, and laboratory research. The criterion for the selection of each area, however, was always its applicability to educational administration, whether or not the administrator is concerned with the problems each poses, and whether or not he can profit from the solutions to these problems that have so far been advanced.

Motivation. A first-year administrator, a junior high school principal, said, "The chief cause of worry is the teachers. I don't understand why they do the things they do. If I could only understand them my job would be so much easier." This hits at a key administrative problem. What is it that causes people to do the things they do? The administrator cannot seek the answer in the area of psychological motives alone; he must consider the sociological, anthropological, and cultural aspects, too. Furthermore, he must be capable of understanding his own motivation in addition to the motivation of the individuals with whom and through whom he works.

Perception. How does the administrator perceive his role in the school and the community? How does the teacher perceive her role? How does the administrator perceive the teacher? Are these perceptions in conflict? Much knowledge has been shed on the problem of perception in the past few years which makes it possible for administrators to "see" the situation in which they are operating much more clearly.

Communication. Roethlisberger has said that the administrator's environment is a verbal one. He is in constant communication with teachers, pupils, board members, townsfolk, salesmen, and so on. He must depend on words to a large degree to reach his staff, and he must be able to use language that will convey his meaning effectively.

Power Structure. All social organizations are held together by some sort of power. Putting this another way, we can say that power is the cement of social organizations. Knowledge of what holds the community together, of what makes it go is vital to the administrator. Lack of knowledge in this area has been the reason for many of the defeats inflicted on school systems.

Authority. The institutional manifestation of power is authority. The state is the source of the authority of the board of education, which, in turn, grants authority to the chief administrator. Although authority is a commonplace topic, it is seldom thoroughly understood in all its ramifications. Of particular importance to school administrators is the question, "How does authority affect the behavior of individuals?"

Morale. The degree to which high morale is present in a group is a measure of the success of the administrator in building good staff relations. Morale is not merely the presence of a happy, joyous spirit; it is acceptance on the part of the group of a common purpose, a determined group effort to attain that purpose and, at the same time, maintain a high *esprit de corps.*

Group Dynamics. Although the administrator must always work with individuals, much of this work is done when the individuals are in groups. Faculty and board of education meetings, for example, are just two of the many group situations common to all school administrators. Knowledge of what contributes to groupness, the dynamics of group action, and skills in working with groups are invaluable assets for a successful administrator.

Decision-making. All the substantive knowledge of the preceding topics is brought to bear on the making of decisions. Decisions are not made in a vacuum; they are made against a background of experiences. In order that each decision be one which advances the school system, the administrator needs to be skilled in the *process* of making decisions, and he must have the broad background of knowledge against which to match alternatives.

Leadership. The literature of leadership still indicates some confusion as to basic theory, but much of a practical nature is known. The school administrator is the educational leader of his community and should be aware of all that this implies. Leadership is essentially a group procedure and, at times, the good leader is the good follower. How one exercises wise and efficient leadership is of vital concern to administrators.

The topics listed above constitute the core of substantive knowledge about which an understanding of human relations can be built. They are certainly not all that could be included, but at the present time and for our purposes, they would seem to have the most to offer. As research continues we will have new hypotheses to examine, new approaches to use, and new truths to validate. We can hold what we know about human relations only in a very tentative manner.

SUMMARY

We have examined the tridimensional concept of the job, the man, and the social setting. We have seen that for the job there is content, process, and sequence; for the man there is capacity, behavior, and time sequence; and for the social setting there is content, process, and time sequence. As we examine this concept of school administration, we see that the administrator functions within its framework through the exercising of three kinds of skills: technical, human, and conceptual. Of the three, human and conceptual skills are much more important to the success of an administrator than are technical skills.

Good human relations in a school system are built on a feeling of good will and mutual respect and faith in the dignity and worth of human beings as individual personalities. The administrator needs to develop skills in relating himself and others to the social setting in which he is placed. These skills are integral parts of the behavior of the administrator and may be developed and improved by an understanding of the content of human relations and by constant practice.

The content of human relations is concerned with the motives of man, communication, perception, power structure, authority, morale, group dynamics, decision-making, and leadership. Through the use of this substantive knowledge and practice in human relation situations, an administrator can develop skills which will make him more competent.

EXERCISES

1. Following are 52 functions of school administration. Go over the list and write *1* in front of those which call for *technical skill*, *2* in front of those which call for *human skill*, and *3* in front of those which call for *conceptual skill*. If the function calls for more than one skill, write *4* in front of it.

_____ Planning and co-ordination of public relations program
_____ Maintaining pupil personnel records
_____ Co-ordinating audiovisual activities
_____ Supervision of professional staff personnel
_____ Purchasing of supplies and equipment
_____ Preparation of reports for the board and state education department
_____ Arranging for substitute teachers
_____ Direction and supervision of pupil activity program
_____ Helping teachers in planning effective remedial instruction
_____ Direction of program for use of school facilities by nonschool groups
_____ Accounting of pupils (census and attendance)
_____ Induction and orientation of nonprofessional staff personnel
_____ Determination of financial needs and construction of the budget
_____ Direction of school lunch program
_____ Counseling professional and nonprofessional staff personnel
_____ Direction and co-ordination of in-service training program
_____ Making recommendations to board for policy formulation and revision
_____ Holding conferences with parents and other lay citizens
_____ Assisting teachers in diagnosing the learning difficulties of pupils
_____ Supervision of nonprofessional staff personnel
_____ Control of the budget
_____ Working with PTA and other lay groups
_____ Administration of the payroll
_____ Maintaining staff personnel records
_____ Scheduling professional and nonprofessional staff personnel
_____ Direction of guidance program
_____ Evaluation and recommendation to the board for promotion and retention of professional staff personnel
_____ Developing procedures for reporting pupil progress to parents
_____ Determining specifications for supplies and equipment
_____ Control of pupil behavior
_____ Induction and orientation of professional staff personnel
_____ Direction of program of plant maintenance
_____ Preparation of information to be disseminated by public communication media

_____ Direction of adult education program

_____ Selection and recommendation to the board for employment of non-professional staff personnel

_____ Inventorying supplies and equipment

_____ Helping the board to determine the educational needs of the community

_____ Making recommendations to the board for the construction and administration of salary schedules

_____ Administering insurance program

_____ Direction of program for exceptional children

_____ Debt service management

_____ Revision of curriculum and selection of curricular materials

_____ Plant planning and construction

_____ Preparation of special reports and bulletins for general distribution

_____ Scheduling pupils

_____ Evaluation and recommendation to the board for promotion and retention of nonprofessional staff personnel

_____ Direction of health and safety program

_____ Supervising and auditing internal accounts

_____ Administering summer recreation program

_____ Distribution of supplies and equipment

_____ Selection and recommendation to the board for employment of professional staff personnel

_____ Direction of program of bus maintenance and operation

2. Take the list of functions mentioned above and categorize them according to the four areas of administration. Write the appropriate letter in front of each function.

A. Maintaining effective interrelationships with the community.
B. Improving educational opportunity.
C. Obtaining and developing personnel.
D. Providing and maintaining funds and facilities.

3. Write a short description of a school situation in which you feel the administrator behaved in a way consistent with good human relations theory. State why you think it is a good example.

SELECTED BIBLIOGRAPHY

A Developing Concept of the Superintendency of Education, rev. ed. (Albany, N.Y., Cooperative Development of Public School Administration, 1955).

BERRIEN, F. K., *Comments and Cases on Human Relations* (New York, Harper, 1951), pp. 3-19.

BILLS, Robert E., "Attributes of Successful Educational Leaders," *Interdisciplinary Research in Educational Administration*, Bulletin of the Bureau of School Services, University of Kentucky, Vol. 26, No. 2 (December, 1953), pp. 16-38.

BOYKIN, Leander L., "Let's Get It Straight: What Are Human Relations?" *The Social Studies*, Vol. 46, No. 2 (1954), p. 59.

COLADARCI, Arthur P., and GETZELS, Jacob W., *The Use of Theory in Educational Administration*, Educational Administration Monograph (Stanford, Cal., Stanford University Press, 1955), No. 5.

FLOWER, George E., "Relationships with People Is the Key," *American School Board Journal*, Vol. 124 (June, 1952), p. 27.

HAGMAN, Harlan, and SCHWARTZ, Alfred, *Administration in Profile for School Executives* (New York, Harper, 1955).

Human Relations in School Administration, Western Washington College Bulletin, (December, 1954), pp. 3-18.

"Human Relations," *Time* (April 14, 1952), pp. 96-97.

KATZ, Robert L., "Skills of an Effective Administrator," *Harvard Business Review,* Vol. 33, No. 1 (January-February, 1955), pp. 33-42.

MAIER, Norman R. F., *Principles of Human Relations* (New York, John Wiley, 1952), pp. 1-18.

OVSIEW, Leon, *Emerging Practices in School Administration* (New York, Metropolitan School Study Council, 1953).

ROETHLISBERGER, F. J., and others, *Training for Human Relations* (Cambridge, Mass., Harvard University Press, 1954).

Ross, Donald H., *Some Arguments for Requiring a More Rigorous Professional Preparation for Chief School Administrators* (Albany, N. Y., Cooperative Development of Public School Administration, 1954).

SEARS, Jesse B., *The Nature of the Administrative Process* (New York, McGraw-Hill, 1950).

STOGDILL, Ralph M., "Personal Factors Associated with Leadership: A Survey of the Literature," *Journal of Psychology,* Vol. 25 (1948), pp. 35-71.

"The Importance of Human Relations in Educational Administration," *Nation's Schools,* Vol. 53, No. 1 (1954), pp. 43-54.

WILES, Kimball, *Supervision for Better Schools,* 2d. ed. (New York, Prentice-Hall, 1955).

CHAPTER **2**

Human Relations and
the Motives of Man

The school administrator finds that most of his time is spent in face-to-face contacts with members of his faculty, board of education members, parents, and students. If he is to be successful in his dealings with these various people, he shortly begins to wonder *why* they behave as they do. Once he arrives at some reason why they behave as they do, he can formulate a path of action and proceed. It can be readily seen that this calls for a knowledge of the motives of man as well as skills in implementing this knowledge. Let us examine some excerpts from case studies that point up various problem situations in which a knowledge of why people behave the way they do would be helpful.

In the first case, that of Mr. Goodyear, we are interested in the behavior of both Mr. Goodyear, a new teacher, and his students. Mr. Goodyear had been having difficulty in maintaining order in his last period study hall, so he put into effect some of his own rules and regulations. The following resulted: [1]

several comments were forthcoming from the students regarding the activities in the last period study hall. One senior girl who had recently been transferred into the study hall has this to relate to one of her teachers, "I wouldn't have missed it for the world. It's as good as a show. He demands perfect silence, then leaves the room. Soon we see him peeking through the window of the door and taking the names of those who are talking. Then he re-enters and puts those students on detention."

One boy said, "I sit with a group of boys in the front of the large study hall. Soon I begin to whistle. Goodyear, whose desk is located in the back of the room, hustles to the front demanding to know who the culprit is. Then someone in the back begins to whistle, and the merry-go-round begins. Gee! It sure is a circus."

Then the students became more vicious. When he was absent from his classroom, they would cover his blackboard with obscene names or throw his books out of the third-story window into the snow. When he was teaching, they would pay very little attention to anything he had to say.

Mr. Goodyear began wearing a path between his classroom and the vice-

[1] The complete text of each of these cases is to be found in Part 3 of this book. They should be read in their entirety.

principal's office, reporting first this and then that. He placed numerous students on detention each day to punish them. Soon the vice-principal suggested that he not place so many students on detention.

Why would an adult behave the way Mr. Goodyear did? One of the undergraduates at our college answered, "He's crazy!" It would be wonderful if such neat and simple categorizations offered the solution. Why is it that the students behaved the way they did when Mr. Goodyear's difficulties mounted? Why didn't they discipline their own membership? Why didn't they co-operate and obey the new rules and regulations? How should the building principal analyze the motives of the teacher and the students?

Consider now the case of Andrew Norwood, who is a principal new to his community. He got into arguments with the faculty and the president of the board of education. This difficulty even extended to the community as follows: [2]

Things were quiet for several weeks. Then one day Mr. Norwood struck a neighbor's child for tripping his small son. News of this incident spread throughout the community, and soon school children began calling him such names as "Big Bully" and "Old Meanie."

Soon after this he slapped the faces of two boys for shoving other students during the exchange of classes. The parents of the boys went to the board. A special meeting was called, where Mr. Norwood, the two boys, and their parents were asked to appear. Mr. Norwood called the county superintendent and asked him to come to the meeting.

What was the motivation behind this kind of behavior? Why should a man in a responsible position of community leadership fly off the handle so quickly?

Another type of motivation is illustrated by an excerpt from the case of Doreen, a teen-aged student. Here again we see the interplay of several drives which culminate in an aggression against family, school, and peer groups. [3]

In subsequent interviews with Doreen's teachers, it was learned that her difficulty was caused by persistent whispering, the fact that she had made it very clear to her teachers that she was not interested in any kind of school work, and that she was merely "marking time" until she could withdraw from school. During the next two years, the counselor attempted to change Doreen's attitude toward school by pointing out that as long as she had to remain there, she could make things pleasant for herself by pleasing her teachers. Her whispering habit did not decrease, but she became more willing to co-operate with teachers and

[2] Prepared in the Department of Education, Ohio University, by H. E. Benz and Walter H. Herriot. Copyright, 1955, by the Ohio University Press. Reprinted by permission of the publishers.

[3] From John W. M. Rothney and Bert A. Roens, *Guidance of American Youth* (Cambridge, Mass., Harvard University Press, 1950), pp. 40-47. Copyright, 1950, by the President and Fellows of Harvard College. Reprinted by permission of the publishers.

counselor. She did so, she said, only on condition that they would recognize her plan to leave school at the age of sixteen. . . .

In several interviews with her near the end of her junior year, the counselor realized that she was serious about her plan to run away from home and go to New York, where she was sure she could become a successful actress.

One last example of administrative behavior that needs to have its motivation analyzed concerns the choice which a superintendent makes between two candidates for the principalship of a new school. The excerpts below indicate the men who are being considered and the choice the superintendent finally made.[4]

"There are some likely-looking candidates, Tom: a couple of them with outstanding records behind them. One man especially impresses me. You probably know him—Smith, from your state department. He came over to see me the other day. He's young and personable and ambitious, with an amazing record behind him for a thirty-five-year-old. His application is highly recommended by your assistant commissioner, among others. The boy seems to have experience, gets along well with people, gets things done. He taught on the summer faculty at Curry College last year. And he is really keen on doing one of those community jobs in the Montgomery School."

The description of Hamilton, the other candidate, follows:

"He's a great conference hound, even though he never contributed anything to a conference or takes any new ideas away from it with him either! He's a Kiwanian, and an official in the Congregational church. He comes of one of the older families in this area; he has a brother-in-law on the board, an older brother is the District Court Judge, and his best friend is the editor of the *Examiner*. He's been principal of Central Junior High for fifteen years or so. . . . A.B. degree in 1911, due for retirement in four years. He looks to Montgomery School as a just reward for thirty-eight years of service: a sort of comfortable, well-paid, 'prestigeful' post from which to retire."

The effectiveness of Hamilton's administration is then summarized:

"He gets by down there. His returns always reach us on time, and his building maintenance costs are low. Never any serious accident or discipline problems to plague me with. Not much ever happens down there, though, other than the traditional day-by-day type of thing. Not much imagination. Our little survey three years ago showed Central with the highest percentage of drop-outs in the city, and the high schools often complain about the students they get from Central. But Hammy points out that his school is on the wrong side of the tracks, and he probably has something there. That may also account for more teachers asking to be transferred out of Central than any other school."

With this evidence for both candidates the superintendent reluctantly decides to nominate Hamilton and states his reasoning:

"I really don't know how hard to fight for Smith. I firmly believe he is the better man for the Montgomery School, both from the point of view of the community and of the children who will attend the school.

[4] From "Principal for the Montgomery School." Copyright, 1951, by the President and Fellows of Harvard University. Reprinted by permission of the Harvard Graduate School of Education.

"But maybe that would be asking too much all at once, making too sharp a break with custom here in tradition-bound Oakville. Maybe I am just getting to feel a bit guilty about letting things drift along as long as I have. I suppose changes have to take place gradually. Probably I should have started it years ago."

What would cause a superintendent to reason his way through the qualifications of two candidates, become thoroughly convinced that one is better than the other, yet reject him? If we tried to analyze this behavior solely on the basis of the superintendent's internal convictions, we would be quite bewildered because it would appear to be antirational. He arrives at a reasonable, defensible solution and then chooses the opposite! However, the internal convictions of all people are modified by other factors, and in the above case this is especially true. The community had many expectations of how the school should be operated and how its problems should be solved. This case is an instance of the community influencing the choice of a school principal and will be discussed in detail later.[5]

In each of the problem situations we have just discussed, knowledge of the underlying motivations would have helped to change the behavior of the participants. Each is an illustration of why an understanding of motivation is important to the administrator. In order to deal with these and similar problems effectively, the administrator must be capable of understanding the motivations of the teachers, students, and members of the board, and using this knowledge to bring their behavior into closer alignment with the purposes and objectives of the school.

THE FRAMEWORK FOR INVESTIGATION

There are many different theories of motivation, each dependent upon the method of investigation used by those advancing the theory and upon the subject of the theory. The theories most concerned with social forces insist that motives are *sociogenic* in nature. Those which emphasize the physiological factors in man and animals insist that motivation is the result of the effort to ease tensions. Others have attempted to relate men's motives to the climate of his habitat, the lack of water (in the case of desert Indians), the chemistry of his body, the cultural history of a race, and so on. It is questionable whether any *one* of the above views is entirely correct. In all probability, the answer most nearly correct is a synthesis of the above views. As Berrien states: "The sciences of man have made it increasingly clear that he is a bio-social-psychological entity on whom chemical, electrical, mechanical, climatic, temporal, social, historical, and psychological factors write a record."[6]

[5] Pp. 40-42.
[6] F. K. Berrien, *Comments and Cases in Human Relations* (New York, Harper, 1951), p. 65.

We shall consider the problem of motivation in human relations from all three of these points of view: biological, social, and psychological. The main emphasis, however, will be on the social origin of motivation. Behavior has varied throughout the ages according to changes in society. Different societies have developed different modes of behavior among individuals comprising the society. An excerpt from Tawney draws a picture of medieval society, in which the implications for motives are clear: [7]

Society, like the human body, is an organism composed of different members. Each member has its own function, prayer, or defense, or merchandise, or tilling the soil. Each must receive the means suited to its station, and must claim no more. Within classes there must be inequality; for otherwise a class cannot perform its function, or . . . enjoy its rights. Peasants must not encroach on those above them. Lords must not despoil peasants. Craftsmen and merchants must receive what will maintain them in their calling, and no more.

When we contrast this society with modern western societies the difference in social motivation is vivid. Although we do have a degree of social stratification, social mobility is an accepted fact. A priori concepts of a man's place in life are not looked upon with much favor. The protective attitudes of the Middle Ages largely have disappeared. There is more stress placed upon the acquisition of material things. The concept of the equality of man, regardless of his social station, is strongly believed in, even though not always practiced.

What Are Motives?

There seems to be little argument as to a definition of motive. It is commonly accepted that a motive or need or drive (the terms are often used interchangeably) refers to a condition of the individual which causes him to act toward the achievement of an end or goal. Since a major consideration of administration is to influence the motives of the members of the staff so as to result in desired activities, it is necessary to introduce the concept of incentives. Viteles states: "The conditions which start or initiate, decrease or speed up, or partially inhibit and direct activities are commonly known as *incentives*." [8] The distinction between incentives and motives is made by Warren as follows: [9]

If the motivation of conduct be conceived as originating in some maladjustment between organism and environment, the organism's efforts are said to be the result of inner *drive* (motive) while the critical environmental conditions are

[7] R. H. Tawney, *Religion and the Rise of Capitalism* (New York, Harcourt, Brace, 1926), pp. 27, 28.

[8] Morris S. Viteles, *Motivation and Morale in Industry* (New York, Norton, 1953), p. 76.

[9] H. C. Warren, *Dictionary of Psychology* (Boston, Houghton Mifflin, 1934), p. 134.

called the *incentive;* i.e., food is the *incentive* to a *hunger driven* animal or person; a badge of honor is an *incentive* to one under the urge of ambition.

Although *motive* and *incentive* are discrete terms, they are usually found to be involved in the same behavior. In other words, incentives act to modify, either positively or negatively, the behavior of an individual as he strives to attain a goal. Motivation is usually thought of in terms of goal-seeking behavior. The norms of behavior which a person sets for himself would be considered the goals. A necessary constituent of a goal is the personalization, or internalization, of the object of motivation. This distinguishes goal-seeking behavior, or motivation, from behavior dictated by incentives. The incentive is from the outside and is not personalized or made the person's "own." The incentive would have to be very potent for it to equal or exceed in effectiveness the behavior generated by the motive.

In our American culture man's position in society is determined in large measure by his occupation and income. The drive to improve one's position in the social strata, that is, to attain status, is a basic motivation. In satisfying this motivation, one has as incentives a better occupational position and increased income. The interrelationship of motives and incentives can be seen in the above example. In school administration the same sort of procedure can be illustrated. Men do not necessarily go into school administration because they like it. Many would prefer to remain teachers. However, administrative positions have a higher status value than does that of teacher.[10] In addition to the satisfaction of attaining a higher pay and better conditions of employment, there is that of attaining a higher social status. We can say, then, that the man going into administration has a basic motivation of improved status and is propelled toward this with incentives of higher pay and better conditions of employment.

One further point to be mentioned is the question of *basic* drives or motives. There has been and still is considerable controversy over which motives are basic and which are not, but such a controversy need not be resolved before we can function intelligently in the area of motivation. For the purposes of this study, it is not of particular value to know whether a motive is basic or not. The important point is to be able to work with the *results* of motivation, whatever their source.[11] The material which follows is very close to the viewpoint expressed by Berrien: [12]

It becomes increasingly clear from the testimony of historians and anthropologists that the dominant drives of a person or a society are the net manifestation of an interaction between a biological substratum (physiological mechanisms having roots in tissue needs) and the climate of opportunity and values existing

[10] Theodore L. Reller, "Administration—City School," *Encyclopedia of Educational Research*, ed. Walter S. Monroe (New York, Macmillan, 1952), p. 16.
[11] K. Lewin, "Frontiers of Group Dynamics," *Human Relations,* Vol. 1 (1947), pp. 5-41.
[12] Berrien, *op. cit.,* p. 67.

at any particular time. The latter can modify the former in diverse and strange ways, so strange that we can place no confidence in any claim that our current dominant motives represent human nature which cannot be altered.

Motivation will, therefore, be considered in terms of what occurs as the result of an interaction between what is "inside" and "outside" an individual.

Motivated Behavior

Practically all writers in the field of motivation attempt to categorize motives in one way or another. Some lists are long, some are short, all are very probably inadequate. The categorization which we shall employ is a short one, suffering from the defects of most lists, but it has some value for us because we can use it to talk about administrative problems. It is suggested by Anderson, who has grouped the drives and needs of man as follows: [13]

1. *Appetites:* This group is concerned with those needs related to the maintenance of life itself such as, thirst, hunger, elimination, and fatigue.
2. *Reproduction of the race:* This drive is latent in the newborn but appears in full force in late adolescence and early maturity. Related to this group are the need for companionship with members of the opposite sex as well as maternal and paternal impulses. More behavior of teachers could be explained by reference to this drive than is commonly believed.
3. *Association with other people:* Human beings are essentially social in nature and the deprivation of human beings from normal associations with others is a powerful punishment.
4. *Curiosity and manipulation:* This group of needs is reflected in the quest for knowledge, scientific inquiry, and invention. It deals with the manipulation of objects in the environment.

Energy and Tension Systems. The way in which the above motives operate can be discussed by reference to the concept of energy and tension systems in man. Since the term *motivation* covers the forces which impel, lead, or force the activity of persons in one direction rather than another, we can see that activity itself is a basic characteristic of man as an energy system. This energy is the expression of life itself. Man as a living system is constantly in action and never really rests—sleep, for instance, is merely a slackening of energy output. Death is the cessation of energy. The problem of motivation, then, is one of direction of energy outlets, preferably self-direction.

It is more helpful if we do not consider the energy system of man as a whole but think in terms of the subsystems, which are called *tension systems.* An example of a simple tension system is thirst. A person becomes thirsty, drinks, loses his thirst, then becomes thirsty again, and the cycle repeats. A general pattern would then be: (1) need appearance, (2)

[13] John E. Anderson, *The Psychology of Development and Personal Adjustment* (New York, Holt, 1949), p. 233.

tension, (3) seeking movements, (4) need satisfaction, (5) disappearance of need.[14] The pattern is then renewed and repeated with another need. The simplest types of tension systems are the appetites, but more complex tension systems develop for the other needs.

We can begin to see the basis for a practical concept of motivation evolving in the study of the appetites. When a person is thirsty, water is, for the moment, the most valuable thing in the world. He knows that water will satiate his thirst, so he places a high value on it when this need arises. After he drinks, the value of water decreases. In this simple example it is easy to see that water has a high value at one time and a low value at another.

Valence. We begin to see, then, that things do not have an intrinsic value but a value in terms of fulfilling needs as these arise. What fulfills a need in one person does not fulfill the need in another person. *Time* carried an interesting article on this recently when they discussed the many cases of acute alcoholism now being discovered among children in France. Many French mothers give their youngsters wine to drink instead of the American diet of milk or water. Wine has highest value in fulfilling the thirst need in France; it is practically unheard of in America. How is it that certain things attain such value in satisfying needs and others do not?

We call this value of things *valence,* and it is a most convenient term. The dictionary defines it as "The degree of power which exists between certain bodies or substances, causing them to unite or produce a specific effect on each other." This term is used most commonly in chemistry, where it refers to the charge on an atom. This charge affects the way in which it combines with other atoms. For instance, the charge on an oxygen atom is -2 and it normally combines with two hydrogen atoms each of $+1$ charge. The application of valence in motivation can readily be seen now. As a need arises, the individual selects some object to satisfy the need. The choice is not merely dependent on the object; it is also dependent on the individual. If the individual repeatedly selects the same object to satisfy a need, we say that the object possesses *positive valence* for him. If the individual rejects a certain object as the satiater of his need, we say that the object possesses *negative valence* for him. Thus valence expresses a *double* or reciprocal relationship between an individual and an object, or between two individuals. This is very important. We should always remember that valence in human relations, just as in chemistry, is defined in terms of a mutual relationship and is never a one-way proposition. Objects of the physical world do not have valences until the individual reacts with them. For example, most American children have not experienced drinking wine. They neither accept nor reject wine and so have not developed any valence in regard to it. Valence develops as the individual's experiences of life develop. In general, though, positive valence is attached to

[14] *Ibid.,* p. 237.

those objects which satisfy or bring pleasure to the individual; negative valence is attached to those objects which bring pain or displeasure to the individual.

A look at a school situation will illustrate the importance of the valence concept in administration. Even though the teacher and the principal are in the same building, they do not have the same perceptions and experiences. Therefore, objects do not necessarily have the same valences for each. In high schools, for instance, we have developed a high degree of specialization among teachers. The principal is a generalist. It is his job to see the whole child in the whole school in the whole community. The teacher perceives her job as, let us say, a teacher of English. For her, because of her inexperience in such matters, the students' activities on the football team are likely to have no valence. The principal, in making decisions regarding students, considers the football activities. For him, there exists a positive valence in football because in his experience he has seen the relationship of the student, football, and the school. This difference in valence becomes more important as the necessity for making decisions increases. Although the above discussion relates to a principal who has developed a positive valence for football and a teacher who has not developed a valence, a more complex situation often exists. This would be the case if the principal had a positive valence for football and the teacher a negative valence. Decisions made by the principal concerning football would then be likely to result in open disagreement with the teacher.

The concept of valence can be used further to describe the relations between people on faculties. Those who work well together have positive valence. Those who work poorly together have negative valence. As two people of the latter category come together in committee meetings, for instance, they seem to disagree and fight on every point. It would be presumptuous to try to explain in detail why the negative valence exists. In general, we may assume that the tension systems and the environmental conditioning of each are different and antagonistic. Each has developed valences that are repelling to the other. Changes in each can be brought about only through a long series of vivid experiences to which each attaches the same meaning.

Field Theory. It can be seen that the motivated behavior of an individual will vary according to his environment and the strength of the valence between himself and the objects in this environment. The theory of psychology which gives most cognizance to this belief is termed the *field theory.* As Allport puts it, "Roughly stated, the field theory of personality regards the total environmental setting as well as the inner structure of the person as decisive in the shaping of conduct." [15] This means

[15] Gordon W. Allport, *Personality: A Psychological Interpretation* (New York, Holt, 1937), p. 364.

that the individual operates within a set of boundaries, the area being called a "field." This field is not physical but psychological.

An illustration might clarify this point. In the case of the Valley Elementary School, Mr. Metcalf, the principal, made a decision concerning pupil behavior.[16] At the time he made the decision his concept of the field, that is, the school community, was an uncluttered one. He thought that he and the students were the only ones involved. Schematically, his concept was this: [17]

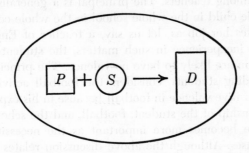

Actually, the field included the teachers, who wanted to have a word in how the decision was to be made. These teachers did not agree concerning the decision. The field, therefore, changes as follows: [18]

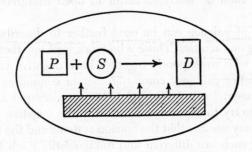

The teachers, who are represented by the barred rectangle, are not perceived to be part of the field by the principal. They have, however, construed themselves to be present and are exerting a force that is changing the field. By the exertion of this force, the effect of the decision will

16 See below, pp. 373-376.

17 In this diagram, P represents the principal, Mr. Metcalf, S represents the students, and D represents the decision. The arrow represents the interaction taking place between principal and students.

18 The field is pictured here as an ellipse, but it could be any geometrical form. The idea is that there is an enclosed boundary in which the individuals must cope with various forces. These forces may have positive or negative valence. The teachers in the Valley Elementary School would have a negative valence.

be changed in that the results will not be what the principal and the students had intended.

If the principal had had a more complete perception of the field, he would have included the teachers in the formation of the decision. The case indicates that the decision would not have been the same as was arrived at by the principal and students alone. The figure, therefore, would be like this:

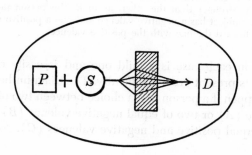

As can be seen, the decision has a barrier to overcome, and in overcoming the barrier, the decision is changed. The teachers in this case are more interested in the process than the outcome and so insist on being consulted. This consultation, merely by adding to the number involved, changes the nature of the decision.

Note the importance of the boundary. If there were no boundary, the principal and students could have excluded the teachers and worked out an independent decision. As it is, the field includes those elements which are bound together to force all of the individuals to interact. This case could be pictured as a series of diagrams showing a gradual weakening of the boundary as the valence between faculty and principal grows increasingly negative, until, at last, the principal leaves the field because the barriers are too great to overcome.

Conflict. We discussed above one of the difficulties in school administration when we pointed out that ignoring or being unaware of forces in the field can bring about unforseen consequences. There are always present in any field a number of possibilities, some of which must be acted upon and some neglected.[19] Very often a choice *must* be made between conflicting alternatives. It has been said, with considerable validity, that the true test of an administrator is the ability to choose between conflicting alternatives, in other words, to make a decision. We can picture the conflict situations most easily by reference to Anderson.[20]

[19] See Ch. 10.
[20] Anderson, *op. cit.*, p. 244.

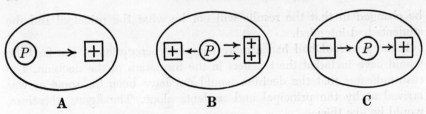

A   **B**   **C**

When one object has a positive valence, as in A, the person moves toward it (or if one object has a negative valence, away from it). If objects have similar positive valences but one is stronger than the other, as in B, the person moves toward the stronger one. If one object has a negative valence and one a positive valence, as in C, the person moves toward the one with the positive valence.

The conflict in each case is a mild one and is easily resolved. More complex conflicts present greater difficulty. The diagram below illustrates what would happen if a person had a choice between two objects of equal positive valence (A) or two of equal negative valence (B) or a choice of one object of equal positive and negative valences (C).

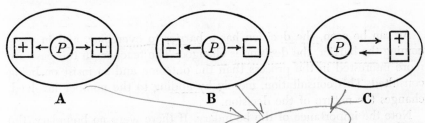

A   **B**   **C**

In all three situations, the administrator *oscillates* back and forth between the choices until he finally chooses in terms of the *structure* of the field. Hunkin's case is an example of the B situation. Here, the administrator found himself forced to choose between defending a decision of his board of education or siding with the public who opposed it.[21] He saw both as possessing negative valence. He made his choice in terms of the field, the violent opposition of the public. He could not "win." It was a choice between two alternatives, both of which were very difficult and meant trouble. The oscillation that he went through gave him an opportunity to see more elements in the field; consequently, his final choice was made on the basis of his broader view of the total field.

MOTIVATION AND MANAGEMENT

Although we usually do not consider educational leadership to be concerned with the *management* of the faculty, this administrative function is always present to some degree. In line with the general thesis of this

[21] See below, p. 222.

Note

chapter, there are two ways in which the behavior of the faculty can be altered in terms of motives of the administration. The first method is concerned with *incentives,* and the second with *changing the atmosphere,* that is, changing the valence of objects in the field.

Incentives involve the attachment of reward or punishment to the behavior of individuals. When this reward or punishment is administered it changes the valence of the object. Many administrators act on the basis that the only effective incentive is that of punishment (defined as any deterrent). Enough is now known about the relative values of incentives to say that positive rather than negative incentives are more effective.[22]

In the field of school administration, we have had little success in the use of tangible incentives. The most extensive attempt to institute a system of merit rating was tried in New York State. The attempt encompassed a statewide trial of merit rating legislatively imposed under the 1947 salary law.[23] This law called for a state salary schedule with periodic merit ratings based upon criteria selected by a committee of representative teachers in each school district. The law has since been repealed, and merit rating is no longer legally implemented, although a few communities continue to practice it.

In terms of what we shall discuss later in this book, the New York State merit rating trial has many interesting implications. We note that two months after the salary law went into effect, the House of Delegates of the New York State Teachers Association (representing practically all upstate teachers) almost unanimously proposed that the number of steps in the salary schedule be increased and that promotions be made automatically available to all who had been teaching long enough to qualify for them. The point is not that teachers found merit rating unsatisfactory but that they were willing to reject it before it went into effect. The teachers' perception of what constituted merit ratings was so negative that they could not believe the system to be anything but detrimental. The thoughts conjured up by the words was enough to make them rebel.

It may be possible, in the future, to use some type of tangible incentive to improve teaching. If such a program is to be successful, however, the preconceived notions of teachers concerning merit ratings must first be offset. The conditions that would have to prevail are:

1. Teachers would have to recognize that real differences do exist among themselves.
2. Teachers would have to have great confidence in their administrators.

[22] Anderson, *op. cit.,* p. 250.
[23] For a discussion of the New York State trial of merit rating, see Arvid J. Burke, "Some Dangers of Merit Measurement," *Nation's Schools,* Vol. 41 (January, 1948), pp. 27-28, and Dwight E. Beecher, "Objections Answered—The New York Plan of Rewarding Good Teaching," *American School Board Journal,* Vol. 19 (October, 1949), pp. 35-37.

3. The basis on which the incentives were paid would have to be acceptable to both teachers and administrators.

With these conditions prevailing, the use of positive incentives probably
would be more successful than it has been up to now. At present, the most
effective incentives are the giving of praise, the improvement of facilities,
and the increase of job satisfaction.

Satisfaction

The satisfaction one derives from the work he does can be the most
effective incentive for good performance. The competent administrator
uses other positive incentives to increase this satisfaction.[24] Parsons, in
discussing this factor in motivation, points out that there are five components of job satisfaction: [25]

1. Self-respect
2. Recognition
3. Satiation of wants
4. Pleasure
5. Affection

Self-respect is treated as the extent to which a person lives up to the
moral norms which he has built into his own personality structure. Moral
norms are often called "levels of aspiration" by other authors. The administrator builds self-respect in the members of his faculty by helping them
to develop a realistic level of aspiration and then providing the means
whereby they can attain this level.

Very closely allied to self-respect is the need for *recognition*. It would
be rather difficult for a person to have self-respect if he did not gain
recognition. All people feel this need to a greater or lesser degree. The
school administrator should be aware that he is the one who can either
give or withhold recognition in his school. Failure to grant recognition
is one of the causes of low morale. How can the administrator show recognition? Probably the best way is for the administrator to know what each
teacher is doing in her work and to let her know this. Although some
superintendents follow the practice of writing a note to each teacher who
does something outstanding, this is not necessary. It is essential, however,
that the administrator be aware of what is going on and acknowledge
this fact.

The third component involves *satiation of wants*. We are all interested in doing a good job "for what we can get out of it." Some of this

---

[24] Note that here we are using the term *incentive* in a sense of reinforcement.
[25] Talcott Parsons, "Motivation of Economic Activities" in *Human Relations in Administration,* ed. Robert Dubin (New York, Prentice-Hall, 1951), pp. 27-38.

"getting" refers to salary, some to recognition; but in all cases, it is necessary to get some satisfaction out of doing a job or we will not do it at all. Gross illustrates this very well with the following case of a Massachusetts superintendent.[26]

I used to get a tremendous satisfaction out of teaching, being near to the kids. You feel you really have done something for them. You can see it in their eyes. But as a superintendent, you get no appreciation from the community leaders for your hard labor, for what you do in the community, for the fact that you have no time for relaxation, no freedom of your own.

Look, I'll show you exactly what I mean. For over a half dozen years I have knocked myself out in getting a new school building for this community. I spent days and days with architects, night after night working with school building committees and speaking to every group in town. I worked like a dog planning and selling them on the need for the new building. And it was for their own children. The need so obvious that it would be a laughing matter if it were not such a serious one. Finally, they built the new building.

At the dedication, every important civic official spoke. School committee members, every important local official and all the "big wheels" made speeches. Not one of them mentioned the position or name of the superintendent. I gave some of my life to that building. But there was not one word of appreciation spoken by the town leaders. Then and there I realized you have to work for money, not for the welfare of the community.

My wife and children went to the dedication. They felt for me. When they got home, they were crying—crying for me. I did not, I could not say a word. I tried to brace them the best I could. It really hurt. The superintendent gives his heart to the job, but there is no appreciation for the job he does. That is when I said to hell with public education. I plan to get out as soon as I can. I've given my community the best that was in me. I'll leave with no regrets. Enough is enough.

This points up very clearly the three components of satisfaction described above. It is obvious that this superintendent failed to receive recognition on the part of community leaders for his role in the construction of the new school. This ruined his self-respect. Underlying his desire to provide a better school building and so better education was an aspiration to be recognized as a community leader. Failure to receive this recognition was evidence that he could not achieve his level of aspiration, and so he lost respect for himself. We further see that he "got nothing out of his endeavor." He now says that he will work only for money, but we notice, too, that he cannot continue to be a superintendent merely for money. Fortunately, most communities give at least a little more recognition to their superintendents than did the community in our case. The point for administrators to remember is that their teachers feel toward them as this superintendent felt toward his community. In New York state, the most frequent reason given for leaving the teaching profession, next

[26] Neal Gross, *The Pressures on and the Dilemmas of the School Superintendent* (Cambridge, Mass., New England School Development Council, 1954), pp. 20-21.

to marriage and pregnancy, is discontent, with particular reference to the lack of job satisfaction.[27]

The fourth point referred to is *pleasure*. This is not to be interpreted as being the sole end toward which a person strives. Pleasure should be construed as "a function of the *total* personal equilibrium of the individual." [28] A person actually should enjoy his work, should get from it actual pleasure of the type that most people derive only from playing games or other sorts of recreation. A highly successful top executive put it this way: "When I come home from the office in the evening, my son likes me to play ball with him, and I do. But while it's a game for him, it's work for me. My job is my game, and I'm happiest when I'm at it." [29]

This probably best illustrates the intense motivation of a successful business executive, but it also illustrates the point that pleasure is an important concomitant of the field of forces of a person and his occupation. The provision of those things which make teaching a pleasure will act as a powerful incentive.

The fifth element in satisfactions is that of *affection*. This has to do directly with the establishment of favorable valences between the administrator and his faculty. The point is made that a very important incentive is friendship between professional associates. Surely the opposite is painfully clear. If negative valences are developed, then low morale and its concomitants, bickering, back-biting, and low production are the result. The teamwork of successful business and educational organizations is, in part, built upon the motivation of friendship or affection.

Atmosphere

To achieve good management we have seen how incentives can be used. Also important is the existence of a good atmosphere. Atmosphere becomes a necessary consideration in view of the fact that certain schools have large teacher turnovers each year but that others never lose a teacher by resignation, that some schools cannot keep a superintendent, although others grant long tenure to their chief administrator. The difference in schools can be described in terms of atmosphere.

The chapter on morale points out the various atmospheres in terms of autocratic, democratic, and other types of administration, and shows how morale is related to the kind of leadership present. Morale is indicative of the atmosphere. In those schools where there is an atmosphere of freedom, a permissive atmosphere, there is creative activity. Since it is safe to con-

---

[27] Lewis Wilson, in an address before the New York State Teachers Association Conference on the Teaching Profession, April 29, 1954.

[28] Parsons, *op. cit.*, p. 33.

[29] Robert H. Wald and Roy A. Doty, "The Top Executive," *The Harvard Business Review*, Vol. 32, No. 4 (July-August, 1954), p. 49.

sider personality in terms of *social stimulus values,* it is necessary that a permissive atmosphere be created to allow teachers to function to their capacity.

THE FUNCTIONAL AUTONOMY OF MOTIVES

Some behavior cannot be explained on the basis of the terms we have been using. In fact, some behavior seems to be without reason or basis. Some of the students' behavior in the case of Mr. Goodyear appears to be of this nature. Once they began, they continued to behave as they did just because they enjoyed it. As Woodworth has put it, "The fundamental drive towards a certain end may be hunger, sex, pugnacity, or what not, but once the activity is started, the means to the end becomes an object of interest on its own account." [30]

The point being made is that although behavior can have an original purpose or motive, it can continue in a manner devoid of any relation to the original motive. The act of behavior *itself* is the reason for continuing the behavior.

This concept of motivation has probably been championed best by Allport in his studies of what he calls "the functional autonomy of motives." He discusses this as a dynamic psychology which "regards adult motives as infinitely varied and as self-sustaining, contemporary systems, growing out of antecedent systems, but functionally independent of them." [31]

This theory of the functional autonomy of motives does not *simplify* our approach to behavior. It would be much simpler if we could apply a Freudian approach, for instance, to all behavior. We know, however, that the Freudian approach does not always work and that even the recognition of the original cause for a certain type of behavior does not always effect a change. The compulsive tic is an extreme example of this point. Knowledge of the original cause rarely, if ever, enables the possessor to stop the movement. Such movements, which some authorities consider symptoms, have set themselves up as independent systems of motivation quite separate from their roots.

One example of behavior that can best be explained by reference to the functional autonomy of motives may help to clarify this point. Thumbsucking is an extremely common practice among young children. It has been explained on the basis of being associated with feeding, with sleeping, with a blanket or some other "feely" object or with insecurity or a host of other causes. It is interesting to note, however, that many children carry the habit to the age of seven or eight (or even later), and none of the presumed causes seems to be involved. True, the habit may have been

[30] R. W. Woodworth, *Dynamic Psychology* (New York, Columbia University Press, 1918), p. 201.

[31] Allport, *op. cit.,* p. 194.

started by one of the above causes, but the thumb is now being sucked because it feels good. Thumbsucking, particularly in older children is an example of an independent system of motivation quite separate from its original cause. This is now recognized by some authorities. Kelly, for instance, describes a method of what he calls "controlled elaboration," which is a method of treating thumbsucking directly, without regard for the cause.[32]

Examples of functional autonomy of motives in school administration are quite common. A superintendent who literally and actually worked himself to death is a case in point. This particular superintendent had a reasonably secure position, a substantial income, the respect of his fellow workers, and the admiration of his community. In developing these forms of recognition, he had worked very hard. His original motivation could be explained on the basis of desire to attain status, more money, and the like; but these motives could not explain the driving behavior which led to his death. Functional autonomy would explain it on the basis that the behavior of the superintendent provided all the motivation that was necessary. "Activities and objects that earlier in the game were *means* to an end, now become ends in themselves."[33]

In the case of Andrew Norwood, it would be very difficult to explain his arbitrary behavior on any grounds other than that he behaved the way he did because the behavior itself was all that was sufficient to keep it going.

The great difficulty in working with people who behave in patterns that are contrary to the efficiency of the organization and that, *because* of the functional autonomy of their motivation, are not easily susceptible to change makes the process of selection all the more important. Administrators with patterns of behavior that are unsuccessful in a situation usually are best advised to move to a position more congruent with their pattern.

ANALYSIS OF CASES

Let us try to analyze two of the cases that were cited at the beginning of the chapter in terms of the material on motivation. Let us also see if we can recommend some procedures or ways of changing behavior so as to bring about a more productive environment.

A Principal for Montgomery School

This case appeared at first to deal with an antirational superintendent, one who first developed a rational solution to his problem and then used

---

[32] George A. Kelly, "Clinical Diagnosis and Psychotherapy," *The Psychology of Personal Constructs* (New York, Norton, 1955), Vol. 2, pp. 995-997.

[33] Allport, *op. cit.*, p. 195.

a solution which was just the opposite. A diagram using the *life-space concept* of Lewin will show us what the superintendent actually considered in making his decision on the appointment.

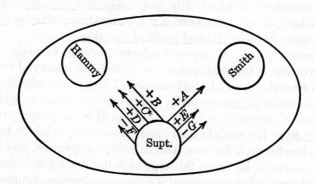

This diagram represents the *life space* of the superintendent, that is, those factors which come into play on his decision regarding the principalship. The diagram consists of circles representing the superintendent, Hammy, and Smith, with vectors indicating the strength and direction of reasons why each man should or should not be appointed. The length of the vectors is arrived at in a very subjective manner, and they should not be used with the precision associated with a physics problem. They will, even though only roughly approximate, give an indication of why the superintendent makes the decision that he does make or appears to make.

Vector A is strongly positive and represents the excellent background of Smith, both in terms of his academic and professional training and in terms of his professional experience. Vector E is also positive but rather weak. It represents the obvious fact that the superintendent is a little ashamed of himself professionally for not recommending Smith immediately. While he is telling a professional friend of this case, the act of telling seems to influence him toward Smith more than he would ordinarily be influenced.

We now need to examine the three positive vectors, all strong, which would lead the superintendent to appoint Hammy. Vector B is the position of Hammy in the community—a Kiwanian, an official of the Congregational church, and so on. He is one of the pillars of the community, strongly entrenched and apparently well liked by the townsfolk. Vector C is the custom of Oakville, which says that such positions as principal of the Montgomery School are given to local people. This also is reflected in Vector D, which is the superintendent's own insecurity. He had left Oakville to take a better job, had received his present post on a split vote, and was very uncertain of his position with the board of education. Vector F is negative and represents the superintendent's own concern for Hammy's lack of ability. It can be seen, however, that this is *not* a very serious concern, for he finds ways to excuse Hammy's failures.

Summing up the vectors, it can be seen that the vectors for the appointment of Hammy far exceed the vectors for the appointment of Smith. This is apparently the reason why, after building such a strong case for Smith, the superintendent switched. His motivation was manysided, and his decision, which should have been a professional one, was based instead on a knowledge of the social and political situation.

The question arises: If superintendents continue to make decisions based on reasons of this sort, can we ever attain an improved profession? There are several answers to this question. The first contains the realization that decisions are always made within a power structure and that the superintendent, generally, is not very influential in the power structure of his community.[34] He can, of course, make a sacrifice, in which he puts his job on the line for each decision. This is living dangerously, and he would be better advised if he saved this type of action for a particularly fitting moment. The second answer contains a more constructive approach. Probably the first task of a superintendent new to the job is to analyze his community. In our case, the superintendent had six years in which to do this before having to make a major appointment. During this time, he could have worked to change the community and modify its views regarding the kind of personnel needed for good schools. He also had time to gain the confidence of people in power positions. By bringing these people into the discussion of school affairs he could have raised the sights of the whole community.

Mr. Goodyear

Here we have behavior based on entirely different motives; in fact, just the opposite motives from those in the above case. As we read over the case, we see that Mr. Goodyear enters his new position with a preconceived idea of what a school *should* be like. He fails to recognize the limitations of the present position and so, in determining how he should act, he fails to take into account the reality of the situation. His resultant behavior could have been predicted by use of the formula

$$B = f(P, E)$$

in which behavior is a function of the person and his environment.[35] The person is comprised of his needs and abilities, and the environment is both that which the person recognizes and that which he does not. In order to analyze the predicament of Mr. Goodyear, we need to depict the situation exactly as Mr. Goodyear perceives it. As Lewin puts it, "Objectivity in psychology demands representing the field correctly as it exists for the

[34] See below, Ch. 5.
[35] Morris L. Bigge, "A Relativistic Approach to the Learning Aspect of Educational Psychology," *Educational Theory,* Vol. 4, No. 3 (July, 1954), p. 216.

individual in question at that particular time." [36] In a school administration situation it is also necessary to look beyond this objective, psychological situation to determine how the situation appears to others in the field of the chief protagonist. The principal, for instance, needs to have an understanding of why Mr. Goodyear is behaving as he is; but he needs also to know why the students are motivated to behave as they do. Let us describe the field of Mr. Goodyear by means of a diagram suggested by Bigge.[37]

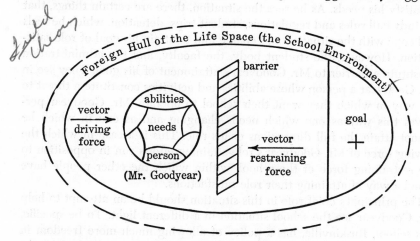

The components of this diagram are defined as follows:

Life Space: The totality of the constellation of interdependent factors which determine the behavior of an individual at a certain moment.

Environment: Everything in which, toward which, or away from which a person can make psychological movement.

Barrier: Dynamic part of the environment which resists movement through it.

Foreign Hull of Life Space: Physical and social raw materials; a complex of all nonpsychological facts that surround the life space; limits behavioral possibilities.

Person-Centered Constructs:

    Needs: States of a person which, if they exist in relation to a goal, have a part in determining behavior toward that goal.

    Abilities: Cognitive—knowing environment; Executive—manipulating environment.

Environment Centered Constructs:

    Valences: Imperative environmental facts; properties which parts of the life space have if the individual goes toward them or away from them.

Cognitive Structure: An environment as known by the person; insight, understanding; it has one dimension—clarity.

[36] Kurt Lewin, "Behavior and Development as a Function of the Total Situation," in *Manual of Child Psychology*, ed. Leonard Carmichael (New York, Wiley, 1946), p. 793.

[37] Bigge, *loc. cit.*, p. 217.

Central to the diagram is Mr. Goodyear as a person. He has a set of *needs* or motives which trigger him into action. These needs relate to Mr. Goodyear's attempt to gain satisfaction from his role in the new school. The components of the attempt to gain satisfaction are self-respect, recognition, satiation of wants, pleasure, and affection. Mr. Goodyear has certain *abilities* which were developed in his previous teaching position. He has a *cognitive structure* of the school situation in which he is attempting to satisfy his needs. As he sees the situation, there are certain things, that is, study hall rules and regulations, student trips, detention, which he feels will cope with the situation and enable him to attain his goal of role satisfaction. However, the student body, the faculty, and the administration constitute a barrier to Mr. Goodyear's attainment of his goal. They see in Mr. Goodyear a person whose abilities and activities constitute a threat to the way in which they want their school to operate. Mr. Goodyear perceives this way as one which needs changing and as one in which he cannot attain the full dimensions of his role. This is a case in which the driving force of Mr. Goodyear's role-attaining efforts run in opposition to the restraining force of the school, within which the other people have found a way of attaining their role satisfactions.

The principal's chief role in this situation should be an attempt to help Mr. Goodyear see the school situation in a different light. To be specific, this school, Ruskinville, has a policy of allowing much more freedom in student behavior than did the school in which Mr. Goodyear had taught previously. It is the principal's job to orient Mr. Goodyear to this type of behavior. Mr. Goodyear needs to know that this behavior is *different* but not necessarily *worse* than that which he had known before.

Back of much of Mr. Goodyear's behavior is a distrust of students. He cannot trust them. Although it will not be easy, if Mr. Goodyear is to become a successful teacher, he must change this attitude. The principal should attempt to have Mr. Goodyear take part in several activities in which the students *can be seen* to be trustworthy and then point this fact out to Mr. Goodyear.

The role of the administrator in this case is very similar to that of a therapist. He must analyze the reasons for Mr. Goodyear's behavior and arrange situations which will cause Mr. Goodyear's attitude, and subsequently his behavior, to change.

SUMMARY

Through the use of case studies we presented a number of behavior problems with which a school administrator must cope. We then established a framework for investigation, in which we distinguished between behavior induced by motives (goal-seeking behavior) and behavior induced by incentives (critical-environmental factors). We noted that the motivated behavior of an individual will vary according to his environment and according to the strength of the valence between himself and the objects in this environment. This synthesis is best represented through the approach of the field theory of Lewin. Field theory holds that the total environmental setting, as well as the inner structure of the person, is decisive in the shaping of behavior. Behavior in conflict situations was investigated through the analysis of field diagrams.

The use of incentives by the administrator in order to increase the effectiveness of faculty members in their job was discussed. We also discussed the five components of job satisfaction: self-respect, recognition, satiation of wants, pleasure, and affection.

It was pointed out that determining the causes of behavior was not an easy task and that some behavior seemed unrelated to reasonable causes. An explanation of this type of behavior may be found in the theory of the functional autonomy of motives. This theory states that adult motives are infinitely varied and are self-sustaining contemporary systems which grow out of prior systems but are functionally independent of them. Behavior for the sake of the behavior itself falls into this category.

Finally, we tested our ideas against two case studies to see if we could gain further insights into the problems presented.

EXERCISES

1. Read the case of Julia Brockton. How could the principal have used incentives to help Julia become a more effective member of the teaching staff?

2. In what way did Julia achieve self-respect? Recognition? Job satisfaction?

3. In the discussion of motivation, it was pointed out that the administrator can use positive incentives to help teachers achieve satisfaction from their roles on the faculty. The components of satisfaction are (1) self-respect, (2) recognition, (3) satiation of wants, (4) pleasure, (5) affection. Give specific examples under each of how the administrator can help teachers achieve these satisfactions.

4. Write a case in which the functional autonomy of motives appears to be the only way in which to account for the behavior of an individual.

5. Analyze the case of Andrew Norwood in the same method we have used in the text.

6. Take a situation in which you as an administrator are working with a member of the faculty to improve that member's effectiveness. What are the teacher's motives that are relevant to the problem between you? What are the incentives that are relevant to the problem between you? What incentives can an administrator use to increase a teacher's effectiveness?

7. Diagram the valences existing among the teachers in a single building or department of your school system.

SELECTED BIBLIOGRAPHY

ALLPORT, Gordon, *Personality: A Psychological Interpretation* (New York, Holt, 1937), ch. 7.

ANDERSON, John E., *The Psychology of Development and Personal Adjustment* (New York, Holt, 1949).

BERRIEN, F. K., *Comments and Cases On Human Relations* (New York, Harper, 1951), ch. 4.

GROSS, Neal, *Human Relations and the Wishes of Man* (Cambridge, Mass., New England School Development Council, 1953).

———, *The Pressures on and the Dilemmas of the School Superintendent* (Cambridge, Mass., New England School Development Council, 1954).

PARSONS, Talcott, "Motivation of Economic Activities," in *Human Relations in Administration*, ed. Robert Dubin (New York, Prentice-Hall, 1951), pp. 27-38.

VITELES, Morris S., *Motivation and Morale in Industry* (New York, Norton, 1953).

CHAPTER **3**

Human Relations and Perception

As an approach to a common background for our discussion of perception, let us consider the following case. The setting is a childrens' institution just outside of Metropolis, and the three people involved are Mrs. Martin, a teacher cottage mother; Mr. Adams, the new executive director of the institution; and Miss Barnes, the director of social service.

"The cottage looks very good," thought Mrs. Martin as she went from room to room. The girls had done a fine job. The windows sparkled, all of the furniture was neatly arranged, and the floors seemed to shine from their recent waxing. Yes, the cottage did look nice. Certainly Mr. Adams could find nothing wrong here. Mrs. Martin wondered what he would be like. She hoped he would be a little easier to work with than was the former director. Well, better not spend the time daydreaming when there was work to be done.

Shortly thereafter, Mr. Adams, accompanied by Miss Barnes, entered the cottage without knocking. Mrs. Martin was introduced to Mr. Adams, and he said, "It is nice to meet you Mrs. Martin. As you know, we are here to inspect this cottage. I would like to see what standards are being maintained at this institution."

During the tour of the cottage, Mrs. Martin tried several times to engage the new director in small talk. Mr. Adams ignored the attempt and started to jot down notes in his notebook. Miss Barnes and Mr. Adams walked through the cottage discussing its condition. No attempt was made to draw Mrs. Martin into the the conversation.

After the inspection tour was completed, the house mother offered to make coffee. Mr. Adams declined, indicating that they had been delayed too long by the cottage parents at the last place they had inspected. However, Mr. Adams did say, "Before leaving, Mrs. Martin, there are several small items I would like to call to your attention. Will you please see to it that the shades are evenly spaced throughout the cottage. I noticed that the shades on the downstairs windows are lower than those on the upstairs windows." With that, he and Miss Barnes left.

On the way back to the administration building, Mr. Adams remarked to Miss Barnes, "On the whole, I think that Mrs. Martin is doing a fine job at her cottage. Please see to it that she receives a note of commendation."

What is going on in the case? Obviously, from Mrs. Martin's point of view things are not very satisfactory. Why not? The answer to this question is the basis for our discussion. Stated very simply, the problem is related to how different people perceive themselves and the situation in which they are placed. These perceptions are fundamental to the human relations skill of the administrator. He is making observations continually, just as was Mr. Adams in our case. We raise the question, What does the administrator perceive when he makes an observation? Does he, as did Mr. Adams, see that the shades are not even? Or does he perceive the importance of this visit to Mrs. Martin? We are concerned, in this discussion, with the problems of perception as they relate to the school administrator. In considering these problems, we will take a look at the theory of perception and some of the experiments that have been carried out recently in the field. Then we will relate this information to the behavior of the school administrator.

THE NATURE OF OBSERVATION

Let us try a few test observations. Take both of these little tests according to the directions and note down your response.

TEST A [1]

Look at each of the following triangles singly and repeat aloud or write down on paper what you see. Take as much time as you like—but do it *before* you read the explanation that follows.

Now that you have written down or repeated aloud each saying, did you notice that each triangle contained an extra word? The first has an extra THE, the second an extra A, and the third an extra THE. If you didn't notice this, don't feel badly. An extensive test has shown that only one out of forty persons can read these triangles correctly. Why is that so? What significance does it have for us?

[1] From Ralph A. Brooks, "The Triangle Game," *This Week Magazine* (May 23, 1954). Copyright, 1954, by the United Newspapers Magazine Corporation. Reprinted by permission of the publishers.

TEST B

Look at the figure below and then jot down on a piece of paper a description of what you see. Take all the time you wish and make your description as long or as short as you desire.

What did you write down? Most people would say, "Two lines, one longer than the other." Is that what you said? Well, let us make an assumption before going any further. Let us assume the two lines are telephone poles. What do you see now? Most people would, of course, respond that they see two telephone poles, one farther away than the other. Notice how the perception changes as you make a change in your assumption? Why should an assumption have anything to do with what you see? Again, what significance does this have for us as school administrators?

Let us think together about two experiences which most of us have had. Have you ever been to a restaurant and picked up your glass of water and have it come up so easily that it nearly showered you? You had expected the container to be made of glass. Instead, it was constructed of plastic and was very light. You had flexed your muscles for something much heavier, and up it came! Or have you had the experience of bending over to pick up a bar of metal? You reached down and heaved up. It came up so easily that you staggered backward. Somehow you had not expected the bar to be so light. Even had you known beforehand that it was made of aluminum, you would have expected a metal bar to be much heavier. What do these experiences mean?

One last description of a perceptual experience. This one is much more sophisticated and lengthy. During the past few years there has been a considerable flurry of interest in the study of perceptual problems. One of the first laboratories to study the problem from a relatively new point of view was the Hanover Institute at Dartmouth College. Under the direction of Adelbert Ames, several demonstrations of perceptual phenomena have been set up. The visitor to the laboratory proceeds through

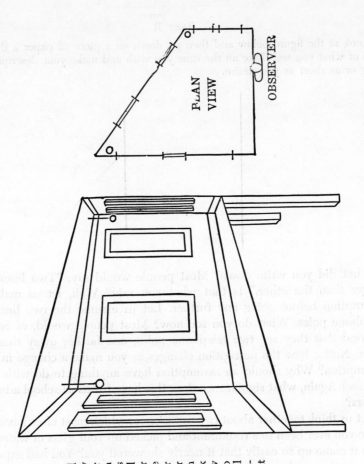

PLAN VIEW

OBSERVER

Fig. A. This is a drawing of the distorted room. It does not show the distortion fully because the back left corner does not appear to be far enough away from us. The reason for this is that there are so many things built into the room which violate the usual rules of perspective. For example, consider the two back windows. If they were the same size, the left one should look smaller than the right one, because it is farther away. It is actually larger, and when drawn larger, the left corner refuses to go back where it belongs. In order to realize how far away the back left corner is, we have to have the plan view, which is a horizontal cross section of the room. For the experiment, the observer is placed nearer the right wall than the left one.

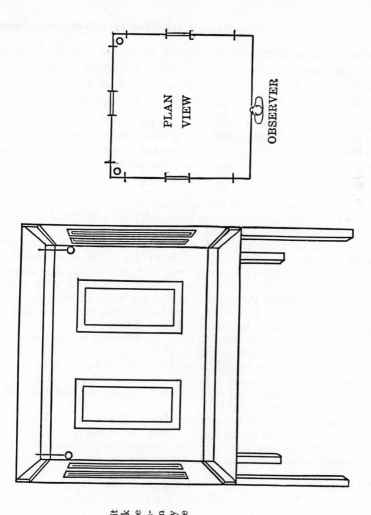

PLAN
VIEW

OBSERVER

Fig. B. This is the distorted room as it appears with the glasses. Note that the back left corner appears to be the same distance away as the back right one. The back windows appear to be the same size. In the plan view, note that while the observer is actually to the right of the center (see *Fig. A*) he seems to be in the center.

a veritable penny arcade of peepshows. Kelly has described one such exhibit, the famous "cockeyed room," which has received wide publicity. His description, which follows, is accompanied by two figures.[2] Study these pictures very carefully as you read the description.

The fact that perception is a directive for action is demonstrated in the laboratories of the Hanover Institute by what is called the distorted room. [*Fig. A*]. It is a box with one side open, so that we can look into it. The right side is small, the left side large, so that the floor, back, and ceiling have to slant away from the right side, to meet the left. The floor therefore slants down to the left, the ceiling up to the left, and the back away to the left. The right-hand corners are therefore much nearer than the left-hand corners.

A metal ball hangs near the ceiling in the left-hand corner, and a similar one hangs in the corresponding right-hand corner.

Now you put on a pair of glasses which shortens the left side, and you see the room as rectangular [*Fig. B*]. (The effect of the glasses is as follows: When you look at the room with either eye alone it appears rectilinear, because it is so built that the binocular clues are similar to those that you get from a rectilinear room. The effect of the glasses is to give you binocular clues that are similar to those that you get from a rectilinear room. These two sets of false clues, supplementing each other, increase your sense of surety that your false impression is a true one.) You are asked to touch the left-hand ball with a stick. You know the ball is far away, but you put the stick where it *appears* to be. This does not touch the ball, so you extend the stick farther and farther until you finally touch the ball. Now you are asked to touch the other ball quickly. You far overreach it and hit the back wall with the stick. Finally you withdraw the stick enough to touch the right-hand ball.

When you saw the room through the glasses, all square, you knew intellectually that the room was not that way. It was the present perception on which you acted. That was your present reality. Because the perception didn't fit the box, your action failed. But you could not act any other way.

We have just been through a series of perceptual experiences in which we have been "fooled." In each case, we acted on the basis of what we saw; but what we saw was not real. We will always act on the basis of our perceptions. What we see is to us real and will form the basis for action, for decisions, for policy-making. The foregoing illustrations demonstrate the importance and value of perception as a factor in administration.

ANALYSIS OF PERCEPTIONS

For a great many years, educational leaders have been trying to find some way of evaluating the effectiveness of teachers. They have been concerned with "merit rating" in one or another of its facets. One point that business and industrial leaders invariably bring up when discussing educational problems is the fact that teachers are not "rated" in the same way that employees in other fields are rated. Reluctance to use the merit rating

[2] Earl C. Kelley, *Education for What Is Real* (New York, Harper, 1947), pp. 38-41. Reprinted by permission.

plan in teacher evaluation does not stem from a lack of interest. The number of studies in the area of rating and evaluation is well over 1300, but the results are highly inconclusive.[3] If we look at the method of procedure in studies of teaching effectiveness, we can see why the results probably always will be inconclusive. After rating devices have been prepared and used, there must always be a validating procedure. These devices must be used on certain teachers, and the results must be compared with ratings made by a separate group of judges. What happens when different judges observe the same teacher? Is it not true that the teachers appear to be "good" to some, "poor" to others, and "mediocre" to still others? As in the following illustration, two administrators observing the same teacher see two entirely different people. As the two administrators observe the teachers, they are watching through the glass of their own experiences. The teacher appears to be "good" to one because her behavior coincides most nearly with what the administrator has known and has been successful with in the past. The same teacher will appear to be "bad" to the other because her teaching does not agree with this administrator's background of experience. As Berrien has stated: "What a person observes is the end result of what he has experienced in the past and what is pressing upon him at the moment of observation."[4]

What a person observes is not necessarily the "real" thing. All of us are so conditioned by our past experiences that we react to clues which are congruent with our past but which are not necessarily what we are looking at in the present. In summarizing the present trend in the literature of perception, Berrien makes the following observation:[5]

[3] A. S. Barr, *The Measurement of Teaching Ability* (Madison, Wis., Dembar Publications, 1945).

[4] F. K. Berrien, *Comments and Cases on Human Relations* (New York, Harper, 1951), p. 38.

[5] *Ibid.*, p. 39.

These reports, which are only a sample of scores, unequivocally support the conclusion that the individual's frame of reference—the network of previous experiences, expectations, beliefs, and attitudes, all related to the current event —is one determinant of what he will perceive and remember. Since these frames of reference cannot, even for identical twins, be identical, it follows that our observations and evaluations cannot be precisely alike from person to person. Each sees and judges the world through his own somewhat distorting spectacles.

The task, then, for those of us who want to improve our human relations in administration, is one of analysis of perceptions. We have established the fact that all people do not see the same event as it occurs, that all individuals see something different in experiences apparently common to all. We could cite innumerable supporting examples. It is not open to debate. We may conclude, therefore, that this perceptual difference is the fundamental cause of human relations problems. In attempting to find some solution to these problems, we must first examine briefly the theory of perception.

THEORY OF PERCEPTION

Once we have looked at some of the controlled experiments in the field of perception, it is necessary for us to draw some generalizations that we can use in our work as administrators. This is the real value of theory. Good theory is actually the most practical sort of thing we have, since it enables us to operate more effectively in a wide variety of situations.

The Transactional Approach

The dictionary definition of perception as "awareness of objects; consciousness," is of very little help to a person who wishes to use the concept of perception operationally. It certainly gives us little insight into the field of perception. We find it much more helpful to consider perception from the frame of reference of a recent study, which uses what is called the *transactional approach.*[6] In working toward a definition of perception, this study presents the major characteristics of perception, the central problem, and ways of studying the phenomena. According to Ittelson and Cantril, the three major characteristics of human perception are:

1. Perception can be studied only in terms of *transactions,* that is, concrete individuals dealing with concrete situations.
2. Perception comes into the transaction from the unique *personal behavioral center* of the perceiver.
3. Perception occurs as the perceiver creates his own psychological environment by identifying certain aspects of his own experience to an environment which he believes exists independent of his own experience. This is called *externalization.*

[6] William H. Ittelson and Hadley Cantril, *Perception* (New York, Random House, 1954).

Since the characteristic most difficult to understand is that of the *transaction,* it would be well to consider it for a moment. Ordinarily, the term *interaction* is used to describe what goes on between an individual and his environment. We say, "Man interacts with his environment and brings about a desired change." This assumes that man and his environment exist as independent entities and that when they interact, they do so without affecting their own identities. The concept of *transaction* uses the content of the interaction as the subject matter to be discussed.[7] Ittelson and Cantril state: [8]

Neither a perception nor an object-as-perceived exists independent of the total life situation of which both perception and object are a part. It is meaningless to speak of either as existing apart from the situation in which it is encountered. The word *transaction* is used to label such a situation. For the word transaction carries the double implications (1) that all parts of the situation enter into it as active participants, and (2) that they owe their very existence as encountered in the situation to this fact of active participation and do not appear as already existing entities merely interacting with each other without affecting their own identity.

The concept of the *personal behavior center* has as its meaning the fact that the person enters into a transaction from his own unique position. He is somewhat different from all others in the transaction. We say, then, that each person enters a transaction from his own unique personal behavior center. To the extent that his perception is common with others we have social activity. Later, we shall discuss some of the interesting ramifications of what is called social perception.

The concept of *externalization* is of recent historical origin. Possibly a look at its history would be the clearest way of explaining it. Early studies in perception were concerned with what the environment did to the individual. The Greeks started this chain of thought by formulating the concept that objects emitted small replicas of themselves which were received by the perceiver. The fact that different viewers received different replicas did not bother them to any great extent. Recently, there has been interest in what the organism does when it perceives. The concept of externalization describes but does not explain how it happens. It states that when we perceive anything, we consider it as external to ourselves. As Ittelson and Cantril say: "When we perceive, we externalize certain aspects of our experience and thereby create for ourselves our own world of things and people, of sights and sounds, of tastes and touches." [9]

The concept of transaction is basic to the concepts of the personal behavior center and externalization. It can be seen readily that each situation will be perceived differently by different individuals and that each

---

[7] A more complete discussion of this concept is to be found in John Dewey and Arthur F. Bentley, *Knowing and the Known* (Boston, Beacon Press, 1949).

[8] Ittelson and Cantril, *op. cit.,* p. 3.

[9] *Ibid.,* p. 5.

individual will assume to be real that which he perceives. He then acts accordingly. This has been neatly summarized as follows: [10]

> The three major characteristics of perception can be summarized by saying that perceiving is that part of the process of living by which each one of us, from his own particular point of view, creates for himself the world within which he has his life's experiences and through which he strives to gain his satisfaction.

Let us stop for a while and consider the meaning of what we have just said. How is this discussion of perception important to the administrator as he works with the school staff? Is there a practical application of this theoretical discussion? We can see some of the meaning of this approach in the case of Valley Elementary School.[11] The portion of the case that is relevant to our discussion follows:

> Mr. Arthur Metcalf, the newly hired principal of the Valley Elementary School, walked briskly up the steps of the red brick school building. It was the last week in August and he had a lot of plans to make preparatory to the opening of school the following week. Hurriedly he entered the building and proceeded upstairs to his office, stopping only long enough to glance at a few new items of playground equipment which had arrived the day before.
>
> Once in his office, he immediately began to write several paragraphs which he added to the bulletin he was preparing for distribution on the first day of school. He was so involved in his work that he failed to hear the footsteps of the man who was approaching the office.
>
> "This room looks familiar," said the man as he entered the office. "I'm Charles Burns, the former principal. I was passing through town and thought I would stop and pick up a few of my books which I forgot when I left the school last spring."
>
> "How do you do, Mr. Burns," said the startled Mr. Metcalf. "I believe you'll find your books right here in this bookcase. This is the opportunity for which I have been waiting. Maybe you can tell me a few things about the school that might help me to adjust a little faster to the new situation. Perhaps it would be a good idea for you to give me a little character sketch of the people I'll be working with this year."
>
> "I'll be glad to give you some information, Mr. Metcalf, but I'm afraid my opinion will be slightly prejudiced. You see, I was the principal here in name only. Because of the aggressiveness of the staff, I had little actual authority. Each teacher in this school is a self-appointed administrator, running his part of the school as he deems necessary. Due to these circumstances, unified school policy and co-operation are nonexistent.
>
> "You will receive very little help from the superintendents. Mr. Bartlett, the county superintendent, visits the school perhaps twice a year—if he happens to be around this way. These visits usually last about an hour. Mr. Rose, the district superintendent who is also the principal of the local consolidated high school, has time only to mail out the schedules for the current school term. The total responsibility of administration is in your hands."

[10] *Ibid.*

[11] Prepared in the Department of Education, Ohio University, by H. E. Benz and Kenneth L. Cleland. Copyright, 1955, by the Ohio University Press. Reprinted by permission of the publishers. For the full text, see below, pp. 373-376.

"That gives me a good picture of that side of the situation. The problem of the aggressiveness of the teachers, which you mentioned, interests me. Although I have been away for four years, I've lived in this community quite a long time and have a speaking acquaintance with all of the teachers, but I know none of them intimately. Some information about their professional abilities would be a great help," suggested Mr. Metcalf.

"The first-grade teacher is Miss Adams," continued Mr. Burns. "Her principal professional asset is her twenty-four years of experience. She is very independent. You will find out sooner or later that she seldom arrives at school on time.

"Mrs. Blair of the second grade has had seven years of experience, has twenty-one college credits and a temporary certificate. She is the mother of two grown sons. She taught here from 1928 to 1930, then quit to get married. Five years ago her husband died and she resumed teaching.

"The third- and fourth-grade teacher is Mrs. Noland. She has a Bachelor of Science degree and four years of experience. She is divorced and her out-of-school life has been criticized by the community.

"Mrs. Perry is the teacher of the fifth and sixth grades. She also has two grown sons who, naturally, are the center of her life and activities. She has had fourteen years of teaching experience. Her instructional methods leave little to the child's imagination, for she covers the textbooks thoroughly. She considers herself an expert disciplinarian. Her husband enjoys a high social position in the community, mainly because of his political activities. Mrs. Perry is more aggressive in assuming the position of a self-appointed principal than are the other teachers.

"There you are, Mr. Metcalf, but don't let me discourage you. Perhaps you will find an entirely changed staff. You've no doubt faced situations such as this before."

"No, I haven't," confessed Mr. Metcalf. "That is why I was anxious to get this information. My experience consists of four years in the army, including both domestic and foreign duty."

"That experience should serve you well on this job. I hope everything goes well, Mr. Metcalf. Good luck!" Mr. Burns took his books under his arms and departed, leaving Mr. Metcalf in deep thought about the problems of the coming year.

In an effort to gain encouragement and reassurance Mr. Metcalf contacted Mr. Rose on the telephone. The busy Mr. Rose had little to say. The only enlightenment from this superintendent was the suggestion that Mr. Metcalf immediately let all his teachers know who was to be "boss."

Discouraged, Mr. Metcalf turned from the telephone muttering to himself, "So this is the introduction to my new job for the coming year."

This case presents a problem which confronts every administrator who moves into a new position. He will receive information about the school staff, the pupils, the community, and the nonteaching staff. In fact, he is advised by his professors of educational administration to learn as much as possible about all of the aspects of his job, including the persons with whom he will come in contact. This is still good advice, providing the information received is interpreted properly. It is in the area of how to evaluate information and observations that the content of the subject of perception is valuable.

As Mr. Metcalf listened to Charles Burns he should have realized that Mr. Burns was relating the incidents of his tenure as principal in a *transactional* manner and from his personal behavior center. In other words, he was telling Mr. Metcalf not only what his experience had been but how he had influenced the other participants in the case to behave as they did. For instance, Mrs. Perry's behavior was at least partially influenced by the behavior of Mr. Burns, as was the behavior of Mr. Rose and the other teachers. Mr. Metcalf did not realize this. He was thinking in terms of an interaction, not a transaction. He thought that the teachers were entities who would interact with their principal without changing their identities. Instead, their identity was dependent, at least in part, on the principal and on others with whom they were participating.

As we read the case in its entirety, we see that Mr. Metcalf's perception of the Valley Elementary School was greatly influenced by Mr. Burns's comments. He believed that the teachers would react to anything he did in the same way they had to his predecessor's actions. The fact that they finally did do just this can be accounted for by observing that Metcalf expected them to, and they knew it.

A different approach to much the same problem is suggested by Purcell.[12] He presents a case in which a foreman had a man assigned to his gang who had been in trouble in another part of the plant. At the time of the transfer, the foreman was warned that the man was a troublemaker. The foreman's procedure was to tell his new employee that what had happened in the past was over, that a fresh start could be made. The foreman then observed the man closely, talked to the other members of the gang about the man, and listened when the man had something to say to him. Through this process, he was able to identify the man's problems and to help him.

Although the foreman would not be able to verbalize what he had done, we know that he was acting under the belief that the behavior of his new man in his old group was not entirely of his own making. He realized that the man behaved in a troublesome manner because of all of the factors in his environment—his home and family, his supervisors, and his fellow employees. The foreman realized that changes in these factors could affect the man's behavior. This type of analysis on the part of the foreman resulted in his gaining a very good worker who did a fine job.

The Validity of Perceptions

Moving back to our discussion of perceptual theory, let us consider the statement that "perceiving is that part of the process of living by which each one of us, from his own particular point of view, creates for himself

---

[12] Theodore V. Purcell, "Observing People," *Harvard Business Review*, Vol. 32, No. 2 (March-April, 1955), pp. 90-100.

the world within which he has his life's experiences and through which he strives to gain his satisfactions." This raises a very serious question in our minds. The question concerns the validity of the world of reality in which each of us gains satisfaction. If we accepted the statement as a definition of perception, we would experience great difficulty in the everyday matters of living. There needs to be some way of evaluating the perceptive experiences of individuals so that norms can be established. We need to be able to make judgments concerning the validity of the perceptions that people report.

A measure of validity that can be applied to perceptions is the degree to which they correspond to the environment as described by numerous individuals. Another way of saying this would be to refer to the concept of norms that are accepted by society.

Three simple examples of perceptive experience that does not correspond to the "real" environment may help to clarify this point. First, there is the case of those individuals who claim to have seen flying saucers which later are identified as balloons sent up by the weather bureau. The second is the case of the color-blind person to whom all clothing looks gray, even though most people are able to distinguish the individual color of each item. Finally, there is the person who hallucinates an object that is nonexistent to everyone else. Notice that in each of these cases we have a *lack of correspondence* between the environment and the perception. Each case represents a departure from the socially acceptable norm that constitutes the "real" description of the environment.

An example of this lack of correspondence in the school situation is contained in the following description of the way in which a teacher may perceive a supervisory visit.[13]

We have all seen school teachers who enjoy teaching when the atmosphere of the classroom is warm, friendly, and spontaneous. However, when these same teachers learn that the school superintendent is going to visit the class (or even more, is already in their classroom), they seem to tighten up; they want the children to be orderly, obedient, and well mannered.

In short, when the superintendent is visiting, everyone must be on his best behavior. This is not surprising, since the superintendent's approval means a great deal to the teacher concerned. For this reason, his presence in the room makes all the difference in the world as to how she behaves, even though her underlying motivation to be a good teacher has not changed in the least. What has changed is the teacher's perception of this external situation. It is no longer a teaching situation with thirty children; it is now a demonstration of her proficiency for the superintendent. Regardless of whether or not the superintendent would disapprove of a spontaneous atmosphere in the classroom, the position he holds over her makes her think not only of teaching but also of her position and her livelihood. Perceiving this possible threat to her position, she may tighten up and feel anxious.

[13] *Fostering Mental Health in Our Schools: Yearbook of the Association for Supervision and Curriculum Development* (Washington, D. C., National Education Association, 1950), pp. 172-173.

We note that this excerpt points out what we have been saying about the validity of perception. In the same school system the teachers have many different concepts of what will satisfy the superintendent. We see that teachers who would ordinarily teach in one way feel that they must teach another way in order to receive the approval of the superintendent. It is obvious that all of the teachers have not made perceptions which correspond to the actual situation. Very probably the most anxious of the teachers are those who are most uncertain of the validity of the way in which they have diagnosed the purposes of the superintendent. Anxiety may also be caused by experiences which the teacher has had with this or other superintendents in the past. She may have been severely reprimanded or highly commended. If her experience with supervisory visitors has been very unpleasant, she has little control over her anxiety and its resulting physical effects. These past experiences give her present experience a particular significance.

The illustrations given above indicate ways in which the correspondence between perceptions and reality occasionally break down. This does not mean that the framework in which we are formulating our concept of perception is wrong. It means that we must increase the amount of correspondence. The superintendent who visits a classroom is responsible for helping the teacher to know what the purpose of his visit really is. Of course, in some cases, this may make her more anxious than ever, but at least she will have a valid reason for her behavior. No one in the system has a greater responsibility than does the superintendent for seeing to it that the faculty has a valid and realistic perception of the purposes and objectives of the school district.

With this discussion as a background we can use the definition of perception which Ittelson and Cantril have formulated: [14]

We have seen that perceiving refers to the process by which a particular person, from his particular behavioral center, attributes significances to his immediate environmental situation. And the significances which he attributes are those which he has discovered from past experiences have furthered his purposes. Under conditions in which this analysis of the significances of the immediate environmental situation provides a correct prediction as to the significances of this environmental situation, there can be said to be correspondence between what is in perceptual awareness and the environmental situation.

Perception and Purpose

We are concerned with the study of perceptions in order to improve the human relations skills of the administrator and to avoid certain of the frictions that are generated by inaccurate perceptual analysis. As our discussion of perception develops, it becomes increasingly obvious that a

[14] Ittelson and Cantril, *op. cit.*, p. 26.

major difficulty has not yet been mentioned. This difficulty has to do with the *purposes* of the participants in a situation, and our earlier description of the supervisory visit will serve again as an illustration. In that instance, the purpose of the teacher is to satisfy the superintendent, regardless of how she deviates from her usual classroom behavior. If the superintendent believes that he is observing the teacher teaching in her usual way, he has made an observation that does not correspond to the actual situation. The same problem confronts us when we observe a father playing base-ball with his little boy. Can we make a valid judgment as to his pitching ability when we observe him lobbing a ball toward the boy and notice that the boy hits the ball at will? Or can we judge the father's batting ability if he allows the boy to strike him out time after time? If we examine the purpose of the father in each of the above situations, we find that our perception alters radically.

The major problem in perceiving other people, then, can be said to be the degree to which the purposes that we attribute to them are actually the purposes that they have.

SOCIAL PERCEPTION

Although we have been discussing what could be called "personal per-ception," there is also a very interesting new field of study called *social perception*. Most discussions of social perception begin with a discussion of an experiment by Sherif.[15] In this classic experiment, Sherif had a group of observers report on their observation of the movement of a point of light. Each person entered a completely darkened room. A point of light was then introduced into the room, and, after a period of watch-ing, each person would make his report *in the presence of all the other observers*. It should be pointed out that they were actually observing what is called the autokinetic movement of a point of light; that is, the light did not actually move at all, it only appeared to move, and the apparent movement varied with each individual. There were bound to be disagreements among observers. However, a very dramatic sort of thing began to happen. As the experiment continued, the reports of the individuals began to coincide, and, ultimately, a group norm was estab-lished. In other words, the observers in each group began to perceive much the same thing when they went separately to observe the illusory movement of a point of light!

At the present time, psychologists are not absolutely certain of the significance of Sherif's experiment.[16] It is clear, however, that this experi-

[15] M. A. Sherif, "A Study of Some Social Factors in Perception," *Archives of Psy-chology*, No. 187 (1935).

[16] James J. Gibson, "Social Perception and the Psychology of Perceptual Learning," in *Group Relations at the Crossroads*, ed. M. A. Sherif and M. O. Wilson (New York, Harper, 1953), pp. 120-138.

ment does shed some light on establishing norms for perception. Even after Sherif's observers were removed from their groups and reported as isolates, their perceptions of the extent that the light appeared to move followed the previously established group norm. Later experiments have verified Sherif's conclusion that social modification of perception did occur.[17]

An experiment of interest to school administrators was performed to follow up some of the leads opened by Sherif. In this experiment, Bovard determined the influence of group structure on setting the social norms of perception.[18] He established two types of groups, one called leader-centered and the other group-centered. There were 504 individuals in twenty groups of each type. The procedure was for each person to estimate anonymously the length of a rectangle. The individual estimates and the average were reported to the groups and then the individuals were asked to re-estimate the rectangle's length. It was found that the members of the group-centered units tended to shift more toward the norm than did the leader-centered units. It was concluded, therefore, that group-centered structure has more power to alter the perceptions of individuals toward a common norm than has the leader-centered structure. A further conclusion adds to the interest of this experiment. It was found that the group-centered structure had a greater dispersion of estimates than the leader-centered structure before the averages were announced. In other words, there was a greater variety of estimates in the group-centered structure before the averages were announced and less of a variety after they were announced. This would mean, to administrators, that when the unit is group structured—that is, the member interaction is at a maximum—it is possible to get a greater range of opinions; yet when the common goal is announced, these groups have the tendency to close ranks. It offers some experimental evidence in favor of the democratic organization of which we have heard so much.

PERCEPTION APPLIED TO SCHOOL ADMINISTRATION

By examining a number of theoretical and experimental cases, we have noted several ways in which an understanding of perception will help an administrator solve the problems he faces. There are several other areas of the administrative job in which perceptive ability has been found to be a particularly important factor. This section will relate perception to these

[17] Rosalea A. Schonbar, "The Interaction of Observer-pairs in Judging Visual Extent and Movement," *Archives of Psychology*, No. 299 (1945).

[18] Everett W. Bovard, Jr., "Group Structure and Perception," in *Group Dynamics*, ed. Dorwin Cartwright and Alvin Zander (Evanston, Ill., Row, Peterson, 1953), pp. 177-189.

areas, discuss the perceptual differences that have been found among administrators, and touch briefly upon the way other people perceive the role of the administrator.

Staff Relations

"In order for an administrator to work effectively with his faculty, he must learn as much as possible about them." This seems to be a straight-forward statement. What does it mean in terms of perception? Learning could well be defined as an increased differentiation of the perceptive field.[19] In other words, learning proceeds as a person is able to see and act upon more and more of the material in a given situation. Reading provides the simplest example. A very young child observes a printed page and can make only the most generalized kind of perception, which does not take into account any of the particular aspects of the page. As he begins to learn to read, he can understand a word here and there. Finally, he can read the whole page and understand each particular part of it. He is able to differentiate the page.

In school administration, learning in staff relations proceeds as the staff is differentiated in the mind of the administrator. Although various stages in the development of understanding of the faculty are really points on a continuum, let us examine three stages for purposes of clarity:

1. At one end of the continuum is the lowest or poorest understanding of the faculty. At this stage the administrator considers all staff members to be the "same." He views the staff as an undifferentiated mass to be dealt with as a whole. He will demand that rules and regulations be rigidly adhered to, that all teachers perform in much the same way, and that no special or different treatment be accorded to any teacher. He may believe in the theory of indi-vidual differences for students, but not for teachers.

2. This stage is in the middle of the continuum. The administrator, in this stage, has differentiated teachers into certain types. He can identify "new" teachers or "old" teachers. He might have certain problem categories into which he can place certain teachers. At any rate, in this stage of "learning the staff," the administrator is beginning to differentiate, to break up the perceptual field into smaller pieces.

3. The highest point on the continuum of understanding the staff is arrived at when the administrator recognizes and acts upon the knowledge that the staff is composed of individuals, all of whom should be treated separately ac-cording to their peculiar needs. We would say that he has achieved a high degree of differentiation of the perceptual field.

We can conclude, therefore, that one aspect of successful staff relations will be achieved in direct proportion to the ability of the administrator to perceive his people as individuals.

[19] Carl R. Rogers, *Client-centered Therapy* (Boston, Houghton Mifflin, 1951), p. 142.

Listening

Listening as it involves perception is not a very difficult matter. In Chapter 4 we will go into considerable detail on the improvement of listening. It is enough to say here that the administrator can more readily understand what is being said to him if he observes carefully. There is usually something left unsaid, something implied but not stated, some hidden meaning in a person's talking. By careful observation, the administrator can interpret motions and facial expressions so that he gets the full intent of the statement.

Self-perception

Inasmuch as the administrator's role requires a considerable perception of other people, it is of interest to know how the administrator perceives himself. Hopper and Bills have recently reported on a statewide study of school administrators in Kentucky.[20] Through the use of a large number of psychological tests, they were able to categorize administrators in three groups based upon the attitudes an administrator holds toward himself and other people. Their findings revealed that administrators [21]

1. Accept their own worth and believe that other people are equally or more accepting of their worth.
2. Reject themselves but believe that other people are more accepting of themselves.
3. Accept themselves and believe that other people are less accepting of themselves.

Hopper and Bills state that the first group constitutes "the ideal type of administrator"; the second group is next most desirable; and the third, least desirable. This study provided some indication of how various administrators see themselves and introduced the theory that self-perception bears certain relations to other types of perceptions. This relationship was investigated, and it is very informative to administrators to consider at least three of the findings: accuracy of perception, scope of perception, and behavior.

Accuracy. It was found that all three types of administrators varied in their ability to make accurate perceptions. Designating the above group classifications as types *1*, *2*, and *3*, respectively, it was found that type *2* administrators were highly accurate, type *3* inaccurate, and type *1* in a position between the two. Administrators of type *2* and type *3* get into difficulty because of their deficient perceptual abilities. Those of type *2* have such a strong need to be accurate that they cannot be creative. They

[20] Robert L. Hopper and Robert E. Bills, "What's a Good Administrator Made Of?" *The School Executive,* Vol. 74, No. 7 (March, 1955), pp. 93-95.
[21] *Ibid.,* p. 94.

cannot go beyond the stimulus as they perceive it. Those of type 3 have such difficulty in making accurate perceptions that they are out of line with others. It may be that since they feel others do not accept them, they continually change their perceptual reports in an attempt to gain social approval.

Scope. In the first chapter we discussed the three-skill approach and noted that there was a hierarchy of skills ranging from technical to human to conceptual. Hopper and Bills report a relationship between their types of administrators and the ability to perceive at the conceptual level. Type 2 administrators feel more secure when they are concentrating on concrete details. Type 3 administrators are unable to see important details, and although they concentrate on organizing events, their efforts may be meaningless because of their difficulty in perceiving important details. Type 1 administrators are able to perceive important details and to organize them into meaningful wholes. This group is the only one able to conceptualize. As Hopper and Bills summarize: "It can be said that a type 2 person cannot see the forest because of the trees, a type 3 cannot see the trees because of the forest, but a type 1 can see both the trees and the forest." [22]

Behavior. The Hopper and Bills study also relates perceptual ability to the behavior of the administrators who were studied. They found that the type 1 administrator responded to the situation as he perceived it and, as a result, had the best relations with people. Type 2 behaved in terms of his perceptions but modified them according to his need to enhance himself. Type 3 was unable to perceive accurately and behaved in terms of his own preconceptions and predilections.

Perception, Personality, and Selectivity

It has generally been accepted for some time that perception and personality are related. The above study which involved a large number of school administrators, offered more specific evidence to this conclusion. Closely associated with the interrelationship between perception and personality is the problem of *selectivity*. This problem is one in which different people select from the environment certain things to perceive and certain other things to ignore. We will examine the following case in order to set the stage for our discussion of selectivity.

Dave Blair was a young college professor at work on his doctoral project. As part of the process of collecting data, he interviewed a large number of school superintendents to determine what they did as they went about their work. He was interested in administrative practices of school superintendents. He was visiting Amos Jones, a superintendent of a small city who had held his position for thirty-five years. As Dave walked into the superintendent's office, Mr. Jones

---

[22] *Ibid.*

was very busy correcting arithmetic papers. He explained that he did this each month, receiving sets of papers from various grade levels. "Best supervision in the world," he told Dave.

Dave had an interview form, and the two men started to talk about what Mr. Jones did. "How about public relations? What do you do in this area?" was the question. Mr. Jones replied, "Nothing. No problems there. The public doesn't need to know what goes on in the schools. Just makes for trouble if they do."

As they talked along they came to the question, how do you co-ordinate the work of the elementary and secondary schools? "Well," replied Mr. Jones, "I handle the elementary grades, and the high school principal has charge of the secondary grades. Co-ordinate—why what is there to co-ordinate? I don't see any problem there, young man!"

Mr. Jones was telling Dave Blair what he perceived as he looked at the school system in operation. As Mr. Jones looked at the schools, there was much that he did not see. As Kelley has said, "We select what we choose to see." [23] Mr. Jones had selected certain aspects of the system *to see* and certain others that he did not see. We might think of Mr. Jones as wearing a set of spectacles which screened out certain things and let others through. It has long been recognized by psychologists that we all do this to a certain extent,[24] but as administrators, our primary concern is *why* people see some things and not others. It may be that Mr. Jones, for instance, did perceive a need for co-ordination between the elementary and secondary grades, yet was so uncertain as to how to accomplish it that he refused to acknowledge his perception. Murphy stated this line of reasoning very well when he said, "For the process of social perception in general, few things are so important as the difference between what we do not perceive and what we do not acknowledge we perceive." [25] Kelley suggests that the answer to this rests in the *purposes* of individuals. If a person perceives a need, but the need runs counter to his purposes, then he will not acknowledge the need. This seems to make a great deal of sense.

Another problem in the selection of what we perceive is that case in which the person actually *does not* see what is obvious to all others. Mr. Jones and the problem of public relations, for instance. Many people in his city attested to the need for better public relations, yet Mr. Jones apparently did not *see* it. Why does this happen? Murphy summarizes the data on this subject as follows: [26]

There is a rather bewildering mass of evidence, both clinical and experimental, relating to the ability to shut out of clear awareness those stimuli which threaten us; some of these studies seem to indicate that, as vague awareness

[23] Kelley, *op. cit.*, p. 45.

[24] Gardner Murphy, "Knowns and Unknowns in the Dynamics of Social Perception," in *Group Relations at the Crossroads,* ed. M. A. Sherif and M. O. Wilson (New York, Harper, 1953), p. 140.

[25] *Ibid.*, p. 149.

[26] *Ibid.*, p. 148.

of a situation tends to become defined, we can arrest the process, so that sharp and explicit awareness does not follow; and perhaps that, after reaching this critical point and effecting this rejection, we actually demolish (repress?) what has begun to take shape.

So we see that the administrator who gets an inkling of a situation which threatens his security *may* act to demolish the perception and so not see it at all. If the administrator does not feel threatened, he accepts the situation, perceives it sharply and clearly, and acts on his perception. This is the type *1* administrator of whom Hopper and Bills talk. These administrators have the personality structure which allows them to "accept their own worth and believe that other people are equally or more accepting of their worth." The administrator with a strong sense of inner security will perceive clearly and accurately and will act on the basis of his perceptions. This is of basic importance in our discussion of the administrator and perception. It highlights the need for careful selection of individuals who have this attribute and for a training program in the colleges and universities that will develop this inner security. We have talked for a long time in education about the need for security. We must have administrators who, by virtue of their own inner security, will perceive their problems clearly and accurately and will have the courage and ability to solve those problems.

Administration Perceived by Others

How do various people in the school system perceive the job of the school administrator? We do not, as of now, have definitive studies to answer this question. There is some evidence to indicate that people perceive the job of the administrator in different ways. They have different role expectations of the administrator, and as he acts to satisfy one group he antagonizes another.

We know some of the conflicts in roles as perceived by different people. Let us list some and see what they are.

The school board expects the administrator to keep costs down.

The teachers expect the administrator to lead the way to higher salaries.

The school board looks to the administrator for sound business management as his first responsibility.[27]

The teachers expect the administrator to improve staff relations and welfare as his first responsibility.

What we are saying is that there is a difference in the way in which the job of the administrator is perceived by different people in the commu-

[27] *School Boards in Action: Twenty-Fourth Yearbook* (Washington, D. C., American Association of School Administrators, 1946), pp. 49-51.

nity. Examples with pupils and parents would further bear this out. It is not enough to know how the administrator perceives his role. We need a series of studies to show how various individuals and groups perceive the administrator.

Decreasing Variability in Judgment

The findings of experimenters in perception have implications for at least two major functions of administration. We noted that Sherif, Bovard, and Schonbar all found that the judgments of individual observers tended to have less variability, tended to become more nearly the same as these observers reported to their groups. Bovard found that group-centered units agreed more than leader-centered units. These findings have significance for both the evaluation of teaching efficiency and the development of faculty cohesiveness.

Teaching efficiency has long been a controversial topic in American education. On the one hand, there is a cultural imperative operating in all areas of American life which tends to reward the most successful, and, on the other hand, there is the reality that educational administrators have not been able to distinguish, reliably and consistently, the good from the poor teacher. The findings of research in perception would indicate that the judgments of administrators and supervisors concerning teacher efficiency could be made to come much closer together.

Agreement could be approximated if administrators, supervisors, and teachers in a given school system could have a series of common experiences centered about examples of teacher efficiency—demonstration lessons, films, role-playing scenes—and then have each report to the group what he observed. This could be followed by discussion of all involved. Experimental evidence would indicate that the administrators, supervisors, and teachers would be closer to agreement following these experiences.

Faculty cohesiveness could be attained in much the same manner as above. In order to have a group of teachers agree they must have common experiences and the opportunity to exchange their judgments on these experiences. As they exchange opinions, the variability will decrease and the group will close ranks. If the faculty is group-centered, it will close ranks more quickly and more completely than if it is leader-centered.

SUMMARY

We have summarized in this chapter some of the observations, experiments, theories, and applications of both personal and social perception. We started by considering some of the observations and were able to conclude that what a person observes is the end result of what he has experienced in the past and what is pressing on him at the moment of observation. People view and judge the world through their own somewhat distorting glasses.

The three major characteristics of perception are the transaction, the personal behavior center, and externalization. We arrived at a definition (p. 60) which synthesized these characteristics and helped us to explain the observations we had made concerning perception. The question of purpose was introduced as a major problem in observing people.

We considered some of the findings in the area of social perception, beginning with Sherif's study. We noted that what people perceive conforms to the social norm, once that norm is known, and that perception is also influenced by personality, group structure, and purpose.

Perception and the findings in perception were related to various aspects of school administration. It was noted that how one perceives himself has a remarkable bearing on how one perceives the situation in which he is placed and how one behaves toward others. The scope of an individual's perceptions is revealed in the kind of plans that he makes. The ability to perceive clearly and accurately is also revealed in the understanding an administrator has of his staff and the ability he has to listen. The findings of personal and social perception were focused on the problem of how people select what they perceive. Those who feel threatened by a situation demolish or repress the perception. Those who perceive situations which run counter to their purposes may choose not to acknowledge the perception. The variability in judgment of teacher efficiency can be decreased if those involved—administrators, supervisors, and teachers—have common perceptions and set group norms. In a similar manner, faculty cohesiveness can be developed.

Much needs to be known about perception and its relation to school administration; however, we can say that some helpful leads have already been uncovered which point the way to further investigation.

EXERCISES

1. Write a description of a situation in which two or more people had widely differing perceptions of what had occurred.

2. Ask several people in your neighborhood what they think of some aspect of the school, i.e., the budget, athletic teams, band teachers, or administrators. Try to account for the different opinions expressed. Relate your findings to the points discussed in this chapter.

3. If you are an administrator, try this exercise. Write a description of the "best" teacher, the "worst" teacher, and the "average" teacher on the faculty of your school. When you finish, ask yourself the following questions.
   a. Did you note the good qualities of your worst teacher?
   b. Did you note the poor qualities of your best teacher?
   c. Did you write more about the "worst" teacher than you did about the "best" teacher?
   d. Did you write least of all about the "average" teacher? Is he average because you know so little about him?

4. What are the three major characteristics of perception? Illustrate them in a school setting.

5. In the case concerning the superintendent visiting a teacher in her classroom, how could the superintendent have allayed the anxieties of the teacher? Be specific.

6. The major problem in perceiving others is determining the purpose of the individual being observed. Give some ways in which you can determine an individual's purpose.

7. As an administrator, do you have some illustrations of the tendency for the individual perceptions of group members to follow a group norm, once the norm has been announced?

8. What are the areas of school life in which you, as an administrator, feel most insecure? List these and ask some teachers to list problems which they see in these areas. Did you know these problems existed? Had you seen them and refused to acknowledge them?

9. Where do you stand on the continuum of knowing your staff? Do you know your staff as individuals or as a group?

10. Ask the chairman of your board of education to list those five responsibilities which he feels are your most important. You list the five you feel to be most important. How do the lists compare?

SELECTED BIBLIOGRAPHY

BERRIEN, F. K., *Comments and Cases on Human Relations* (New York, Harper, 1951), ch. 3.

BILLS, Robert E., "Traits and Abilities Needed for Successful School Leadership," in *Interdisciplinary Research in Educational Administration,* Bulletin of the Bureau of School Service, College of Education, University of Kentucky, Vol. 26, No. 2 (December, 1953).

CARTWRIGHT, Dorwin, and ZANDER, Alvin, *Group Dynamics* (Evanston, Ill., Row, Peterson, 1953), ch. 14.

CORNELL, Francis G., "Socially Perceptive Administration," *Phi Delta Kappan,* Vol. 36, No. 6 (March, 1955), pp. 219-223.

HOPPER, Robert L., and BILLS, Robert E., "What's a Good Administrator Made Of?" *The School Executive,* Vol. 74, No. 7 (March, 1955), pp. 93-95.

ITTELSON, William H., and CANTRIL, Hadley, *Perception: A Transactional Approach* (New York, Random House, 1954).

KELLEY, Earl C., *Education for What Is Real* (New York, Harper, 1947).

PURCELL, Theodore V., "Observing People," *Harvard Business Review,* Vol. 32, No. 2 (March-April, 1955), pp. 90-100.

SHERIF, M. A., "A Study of Some Social Factors in Perception," *Archives of Psychology,* No. 187 (1935).

———, and WILSON, M. O., eds., *Group Relations at the Crossroads* (New York, Harper, 1953), chs. 5 and 6.

CHAPTER 4

Human Relations and Communication

THE VERBAL ATMOSPHERE OF ADMINISTRATION

Of all the things an administrator does during the course of a day, *talking* takes first rank. He talks to teachers, students, parents, patrons, board members, book salesmen, architects, and a host of other people. As we observe the administrator, we note him talking on the telephone, holding conferences, meeting teachers and students in the halls, greeting citizens, expressing ideas and attitudes to friends and associates. The atmosphere which surrounds a school administrator is *verbal*. It is not only a talking variety of verbal atmosphere. The school administrator must also write a great deal. He must compose, dictate, or write letters, bulletins, notes to parents, prefaces to the printed materials published by the school system, and many other kinds of verbal communication. The administrator leads through the use of words.

On the other hand, the administrator needs to have great skill in listening. Most of what he learns of his school system comes to him from the people who surround him. As they report at their daily conferences, as they discuss in committees, or as they talk together, the people in the system give the administrator information relative to both situations and the way they feel about these situations. This latter consideration, how the teller feels about the situation, may be more important than a recitation of the facts of the situation. The administrator needs to listen carefully and well in order to grasp these emotions. Roethlisberger sums up what we have been saying when he states: "It seems obvious to me ... that the higher the executive goes in an organization the more important it becomes for him, if he is to handle effectively one aspect of his job, to deal competently with his verbal environment." [1]

[1] Fritz Roethlisberger, "The Executive's Environment Is Verbal," in *Human Relations in Administration*, ed. Robert Dubin (New York, Prentice-Hall, 1951), p. 306.

Examples of Administrative Communications

Before we go any further, let us look at some examples of administrative communications in the public schools. All those cited here have been taken from bulletins, notices, handbooks, or other types of communicative documents. Each is an attempt on the part of the administrator to inform the members of the faculty of some rule or policy or regulation. These examples do not reflect the way in which the rule or policy was arrived at; they attempt merely to communicate the intent to the faculty. These examples will not be taken out of context, and no attempt will be made to evaluate them, although the student may evaluate them for himself when he has completed this chapter. The first example comes from a bulletin that is given to teachers at the beginning of the school year and is entitled "Miscellaneous Notes." There is no explanatory or introductory material.

Continue making salary claims as you did last year. The claim will be for a one-week period the first time and for two-week periods thereafter. The period of claim should always terminate on the Friday night of the week before the pay check is due.

Special teachers: Please arrive on time, leave on time, and clean up before you leave. Don't run away from meeting disciplinary problems while you are in charge of the class, and don't chase pupils away from your disciplinary control.

Building principals should get all the duplicate promotion lists left in their buildings before the first day of school. These lists will help the principals to know the sizes of the various grades, a fact that will be helpful in determining into which grades to place new pupils. Miss White is asked to compile a statement giving the number of boys, girls, and total pupils registered at the end of the second day of school. The rural teachers and grade principals should bring this report by grades. Names are not required on this report.

Check your census the second day. At the end of the day the people mentioned above should give to Miss White the *names* of all people who according to the census or common knowledge should be in school but were not. Try to make a statement concerning the reason for absence in every case. If the pupil's absence is illegal, the people mentioned above should get information to the parents that these children will be expected in school right away and that if they do not present themselves within a reasonable time penalties for such illegal absence will have to be imposed when they return.

The following is an excerpt from a handbook that was distributed to all teachers in "an attempt to clarify those regulations that every school must have in order to operate with minimum confusion." This section is reproduced exactly as it appeared in the handbook. Under the heading "Nonacademic Activities" we find:

Every teacher who has experienced a successful school program knows that there are many activities which are entirely non-academic, yet fully as important as routine planning and carrying out of the classroom sessions. IT IS UP TO EACH INDIVIDUAL STAFF MEMBER TO REALIZE THAT WHEN YOU DO NOT DEMAND PASSES FROM PUPILS (as an example), YOU ARE AUTOMATICALLY ADDING TO THE BURDENS OF ALL OTHER TEACHERS WHO SOON FIND IT A PROBLEM TO LOCATE PUPILS SINCE

SOME TEACHERS DO NOT DEMAND THE RECOGNIZED NECESSARY PASS. A teacher who demands that pupils live up to minimum regulations is not therefore, a crab so to speak. Rather, that teacher is helping pupils to realize that every community necessarily sets up a list of minimum regulations in order to protect the whole group from confusion and at the same time safeguard the rights and property of each one in the group.

It is clear, therefore, that each teacher must have a flexible type of authority which extends over ANY CHILD IN THE SCHOOL AT ANY TIME WHEN NO OTHER TEACHER IS PRESENT WHO SHOULD MORE RIGHTFULLY HANDLE A GIVEN SITUATION. THE TYPE OF AUTHORITY SHOULD BE DIRECTED TOWARDS GUIDANCE OF THE PUPIL AT ALL TIMES.

It is also clear, that all teachers are working for the same objectives and should, therefore, be willing to take on thos [*sic*] extra duties which will aid the whole program and which he or she is most capable of handling.

All teachers are RESPONSIBLE for maintaining ORDER AT ALL TIMES AND IN ALL PARTS OF THE BUILDING!

During the first few weeks of school teachers shall stand at the door of their class room to supervise the corridor while classes are passing. ALLOW NO DISORDER!

Finally, let us compare two sets of instructions to teachers concerning make-up work. The first is very brief:

INCOMPLETE WORK. All incomplete work due to illegal absence, tardiness, etc. should be completed. One teacher's failure to do this makes an additional burden on the teachers who do demand complete work.

The second is more specific:

MAKE-UP-WORK

a. No make-up work will be allowed except for absences caused by illness, death in the family, or an equally serious reason. The only exception will be for absences arranged in advance with the Principal.

b. The responsibility for all make-up work will rest on the pupil, not on the homeroom teacher or the subject teacher.

c. If the pupil has not made up his work or made the necessary arrangements within five days, no credit can be given for work missed.

d. Pupils whose absence warrant scheduling of make-up work from the Guidance Department will be referred there. Such pupil will have his regular Guidance Department schedule to present to the teacher.

e. The entire responsibility for making up the school work missed during legitimate absences and the procedure as outlined above rests with the pupils.

f. At the end of a marking period no incomplete marks are to be handed in on teachers' grade cards. Grades subject to change later are to be in pencil.

g. If a pupil makes up work in accordance with the above rules after the close of a marking period, corrections will be made on the teachers' grade card and on the office record card.

Some of the foregoing samples of administrative communications are good and some are not so good; but as we consider them we realize how constantly we are involved in trying to understand what people are saying to others. It must seem strange to many that such handbooks, notices, and the like occasionally contain misspellings and typographical and grammatical errors. Even though we recognize these mistakes and make every effort to correct them, we often find that the meaning of the written words remains obscure. Communication, though commonplace, is not simple. In fact, it is so difficult that Roethlisberger has said: "In thinking about the many barriers to personal communication, particularly those that are due to differences of background, experience, and motivation, it seems to me extraordinary that any two persons can ever understand each other." [2] This statement pinpoints the principal reasons for the inherent difficulties of communication among people. With these factors of background, experience, and motivation bearing on the problem, we can see the need for an approach that will synthesize what is known in these areas and focus this knowledge on administrative communication.

We raise the question at this point: What are the criteria for evaluating communications? Where can the administrator get some help in improving his communications? One recent movement has given us a great deal of knowledge and a tremendous number of insights into the problems of communications. This movement is called *general semantics*.

GENERAL SEMANTICS

Historical Background

Perhaps the best way of beginning our discussion of general semantics is to approach the topic historically. Although very probably there have always been people who are concerned with the problems of semantics, the movement known as general semantics is one of relatively recent origin. Those premises, postulates, and formulations that are unique to this movement have been traced to Horace Bushnell and a book which he published in 1849 called *God in Christ*.[3] Although many of the now recognized bases were discussed at that time, it was not until some seventy years later that the organized movement really got underway. The founder of the movement was Alfred Korzybski, a man who was trained as an engineer—a fact which is quite relevant to some of the questions that he raised which became the basis for general semantics.[4]

[2] Carl R. Rogers and F. J. Roethlisberger, "Barriers and Gateways to Communication," *Harvard Business Review*, Vol. 30, No. 4 (July-August, 1952), p. 50.

[3] Wayne C. Minick, "Horace Bushnell: Precursor of General Semantics," *Etc.: A Review of General Semantics*, Vol. 5, No. 4 (1948), pp. 246-251.

[4] Korzybski's main work, which encompasses the systematic approach to general semantics, is called, *Science and Sanity: An Introduction to Non-Aristotelian Systems and General Semantics* (Lakewood, Conn., Institute of General Semantics, 1948).

There have been many descriptions of how Korzybski became interested in the problems of communication. Lee, perhaps, has done the best job of recounting this to date: [5]

The question that Korzybski then posed was this: If both the physical structures and the social institutions are products of human nervous systems, what does an engineer do when he builds a bridge that the social scientists do not as invariably do when they go to work? He put the answer in terms of the most easily observed activities of each—their talking. The engineer talks to himself (or calculates) in varied languages (words or figures) which are appropriate or similar in structure to the facts and then makes what he has to say fit. His major effort is to make his talk, formulas, equations, etc., adequate to represent the facts. And when that is achieved, the bridges don't break down. But what of our everyday language habits in our personal affairs, in matters of community and national importance? Do we follow the efficient patterns of the engineers? Korzybski's investigations led him to a negative answer. In dealing with direct experience in the business of daily living, men were too frequently speaking in ways that did not fit the situations they were speaking about. If reliability was not consistently found, it was because the utterances too often did not fit the facts.

Some may question the validity of making an analogy between the physical and social sciences, yet one point does stand out clearly and distinctly: the language of the physical scientist is precise; it is clear in its intent and meaning, and it is reliable. Can we say the same for the language of education? In particular, can we say it of school administration? These questions are rhetorical in nature. Since our environment as administrators is verbal, we should exert every effort to improve our communications. We may never reach the precision of the physical scientist, but we can do much to improve our present habits of communication. The administrator's use of language takes place in a locale so different from that of the physical scientist's that the problem becomes a much more difficult one. In fact, it is well documented that physical scientists themselves are notoriously nonscientific outside of the laboratory.[6] When these scientists try to verbalize their human relations, they, too, do a very poor job of it. This would seem to indicate that there is more to our problem than automatically transferring scientific language to everyday situations. There must be some other use of language which we can apply to relations between people.[7]

[5] Irving J. Lee, *Language Habits in Human Affairs* (New York, Harper, 1941), p. 8.

[6] *Science Education in American Schools: Forty-Sixth Yearbook of the National Society for the Study of Education* (Chicago, University of Chicago Press, 1947), Pt. 1, ch. 2.

[7] For an account of the social scientist's attempts to use mathematics in his work see, Abraham Kaplan, "Sociology Learns the Language of Mathematics," *Commentary* (September, 1950), pp. 274-284.

Definition of General Semantics

With this problem in mind, we should ask the question: On what basis does general semantics propose to aid the situation? Johnson has posed the basis of general semantics as follows: [8]

General semantics may be regarded as a systematic attempt to formulate the general method of science in such a way that it might be applied not only in a few restricted areas of human experience, but *generally* in daily life. It is concerned with science not as specialized laboratory techniques, not science as it depends upon highly refined precision apparatus, not science in the form of esoteric theories concerning the moons of Jupiter or the chemical composition of spot removers, not science as compilations of facts and statistics with regard to everything from wind velocities to petroleum—not science as technology—*but science as a general method, as a basic orientation, as a generalized way of solving problems*—and with due regard for the language of science; it is science in such a sense with which general semantics is concerned.

General semantics, then, is an attempt to deal with human problems through the use of the methods of science. Through the application of scientific methods to human problems many of the language problems we now face will be remedied. Hayakawa was talking of science in much the same manner when he stated that "Science is a social and linguistic product, the result of co-operative endeavor made possible by observations accurately made and by communications accurately given and understood." [9]

General semantics is concerned with pointing out errors of fact, opinion, and logic in communications, that is, with improving verbalizations. It is, however, much more concerned with what is back of a person's verbalizations, that is, his pattern of reaction. The founders of general semantics believed that the metaphysics of man, his philosophies, his theories of knowledge end up in his nervous system. They further believe that these are reflected in the language which they use. Korzybski noted that in the area of the special sciences men have been able to escape the difficulties of their language.[10] This is true because these scientists can communicate only through the use of words which have but one meaning. It is also possible to communicate only through the use of these words, since the meaning has but one word to describe it. A person using a word without its proper meaning would not be understood. As each science has advanced, its language has become more and more mathematical and specialized. This has enabled the initiated to understand one another better.

---

[8] Wendell Johnson, *People in Quandaries* (New York, Harper, 1946), p. 33. Italics mine.

[9] S. I. Hayakawa, "Semantics, General Semantics," *Etc.: A Review of General Semantics*, Vol. 4, No. 3 (1947), p. 165.

[10] *Ibid.*

On the other hand, it has prevented the uninitiated from understanding at all. As an example, we can take the formula:

$$e = mc^2$$

This very famous formula has one precise meaning to the physicist but no meaning at all to the scientifically unsophisticated layman.

General Semantics and Administrative Communication

It is obvious, of course, that this problem of language is a real one for the school administrator. He must be able to communicate with others in the field of education; but he must also be able to communicate with lay people. Since so much depends on "getting through" to the lay citizens of the community, it might almost be said that this is of prime importance. It is not enough that we, as school administrators, follow the physical scientists in their conquest of communication, that is, that we invent our own language. We must solve our problem by refinements in our present language, by precision, and by mastering ourselves so that our emotions do not ruin our meanings.

Let us now look at some specific findings of general semantics and apply them to school administration.

WHAT ARE WORDS?

Just what is a word? We could start with the dictionary, which defines "word" as "That which is said; esp., a brief remark or expression. . . . An articulate sound or series of sounds which symbolizes and communicates an idea; the smallest unit of speech that has meaning when taken by itself." Although this is somewhat helpful, it does not really clarify the concept for us. A more helpful definition might be found in the concept which Korzybski originated. He perceived words as *maps of territories*. This concept indicates very clearly the symbolic nature of words. Words are not things but may represent things. Many times we confuse words with the things they represent and so add to the confusion of our discussions.

What do we mean when we say that we sometimes confuse words with what they mean? We are really trying to say that words have no meaning in and of themselves. They represent something, but they are *not* something. A little story which Hayakawa tells illustrates this point: [11]

a chimpanzee can be taught to drive a car, but there is one thing wrong with its driving: its reactions are such that if a red light shows when it is halfway across a street, it will stop in the middle of the crossing, while if a green light

[11] S. I. Hayakawa, *Language in Action* (New York, Harcourt, Brace, 1941), p. 26.

shows while another car is stalled in its path, it will go ahead regardless of consequences. In other words, so far as a chimpanzee is concerned, the red light can hardly be said to *stand for* stop; it *is* stop.

It has been observed that it is not possible, except in very rudimentary forms, for animals to understand that certain things *stand* for other things. In humans, this ability is present, although not fully developed. The story of the young child who was told to come directly home from school each day is an example. Each day, when school was dismissed, she would run home. One day it was raining very hard. She dashed out of school and ran all the way home. Her mother was waiting outside, but the child ran right past her. She had been told to come directly home! She had not understood that she should rush home—when conditions warranted. To her the words were the thing.

Symbol-Signal

The difference between the way the chimpanzee behaved and the way in which a mature driver would behave at the sight of a red signal light is the difference between a *signal reaction* and a *symbol reaction.* The first is the reaction of the chimpanzee's nervous system, which reacts completely and invariably whether or not the conditions warrant such a reaction. On the other hand, the nervous system of the mature driver would have a delayed reaction contingent upon the circumstances. The mature adult would consider the red signal light a *symbol.*

Words are the most advanced kinds of symbols. Without them we would be little better than animals. These symbols, words, all stand for something. This something is a territory. A word is a *map* of a territory. We know that some maps are precise and some are not. Some maps truly depict the territory that they represent. A road map which does not include all of the roads in an area is not a true map. The man who attempts to go on a trip and reach his destination by reference to this map may well lose his way. In the same manner, if he uses words whose territory he does not know, he will probably lose his way on his verbal journey. The words one uses should have the same relationship to reality as that which exists between a true map and its territory.

Words and What They Refer to

In the discussion of what words mean, the semanticists use a very interesting concept. They talk about the *referents* of words. Referents are actually the relationship between the map of a territory and the word. A referent can be defined as the term which is used to designate the object or situation in the real world to which the word or label refers. This concept is so important that Stuart Chase has said, "Indeed the goal of semantics might be stated as find the referent," and "When people can agree on the thing to which their words refer, minds meet, the communication line is cleared." [12] There can be several combinations of words and referents as we shall see. We know that there are some words which refer to several things and that there are some things that are called by several different words. We also have the interesting but very confusing situation in which we have words with no referents. Let us look at some of these combinations.[13]

One Referent—Several Words

As one moves about the country, one is struck by the use of many popular terms to describe the same thing. The words *soda, pop,* and *tonic* are all used in various parts of the country to designate a carbonated beverage. Here we have one referent with several words. In the field of education, we have several examples of this sort of thing. In fact, this is one of the sources of confusion within our ranks and a source of constant criticism from without. On the other hand, it should be recognized that the meanings of words constantly change and that the exact meaning of a word usually is found in the context of the sentence. Some of the common examples of the concept of one referent with two or more words are core, evaluation, curriculum, and foundation program.

The field of education is not alone in this kind of talking; the field of psychology furnishes us with the prize example. Allport reports that for the referent *personality* there are no less than fifty meanings.[14]

Here we have the case, then, of a territory (that is, core, personality, etc.), with several different maps.

One Word—Several Referents

In this instance, we have a word which refers to several real objects. An example is the word *deck.* This word, at different times and in different places, means a complete set of playing cards, the flooring of a ship, the flooring of a naval dormitory, the platform-like structure of an elevator, or the shelf from which paper is fed into certain types of printing presses.

In education we have a similar example of this type of word usage. We might use the word *book* to mean text, primer, or reader.

We see, then, that a single word may refer to several real objects. These real objects may differ substantially from each other. In order to communicate our thoughts when using this kind of language, it is necessary that

[12] Stuart Chase, "Tyranny of Words," *Harper's Magazine,* Vol. 175 (November, 1937), p. 563.

[13] For a further discussion of this topic, see F. K. Berrien, *Comments and Cases on Human Relations* (New York, Harper, 1951), pp. 23-26.

[14] Gordon Allport, *Personality* (New York, Holt, 1937), pp. 24-48.

the *context* of the statement make clear what is in the mind of the speaker or writer.

Words Without Referents

This is one of the most interesting uses of words. On the one hand, we might say that the ability of man to use words without referents is an example of the great intellectual development which has evolved over the centuries. On the other hand, it serves to point out that we have not really advanced very far after all. A few examples are necessary to point this up.

Our nuclear physicists have made rapid strides in their conquest of the atom through the use of words without referents. In attempting to explain why certain things happen within the nucleus of the atom, they found it necessary to invent certain particles such as the meson and the neutrino. There was no proof that these existed, but, by hypothesizing their presence, the physicist was able to explain the observations which he had made. These "inventions" have been so successful that the inventors are considered to be our top physicists. Consider some rather early scientific inventions of the same nature. In the search for an explanation of the nature of heat it was found convenient to invent the term *caloric*. It was thought that when a colorless, odorless, weightless, invisible fluid (caloric) was present, a room, for example, would be warm. If the caloric was absent, then the room would be cold. Here we had a word with no referent which was accepted for a time. Today, however, no one believes there is such a thing, and its inventor is no longer even thought of as a scientist.

In our own field, we have had a constant battle over many words without referents. One very obvious term is *mental discipline*. This is a concept which has no basis in objective reality at all. Although its adherents are somewhat fewer than in past years, there are still many who find comfort in the concept. Inventions of this sort have an appeal based upon a primitive approach to thought. Korzybski called this kind of thinking *prescientific*. The degree to which the use of words without referents is scientific or prescientific would seem to be based upon the usefulness of the word in attaining an acceptable goal. Thus, one may be a quack or a genius, but in either case he will have much trouble in communicating.

In summarizing our discussion of words and what they refer to we find Berrien's statement very helpful: [15]

It becomes clear that words are first of all symbols only. The symbols represent objects and events with varying degrees of accuracy. Some words are, for nearly all practical purposes, unambiguous (chair, floor, electric light bulb), depending upon the circumstances surrounding the utterance. However, a given object or event may be referred to by two or more words . . . Secondly, a given word may have multiple referents . . . Finally still other words are pure inven-

[15] Berrien, *op. cit.*, pp. 25-26.

tions, like imaginary numbers in mathematics, that for one reason or another some people have found convenient, but for which no referent in direct experience exists.

Extensional Meanings

We have just been talking about words and their referents and have *concrete* known in some instances what the referents were. When we know this *clear* much, we are using the *extensional* meaning of the word. As was pointed out, there are certain words, such as chair and floor, the meaning of which is seldom ambiguous. Such words are generally clearly understood and give us little or no trouble in human relations. When an administrator uses words with extensional meanings, he will be understood.

Intensional Meanings

hidden meanings in words

There is another meaning of words, however, and that is the hidden meaning. The general semanticists say that words with hidden meanings have *intensional* meanings. These words with intensional meanings are the ones which cause a great deal of trouble in human relations. Very often the meaning of a word has a particular emotion attached to it. Practically everyone has a special word which he uses when expressing interest or disgust or merely passing comment. This emotional meaning is particular to him, and for him it has great importance. Another person might not understand him at all when he uses the term.

The problem for us is to be able to understand a person when he is using intensional referents. It is very important for the administrator to know what it is that a board member or a teacher is saying when he talks to him. We have gone far enough in our discussion so that it is clear that we do not always say what we mean or mean what we say. There are two profitable approaches to this problem. They are both based upon careful observation and interpretation and the ability to listen carefully and with alertness. The first approach is through *cultural* referents, that is, the particular meanings each culture has for the words it uses. And the second approach is through *personal* referents, that is, the particular meanings each person has for certain words. These meanings are quite separate from the cultural meanings. Let us look at cultural referents first.

Cultural Referents. There are many implications of the use of cultural referents on the part of individuals. We will start with some of the more obvious ones and then move to the more sophisticated. First of all, there are words which the members of one culture use to discuss members of another culture. Some of these words are *nigger, coon, gook, frog,* or *wop.* None of these is particularly complimentary; yet they are not all equally derogative. A southerner may use the term *nigger,* for instance, with far

less heat than a northerner. Likewise, a Korean veteran may use the term *gook* in a rather neutral manner and have it be interpreted by a statesider as an inflammatory word. Although it is possible that an individual using these cultural referents might be implying the full contemptuousness of the term, it is more likely that he is using these terms because they are in the language pattern of his particular culture.[16] In this way he gives meaning to words almost unconsciously. In this unconscious use of words, however, he is reflecting the way he feels about the topic. When he listens, he hears through this screen of cultural referents and so attaches emotions to the words as he receives them.

There is another important type of cultural referent, which consists of the hierarchial meanings that are applied to certain words by the culture as a whole. Below are some words which we in the American culture have accepted. These words are categorized according to whether the word "up-grades" the referent, neutralizes the referent, or "down-grades" the referent. The referent, in all cases, will be clear.

Up-grading	Neutral	Down-grading
Official	Officeholder	Bureaucrat
Statesman	Policy maker	Politician
Investigator	Detective	Flatfoot
Orator	Influential leader	Rabble-rouser

Or consider this set of words:

Up-grading	Neutral	Down-grading
Loyal	Obedient	Slavish
Tolerant	Nondiscriminating	Nigger-lover
Realistic	Suspicious	Cynical
Humanitarian	Idealistic	Do-gooder [17]

How, for example, would you talk about Eleanor Roosevelt if you were restricted to the last set of three words? We have heard each word applied to her by people of various cultural groups. Such connections as political affiliation, wealth, race, and status are important in identifying the intent of people as they communicate. Through a knowledge of cultural referents, the administrator can determine to a greater extent what the people with whom he is working are driving at. This is particularly applicable to the educator working in a large city which invariably has a multicultural population. He must be particularly alert to the use of words which will be heard differently by different groups. He must also listen for the intensional meanings of the different cultural groups which talk to him.

Personal Referents. Just as cultures have given certain meanings to certain words, so have individuals or small groups of individuals. These spe-

[16] Felix S. Cohen, "The Vocabulary of Prejudice," *Christian Friends* (January-February, 1954), p. 4.
[17] *Ibid.*, p. 5.

cial meanings are called personal referents. Probably all of us have an acquaintance who always reacts to a new proposal in a very pessimistic, negative manner. The words he uses, when falling on a stranger's ears, indicate that he will never go along with the proposal. We know, however, that this is his way of responding, that his reaction is not so drastic as it sounds, and that in the long run he ends up supporting the measure. Not knowing the personal referents of this person is a serious handicap to understanding him. In fact, if one did not know how he used his words, a very serious error could occur. This is one of the difficulties encountered by a new administrator. He does not know the intensional meanings, especially those that are personal, of his new staff and is apt to not be able to communicate with them in the early days of his tenure.

One of the clues to interpreting the intensional meaning of words is the context in which the word is used. Some words used in particular context take on a meaning quite different from the meaning a person intends in another context. Hunkins cites a case which illustrates this point quite clearly.[18]

I (Superintendent E) had been elected in April to a new position. Later in the spring I took a trip to the new place to look over the situation in preparation for taking over in the fall.

I found the one school building badly in need of cleaning and repair. That evening I met with the board. We spent some time getting better acquainted. A new high school teacher was employed in the course of the session. I presented some suggestions, which were favorably considered. Encouraged by this favorable attitude, I decided to bring up the matter of the condition of the building. But this suggestion did not go so well. The members were not quite discourteous on the point but they passed it off without action and without discussion. I was not yet well enough established in their graces to be insistent. I left the meeting with a sense of defeat about the matter. Besides that distress I had visions of working the following year in an unsightly building.

Superintendent E went on to say, however, that when he came to work in the late summer, the building had been painted inside and out, had been thoroughly cleaned, and was in first-class shape. The action of the board in their reception of Superintendent E's suggestion was based on the frame of reference of the board of education. They hired teachers in the spring but did not discuss building repairs. It was simply not the time to do it. They discussed building repairs in July. They always had, and as far as they were concerned, always would. If Superintendent E had realized the basis of operation which this board had, he (1) would not have taken the refusal to discuss his suggestion as a personal rebuff, or (2) would not have proposed the building renovation. This case illustrates quite clearly the point that the intensional meaning of words can often be made clear by knowledge of the background of the people mak-

[18] Ralph V. Hunkins, *Superintendent and the School Board* (Lincoln, University of Nebraska Press, 1949), pp. 38-39.

ing the statements. In the field of human relations, there must be this deep sensitivity to background contexts, for these are the stuff from which good human relations are made.

Projection and Ventriloquizing

We have now made some progress in our study of the hidden meanings in the words which people use. We have two other types of phenomenon of communication to investigate. On the other hand, perhaps we should reconsider the use of the word *phenomenon*. These two ways of talking are really much too common to be considered phenomena, although very few of us would admit to ever having indulged in either. Almost everyone would say that he had observed this type of behavior in someone else but definitely not in himself.

Projection. Let us consider the first type of talking. We might start with the statement of almost any young male on almost any spring day as he views almost any young lady, "Boy, what a beauty!" Or we might put it into academic discussion. The high school principal might ask the superintendent of schools, "How was the conference yesterday?" and the superintendent might reply, "It was wonderful. That speaker certainly knew what he was talking about!" What we actually have in both cases, is a projection of the individual into the situation being reported.

In the first case, the young man is not describing the young lady so much as he is describing himself and his mental and emotional set at the time. As for the superintendent, he is doing much the same thing. He is reflecting, not so much the virtues of the conference and the speaker as the way the whole thing struck him. It may be that the seats were comfortable, the room well aired, the food good, and the speaker agreed with his point of view! We have observed two cases of what the general semanticists call *projection.*

Many of us may be familiar with the term *projection* as it is used in the field of psychology. A common definition, in psychology, is that used by Shaffer: "A form of defense somewhat allied to rationalization is that called projection, in which persons perceive in others traits or motives in which they feel their own inferiority." [19]

This is quite different from the concept which we are discussing. To the general semanticist, projection takes place whenever an individual observes or evaluates or participates. This takes place practically all of the time. As Johnson has said, "Projection is as natural as breathing." [20] In school administration this is particularly true—and this is why we are stressing projection in this discussion. There are so few standards that are

[19] L. F. Shaffer, *The Psychology of Adjustment* (Boston, Houghton Mifflin, 1936), p. 170.
[20] Johnson, *op. cit.*, p. 60.

backed by substantial research upon which an administrator can lean that he must make innumerable decisions on the basis of "what suits him." If he were asked to justify his decision on the basis of substantive knowledge, he would be unable to do so. However, he generally states the decision in terms of the verb *to be*. He states, "This *is* so," "We *are* going to," and the like. This, in turn, gives rise to innumerable squabbles and fights because someone else—board member, citizen, principal—has a different point of view and states his opinion in terms of the verb *to be* also. Neither has any evidence, and so the fight is on. This kind of situation usually develops in conferences where decisions are being shaped.

With projection so common and yet so inviting of disaster, what should be done? The most important thing about projection is that we need to be *aware* of it. We need to because, as it has been said, "the universe, as we know it, is a joint product of the observer and the observed." [21] This means that as we describe any situation, state a fact, or react or evaluate, we are injecting ourselves into the words we use in verbalizing the experience. We are, of course, also injecting ourselves into the situation to the extent that it would not be the same situation if we were not present. What is needed, on the part of the administrator, is an awareness of the fact that we project ourselves and an awareness and use of the mechanism of *to-me-ness*. [22] In the above cases, the young man would have said, "Boy, what a beauty!" and added *to me;* the superintendent would have said, "It was wonderful," and added *to me.* In matters of administration, where human relations are of the essence, it is particularly important that one use this concept of to-me-ness at all times. In conferences, it is necessary to preface one's remarks with, "It seems to me," "As I understand it," and the like. More understanding would be brought about if participants would state, "As I heard you," or "I heard you say," or "It seems to me you said," instead of making declaratory statements about what you thought someone said. In this way, personalities are not constantly coming to the foreground, and the discussion stays in the context. [23]

Projection is a very natural mechanism of human behavior. An individual needs to be aware that this is taking place at all times and needs to compensate for it by the use of to-me-ness.

Ventriloquizing. The second kind of talking is very closely allied to projection. It involves one individual speaking through another, as in the following situation:

During lunch period the men teachers of High School A would eat in a small room designated as a men's faculty room. Since the lunch period was only

---

[21] *Ibid.*

[22] *Ibid.*, p. 61.

[23] A good description of this matter of projection and its relation to industrial management is to be found in Verne J. Kallejran, Irving R. Weschler, and Robert Tannenbaum, "Managers In Transition," *Harvard Business Review*, Vol. 33, No. 4 (July-August, 1955), pp. 55-64.

twenty minutes long and some men had a free period following lunch, they would remain after the period was over to smoke a cigarette and then go about their business. The principal objected to smoking, but did not quite dare tell the men on the faculty to stop. One day there appeared in the men's lunch room a small typed note reading, "The Board of Education has indicated that there is to be no smoking outside of the regular lunch period."

What is going on in this situation? Did the board of education really have a rule forbidding smoking? Well, they might have; but in this case it is safe to assume that they did not. Actually, the principal felt inadequate to handle the situation in any other way than to call upon an authority greater than himself. He could have done this by requesting the board to make a ruling, but he chose instead to pretend that he spoke with the voice of the board. This type of evasion in speech communication is called *ventriloquizing*.

Ventriloquizing can be unconscious and, in fact, very often is. One outstanding example is the case of a well-known and honored college professor. He has several assistants who work very closely with him on his research projects. They work so closely, in fact, that when they speak publicly of their work, one might close his eyes and think that he is listening to the professor. Unconsciously, they have adopted the ideas, speaking voice, and mannerisms of the man with whom they work.

On the other hand, ventriloquizing can be conscious, and, unfortunately, in the broad field of education, it is indulged in to a rather large degree. The principal in the foregoing case, for example, might have used the voice of the board quite consciously. Ventriloquizing also becomes a conscious tactic when the administrator uses the voice of authority rather than evidence to support his argument. For example, in advocating the use of a certain reporting system, he claims, "So-and-so (naming a recognized authority) says it should be done this way." If his statement is questioned, he repeats his statement—in a louder voice, of course. Clearly, the administrator needs to guard more against using this mechanism himself than against having others use it. He should, however, help his associates avoid picking up his habits of thought and speech, and he should make every effort to help each person be creative and productive in his own way.

LISTENING

When a group of teachers were asked what they would like to tell their administrator about improving staff relations, they came up with some very interesting observations. For one thing, they said, "Administrators should listen more than they do." [24] They might have added, "They should listen *better* than they do." As we have discussed the differences between

[24] Daniel E. Griffiths, "Staff Relations," *Nation's Schools,* Vol. 52, No. 2 (August, 1953), p. 41. and *The Education Digest,* Vol. 19, No. 3 (November, 1953), pp. 12-13.

intensional and extensional meanings of words, it must certainly have occurred to us that we need to improve the way in which we *listen*. Some administrators will have to learn first of all that they should listen. The "team" concept of school administration calls for a sharing of information and ideas. It calls for careful listening by all administrators before decisions are made. If the knowledge of highly professional teachers is to be made use of, then administrators must listen to what they have to say. To be a good listener is as important to a school administrator as is the ability to be a good speaker.

Blocks to Good Listening

What are the blocks to good listening? What is it that prevents an administrator from "hearing" what is said by the teacher? There are probably four major types of blocks to good listening.

1. Preoccupation.
2. Emotional blocks.
3. Stereotypes.
4. Two-valued thinking.

Preoccupation. The busy school administrator is usually concerned about several problems at one time. Although this in itself can be the cause of much inefficiency of operation, it is particularly harmful to good listening. If Superintendent A is puzzling over the type of desk he should purchase for the new elementary school which is being built, he cannot hear what Teacher A is saying about her need for science equipment.

Another type of preoccupation has been discovered through naval research in the field of listening. They report that men who most often failed to "get" the message were those who were overly tense and strained. They strained to get each word and syllable. They were preoccupied with *parts* rather than wholes.[25]

Preoccupation as a block to good listening has two aspects: (1) preoccupation with another subject and (2) preoccupation with words and syllables instead of the total meaning.

Emotional Blocks. Kelly indicated one of the major blocks to good listening when he said, "Most of us are incapable at times of looking at facts, because our thinking is obstructed by mere words."[26] Many of us have emotional blocks which become activated at the sound of certain words. Chase reports two studies which indicate that students, for example, clearly comprehend only about 25 per cent of what they hear.[27]

---

[25] Wendell Johnson, "Do You Know How to Listen?" *Etc.: A Review of General Semantics*, Vol. 7, No. 1 (1950), pp. 4-5.

[26] Fred C. Kelly, "Do Words Scare Us?" *Saturday Review of Literature*, Vol. 24 (November 22, 1941), p. 11.

[27] Stuart Chase, *Power of Words* (New York, Harcourt, Brace, 1953), p. 166.

Since students listen under somewhat ideal conditions, it is highly dubious
if adults in the educational world comprehend any more than 25 per cent.
Some people have "blind spots" in their listening which are related to
areas of little knowledge. For example, if statistics are quoted, many
people just stop listening. They have a generalized emotional response to
statistics, and they refuse to listen to them. Others have emotional blocks
built around single words or phrases. An acquaintance of ours rebels at
the phrase "social engineer." He says it literally makes him see red, and
he stops thinking and listening when he hears it.

Emotional blocks are also set up by personal prejudices. If the listener
hears words which symbolize his prejudice, then he fails to listen. Prejudice is a strong block to good listening.

Stereotypes. One of the most common blocks to good listening is the
tendency of the listener to invoke stereotypes. This is a type of signal
reaction in which the listener responds to the word as if it were the thing.
We might consider the case of the elementary school principal who is
talking with a student who has become involved in some difficulty concerning classroom conduct. Upon looking at the cumulative record, the
principal discovers the child is from a broken home. Many principals
would stereotype the child as "the broken-home type," and for all intents
and purposes that would close the discussion. Stereotypes have been built
up in our culture around all sorts of people and enterprises. These stereotypes block good listening and prevent people from understanding differences. Certainly, the "broken-home" stereotype is of this order, because
all children from broken homes are different with different problems, and
typing them prevents us from seeing their problems clearly.[28]

Two-valued Thinking. How many times, in the discussion of an administrative problem have we heard, "Let's listen to both sides of the question."
We then proceed to discuss the pros and cons. We see what is *for* and
what is *against*. This is a very neat way of eliminating most of the possible
solutions to the problem at hand!

Whenever we resort to this procedure, we have what the general
semanticist calls a two-valued orientation. We are saying that there are
only two sides to a question and thereby setting up one of the greatest
blocks to communications for both the speaker and the listener. Basically
this is so because of the way in which two-valued thinking hems in the
mind. The two-valued thinker cuts off many of the possible solutions
needed to solve his problems. He tends to be a rigid rather than a flexible
individual. When a two-valued thinker is supporting his conclusion, he
cannot accept criticism, he cannot safely change his position. If he moves
from his contention that "all school buildings must be made of brick," he

---

[28] A further discussion of this topic is contained in H. C. Lindgren, "General
Semantics: A Tool for the Counselor," *Occupation,* Vol. 27 (January, 1949), pp. 229-
233.

finds himself supporting the contention that "no school building should be made of brick." There is nothing between the two positions for him.

In administrative listening, this kind of thinking occurs a great deal. Administrators have to make many decisions. They are prone to put all discussions into a form that is conducive to easy decision-making, even though listening to only two sides of a question can often eliminate the possibility of arriving at a really good decision.

How to Improve Listening

With the blocks to good listening clearly in mind, let us take a look at some ways of improving our ability to listen. We have many clues from our description of the blocks to listening. Probably the most important point in good listening for the school administrator is that he must make it possible for his subordinates to talk to him. Many an administrator has raised the question, "Why is it that my teachers and principals don't speak up when we are in conference?" Very probably it is because his subordinates feel that they will not be listened to. The administrator needs to set up an atmosphere, call it permissive if you like, which allows and encourages others to talk. The first step to good listening is to have something to listen to.

Developing a Listening Atmosphere. There are several techniques which an administrator can use to help set the atmosphere for listening. When he finds himself in a listening situation, he should sit back and relax. He should hear a person out before he asks questions. Several studies and articles support this technique. Both Chase and Whyte emphasize its usefulness in emotion-ladened atmospheres.[29] Wynn cites the following case to illustrate the value of this approach in talking with irate parents: [30]

Into Superintendent Samuels' office stormed an irate citizen overflowing with invective because his son had been declared ineligible for the varsity football team. The upset father stalked about the office, pounding the furniture and exclaiming his criticism not only of athletic policy but of a whole variety of other topics. After a while he lowered his voice and sat down. Mr. Samuels calmly asked his opinion on several other matters and called for his suggestions as to how some of the problems he raised might be solved. The father began to assume a more rational tone and a constructive approach. Finally the father rose and prepared to leave. Mr. Samuels thanked him cordially for bringing these problems to his attention and promised to consider them thoroughly.

You will note that the superintendent _listened_ and did not talk until the parent had had his say. The parent felt a certain therapeutic value in

[29] Stuart Chase, "How to Argue," _Reader's Digest_ (November, 1952), and William Foote Whyte, "Listening and Disagreeing," _Pattern for Industrial Peace_ (New York, Harper, 1951), pp. 181-184. Both these works have been reprinted in Irving J. Lee, _Customs and Crises in Communication_ (New York, Harper, 1954), pp. 309-316.

[30] Richard Wynn, "The Application of Good Human Relations," _Nation's Schools_, Vol. 53, No. 1 (January, 1954), p. 53.

being able to speak his mind. When he finished, the superintendent raised some questions which enabled the parent to voice further criticism. The parent was then encouraged to give his opinions on other issues and gradually had become quite reasonable.

Listening for Clarity. In the actual process of listening there are several things a person can do to make more clear to himself what the speaker is trying to say. Johnson has suggested three questions which the listener should ask himself.[31] The first of these is very simple: "What does the speaker mean?" The emphasis here is on the word *mean*. Knowing, as we do, that words have different meanings to different people and that the meaning of the word rests with the person and not the word, the listener pays special attention to the context and the circumstances. In addition, the listener notes that whatever meaning he does get out of the message has a "to-me" tag attached to it. So the astute listener is always raising the question, "What do you mean?" He might direct the question either to himself as he listens or to the speaker at the opportune time.

The second question the listener raises is: "How do you know?" What is wanted here is evidence. The listener asks himself continually as he receives messages, "How does he know that?"

The third question is more difficult to answer than the others. It is: "What is the speaker leaving out?" As Johnson points out, the speaker may fail to mention three different kinds of matters. "He may leave out important factual details; he may fail to draw certain possible conclusions, while overstressing the ones he favors; and he may neglect to develop the implications of the conclusions he does draw." [32]

What the speaker does not say may be more important than what he does say. When the listener feels that much is being left unsaid, he may decide to do one of two things. His first procedure might be to raise questions which would tend to bring out the whole story. This might, however, tend to embarrass the speaker and cause him to cover up even more. The administrator's second procedure would be to secure the information elsewhere or to infer it from what has been said. In many situations, this may be the preferred alternative.

With the answers to these three questions, the listener can be much more confident about what he has heard.

Responding to Stereotypes. As was pointed out above, the stereotype is a serious block which must be overcome if the administrator is to achieve good communications. D'Arcangelo indicates that the person who is schooled in general semantics realizes that no two persons interpret similar events or environmental background in the same way. Likewise, the general semanticist realizes that all people are different, and this leads him to discard the use of stereotypes. The good listener does not allow

[31] Johnson, *loc. cit.*, pp. 3-9.
[32] *Ibid.*, p. 7.

words or phrases to create prejudicial stereotypes because of previous experiences. He also realizes that most individuals, when talking, tend to evaluate and react in terms of more or less emotionalized signal reactions or stereotypes.[33] The careful listener, therefore, not only guards against his own use of stereotypes but is alert to their use by others. The administrator should develop a reflex action which is activated whenever a speaker appeals to a stereotype. He should immediately raise such questions as: What specific information do you have? What evidence is there that the stereotype is true? Guarding against stereotypes is not easy, but it can be accomplished through practice.

Multivalued Orientation. Opposed to the two-valued orientation that we discussed earlier is multivalued orientation, which is most common among scientists. The layman speaks of the weather as cold or very cold or hot or very hot, but the scientist uses both degrees and fractions of degrees. For him, the temperature is a continuum. In both talking and listening, the administrator needs to avoid the use of the certain fact, of the incontrovertible position. He needs to have his values oriented to a changing world while he takes his position along the continuum. Hayakawa has put this very well: [34]

The mature mind . . . knows that words never say all about everything, and it is therefore adjusted to uncertainty. In driving a car, for example, we never know what is going to happen next, no matter how often we have gone over the same road, we never find exactly the same traffic conditions. Nevertheless, a competent driver travels over all kinds of roads and even at high speeds without either fear or nervousness. As driver, he is adjusted to uncertainty . . . and he is not insecure. Similarly the intellectually mature person does not "know all about" anything. And he is not insecure because he knows that the only kind of security life offers is the dynamic security that comes from within; the security derived from infinite flexibility of mind—from an orientation that is infinite-valued.

In discussing the ability to talk as well as to listen, we could substitute "administrator" for "driver" and complete the analogy. Multivalued orientation will help the administrator listen to all those who can help in improving the system and it will enable him to understand the person who is talking. The administrator finds, early in his career, that few, if any, situations are black or white, good or bad, true or false. In practically all human relations situations, he will find some "good" and some "bad" in each of the participants. If the administrator has a two-valued orientation he will constantly frustrate both himself and those with whom he works. What is needed is the realization that conditions are rarely black or white but most often gray. In a controversy between a student and a

[33] Marvin J. D'Arcangelo, "General Semantics: A Tool for Improving the Employment Interview," *Personnel,* Vol. 29 (1952), pp. 56-61.

[34] S. I. Hayakawa, "Words and Their Importance," *Science Digest,* Vol. 11 (April, 1952), pp. 55-56.

bus driver, neither is all right or all wrong—probably each is a little wrong. Having a multivalued orientation means that the administrator seeks the solution to human relations problems along the continuum which lies between the extremes.

Questions to Raise As You Listen. There are three other things which the careful listener should note. These are somewhat related to Johnson's three questions above; but in writing them down, we can make certain we look specifically for them. The first of these is to determine the speaker's motive, the driving force behind what he is saying. If we understand a man's motives, we can more easily understand what he is talking about. The second deals with the nature of the referents the speaker is using. We might first ask if his words do have referents or if he is using words which are not related to anything in reality. And if he is using referents, at what level of abstraction they are. Can we understand what they are? Last of all, we must ask if the speaker is dealing in facts, inferences, or value judgments. Knowing this will enable us to evaluate the speaker and what he is saying.

OUTLINE OF LISTENING AIDS

The administrator's ability to listen will be improved by:
1. Setting an atmosphere in which people feel free to talk to him.
2. Being relaxed.
3. Listening for the whole idea, not words and syllables.
4. Asking these questions:
    a. What does the speaker mean?
    b. How does the speaker know?
    c. What is the speaker leaving out?
5. Not allowing words or phrases to create stereotypes.
6. Realizing that others use stereotypes.
7. Having a multivalued orientation.
8. Being alert to the speaker's motives.
9. Being aware of the speaker's referents.
10. Being alert to the difference among facts, inferences, and value judgments.

SUMMARY

We started our discussion of communications by introducing the concept of the verbal atmosphere of the school administrator. How he talks, writes, and listens is of great importance to his success in human relations and in administration. Our study of communication was oriented to general semantics with its particular frame of reference. General semantics is defined by the International Society for General Semantics as the study of human evaluative processes with special emphasis on the relation of these to signs and symbols, including language.

We discussed words as maps of territories. We noted that some people use words as symbols of reality and that others use them as the object (signal reaction). The referents of words are very important to the meaning that a person wishes to convey. It was pointed out that some words have several referents, some words have no referents, and some referents have several words to represent them. The search for referents is a major goal of the good communicator.

Central to the task of the administrator striving to improve his human relations skills in communicating is the search for the hidden or intensional meanings of words. Clues to these intensional meanings are found in the cultural and personal referents employed by various people. Two other devices of which we need to be aware are projection and ventriloquizing. In the case of projection, we have an inaccurate picture presented because the speaker has not been aware of the to-me-ness of his report. In ventriloquizing, the speaker talks as if with the voice of another, and those listening to him can be deceived about the source of his statement.

We noted that listening can be improved by setting a permissive atmosphere in which a person feels that he can speak freely; by hearing him out; by remaining relaxed; and by focusing on total content, not individual words and symbols. The listener should ask himself questions regarding the speaker's meaning, evidence, omissions, and the level of abstraction at which he is speaking. The listener should also be alert to the value orientation of the speaker, his motives, his referents, and his use of stereotypes.

EXERCISES

1. Formulate a rating scale from the Outline of Listening Aids (p. 92). Use this scale in rating a speaker in the fields of education and politics, a minister, a priest, or a rabbi. Note the use of words without referents, stereotypes, ventriloquizing, projecting, and so forth.

2. Make a tape recording of your next speech or conference discussion. Rate it, using the outline above.

3. Using the materials in this chapter for reference, how would you deal with (*a*) an irate parent, (*b*) an angry board member, (*c*) a teacher who talks too much during a faculty meeting?

4. What, in your opinion, are the chief contributions of general semantics to school administration?

5. Rewrite the bulletin which appears under the heading "Miscellaneous Notes" (p. 72).

6. Write a case involving the misinterpretation on the part of an administrator of the referents in a teacher's conversation.

7. List all of the words in education which, to you, have no referents. List those words which, to you, have several referents.

8. What are the most common cultural referents in use in your school community? Have they caused you to have faulty communications with the faculty, the students, the public?

9. Outline a procedure for learning the personal referents of each member of the board of education in your school district.

10. Indicate the evidence which leads you to believe that certain members of the administrative staff are ventriloquizing.

SELECTED BIBLIOGRAPHY

BERRIEN, F. K., *Comments and Cases on Human Relations* (New York, Harper, 1951), pp. 20-35.

CHASE, Stuart, *Power of Words* (New York, Harcourt, 1954).

DOOHER, M. Joseph, ed., *Effective Communication on the Job* (New York, American Management Association, 1956).

DUBIN, Robert, *Human Relations in Administration* (New York, Prentice-Hall, 1951), pp. 304-308.

GLICKSBERG, C. I., "General Semantics and the Science of Man," *Scientific Monthly*, Vol. 62 (May, 1946), pp. 440-446.

HAYAKAWA, S. I., *Language in Action* (New York, Harcourt, Brace, 1946).

———, "Semantics, General Semantics," *Etc.: A Review of General Semantics*, Vol. 4, No. 3 (Spring, 1947), pp. 161-170.

———, "Words and Their Importance," *Science Digest*, Vol. 11 (April, 1942), pp. 53-6.

JOHNSON, Wendell, "Do You Know How to Listen?" *Etc.: A Review of General Semantics*, Vol. 7, No. 1 (Fall, 1949), pp. 3-9.

———, *People in Quandaries* (New York, Harper, 1946), chs. 1-8.

KELLY, Fred C., "Do Words Scare Us?" *Saturday Review of Literature*, Vol. 24 (November 22, 1941), p. 11.

KORZYBSKI, Alfred, *Science and Sanity*, 1st ed. (Lancaster, Pa., Science Press Printing Co., 1933), pp. 371-561.

LEE, Irving J., "General Semantics and the Case Method," in *The Case Method of Teaching Human Relations and Administration*, ed. Kenneth Andrews (Cambridge, Mass., Harvard University Press, 1951).

LINDGREN, H. C., "General Semantics: A Tool for the Counselor," *Occupations*, Vol. 27 (January, 1949), pp. 229-233.

CHAPTER **5**

Human Relations and Power

It may seem strange to introduce into the study of human relations a concept such as *power*. It is not commonly discussed as a topic in a human relations text, although there is some interest on the part of those working in group dynamics. Power has been one of those concepts that has been uncomfortable to discuss. After all, if we desire a permissive atmosphere to prevail in a school system, if we wish to have a democratic environment, the introduction of such a concept as power is like introducing a lion to a flock of sheep. Yet, if we are to be realistic, we must face the facts of life, and power is fundamental to these facts.

We are concerned, in this book, with all of the aspects of administration which influence the way in which people behave. We will see what power really is, how it is manifested, how it can be controlled. We will find that the administrator must be able to diagnose his community, determine who the leaders in its power structure are, and how to behave with this knowledge at his control. Power structure is not confined to the community, as we will discover. It is present in *any* type of human enterprise. The school itself has a power structure that controls the way in which people will behave. There is a power structure present in each committee, each small discussion group, at each coffee break. The way in which power influences the behavior of individuals in school administration will be fundamental to our discussion.

Chapter 6 will deal with *authority*. Since power and authority are interdependent, the reader will find that certain topics related to power have been reserved for discussion there.

WHAT IS POWER?

Let us try to determine just what power is in a human relations situation. How would we recognize and identify power in a school? Is it something which we can see or hear or feel? What are the outward manifestations of power?

Dubin introduces the discussion of power by raising some very commonplace but incisive questions.[1] He asks, "Why does any one submit to the

[1] Robert Dubin, ed., *Human Relations in Administration* (New York, Prentice-Hall, 1951), pp. 172-173.

discipline of an organization?" "What is the basis upon which the control of an organization can be exercised over an individual?" Why indeed, do we submit ourselves to the innumerable organizations, both formal and informal, in our culture? We Americans are reputedly the greatest joiners in the world. The various groups that we join exert a certain amount of ordering of our lives. They set up restrictions in terms of our time, our activities, and, in many cases, our thoughts. They demand money for their support and energy for their activities. We join most of these groups because we want to, because we have a definite purpose in mind, and because each group helps us to achieve our purpose. But our major consideration is how these reasons relate to the power structure of school groups.

Well, we do join school faculties as teachers or administrators with definite purposes in mind. It is obvious that many of these purposes could not be attained readily in other ways. We might start a school of our own, but many things militate against this. We may not have the money or facilities. The opening of our own school involves more than the attainment of the purposes for which we join a school faculty. It appears that if we desire to achieve certain purposes, it is imperative that we join the faculty of some school. No one says we must, and there seems to be no obvious force compelling us to do so; nevertheless, we do become members of a faculty! It is important to note that the person who wants to teach has very little choice in selecting the type of organization in which he teaches. We can note, then, that in this specific case, society has an ordered procedure for teaching its young. The relationship between the teacher and the young is an ordered one; it is institutionalized. Underlying the ordering of these interactions of teacher and the student is power. Bierstadt states this concept of power very well: "Power supports the fundamental order of society and the social organization within it, wherever there is order. Power stands behind every association and sustains its structure. Without power there is no organization and without power there is no order." [2]

When we say that power stands behind every organization and association, we are introducing the concept that power is a latent force. That is, we never see the power itself; we see the results of power. Power is the ability to employ force or to produce action; but it is not the force or action itself. Likewise, power is not authority; but behind all authority there is power. It is power which makes the authority significant, and the authority is that which we see and with which we deal. In this sense, it is easy and quite clear to talk about the concept of power. Although the concept is abstract, it is neither ephemeral nor reified. To clarify the concept further, we turn to Hunter, who defines power as a latent factor: "Power is a word that will be used to describe the acts of men going about

[2] Robert Bierstadt, "An Analysis of Social Power," *American Sociological Review,* Vol. 15 (December, 1950), pp. 730-736.

the business of moving other men to act in relation to themselves or in relation to organic or inorganic things." [3]

We might develop this concept of the latency of power with an analogy. In taking a picture with a camera, we obtain a "latent image" on either a glass plate or a nitrocellulose film that is covered with a suspension of crystalline silver halide particles. Examination of the exposed film would fail to reveal any image or picture. But if the exposed film is developed, that is, put into a situation designed to be "ordered," the image appears. The "latent image" on the film puts order into the suspension and developer so that a picture results. Although not visible, it nonetheless is the factor which makes the picture emerge. The power structure of a community is similar to the latent image. It cannot be seen, and its effects are noticed only when the situation needs "ordering." A vote on a school-building bond issue might well be the situation. The power structure of the community determines, to a very large extent, whether the vote succeeds or fails.

Since the concept of power is difficult to understand but vital to the study of human relations, let us consider it from a different point of reference. Lippitt and others approach the discussion of power from the point of view of *potentiality*. They stress power as the potentiality to exert influence. In fact, they state that the concept can be differentiated into units as follows: "*Social power* is (*a*) the potentiality (*b*) for inducing forces (*c*) in other persons (*d*) toward acting or changing in a given direction." [4]

They are using the term *social power* as we use the term *power*. Notice the close similarity between their definitions and Hunter's. In stressing the potentiality of power, the concept is made somewhat clearer. We are trying to get the idea across that one can never *see* power in action. One sees the results and the effects, but power itself is always latent or potential. The term *potential* is also helpful, because we can never be certain as to the full dimensions of power. Although there have been attempts to measure power, these attempts are strictly limited in their scope, and those who are engaged in such research are fully aware of the limitations of their techniques. [5]

It is like this with power in school situations, since we observe the results of power rather than power itself. If the power resides with the board or one member of the board or the superintendent or some "boss" in the community, this power will be revealed through the exercise of authority. As students of human relations, we must examine further the

[3] Floyd Hunter, *Community Power Structure* (Chapel Hill, University of North Carolina Press, 1953), pp. 2-3.

[4] Ronald Lippitt, Norman Polansky, Fritz Redl, and Sidney Rosen, "The Dynamics of Power," in *Group Dynamics,* ed. Dorwin Cartwright and Alvin Zander (Evanston, Ill., Row Peterson, 1953), p. 463.

[5] *Ibid.,* pp. 463-466.

concept of power, since it sets the frame of reference for a study of leadership and followership.

RESIDUAL CATEGORIES OF POWER

When talking about power, we can readily notice the influence of the
acts of men in power positions; but there are three categories of power
influence in any culture which one must be aware of in order to understand the total power structure. Hunter indicates that these three categories might be called: (1) historical references, (2) motivation and other
psychological concepts, (3) values and moral and ethical considerations.[6]

Historical Reference

Let us consider the historical references to a power structure in the
public schools. This historical reference is found in the writings of the
educational philosophers of the past: Plato, Aristotle, Thomas Aquinas,
and on down to John Dewey and William Kilpatrick. We could also trace
this historical reference through the study of the history of education as
written by Ellwood Cubberly or John Brubacher. More particularly, we
might find some enlightment in the work of Willard Elsbree.[7] In Elsbree's
work, we can see the development of the frame of reference which Americans have shaped for their teachers. It is not one of immense power in the
community. This is borne out by subsequent empirical studies of the power
structure of communities.[8] Hunter, in the most ambitious of these studies,
describes the power structure of a city of a half a million people but does
not even mention a public school person as being nominated to any power-
wielding position in the community. Armstrong found that although the
school superintendent is expected to be a community leader, he is considered to be one by only 50 of the 105 community leaders in ten school
districts surrounding New York City. In addition, he noted that a large
proportion of the governmental officials and presidents of chambers of
commerce failed to name the school administrator as a leader at all. The
conclusion to be drawn from the Armstrong study is that school superintendents are not very high in the power structure of a community.
Griffiths and Vickery found very much the same thing when they interviewed citizens to determine who the community leaders were. In one of
the two communities studied, the chief school officer was mentioned twice

---

[6] Hunter, *op. cit.*, p. 3.

[7] Willard Elsbree, *The American Teacher* (New York, American Book Company,
1939).

[8] Hunter, *op. cit.;* Louis W. Armstrong, "Community Expectancy Concerning the
Superintendency." (Unpublished doctoral project, Teachers College, 1951); and Dan-
iel E. Griffiths and William Vickery, *Communities Look at Their School Principals*
(Albany, N. Y., Capital Area School Development Association, 1953).

in a listing of 114, in the other he was mentioned twelve times in a listing of 169 leaders. Thus, in the historical perspective, we find educational leaders generally to be very low in the power structure of their communities. This conclusion has been verified by a recent study by Kimbrough.[9] But it has been questioned in a study by Gleazer, who found that the superintendent does have some influence in the power structure.[10] We need to point out that there are some men in the superintendency who because of factors *outside* of their positions, gain a position of strength in the power structure. We will consider this point at length later.

In considering the historical reference of power, we must also consider a subgroup of the community, the school itself. Here we find that the power structure is one of a hierarchical nature, following rather closely the line and staff organization of industry. Although there is a strong trend now underway to bring change to this structure, it has not yet made significant progress. Historically, power is vested in the school board and exercised through the superintendent. Each of the administrative officers wields power in direct proportion to his position. This is particularly true in large city systems and can be found in any school system which has been formally organized for any length of time.

The impression should not be gained that the above description holds true invariably. It is a general description of a general situation. There are many variables in each situation which act to modify the power structure. One might be examined briefly. In the case of a newly organized school district, we might well find numerous modifications. If, for example, we had a new consolidated district formed where there were previously some fifty one-room schoolhouses, we would find a large number of people operating in an organization, the framework of which is unfamiliar to them. The people would still look to their trustee rather than the central school board for leadership. The teachers, assuming they were gathered together in one central building, would be unaccustomed to co-operation. Their historical reference might well be "Every teacher is a king in his own room." In this time of change, a new power structure would take shape, but it might not follow the above pattern. There could be many other variables also present, and some of these will be examined later.

The historical reference, then, gives us insight into the way in which a culture is accustomed to looking at its power structure. Much of the behavior of the community will be in conformity with the customs and mores of its people, without any apparent overt action on the part of its power wielders.

[9] Ralph B. Kimbrough, "The Operational Beliefs of Selected Leaders in a Selected County" (Unpublished Ph.D. dissertation, University of Tennessee, 1953).

[10] Edmund J. Gleazer, Jr., "The Identification of Certain Alignments of Social Power Impinging upon Decision-making of School Committee and Superintendent in a New England Community" (Unpublished Ed. D. project, Harvard University, 1953).

Psychological Concepts of Power

The psychological and motivational concepts of power are probably classed as residual more because of our lack of knowledge about them than because of any other reason. Although we are quite certain that these exist as causes of power-seeking in a community, it is difficult to analyze them; and very little definitive work has been done in this area. This has been expressed by Gardner Murphy in his discussion of the need for more knowledge in the area of social needs. He wonders if status and power needs operate according to the same laws as the simpler visceral needs but observes that we do not have any evidence at the present time. Some of what he has to say bears on our discussion.

We do have some studies . . . which suggest that desire for status is a measurable continuum . . . comparable to the desire for food; but we also have some evidence that prestige and power needs are never satisfied, put to rest, and rendered temporarily inoperative as are the visceral drives when satisfied. Indeed, we have some rather strong evidence both from history and from the clinic that there is no limit whatever to the amount of prestige or the amount of power which may be sought if there is some feasible way to seek it. We live in a status and power-motivated society, and we perceive our fellows and the social order largely in terms of the status and power which others possess; but actually we have almost no information about the way in which prestige and power govern the daily perceptual acts by which we apprehend social reality.[11]

Although there is little or no precise work to substantiate the above contentions, those writing in the field seem to agree with Murphy's conclusions. In a very interesting article, Lee examines some of the underlying motivations of those who pursue power. He takes a stand somewhat similar to that of Murphy and states: "The contention here is simply to recognize that the acquisition of greater personal power is one of the common outlets for human aspirations and energies and that some become more absorbed in that outlet than do others." [12]

It appears that the quest for power is circular. The more power one has, the more he wants. It feeds upon itself, and, paradoxically, the more one feeds on power, the hungrier he becomes. Kiplinger puts this concept in the framework of a game when he says: [13]

As a business man rises in the scale of material success he tends to work more and more for the sport of the thing. Business becomes a game. He wants to be a player in the next bigger league—up the scale. Money becomes more important to him for the pile of chips it will buy in the game of business. It isn't the money he's after; it's the power, influence, prestige, standing, rank.

[11] Gardner Murphy, "Dynamics of Social Perception" in *Group Relations at the Crossroads*, ed. M. A. Sherif and M. O. Wilson (New York, Harper, 1953), p. 148.
[12] Alfred McClung Lee, "Power-Seekers," in *Studies in Leadership*, ed. Alvin W. Gouldner (New York, Harper, 1950), p. 667.
[13] W. M. Kiplinger, "The Business Man: What He Is and Why," *New York Times Magazine* (January 23, 1938), p. 2.

In education, this drive for more and more power is manifested by the acquisition of positions of prestige outside of the localized educational situation. Thus we see school administrators broadening their scope to such activities as the Boy Scouts, Rotary, Lions, Kiwanis, the churches, and Red Cross or Community Chest fund drives. Most school administrators claim that they do not willingly take over these posts, yet they do so in such large numbers as to cast some doubt on their protestations. Witness too, the national and state posts held by these men in a myriad of professional and service organizations. And these posts are not held in an evenly distributed manner. Those men holding the best, that is, the highest-paying school jobs are the ones holding the largest number of outside positions.

Another example of this power-seeking on the part of superintendents is the urge to move to larger and larger communities. In many instances, of course, there is the incentive of higher salary; but there are many other instances in which this incentive is not present, and many still apply. In education, just as in business and industry, the prestige and power is in the hands of the superintendents of the largest cities.

We can summarize this aspect best by quoting Stefan Zweig: "Power is like Medusa's head. Whoever has looked on her countenance can no longer turn his face away, but remains for always under her spell."

Values and Moral and Ethical Considerations

The third residual category of power is that of values and moral and ethical considerations. There are times when we are moved to behave in a certain way by the force of the values that we hold in common. We will behave in such a way because it is the "good" way. Our society has attached high value to this type of conduct. On the other hand, our society frowns on certain kinds of behavior, and so we do not behave in that manner. We in education are acutely aware of the values which our communities hold. And we are just as aware of moral and ethical considerations, which are particular kinds of values.

Each culture has worked out a code of values for itself. Some cultures have established more formal codes than others, but all have them. Counts makes this point abundantly clear. He demonstrates, through a series of case studies, how decisions in school administration are influenced by the values and moral and ethical considerations that we adhere to in America. An examination of one case will illustrate this concept: [14]

A teacher belonging to a certain religious sect applies for a position in the school of a community populated overwhelmingly by another denomination. In terms of professional preparation, teaching experience, and personal traits she

[14] George Counts, *Decision-making and American Values in School Administration* (New York, Teachers College Bureau of Publications, 1954), p. 22.

appears to be the best qualified of all the applicants. But the community is vigorously intolerant in matters of church affiliation and has never employed a teacher of her persuasion. Nevertheless, the superintendent of schools, who is relatively new on the job, recommends the appointment at a regular meeting of the board of education.

The president of the board, who is himself a devout member and an elder in the dominant local church, asks the superintendent to withdraw his recommendation or at least agree to postponement of action until the next meeting. In the meantime members of the community learn of the incident, take sides, and enter into violent controversy. Some citizens presume to see the hand of an ecclesiastical conspiracy in the affair. Others contend that the church affiliation of the applicant is entirely irrelevant. While the dispute is raging the board meets again.

Counts discussed this issue in terms of basic American values. He pointed out some of those values which are pertinent, namely:

1. Separation of church and state is the fundamental law of the land.
2. Public school welcomes children of all denominations as well as those from no denomination.
3. People of differing opinions in the realm of religious belief can live together in harmony, tolerance, and mutual respect.
4. Minorities shall be protected from the tyrannies of the majorities.

After some discussion both the board and the community accepted the appointment of the teacher. They based their decision on the values which this country had established and maintained over the years.

TYPES OF POWER

As we have discussed the meaning of power, its ramifications, and, to some extent, its etiology, it must be evident that there are several different types of power. Remembering that we define power in terms of the acts of men going about the business of moving other men to act, we can say there are three major types of power in terms of the kind of influence brought to bear on the individual who is being moved to act in a certain direction.[15] These three major types are:

1. *Force*—the influence is brought to bear through the use of physical force.
2. *Domination*—the influence is brought to bear through the use of commands or requests. It should be noted that "Right face!" and "Please turn around" are both forms of domination so long as the person commanded actually complies with the command. There are times when a polite request brings about greater compliance than a brutal command.
3. *Manipulation*—the influence is brought to bear without making explicit the behavior the power-holder wants the subordinate to perform. Manipulation may take place by utilizing symbols or performing acts. A person can manipulate through symbols by the use of propaganda. An

[15] Herbert Goldhammer and Edward A. Shils, "Types of Power and Status," *American Journal of Sociology*, Vol. 45 (September, 1939), pp. 171-178. Reprinted by permission of the University of Chicago Press.

example of manipulation through acts would be the sabotaging of an enterprise's activities, thereby undermining the confidence of its employees.

The difference between domination and manipulation is the degree to which the power-holder makes explicit his intention to the person whose behavior he is trying to influence. It can be seen that at times one will shade off into the other and that it is very difficult to distinguish between the two. The use of these three types of power will be discussed at length later in this chapter and in Chapter 6, but they are contrasted by Goldhammer and Shils as follows: [16]

A person whose general position as a power-holder is recognized as legitimate may exercise force, domination, or manipulation. But, as far as the recognition of the legitimacy of individual acts of power is concerned, it is clear that manipulation cannot be legitimate power, since in the case of manipulation there is no recognition by the subordinated individual that an act of power has been effected. Persons who are subject to force (especially as an initial form of influencing behavior and not as a sanction) frequently do not recognize the legitimacy of such acts of power. Generally, therefore, the recognition of a power-holder as a legitimate exerciser of power rests on the recognition of the legitimacy of his acts of domination. However, this does not mean that he may not also exercise force or manipulation.

POWER POSTULATES AND HYPOTHESES

We have discussed thus far a basic definition of power ("the acts of men going about the business of moving other men to act"); the three residual categories of power (historical reference, motivation, and values and moral and ethical considerations); and the three types of power (force, domination, and manipulation). Let us now consider in more detail the concept of power in terms of our basic definition. Some questions which need to be raised are:

1. Is power necessary in social organizations?
2. How can the school administrator diagnose the power structure of the community into which he moves?
3. What is the power structure in a school system?
4. How can the administrators and teachers act to protect themselves in the power structure in both the school and the community?

At this point let us look at a set of postulates and hypotheses which frame a point of view from which we can examine several examples of power in action. In our later discussion some of these statements will be referred to specifically and others will be inferred. These statements have to do with the way in which power affects relationships between individuals and groups, the way in which power is structured, the relationship between power and policy, and the way in which power can be gained by

[16] *Ibid.*, p. 183.

individuals. The statements are short and to the point. They will also aid us in our study of authority which follows.

In addition to giving us some information about how power affects us, these postulates also help us to further define the concept of power. Keeping in mind that a postulate is a self-evident truth, let us examine Hunter's statements.[17]

1. Power involves relationships between individuals and groups, both controlled and controlling.
> Corollary 1. Because power involves such relationships, it can be described structurally.

2. Power is structured socially, in the United States, into a dual relationship between governmental and economic authorities on national, state, and local levels.
> Corollary 1. Both types of authorities may have functional, social, and institutional power units subsidiary to them.

3. Power is a relatively constant factor in social relationships with policies as variables.
> Corollary 1. Wealth, social status, and prestige are factors in the "power constant."
> Corollary 2. Variation in the strength between power units, or a shift in policy within one of these units, affects the whole power structure.

4. Power of the individual must be structured into associational, clique, or institutional patterns to be effective.
> Corollary 1. The community provides a microcosm of organized power relations in which individuals exercise the maximum effective influence.
> Corollary 2. Representative democracy offers the greatest possibility of assuring the individual a voice in policy determination and extension.

Following his presentation of these self-evident truths, Hunter gives a set of hypotheses which he then proceeded to test. He found that these hypotheses stood the test and could be considered valid for the person wishing to study power relations. Notice that these are of particular value from an operational point-of-view, that is, from the point-of-view of a person such as a superintendent of schools. Hunter is saying that power is necessary in any kind of social organization; it is a fact, and we must learn to work with it. He also says that the exercise of power is not unlimited but is exercised under a social policy within the framework of social authority. He also points up an interesting fact that behind the power exercisers are a smaller group of men who frame the policy for the exercise of power. Let us look at this set of validated hypotheses: [18]

1. Power is exercised as a necessary function in social relationships.
2. The exercise of power is limited and directed by the formulation and extension of social policy within a framework of socially sanctioned authority.

[17] Hunter, *op. cit.*, p. 6.
[18] *Ibid.*, p. 7.

3. In a given power unit (organization) a smaller number of individuals will be found formulating and extending policy than those exercising power.

Corollary 1. All policy makers are "men of power."

Corollary 2. All "men of power" are not, *per se*, policy makers.

In formulating our conclusions in this chapter these postulates and hypotheses will be the guidelines. They are not only the result of Hunter's extensive study but are generally agreed upon by other workers in this field and are extremely helpful generalizations for us to use.

Is Power Necessary?

Is power a necessary constituent in our modern society? We might ask if power is a necessity in any society. The general consensus would seem to indicate that power is necessary. Without it, no society could exist. We are all aware of the evidence supporting this contention. The decisions of the power command as voiced through the duly constituted authorities are obeyed habitually even in our democratic society. The bulletins distributed by principals to their teachers are generally followed almost to the letter. In fact, we hardly have to have bulletins distributed at all; the teachers look for innuendos indicating what those in power want to have done. Although this is the general case, there are, of course, exceptions. The point is that our democratic society depends on a multiplicity of habitual responses for the bulk of its activity. Power is the cement which holds our society together.

The question, then, is not so much "Is power necessary?" as "How can we control power?" and "How can we control the power-holders?" In the democratic society, questions of this sort are of prime importance. If power is held by a small group of men and is not subject to the control of all the people, then we have a totalitarian situation, regardless of what it is called. The problem is how to handle power in such a way as to benefit all of the people. Let us consider ways of doing this in our school systems. We will first contrast the democratic and totalitarian concepts of power and then look at our schools.

We have said that power is the cement which holds our society together. It is also the cement which holds other types of societies together, including totalitarian states like Soviet Russia and Nazi Germany. But there are substantial differences between the power concept of a democratic state and that of a totalitarian state. One difference rests in the *degree* to which the power command is decentralized and diffused throughout the society. *A democratic society is one in which the power command is held by a large number of people and is susceptible to the will of all of the people.* An authoritarian society is one in which the power command is in the hands of one person or *very* few people and is not susceptible to the control of all the people. A second difference is in the *type* of power exercised. In the democratic society, the *only* kind of power which should be exerted is *domination*. Democratic leaders influence the behavior of others by making *explicit* commands or requests. In the totalitarian society, both *force* and *manipulation* are widely used types of power.

Use of Power in the Schools

On the basis of these two criteria, let us look at the administration of our schools and see how power is used to influence the behavior of those in the schools. We will also examine ways in which power *should* be used in the schools.

What is being said is this: in a democratic society, ways and means must be found to enable larger numbers of people to exercise power. Studies of American communities indicate that the majority of individuals in these communities have no say in policy determination.[19] Although no comparable studies have been made of American public schools, the general literature in the field indicates that the situations are comparable. Teachers as a group have little or no say in the formulation of school policy. They are not an integral part of the power command. Several writers, notably Griffiths and Ovsiew, have found school systems that have attempted to involve teachers in policy making.[20] Griffiths found that those superintendents who were rated most successful by a committee of judges had teachers formulating policy to a much greater degree than did those superintendents who were rated least successful. Both Griffiths and Ovsiew found among this top group of superintendents a strong trend toward establishing what could be called the "superintendent's cabinet." Such a cabinet is usually selected or elected from units of teachers, buildings, grades, or subjects; it meets frequently in informal settings, considers relevant facts on problems of concern to the system, and makes recommendations to the superintendent, the board of education, or both. In this way, the teachers are given the opportunity to make a niche for themselves in the power structure of a school. Ovsiew found some school administrators using a "student cabinet." [21] Here, elected representatives of student groups meet with the superintendent to discuss problems of concern to students. Although these meetings are of an advisory nature, they provide the basis for revision of old policy and the formulation of new policy in such areas of student life as intramural athletics, school

[19] Hunter, *op. cit.* and A. B. Hollingshead, *Elmtown's Youth* (New York, John Wiley, 1949).

[20] Daniel E. Griffiths, "An Evaluation of the Leadership of the School Superintendent" (Unpublished Ph.D. dissertation, Yale University, 1952), and Leon Ovsiew, *Emerging Practices in School Administration* (New York, Metropolitan School Study Council, 1953).

[21] Ovsiew, *op. cit.*, p. 85.

intervisitation, student government, and other curricular, cocurricular, and social activities. This serves to broaden the base of power by including students in at least one phase of policy making.

These developments in school life fulfill the postulate that "power of the individual must be structured into associational, clique, or institutional patterns to be effective." We see that the faculties and student bodies of the above schools have so organized the individuals as to enable them to participate more effectively in policy making. This is a positive step toward the democratization of our schools.

What type of power is used in school administration? We can state with certainty that *force* as we defined it earlier is not used—at least not with the faculty! It would be very difficult to discuss definitively the other types of power being used. There have been no studies that attempt to determine the extent to which domination and manipulation are used to influence behavior. From observation, it would appear that there is still too much manipulation; too many administrators exert power through indirection and propagandistic measures. Many administrators, for instance, deprecate the efforts of the local teachers' association. They will not say in so many words that they are opposed to the association, but they indicate in many ways that they do not approve of various aspects. The following case illustrates this:

It was time for the annual Teachers Convention in the state. Since the state was quite small there were only two meetings. The teachers in Matsaw, a city of 25,000 were to go to the state capitol for their meeting. The state association sent an envelope of materials to each superintendent in the state and requested them to distribute them to each teacher. The superintendent in Matsaw distributed the envelopes as requested. When he opened his, he noted that it contained a sticker. This sticker was to be pasted on the windshield of his car and indicated that he had special parking privileges. He exploded at this. He declared openly: "I'll never put that on my windshield! I'd rather be dead than go around advertising that I am a member of this association! Just who do they think they are? It's bad enough to go to the convention without advertising it too!"

Here is an example of manipulation through propaganda. By voicing criticism of one aspect, the superintendent is capable of undermining the belief of the teachers in the total program. Power-holders have great influence upon their subordinates and can wield that influence in apparently innocent ways.

The use of power by school administrators constitutes a fertile area for research. At the present time we have practically no material on the subject. All we can say is that there is evidence of manipulation of the faculty and student body, even though the use of force and manipulation to influence the behavior of subordinates is not consistent with democratic administration.

Why Diagnose Power Structure?

Before we ask how the school administrator can diagnose the power structure of the community in which he is working, we must ask why he should want to know the power structure of that community. Two recent publications shed some light on this question. It is hoped that the substance of the chapter thus far has indicated many reasons why the school administrator needs to know who the community power-holders are.

In a very exhaustive study of the power structure of a small community (Central Forks) and its relation to the board of education, Goldhammer draws some conclusions of great interest to school administrators. He states: [22]

1. ... Four of the elected board members, in this instance, were individuals either proposed by or acceptable to the power structure. It would appear that the degree to which the board is a self-perpetuating governmental entity is a variable of (a) the acceptability of candidates to the dominant power structure, (b) the general apathy of the electorate to school board politics, and (c) the strength of the power structure to confront challenges to its supremacy.
2. ... Each candidate was handpicked by some group, either formally or informally constituted, which looked for the candidate to achieve certain specific ends through his school board membership.
3. In many instances the school board candidate represented the power aspirations of some particular group within the community. Hence, a church group wanted to control certain school policies; consequently, it endeavored to secure the election of its members to school board positions. ...
4. For the most part, school board members represented men of substance in the community. Length of residence, relative economic security, acceptance of the values and moral codes of the community—all were important qualifications for school board candidates.
5. Although school board members felt that they represented the "community" a careful examination of their contacts and perspectives leads to the conclusion that they represented only narrow segments of the community. ... For the most part minority groups failed to achieve consistent representation, and their interests were frequently looked upon either as hostile or unimportant.
6. It would appear as though the school administrator needs to develop a consistent perspective of power or leadership functions within the community. ... The American generally assumes that power operates "through fair means or foul," but the power utilized in a community like Central Forks need not necessarily be arbitrary or abusive.

To the administrator who is naïve enough to think that his school is free from the community power structure these findings should be quite revealing. A recent article by Dodson follows up the arguments made by Goldhammer by relating the community power structure to the schools

[22] Keith Goldhammer, "Community Power Structure and School Board Membership," *American School Board Journal*, Vol. 130, No. 3 (March, 1955), pp. 23-25.

in the matter of desegregation, although the same analysis could have been made of any other major problem which faces society. Dodson not only presents the relationship of school administrator and power structure but indicates some paths of action for the administrator. He introduces the discussion by describing a study by Louis E. Raths of the teacher and the power structure of his class. Raths reported that teachers who had a productive climate in their classes sensed the power structure and played to it but that teachers with poor classroom climate were unable to sense the power structure of their classes. With this background, Dodson states: [23]

Likewise with us all, I suspect, in more ways than we would care to admit even if we were conscious of it, this catering to power is something with which we must deal. The success of an administrator depends upon his having a radar-like equipment which senses who the power people are, and caters to them. In desegregation programs the superintendent of schools will know who such people are in his community and he will pretty much behave as those power persons desire. It is for this reason that Laswell says the leader is least free to change of most persons in a group situation. The leader's problem is largely that of staying a leader. Hence he is tied to the wheel of what power desires. Most often, it should be realized, the power persons in a local community are the status people, who never participate actively in community life, persons who never hold office, individuals who operate behind scenes. It is they, rather than elected officials, who will decide how social process moves. In some instances we will be able to "run it over" such persons. In others they will "go along," but in others movement will depend unfortunately on funerals.

When speaking of how administrators will have to act in the face of struggles with the power structure (in this case the issue is desegregation) he states: [24]

It is also at this point that administrative and institutional leadership of institutions must either "fish or cut bait." They are today confronted with the necessity of taking a position on the race issue in their local community. They can either move creatively or be pushed to move defensively. In the changing pattern of power they can help interpret to the power structure, or they can play dissident aspects of power against each other to move the community toward more democracy.

These two statements point up the need for the administrator to know the power structure of the community in which he works. Let us summarize the points which have been made thus far.

The school administrator should know the power structure of his community because:

1. The ultimate direction of the schools will be influenced to a great extent by the community power-holders.

[23] Dan W. Dodson, "For Those of Us Who Teach," *American Unity,* Vol. 13, No. 5 (May-June, 1955), p. 5.
[24] *Ibid.*

2. Members of the board of education are generally either power-holders or representatives of power-holders.
3. The school administrator will be unable to exercise community leadership without the aid of the power-holders.
4. Since decisions affecting the community as a whole will be made by a small group of power-holders, the school administrator needs to know who they are and how they operate in order to assess public opinion.

How to Diagnose Power Structure

Various techniques can be used to aid the school administrator in his analysis of the community power structure. Although these techniques are all quite helpful, they should be used to supplement the observations which the administrator has been making since he first entered the community. Great care should be exercised in using these techniques because there is danger of their backfiring. If an analysis of the power structure is undertaken while the community is under stress, more harm than good might result. Proper timing is essential to the success of any of the following techniques.

Outside Survey Group. Superintendent A desired a list of the power-holders in his community. He and the board of education were in the process of forming a citizens committee to study an aspect of the school program. Although he had been in the community for three years and felt he knew the community structure fairly well, he wanted to check his knowledge. He enlisted the aid of a nearby college, and together they planned the survey. A team of graduate students was trained to do the interviews. A sampling design was constructed, and the interview guide was formulated. In this particular study, it was decided to interview every fifth household. Such questions as the following were asked.

1. Would you please name the people whom you consider to be community leaders?
2. If you wanted to bring about a change in the community to whom would you talk?
3. Do you consider the superintendent of schools to be a community leader?

This method has the advantage of having trained interviewers collect the data and trained professionals analyze the data. It provides the superintendent with reliable objective data. It also provides supplementary information on the attitudes of the public, since the trained interviewers are sensitive to innuendoes and other signs of public opinion.

Student Reports. This method, which has been tried by some schoolmen, is very interesting but has not been validated by research. It calls for asking students in the fifth or sixth grades to list the people whom they consider to be community leaders. In most cases, of course, they report names of the people whom their parents talk about as community leaders.

This is a very simple procedure, and those school administrators who indicate that they have used it feel it has some merit. It should be just one device and the administrator should not depend upon it exclusively.

Sociological Analysis. This type of analysis deals with determining the prestige groups in a community and the leaders of these groups. It is the procedure used in the case study of Riverdale and is also the basis for such studies as Yankee City and Elmtown's Youth. In the Riverdale case (to be found in Part 3 of this book), we note the hierarchy of ethnic groups running from the "native" American to Swedish on down to the Italians and, below these, the southern whites and the Negroes. The community is divided into seven distinct social classes: the "fine old families," the "nouveau riche," the "well-to-do professional class," and on through the "poor, but respectable" and the "no goods." The case also points out that certain clubs have a high prestige rating and that certain families are easily identified as the most influential.

The school administrator can make such an analysis of his community as is mentioned above through the use of the booklet, *Student Status and Social Class.*[25] Although this booklet was intended primarily for the use of classroom teachers in diagnosing the social structure of his classes, it can be used by administrators for community analysis. The booklet contains a section, "Social Class in America," which describes the characteristics of each class and two methods of determining social class, including Warner's Index of Status Characteristics. There is also a section, "The School and Social Class," which indicates how social structure affects the classroom. By following the procedure outlined, the administrator could make an analysis of his community to determine its power structure.

Power Structures Affecting the Schools

Our all too brief description of power structure in the case study of Riverdale leads us to raise the question: Is there a similar power structure in a school system? The answer is categorically yes, but it is altogether inadequate. There are several power structures which influence a school system, and we will look at each briefly.

The State. Since education is a state function in the United States there is behind each school the power of the state. This is reflected in the orderliness of the programs. In New York State, for example, the school year is 190 days long. All schools have a 190-day school year. There is no bickering or argument about it, each school system plans for a school year of 190 days. The business of the district is transacted at an annual meeting held either in May or July, not September or December. Certain aspects of the course of study are prescribed, such as the teaching of American

[25] Louis E. Raths and Stephen Abrahamson, *Student Status and Social Class* (Bronxville, N. Y., Modern Education Service, 1951).

history and New York State history. Behind each local board of education is the state, and the rulings the board makes can be backed up with this irrepressible power.

The Local Community. Although the state has primary control over the schools, the local community determines in large part the nature of the school. Its mores and customs dictate the attitude of teachers toward students, of administrators toward teachers, and the atmosphere of the school. The local community can withhold funds or can be very generous. It determines the course of events in the classroom, that is, the extent to which controversial issues will be discussed. Although it does this through its authorities, the board of education, there is always present, though not verbally, the power of the community.

The Board of Education. The chief power force in a school system is generally the board of education. Through it, the school administrator derives his authority. The source of the power which the board exercises over the staff is generally the state education law and the rules and regulations of the board itself. The power may also reside in some of the members of the board itself whose power in turn stems from their position in the community or, in some cases, from their personalities. Let us consider the source of power in particular. What are some of the specific reasons why the board can exercise such power over the faculty and student body of a school?

The board gives its first demonstration of power over the teacher when it *hires* him. This in itself is the key to the power situation. In addition, the board holds the power to discharge the teacher. The body which holds the power to hire and fire carries considerable weight with regard to any of its rulings, suggestions, or comments it might advocate. Its slightest suggestion will be considered to be most important.

There are several other ways in which the board controls those factors that tend to make its employees submissive. One of the factors which has the most immediate effect upon the lives of teachers is salary. Final judgment on salary raises rests with the board of education. The salary schedule in effect in a school district is at the discretion of the board (sometimes within state-prescribed limits). Any change in the schedule requires the consent of the board, which means that relations between the board and the teachers must be good in order to persuade the board to act favorably on salary issues. The alternative to this is for the teacher to persuade the community to force the board to increase salaries. The former course of action is so much preferred by the teachers that the latter is rarely taken. In those school districts which have tenure laws, tenure is granted by a vote of the board. Although boards normally act on the recommendation of the administrator, they do take the final action and are the ultimate power-holders. The conditions of employment are also largely the province of the board. Such things as classroom equipment, amount of heat and light, and even the building itself are determined by board action. These factors have so much meaning to the individual teachers that they influence the way in which teachers regard the board and what it does. Rather than critically evaluating the work of the board, teachers are prone to accept any of its statements on school matters without judgment.

Another source of power of the board is the power of the individual members of the board. This was mentioned above in reporting Goldhammer's study of community power structure and the board of education. An early study by Counts pointed out that board personnel consists predominantly of managerial, professional, and business groups.[26] Brown, in a recent study, generally substantiated these findings.[27] It is clearly established that members of boards of education are members of the upper social classes. These are the groups which hold the power in communities. On the other hand, teachers are generally members of the lower middle and upper lower classes.[28] A recent study by Newbill examined the social role of the teacher. He found that teachers were relatively isolated and, in spite of the high value placed on education in this country, suffered low prestige. He further pointed out that they were the object of lower middle class hostility and were not effective in the community power structure.[29] This accounts in part for the attitudes of teachers toward their board of education. We may explain this further by pointing out that the board is looked up to by members of the community since it is composed of the representatives of the upper classes—those people whom the parents of the community would like to have their children emulate. The teacher, on the other hand, is an upward mobile person socially. He does not come from a class which is looked up to; in fact, he himself usually looks down on his class. In most cases, he moves upward from it. Much of the present drive toward "professionalism" in teaching probably could be traced to the above. It is implicit in the reasoning of teacher groups that if they could attain a professional status like that enjoyed by doctors and lawyers, they would rise in the eyes of the public. The belief is that this would bring about a position on a higher rung on the social ladder. This is not the place to debate the issue of professionalism. The point being made is that the drive is present, indicating a desire

[26] George Counts, *The Social Composition of Boards of Education,* Supplementary Educational Monographs (Chicago, University of Chicago Press, 1927), No. 23.

[27] Robert H. Brown, "The Composition of School Boards," *American School Board Journal,* Vol. 129 (August, 1954), pp. 23-24.

[28] See Hollingshead, *op. cit.,* p. 192; Wilbur B. Brookover, "Teachers and the Stratification of American Society," *Harvard Educational Review,* Vol. 23 (Fall, 1953), pp. 257-267; Robert W. Richey, "The United States," *The Yearbook of Education: 1953,* ed. Robert K. Hall, N. Hans, and J. A. Lauwerys (London, Evans and Brothers, 1953), pp. 203-228.

[29] Esko E. Newbill, "The Social Role and Prestige of the Public School Teacher in the Social Structure" (Unpublished Ph.D. dissertation, Syracuse University, 1952).

to improve the social status of the teacher. Certainly a higher social status would improve the power relationship of the teacher with the board of education.

The School Administrator. The school administrator derives his power directly from the board of education. He is "strong" to the degree that the board allows him to use the power which it has by law and by virtue of its position in the community.

In all the examples of board-controlled factors mentioned above, the school administrator acts as liaison between the board and the faculty. From the beginning of a teacher's career, the administrator is the one who *selects* a teacher from a group of candidates and *recommends* him to the board of education. Likewise, the recommendation to put a teacher on *tenure* or to *discharge* him or to withhold or increase the salary increments is always made by the school administrator. By having control of these vital influences, his power over the teachers becomes very great. More than one teacher, upon having an argument with his principal, comes up short with the thought, "He can fire me!" This control needs to be used wisely and judicially by the administrator if he is to release the creative talents of his staff. He should act in such a manner as to ease the threat to his teachers that this control gives him.

It was noted earlier in this chapter that there is some disagreement in the literature as to the amount of power that a superintendent exercises in a community. The fact that the amount of power exercised by superintendents does vary from community to community immediately causes us to ask why some superintendents exercise more power in the community than do others. An answer to this might be found by applying Hunter's postulates and the other information we now have about power-holders in general. Let us construct two paradigms, one of a superintendent holding much power in the community and the other of a superintendent holding little power in the community. These paradigms, however, are in the nature of hypotheses based upon present knowledge and would need to be tested further.

SUPERINTENDENT: HIGH POWER-HOLDER	SUPERINTENDENT: LOW POWER-HOLDER
1. Has had long tenure in position. (May be lifelong resident of community.)	1. Has had short tenure in position. (Has been nomadic, having been in several communities.)
2. Is financially independent.	2. Is financially dependent upon his salary.
3. Has the backing of one or more powerful groups in the community.	3. Attempts to represent all of the people.
4. Has high social standing, probably in lower upper class.	4. Has social standing in the upper middle class but originated in a lower class.

In these paradigms, the key point might very well be the first. The school superintendency has been a highly nomadic position. The pattern has been for men to start in small communities and work their way into larger ones, serving only as much time in each as was needed to build a satisfactory record. They stay in the smaller communities only long enough so that it does not look as though they were fired. It could be mentioned that all forty leaders listed by Hunter [30] had lived in the community for a long period of time and that most were lifelong residents. It appears that an obstacle to superintendents' achieving a power status in the community is the nomadic trend which the position seems to have taken.

Administrative power over subordinates has been misused by many. Hunter describes ways in which those in authority treat the relatively powerless group which he calls the understructure. Although he describes the power structure of a community, his words are of value to use in our analysis. He states: [31]

The method of handling the relatively powerless understructure is through the pressures previously described—warnings, intimidations, threats, and in extreme cases, violence. In some cases the method may include isolation from all sources of support for the individual, including his job and therefore his income. The principle of "divide and rule" is as applicable in the community as it is in larger units of political patterning and it is as effective.

Conditions Modifying the School Power Structure

We should not get the idea that the power structure which we have been describing is fixed and unchanging. It is, just as is society, in a state of constant flux. There are many conditions now in operation which affect the power relations of school people. There are also some indications of conditions which will modify the power structure in the future. Let us take a look at some of these modifying conditions.

Teacher Shortage. This one factor is of great importance in changing the power structure of education. You will note, in many of the cases in Part 3, that whenever the administrator has to make a decision about letting a teacher go, he must always consider the difficulty he will have in replacing him. This scarcity has increased the value of the teacher and has brought about a change in the viewpoint of the administrator, the board, and the community. In the 1930's, the tremendous oversupply of teachers gave rise to the attitude that anyone could teach. This attitude carried with it a certain amount of depreciation. The present shortage is demonstrating the value of the teacher and is adding to his prestige.

The shortage is also a factor (possibly the only *real* factor) in bringing

[30] Hunter, *op. cit.,* p. 11.
[31] *Ibid.,* pp. 247-248.

about salary increases. Clark has indicated that the average salary of instructional staff members has risen $806 in the past five years.[32] There is no indication that the trend toward higher salaries has slackened off. In terms of salaries and power structure, we have one other very significant fact to note. This is the decrease in the gap between salaries paid to classroom teachers and administrators.[33] Decreasing the gap while increasing the general level of salaries will tend to improve the status of the teachers in the power structure of both the school and the community.

Teacher Tenure. The granting of tenure to teachers and some administrators has acted to decrease the arbitrary use of power on the part of the board and school administrators. Since a teacher on tenure cannot normally be discharged unless cause is demonstrated or the position abolished, the power of the teacher has been strengthened. This power is reflected in at least two ways: the first, and most important, has been the over-all increase in spirit, aggressiveness, and confidence which has come with job security; the second has been the change in the way the administrator treats the teacher.

In some cases, it would seem that the teacher has abused the newly acquired power of tenure. In some cases, the teacher has as much as said, "I have tenure. You can't fire me. In fact, you don't have any control over me any more!" Since the courts have demanded precise showing of cause for dismissal and administrators have found it difficult to collect the necessary evidence, there have been few such cases. Much of the increase in the power of the teacher has been used to resist the control of the board and the administrator. This has acted to change the relationships of the board, administrators, and teachers. It has meant that all are on somewhat more common ground and that the relationship, of necessity, more closely approaches a partnership than was formerly the case.

Improved Preparation of Teachers. The amount of preparation required for those going into teaching has increased steadily over the years. We are approaching the time when schools will be staffed by teachers who are fully prepared, competent, professional people. The only difference in preparation between the teachers and administrators will be of kind rather than degree. The difference which once existed, in which the teachers were poorly educated and the administrators well educated (not necessarily in terms of administration), is now on its way out. This is now influencing the status of teachers and will continue as a factor in moving them up in the power structure.

[32] David L. Clark and Arvid J. Burke, "Economic, Legal, and Social Status of Teachers," *Review of Educational Research*, Vol. 25, No. 3 (June, 1955), p. 239.

[33] Frank W. Hubbard, "Salaries and Salary Schedules of High School Principals in 1952-53," *Bulletin of the National Association of Secondary School Principals*, Vol. 37 (December, 1953), pp. 1-9; Theodore L. Reller, "Finance and Personnel," *Problems and Issues in Public School Finance* (New York, Teachers College, Bureau of Publications, 1952), pp. 359-396.

Increased Community Interest in Schools. There are at the present time somewhat more than 10,000 citizen groups in the country. They are interested in and are studying the problems of education and are coming to realize more and more the importance of good teaching. As these community groups act to solve the problems of the teacher shortage, they will act to increase salaries, improve working conditions, and raise the status of teachers.

Human Relations Trend. There has been an increased emphasis on human relations in industry and business which has been reflected in our schools. This movement has encouraged a fuller awareness of the value and worth of individuals and has caused all concerned to try to improve relations between administrator, teacher, and board members. The biggest result of the movement has been the general improvement of the atmosphere in the schools.

Teacher Organizations. There has been considerable growth in the membership and power of teacher organizations in recent years. This point is interesting in light of Hunter's postulate concerning power structure. He points out that since power is a necessary part of any social organism, we must learn to use it rather than try to eliminate it. To repeat his postulate: "Power of the individual must be structured into associational, clique, or institutional patterns to be effective." [34] Apparently, teachers are beginning to realize that Hunter is right.

It has been demonstrated that teachers actually increase the amount of power they can wield when they band together into organizations. Male has demonstrated that when teachers act through a state education association, they can resist pressures at the state and local levels and can exert pressure of their own.[35] As Hunter has pointed out, people can only be assured a voice in policy determination and implementation when they do band together. Where these groups are not present, we find a lack of power influence.

The increase in membership and activity has brought with it a change in relations between teachers and administrators. The trend since 1946 has been toward greater interaction between teachers as a *group* and the administration. Many administrators deplore this tendency because they want to feel that they are a part of the teacher's group. They never can be because of the power they wield as the head man in their school. This trend toward group bargaining with administration in all probability will grow rather than decrease. It is only as a member of an organized group that the teacher will acquire the power necessary to talk on even terms with the administrator. School administrators should recognize the role of these groups in the power structure of a school and learn to work

[34] Hunter, *op. cit.*, p. 248.
[35] George A. Male, "The Michigan Education Association as an Interest Group: 1852–1950," in *Dissertation Abstracts*, Vol. 12, No. 2 (1952), pp. 152–153.

with them. This has been the pattern in other aspects of our society and there is every indication that it will be the pattern in education.

SUMMARY

Power is the word we use to describe the acts of men going about the business of moving other men to act in relation to themselves or in relation to organic or inorganic things. As such, it is one of the most basic concepts to understand if we are to discuss human relations in an administrative frame of reference. Power is not always seen in the same guise. There are three definite types of power: force, domination, and manipulation. There are also three categories of residual power in a culture. These are the historical reference, which indicates how the culture has considered a particular group in reference to power in the past; psychological concepts of power, which deal with power in relation to motives; and the values and moral and ethical considerations, which have to do with the code of conduct which the culture enforces.

The discussion of power was based upon Hunter's four postulates and three hypotheses. It was pointed out that in a democratic society power should never be exercised through force or manipulation. The democratic leader makes explicit his desires with regard to the behavior of his subordinates. In a democratic society, the power command is held by a large number of people and is susceptible to the will of all of the people.

The need for ability to diagnose the power structure of the community in which the school administrator works was pinpointed. Power-holders in the community influence the direction which the school will take; are either on the board of education or influence its membership; will not allow the superintendent to be a community leader if he is seriously at odds with them; and control the making of important decisions concerning community life. With this in mind, three methods of learning about community power structure were presented.

The chapter concluded with the diagnosis of the power structure within a school and a consideration of current conditions that are modifying the power structure.

EXERCISES

1. Using the techniques indicated, make an analysis of the power structure of your community.
2. Make a study of major decisions made by your community in the past five years. Can you relate these decisions to the interests of any group in your community?
3. Take the four postulates and three hypotheses of Hunter and illustrate them from your own experience.
4. How does the democratic power-holder differ from the authoritarian power-holder? Are these differences readily noticeable in our public schools?

5. Work out a method of involving more people in the power structure of your school.

6. Do Goldhammer's conclusions about the board of education in Central Forks hold true for your board of education? If not, how do they differ?

7. On what community issues do you, as an administrator, have to "fish or cut bait"? What group (or groups) is forcing your hand?

8. How do you, as an administrator, feel about the increasing power of teachers organizations?

9. What particular factors have increased or decreased teacher prestige in your community in the past five years?

10. Will teachers organizations ever become as strong in education as the unions are in industry? If not, why not?

SELECTED BIBLIOGRAPHY

BROOKOVER, Wilbur B., "Teachers and the Stratification of American Society," *Harvard Educational Review*, Vol. 23 (Fall, 1953), pp. 257-267.

BROWN, Robert H., "The Composition of School Boards," *American School Board Journal*, Vol. 129 (August, 1954), pp. 23-24.

CARTWRIGHT, Dorwin and ZANDER, Alvin, eds., *Group Dynamics* (Evanston, Ill., Row, Peterson, 1953), pp. 428-492.

DODSON, Dan W., "For Those of Us Who Teach," *American Unity*, Vol. 13, No. 5 (May-June, 1955), pp. 3-8.

DUBIN, Robert, ed., *Human Relations in Administration* (New York, Prentice-Hall, 1951), pp. 172-187.

GOLDHAMMER, Keith, "Community Power Structure and School Board Membership," *American School Board Journal*, Vol. 130, No. 3 (March, 1955), pp. 23-25.

GOULDNER, Alvin, W., ed., *Studies in Leadership* (New York, Harper, 1950), pp. 667-678.

HUNTER, Floyd, *Community Power Structure* (Chapel Hill, University of North Carolina Press, 1953).

LOOMIS, Charles P., "Tapping Human Power Lines," *The Leader Digest* (Chicago, Adult Education Association, 1954).

RATHS, Louis E. and ABRAMSON, Stephen, *Student Status and Social Class* (Bronxville, N. Y., Modern Education Service, 1951).

Human Relations and Authority

In the preceding chapter, we investigated the power structure of communities and schools. We noted that power is a latent force which brings about certain behavior on the part of those individuals in the power structure. This behavior will be the subject of our investigation in this chapter.

Many questions of major importance arise when the school administrator considers the question of authority. He is faced with such questions as these: How is authority exercised in a democratic state as contrasted with a totalitarian state? How does the exercise of authority influence people in leadership positions? Why and to what extent will a subordinate accept the decision of another as governing his own conduct? Can authority be delegated and, if so, how? Does authority reside in a position or in a person? How do people behave under different conditions of authority?

WHAT IS AUTHORITY?

There seems to be some confusion in the literature as to the exact meaning and use of the term *authority*. Many people confuse it with the term *power*, use it interchangeably with the term *authoritarian*, think of it as a psychological term or as a legal term. There is also a tendency to think of authority only in terms of a totalitarian situation. For instance, the Catholic church is usually discussed in terms of the degree of authority which the hierarchy holds, but it is relatively rare to hear the various Protestant churches discussed in these terms. If, however, we adhere to Hunter's definition of power as "the acts of men going about the business of moving other men to act in relation to themselves or in relation to organic or inorganic things," [1] we can see readily that power is present in each of the two types of religious institutions. It differs only in outward appearance, and it is this outward manifestation of power that we will consider as *authority*. All formal and many informal organizations, then, are the visible signs of power and therefore constitute authority. It would be entirely misleading to consider authority as limited to one variety of political or religious belief.

[1] Floyd Hunter, *Community Power Structure* (Chapel Hill, University of North Carolina Press, 1953), p. 2.

According to the concept of authority that we have just formulated, we note that authority, or the outward manifestation of power, takes the form of institutions. Therefore, it would be more nearly correct to state, as does Dubin, that "authority is institutionalized power."[2] Going one step further in our analysis, we can state, with Hunter, that "authority, as institutionalized power, sits astride latent force."[3] In other words, when we speak of authority, we are talking about the institutionalized form which the latent forces in community living assume. We have forces that cause people to live together under law, and the police force is the institution which has been created to see that this is done. The people have desired to have their children educated, and the school is the institution which has been formed to do the job. These are two examples which illustrate the point. There is a latent force, power, and there is the institution riding astride the power, authority.

AUTHORITY IN THE SCHOOLS

It may be that we have oversimplified the concepts of authority and power and conveyed the impression that there exists naked power, with its institutions exerting overwhelming and uncontrollable force. In this connection, let us look at the school. We know that education is a state function and that in the local school district the board of education is the agent of the state. We say that the state holds the power to act in the field of education. It creates boards of education, which are institutions. These boards hire administrators, teachers, and nonteaching personnel to implement the authority of the boards. The board establishes policies, and the chief school administrator is responsible for the execution of these policies. The authority of the administrator flows downward through a chain of command composed of assistant or associate superintendents and principals. Within the framework of board policy, the will of the chief school administrator is the will of the school system.

Anyone familiar with schools knows that the above pattern rarely holds true. There are often modifications in the authority of the administrator in terms of the push and pull of the community forces which are brought to bear on a particular issue. The authority of the school administrator is also conditioned by the degree to which the faculty and, for that matter, the student body accept his leadership. It can be readily seen that although the school is the authority which is created by the power of the state, this authority is not a simple thing. The ultimate authority of the school is as much a function of delegation by the state as it is of delegation by the community, the faculty, and the students. The administrator

---

[2] Robert Dubin, ed., *Human Relations in Administration* (New York, Prentice-Hall, 1951), p. 188.
[3] Hunter, *op. cit.*, p. 164.

accepts the delegation of authority from the board to much the same extent as he accepts authority from those whom he leads. The democratic leader must gain the consent of the governed.

The authority to which a school administrator is subjected is a complex and many-handed organism. According to Hagman and Schwartz there are nine factors of the school-community matrix which bear on the authority of the school administrator. These are stated as follows: [4]

1. The board of education is a principal conditioning body of administrative decision and action. Through policy, formally and informally established, the board holds control over the administrator's activity and at the same time delegates to him authority which he may use in meeting his assigned responsibilities.

2. The instructional staff, through which the administrator must work to accomplish the purposes of the school system, applies subtle or obvious sanctions against the administrator's activity. His authority as titular leader of the schools will not be challenged because the authority is thought attached to the position not to the person. But in order that his leadership may be effective, he must secure his authority in the teaching group by grant of authority from it. The authority of the group is therefore the source of the authority which gives him the role of leader in fact as well as in name. Should he fail to win his place in the group, to the extent that he fails, the group will subvert his will that they perform in the direction of the ends which he holds as ends for the school organization.

3. The noninstructional staff, clerks, bus drivers, custodians and others, if co-operating fully with the general school effort can assist greatly in the accomplishment of school tasks and the co-operation of the noninstructional staff is desirably to be won by the administrator.

Concerning this third factor, there are two points to bear in mind. First, because of the lack of professional restraints which the nonteaching staff experiences, its members are capable of exercising far greater negative authority in a school system than are the faculty members. The community contacts, the fact that many of the noninstructional jobs are political appointments, and the nature of the tasks performed give this group a peculiar kind of status in a school system. They very often see the school from the point-of-view of how clean the floors are and whether or not the busses are on time. They do not have general loyalty to the educational policies of the system and can exert a negative authority on administrative decision and action. A further point is that in some states the noninstructional employees have civil service status, and, consequently, they look to a source beyond the local school district for policies, decisions, and actions that influence their welfare. This serves to remove them even further from the authority of the local district and could tend to increase whatever negative authority they may exercise.

[4] Harlan L. Hagman and Alfred Schwartz, *Administration in Profile for School Executives* (New York, Harper, 1955), p. 111.

The next five factors are listed in the following order: [5]

4. The parents of the children in the schools exert both friendly and unfriendly pressures upon the administrator and he cannot escape their influence upon his decisions and actions.

5. The children in the schools exercise an influence upon the administrator's activities in many ways, most of which are desirable but some of which are potentially undesirable. He must win their co-operation also because without it some of the objectives of the school system will obviously be defeated.

6. All the people of the school district exercise their authority at times of school elections and at all other times through the sensitivity of the administrator and the school board to public opinion in the community. . . .

7. The state school law is authority which the school administrator must acknowledge as basic to public education, and as a primary conditioner of his activity.

8. The customs and traditions of society, with particular reference to the local community, control much administrative behavior. It is authority which ordinarily is not to be challenged with impunity. In introducing changes in school practice, the administrator must move with care in those matters which seem to be rooted deeply in community life.

The importance of the eighth factor cannot be overemphasized and will be dealt with in greater detail in other sections.[6] Some indication of its importance can be gained from Niblett, who goes so far as to say: [7]

The culture within which we live shapes and limits our imaginations, and by permitting us to do and think and feel in certain ways makes it increasingly unlikely or impossible that we should do or think or feel in ways that are contradictory or tangential to it.

It should be observed that Niblett's statement is somewhat extreme. However, it is more true for people who hold high positions of responsibility than for those who do not, and school administrators are particularly referred to as those who are unlikely to behave in a way not approved by the culture. That school administrators are further bound to the educational *status in quo* is pointed out in Niblett's statement that "Those who come into positions of authority in the public school system have been shaped by the spirit and tradition of the educational system of the past." [8] The influence of past as well as the present culture, then, is clearly a source of authority which conditions administrative behavior.

With regard to the final factor of authority, Hagman and Schwartz make the following observation: [9]

9. The educational profession exerts an authority over school practice and administrative activity. Professional opinion, widely held, is apt to influence

[5] *Ibid.*, pp. 111-113.
[6] See below, Ch. 11.
[7] W. R. Niblett, "Authority in Education," *Journal of Education* (London), Vol. 84 (January, 1952), pp. 5-6.
[8] *Ibid.*
[9] Hagman and Schwartz, *op. cit.*, p. 113.

the administrator more than lay opinion, locally held, even if the latter results in considerable pressure upon the schools. The school activity is likely to reveal in every area the attention paid to what is thought to be professionally approved.

It can be seen that the behavior of the school administrator is both restrained and encouraged by a variety of factors. Of course, there is the added factor of the administrator himself. He does not ride astride these influences without influencing them to some extent. He is not a neutral factor; nor is he strictly a catalyst. He does not influence events without himself being influenced; nor does he act solely as a result of outside factors. The success of the administrator is a function of his skill in working with the diverse authorities of the school-community matrix. His task is not merely that of a compromiser but that of an engineer. He needs to see where the school is going and then weigh the influences upon its direction and act so as to attain the objective in the most expeditious manner.

The demands of the various authorities in the school and community have been summarized by Neal Gross, director of the Harvard School Executive Studies. He solicited information from school board members concerning the demands with which they were confronted in their positions. He reports the following: [10]

Of 500 school board members questioned, 53% said that citizens had demanded they put more emphasis on the 3 R's, while 43% received demands for other types of courses; 41% received protests over the opinions of certain teachers, while 12% were confronted with demands that teachers be allowed to speak more freely; 69% received complaints about the amount of school taxes; while 51% received demands that the schools get more money.

Although it is very important that the school administrator be able to assay the opinion of his community, he can rarely decide an issue merely by taking a vote. As noted under factor 9 above, there is an observable tendency for administrators to be influenced more by the authority of the profession than by that of the local community in *some areas*. Certainly, in educational matters, which have been subjected to long and penetrating research, a sounder judgment can be made on the basis of the authority of the profession than on the authority of the local community. The skill of the administrator is contingent upon his ability to determine a heirarchy of authority in a particular situation and to act on the basis of this judgment. He must turn the forces acting upon him and through him to the accomplishment of the aims and purposes of the school system. This is the test of leadership.

In summarizing this section of the chapter we can state that authority is the outward manifestation (usually institutionalized) of power. The authority of an individual is governed to a large extent by his acceptance

[10] *Time* (April 11, 1955), p. 48.

by the group in which the authority is being exercised. This has been well stated by Benne: [11]

Authority always involves the exercise of power, but this power depends ultimately in some degree upon the acceptance by the subjects of the right of the bearer to obedience within some definable, though not always clearly defined, field of conduct or belief. Those who define authority as "power to enforce obedience" often neglect this peculiar character of "human" power. And those who define authority as the "right of the bearer to obedience" often neglect the power of compulsion which operates in the widespread acceptance of some bearer of authority as "right" and the power of the sanctions which this acceptance authorizes.

BEHAVIOR AND AUTHORITY

The importance of the topic of authority to the study of human relations is evident in observing the behavior of people both in positions of authority and in subordinate positions. We are concerned with the general question, What are the differences in behavior which are due to differences in authority roles? Does the fact that a person is superintendent of schools alter his behavior because he fills a higher authority role than does a teacher? Does the fact that a teacher fills a lower authority role than does the superintendent affect the teacher's behavior? It is not only the behavior of the two in relation to each other that concerns us; the behavior of each in relation to others in the community is also of importance. We will not be able to test the differences between groups of teachers and superintendents in any statistical manner, but we will be able to note studies in which differences in behavior have been observed.

Behavior of People in Authority

As school administrators we need to consider the proposition that the filling of a role high in authority will cause a difference in behavior. Simon has defined authority in terms of behavior of a superior and a subordinate. This use of the term *authority* as descriptive of behavior gives us our lead into the discussion. He states the behaviorial relationship as follows: "The superior frames and transmits decisions with the expectation that they will be accepted by the subordinate. The subordinate expects such decisions, and his conduct is determined by them." [12] Simon goes so far as to indicate that unless this type of behavior is exhibited, there is no authority relationship regardless of the "paper" theory of organization.

It is obvious, however, that not all holders of authority react to their

[11] Kenneth D. Benne, "A Conception of Authority," *Teachers College Record*, Vol. 44 (February, 1944), p. 350.

[12] Herbert A. Simon, *Administrative Behavior* (New York, Macmillan, 1950), p. 125.

roles in the same manner. In fact, because of individual differences, they would seem to react in different ways. There are, however, some general groupings within which we can place various kinds of authority holders in order to examine some of their characteristic behavior. It should be borne in mind that there is, most often, an overlapping of types of authority. One type in its basic form is rarely observed. Dubin distinguishes three types of authority in his discussion of this topic: [13]

1. that which is based upon rational grounds;
2. that which is based upon traditional grounds;
3. that which is based upon charismatic grounds (derived from *charisma*, the "gift of grace").

Authority based upon *rational* grounds rests on the belief that the position is the center of authority and that the sanction for this authority rests in duly constituted law and order. The personal characteristics of the individual theoretically do not influence the amount or type of authority that is present. Herman Wouk's Pulitzer Prize novel, *The Caine Mutiny*, illustrates this rational type of authority. In it, Captain Queeg exercises his authority because it is inherent in his *position*. His own weaknesses are not supposed to be considered as factors affecting the subordination of his officers and men. However, one of his men does not thoroughly subscribe to this concept of authority and incites the men to mutiny. The authority structure of the entire formal organization, which in this case, happens to be the Navy, is thereby threatened. When an organization is based upon rational authority it has a great responsibility to itself to choose men to fill its top positions who will live up to the expectations of the position.

Authority based upon traditional grounds derives from a long history and a legitimate sense of "rightness." Any monarchy is the prime example of this type.

Authority based upon *charismatic* grounds rests upon the belief of followers that the leader has exceptional personal characteristics. They may, and usually do, believe that these qualities set the leader apart from other people, that he is over and above all others.

In education we would expect the typical, in fact, the only, type of authority to be the *rational*. In other words, we would expect the superintendent to exercise his authority because he holds a position with clearly defined powers and responsibilities. He also holds the position because he has the required knowledge and skills. His authority is rational because the position is clearly defined and he has the knowledge and skills necessary to fill that position. His authority should not be conditioned by his personal characteristics. This, however, is rarely the case. The authority of most administrators is both rational and charismatic. The authority which a school administrator exerts is due to his position, but the ac-

[13] Dubin *op. cit.*, p. 196.

ceptance of his authority by others is, in part at least, conditioned by his personal characteristics. Some administrators inspire great faith and confidence in their followers and, as a result, can exercise far more power than their position normally permits.

The typical staff organization, mode of exercising authority, and staff obedience for each of the three types of authority is depicted by Dubin in the following chart. [14]

Type of authority	Typical organization of staff	Typical mode of exercising authority	Staff is obedient to
Rational	Bureaucracy	Rational delegation	Legally established, impersonal order
Traditional	Retainers	*Ad hoc* delegation	Person of leader
Charismatic	Personal staff, servants	Directly, no delegation	Idealized person of leader

The development of Western civilization has been marked by the ascendency of the rational type of authority and the gradual decline of the traditional and the charismatic. So, too, has the organization and administration of the American public schools. This has given rise to the bureaucratic organization of the staff, the rational delegation of authority, and obedience to the legally established, impersonal order. When discussing bureaucracy, we should be careful of the connotation implicit in the term. To most people, bureaucracy smacks of inefficiency and waste. As it is used here, the direct opposite meaning of the term is intended. In terms of wide historical perspective, modern-day bureaucracy is the most advanced system of organization yet devised to do the work of man.[15] Nevertheless, it is obvious that there are many weaknesses in the bureaucratic organization. One of these weaknesses is vitally important to us in educational administration.

Impersonality of Bureaucratic Behavior

Administrators in a bureaucratic organization owe their authority to the position and not primarily to their own talents. Their subordinates owe allegiance primarily to the position and not to the man in the position. In the public schools, the administrator derives his authority from the position, be it superintendent or principal. Teachers owe allegiance to the position of superintendent or principal and not the man. Considering the mobility of superintendents, this is not entirely without virtue. This condition brings about one of the most serious of the problems faced by American school administrators—the lack of good human relations with

[14] *Ibid.*, p. 197.
[15] Alvin W. Gouldner, ed., *Studies in Leadership* (New York, Harper, 1950), p. 57.

the staff and community.[16] It has been reported in several studies, notably those of Bakke [17] and Horney,[18] that bureaucracy breeds *impersonality*. This has given rise to an evil which is just being recognized in the public schools. The administrator, being tuned to a norm of impersonality, behaves in such a way as to minimize personal relationships with teachers, parents, and students. He categorizes instead of dealing in a personal manner with each problem. The individual becomes lost as the superintendent deals with "a first-year teacher" or "a truant" or "a trouble-making parent." Merton summarizes this problem as follows: [19]

> Since functionaries minimize personal relations and resort to categorization, the peculiarities of individual cases are often ignored. But the client who, quite understandably, is convinced of the "special features" of *his* own problem often objects to such categorical treatment. Stereotyped behavior is not adapted to the exigencies of individual problems. The impersonal treatment of affairs which are at times of great personal significance to the client gives rise to the charge of "arrogance" and "haughtiness" of the bureaucrat.

If we substituted "teacher" or "pupil" for the word "client" here, we would have a description of the reaction of the school-oriented person to the bureaucracy of the school. The parent who visits the school is not content with being treated as one of a large group of the public or even as a kindergarten parent. He expects, instead, to be regarded as an individual, and he wants evidence that the school is treating his child as an individual. To the extent that school administrators practice good human relations, this major weakness of bureaucratic organization is being overcome.

Behavior and Amount of Authority

Recent research has been very helpful in clarifying the relationships that exist in the power structure of an organization. Suppose we look in on a meeting of the superintendent's council in a rather large school system. The council is composed of the superintendent, two assistant superintendents, and seven principals. One of the principals is a young man, thirty years old, who has just been appointed to his position. During the course of the meeting, the new principal doesn't say very much. When he does talk, he directs his comments to the superintendent. He is very careful not to be critical of the other people at the table. He listens very intently to the superintendent and agrees with him on practically every point. On the other hand, the superintendent behaves quite differently.

---

[16] See above, Ch. 1.
[17] E. W. Bakke, *Unemployed Man: A Social Study* (New York, Dutton, 1934).
[18] Karen Horney, *The Neurotic Personality of Our Time* (New York, Norton, 1937).
[19] Robert K. Merton, "Bureaucratic Structure and Personality," *Social Forces*, Vol. 18, No. 4 (May, 1940), p. 566.

When he speaks, he addresses the whole group. He doesn't listen too closely to the comments of the other members of the council. Whenever he makes a point, he is very careful to defend himself. His reaction to their comments on his argument is one of self-defense.

In considering the behavior of the two men, we might, at first, be inclined to attribute these differences in behavior to differences in personality. But this is not so; for if we were to look in on a meeting of the new principal and his faculty, we would find him acting in very much the same way that the superintendent acted in his council meeting. There would be some small differences to be sure, but basically their behavior would be the same.

The reasons why the two men behaved differently in one situation yet similarly when each occupied a similar position are provided, in part, by current research. Bales, in his study, observes that groups may display differentiation according to several criteria and that each member of a group will occupy a position with regard to these criteria. The following are adopted from his bases: [20]

1. The differential degree to which members have access to resources.
2. The differential degree to which they have control (power) over other persons.
3. The differential degree to which they have importance or prestige.
4. The differential degree of solidarity or identification each has with the group.

It is clear that in the council meeting the new principal has no access to resources that are not available to everyone else. He has little or no power over anyone else in the group; he has little or no importance or prestige as far as the council is concerned; and, since he is new, he has not yet achieved a feeling of solidarity or identification with the group. Within his own faculty group, his position is quite different. His role here is more like that of the superintendent in the council meeting. If we review his position in the faculty group in relation to Bales's bases of differentiation, we note, first of all, that he has more access to resources than does any member of his faculty. In fact, he *is* the one through which they receive their supplies and so forth. In the preceding chapter we discussed the power of the administrator over subordinates and that discussion would be applicable here.[21] The principal is the head man in a school and so he has the most prestige as far as formal structure is concerned. He has had the opportunity to identify himself with his school group and therefore has identified more with his faculty than with the council.

Cartwright and Zander, in reviewing the research on position in the

[20] Robert F. Bales, "A Theoretical Framework for Interaction Process Analysis," *Group Dynamics*, ed. Dorwin Cartwright and Alvin Zander (Evanston, Ill., Row, Peterson, 1953), pp. 33-36.

[21] See above, pp. 114-115.

power structure, discuss the different behaviors of various position hold-ers.[22] They point out that a person's position in the communication struc-ture determines to whom he can speak and from whom he can receive information. How well an individual can satisfy his needs for acceptance and affection will depend, at least in part, on his position in the power structure. Likewise, his position determines what he can do, his space of free movement, how autonomous he can be, and how subject he is to arbitrary control by others.

We have noted the general effects of position in the power structure on behavior. We shall now observe how top executives, people with a great deal of authority, behave and contrast this with the way in which people with very little authority behave. We shall also try to indicate ways in which the negative effects of this behavior can be offset.

Behavior of Top Administrators

What happens to a man as he advances higher and higher on the scale of leadership in an organization? Does his behavior change? Do people regard him differently? These questions apply equally as well to the chief school administrator as to the head of a large business, industrial, or mili-tary organization. One of the first things which a newly appointed chief school administrator learns when he steps into his job is that his rela-tionships with the other members of the faculty undergo an abrupt change. If he attempts to maintain the relationship he had established before assuming his new position, he finds constant rebuff. When he walks into the men's faculty room, for instance, he notices that the topic of con-versation changes quickly and that the atmosphere of the group also changes. Then, too, the duties of his position make demands on his time which preclude contacts with the faculty and his previous associates.

As men rise in the hierarchy of authority, there is considerable evidence that they become more and more removed from the human beings in their organization. But the increased demands on their time are not wholly responsible for this predicament. Zilboorg, for example, has found that in our society the greater the authority of a given leader, the more sheltered he is from the impacts of reality.[23] This same phenomenon is discussed by Moley in a very interesting commentary on a typical day in the life of former president Harry Truman.[24] This brief article points out that the president read newspapers favorable to him, received reports from people who knew what he wanted to hear,[25] talked to others who wanted favors

---

[22] Cartwright and Zander, *op. cit.*, p. 424.

[23] Gregory Zilboorg, "Authority and Leadership," *World Federation of Mental Health*, Vol. 2, Bull. No. 5 (1950), pp. 13-17.

[24] Raymond Moley, "Presidential Isolation," in Dubin, *op. cit.*, pp. 236-237.

[25] This behavior is called *anticipated reaction* and will be discussed later in this chapter.

from him, and never had to face reality squarely. (This routine was broken occasionally as we know; the storm following the dismissal of General MacArthur is a case in point.) Moley was led to comment that "a president, despite ample facilities, lives in an atmosphere of unreality—a never-never world." [26] Katz, in his study of top executives, was led to a similar conclusion: [27]

> As we go higher and higher in the administrative echelons, the number and frequency of these personal contacts decrease, and the need for human skill becomes proportionately, although probably not absolutely, less. . . . The human skill of dealing with individuals then becomes subordinate to the conceptual skills of integrating group interests and activities into a co-ordinated whole.

The paradox which is constructed is discussed by Zilboorg.[28] What is happening is that as a person rises in an institutional structure, his power over the people in the ranks increases. In fact, the increase in power over people is probably proportional to the increase in position. At the same time, he is becoming increasingly farther removed from the people over whom he is exercising this power. This tends, then, to relieve him of the sense of responsibility in the same proportion as he receives authority, which can lead to a disregard for the individuals within the organization, although this need not be a certain outcome.

Subordinates in Authority Systems

We have seen the effects of an authority role on persons in leadership positions. What is the effect of authority on people in a subordinate position?

Simon has used the definition which states that " 'authority' may be defined as the power to make decisions which guide the actions of others." [29] In discussing this concept, he points out that in every authority situation there is a superior and a subordinate. The superior frames decisions and anticipates that they will be followed. "The subordinate expects such decisions, and his conduct is determined by them." [30] The characteristic behavior of a subordinate is expressed in this last sentence. His behavior is such that he holds in abeyance his own critical facilities and waits for his superior to express his beliefs or to make a decision. It should be noted that this is not always a continuing relationship. In other words, there are times when the superior and subordinate exchange places. In certain situations, one person may be in authority over another; then,

[26] *Ibid.*, p. 236.

[27] Robert L. Katz, "Skills of an Effective Administrator," *Harvard Business Review*, Vol. 33, No. 1 (January–February, 1955), p. 37.

[28] *Op. cit.*, pp. 13-17.

[29] Simon, *op. cit.*, p. 125.

[30] *Ibid.*

with a change in situations, the relationship may be reversed. However, although this is an accurate theoretical statement, it is not generally observed to occur in formal organizations. As was pointed out in Chapter 5, the hierarchical structure in most formal organizations cannot easily be forgotten or changed. So it is with authority. The superintendent of a school, for example, is the person in authority. Even though he might indicate that he would like to assume a subordinate role in a particular situation, it would be very difficult for one of his faculty members to assume the superior role.

We can see two conditions of authority emerging as far as the behavior of subordinates is concerned. One condition occurs when authority is exercised intermittently; the other when authority is exercised continually. In the first case, we have the situation which prevails among peers. As the situation changes different persons emerge as being in authority. At one time or another all will probably be in a position of authority, and no conditioning toward obedience or the expectance of obedience will occur. On the other hand, if authority is exercised continually by one person or set of persons, then a *willingness to obey* on the part of the subordinates can be observed.[31] The development of this willingness to obey is of great concern to school administrators, for it can be seen that if subordinates in school adopt such an attitude toward their superiors, they are giving up their right to express free ideas. The only opinion, then, which will receive any consideration, and, in extreme cases, the only idea advanced, would be that of the one in authority. The method of intelligent, critical thinking would be abandoned. The school administrator should strive to develop a receptiveness to the ideas of his subordinates by exchanging positions of authority whenever it is feasible. This practice would permit his subordinates to exercise their power of critical thought freely whenever decisions and ideas were referred to them.

Rule of Anticipated Reactions

In the summer of 1953, the Central School Study, a co-operative study group composed of the central schools [32] of New York State were studying the problem of financing public education. They were getting ready an appeal to the state legislature for an increase in the state-aid appropriation. It was thought that one way in which the case for more state aid could be made was to ask all of the central schools to send data on all of the items which were cut from the budget by the annual meeting. It was thought that this would constitute a list of all of the things which schools

[31] Jeanne and Jack Block, "An Interpersonal Experiment on Reactions to Authority," *Human Relations,* Vol. 5 (1952), pp. 91-98.

[32] A central school district is a consolidated school district usually composed of several small governmental units.

needed, but which they could not have because of a lack of ability to pay on the part of the local district. All schools were requested to send this data to the research office. Of the 450 central schools, *not one* school reported a single item cut from the budget.

Does this incident indicate that the central schools of New York State were adequately financed? Does it mean that the schools could get any amount of money they desired merely by asking for it? Not at all. What actually happened was this: all of the school administrators and boards of education had cut out of their own budgets everything to which they thought the public would object. In other words, they had anticipated that the public, in annual meetings, would object, although there had been no overt indication of such an objection. This type of behavior is called the "rule of anticipated reactions." [33]

This "rule" is common to all power situations. It occurs when the exercise of authority has been continual and the subordinate gets to the point where he asks himself, "How would my superior expect me to behave under these circumstances?" The subordinate then acts on the basis of previous experience. If the circumstances are similar to a preceding situation and the response was previously acceptable, he will respond in the same way again. Thus we see how many administrative decisions are made in education. The above case was clearly such an illustration. The authority of the public was so great that it did not need to be overtly exercised. This is an important point in our discussion of the effects of authority on the behavior of subordinates. Many times we believe that no authority is being exercised unless sanctions of some sort have been applied. The more power an authority has and the more obedient a subordinate is, the less the need for a show of authority. We would then need to consider and observe the way in which people *anticipate* what the superiors might want and, in so doing, surrender their right to critical thought.

The subordinate in a power structure exhibits some other characteristics which should be noted. There are times when the subordinate wants to influence the power-holder to change his behavior. This is usually undertaken in a nondirective manner.[34] In other words, the subordinate does not "come right out with it." He tends to indicate by indirect methods that he would like the power-holder to change. He is quite deferential and will not directly state his intent. This is often interpreted as a sign of weakness and indecision by the power-holder and tends to make him disregard the subordinate.

There is also a tendency for subordinates to ape the behavior of those in power.[35] In school systems, we often note a similarity in the behavior

[33] Simon, *op. cit.*, p. 129.

[34] Ronald Lippitt, Norman Polansky, Fritz Redl, and Sidney Rosen, "The Dynamics of Power" in Cartwright and Zander *op. cit.*, pp. 470-471.

[35] *Ibid.*, pp. 468-470.

of the superintendent and members of the central staff, which extends to mannerisms, voice, gesture and, sometimes, clothing. This is known as the tendency of subordinates to "contage" from superiors.

DELEGATION OF AUTHORITY

The delegation of authority is the *sine qua non* of successful institutional operation. As was discussed above, the highest type of organization yet attained is the bureaucratic organization, in which there is *rational delegation* of authority. As contrasted with this method of delegation we have either *ad hoc* delegation or no delegation by the leader of the organization.

Studies of how school administrators, particularly chief school administrators, spend their time are quite revealing in relation to this topic. Fitch, for example, found that supervising principals in Pennsylvania spent 53 per cent of their time performing or supervising the performance of operational functions.[36] Since these operational functions were related to the business and plant-management aspects of administration, there was insufficient time left for leadership of the instructional program or for human and public relations.

With the current growth in the size of school districts, due to an increase in the birth rate and consolidation of small districts, the problem of delegation of authority must be given greater attention. Let us turn, then, to a consideration of basic administrative functions and the ways in which these are being delegated by school administrators.

What Is Delegated?

Although this is another area of school administration in which research is almost completely lacking, one major study of delegation of authority has been reported. This is a statewide study conducted in New York which shows how functions are delegated in that state.[37] A questionnaire was sent out to chief school administrators in the state in which the respondents were requested to indicate by whom fifty-two important functions of administration were performed. These functions were subdivided into four areas of school administration:

1. Maintaining effective interrelationships with the community.
2. Improving educational opportunity.
3. Obtaining and developing personnel.
4. Providing and maintaining funds and facilities.

[36] George E. Fitch, "A Survey of Administrative Operational Techniques Used by Supervising Principals in Pennsylvania" (Unpublished doctoral dissertation, Pennsylvania State College, 1953).

[37] *Your School and Staffing: Current Practice in Administrative Staffing in New York State* (Albany, N. Y., Cooperative Development of Public School Administration, 1955), Report No. 1, pp. 10-15. Basic data for this study were collected under the direction of Lloyd Elliott of Cornell University.

However, the patterns of operation in delegating and sharing functions cut across these four arbitrary classifications of duties. A clearer picture was drawn by describing general patterns of delegating and sharing and then listing the individual functions which formed the pattern. Thus, the following five charts and brief descriptions are generalized patterns that chief school administrators follow in handling certain functions. The functions so handled are listed in random order following the description of each pattern. The legend for the five charts is as follows:

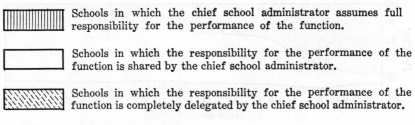

Schools in which the chief school administrator assumes full responsibility for the performance of the function.

Schools in which the responsibility for the performance of the function is shared by the chief school administrator.

Schools in which the responsibility for the performance of the function is completely delegated by the chief school administrator.

ADA   Average daily attendance.

General Pattern A

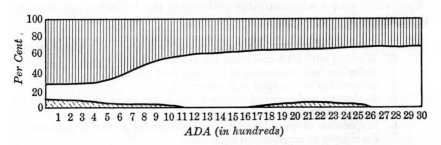

ADA (in hundreds)

In only a few isolated cases does the chief school administrator completely delegate these functions. In the smaller schools, he generally performs them himself. Even in the larger schools, about 30 per cent of the administrators assume sole responsibility for the following twelve functions:

1. Helping the board of education to determine the educational needs of the community.
2. Planning and co-ordination of public relations program.
3. Determination of financial needs and construction of the budget.
4. Selection and recommendation to the board for employment of non-teaching staff personnel.
5. Selection and recommendation to the board for employment of teaching staff personnel.
6. Recommendations to the board for policy formulation and revision.
7. Preparation of information to be disseminated by public communication media.
8. Counseling teaching and nonteaching personnel.

9. Preparation of reports for the board and the state education department.
10. Recommendations to the board for the construction and administration of salary schedules.
11. Evaluation and recommendation to the board for promotion and retention of teaching staff personnel.
12. Plant planning and construction.

General Pattern B

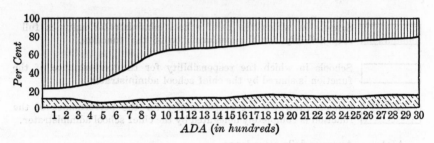

ADA (in hundreds)

In schools below 1000 ADA, this pattern is similar to A. Above 1000 ADA, there is a greater degree of delegation than in A, with only 20-25 per cent of the chief school administrators performing the following functions by themselves:

1. Direction of program for use of school facilities by nonschool groups.
2. Working with PTA and other lay groups.
3. Induction and orientation of teaching staff personnel.
4. Supervision of teaching staff personnel.
5. Evaluation and recommendation to the board for promotion and retention of nonteaching staff personnel.
6. Preparation of special reports and bulletins for general distribution.
7. Purchasing of supplies and equipment.
8. Direction and co-ordination of in-service training program.
9. Determination of specifications for supplies and equipment.
10. Control of the budget.

General Pattern C

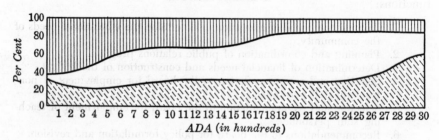

ADA (in hundreds)

Pattern C indicates those functions which many chief school administrators share or delegate. As in patterns A and B, some chief school administrators continue to assume sole responsibility, regardless of the size of the school, but the number assuming such responsibility is less. In the smaller schools about 60 per cent, and in schools above 1600 ADA about 20 per cent, handle the following functions alone:

1. Maintenance of staff personnel records.
2. Administration of insurance program.
3. Induction and orientation of nonteaching staff personnel.
4. Debt service management.
5. Direction of school lunch program.
6. Direction of program of plant maintenance.
7. Supervision of nonteaching staff personnel.
8. Direction of program of bus maintenance and operation.
9. Administration of the payroll.
10. Supervision and auditing of internal accounts.

General Pattern D

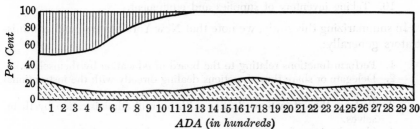

ADA (in hundreds)

This pattern is characterized by increased sharing of responsibility. In the smaller schools, the chief school administrator may perform the function alone, but above 1200 ADA, this is rarely the case. There is a uniform pattern of delegation involving 10-30 per cent of the schools of all sizes. The functions which most chief school administrators share with other members of the staff include:

1. Conferences with parents and other lay citizens.
2. Revision of curriculum and selection of curricular materials.
3. Development of procedures for reporting pupil progress to parents.
4. Scheduling of teaching and nonteaching staff personnel.

General Pattern E

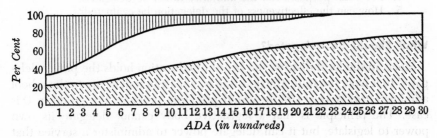

ADA (in hundreds)

The chief school administrator tends to delegate the responsibility for performing these functions:

1. Assisting teachers in diagnosing the learning difficulties of pupils.
2. Control of pupil behavior.
3. Accounting of pupils (census and attendance).
4. Direction of adult education program.
5. Direction and supervision of pupil activity program.
6. Direction of health and safety program.
7. Co-ordination of audiovisual activities.
8. Arrangements for substitute teachers.
9. Helping teachers in planning effective remedial instruction.
10. Scheduling of pupils.
11. Maintenance of pupil personnel records.
12. Direction of guidance program.
13. Direction of program for exceptional children.
14. Administration of summer recreation program.
15. Distribution of supplies and equipment.
16. Taking inventory of supplies and equipment.

In summarizing this study, we note that New York State school administrators generally:

1. Perform functions relating to the board of education by themselves.
2. Delegate or share those functions dealing directly with the instructional program.
3. Perform those functions dealing with over-all administration by themselves.
4. Share business functions or perform them by themselves, even though they have an assistant for business affairs.

When we say we are delegating authority, we really mean that we have some *power* and that we are delegating the right to use this power. Briefly, the state is the power behind public education. Through legislative action, the right to use this power is delegated to local boards of education. In turn, local boards delegate the right to use their power to professional administrators. Basic to any discussion of the delegation of power in school administration are the following questions:

1. What powers does the delegator possess?
2. What powers can be delegated?
3. To whom can the authority to act be delegated?
4. For what purposes can the authority to act be delegated?
5. How can the effectiveness of the delegation be evaluated?

What Should Be Delegated?

Since, in the local district, the board of education holds the power delegated to it from the state, the question is, what can it delegate to the school administrator. A very simply stated principle provides the guide in this case. The principle is that a legislative body cannot delegate its own power to legislate, but it can delegate power to administer a service that it has the authority to provide.[38] In the case of boards of education, the superintendent could select teachers, but the board would have to hire them; the superintendent could write a set of policies, but the board would have to adopt them. The board of education can delegate to administrators the power to perform the services which it has the power to provide. Fitch demonstrated in his study that boards were delegating to the chief school administrators, but that these were not delegating to others.[39] In not doing so, the administrators failed to function as educational leaders.

In order that delegation be a rational process, it is recommended that all boards of education prepare a set of rules and regulations which will cover the *functions* of the educative process for which the board is responsible and indicate the people who should perform these functions. There are several ways of defining the functions of education, but Sears offers a very convenient system: [40]

1. Legislation—making policies, deciding cases, contracting. Performed by the board, but with aid of the superintendent.
2. Administration—directing operation in terms of board policies and decisions. Performed by a hierarchy of executives, varying with size of the school system.
3. Supervision—a staff service devoted to development, co-ordination, and improvement of instruction. Performed by supervisors or by employees having some supervisory duties ...
4. Teaching—instruction, care, and management of children. Performed by teachers, coaches, counselors, and supervisors.
5. Health care ... performed by medical experts, nurses, physical education directors, and coaches, in co-operation with teachers and principals.
6. Research—staff service—devoted to study of problems, preparation of data and reports for use in the system, evaluating, experimentation, and planning. Handled by specialists with staff powers only.
7. Library service ... service, in part, line and, in part, staff in character.
8. Clerical and secretarial service for all divisions of system as work requires.
9. Operation and maintenance—technical, trade, and common labor, covering development, care, and operation of buildings, lawns, and gardens.
10. Business and accounting—to cover financial accounts and budget control, purchase, storage, and distribution of materials and supplies. Performed by accountants and business experts.

This gives us a list of functions and the appropriate people to whom the function can be delegated. The thing to note is that administrators should operate directly in only *two* of the functions. The rest should be delegated. This listing provides a rational and reasonable distribution of functions to the various personnel of the system.

[38] Jesse B. Sears, *The Nature of the Administrative Process* (New York, McGraw-Hill, 1950), p. 291.
[39] Fitch, *op., cit.*
[40] Sears, *op. cit.*, pp. 295-296.

Evaluating the Delegation of Authority

The best way to guarantee that this matter of delegation of authority will work successfully is to make certain, first of all, that safeguards are built into the structure. The admonition of Zilboorg should be noted: "Only so-called psychologically normal leaders are capable of good and wise leadership, and only the hypothetically normal leadership is capable of bringing about a desirable social order." [41] The selection of leaders who will add psychological and moral authority to the authority of the school will be a major safeguard.

The second device is the clear definition of the powers that are to be delegated. Although the area of authority should be clear and unmistakable, it should not be so minutely described that the person feels completely circumscribed and not able to move about as he should.

With adequate leaders whose duties are closely defined, the delegator of authority then observes the way in which the organization functions. Frictions are danger signals and occur either when the delegatee moves into an area that is not his own or does not perform his assigned tasks competently. At the first indication of friction, the person or persons delegating authority should move into action, for the problem may be a simple one of resolving a difficulty between two people or refining the function of one of the individuals.

The whole process of evaluation, in the delegation of authority, is the devising of safeguards and the observation and eradication of frictions. In summarizing this section, a statement from Hagman and Schwartz seems appropriate: [42]

In the delegation of authority, the administrator does not lessen his own authority but rather places it in relationship to other persons so that . . . it can be used more effectively. He retains his power while attaching authority to someone else who may consequently also exercise effective power in situations covered by the authority given him. If the delegation is badly done, the person to whom authority is attached may not have effective power. If the delegation of authority is well done, the administrator has in effect extended himself and his power through the persons to whom delegation has been made.

DEMOCRATIC VS. TOTALITARIAN AUTHORITY

An assumption to which most people in public education claim adherence is that institutions in a democratic country should be democratic in nature. As Simon has said: [43]

There has been much speculation that the central attitudes of a society must be reflected in administrative organization, so that administration in a democracy

---

[41] Zilboorg, *loc. cit.*, pp. 13-17.
[42] Hagman and Schwartz, *op. cit.*, p. 125.
[43] Simon, *op. cit.*, p. 131.

will be in some sense "democratic" while administrators in a totalitarian system will be "authoritarian." Thus far, the thesis has been expounded, but by no means demonstrated.

Let us examine the fundamental differences between a democratic and a totalitarian concept of authority and then determine whether or not a definite effort should be made to reflect a democratic concept in school administration.

Totalitarian Concept of Authority

What seems to be the foundation for authority in a totalitarian state? How is the power of the state exercised as far as individuals are concerned? Friedgood, in analyzing a mass of data on the behavior of the Russian people, has concluded that the authority of the Russian state is based upon an appeal to the unconscious.[44] He demonstrates that an authoritarian government is one in which an individual is reduced to a state of dependence upon, and submission to, the power and authority of the state. To achieve their ends leaders of an authoritarian government exploit the primitive, unconscious drives that stand in constant need of expression and satisfaction. In stimulating these, and, at the same time, repressing them by refusing to grant individual freedom, the Russian state, for example, has been able to manipulate its people by means of governmental propaganda with no little success.

Herbertz has made much the same observation concerning Prussian militarism.[45] On the premise that *Kopenick,* or uncritical yielding to authority, is present to some extent in all men, he demonstrates how deliberately this element of passive dependency was appealed to in the Prussian armies.

Democratic Concept of Authority

The democratic concept of authority differs most noticeably from the totalitarian in that it encourages the rational thinking of the individual and allows him the right to adhere to whatever conclusion he may reach. In a democratic environment, every effort is made to stimulate critical thinking on the part of those in subservient roles. This is accomplished by attempting to allow all individuals to assume leadership roles when their talents permit.

The American public schools have no choice but to adhere to a democratic concept of authority. This means that school administration should

[44] Harry B. Friedgood, "On the Psychological Aspects of Authoritarian and Democratic Political Systems," *American Scientist,* Vol. 39 (1951), p. 440.

[45] Richard Herbertz, "Die Kopenickiade in Leben Des Mannes" ("The 'Kopenick' Element in the Life of the Male"), *Psychd. Berater Gesunde Prakt Lebengestalt,* Vol. 4 (1952), pp. 318-325.

appeal *not* to the primitive, unconscious drives in man but to the rational thinking of individuals as the justification for their authority.

SUMMARY

Authority is institutionalized power. It is the outward manifestation of power, which we cannot see. Although there is a line of authority in each organization, there are also modifying conditions which change the effectiveness of the power being exerted. We note that the authority of an administrator is affected and modified by the board of education, the teachers, nonteaching staff, parents, students, patrons, the state school law, the customs and traditions of the community, and the authority of the profession. The job of chief school administrator is made more difficult because of the conflicting nature of the demands of these various pressure groups.

We find that the behavior of individuals in the power structure is affected by their position in the structure. There are three types of authority: the rational, the traditional, and the charismatic. Western civilization has brought into being the bureaucratic organization, with its resulting rational distribution of authority. A democratic state could not operate under any other kind of governmental organization. Although democratic government is devoted to the benefiting of all of the people, bureaucratic organization becomes highly impersonalized. This is a weakness which school administration must combat.

The behavior of men in high positions of authority is quite different from the behavior of men in low positions of authority. The top executive expects others to defer to him, becomes relatively isolated from those he leads, and acts toward others on the basis of information which those around him slant toward his desires. Men in low positions are characterized by a willingness to obey; they will anticipate the reactions of their superiors and then act accordingly.

Delegation of authority means that the power-holder transfers the right to use this power to another person. The administrator needs to know what can be delegated, to whom it can be delegated, and then how to evaluate the use of the authority which has been delegated.

Authority in democratic organizations differs widely from that in totalitarian organizations. In totalitarian organizations, authority is exercised through an appeal to the unconscious; in democratic organizations it is exercised through an appeal to reason.

EXERCISES

1. Rank the administrators in your school system in terms of their status in the hierarchy of administration. With this list before you, write down examples

of how they behave toward one another. Note who seems to be the one most deferred to in meetings, etc. Next, take Bales's list of bases of differentiating a group and rank each administrator on each base.

2. Is authority in your school system exercised in a democratic or authoritarian manner? What evidence did you use to form your opinion?

3. Using the list of administrators collected for question 1, indicate beside each name whether they exercise authority in a "rational," "traditional," or "charismatic" manner. What evidence did you use to form each decision?

4. How do you distinguish between "power" and "authority"?

5. How is the chain of authority modified in your school system?

6. Does your school system operate as a bureaucracy?

7. Give an example of "anticipated reaction" as it occurred in your school system.

8. What can an administrator do to overcome the negative effects of the "anticipated reaction"?

9. What could be delegated in your school system which is not now being delegated?

10. How can you evaluate the effectiveness of your system of delegating authority?

SELECTED BIBLIOGRAPHY

BENNE, Kenneth D., *A Conception of Authority,* Teachers College Contributions to Education (New York, Teachers College Bureau of Publications, 1943), No. 895.

BLOCK, Jeanne, and BLOCK, Jack, "An Interpersonal Experiment on Reactions to Authority," *Human Relations,* Vol. 5 (1952), pp. 91-98.

CARTWRIGHT, Dorwin, and ZANDER, Alvin, eds., *Group Dynamics* (Evanston, Ill., Row, Peterson, 1953), pp. 415-534.

CLAY, Lucius D., "The Art of Delegation," in *The Management Team,* ed. Edward C. Bursk, (Cambridge, Mass., Harvard University Press, 1955), pp. 6-16.

COLADARCI, Arthur P., and GETZELS, Jacob W., *The Use of Theory in Educational Administration* (Stanford, Stanford University Press, 1955).

DUBIN, Robert, ed., *Human Relations in Administration* (New York, Prentice-Hall, 1951), pp. 188-198.

FRIEDGOOD, Harry B., "On the Psychological Aspects of Authoritarian and Democratic Political Systems," *American Scientist,* Vol. 39 (1951), pp. 432-440.

GOULDNER, Alvin W., ed., *Studies in Leadership* (New York, Harper, 1950), pp. 67-79, 679-701.

HAGMAN, Harlan L. and SCHWARTZ, Alfred, *Administration in Profile for School Executives* (New York, Harper, 1955), ch. 5.

HUNTER, Floyd, *Community Power Structure* (Chapel Hill, University of North Carolina Press, 1953).

NIBLETT, W. R., "Authority in Education," *Journal of Education* (London), Vol. 84 (January, 1952), pp. 5-6.

REED, Warren, "Social Control in the Newsroom: A Functional Analysis," *Social Forces,* Vol. 33 (May, 1955), pp. 326-335.

SEARS, Jesse B., *The Nature of the Administrative Process* (New York, McGraw-Hill, 1950), chs. 7, 8.

SIMON, Herbert A., *Administrative Behavior* (New York, Macmillan, 1950), ch. 7.

CHAPTER 7

Morale

"Morale is when your hands and feet keep working when your head says it can't be done." This is what a seabee told Adm. Ben Moreell about morale, and, in spite of the many refinements in definition which we can now make, this statement comes very close to telling us what morale really is.

It is very interesting to note how little attention has been paid to the subject of morale in the past. Research reveals no book or periodical reference on morale prior to 1918, when Harold C. Goddard published his study entitled *Morale*.[1] The first sentence of Goddard's book can now be looked upon as prophetic: "Morale is a war word but its mission will not end with the war." World War I marked the beginning of systematic inquiry into the subject of morale and produced some findings which have since become fundamental in industrial management. It was found, for example, that when workers received more benefits, production increased. It was found also that the partial failure of production in Great Britain in the early years of World War I was due to ignorance of human rather than technical factors.

In our investigation of the subject of morale we are concerned particularly with the morale of the teaching staff and the school administrator. It seems strange that in a social enterprise so dependent upon interpersonal relationships as education there has been such little progress or interest in the study of morale. Shortly after World War II, Benjamin Fine, writing in the New York *Times,* made the widely publicized statement: "never before has the morale of the teaching staff in this country been so low as it is today." Since that time, there has been some improvement in the situation. Citizen interest is at an all-time high, as is evidenced by the more than 10,000 lay advisory committees now functioning. A study of the *Education Index* reveals that well over eighty articles on morale were written between 1947 and 1955. Teacher salaries have been increased since 1947, although not so greatly as those of the rest of the employed people in the country.

[1] Reference to the historical background of morale is from Ellsworth Tompkins and Galen Jones, "The Genesis of Morale," *School Review,* Vol. 58 (March, 1950), pp. 156-161.

If we assume that the prime job of the school administrator is to release the creative capacities of the teachers on his faculty, then more and more attention must be paid to factors of morale. If anyone needs more evidence that we have not faced up to the problem of morale and staff satisfactions, let him remember that some 350,000 teachers left the profession during the war years. It was their first opportunity to get out and they did.

Morale is something which we all tend to *talk* about without any precise definition of what we mean. We *feel* about morale without really seeing it or measuring it objectively. This is not to say that there is no possible way in which morale can be measured. It means that we do not know enough about it to measure it conclusively at the present time. The methods of measurement now being used will be discussed later in this chapter. At this point, however, it would be helpful to ascertain the meaning of morale.

WHAT IS MORALE?

In his study of group relations, French seems to have arrived at a good general definition of morale: [2]

Morale refers to the condition of a group where there are clear and fixed group goals (purpose) that are felt to be important and integrated with individual goals; where there is confidence in the attainment of these goals, and subordinately, confidence in the means of attainment, in the leaders, associates, and finally in oneself; where group actions are integrated and co-operative; and where aggression and hostility are expressed against the forces frustrating the group rather than toward other individuals within the group.

There are numerous examples of morale which tend to support the above definition. Perhaps the one most commonly referred to is that of the United States Marine Corps. The extreme pugnacity of the marines toward all "outsiders" is historical and famous. When taking part in joint maneuvers with other branches of the armed services, the marine detachments exhibit almost as much animosity toward them as they do toward a wartime enemy. Although some of this belligerent attitude may be marked up to jest, most of it is directly related to an intense pride in the Marine Corps and a sense of unity which can be possessed only by a group which sees clearly its goals and has confidence in its ability to achieve these goals. This high degree of morale is inculcated in marine inductees and transmitted to the general public. Faris points up the extreme to which high morale may carry a group when he says that morale represents the domination of group purposes over individual purposes to the extent, in some cases, of overriding the so-called most powerful human instinct—self-preservation.[3] This is seen not only in the Marine Corps but in other

[2] John R. P. French, Jr., "The Disruption and Cohesion of Groups," *Journal of Abnormal and Social Psychology*, Vol. 36, No. 3 (July, 1941), p. 376.

[3] Robert E. L. Faris, "Small Group Research Movement," *Group Relations at the Crossroads*, ed. M. A. Sherif and M. O. Wilson (New York, Harper, 1953), p. 180.

branches of the armed services, in police and fire departments, and other like organizations.

Roethlisberger also defines morale in a way which is clear and convincing. He discusses morale in terms of health, the health of a co-operative system: [4]

It is our thesis that what physical health is to a physical organism, morale is to a co-operative system. Lack of morale, like lack of health, cannot often be reduced to some one simple cause. Just as problems relating to health require a simple and useful way of thinking about the physical organism as a physico-chemical system, so an understanding of problems relating to morale requires a simple and useful way of thinking about human beings in their associations with one another as a social system.

He then points out that the problems of morale in a business organization break down into two major parts: [5]

(1) the daily problems of maintaining internal equilibrium within the organization, that is, maintaining that kind of social organization in which individuals and groups through working together can obtain human satisfactions that will make them willing to contribute their services to the economic objective of co-operation; and

(2) the daily problems of diagnosing possible sources of interference, of locating sore spots, of liquidating human tensions and strains among individuals and groups, of helping people to orient themselves to their work group, of spotting blockages in the channels of communication.

Although Roethlisberger makes specific reference to the business group, his breakdown of morale problems applies equally well to the education group with which we are most concerned. Teachers, possibly more than industrial workers, need an organization in which and through which they can derive satisfactions in carrying out the educational philosophy of the school system. The gratifications accruing to the teacher in his work are few and far between. In many respects, teaching is the least satisfying of all the professions because it is so difficult to see the results of one's labors. The lawyer wins a case, the doctor cures a patient, the artist paints a picture, but the teacher rarely sees any concrete, tangible results of his work. The development of morale in a school faculty is directly related to the degree to which the administration can help individuals to achieve satisfaction in their work. We have recognized of late the need for administrators to be sensitive to the human needs of faculty members. There exist among faculty members, just as among employees, those tensions and strains between individuals and cliques. Teachers need to be moved about, placed in situations in which they can be more effective, so that both the teacher and the school system will profit. Administrators need to be certain that communication channels are kept clear. Probably there is little so

---

[4] F. J. Roethlisberger, *Management and Morale* (Cambridge, Mass., Harvard University Press, 1941), p. 192.

[5] *Ibid.*

damaging to faculty morale as lack of information about what is going on. Faculty members, if they do not have information about things which concern them, will speculate and conjure up rumors that are usually far more drastic than the truth. In many systems, the students have more information than the teachers. A good practice, which some schools have adopted, is to make certain that the faculty is notified of all important developments before the newspapers, radio, or the public receive the news. This not only gives the teachers the information but increases their sense of importance in the organization.

It can be seen readily that morale, in the sense in which we have been using the term, refers to a "dynamic relation of equilibrium between individuals and the organization they serve." [6] In order to preserve and strengthen this dynamic relationship, the administrator needs skills in diagnosing human situations. It would be well to look at the framework within which the administrator operates before we consider the skills he needs.

MORALE AND SCHOOL ADMINISTRATION

If we observe a faculty carefully, we can find some indication of its morale. We can observe the amount of work its members do. In cases of high morale, production is high; in cases of low morale, production is low. When observing the amount of work the teachers do, we should seek for answers to such questions as: Does the teacher give freely of his time to after school activities? Does he resent coming to PTA meetings and similar school functions? Does he waste time at work loafing? Is there constant bickering among staff members so that there is no co-operative effort toward common goals? These are signs or indications of low morale. Evidence of high morale would be found in teachers who are cheerful, prompt, dependable, and co-operative. They are willing to work after the regular school hours, knowing that this work will make the total educational program a better one. They show signs of hostility toward those who attempt to harm their group but little toward each other. To an outsider, many teacher groups of high morale appear to have low morale because of this latter factor. For instance, the in-service consultant who attempts to work with a high morale faculty often has great difficulty in "reaching" the group. The group "feels" that it has attained a high level, and the consultant appears to be someone who wants to change the group. Too often the consultant tries to bring about changes by attacking those things in which the group takes great pride, and so the group closes ranks. High morale groups must be worked *with* and not *on*. Change must come from the inside.

Most of the studies investigating morale in the field of education attempt

[6] *Ibid.*, p. 193.

to determine the conditions which teachers report as irritating or annoying and the conditions which they like. Scates has suggested that a more profitable approach would be to compare the characteristics of groups of teachers with varying levels of morale.[7] We will follow both procedures, since, at the present time, it seems that we can gain much information from each. In both instances, the data are gained from a survey of the literature on morale which includes industrial, business, theoretical, and educational studies.

We will first compare morale in four types of groups. These groups are categorized according to the *type of administration* with which each group of teachers is working, inasmuch as recent studies indicate that the administrator sets the climate for morale in the school. Each of the types is a composite drawn from a number of sources.[8] The composite sets forth a description of the type of administration, the climate of the school, and the resulting morale.

Laissez-faire Administrator

The researchers in educational administration, business, and industry are unanimous in their conclusion that the laissez-faire situation is one in which morale is at its lowest ebb. It is the situation which is least satisfying to teachers and least successful in realizing educational goals. In terms of French's definition referred to above, the laissez-faire group exhibits an almost complete absence of clear-cut purposes. Lacking definite leadership, the group finds no way to function to define its goals or purposes. The laissez-faire group is further characterized by a lack of confidence in the attainment of goals which individual members of the group might hold, a lack of confidence in the head men in the group, and a lack of confidence in themselves as members of the group. This last point is probably the most disastrous result of laissez-faire leadership. In other types of

[7] Douglas E. Scates, "Stresses and Strains of Teaching: Do We Understand Them?" *Journal of Teacher Education,* Vol. 2 (December, 1951), pp. 302-305.

[8] The descriptions are composites drawn from the following sources: Alex Bavelas, "Morale and the Training of Leaders," in *Civilian Morale,* ed. Goodwin Watson (New York, Reynal and Hitchcock, 1942), ch. 8, and "An Analysis of the Work Situation Preliminary to Leadership Training," *Journal of Educational Sociology* (March, 1944), p. 17; Arthur Coladarci, unpublished CPEA Center studies, at Stanford University; K. Lewin, R. Lippitt, and R. K. White, "Patterns of Aggressive Behavior in Experimentally Created Social Climates," *Journal of Social Psychology,* Vol. 10, No. 2 (1939); Ronald Lippitt, *An Experimental Study of Authoritarian and Democratic Group Atmospheres,* University of Iowa Studies in Child Welfare, Vol. 16, No. 3 (1940); Ronald Lippitt and R. K. White, "An Experimental Study of the Social Climate of Children's Groups," in *Child Behavior and Development,* ed. Roger Barker, Jacob Kounin, and Herbert Wright (New York, McGraw-Hill, 1943); Leland P. Bradford and Ronald Lippitt, "Types of Group Leadership," in *Human Relations and Curriculum Change,* ed. Kenneth D. Benne and Bozidar Muntyan (New York, Dryden, 1951), pp. 118-132; Roethlisberger, *op. cit.;* French, *loc. cit.*

leadership there is some confidence exhibited in someone, so there is the necessary drive to produce something. The laissez-faire group presents an attitude approaching hopelessness on the part of individual members.

Aggression and hostility of group members is exhibited against other group members, not toward critics of the group. This may well be one of the reasons why criticism of public education is successful. A large number of faculties could be characterized as laissez-faire groups, and when they are attacked, they have nothing which causes them to close ranks. Many members of these faculties feel that the critic must be right because he expresses the hostility toward members of the group which they themselves feel. Of course, each of these individuals fails to see *himself* as being attacked! It is only the other members who are being criticized. Therefore his criticism is even more severe than the critic's.

In terms of Roethlisberger's definition of morale as given above, we see that the laissez-faire group does not offer its members a *social system* which leads to the gratification of their needs. The teacher in a laissez-faire group does not derive any satisfaction from membership in the faculty. He may derive some from his experiences with children, but none as a faculty member. Then, too, in a laissez-faire group, the administrator does not act to resolve the daily problems of morale outlined by Roethlisberger. Faculty members are continually hampered by such "little" things as inadequate supplies, facilities, clerical help, or petty cash to purchase materials on the spur of the moment. The effect of these recurrent irritations is cumulative. Tensions mount, and communication becomes increasingly difficult.

Hard-boiled Autocrat

In terms of productivity, the next highest administration on the morale scale is that of the hard-boiled autocrat. The attitude of this type of administrator toward the teaching staff is "If you don't like it here, why don't you leave?" He also maintains and acts upon the concept that inasmuch as the teacher is being paid, he should do everything he is told to do and should do it unquestioningly. He has no regard for such things as teachers' advisory cabinets because he knows everything that goes on in his building. And no one can ever convince him that he doesn't! A quotation from Turner illustrates the way workmen feel about hard-boiled bosses, and their attitude is not too different from the attitude of teachers toward hard-boiled principals: [9]

"My foreman is pretty rough. He is inconsiderate even of his friends. He don't think anything of driving you.... The job I had before, I always respected the foreman. He knew everything about the job, and the men looked up to him.

[9] Arthur N. Turner, "Foreman—Key to Worker Morale," *Harvard Business Review* (January–February, 1954), p. 77.

Here, it doesn't work out that way; they make anybody a foreman. You can't be a good foreman (in the eyes of management) until the men call you names."

Note here the transfer of feeling from the driving, inconsiderateness of the foreman to reflections on his ability and then to reflections on the management of the whole company. The way in which foremen or principals act in their face-to-face relations with subordinates sets the emotional climate or morale for the whole enterprise.

Some comments from teachers in systems which are administered by hard-boiled autocrats and which had low morale scores on the *Administrative Behavior Checklist* [10] reveal much the same attitude. One teacher stated: "He never mentions or says anything in regard to something well done."

Another teacher made these responses to the following items in the checklist:

14. He is a follower on occasion and lets more competent individuals lead. "Is there anyone more competent to lead than a school superintendent (in his mind, at least)?"
15. He is solicitous concerning his new teachers. "Get 'em by hook or crook."
19. He has insight into himself. "Am I to judge God!"

The administration of the hard-boiled autocrat is characterized by close supervision, exertion of pressure, lack of compliments to teachers, and reliance on directives, memoranda, and the like, instead of conferences. The hard-boiled autocrat is himself egocentric and aggressive. His behavior results in submission on the part of the faculty, together with a smoldering resentment which is not always recognized by the subordinates. There is some irritability and unwillingness to work together, but not so much as in the laissez-faire group. There is considerable backbiting, and members disparage each other's efforts.

There are, however, many teachers who feel secure in this type of school system, who are willing to accept the goals and purposes of a strong head man. In line with French's definition, these teachers do have confidence, both in the merit of the goals and in the way in which the leader proceeds to fulfill the goals. These teachers also rise to the immediate defense of their leader, regardless of the grounds upon which he is criticized. In terms of Roethlisberger's analysis, there is a social system of sorts in which the teachers gain a certain amount of satisfaction. This is possible because the hard-boiled autocrat does alleviate the sources of interference and other daily problems, but only to the point where they do not hamper him and where the school again functions "smoothly."

[10] Daniel E. Griffiths, *Administrative Behavior Checklist* (Albany, N. Y., Capital Area School Development Association, 1952).

Father Type

The next highest on the scale of educational productivity is the faculty administered by the so-called "father" type, or benevolent autocrat. The administrator, in this case, works toward developing a happy family group with himself as the father. He demonstrates great and sincere evidences of interest in his staff. He wants them to bring their problems to him because he knows very well that he is far more capable of working out a solution than they are.

The benevolent autocrat secures the complete dependence of the staff on his judgment and ability by using the technique of relating the success or failure of all enterprises to his reaction. He will indicate his approval of a school play, for instance, not by saying to the director, "You did a fine job, Miss Brown," but by saying, "That's the kind of a play I like," or "Miss Brown, I liked that play." The teachers get into the habit of waiting upon his responses in terms of his own likes and dislikes. In this manner, he makes himself the source of all standards of production.

Faculties operating under this type of leadership exhibit many of the characteristics of a high morale group. The faculty members demonstrate a sense of belongingness and personal achievement. In general, they bask in the reflected glory of their administrator. Since he gives forth with slaps on the back and a great deal of encouragement, they feel wanted and as though their efforts are worthwhile. These are probably the biggest differences between the hard-boiled autocrat and the benevolent autocrat. Another observable difference is the lack of frustration exhibited in the benevolent autocrat's faculty. Since this type of administrator exercises subtle manipulation, which is generally accepted, there is little to frustrate the teacher.

What are the negative aspects of this type of leadership? At first glance, it would seem to inspire a fine type of group; it engenders high morale, high production, security, freedom from frustration, and satisfies the needs for belongingness and personal achievement. The weakness of this type of leadership lies in the increasing dependence of the faculty upon the judgment and wisdom of the administrator. Teachers, as they acquire more and more years of experience, become less independent and more reliant on their administrator. These faculties regress to a childlike level of dependency. The loss in initiative, in creativity, is beyond all calculation. A faculty of this sort is probably operating at no more than 5 per cent of its potential, even though it has a fairly high production relative to the above groups.[11]

We might speculate for a moment as to why this benevolent autocrat should be a rather popular kind of school administrator in the American

[11] Auren Uris, *How to Be a Successful Leader* (New York, McGraw-Hill, 1953), p. 154.

public schools. Looking at him again, we see a man who fulfills our expectations of the ideal father. He is kindly, wise, and sincere. He looks after us when we are in trouble. He inquires as to the health and prosperity of the other members of our family. He always congratulates us when we do something well and chastises us when we are wrong. He notices when we need some special equipment or extra material and then he provides it. If we have not been performing as he desires, though, we may not get it! Since he is the father, the faculty are the children and, as such, are immature, cannot be trusted to exercise much judgment, and so must depend upon him. This is a portrait of the benevolent autocrat as he administers his school. He is probably the most numerous of all administrators in American schools. Why is he so popular? One easy and quick answer lies in the composition of our faculties. Women comprise approximately 90 per cent of our faculties. Of the women, over half are married. In the American culture, women, as a group, have never occupied a high place in the power structure. Although woman seems to be acquiring higher cultural status, this is not evident to any great extent in our schools. The subordinate role of woman in western culture and their predominance in the field of teaching partially explain the father type of school administrator. Another explanation is related to the fact that a very large number of people enter teaching because of the security it offers. This has been more true of late, since the recruitment campaigns have stressed steady pay, tenure, retirement pensions, and long vacations. This, together with the bitter experience of the Great Depression, has created a group of security-minded teachers. The third probable cause is the second-rate nature of teaching. Many people are in teaching as a second choice. Having been unsuccessful in becoming a doctor or lawyer, the individual turns to teaching. All of these may be reasons for the popularity of the father type of administrator.

Democratic Administrator

The term *democratic* has been more maligned in education than any other, except possibly the term *progressive*. This has been especially true in school administration. Democratic administration has been confused with many of the techniques that are sometimes used by autocratic administrators. The belief is prevalent that to be democratic it is necessary to have the faculty vote on *all* issues confronting the school. It is often felt that a democratic administrator cannot make a decision alone; he must *always* consult his faculty. Neither of these techniques is characteristic of the nature of true democratic administration.

Bendix has some concepts of democratic administration which help to clarify the issue. He advances the idea that in democratic administration, commands or orders are given which have a far greater latitude than commands or orders given in authoritarian setups and that these commands or orders are subject to a rather diffuse supervision. He then states a very interesting concept of democratic administration: [12]

The democratic official is ideally expected to be obedient to his superior, but he does not thereby express his loyalty to the people's mandate. On the other hand, he is to exercise his authority in the spirit of service, not of mastery. The democratic administrator stands, therefore, in an ambivalent relationship to his superior and his subordinate. His compliance, his orders and his initiative are tempered by a sense of direct, if imponderable accountability to the people. In this respect, superior and subordinate are equals before the public, although they are unequal within the administration hierarchy.

This is getting into the difference between the benevolent autocrat and the democratic leader. The democratic leader does not solicit loyalty to himself as a person. The loyalty is to the cause; in our case, to public education. In this way, the overwhelming influence under which administrators and teachers operate is the responsibility to the public to provide the best education possible. The basic motive is not to please the superintendent. The heart of the difference, however, is found in the statement that "he is to exercise his authority in the spirit of service, not of mastery." We have noted in our preceding descriptions of administrative types a decided lack of the concept of administration as a *service* profession. There has been implicit in each the concept that the administrator is above his teachers. He is a master. The concept of administration as a service function clearly undercuts the prevalent concept of the other three and is the characteristic which marks most clearly the basic difference. The administrator must believe that his is a *service* role if he is to be democratic.

This assumption leads to the practices of democratic administration and gives them meaning. The democratic administrator shares with his faculty the making of decisions concerning work planning, assigning, scheduling, and promotions whenever this is feasible. Where it is not feasible, he strives to explain the reasons for his actions to the faculty. It is not possible to have the faculty share in all decisions, and this, together with the reasons, should be made clear to the faculty. The democratic administrator strives to make certain that the credit for success and failure of the work is shared by those who participate in the work. In this way his do not become the sole standards against which the work of the group is judged. Faculty members grow as *they* assume the responsibility for their behavior. The administrator judges the work of the staff in terms of objective rather than personal standards. This keeps him out of the way and allows the teacher to work and to be judged in terms of standards which are in the open and understood by all.

[12] Reinhard Bendix, "Bureaucracy: The Problem and Its Setting," *American Sociological Review*, Vol. 12 (October, 1947), p. 505.

The democratic group displays more enthusiasm for its work and produces at a higher rate than does any of the three other groups studied.
Less frustration is noted because the teachers are free to move and initiate action within limits which, although broad, are clearly understood.
It is noted that in the laissez-faire situation the limits are much broader;
in fact, they are probably nonexistent, and this brings about frustration
and lack of production. The limits must be broad but they must exist and
be understood. The need to belong to a cohesive group is fulfilled in a
democratic faculty, especially the need to be regarded as an individual
who has meaning and importance to others. Security is high, and it increases because the individual grows in his membership as he participates
and accepts more responsibility.

Factors Affecting Morale of Teachers

Many articles have been written which discuss the factors which affect
morale in a school system. These factors have been spelled out in more
detail than those presented under the composites presented above. It
should be noted that although the number of articles concerning morale
is large, there are not many research studies on the subject; and the greater
proportion of these leave much to be desired in the way of techniques used
and in the treatment of data. There also seems to be a tendency to regard
morale as some sort of a segregated unity. Morale is being studied in
somewhat of a vacuum. Most of the studies are of the questionnaire type,
and the respondent is asked to indicate whether or not the particular item
is important in morale. The reason why a person answers a question is
sometimes more important than the answer he gives. From our discussion
of perception, general semantics, and motives, we know that each individual sees something different in each question. One superintendent,
whose faculty took a commercially prepared test of morale, indicated that
when his faculty sat down together after having taken the test individually
and arrived at a common agreement as to what the questions meant, several answers were changed.

Looking at this problem of determining morale factors from the background of our study of perception, we have two reports which indicate
some of the difficulties that are encountered. In one study of industrial
morale, employees were asked to identify, in order of importance, five
morale factors out of a list of seventy-one. Executives and labor leaders
were asked to predict the ranking of employees' morale factors. The employees ranked the factors in the following order: (1) job security, (2)
base pay, (3) opportunities for advancement, (4) employee benefits, (5)
information as to job status. The executives were able to predict three
factors: job security, base pay, and opportunities for advancement. The
labor leaders were able to predict only two factors: job security and base

pay.[13] Both the executives and the labor leaders were viewing employee morale from different personal behavior centers. What seemed important for employee morale was different for each group.

A similar attempt was made to predict teachers' rankings on the Educators Opinion Inventory, distributed by Science Research Associates at the Southbury, Conn., Training School. The director and four supervisors attempted to predict the teachers' rankings. It is reported that the "supervisors were close to the actual results in over 40% of the cases. The Director and one other individual came out with anticipated results which approximated the actual scores in 60% of the cases." [14]

Several studies have indicated that morale was dependent upon "a lot of little things" and was apt to fluctuate from time to time. One superintendent whose school also used the Educators Opinion Inventory stated:

> In talking with other superintendents about the Inventory from the administrative point of view, we are convinced that the time to conduct the survey is when there is peace and quiet prevailing in the force, since any little disturbance is apt to throw the whole survey out of balance.

This superintendent is saying very well what others have found in their study of morale. Morale is not a steady, pervasive sort of thing. One cannot "build good morale" and then sit back and enjoy it. When you get seated, it may very well be gone! We need also to reckon with the fact that morale needs to be studied when staffs are in turmoil as well as when they are placid. We need to know whether the data available to us have been collected while the staff was in turmoil or while it was placid. In other words, we need another set of variables against which to match our morale factors.

We must not think that we have found all the factors which cause morale to be high or low. We are but beginning our job in this area. With this understanding that the findings to be discussed are tentative and incomplete, let us look at some of the factors which affect morale.

Four texts have been published within the past year, each by experts in the fields of administration and supervision. Each of these texts contains lists of factors concerning morale and indicates that these factors are generally agreed upon by researchers in education as well as the other social sciences.[15] We will construct a composite of factors which affect

[13] S. Avery Raube, *Factors Affecting Employee Morale* (New York, National Industrial Conference Board Report, 1947), No. 85, 35 pp.

[14] Robert M. Porter, "A Report on a Survey of Factors Affecting the Morale of Personnel in the Department of Education and Training of the Southbury Training School" (Southbury, Conn., The Southbury Training School, 1955), p. 5, mimeo.

[15] William H. Burton and Leo J. Brueckner, *Supervision*, 3d ed. (New York, Appleton-Century-Crofts, 1955), pp. 555-559; Daniel R. Davies and Kenneth F. Herrold, *Leadership and Morale* (New London, Conn., Arthur C. Croft, 1955), 55 pp.; Kimball Wiles, *Supervision for Better Schools* (New York, Prentice-Hall, 1955); Willard S. Elsbree and E. Edmund Reutter, Jr., *Staff Personnel in the Public Schools* (New York, Prentice-Hall, 1954).

morale and supplement the composites with data from recent research.

Key to the Morale Problem. The administrator is the key to the morale problem. He sets the climate for morale in his school. All four texts list him as a basic factor in building morale, with three texts specifying him as *the* most important factor. This is also the finding of many of the studies reported in the journals. Schultz studied the morale of recent University of Illinois graduates. He included many items to be checked, and he also asked for free responses. He concluded: "On the basis of these free responses, the factor that these teachers identify as being most crucial to happiness in their position is the administrator." [16]

Teachers expect the administrator to actively and aggressively seek to provide better working conditions, including equipment, supplies, and buildings. They expect him to provide leadership in establishing a satisfactory salary schedule. They expect him to lead in the development of good community relations, particularly in gaining recognition for the schools and in providing good living conditions and opportunities for desirable social life. He should employ consistent policies in the selection, orientation, promotion, and placement of teachers. He should include teachers in the process of policy-making. He should, above all, treat teachers fairly and squarely. He should inspire confidence in himself.

Satisfaction of Teacher Needs. Teacher needs, such as security (financial and emotional), recognition, job satisfaction, and knowledge of advancement, must be recognized and met. Teachers need to know that they are accepted as professional peers by other members of the faculty, that their efforts are being appreciated by the staff, the community, and the students. Teachers need to feel secure and confident that they will get a fair deal from the administration. They need to feel that they are contributing to the success of the school.

Participation in Team Effort. Morale requires the establishment of a real team spirit on the part of all members of the staff, administrators and teachers. A team spirit includes the feeling that all members are pulling together to achieve a commonly held purpose, all members have common experiences, all members share in success, and all members are striving to meet a significant challenge. The need for clear communications channels must be met.

Mature Staff. Although morale is essentially a group concept, it is necessary that the staff be composed of mature individuals. These individuals need to have a tested and reliable set of personal values. They need to be well-adjusted individuals who can take success or failure in stride and move ahead to meet each challenge as it arises.

[16] Raymond E. Schultz, "Keeping up Teacher Morale," *Nation's Schools*, Vol. 50 (October, 1952), p. 56.

Factors Affecting the Morale of Administrators

Whenever morale is discussed in education it is done so in reference to teachers or students. The factors which affect the morale of school administrators have not received the same attention. Barry undertook a study of these factors in 1955.[17] He formulated a series of hypotheses and tested them by means of an elaborate interview process. A jury of eighty-five judges rated New York State school systems for high and low administrator morale. Schools in these categories were then paired with reference to such factors as size, wealth, and organizational structure. The administrators in these sets of paired school systems were interviewed. A review of Barry's data reveals seven factors which have a statistically significant relationship to high administrator morale. In order of their significance these factors are:

1. Administrators receive *recognition* for the ideas which they have concerning education in the community.
2. The relationship between the administrator and the board of education is characterized by co-operation, mutual respect, and an understanding of each other's roles.
3. The relationships among administrators within a school district are characterized by free and open exchange of ideas and mutual respect for each other's personality.
4. Administrators are among the prestige people in the community, being appointed to important community committees, sought out for community projects, and are considered on the same plane as such professional people as doctors and lawyers.
5. Administrators are active participants in projects which improve the quality of education in the school.
6. Administrators are quite satisfied with such material factors as salary, facilities, secretarial help, and supplies.
7. Administrators receive stimulation through working with consultants, attending professional meetings, and studying the problems of their own district.

How Can a School Study Its Morale?

On the question of how a school can study its morale, we are going to take the position that an outside agency should make the morale study. There are several reasons for this, the most important being: (1) the difficulty in constructing a morale instrument, (2) the difficulty in interpreting data, (3) the difficulty in getting teacher co-operation in a self-study, (4) the skill of commercial agencies, and (5) the difficulty of the administrator in perceiving his own situation.

[17] Franklyn Barry, "Factors Affecting Administrative Morale" (Unpublished Ed.D. project, Syracuse University, 1956). An abstract of this study is available from the Cooperative Development of Public School Administration, Albany, N. Y.

A school system should not wait until the obvious signs of low morale appear (rapid teacher turnover, excessive griping, lack of faculty co-operation, high absentee and tardiness rates) but should have the study made while the situation appears to be somewhat normal. It is suggested that such time of the year as Christmas and the opening and closing weeks of school be avoided, but almost any other time of year would be appropriate. The morale study could be made while the staff is embroiled in some sort of controversy, but one could not then generalize from the results.

The teachers should be in on all of the discussion of the survey from the outset. If they do not fully understand and appreciate the values to be derived from the morale survey, it will not be worth the effort. Being in on the discussion from the beginning will help to insure their support. The planning stage should also take into consideration the way in which the results will be used. Plans should be made, in tentative form, for a series of meetings to consider the results of the survey, and a plan should be considered for putting the recommendations into action. This will help to convince the teachers that the administration is being completely honest and straightforward about the proposal.

A group of five school systems in Connecticut held morale surveys in 1954. This was done as part of the Connecticut CPEA study, and the Educators Opinion Inventory was used. The five superintendents were contacted and replies were received from four of them. These four were unanimous in their commendation of the procedure and recommended that other schools follow it. The comments of one superintendent regarding the values of the survey were particularly apt:

At least three different purposes are served by the use of the inventory. The least obvious but probably not the least valuable is the cathartic effect. It seems to help build and maintain morale when workers have the opportunity to express their feelings anonymously in a way which is certain to come to the attention of the administrator.

In the second place we received assurance that some of our personnel policies are paying dividends in increased morale. Our strong points were revealed. We became aware of practices and policies which, like Topsy, had just growed, but which have been contributing to high morale. We now know enough to build on the successful policies and to reinforce them.

We also found some spots which need further study and improvement, e.g.— "distribution of teacher-load and extracurricular assignments—especially at the high school level"—appear to require study. (Through our Council on Administrative Problems a group has been set up to work on this problem.)

Morale surveys have become fairly common in business and industry. They should become equally common in the public schools.

Effect of Faculty Morale on Students

Many may have wondered what the effect of teacher morale is on the students. We may have thought, "Yes, it's nice to have good teacher morale, but does it really make any difference to the students?" Anderson attempted to answer the question of how low teacher morale affects the outcomes of instruction. He studied twenty Iowa schools, which were selected on the basis of student achievement on the Iowa Test of Educational Development. The schools fell in such a way as to have ten above the 75th percentile and the other ten below the 30th percentile. The teachers were then tested and interviewed so as to determine their morale. Anderson's conclusion was that "Teachers in secondary schools whose pupils achieve relatively high scholastically, appear to have higher morale than do teachers in schools with relatively low pupil achievement." [18] This is an indication that morale is even more important than it appeared to be earlier in our investigation. Low morale has a measurable influence on the achievement of students. The students of low morale teachers do not achieve as well as do the students of high morale teachers. If administrators are complacent in the face of low morale, this fact should certainly stimulate them to action.

Special Morale Problems

Before concluding our discussion of morale in the school we should take a look at two problems which are particularly important. Both are extremely difficult to solve, and possibly for this reason, very little attention has been focussed upon them. Some questions have been raised concerning these problems, but little, if anything, in the way of answers has been gained.

A Paradox. The first problem is somewhat of a paradox. As one reviews the research on teacher morale, one is overwhelmed by the importance of the administrator. The studies reported have all queried teachers on how they feel about morale, and all indicated that the most important factor in the morale situation is the administrator. What does this mean? Some of the writers give the impression that the superintendent should play the role of the "Great Provider." He will work for higher salaries, greater security, be a psychological counselor, and meet all of the needs of the group. In other words, what actually happens is that the staff becomes more and more dependent upon the administrator. Instead of the group becoming stronger, it becomes weaker as it depends on the superintendent for its strength.

Spalding discusses a facet of this paradox. He speaks of the relationship

[18] Lester W. Anderson, "Teacher Morale and Student Achievement," *Journal of Educational Research*, Vol. 46 (May, 1953), pp. 693-698.

between the superintendent and the so-called "cohesive group" in the faculty and the "independent" members of the faculty. He points out that the independent members look to the superintendent to protect them against encroachments from the cohesive group. He concludes: "Hence the entire faculty comes to feel that the more 'democratic' the school becomes the more it depends upon the superintendent to protect its democracy." [19]

Throughout the available studies there seems to be confusion between the group achieving "democracy" but having the administrator "give" the group those factors which will insure a high morale. It may be that the research techniques are at fault here. Most studies fail to differentiate among the respondents. No attempt is made to indicate whether the respondents are young or old, male or female, married or single, financially independent or impoverished. One study which did differentiate arrived at some radically different conclusions. Shilland found that women teachers ranked "fair compensation" tenth on a list of thirty factors, although men ranked this item second. Since in this study there were two and a half times as many women as men sampled, "fair compensation" ended up in eighth position. [20]

The Classroom Teacher. Recurrent throughout the studies is the concept that a person—to have high morale—must feel that there is a future in his work. At the same time that we grant this to be an entirely reasonable and valid factor, we must admit that our schools are not organized in such a way as to grant the conventional types of future. In business and industry, there appears to be such a hierarchy of positions that a man can see "something ahead" for him. In our schools, we have organized in such a manner that a teacher must leave the classroom if he is promoted. Promotions in education take the form of administrative and supervisory positions. The ambitious young teacher cannot look forward to a future in classroom teaching. Hedlund and Brown put the problem this way: "How can schools be organized to give ablest teachers greater opportunity to teach? Why must promotional paths lead them out of the work for which they are best suited?" [21]

A few schools have found a partial answer in the *helping teacher.* This enables the master teacher to step up a rank and to work with the teachers who are having difficulty. He works on a consultive basis and has no line authority. He receives a higher salary and has a higher status than regular classroom teachers. Most colleges have gotten at the problem through the use of ranks. The conventional number is four, and they are usually called

[19] Willard B. Spalding, *The Superintendency of Public Schools—An Anxious Profession,* The Inglis Lecture (Cambridge, Mass., Harvard University Press, 1954), p. 47.

[20] Peter D. Shilland, "A Teacher Morale Survey," *Educational Forum,* Vol. 13 (May, 1949), pp. 479-486.

[21] Paul A. Hedlund and Foster S. Brown, "Conditions That Lower Teacher Morale," *Nation's Schools,* Vol. 48 (September, 1951), pp. 40-42.

instructor, assistant professor, associate professor, and professor. In this way a man can look forward to a life of classroom teaching but receive salary increments *and* increases in rank. Oppenheimer indicates the importance of attaining higher rank when he writes: "We re-emphasize that the goal in achieving academic rank is more than the monetary returns of the higher position; perhaps equally important is the social recognition such advancement can bring." [22]

It would seem that some such reorganization as that proposed above will have to occur if faculty morale is to improve. These two problems have been posed to point out that even if we have found the factors which lead to higher morale, the methods of attaining the factors may entail more difficulty than the public schools are willing to meet.

SUMMARY

Since World War I there has been considerable interest in the human factor called morale. We began by defining morale in general terms, but we can redefine it in operational terms as follows:

If it can be shown that groups which achieve their goals efficiently exhibit a high degree of cohesiveness, think well of their leaders, do not fight much among themselves, agree on their objectives, have confidence in their equipment, and so on, then these manifestations represent high morale; but only if a relationship to goal achievement can be shown.

Our investigation into morale was organized into two sets of composites. One set was built around four groups categorized according to the type of administration and indicated the type of administration, the behavior of the administrator and the teachers, the morale, and the production of each group. The production of the groups increased with the type of group in the following order: laissez-faire, hard-boiled autocrat, father type, and democratic. In the second set, we categorized the factors which contribute to morale, noting that the most important factor is the administrator. He sets the climate for the school and is the key to faculty morale. Some suggestions were made concerning the way in which to survey morale, and two problems of particular difficulty were discussed.

EXERCISES

1. As a building principal what would you look for as indications of morale?
2. In terms of the four types of administration in the composites, what are you? Does the behavior of your teachers agree with the text?

[22] J. J. Oppenheimer, "Faculty Morale," *Journal of Higher Education*, Vol. 23 (October, 1952), p. 386.

[23] R. L. French, "Morale and Leadership," in *Human Factors in Undersea Warfare* (Washington, D. C., National Research Council, Committee on Undersea Warfare, 1949), p. 465.

3. Write a case covering a teacher whom you know to be having morale trouble. What factors do you notice? How could you help the teacher?

4. As an administrator itemize those things you do which you feel make for high morale.

5. Is there an observable change in the morale after a salary increase has been granted in your system? Is there a difference in the way in which the men and women react to the raise?

6. Read one of the studies in morale listed in the selected bibliography. Criticize the study from a research point of view.

SELECTED BIBLIOGRAPHY

ANDERSON, Lester W., "Teacher Morale and Student Achievement," *Journal of Educational Research*, Vol. 46 (May, 1953), pp. 693-698.

BRADFORD, Leland P., and LIPPITT, Ronald, "Types of Group Leadership," in *Human Relations and Curriculum Change*, ed. Kenneth D. Benne and Bozidar Muntyan (New York, Dryden, 1951), pp. 118-132.

BURTON, William H., and BRUECKNER, Leo J., *Supervision*, 3d ed. (New York, Appleton-Century-Crofts, 1955), pp. 555-559.

DAVIES, Daniel R., and HERROLD, Kenneth F., *Leadership and Morale* (New London, Conn., Arthur C. Croft, 1955), 55 pp.

ELSBREE, Willard S., and REUTTER, E. Edmund, *Staff Personnel in the Public Schools* (New York, Prentice-Hall, 1954), pp. 262-288.

FRENCH, John R. P., Jr., "The Disruption and Cohesion of Groups," *Journal of Abnormal and Social Psychology*, Vol. 36, No. 3 (July, 1941), p. 376.

HEARN, Arthur C., "Staff Morale," *National Association of Secondary School Principals Bulletin*, Vol. 34 (December, 1950), pp. 150-157.

HEDLUND, Paul A., and BROWN, Foster S., "Conditions That Lower Teacher Morale," *Nation's Schools*, Vol. 48 (September, 1951), pp. 40-42.

JUCKETT, Edwin A., "Staff Morale," *National Association of Secondary School Principals Bulletin*, Vol. 34 (December, 1950), pp. 158-166.

LIPPITT, Ronald, *An Experimental Study of Authoritarian and Democratic Group Atmosphere*, University of Iowa Studies in Child Welfare, Vol. 16, No. 3 (1940).

——, and WHITE, R. K., "An Experimental Study of the Social Climate of Children's Groups," in *Child Behavior and Development*, ed. Roger Barker, Jacob Kounin, and Herbert Wright (New York, McGraw-Hill, 1943).

LOWE, Joe, "Five Steps to Higher Staff Morale," *School Executive*, Vol. 74 (September, 1954), pp. 54-55.

OPPENHEIMER, J. J., "Faculty Morale," *Journal of Higher Education*, Vol. 23 (October, 1952), pp. 383-386.

RAUBE, S. Avery, *Factors Affecting Employee Morale* (New York, National Industrial Conference Board Report, 1947), No. 85, 35 pp.

ROETHLISBERGER, F. J., *Management and Morale* (Cambridge, Mass., Harvard University Press, 1941).

SCHULTZ, Raymond E., "Keeping up Teacher Morale," *Nation's Schools*, Vol. 50 (October, 1952), pp. 53-56.

SHILLAND, Peter D., "A Teacher Morale Survey," *Educational Forum*, Vol. 13 (May, 1949), pp. 479-486.

TOMPKINS, Ellsworth, and JONES, Galen, "The Genesis of Morale," *School Review*, Vol. 58 (March, 1950), pp. 156-161.

TURNER, Arthur N., "Foreman—Key to Worker Morale," *Harvard Business Review* (January-February, 1954), pp. 76-86.

WATSON, Goodwin, *Civilian Morale* (New York, Reynal and Hitchcock, 1942), ch. 8.

WILES, Kimball, *Supervision for Better Schools*, 2d ed. (New York, Prentice-Hall, 1955), pp. 50-75.

CHAPTER 8

The Structure of Groups

To this point we have been concerned primarily with the problems that arise in face-to-face relationships between the administrator and individuals. Today, however, administrators are finding that a great deal of their time is being spent in working with people in *groups*. This requires a somewhat different knowledge and skill from those required in working with individuals. Have you ever noticed that some administrators exercise great skill in discussion when working with one person but seem highly inadequate when working with a committee or a department staff or other groups? The problems faced in each type of situation are quite different. It is our intent, in the next two chapters, to discuss the relevant research on the nature and structure of groups and the skills needed in working with these groups. When we consider the vast amount of time the administrator spends with groups—committees; faculty; formal community groups, such as the Rotary, the Lions, the various churches; affiliated school groups, such as the PTA; and that very important group, the board of education—we can begin to appreciate the value of knowledge about groups.

The administrator faces a number of general problems concerning the structure of groups. Probably more important than any other problem is the answer to the question: Just what is a group, and how can I identify one? He also wonders if all members of a group are the same and whether all people belong to a group for the same reason? If the school administrator is associated with a set of people who should be a group, that is, a faculty, but are not, what can he do about it? How do you bring a set of people to the point where they become a group? What about membership in groups from the point of view of different roles played by the participants? In other words, in considering the make-up of a group, should special care be taken to have people with particular talents in the group? What are these talents? These last three questions are of value to the administrator not only in the matter of appointing committees but in the selection of new faculty members. Then there are some questions which refer to the matter of group atmosphere. Is there such a thing as group atmosphere? Can it be measured? Can it be changed? The question of how large a group should be is another important consideration. In forming a committee for the study of the kindergarten, for example, it would be helpful to know what size would be best for its particular purpose. Information about group size is also valuable to the administrator in setting up faculties for new schools and working with community or other groups outside the school.

WHAT IS A GROUP?

Since the literature abounds with references to characteristics of groups, it must be obvious that just any gathering of two or more individuals does not constitute a group. There must be some way in which a group can be identified, some set of characteristics which delineate the group from the nongroup. Determination of what we mean when we use the term *group*, then, should be our first consideration.

Definition

In our search for an adequate definition of a group, we might do well to begin with the psychological definition formulated by Krech and Crutchfield.[1]

The term group ... refers to two or more people who bear an explicit *psychological relationship to one another*. This means that for each member of the group the other group members must exist in some more or less immediate psychological way so that their behavior and their characteristics influence him.

This definition of group holds for small groups, where there is the genuine possibility of face-to-face contacts and where the behavior of one member will affect the behavior of all others in the group. This is the sort of conceptualization about groups which is of value in the formation of committees, where it is important for the members to be psychologically compatible. They would have to be able to get along, strive for a common goal, receive somewhat the same benefits from a common type of recognition. If the behavior of one were of such a nature as to distract the others, they could not work together as a group.

Cattell has a brief, more general definition which will give us some help. He states that a group is "a set of people who satisfy their needs consciously and unconsciously through the existence and instrumentality of this set of people." [2] This concept is important because it points out that groups must operate as the best means by which each member can satisfy certain individual desires. It is very interesting to note that it is not neces-

---

[1] D. Krech and R. Crutchfield, *Theory and Problems of Social Psychology* (New York, McGraw-Hill, 1948), p. 18.

[2] Raymond B. Cattell, "Determining Syntality Dimensions as a Basis for Morale and Leadership Measurement," in *Groups, Leadership and Men,* ed. Harold Guetzkow (Pittsburgh, Pa., Carnegie Press, 1951), p. 19.

sary for the group to satisfy *common* desires, only *certain* desires. This means that so long as the group serves the purpose of satisfying in some way or other the desires of the individuals within the group, the group will, to that degree, succeed. The school administrator should keep this in mind in forming a committee. Suppose one is to be formed to study the status of the school plant. Member *A* might work hard because he has an interest in school buildings; member *B* because he wishes to do a good job and raise his status in the eyes of the administration; member *C* because she is interested in member *A*!

In discussing the question of group formation in group therapy, Jennings gets at the question of when a set of people constitutes a group. She states: [3]

Any group psychotherapy faces the question of what constitutes a group. Since it is obvious that no "group" is a group in any basic sense which develops little or no positive relationships among its members, it would follow that group therapy must start out with whatever grouping can be arranged which maximizes within each group a sociometric structure which reflects the capacity of the patients to warm up to one another.

Jennings is raising the point, expressed in a somewhat different manner by Krech and Crutchfield when they referred to psychological relationships, of how to form a group which will "warm up" rapidly. This is important in group psychotherapy, but it is also very important in school administration. If a committee is formed of individuals who lack a positive relationship, a long period of time will elapse before they can function together smoothly.

Group Bonds

Sorokin's discussion of what constitutes a group from a sociological point of view is very enlightening. It stresses the point that "The real social group ... exists only when it *lives and functions as a unity*" [4] and that this unity comes about when certain ties or bonds are present. These ties or bonds are defined as those which "make their lives and behavior closely interdependent, and infuse into their minds ... feelings of oneness, solidarity, and community of interests." [5]

There are fourteen of these group-creating ties or bonds, not all of which are relevant to the discussion of groups in education. Those which appear to be most relevant are (*a*) common responsibility for the maintenance of order, (*b*) community of occupational interests, (*c*) attach-

[3] Helen H. Jennings, *Leadership and Isolation*, 2d ed. (New York, Longmans, Green, 1950), pp. 310-311.

[4] P. A. Sorokin, C. C. Zimmerman, and C. J. Galpin, *A Systematic Source Book in Rural Sociology* (Minneapolis, University of Minnesota Press, 1930), p. 307.

[5] *Ibid.*

ment to the same social institutions or agency of social service and control, (*d*) mutual aid, and (*e*) general living, experiencing, and acting together.[6] Two others are mentioned which many teachers would undoubtedly say were present in their situations: (*f*) subjection to the same lord and (*g*) common defense! It can be seen that although this is a sociological definition, it has much of the psychological in it. Such things as mutual aid and general living, experiencing, and acting together are related to the psychological relationships referred to above.

These group-creating bonds have a crude quantifying value in addition to their descriptive values. It is explained that a group with one tie or bond is called an *elementary* group and a group held together with two or more ties or bonds is called a *cumulative* group.[7] Sorokin, Zimmerman, and Galpin point out that the members of a cumulative group are like-minded, have a well-developed community consciousness, and exhibit a feeling of oneness and solidarity that is deeply rooted.[8] It would seem to be the function of administrative leaders in the public schools to move their groups from elementary to cumulative groups. Each group (faculty, committee, department) is an elementary group in the sense that it is held together by occupational interests, and, as such, it operates on an extremely low level. The job of the administrator is to move his group by introducing as many additional bonds as he can. Good group activities, such as the co-operative development of policy create these bonds and help develop a stronger group. This was demonstrated recently in one rural school that worked out the problem of developing a promotional policy which would be acceptable to the whole faculty. The approach used involved the entire faculty operating as a group which occasionally was divided into subgroups that worked with the aid of consultants. Evidence seemed to accumulate to support the contention that such bonds as mutual aid and general living, experiencing, and acting together emerged and were made stronger. This, in turn, had the effect of strengthening the "groupness" of the faculty. An approach by an administrator which establishes and strengthens these group-creating bonds builds a productive group in which the members have a strong feeling of unity, have strong psychological relationships with one another, and can satisfy their needs.

TYPES OF GROUPS

We are concerned, in this discussion of groups, with relatively small groups. Although the school administrator may have contacts with, say, the National Chamber of Commerce and similar organizations, we will not discuss these as groups, although we are interested in smaller local units.

[6] *Ibid.*, pp. 307-308.
[7] *Ibid.*, pp. 308-320.
[8] *Ibid.*, pp. 321-327.

Haiman has distinguished between two sets of groups which can be differentiated into pure types.[9] He discusses groups which are formed so that the members can *learn* from each other and groups which are formed so that the members can *act* together. The first he calls *learning* groups; the second, *action groups.* He further states that the motivation in these two types of groups is quite different. In the learning group the purpose is individual growth; in the action group, the purpose is group productivity. It is quite obvious that one would rarely find these groups in their pure form, especially if one is viewing groups from the point of view of an administrator. A faculty would be considered a learning group while participating in an in-service program, but an action group while attempting to incorporate into the curriculum what it had learned. The differences in the groups as they change their functions are important in that they help to determine the way in which the administrator should behave. He should use one type of leadership technique with learning groups but another type with action groups.

It would help to clarify this concept if we could consider a diagram on which there were two types of pure groups and then some intermediate groups spread out as the continuum from learning to action.

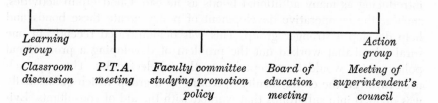

| Learning group | | | | Action group |
| Classroom discussion | P.T.A. meeting | Faculty committee studying promotion policy | Board of education meeting | Meeting of superintendent's council |

This diagram [10] shows that only a classroom group can be a pure type of learning group. The PTA in its meetings exemplifies a group which takes some action, but most of its meetings are devoted to individual growth of the members. A faculty committee studying promotion policy is just about in the middle of the continuum in that it must first aid in the growth of each individual member and then take some action. The board of education approaches the pure action type, but inasmuch as the members are lay people, they must do some studying on each item of business before taking action. The superintendent's council is the nearest thing to a pure action group that we have. It is a professional group, the main function of which is to advise the superintendent in the area of policy making. They do little investigating as individual members and devote practically their entire time to action.

[9] Franklin S. Haiman, *Group Leadership and Democratic Action* (Boston, Houghton Mifflin, 1951), pp. 79, 80.
[10] Adapted from Haiman, *op. cit.,* p. 40.

GROUP SIZE

The problem of group size is a very important one but very difficult to discuss because of the lack of research data. Indeed, the very nature of the problem is such that there may never be any definitive research in this area. We will examine what little evidence there is and then attempt to draw some conclusions. Some criteria for group size have been given by Thelen. He states: [11]

1. The smaller the learning committee, the more time is available for each person to test his ideas directly through overt participation.
2. The smaller the learning committee, the less clearly defined the problem has to be for them to be able to work on it.
3. The smaller the learning committee, the greater pressure each individual feels to participate, and the more visible is his nonparticipation.
4. The smaller the working committee, the easier it is to express intimate thoughts and feelings.
5. The smaller the working committee, the less are its potential resources, but the greater is its motivation.
6. The smaller the working committee, the greater the influence of each individual, including the "blockers" and "wreckers."

These criteria indicate that the group should be small. Other bits of evidence indicate that the membership of a group (that is, a discussion group) should not exceed fifteen. Probably a group should range in size from six to fifteen, depending upon such factors as purpose, type of individuals, and so forth.

GROUP MEMBERSHIP

In discussing group membership, we would do well to start with a very common fallacy which was stated by Gross as follows: [12]

Most people who participate in a given group are basically similar—they want to be members of the group for the same reason. The members of a club, those who accept appointments to committees or who seek election to a city council have the same reasons for being members of the organization.

Gross goes on to make very clear that this statement is not true and that to think of groups in terms of commonness of purpose is to invite disaster. People belong to the same group for a vast number of different reasons. Both from the point of view of the group leader and that of the group member, we must take the attitude that others can have different ways of looking at problems that are as honest and respectable as our own. As

[11] Herbert A. Thelen, *Dynamics of Groups at Work* (Chicago, University of Chicago Press, 1954), p. 63. Copyright, 1954, by the University of Chicago.
[12] Neal Gross, *Human Relations and the Wishes of Men* (Cambridge, Mass., New England School Development Council, 1953), p. 13.

Gross says: "I am trying to understand your feelings, I give you the right to have those feelings, I give you recognition." [13]

The individual accepts a committee appointment or joins a group so that he can satisfy some specific need. This need does not have to be the same as the need of any other individual in the group. The group can achieve its common purpose, even though all of the individual members are filling needs which differ from each other and from the common need. The concept of the "group mind" is no longer accepted for the reasons outlined above. The group leader is demonstrating his skill to the degree that he can co-ordinate the diverse needs of the group so that the group purpose can be accomplished at the same time that individual needs are met.

DISCUSSION GROUP: SERVICE ROLES

The school administrator needs to have an understanding of how all groups function, but most of all, he needs knowledge concerning discussion groups, because whether the group is a learning, an action, or an intermediate group, it will accomplish its purpose through discussion. We will discuss this form of group through a study of its membership. Generally speaking, the membership of a discussion group can be categorized as filling *service* roles or *functional* roles. It is possible for some overlap to occur, but in some places, which are indicated, this should be avoided. Let us start with a consideration of the service roles in a discussion group. There are four service roles to be filled: group discussion leader, group recorder, group observer, and group consultant.

The Group Discussion Leader

Although there can be no group discussion without a leader, there can be very poor group discussion with a leader. Willey characterizes four kinds of leaders, only one of which he believes to be effective.[14]

First, there is the "policeman" type who looks at his function as one of keeping order. He parcels out assignments and expects to get action quickly. He answers questions with finality. He is the group boss.

Second, there is the "we-must-get-results" leader who is afraid that the group will not act swiftly enough. He has little faith in the group's ability to think. He has carefully prepared an agenda. He works out the questions and answers in advance of meeting. A *third* type is the "good fellow" type who believes that since two heads are better than one, ten heads must be even better. He believes he has served satisfactorily if he lets the group talk and carry on under its own

---

[13] *Ibid.*, p. 14.

[14] Gilbert S. Willey, "Effective Group Discussion," *Proceedings of the Annual Summer Conference and Institute* (Bellingham, Wash., Western Washington College, 1951), pp. 39, 40.

momentum. He is known as the "laissez-faire" leader and usually fails to inspire or direct the group.

He then discusses the leader whom he calls "democratic," who realizes that leadership is a set of functions requiring thought and skills, and whose chief function is to create a "permissive" atmosphere in which the creative abilities of the group can be released.

The literature on leadership is so voluminous as to defy a brief summarization. An inclusive consideration of the qualities of leadership would require tremendous detail. We are, however, somewhat agreed on the premise that leadership is a function of the *situation* and shall talk about the discussion leader from this point of view. First of all, we should bear in mind the fact that the discussion leader is a *designated* leader. He is the formal or appointed leader of the group. This means that he has certain duties which he must perform. He is responsible for the group getting squared away, for keeping on the subject, for getting something accomplished, but his chief duty is to maintain an atmosphere in which all of the people in the group will be able to participate to the full extent of their abilities. In the course of the discussion he frequently will relinquish his leadership role to those who have more knowledge or greater skill in meeting the needs of the group at that particular time. The leadership of the "democratic" discussion group moves from person to person. The group is member centered rather than leader centered. In terms of a diagram, the two types of groups look like this:

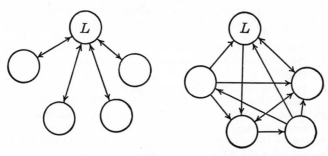

Leader-centered Group   **Member-centered Group**

In the leader-centered group, the discussion is more of a question-and-answer variety. In the member-centered group, the discussion takes place between members as well as with the leader.

Within this frame of reference, the discussion leader can operate to develop a full and complete discussion of the topic at hand. A listing of his duties would include:

1. Assembling and introducing the members of his group. A good technique to use is to have each person have a roster in which he writes the name, position, and remarks as each person introduces himself. Each

person should also have a sign placed in front of him to identify him easily.

2. Getting the discussion going. This might be done by having a problem census in which group members give their ideas on what should be discussed. The leader should aid in selecting and defining the problems which emerge.

3. Mediating arguments. When a difference of opinion emerges, the leader should try to keep the discussion as objective as possible and find the common ground on which members can agree.

4. Keeping the group on the point. He might comment on the wandering or ask the recorder to summarize and bring the group back to the point.

5. Keeping the group from bogging down. He might do this by asking the observer to give some reasons why this has happened and to suggest a remedy.

6. Recognizing and utilizing all of the individuals within the group.

7. Making certain that a permissive atmosphere is maintained.

8. Devoting time to periodic summarizations by the recorder. He should take this time to ask, where are we? What have we been doing? Do we have an answer?

The Group Recorder

The job of the recorder is to keep a concise record of the content of the discussion so that he can report back to the group what has been discussed. He should not act as a stenographer or a secretary. He should record the important phases of the discussion, not all that has been said. It would be well to omit names from the report, since the emphasis would then be on *who* said something, rather than *what* was said. The following guide for the group recorder is offered by Benne and Muntyan: [15]

1. Keep track of major contributions to the discussion:
   a) Points upon which group agreed or on which formal action was taken;
   b) Points upon which there was cleavage of opinion in the group;
   c) Points where the recorder is not sure of the group opinions;
   d) Points mentioned but not discussed which the group may wish to consider later.

2. Report to the group—what was discussed and concluded rather than merely what the discussion was *about*.

3. Be ready to report at any time and to make an inclusive report at the end of the session.

4. Ask for suggestions from the group as to how the recorder's work may be made more helpful.

The Group Observer

The group observer is primarily interested in the *process* that is being used by the group. It is his job to note how well the group is working. He

---

[15] Kenneth D. Benne and Bozidar Muntyan, eds., *Human Relations in Curriculum Change* (New York, Dryden, 1951), p. 158. Copyright, 1951, by The Dryden Press, Inc. Reprinted by permission.

notes what the leader is doing and what effect this has on the members of the group. He also notes the members. He tries to determine whether each person is pulling his own weight, whether all are contributing, and what the *quality* of their contributions are. He should always be ready to comment to the group on their process with the aim of improving the discussion. He should be called on at the end of the meeting to give a summary statement on the way the group has functioned. This is in addition, of course, to the times during the meeting when he can be called on.

Willey points out that the group observer should be selected rather carefully and should be a person: [16]

1. Who is accepted freely and easily by the group.
2. Who is sensitive and objective in noting aspects of group operation which can be improved.
3. Who is able to report his observations to the group in a simple, objective manner without creating confusion.

A helpful checklist for an observer would include the following:

1. He tries to observe what goes on in an objective manner.
2. He makes notes as he goes along for his summary statement.
3. He checks to see that the leader does what he is supposed to do.
4. He identifies the role(s) which each member of the group is playing.
5. He does not talk down to the group when he makes his report.
6. He is ready to report to the group at any time.
7. He remembers he is part of a leadership team consisting of the group leader, recorder, consultant, and himself which is dedicated to improving the group.

The Group Consultant

Many groups realize that they need a person in the group who has a greater knowledge of the problem under discussion than does any other group member. This person is called the consultant or resource person. He should not be the same person who leads the group discussion. In cases where the administrator feels that he is the expert in the problem under discussion, he should designate himself the resource person and have someone else assume the role of group leader. Whyte indicates very clearly the difference between these two roles: [17]

The leader originates activity for the group. He co-ordinates the discussion, he responds to individual group members, but the group does not act until he originates activity for it. The resource person, on the other hand, is expected to be an individual who possesses expert knowledge, but who does not introduce that knowledge to the group unless he is called upon.

[16] Willey, *loc. cit.*, pp. 40, 41.

[17] William Foote Whyte, *Leadership and Group Participation* (Ithaca, N. Y., New York State School of Industrial and Labor Relations, Cornell University, 1953), p. 24-25.

If the same person tries to fill both roles, the group will become confused and will be unable to utilize the expert knowledge. A checklist for consultants would include:

1. Helping in the problem census.
2. Clarifying the problem under consideration.
3. Contributing specific information when needed.
4. Helping to evaluate the progress of the group.
5. Inspiring the group to attain higher levels of achievement.

DISCUSSION GROUP: MEMBER-AT-LARGE

We have just discussed the so-called service roles of various group members who comprise the *leadership team*. The real team, however, is the remainder of the group. What roles do these members fill? What do they do? What should they do to bring about the best possible group action? We will consider each member of a group as a specific individual in terms of his contribution to the group in the next section. Let us first consider the group member as a group member and arrive at some definition of his responsibilities.

We could talk in general terms and say that each group member should feel a definite responsibility for the progress of the group; that is, he should have a definite feeling of *involvement*. Each group member should display this concept of involvement by participating in the group activities. This does not mean that he should submerge his own personality in the group and lose his identity; rather, he should enhance his personality by developing it as the group develops and moves toward the attainment of its goals. Group growth is also individual growth.

Willey has set up some very practical guides for individual members of the group. These guides would prove useful to an administrator who is attempting to work with his faculty in group procedures. They might serve also as "rules of the game" for the faculty in their meetings.

A group member to be most helpful does the following: [18]

1. Speaks his mind freely. He recognizes that every idea counts.
2. Listens thoughtfully to others—tries to get the other man's point of view. It is said that there are three points of view on every question—yours, mine, and the right one.
3. Keeps his seat when speaking—speeches are out of place in group discussions. Informality is the rule.
4. Does not monopolize the discussion—speaks not longer than a minute at a time, giving others an opportunity to speak.
5. Does not let the discussion get away from him. Is not hesitant to ask for examples and illustrations to clarify points of the discussion.

[18] Willey, *loc. cit.*, p. 41.

6. Indulges in friendly disagreement. Good-humored discussion helps to find the truth everyone is seeking.
7. Strikes while the idea is hot—frequently not waiting for the leader to recognize him before speaking.
8. Comes to the discussion with questions in mind. Advanced readings frequently raise questions which form the basis for profitable discussion.
9. Follows the discussion period with continued study. Discussion is just the first step—materials for further study on the problem should be formed or made available.

We see in this listing an inclination toward informality in groups and away from formality. The group member is advised to not make speeches, remain seated, and speak up when the spirit moves him. The advice to seek friendly arguments is particularly helpful. The feeling seems to be prevalent in many groups that a participant can not differ with the other members of the group. This stifles many group discussions and does not stimulate the give-and-take so necessary to the creation of new ideas. The group leader should attempt to involve the members in friendly arguments, out of which he can pull real meaning. It is also pointed out that good group work is not limited merely to the meeting itself. Good group work is preceded by reading, investigation, and the formulation of questions to be raised at the meeting. It is followed by further reading and investigation along the new lines that were suggested at the meeting. This points up one of the real advantages of group work for the individual. The individual grows as a "self," as the result of working in a group. The growth of the group is reflected in the growth of the individual. The individual can and does grow through participation in the group.

DISCUSSION GROUPS: FUNCTIONAL ROLES

There are several ways of looking at groups. One way which seems to be very practical is to look at what the individual group members *do* in the course of a discussion. This study of the *roles* which people play during a discussion accomplishes two purposes: (1) it enables the leader to identify sources of problems and (2) suggests a way of solving problems. As we study these roles, we notice that they fall into three categories: (1) group task roles, (2) group building and maintenance roles, (3) individual roles. It should be noted that these are not assigned roles but roles which reflect the "self" of the participants. At various times it is possible that one individual will play several different roles. As the purpose of the group changes an individual may move from a group builder to a group leader. The leader himself will play different roles. These roles are described to show how people do various things when in a group. Some individuals are more consistent in the roles which they play than are others. As we describe the roles you will, no doubt, identify certain individuals whom you have observed filling these roles. Keep in mind that these are not hard and fast categorizations, but are meant to help in the analysis and operation of group activity.

Group Task Roles

The first of the functional roles for us to consider are the group task roles. Benne and Sheats summarize these as follows: [19]

The following analysis assumes that the task of the discussion group is to select, define, and solve common problems. The roles are identified in relation to functions of facilitation and co-ordination of group problem-solving activities. Each member may of course enact more than one role in any given unit of participation and a wide range of roles in successive participations. Any or all of these roles may be played at times by the group "leader" as well as by various members.

   a. The *initiator-contributor* suggests or proposes to the group new ideas or a changed way of regarding the group problem or goal. The novelty proposed may take the form of suggestions of a new group goal or a new definition of the problem. It may take the form of a suggested solution or some way of handling a difficulty that the group has encountered. Or it may take the form of a proposed new procedure for the group, a new way of organizing the group for the task ahead.
   b. The *information seeker* asks for clarification of suggestions made in terms of their factual adequacy, for authoritative information and facts pertinent to the problem being discussed.
   c. The *opinion seeker* asks not primarily for the facts of the case but for a clarification of the values pertinent to what the group is undertaking or of values involved in a suggestion made or in alternative suggestions.
   d. The *information giver* offers facts or generalizations which are "authoritative" or relates his own experience pertinently to the group problem.
   e. The *opinion giver* states his belief or opinion pertinently to a suggestion made or to alternative suggestions. The emphasis is on his proposal of what should become the group's view of pertinent values, not primarily upon relevant facts or information.
   f. The *elaborator* spells out suggestions in terms of examples or developed meanings, offers a rationale for suggestions previously made and tries to deduce how an idea or suggestion would work out if adopted by the group.
   g. The *co-ordinator* shows or clarifies the relationships among various ideas and suggestions, tries to pull ideas and suggestions together, or tries to co-ordinate the activities of various members or subgroups.
   h. The *orienter* defines the position of the group with respect to its goals by summarizing what has occurred, points to departures from agreed upon directions or goals, or raises questions about the direction which the group discussion is taking.
   i. The *evaluator-critic* subjects the accomplishment of the group to some

[19] Kenneth D. Benne and Paul Sheats, "Functional Roles of Group Members," *Journal of Social Issues,* Vol. 4 (Spring, 1948), pp. 41-49.

standard or set of standards of group-functioning in the context of the group task. Thus, he may evaluate or question the "practicality," the "logic," the "facts," or the "procedure" of a suggestion or of some unit of group discussion.

j. The *energizer* prods the group to action or decision, attempts to stimulate or arouse the group to "greater" or "higher quality" activity.

k. The *procedural technician* expedites group movement by doing things for the group—performing routine tasks, distributing materials, or manipulating objects for the group, e.g., rearranging the seating or running the recording machine, etc.

l. The *recorder* writes down suggestions, makes a record of group decisions, or writes down the product of discussion. The recorder role is the "group memory."

Group Building and Maintenance Roles

Continuing their discussion, Benne and Sheats define the second category of functional roles and list the types of members who fall most nearly into this classification: [20]

Here the analysis of member-functions is oriented to those participations which have for their purpose the building of group-centered attitudes and orientation among the members of a group or the maintenance and perpetuation of such group-centered behavior. A given contribution may involve several roles and a member or the "leader" may perform various roles in successive contributions.

a. The *encourager* praises, agrees with, and accepts the contribution of others. He indicates warmth and solidarity in his attitude toward other group members, offers commendation and praise, and in various ways indicates understanding and acceptance of other points of view, ideas, and suggestions.

b. The *harmonizer* mediates the differences between other members, attempts to reconcile disagreements, relieves tension in conflict situations through jesting or pouring oil on the troubled waters, etc.

c. The *compromiser* operates from within a conflict in which his idea or position is involved. He may offer compromise by yielding status, admitting his error, by disciplining himself to maintain group harmony, or by "coming half-way" in moving along with the group.

d. The *gate-keeper and expediter* attempts to keep communication channels open by encouraging or facilitating the participation of others ("we haven't got the ideas of Mr. X yet," etc.) or by proposing regulation of the flow of communication ("why don't we limit the length of our contributions so that everyone will have a chance to contribute?" etc.)

e. The *standard setter* or *ego ideal* expresses standards for the group to attempt to achieve in its functioning or applies standards in evaluating the quality of group processes.

f. The *follower* goes along with the movement of the group, more or less passively accepting the ideas of others, serving as an audience in group discussion and decision.

[20] *Ibid.*, pp. 44, 45.

"Individual" Roles

The third category of functional roles that the administrator should learn to recognize consists of "individual" roles, about which Benne and Sheats comment: [21]

Attempts by "members" of a group to satisfy individual needs which are irrelevant to the group task and which are nonoriented or negatively oriented to group building and maintenance set problems of group and member training. A high incidence of "individual-centered" as opposed to "group-centered" participation in a group always calls for self-diagnosis of the group. The diagnosis may reveal one or several of a number of conditions—low level of skill-training among members, including the group leader; the prevalence of "authoritarian" and "laissez-faire" points of view toward group functioning in the group; a low level of group maturity, discipline and morale; and inappropriately chosen and inadequately defined group task; etc. Whatever the diagnosis, it is in this setting that the training needs of the group are to be discovered and group training efforts to meet these needs are to be defined. The outright "suppression" of "individual roles" will deprive the group of data needed for really adequate self-diagnosis and therapy.

    a. The *aggressor* may work in many ways—deflating the status of others, expressing disapproval of the values, acts or feelings of others, attacking the group or the problem it is working on, joking aggressively, showing envy toward another's contribution by trying to take credit for it, etc.

    b. The *blocker* tends to be negativistic and stubbornly resistant, disagreeing and opposing without or beyond "reason" and attempting to maintain or bring back an issue after the group has rejected or by-passed it.

    c. The *recognition-seeker* works in various ways to call attention to himself, whether through boasting, reporting on personal achievements, acting in unusual ways, struggling to prevent his being placed in an "inferior" position, etc.

    d. The *self-confessor* uses the audience opportunity which the group setting provides to express personal, nongroup oriented, "feeling," "insight," "ideology," etc.

    e. The *playboy* makes a display of his lack of involvement in the group's processes. This may take the form of cynicism, nonchalance, horseplay, and other more or less studied forms of "out of field" behavior.

    f. The *dominator* tries to assert authority or superiority in manipulating the group or certain members of the group. This domination may take the form of flattery, of asserting a superior status or right to attention, giving directions authoritatively, interrupting the contributions of others, etc.

    g. The *help-seeker* attempts to call forth "sympathy" response from other group members or from the whole group, whether through expressions of insecurity, personal confusion, or depreciation of himself beyond "reason."

    h. The *special-interest* pleader speaks for the "small business man," the "grass roots" community, the "housewife," "labor," etc., usually cloaking his own prejudices or biases in the stereotype which best fits his individual need.

[21] *Ibid.,* pp. 45, 46.

There are three other "individual" roles which are played in groups which need to be understood by the group leader if he is to help the group achieve its goals. One of these is the *withdrawer*. This is the person who never seems to have anything to say. He is in the group but, to all intents and purposes, is not of the group. He is difficult to work with, because although he may be profiting greatly, the rest of the group does not profit from him. It may be that this person is afraid to talk for fear of being laughed at or having his point ignored or defeated. If this is the case, the leader needs, more than ever, to try and make the withdrawer feel secure.

The *rationalizer* is another type of individual role which is often found in a group. This person usually acts to block group process because his behavior will result in antagonizing others. Haiman gives a good example of an individual who rationalizes: [22]

Mr. X harbors a deep resentment against Jews. The real reason for this prejudice is that, at one time he had his heart set on a job to which a member of that minority group was appointed. Mr. X is an intelligent man and recognizes two hard facts: (1) that the other man was more deserving of the job than he, and (2) that the other man is only one Jew, not all Jews. However, the jealousy and frustration of X is so great that emotionally he is unable to admit these facts to himself. He has worked out a rationalization for his prejudice toward Jewish people—one which is more "socially acceptable" than his jealousy. He claims that the "reason" for his prejudice is that the Jewish faith denies the divinity of Christ, and that his religious convictions on the subject are so strong that he cannot help resenting this point of view.

Another individual role is filled by the person who fills a strong need to compensate for a weakness, either real or imaginary. In our listing above, three fit this category, namely, the recognition-seeker, the dominator, and the playboy. Two others are quite interesting and they are described by McBurney and Hance: [23]

Mr. Blue-Nose. His sensibilities are easily shocked. He is straight-laced and conventional. He has an amazing nose for moral issues and moral implications, and an amazing lack of warmth and magnanimity. His chilling influence is felt whenever the discussion is earthy, gustful and vigorous. . . . Mr. Suspicious. He finds it difficult to believe that anyone can be frank and honest. He suspects hidden motives and selfish purposes. He sees sinister designs where none exist. . . . As a result he is a cynical, unhappy person and a troublemaker.

In summarizing this section we can say that we have attempted to suggest a medium through which an administrator can take a look at the group with which he is working. This medium is one which asks what the group members are doing and applies to these activities certain descriptive names. If the administrator can identify the nature of the role

[22] Haiman, *op. cit.*, p. 87.
[23] James H. McBurney and Kenneth G. Hance, *Discussion in Human Affairs* (New York, Harper, 1950), pp. 263-265.

being played by each of the group *members,* he can help the group to achieve its goals.

SOLVING THE PROBLEMS OF GROUPS

As groups get down to work there are many problems that crop up constantly. It is our purpose in this section to look at these problems and to suggest ways of approaching and solving them. Thelen has classified those problems that appear to be recurrent as follows: [24]

    a. the publicly stated problem the group was brought together to solve;
    b. the hidden problems of dealing with shared anxieties which usually are
        not explicitly formulated (problems within the "group mentality").

The Publicly Stated Problem

Any time that a group is called together there is some expressed reason for doing so. Occasionally, school groups are called together to hear announcements. This should not be considered a valid reason for a group meeting—some other method that is less costly of manpower should be used to meet this need. Assuming that this is not the reason for the meeting, we are interested in helping the group to solve the announced problem. In surveying the literature on groups, there seems to be little disagreement about the general approach to be used. Several writers have outlined a recommended procedure for groups to follow. Haiman makes a good point when he indicates that the exact method to be followed is not as important as the fact that the group does have a systematic procedure to follow. Most of the proposals are very close to John Dewey's problem-solving process. An outline of a method for groups to use should be some variation of the following plan.

Define and Limit the Problem. The first job which faces a group is the defining and limiting of the problem before the group. The group should know the answers to such questions as: What is the problem? How broad a look do we take at the problem? What kind of an answer should we seek? These answers will set the framework within which the group will work. Properly defined, they will prevent the group from attempting to accomplish more than it can with the time, facilities, and abilities at its disposal. If this step is not accomplished satisfactorily, the group is almost certain to flounder.

Clear Up the Semantic Differences. All discussion groups are primarily and vitally interested in the words they use. As we know, words mean different things to different people. They are maps of different territories. The group must determine what the most important words that it will use

24 Thelen, *op. cit.,* p. 276.

are going to mean to each member of the group. A faculty committee studying a revision of the course of study in mathematics should establish a common meaning for such terms as *curriculum, mathematics needs, graphs,* and *subtrahend.* In other words, a group will not get far if there is lack of understanding on the words vital to the discussion. The maps the group is using should guide all of the members to the same destination.

Determine the Group Objective. It is important for the group to know where it is going. It is possible to analyze, define, and limit the problem, clear up the semantic problems, and still not get anywhere. The group needs to determine its purpose in holding its meeting. Many meetings appear to be fine—the discussion is lively, everyone participates—yet the group gets nowhere. The group should determine the objective toward which it is striving. It should ask itself the following questions:

> Do we want to come up with a plan?
> Are we discussing the question just to inform ourselves?
> Are we expected to put a plan into action?
> Who expects a decision from us and what will he do with it?

The group needs a clearly defined objective so that it will spend its time and energy in the most constructive manner possible.

Collect the Evidence. The group is now ready to settle down to the task of accumulating the evidence upon which it can make its decision. It asks itself: What are the facts? Where can we get them? Who can help us to solve our problems? At this stage, it is appropriate for the group to seek consultant help in order to utilize all pertinent methods of collecting facts, causes, and results.

Re-evaluate the Objective. After the evidence has been collected, it is often necessary to restate the objective of the group. The author worked recently with a teacher-citizen committee which had set as its goal the preparation of a new system of promotion and reporting in the school system. After collecting some of the tremendous amount of evidence available in this field, the group decided that it should deal with promotion and reporting at the seventh-grade level only. This was the crucial grade in this particular system, since it marked the point at which the students moved from one type of grading to another entirely different type. The group decided that during the next year, it would look at the other grades. This committee re-examined its goals in light of the evidence and set a new goal which was more realistic and possible of achievement.

Arrive at a Solution. With the evidence collected and a new goal established, the group needs to consider the possible solutions to the problem it has set itself. A good procedure is to put all the possible solutions before the group. A blackboard presentation could be used for this purpose. No solution should be disregarded by the group during the "solution-census" period. Often a solution which seems ridiculous at first has a great deal of merit. Once all of the possible solutions are put forth, *one* should be se-lected. At this stage, the group should strive for an unanimous decision. This is particularly true if the group is to put its decision into action. Although such a decision may result in a solution which is somewhat "watered down," the long-range benefits of full support from the group should outweigh this drawback. The group should settle for less than complete consensus only when it is obviously impossible to get all to agree. If a very small number of members remains adamant, then it should proceed with the majority point of view.

The Hidden Agenda

The second problem the administrator is called upon to solve is that of the *hidden agenda*. Since by their very nature hidden agenda under-mine the stated purpose of the group meeting, the administrator needs to develop skill in sensing hidden agenda and taking appropriate action. Let us consider a case in which this problem is present.[25]

An assistant superintendent of schools believed that many of the teachers in her city needed further training. The superintendent accepted her idea and sug-gested that such training be started either by conducting a two-day training institute on Fridays and Saturdays or by having hour-and-a-half meetings once a week for ten weeks. Either plan placed the training period on the teachers' own time.

At a meeting the principals agreed at once on the value of such training and appeared at first to like either of the alternative plans. However, difficulties then arose. Some wanted one plan, some the other. All the teachers could not meet at the same time. Hidden agendas were never mentioned. Many of the princi-pals resented being given only two choices. Others suspected that the super-intendent believed their schools were backward. They thought that the train-ing program was really aimed at showing up their schools.

Two of the principals were younger; they felt they were better liked by the superintendent and they wanted to support him in anything he wanted. Two other principals had a number of older teachers who they knew would object seriously to the whole idea.

The situation was further complicated by the assistant superintendent who was new to her job and not entirely accepted by the principals. At the meeting she made the weight of the superintendent too obvious. She implied that she thought the system was behind the times. The principals hoped secretly that something would happen to eliminate the entire idea, so they delayed matters, waiting for a miracle.

We can see what is going on here. The group of principals, lead by the assistant superintendent of schools, is meeting to determine some of the particulars of an in-service training program for teachers. This is the publicly announced purpose of the meeting. However, both the leader

[25] Leland P. Bradford, "The Case of the Hidden Agenda," *The Leader's Digest* (Chicago, Adult Education Association, 1955), pp. 12-13.

and the principals have some other purposes which they carry with them to the meeting. These other purposes keep coming to the fore as the meeting progresses. Each time a point is presented, the secret purposes of one or more of the group members comes out to thwart the point.

These secret purposes of group members are appropriately called hidden agenda. The practicing school administrator will recognize the hidden agenda as one of the most serious obstacles to good group meetings. The private prejudices, likes, and dislikes of each member condition the way in which the member reacts to points as they are discussed. Often, the published purpose of the meeting is entirely forgotten as these private purposes take over. Let us consider some further examples:

A college professor was invited to talk to a high school faculty on the topic, "What should the high school graduate be like." It was a rather difficult topic, but he prepared as best he could. When he arrived at the high school, he was told the meeting would take place in a classroom. Noting that the furniture was screwed to the floor, he objected and suggested meeting in the library. The superintendent indicated that he thought it a lot of foolishness but agreed after some discussion. The professor was introduced, and the superintendent left the group. The faculty was attentive and seemed to follow the talk. There was some indication, however, that this was not really the interest of the group. After the talk there were a few perfunctory questions. The professor felt that there was something being hidden from him, so he probed the subject. Finally, one of the teachers started to talk, and a long list of really important questions came out.

Here was a case of an administrator planning a meeting without consulting the group. The teachers entered the meeting with many hidden agenda. Careful questioning and a permissive atmosphere brought them out.

A second example definitely shows how one agendum affects the other:

A new high school teacher was attending his first faculty meeting. The high school principal had been in the school for one year, but the rest of the faculty were veteran teachers, most of whom had been in the system for some twenty years or more. The principal presented a plan for the study of the curriculum of the school. It was obvious to the new teacher that the principal had consulted the teachers beforehand on the plan he was presenting. As soon as the plan was presented, the members of the faculty began to raise objections to the plan. The objections were not intended to clarify the plan nor to implement it. Finally, the faculty voted, almost unanimously, to reject the entire plan.

After the meeting the new teacher walked home with one of the older teachers. The new teacher tried to find out what was behind the meeting. The older teacher chuckled, "Well, served him right. The plan was okay, but you have to treat these administrators rough. We've been kicked around a lot by other administrators we have had, so we aren't going to give this one a chance!"

In this case, the hidden agendum, the feelings of the faculty toward its past administrators, prevented the publicly announced agendum from being considered on its merits.

What can be done about hidden agenda? Well, it does no good to ignore them or to ride roughshod over them. Probably a basic attitude on the part of the leader which tends to make him sensitive to the needs of his group is the most helpful step toward eliminating this problem. If the leader can sense the factors in the hidden agenda and then act to reassure, to answer the unasked question, to make members feel secure, then he will do much to offset the harm of hidden agenda. Some hidden agenda should not be brought into the open because of their explosive character. In this case, the administrator should keep them quiet, but try to work with the individual so that the wants of the individual can be lessened and redirected to conform more to those of the group.

SUMMARY

We started our discussion of groups by looking at some basic definitions. We noted that there are "elementary" and "cumulative" groups which differ in the number of bonds holding their members together. If the school administrator desires to build a strong group, he must set up situations in which group-creating bonds can be developed to the point where the group members have a strong feeling of unity, have strong psychological relationships with one another, and can satisfy their needs through the group of which they are members.

Our concern is with the small group, sometimes called the talking group. Although the research on group size is highly inadequate, so that it is impossible to draw definite conclusions, it would seem that talking groups should range in size from six to fifteen members. There are two pure types of talking groups: action groups and learning groups. These groups achieve their purposes through a process of discussion. Each discussion group should have a leadership team consisting of a leader, recorder, observer, and consultant. Each member of the group has one or more roles to play. We discussed the general responsibility of the group member under the heading of member-at-large. We also noted that group members fill other roles categorized as group task roles, group building and maintenance roles, and "individual" roles.

We concluded our investigation of groups by discussing the problems which groups face in achieving their purposes. These were summarized under the headings of the publicly stated problem of the meeting and the hidden agenda.

EXERCISES

1. Analyze the faculty of your school to determine the number of bonds which are evident. Is your faculty an elementary group? A cumulative group? What bonds could be strengthened?

2. In the next faculty meeting, try to identify the roles that various faculty members play. Does the list you compile compare with the list in the text?

3. In your next faculty meeting, watch for signs of hidden agenda. What are the evidences of these agenda? What can you do about them?

4. Does your faculty have a systematic procedure for attacking its problems? Most people do not work out their problems in a scientific manner. If your group does not have such a procedure, how can you help it to attain one?

5. How should the leadership techniques vary in the two pure types of groups: the learning group and the action group?

6. Make a diagram of your next faculty meeting showing how the discussion moves. Use circles for each faculty member and draw arrows to show the direction of discussion. Analyze the completed drawing and make recommendations for improving the discussion.

7. Using the diagram you constructed for question 6, can you determine the power structure in your faculty?

8. How would you go about involving a withdrawer in the discussion?

9. How can the group leader work with the senior member of the group who has a high amount of prestige and wishes to have a privileged role in the group?

10. What are some specific activities that a leader can initiate to improve group atmosphere?

SELECTED BIBLIOGRAPHY

BENNE, Kenneth D., and MUNTYAN, Bozidar, eds., *Human Relations in Curriculum Change* (New York, Dryden, 1951), pp. 66-215.

CARTWRIGHT, Dorwin, and ZANDER, Alvin, eds., *Group Dynamics* (Evanston, Ill., Row, Peterson, 1953).

CHASE, Stuart, *Roads to Agreement* (New York, Harper, 1951), pp. 56-82.

GROSS, Neal, *Human Relations and the Wishes of Men* (Cambridge, Mass., New England School Development Council, 1953), Pamphlet.

HAIMAN, Franklyn S., *Group Leadership and Democratic Action* (Boston, Houghton Mifflin, 1951).

McBURNEY, James H., and HANCE, Kenneth G., *Discussion in Human Affairs* (New York, Harper, 1950).

MACKENZIE, Gordon N., COREY, Stephen M., and others, *Instructional Leadership* (New York, Teachers College Bureau of Publications, 1954), pp. 137-167.

MAIER, Norman R. F., *Principles of Human Relations* (New York, Wiley, 1952), pp. 43-86.

SHERIF, M. A., and WILSON, M. O., eds. *Group Relations at the Crossroads* (New York, Harper, 1953).

The Leader's Digest (Chicago, Adult Education Association, 1955).

THELEN, Herbert A., *Dynamics of Groups at Work* (Chicago, University of Chicago Press, 1954).

WHYTE, William Foote, *Leadership and Group Participation* (Ithaca, N. Y., New York State School of Industrial and Labor Relations, Cornell University, 1953).

WILLEY, Gilbert, "Effective Group Discussion," *Proceedings*, Annual Summer Conference and Institute (Bellingham, Wash., Western Washington College, 1951).

CHAPTER 9

Group Dynamics Techniques

During the last few years there has appeared on the educational horizon a new movement called *group dynamics*. There appears to be as much confusion regarding it as there is regarding the term *human relations*. Group dynamics, as a movement, has aroused reactions all along the continuum, from those who see it as the salvation of administration to those who consider it a complete hoax. It may be that there are some who have not heard of group dynamics and so are unable to form an opinion; but it seems to be true that no one who knows of the movement has managed to stay neutral. Such wide divergence of opinion is one way to judge the vitality of an intellectual movement. A movement that does not enlist enthusiastic supporters and vociferous opponents seldom achieves significance. This, however, is not true of group dynamics. It has "caught on."

WHAT IS GROUP DYNAMICS?

Perhaps if we can establish what the term *group dynamics* refers to, we will be able to discuss it intelligently and evaluate it in terms of its relevance to school administration. Bienenstock defines the term rather clearly as follows: [1]

The confusion aroused by group dynamics is partly due to the fact that it covers two areas of inquiry, one theoretical and one practical. On the theoretical side, group dynamics tries to establish the basic principles governing the behavior of individuals in groups. On the practical side, it seeks to develop ways and means by which learning and work of groups can be improved and made more effective.

This definition seems to have rather general acceptance. Both Jenkins and Thelen, writing on this same topic, offer definitions which are almost identical.

Let us follow up this definition by raising the question of what topics group dynamics includes. When we note that group dynamics is concerned with the behavior of people in groups, we see that there are forces acting

[1] Theodore Bienenstock, "Group Dynamics and the Classroom Situation," *Impact of Social and Economic Forces on Education* (Albany, N. Y., State Education Department, n.d.) p. 1.

on people from a variety of sources. To investigate all of the sources we would have to examine such things as the power structure of the group. We should certainly be interested in the motives of the various people as they interact. We would have to be concerned with the values which each member holds and also the values common to the group. As a corollary of power structure we would be concerned with status relationships. The problem of communications and semantics is always difficult to an investigator in group dynamics. The problem of how group members perceive the situation is a continuing one. We can see that the topics which are included in the study of group dynamics are very similar to the problems which we have been studying thus far. We have looked at the problems of the group dynamics researcher from the broad frame of reference of the social sciences. We have also been interested in these problems as they affect people who are not in groups.

It may be obvious now that a person cannot *use* or *not use* group dynamics as it suits his purpose. Every group has its own dynamics, and whenever a group comes together, there will be problems of structure, communication, and the like. A knowledge of group dynamics will help a person to understand how a group functions. It is obvious that although we cannot "use" group dynamics, we should *understand* group dynamics.

CRITERIA FOR SELECTING TECHNIQUES

Since most of the topics included in a formal study of group dynamics already have been dealt with at length, this chapter will be chiefly concerned with the *techniques* or practical applications of group dynamics. This bears repeating, since many people criticize those who work in group dynamics on the grounds that they are overly impressed by techniques and are not concerned with basic theory. We do not feel this to be true. We are emphasizing the techniques in this chapter merely because we have discussed much of the theory in previous chapters.

Techniques of group dynamics are the tools of the trade to those who work with groups of people. Each person who works with groups should be familiar with a variety of these techniques or skills to use in case the first one he tries is not successful. In the use of group dynamics techniques we should maintain an experimental point of view. Group dynamics has not reached the point where it can be said with any degree of certainty that any one technique will be certain to work. In this respect, the group dynamics worker is much like the medical doctor, who has a large number of medicines and treatments at his command and realizes that (1) he may have made the wrong diagnosis or (2) the treatment may not work because of individual differences in patients. With this in mind, he has no difficulty in shifting from treatment to treatment, medicine to medicine. His only absolute is the scientific or experimental method.

Keeping this experimental attitude uppermost in our minds, what are the criteria for selecting techniques to be used with groups? The first criterion deals with our diagnosis of the situation. Techniques are tied closely to situations as they occur so that we can "prescribe" the correct "treatment." Jenkins, in discussing whether to use role-playing or the formal lecture in a situation, has pointed out that "one cannot readily talk about the relative values of two such techniques except in terms of the dynamics and goals under which each makes the better contribution." [2]

The technique used should fit the situation, both in terms of the forces present in the situation and the forces one wishes to loosen in the situation. In the case of the role-playing, it is possible to loosen the forces of contributions from many different people. In the case of a formal lecture, one person may have information which all of the others in the group need. Consequently, the lecture may eventually act to create a greater force than some technique which calls for wide active participation. It is unfortunate that many people have come to think of a lecture as "authoritarian" and, as such, undesirable. In some places, it is considered almost a "dirty" word. The lecture is a technique for imparting information to a gathering of people. Like other techniques, it should be used when a careful analysis of the situation indicates that it will do more good than any other technique which might be used.

The second criterion has to do with the goals that the group has set for itself. The technique that the group leader wishes to use must be the one that will help the group to attain its goals. Tied in with the goals of the group will be its value system. The third criterion indicates that one should not violate this value system while trying to achieve the goals of the group. The use of a particular technique may help a group to reach its goals, but it may run counter to the group's value system. The following case illustrates this point:

A high school faculty had just lost its principal. He had resigned to take another job in the middle of the year. The faculty met with the superintendent and discussed ways of selecting a new principal. It was agreed that they would have an acting principal appointed to serve out the remainder of the school year. In the meantime they could search for a new principal in an orderly manner. The superintendent proposed that each teacher on the staff write the names of any candidates they might want to have considered for the position and send them to him. He would then select the candidate to be recommended to the board. The faculty objected saying that they wanted to do this democratically. They insisted that a committee of three be elected from the group to screen all applicants. This committee would then recommend three candidates to the superintendent, and he could make his choice from the three.

---

[2] David H. Jenkins, "What Is Group Dynamics?" *Adult Education Journal,* Vol. 9 (April, 1950), p. 59.

Thus we have an example of how a technique chosen by the superintendent violated the values held by the group. The technique chosen must be congruent with the values and ethics held by the group.

The criteria for the selection of techniques are summarized by Jenkins as follows: [3]

To select appropriate techniques for use in a particular group, then, we need to know (1) the dynamics of the group at this particular time, (2) the goals, values, and ethics of the group and its members, and (3) the dynamics of the particular techniques we are considering.

ROLE-PLAYING

Of all the techniques used by practitioners of group dynamics, role-playing is, in our opinion, just about the most significant. This value judgment is made in view of the wide application of the technique, the large number of benefits which can accrue from its use, the ease with which it can be used, and its general applicability. In spite of its many virtues, it is almost unheard of as an administrative technique in the public schools. This is understandable in view of the recent introduction of the practice and the fact that it has not been included in the training program of administrators. Role-playing has been introduced into the training of supervisors and executives in business and industry, and there are many reports concerning its use. Role-playing, in its many ramifications and modifications, has a bright future in school administration.

What Is Role-playing?

It is generally conceded that role-playing was originated by Moreno in a somewhat different form from its present common use.[4] He originated the method of role-playing in what he called the *psychodrama,* in which he had a mentally disturbed patient who had serious conflicts with other individuals *act* out his conflicts. Other members of the group played the parts of the conflict individuals. The disturbed person then changed roles, and so, too, did the audience. This was all done under the observation of a trained therapist. Moreno also devised another process which he called *sociodrama.* This is a method for testing ideas before they are put into operation. It calls for rehearsing action, diagnosing the action, and correcting the observed flaws before the idea is actually put into action.

Role-playing, in its many modern forms, developed out of the sociodrama. One of the names which has been applied to role-playing is *reality-*

---

[3] *Ibid.,* p. 59.

[4] J. L. Moreno, "Inter-personal Therapy and the Psychopathology of Inter-personal Relationships," *Sociometry,* Vol. 1 (1937), pp. 9-76.

practice.[5] This name is particularly appropriate because it describes precisely what is going on. The individuals taking the roles in the role-playing situation are actually practicing for reality. In discussing role-playing, it would be inaccurate to indicate that there is only one procedure to follow in this technique. The value of the technique lies in its great flexibility. Each group leader can adopt role-playing however he sees best.

Describing role-playing in its simplest form, we would say that it is the acting out of a problem situation by the members of the group which is attempting to solve the problem. This leads us to many different situations, problems, and benefits. There are two practices which are common to all role-playing situations: namely, the problem and the fact that there is no script. The players are placed in a situation which has been explained to them. They are then allowed to make up their own conversation, motions, gestures, and so forth. As they act out the situation, they reveal the way they feel. In some cases, each player is urged to "be himself"; in other situations, he is told to take the part of somone else. This is done for two reasons: (1) so that he may gain an insight into how another person views the situation; (2) so that the person whose role he is taking can see how another person views him. Thus insights into the behavior of all participants in the problem situation are gained.

Uses of Role-playing

Thelen, in an excellent discussion of role-playing, suggests four major uses for this technique.[6]

1. To "warm-up" an audience; to get "involvement."
2. To help communicate a specific problem so people will have something "real" to talk about as the basis for discovering their own problems.
3. To test various ways of dealing with a problem situation.
4. To develop "sensitivity."

Achieving Involvement. The first use, to get audience "involvement," is the least spontaneous of all of the uses of role-playing. Its use, however, is an excellent one for faculty meetings, in particular, and other meetings in general. Very briefly, the idea here is to present an impromptu play so that the audience can start a discussion with a common background. It also stimulates interest and provides a somewhat novel approach to a faculty meeting. In this case, although there is no script, the roles are cast sometime before the meeting, and there are rehearsals. A discussion of handling discipline cases could get off to a good start if a role-playing

[5] Charles E. Hendry, Ronald Lippitt, and Alvin Zander, "Reality Practice As Educational Method," *Psychodrama Monographs*, No. 9 (1944), pp. 9-24.

[6] Herbert A. Thelen, *Dynamics of Groups at Work* (Chicago, University of Chicago Press, 1954), pp. 191-201. Copyright, 1954, by the University of Chicago.

scene depicting one or more typical cases were acted out at the beginning of a faculty meeting.

Communicating a Specific Problem. In this second use, role-playing becomes much more spontaneous. When, in a discussion, a person attempts to make a point by saying, "I did it like this," he is asked to act out what he said and did. Casting is done on the spot; the situation is described very briefly; and the scene is presented. All those involved in the discussion can then see and feel what went on. This gives them a much better basis on which to discuss the situation.

Testing Ways of Dealing with Problems. This is the most common and probably the most successful use of role-playing. This technique has been used innumerable times over a period of years in the training of business and industrial personnel. There has also been some use of this technique in working out faculty problems. The advantage of role-playing is that it brings out into the open an emotionally charged situation, which could not ordinarily be discussed. Let us consider the following case:

For years, Quistano Elementary School had an all women faculty, except for the special shop and gym teachers, who came twice a week. Last year, three men teachers were appointed to teach the seventh- and eighth-grade classes. Mr. Appleby was appointed the science teacher, Mr. White the math teacher, and Mr. Gray the social studies teacher.

Miss O'Toole, the English teacher, was a middle-aged woman who was the leader of one segment of the faculty. She was a powerful woman who didn't care what she said or whom she antagonized. For the ten years that she had been in this school, she and her clique had monopolized the faculty room which was adjacent to the principal's office. The faculty room was a comfortable room, with a desk, lounging chairs, and a toilet. Except for the janitors' room, which was not too conducive to working or relaxing, this was the only room where a teacher could go for a smoke or to do some work.

On Tuesday morning, Mr. Appleby and Mr. White both had a free period at the same time. They decided to go to the faculty room for a smoke. While they were there, Miss O'Toole walked in, looked about, and walked out. The same afternoon, the three men teachers went in for a smoke after their lunch. The three faculty women who were sitting there walked out as soon as the men came in.

The next day there was a sign on the faculty door, "Women Only." The men looked at each other in surprise and decided to ask Miss Stewart, the principal, what she knew about it. She said she didn't have anything to do with it. Mr. Appleby decided to take the sign down, crossed out the "W" and the "O" so that the sign read "Men Only," and put it back on the door.

The next day there was another sign on the door, "Women Only." Mr. Appleby thought that this was enough of this childish game and went to see the principal again. Miss Stewart said that Miss O'Toole has spoken to her on behalf of the women teachers and requested her to ask the men to stay out. It seemed that some of them were embarrassed to go to the bathroom while the men were there. Miss Stewart said she offered to let them use the one in her office, but they refused and wanted the room to themselves.

This problem is causing friction and threatens to split the staff wide open. It is obvious that this situation could not be discussed in an open faculty meeting in the conventional manner. The principal could not simply state the problem and ask for suggestions. Such factors as the toilet, Miss O'Toole's personality, the taking down of the sign, and the like could not be mentioned yet would constitute the hidden agenda. This situation, however, could be role-played. During a faculty meeting, the principal could mention the problem and set the stage for role-playing. Although this problem has been left in her lap, the solution actually rests with the faculty itself. After stating the problem, she could say, "Now, if you were the principal what would you do?" The group could then choose the people to play the roles. It would be wise if the men took the women's roles and vice versa. It would also be a good idea if Miss O'Toole took the role of principal. This scene could be role-played several times with several different solutions being offered and with different people taking the roles. In the course of the role-playing, the men would be forced to look at the problem from the women's point of view, and the women from the men's point of view. All of the staff would see the problem from the principal's point of view. These different insights into the way in which all of the staff members view the problem would ease the friction. Following the role-playing, a general discussion could be held concerning the merits of the suggested solutions.

This type of role-playing has a great many possibilities for use by school administrators. As in the case above, it can be used in the solution of faculty problems. It can be used in meetings of the superintendent's cabinet or in meetings with principals. It is of value both as a training device and as a way of solving problems. It can be used with PTA groups, student groups, or adult groups, such as home-room mothers. The uses of role-playing are legion.

Thelen has summarized the procedures to be used in this type of role-playing: [7]

1. Pick a typical, familiar, and problematic situation.
2. Demonstrate different ways of dealing with it, without trying to make one "bad" and another "good."
3. Prepare the audience to look for differences in the way the characters act (descriptive) and how they feel (inference, usually).
4. "Cut" each scene as soon as it has made its point or presented an adequate sample of behavior.
5. Discuss the scenes, writing on the blackboard the group's answers to the questions.
6. Check the various ideas as to how the characters felt against the testimony of the characters themselves.
7. Go from this point into discussion of the different assumptions on which action was based, or into generalizations that may be true of other situa-

[7] *Ibid.*, p. 199.

tions "like" these, or into incidents in the history of the group that come to mind, or into possible explanations of why people react the way they were portrayed.

Developing "Sensitivity." This fourth use of role-playing is particularly helpful in developing individual sensitivity to ideas, situations, or concepts. This is a particularly effective technique for school administrators to use. One of the most difficult jobs of the administrator is to attempt to have the faculty do something new. Formal groups are very reluctant to change, and this is especially true of faculties. This technique of role-playing has been used to help change faculty thinking with regard to such innovations as the parent-teacher interview. In order to introduce the idea, a role-playing situation could be set up with two teachers playing the roles of a parent and a teacher. It might be well to have the teacher who is most opposed to the idea play the role of the teacher. She would then see very quickly that she could talk over with the parent some of the problems with students which give her most trouble. Acting in front of the whole group would also be a stimulus toward doing a good job of interviewing.

In reviewing role-playing in its major uses, we can say that here is a technique, which, if properly used, can be of great help in the solution of human relations problems. It causes people to think in terms of how others see the situation. This is the key to good human relations. When we see the situation only from our own center of reference, we are not sensitive to the needs of others. Putting ourselves in someone else's position helps us to achieve the necessary insights.

Steps in Role-playing

The administrator who wants to use role-playing successfully must be willing to experiment with the technique. Through experimentation, he will develop skill in its use and sensitivity to the situations in which it should be used. Whenever he uses the technique he should have firmly in mind the steps necessary in the development of a role-playing situation.

Group Recognition of Problem. The group must be made to recognize the need for a role-playing situation. This can be done by describing the problem in detail and presenting several observations of the effects of the problem. The point is to make the group aware of what is facing them.

Setting the Stage. This step in the development of the role-playing situation calls for the casting of the roles. People can either volunteer for the various roles, or the group can select each person for the role they would like to see him play. The players should then be briefed as to the situation and the kind of role they are playing. The players should also spend a minute or two together to iron out details before they go into their acting.

Helping the Audience to Observe. It is very important that the audience *see* what is going on in the role-playing situation. This could be done by an oral briefing in which attention is called to the things which should be observed or inferred. It is also a good practice to prepare guide sheets which list the sort of things the audience could look for.

Reversing the Role-playing Situation. Since some of the most valuable experiences in role-playing come from seeing the other fellows' point-of-view, it is well to do the role-playing several times. Have the players change roles and re-enact the scene.

Group Discussion and Evaluation. Following the role-playing, the group should settle down to a discussion of what they saw and the way they interpreted it. At this time the leader could make wide use of the blackboard noting questions, answers, and other pertinent facts.[8]

We can summarize the importance and value of role-playing by referring to Maier, who says:[9]

Generally speaking, the function of the role-playing method is to train for action. There are what may be called *barriers to action,* and role-playing as well as the group-decision method is effective for reducing these barriers. . . .

The values of role-playing . . . reside in the ways in which perceptions and attitudes can be changed, the ways in which frustrations may be expressed in harmless manners and thereby reduced, and the ways in which a variety of skills may be developed to replace previous behaviors.

THE BUZZ SESSION

The success of small group discussions is well known to all those who have had experience with them. The lack of success with large groups has been just as obvious. It seems as though people who sit through lectures or speeches or panel discussions come for just that reason—to sit. There is little or no interaction with the speakers or with other members of the audience. The lack of personal participation on the part of audiences has long been recognized as a serious drawback to large meetings.

A plan has been devised to overcome this lack of participation, and, in the few years since its origin, its use has become widespread. This plan was first described by J. D. Phillips and, as a result of his description, is sometimes called *Phillips 66.*[10] The basic idea was to divide an audience up into groups of six and have each group discuss a question for six minutes. Since the time of its origin, however, both the prescribed size of the group and the length of time have been largely ignored. The size of the

[8] For examples of how to develop role-playing situations in detail, see Hendry, Lippitt, and Zander, *op. cit.,* and Norman R. F. Maier, *Principles of Human Relations* (New York, Wiley, 1953), pp. 102-171.

[9] Maier, *op. cit.,* p. 101.

[10] J. Donald Phillips, "Report on Discussion 66," *Adult Education Journal,* Vol. 7 (October, 1948), pp. 181-182.

group varies with the size of the total group, and the length of time is dependent upon the interest of the buzz groups. We have seen some buzz groups work for forty-five minutes or more.

The method of procedure for the basic buzz session is very simple. It can be used with large groups (over fifteen people), regardless of their size. The chairman divides the group up in a convenient manner. He might ask everyone in the odd-numbered rows to turn around or use some other convenient method. In more formalized buzz sessions the members of the audience are given cards with letters or numbers on them. When it is time for the buzz session all those holding the same lettered or numbered card go to the same room. (All the A's go to room 20, for example.) In this way, the groups are divided equally and have private discussion rooms. Before the buzz sessions are actually formed, the total group is charged with the question or issue which it is to discuss. The charge to the groups should be simply worded and clear to all concerned; there should be no ambiguity of language. It should be a *discussable* charge. If the groups form and do not know what to discuss, the whole thing will be a failure. When the group convenes, it selects a chairman and a recorder. The recorder is the one who reports back to the total group.

The chairman of each group is responsible for introducing the buzz-session members to each other and for getting the ball rolling. It has been found to be very satisfactory if each member of the group be given a chance to say something before the general discussion starts. The recorder is usually given one or two minutes to report back to the main group and to ask the questions which his buzz group raised.

Value of the Buzz Session

Although it is difficult to measure the value of such a procedure as the buzz session, there are several observable benefits to be derived from its use. The most obvious value is in determining what the group is thinking about. It gives individuals a chance to blow off steam, and groups to question what has been said. It is much better than having questions from the floor because (1) not every one would have a chance, and (2) many people are afraid to ask questions. Through the buzz group, however, each person remains anonymous.

Those who have used the technique agree with Maier in his appraisal of the amount of interest and involvement when he says: [11]

Evidence of involvement and interest is seen by (a) the businesslike manner in which various groups discuss and argue; (b) the repeated use of "we" in the reports; (c) later comments of individuals who have participated; and (d) the disappointment registered when another group has already covered a group's major items.

[11] Maier, *op. cit.*, p. 75.

This technique has added a great deal of life and enthusiasm to the large group meeting.

Special Uses of the Buzz Session

School administrators are very anxious to obtain the opinion of their faculties on all sorts of things. It has been a most exasperating experience to many administrators to present some material to a group, ask for an opinion, and be greeted with an overwhelming silence. The buzz session could be a solution to this problem. One of the reasons why there is little response to this type of request is that teachers do not feel secure in criticizing the work or word of their superiors. Another reason is that they are not certain what to listen for in order to criticize. Both of these objections can be overcome by the buzz-session technique. Since the questioner remains annonymous, his security is not challenged. If the buzz sessions are arranged properly, the second objection is overcome also.

Stuart Chase in his very interesting book, *Roads to Agreement,* tells of an experience of the sort we have described above. While preparing material for his book, he visited the National Training Laboratory in Group Development at Bethel, Me. The staff there wished to experiment with a new type of relationship between the audience and the speaker. Most speakers are greeted with polite applause and little else. This time, they wished to set the stage for a different kind of response. Chase was asked to lecture to an audience of some three hundred people. Prior to the lecture, the three hundred were divided into six large groups. This was done by chalking the floor at appropriate spots. Each group was then told to listen for something different in the lecture. The instructions were: [12]

> Group 1 was to listen for implications in the lecture which might prove useful to Bethel.
>
> Group 2 was to listen for ideas which the speaker should elaborate later, things he had slurred over. (This was the "probing" team. In an ordinary question period certain individuals in the audience do this.)
>
> Group 3 was to listen for high points of the talk and later emphasize them to the audience.
>
> Group 4 was to think about additional data for possible inclusion in Chase's book.
>
> Group 5 was to listen to his description of areas of human conflict and see what areas could be added.
>
> Group 6 was to concentrate on suggestions for making the book more readable. Given this subject, where should the emphasis be placed; what treatment would best hold the reader's interest?

Following the lecture, each of the six sections divided into three or four buzz groups. Each selected a chairman and a recorder. The recorders for

[12] Stuart Chase, *Roads to Agreement* (New York, Harper, 1951), p. 94.

each of the six groups got together at the end of the buzz session to compare notes and to form a single report. They then proceeded as in a regular buzz-session meeting.

Did it work? Chase thought so. He was thoroughly convinced that this method had a great deal of merit and should be used more often. It had the effect of doing what every lecturer or speaker would like to see happen. As Chase said: [13]

> The audience gave me a different feeling from any I had ever encountered. The words did not bounce back as they often do from a bored or an indifferent aggregation. . . The words went home but were turned around and examined before being taken in. The audience was listening as I never have been listened to from a platform—not agreeing, not disagreeing, neither hostile nor especially friendly, weighing and thinking.

Thelen suggests another adaptation of the buzz session which seems to have great merit. This approach is to *start* the meeting with buzz sessions. Divide the group up into buzz sessions and charge them with raising questions which they want to have answered in the course of the meeting. This is a type of problem census by means of the buzz session.[14]

THE QUAKER MEETING

A technique which is gaining in usage at the present time is called the *Quaker meeting*. The concept of the Quaker meeting is an old one, going back to the founding of the Society of Friends in about 1650. Although the Quakers rebelled against all ceremonials that the Protestants had retained in their rebellion from Catholicism and stood for the ultimate in individualism, they worked out a plan for group action and group decision which has seldom been matched in history. Their meetings seem peculiar to most Americans because there is no chairman in the usual sense of the word, no voting (all decisions are unanimous), and apparently no recognition of status. In spite of these apparent lacks, or possibly because of the lacks, the meetings have been used for three hundred years to carry on the business of the Quakers.

Let us examine some of the major principles upon which the Quaker meeting is based and then see how we can apply it to educational meetings. There are nine basic principles, all of which are directed toward a specific goal: How can we settle this problem so that it will stay settled, so that it is settled right? These principles will not be seen in all meetings; nor are they mutually exclusive. Chase lists them as follows: [15]

1. *Unanimous decisions.* There is no voting, no minority to nourish grievances and so prevent a real settlement.

[13] *Ibid.*, pp. 94-95.
[14] Thelen, *op. cit.*, pp. 205-207.
[15] Chase *op. cit.*, pp. 51-52.

2. *Silent periods,* always at the opening and closing of meetings and whenever two opposing parties begin to clash.
3. *A moratorium* (cooling-off technique) for questions where agreement cannot be reached unanimously, where opposing parties start to form. If they are important questions, they will come up again at further meetings until disagreement ceases and unanimity is found. . . .
4. *Participation* by all members who have ideas on the subject. Experience has demonstrated, says the Book of Discipline, "that the final decision of the group is usually superior to that of the individual." Members pool their knowledge and experience.
5. *Learning to listen.* Again to quote the Book of Discipline: "It behooves them in their meetings to hear with attentive and tolerant minds the messages and views of all members present." Quakers do not go to meetings with minds made up; they go to learn, expecting the right solution to crystallize from the experience of all.
6. *Absence of leaders.* The Clerk does some steering, but he must not interpose his ego or take a dominant role.
7. *Nobody outranks anybody.* Rich and poor, men and women, old and young, have equal status and are expected to participate equally. Everybody has had past experiences, and so everybody has something to give.
8. *Consider the facts.* As emotions are at a minimum, facts and their cool consideration can be at a maximum.
9. *Keep meetings small.* The best size for solving problems is a face-to-face group of not more than twenty persons. Yearly meetings of several hundred, however, are able to use the method.

Although the Quakers are somewhat of a special case in that they are a closely knit, homogeneous group with long years of experience with this method, there are some principles of general applicability. This is demonstrated by the use which one educational group, The National Conference of Professors of Educational Administration, make of the Quaker meeting. N.C.P.E.A. meets each year for a week-long work conference. One morning each year is devoted to a Quaker meeting. Since the group has no officers, the meeting is "led" by a member of the planning committee. The job of the leader is to open the meeting, explain the nature of the Quaker meeting, and then recognize those people who want to talk. Anyone can say anything, since there is no agenda, no order of business, or similar restrictions. People are limited as to the amount of time which they can use; this is necessary because the group numbers over 120. Professors cannot argue with each other either, since one of the major purposes of this form of the Quaker meeting is to get people to talk and to present ideas to the group. If one individual wants to argue with another, he has to see him after the meeting. Over the years, the N.C.P.E.A. has found the Quaker meeting to be very valuable. It has provided many professors with an opportunity to "let off steam." Many of the ideas first expressed at a N.C.P.E.A. Quaker meeting have found their way into the regular work schedule of the conference. It has been a stimulating experience to the group.

It is suggested that the Quaker meeting could very well be adopted for use with public school faculties. It is probably true that most faculties could not shift from meetings under parliamentary procedure to a Quaker meeting to accomplish their business; but the Quaker meeting could be used for other purposes. There are many worries, ideas, problems which are carried around "inside" of people all year round. Most of the time, these develop into frustrations which lead to aggressive behavior. There should be a time when the faculty can get together and unload whatever ideas, worries, and problems they might have. The meeting should be led by a teacher—someone with no more status than any other teacher. The atmosphere needs to be permissive—notice that while the Quakers do not use the term they have built permissiveness into the very structure of their meetings. There need not be any action taken at the meeting itself, the main purpose being the opportunity for everyone to speak what is on his mind.

The Quaker meeting is a technique for which we should find many uses. It offers much to the administrator who really wishes to unloosen the creative forces which are present in the school faculty.

THE GROUP INTERVIEW

This technique is related to other techniques mentioned but is of particular value when used with buzz sessions. Each of us, at one time or another, has probably been quite bored when listening to several group recorders giving their reports. It seems as though all the groups have discussed the same topics and come up with the same ideas and questions. A variation on this method is to have all of the recorders sit before the group and be interviewed by the chairman of the meeting. He asks the recorders for their ideas and questions. By using this approach there is no overlapping or duplication of reports.

THE ROVING OBSERVER

One last technique, which has proved to be of great value at formalized buzz sessions that last for some time, is that of the *roving observer*. The concept is very simple: one person is selected to sit in on all of the buzz sessions (this is practical if there are only four or five) and then summarize their activities to the whole group. The person selected should be as expert as possible in the topic being considered. He should visit all groups to get the gist of their discussion. He should also meet with the group recorders for a while before the summary session. He is then prepared to give back to the total group a compendium of what each buzz group has been talking about. The roving observer also has the opportunity to project what the groups have been talking about. This plan of using a roving observer has been quite satisfactory because it eliminates the need for reports from several recorders. It also adds a fresh viewpoint to what has been discussed, and it compares the contributions of the group with authoritative knowledge as presented by the expert summarizer.

SUMMARY

We have taken a look at the use of several techniques that are promising in the kind of contribution which their use can make to group work. Techniques are not the basis of the group dynamics movement, but they are important to the group worker. Techniques have no value in and of themselves. In order to select the technique which will do the job, it is necessary to know the dynamics of the group; the goals, values and ethics of the group and its members; and the dynamics of the techniques being considered.

With this as our frame of reference, we discussed the use of role-playing, buzz groups, the Quaker meeting, the group interview, and the roving observer. Each of these was discussed from the point-of-view of its value to school administrators. No attempt was made to present *all* of the possible techniques. This chapter, together with chapters 8 and 12, constitutes a rather complete discussion of the concepts and techniques of group dynamics that are of interest to the school administrator.

EXERCISES

1. Ask several of your coworkers the question, "What do you think of group dynamics?" What is the reason for each of their answers?

2. Arrange a role-playing situation for your next faculty meeting. Use it to stimulate interest in the discussion of a common problem with which you have been faced. Sketch the details briefly.

3. Can you work out an acceptable meeting plan based upon the Quaker meeting idea? What obstacles do you see in the adoption of the pure plan of the Quaker meeting?

4. Prepare a role-playing situation to be used in a faculty meeting in which you try to solve a problem. Re-enact the role-playing several times to gain insights. Evaluate the role-playing in terms of other procedures you have used.

5. What are the advantages and disadvantages of buzz groups as you view them?

SELECTED BIBLIOGRAPHY

BARNES, Fred P., "How Can Group Dynamics Be Applied to the School Staff?" *National Association of Secondary School Principals Bulletin*, Vol. 34 (April, 1950), pp. 40-45.

BENNE, Kenneth D., and MUNTYAN, Bozidar, eds., *Human Relations in Curriculum Change* (New York, Dryden, 1951), pp. 223-249.

BIENENSTOCK, Theodore, "Group Dynamics and the Classroom Situation," *Impact of Social and Economic Forces on Education* (Albany, N. Y., State Education Department, n.d.).

BRADFORD, Leland, and FRENCH, John R. P., Jr., eds., "Dynamics of the Discussion Group," *Journal of Social Issues*, Vol. 4, No. 2 (Spring, 1948).

COREY, Stephen M., HALVESON, Paul M., LOWE, Elizabeth, *Teachers Prepare for Discussion Group Leadership* (New York, Teachers College Bureau of Publications, 1953).

CHASE, Stuart, *Roads to Agreement* (New York, Harper, 1951), pp. 45-55.

GRIFFITHS, Daniel E., and WILEY, William T., *The Administrator and Group Dynamics* (Albany, N. Y., Capital Area School Development Association, 1952), 24 pp.

JENKINS, David H., "What Is Group Dynamics?" *Adult Education Journal*, Vol. 9 (April, 1950), pp. 54-60.

MAIER, Norman R. F., *Principles of Human Relations* (New York, Wiley, 1953), pp. 43-172.

MORENO, J. L., "Inter-personal Therapy and the Psychopathology of Inter-personal Relationships," *Sociometry*, Vol. 1 (1937), pp. 9-76.

PHILLIPS, J. Donald, "Report on Discussion 66," *Adult Education Journal*, Vol. 7 (October, 1948), pp. 181-182.

RUSSELL, Edward J., "The Superintendent and Group Dynamics," *School Executive*, Vol. 71 (June, 1952), pp. 77-78.

THELEN, Herbert A., *Dynamics of Groups at Work* (Chicago, University of Chicago Press, 1954), pp. 181-217.

WHYTE, William Foote, *Leadership and Group Participation* (Ithaca, New York State School of Industrial and Labor Relations, Cornell University, 1953).

CHAPTER 10

The Art of Decision-making

School administration has had many definitions, but one which rings true is that it is the making and carrying out of decisions about schools.[1] We have investigated many facets of the relationship between administrators and the people with whom they work. We now come to the point at which all of the substantive material discussed previously must be focused upon the *decision-making* process. It must be understood that the content areas that we have discussed so far are relevant to administration only to the extent that the decisions made by the administrator reflect the influence of these content areas.

THE DECISION-MAKING PROCESS

There has been much discussion, in past years, of a somewhat mechanical process which one must follow if he is to make a decision. Let us back up for a moment and make clear our meaning of decision-making. The dictionary tells us that a decision is "a settling or terminating, as of a controversy, by giving judgment on the matter; also, a conclusion arrived at after consideration." Decision-making is the process which one goes through in order to be able to pass judgment and terminate a controversy. So we see that decision-making can be called problem-solving or some other term with the same connotation. There have been many methods suggested which tend to define the process of problem-solving or decision-making. One of these suggested methods, which is quite typical, is the following: [2]

1. Define and limit the problem.
2. Analyze and evaluate the problem.
3. Establish criteria or standards by which solutions will be evaluated or judged as acceptable and adequate to the need.
4. Face the consequences of each available solution.
5. Select the preferred solution or solutions. Test them in advance.
6. Put into effect the preferred solution.

[1] Van Miller and Willard B. Spalding, *The Public Administration of Public Schools* (New York, World Book Company, 1952), p. 203.
[2] R. H. Wagner and C. C. Arnold, *Handbook of Group Discussion* (Boston, Houghton Mifflin Company, 1950), pp. 70-72.

This type of guide to the making of a decision is quite helpful if one keeps in mind certain factors. Probably the most important factor is that it is possible for each person following such a procedure to come up with a different solution to a common problem. In each step, there are one or more human factors which need to be considered. Let us take each of the steps suggested above and note the substantive knowledge bearing on it. We will then understand all that is involved in each step, and, in this way, make the guide more useful.

Define and Limit the Problem

This, of course, must be the first step. If we are to have a decision, we must know the problem. The problem is not a matter of cold, objective reality. We know from our study of perception that what is a problem to one person is not a problem to another person. The chairman of an eastern university department of education delighted in telling the story of his visits with the principal of a large urban high school. He would come to the high school at least once each year and, after a few remarks, would ask, "Well, what problem are you working on this year?" The answer invariably was, "We don't have problems, we have answers!" Needless to say, the principal never did see the problems which were so obvious to so many others.

One may either fail to see a problem or to see only a gross problem, that is, only one facet of the perception. A person may perceive a problem in its gross form but not see it in its detail or with its ramifications. For example, in the United States some 50 per cent of those entering the ninth grade are not graduated from the twelfth grade. One may recognize this fact—and as a fact it cannot be controversial—but whether or not it is a problem is another matter. It is still another consideration as to what *kind* of problem it is. It may be perceived as a weakness in the curricula of the public schools, or it may be considered a weakness in the students. Others may see the results of an economic situation and look for solutions in the economic situation; still others may look for solutions in the economic background of the students and their families. Others may look to social conditions for their solutions. We could carry this analysis much further, but the point is this: in defining and limiting the problem, it should be observed that we are dealing with a perceptual problem.

In order to define clearly and limit the problem, the administrator needs to recognize that his own personality and his experiences condition him so that he does not see the same problems as do others. It is in this area that group definition of education problems is most valuable. In this process, the administrator is able to overcome his blind areas. He is able to perceive the total situation more clearly because the viewpoints of many people are brought to bear on the definition of the problem.

It is also necessary at this step to be aware of the *semantic* difficulties. Inaccurate wording of the situation one is facing can create more problems and can also give rise to many people getting different impressions of the same problem. The problem should be stated clearly and precisely in words which have objective reality for the listeners. Words with cultural referents and intensional meanings should be avoided.

Analyze and Evaluate the Problem

Probably the first thing of which we should be aware at this stage of decision-making is that we analyze the problem *as we see it* and evaluate the problem according to our own *value system*. We indicated above the differences in the perception of problems, and the same considerations hold for this stage of the discussion. In analyzing the problem, different people will perceive different aspects, so that the analysis of any one person is very apt to be incomplete. Here again, group analysis may be very helpful.

In evaluating the problem, we need to consider such points as: What does this problem mean to me? What does this problem mean to the school system? What can I do about it? What do I want to do about it? In other words, How do I "size up" the situation?

Let us look at a short case to see what is involved in the analysis and evaluation of a problem in the eyes of those who must make a final decision.

The Glider Central School is a fast-growing suburban school district. It is fiscally independent in that it sets its own budget, fixes the tax rate, and collects its own taxes. The district includes one large town and small parts of several other towns. In the state where Glider Central is located the power to assess property is in the hands of local assessors, so there are several people assessing property in the school district. These are political positions, and the people who hold them generally owe their positions to an elected official known as a supervisor.

The school officials have had to raise taxes constantly over a period of time. The tax rate has risen from 20 mills to 60 mills in a five-year period. This has brought about much complaining, particularly on the part of the new people who have recently come into the district. Their homes are assessed at a higher rate than are the older homes. The school district officials have been urged to encourage the supervisor to do two things:

1. Reassess property so that everyone will pay on the same basis.
2. Encourage industries to settle in the community.

Thus far the school officials have not done either.

The question is, Why not? In the first phase of problem-solving, the officials perceived the problem and defined it. However, in analyzing and evaluating, they felt that they saw several other aspects of the problem which precluded action at the time. Although they noted an injustice being done to the new residents, they observed that the latter were not so powerful as the old residents. A reassessment would alienate the old residents and thereby create a new set of enemies for the school. This was also the argument for not encouraging industry. Most of the older residents came to the district to escape the more industrialized localities and opposed the idea, even though it meant higher taxes. In "sizing up" the problem, or in evaluating it, the *ramifications* of the problem become clear. These ramifications determine the ultimate course of action.

Establish Criteria of Judgment

At this point, we consider the question, How will I know if the solution I arrive at is a satisfactory one? Here we become involved with such concepts as the value system of the individual or group. This may be expressed as the level of aspiration of the individual or group. An example of this was the well-to-do community whose school applied a standardized set of achievement exams to its students. Although it found that its students were above the national norms, it did not believe they were high enough above the norms. Through a process of discussion among teachers, administrators, and lay people, the community set a standard at which it thought its children should be achieving and then went to work to reach that standard. In analyzing the setting of standards by this community, we note the existence of a philosophy of education and a level of aspiration. There is also a reflection of the social and economic status of the community, in that it felt it had the money to do what it wanted to do.

Examine the Consequences of Each Solution

This is the step at which each possible solution is weighted against the standards or criteria set previously. We should note that this is not a black or white situation. One individual who is weighing his solution might find that the solution "works" but not to the degree desired, though another person might be satisfied with that degree. The consequences are also evaluated on the scale of values to which a person or group subscribes. When, for example, a group of faculty members is assigned to supervise the lunch period, their behavior during that time can be evaluated along a continuum. Is their solution of "keeping the students quiet and orderly" a satisfactory solution? In some schools it would be. Is the solution of using the lunch period as a phase of the educational process, so that the students acquire the practice of etiquette and good manners, the desired solution? In many schools this would be a more acceptable solution.

Select the Preferred Solution

This is the outgrowth of the fourth step. When the consequences of each solution have been weighted against the preceding criteria, one or more will seem to "fit" the individual or group better than the others. It is not always crystal clear why the solution is preferred. It appears to the individual that this solution will be satisfactory and so he tries it. There are times when more than one solution seems satisfactory. In this case, all that can be done is to try the solutions to determine which one works best.

Implement the Preferred Solution

If the process of evaluation has been realistic, that is, has been considered in operational terms, this step will have been anticipated. At this stage we say, "We have arrived at our solution, let us proceed to implement it." If the solution has not been carefully worked out, it may be necessary to go back and choose another solution. In that case, the process starts all over again.

The foregoing points present a general overview of the decision-making process. It is necessary that we have an understanding of this fundamental process. We need now to move into other phases of decision-making. Some very important questions for us to answer are: What kinds of decisions are administrators called upon to make? What are the limits on decision-making? Who should make what decisions? When should decisions be made? Can a group make a decision?

KINDS OF ADMINISTRATIVE DECISIONS

A mere listing of typical questions will serve to introduce the complexity of this aspect of our study. Here is a random list of problems:

1. Is it snowing too hard to have school today?
2. With only three students enrolled in fourth-year Latin, should we offer the course?
3. Should the new high school building have terrazzo flooring or tile flooring?
4. Should Miss Brown be recommended for tenure?
5. Should a fourth-grade class of thirty-nine students be divided into two sections?
6. How many rooms will be needed in the high school addition which must be built?
7. Should a citizens committee be formed to advise the board on budget making?
8. Should the high school explore the possibility of a core curriculum?
9. Should all ninth graders take music?
10. Should Miss Smith's increment be withheld?

11. Which of the three textbooks recommended by the committee on senior high mathematics shall I choose?

As we read the list of questions and problems on which decisions must be made, we are struck by the complexity of the list. The variety is so great that it seems no one person should ever be expected to be able to make decisions on all of them. This gives us our clue for studying the area of decision-making. There are some decisions which should be made by a group, such as the faculty. There are others which should be made by an individual. Our discussion of decision-making will be divided into two parts: one part dealing with individual decisions; the other, with group decisions.

THE FRAMEWORK OF DECISION-MAKING

Prior to our discussion of how various people make decisions or do not make decisions we should examine the framework within which decision-making takes place. It is necessary to see how people come to make or not to make a particular decision. What is it that prevents individuals from participating in the decision-making process at one time, although at another time they plunge in wholeheartedly? For purposes of clarity, we shall separate the chief school administrator from the other administrators in a system in this discussion. We shall consider the limits placed on each group which plays a part in the decision-making process in American education. These groups are students, teachers, supervisors (including principals, subject supervisors, and assistant superintendents), the superintendent, the school board, and the public.

Before going into detail concerning the restrictions on the way in which each of these groups makes decisions, it would be well to spell out a set of general considerations applicable to all groups within a school system. In many instances, these limitations are intended primarily for boards of education but actually affect the decision-making capacities of the entire staff. And not in all instances do they appear to be directly related to human relations. However, the relation of this general frame of reference to the operation of a teaching staff is one which sets up conditions under which people work and have ideas and feelings. We will see, too, that governing boards interpret these laws and rules and regulations in vastly different ways, with the result that they exercise different degrees of control over the people in their systems.

The Legal Framework of Education

From whence does the right to make decisions in the American public school originate? By a process of oversimplication we can arrive at an answer. Since we operate in a free society, it is never easy or clear to trace lines of responsibility. The whole process is "necessarily blurred and complicated by the wide distribution of power, the respect for differences, and the regard for the creative mind." [3]

As with the search for any authority in the United States, we begin with the federal Constitution. A search of this great document fails to reveal any reference whatsoever to education. Omissions of this sort gave rise to the first amendments to the Constitution, and, in Article X of the Bill of Rights, we find that the "powers not delegated to the United States by the Constitution, nor prohibited by it to the states, are reserved to the states respectively, or to the people." Even though the federal government has appropriated large sums of money for education and the Supreme Court has intervened through judicial interpretations of the Constitution so as to affect public education, education is commonly considered to be a function of the state.

The manner in which the state acts to control education is put most concisely by Miller and Spalding: [4]

The public school is (a) based on the authority of the whole people in the state who (b) delegate authority to the legislature who (c) delegate authority specifically to local boards of education chosen freely by the people in the local school district; these boards (d) select professional employees who (e) are responsible directly for the educational program.

The legal process is quite clear, as it is obvious that the authority for pursuing the educative process rests with the people of the state who have evolved a method of delegation of authority while holding the final responsibility in their own hands. It would be erroneous to stop here, however, since many factors other than those presented actually come into the picture. Although it is true that no decision can be considered from its origin because of the legal structure of the school district, the state, and the country, it must be remembered that this legal structure is subject to continual change. This change is not always through the process of amendment to the various constitutions or the writing of new laws but usually through the process of interpretation. In this manner, old laws and old constitutions are applicable to modern situations.

The process of interpretation is the result of social pressure brought about by the interaction of many social groups. A most pertinent illustration of this is the Communist teacher. In the 1930's there were some Communist teachers and no one was particularly concerned about them. Today, no superintendent of schools would knowingly recommend to his board of education the appointment or retention of a single Communist teacher. This has come about without the passage of a single federal law or amendment to the Constitution concerning the legality of the Commu-

---

[3] George S. Counts, *Decision Making and American Values in School Administration* (New York, Teachers College, Bureau of Publications, 1954), p. 3.

[4] Miller and Spalding, *op. cit.,* pp. 208-209.

nist party. The great change, rather, has been brought about by social pressure, which acts in contradistinction to the legal framework of education and eventually produces a change in the framework.

The Social Framework of Education

More important in the day-to-day operation of the schools than the legal framework is the value system to which the administrator adheres. Perhaps it would be more accurate to state the value system to which the community adheres. The administrator must not be too far from the values which the community holds or he will find that he is not its educational leader.

What is this system of values which is more important than the legal framework which should support it? Probably the phrase *American way of life* best expresses what we mean; yet it is used in such diverse ways that often it is not possible to derive much meaning from it. Still, the phrase has much value, in spite of its misuse. This misuse is analogous to the use of the term *democratic* by the Russians. We find such groups as the Sons of the American Revolution and the Americans for Democratic Action each proclaiming to be the guardians of the American way of life. It would be difficult, from their allegations, to determine just what this way of life is; yet many contend that it is possible to do just that. Counts contends that there is an American way of life which persists amid and through change and which should play a central role in all decision-making in education.[5] He points out that although never fully accepted by all our people, this way of life is spelled out in our basic institutions, processes, conceptions, principles, and ideals. It is exemplified in the democratic process perhaps to a greater degree than any other. And it is not so much exemplified in the democratic process as we actually practice it as it is in the process to which we aspire. Counts has recently stated this concept of our democratic heritage in a manner difficult to improve upon.[6]

This heritage is derived from many sources, ancient and modern. It embraces the ideas of individual worth and dignity, of human equality and brotherhood, of mercy and compassion, of the Hebraic-Christian ethic. It embraces the conception of a common humanity, the faith in the creative power of the free mind, and the affirmation of the perfectibility of man and his institutions, of the humanistic spirit. It embraces the idea of untrammeled inquiry, the devotion to the intellectual virtues of precision, integrity, and love of truth, of science and scientific method. It embraces the commitment to the orderly and peaceful adjustment of disputes and conflicts of interest of the British political tradition. It embraces finally the bold affirmation of the democratic faith that the people, all of the people, should participate in the selection of their rulers and in the framing of the broad policies of government; that, in a word, they should be

[5] Counts, *op. cit.*, p. 11.
[6] *Ibid.*, p. 12.

free and be entrusted with both power and responsibility. Here is the body of values which should be understood and applied by all who make decisions in the realm of public education. It should be regarded as an indispensable part of the equipment of every educational administrator.

This, then, is what we can call the American way of life. It is clear that although we do not always attain these ideals, we do aspire to them. Much has happened to our society to make it difficult to bring about the full realization of these concepts. It is not so easy now to achieve; nor is it so clear what democratic living and the American way of life means. We find ourselves weighing relative values at all times. We weigh the value of "untrammeled inquiry" against security, individuality against the values of group living, free election of city officials against the efficiency of city managers. Much of our confusion has come about through our increase in size. Tead has contrasted the elements which made for our confusion.[7]

We are less sure and less agreed as to how to achieve freedom, equality, and friendliness in big cities, big schools, big corporations, big hospitals, etc., than was true when the economy was less urban, less industrial, less characterized by organizations in and through which so many phases of our lives have now to channel.

These developments have made the emergence of the human relations movement one of great urgency. The growth toward bigness in all institutions has made difficult the treatment of people as human beings in a democratic society. It is the task of the school administrator to be thoroughly immersed in this democratic concept, so that all of his decisions will be made in reference to it. When he chooses among alternates he will choose because of a commitment to a set of democratic values.

We can see that the board of education operates within a legal framework and also within a social order. These two concepts provide the atmosphere in which the decisions of the school district are formulated. They provide the background—the apperceptive mass, if you like—which is always present and always bears directly on the situation demanding a decision. It can be said that these are the chief limiting factors in the decision-making of school boards and of chief school administrators.

LIMITING DECISIONS OF SUBORDINATES

We have indicated that boards of education and chief school officers are limited in the kind and magnitude of decisions which they can make by the legal structure of the local district, the state and federal government, and the mores and values of the American society. Other people in the school system, such as principals, teachers, students, and nonteaching employees, are limited in the decisions which they can make by these

[7] Ordway Tead, *The Art of Administration* (New York, McGraw-Hill, 1951), p. 65.

factors as well as several others. Before getting into these factors, let us see what we mean by *limiting* the decision-making power of individuals.

The chief purpose of setting limitations on decision-making power is to improve the caliber of decisions made. When limitations are set up, ways and means of making decisions are prescribed. This is usually done through the setting of policy. As policy is set, it should indicate *who* is to make a decision, *what* the decision should be concerned with, and some information as to *how* the decision is to be made. Some examples of this will follow below. All employees of a school system, both teaching and nonteaching, should have the security which good policy contributes to the type of decisions that are made. One of the chief causes of confusion in the network of human relationships in a school system is the lack of clear policy.

We will now examine in detail the way in which members of a school system are limited (actually aided) in the making of decisions. The frame of reference which we will use is provided by Tannenbaum, who listed eight major sets of limitations.[8] We will attempt to adapt these to the administration of public schools and show how the decisions of individuals in the schools are limited and guided. This adaptation has resulted in the following six categories of limitation:

1. Definition of purpose.
2. Criterion of rationality.
3. Conditions of employment.
4. Lines of formal authority.
5. Relevant information provided.
6. Time limits.

Definition of Purpose

Basic to the making of any decision is an understanding of the *purpose* of the school. If faculties had a clear understanding of what the purpose of their school was, there would not be so much difficulty as is now experienced in arriving at decisions. Recently, a committee of teachers, administrators, and lay citizens attempted to arrive at a systemwide promotion policy for students. The major difficulty that they encountered was the vast difference in the purposes held by the elementary teachers, the secondary teachers, and the administrators. With these different purposes there was little hope of arriving at a decision about promotion policy. Purpose is basic even to policy. Policy must be built upon a clearly understood purpose. In many schools, the confusion is compounded because of different purposes held by teachers in adjoining rooms. If wise decisions are to be made in school systems, there must be clearly understood and commonly accepted purpose.

[8] Robert Tannenbaum, "Managerial Decision-Making," in *Human Relations in Administration,* ed. Robert Dubin (New York, Prentice-Hall, 1951), pp. 206-211.

Establishing the Criterion of Rationality

This is commonly accomplished in school systems by the adoption of written rules and regulations by the board of education. These rules and regulations deal with all aspects of school life and work toward focusing the activities in a school system in a particular direction. Although the responsibility for preparing the rules and regulations generally is delegated to the chief school officer by the board of education, he should prepare these rules and regulations with the aid of the faculty. This group approach will result in better rules and regulations and also in greater adherence to the letter and spirit of the regulations.[9]

Many of the rules and regulations that apply to teachers and administrators are reproduced in faculty handbooks. Every school system should have such a book. Let us consider some excerpts from the East Greenbush, N. Y., Central School Teachers' Handbook. These excerpts illustrate the point that rules and regulations should indicate *who* will make decisions, on *what* subjects they will make them, and *how* they will make them. There should, of course, always be some leeway for individual initiative and originality, but within certain bounds.

All students becoming ill during school hours should be referred to the nurse who will make the decision regarding disposition of the case. No child should ever be excused to go home due to illness until he has been seen by the nurse. Parents must be contacted and transportation provided.

Concerning use of the public-address system:

There is little excuse for announcements being made during the school day. They interrupt classroom procedure and are an annoyance to teachers and students. Any announcements to be made should be written out on the forms provided in the main office by 8:45 A.M.

Concerning elementary school marking:

Marks given should be based upon the child's capacity to achieve. Therefore capacity must be known. It may be determined by a study of the records or by contacting persons who have previously worked with the child. It may even be necessary to test and observe performance for a period before marking definitely. In many cases a pupil will be doing work below the designated level of his grade. The teacher should mark him to show how well he is doing what he can do. When reporting to parents, however, we must be sure to inform them of the level of the work on which the mark is based.

What is indicated for decision-making is simply this. In these areas, the faculty has a set of guiding regulations. In the above examples, many of the ideas originated with the teachers and principals and are now codified

---

[9] Jacob Levine and John Butler, "Lecture vs. Group Decision in Changing Behavior," *Journal of Applied Psychology*, Vol. 36, No. 1 (February, 1952), pp. 29-33.

so that all will act within the same framework. Tannenbaum points out that although this sort of thing restricts the areas in which individuals can make decisions, it also tends to increase the rationality of the behavior of subordinates insofar as the organization is concerned. Through the process of preschool orientation for new teachers and in-service sessions for experienced teachers, the necessary indoctrination for the acceptance of these provisions can be assured. The whole school system will then function in a more uniform and orderly manner with regard to these common elements.

Conditions of Employment

When an individual is employed by a school system, he is employed as a particular kind of teacher: that is, mathematics, science, English, or the like. The very fact that he is employed as a particular kind of teacher, or specialist, effectively limits the kind of decisions that he can make. He is expected, if he is a science teacher, for instance, to make certain decisions regarding the teaching of science. He is not, without special permission, expected to have much to say about the teaching of English. He may be invited, from time to time, to discuss the English offerings; but it is not his prerogative to originate discussions concerning them.

This distinction in who is to make decisions on what topics increases the rationality in one respect: namely, that decisions are made in areas by those most concerned and best informed. On the other hand, the school is concerned with students more than subject matter, and decisions on curriculum problems might very well be better made if they were made by all those concerned with and informed about students.

Determination of Lines of Formal Authority

By establishing lines of formal authority and having them clearly understood by all, each individual knows who will make decisions that will affect him directly. This prevents the ambiguity of authority which exists in many schools. The diagram which follows is a very simple one and illustrates this point.

Keep in mind that this diagram is for discussion purposes only, although it does illustrate the point we are trying to make. The solid lines represent lines of authority while the dotted lines represent lines of co-operation. Note that no one is directly responsible to more than *one* person. As we follow the diagram through, we note that the principals, the curriculum co-ordinator, and the administrator for business affairs report directly to the superintendent of schools. *All* teachers report *directly* to principals, whether they are "specials" or not. Likewise, all custodians report directly

Lines of Authority in a School System

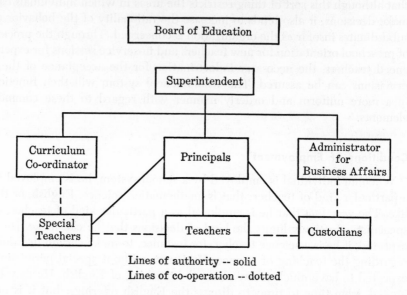

Lines of authority -- solid
Lines of co-operation -- dotted

to principals. The special teachers and the custodians have a co-operative relationship with other teachers and with the curriculum co-ordinator and administrator for business affairs, respectively.

Providing Relevant Information

This concept can be looked upon in three different ways. In the first, if the administration is desirous of involving the faculty in the decision-making process, it can insure good decisions by providing a wealth of information. It can send bulletins, hold meetings at which relevant data is presented and discussed; in fact, it can, at all times, make certain that the faculty gets pertinent information, gets it first, and gets it in a manner which shows that the administration is pleased that they do get it.

Secondly, the administration can circumvent any effective decision-making by preventing the faculty members from ever getting information on which they can act. In this procedure, the faculty feels itself to be in the dark on all matters, and this is demonstrated in at least two ways. The first result of this approach is for the faculty not to respond to the suggestion to take action on matters on which they have no information. This might occur during a faculty meeting, for instance. The superintendent, who has withheld information, asks for an expression of opinion on the part of the faculty, and none is forthcoming. The second result is a continuous deterioration of morale on the part of the faculty. They feel that since they are not informed, they are not wanted, and they develop the attitude that the administration can "do it all." The feeling, "Let the teachers teach, and the administrator administer," is the one which develops here.

The third way involves administrators who wish to give the appearance of co-operating with their faculties, of being democratic administrators, but do not believe that a decision arrived at with the full participation of the faculty is a better one than one arrived at by the administrator alone. They dole out the information in little bits and in such a manner as to manipulate the group with which they are connected. The manipulative administrator also gives bits of information at exactly the right time to influence a vote or faculty opinion. A case in point:

> In an elementary school building the faculty had been vitally concerned with the problem of noon-hour supervision. After a month of controversy, the faculty seemed to have arrived at a decision concerning rotation of playground supervisors. This decision was one in which the principal had little faith, and it was obvious that he opposed it. The faculty appeared as though it would support the decision regardless of the principal's views. On the morning prior to the faculty meeting which would decide this issue, each teacher received a notice which read, "In view of the fact that the Central Office will shortly consider the problem of noon-hour supervision on a system wide basis, I believe it would be wise to drop all consideration of the matter," signed by the principal.

Needless to say, the dropping of this bit of information at this strategic point stopped the faculty from further consideration of the issue.

In summary, we can say that the free flow of information of concern to the faculty increases the rationality of the decisions which the faculty should be expected to make. The decision-making power and ability of the staff is abridged when there is no information forthcoming or when the information is distributed in a manipulatory manner.

Setting a Time Limit

This is a method of forcing action on the part of subordinates. It is particularly effective when used with individuals who are not sufficiently self-motivated to act on a particular topic. They may lack motivation for at least two reasons: 1) a strong interest in another area which precludes interest in the area under consideration, and 2) being a member of a faculty which never has had the opportunity to make a decision and so would tend to dally under new freedom or inability to choose among several possibilities. When work is delegated to individuals or groups, the time element should always be stated. A committee, for instance, should not be created to study the mathematics curriculum and not be told that its report is expected at a certain time. Such a complex subject as this could intrigue the committee for years. Obviously, the time limit should not be so short as to result in a shoddy job.

INDIVIDUAL DECISION

When we talk about decisions made by individuals, we have created a somewhat arbitrary category. There are actually very few, if any, decisions made entirely by one person. There are, however, many decisions for which the school administrator collects evidence from several people prior to actually making his decision. This is one of the phases of the decision-making process which we will want to investigate. Then, too, there are many decisions which should be delegated to others in the system. The problem is to determine which decisions should be delegated and which decisions should be made by the chief school officer.

Personal vs. Organizational Decisions

Barnard is able to distinguish between decisions which can be delegated and those which cannot be delegated. He indicates that there are two general types of decisions: *personal* and *organizational*. Of these he states: [10]

These two kinds of decisions—organizational decisions and personal decisions—are chiefly to be distinguished as to process by this fact: that personal decisions cannot ordinarily be delegated to others, whereas organizational decisions can often if not always be delegated.

What is a personal decision? And what is an organizational decision? Barnard offers the following differentiation: [11]

Every effort that is a constituent of organization, that is, every co-ordinated co-operative effort, may involve two acts of decision. The first is the decision of the person affected as to whether or not he will contribute this effort as a matter of personal choice. . . . This act of decision is outside the system of efforts constituting organization . . .

The second type of decisions has no direct or specific relation to personal results, but views the effort concerning which decision is to be made nonpersonally from the viewpoint of its organizational effect and of its relation to organizational purpose. This second act of decision is often made in a direct sense by individuals, but it is impersonal and organizational in its intent and effect. . . . The act of decision is a part of the organization itself.

Barnard is saying that organizational decisions are those that are assigned to an individual because of his place in the organization. This is what Davies and Herrold are talking about when they raise the question, Whose problem is it? As they point out: [12]

[10] Chester I. Barnard, *The Functions of the Executive* (Cambridge, Mass., Harvard University Press, 1938), p. 188.
[11] *Ibid.*, pp. 187-188.
[12] Daniel R. Davies and Kenneth F. Herrold, *Problem Solving for the Executive* (New London, Conn., Arthur C. Croft, 1954), pp. 18-19.

Most problems of this order are relatively easy to handle. For example, an inventory shows that you are running low on some type of instructional supplies, such as chalk, pencils, paper, etc. The policy of the school is to provide such supplies, and the budget includes a reserve for such emergencies. The decision to purchase does not require a conference. Indeed, in a school system which includes a business manager or some similar executive in charge of supplies, the problem should not even come to the top executive except in the form of a report of the problem solved.

Note the important parts of this analysis as far as decision-making is concerned. First, there was a *policy;* second, there was money *allocated* in the budget for the purpose; and third, there was a *person,* the business manager, who was to make the decision. No one had to worry about this case. The organization had it all arranged!

Now let us look at another case and see what kind of a decision was made here.[13]

One day while Superintendent White was out of town, an early morning snowfall made transportation difficult. Under such circumstances, it was customary for the district's bus drivers, before starting their runs, to call the superintendent at his home to inquire whether school would be held. In the event of the superintendent's absence, the drivers would call the high school principal.

A new driver, uninformed as to the latter part of the procedure, decided to make his trip as usual after he had been unable to phone the superintendent. As a result, many youngsters were needlessly hauled around the district and home again. Several board members and parents inquired of Superintendent White how this happened.

Mr. White immediately assumed all responsibility for the error, explaining that he was responsible for the operation of the schools even in his absence. While a case might have been made for the poor judgment of the driver in failing to call the principal, the superintendent held that it was his responsibility to keep all of his staff informed on emergency procedures.

Here is a case in which there was an organizational arrangement to take care of the situation. The superintendent, when asked why this had happened, could have said, "Well, the bus driver should have called the principal. That's our arrangement." Instead, he *chose* to make this a matter of personal responsibility. He chose to take this upon himself in order to protect a subordinate.

A very good point could be made by demonstrating that poor judgment was used by the bus driver. It would seem that he certainly should have checked with the principal or at least called another bus driver. No one would have blamed the superintendent if he had squeezed out of this one, but the fact that he did not earned him the increased respect of the entire staff, the board, and the public. By interpreting the concept broadly, Superintendent White went so far as to take the responsibility for a deci-

[13] Richard Wynn, "The Application of Good Human Relations," *Nation's Schools* (January, 1954), p. 53.

sion he would have made had he been present, even though he was absent. This unwillingness to pass the buck tends to build high staff morale.

By way of expanding on the wisdom of Superintendent White's shouldering of responsibility we can draw some more conclusions. In any situation in which the dignity of an individual is at stake, he deserves the most protection possible. This principle is recognized in our judicial system through its process of appeal. In the most serious cases—those involving death as the sentence—the highest authority is the state, the governor, or, in case of federal crimes, the president. The point is, the final decision in matters of human rights is the responsibility of the chief administrative officer. In matters of human relations, then, we protect human dignity when the highest officer makes the final decision. The bus driver, no doubt was, "raked over the coals" by his neighbors and the other bus drivers before the superintendent took the responsibility. This taking of responsibility saved face for the employee.

In terms of the difference between organizational and personal decisions, we see that a school system should have a written policy indicating *who* should make *what* decisions and *how* they should proceed to do so. Decisions made because they are assigned and because the individual is making them as a member of the organization are called organizational decisions. When the individual goes beyond this assignment and gives of himself, then he is making a personal decision. The latter, of course, cannot be delegated.

Interpretation and Development of Policy

Davies and Herrold indicate that two other areas of decision-making cannot be delegated.[14] The first of these is the *interpretation of policy,* and the second is the *development of policy.*

There is one further point to be made in this consideration of what should be delegated and what should be retained. In the writing of policy, there are certain types of decisions that should be reserved for the chief school administrator. These decisions have to do with the areas of human relations and conceptual areas that we discussed in Chapter 1. Problems which have to do with matters of vital interest to human beings should not be delegated to administrators on a subordinate level. As an example, consider the matter of recommending a teacher for tenure. During the probationary period, the superintendent must gather information concerning the teaching efficiency of the candidate. These data come from the teacher's principal. Now, in a sense, the principal is passing judgment on the new teacher but cannot and should not make the final decision of recommending this teacher to the board. The decision to recommend or not belongs to the superintendent, and he alone can exercise it.

[14] Davies and Herrold, *op. cit.,* p. 19.

Decisions Requiring Conceptual Skill

Decisions which fall into the category of conceptual skill of administration should also be reserved at the highest possible level. As we have seen, each individual in a school system is restricted in his perception of the total situation. In most cases, the chief school administrator is the only person in a position to see the entire system with all of its component parts in proper relation to each other. Since he is the only one to see the situation in its entirety, decisions affecting the whole system need to be made by him. (He should certainly collect evidence from many people; but the final decision on matters of systemwide import should rest with him.)

This consideration of the human relations and conceptual areas of administration also offers a way in which the building principal can determine which decisions to delegate and which decisions to retain. There are many individuals in each building, each interested in his own particular part of the program. The building principal is charged with the responsibility for making decisions which take into account all of these various opinions, attitudes, and purposes and for acting in the interest of the whole school.

Decisions of this type take into account a problem which has been growing in importance in recent years, but which has received no systematic study. This is the problem of specialists on the school staff, of using the considered judgment of these people to further the educational aims of the school. The concept which some specialists hold regarding the importance of their specialty to the total school program is at times frightening. Many of them have assumed the role of kingdom builders and have exerted pressure far out of proportion to the worth of their specialty. A case will sharpen the discussion of this point.

High School A was going to participate in a music festival to be held one week from today. The choir had not been doing as well as the music director had expected. Normally, the choir practiced during one activity period a week and also for an hour after regular school classes each week. The director went to the principal and requested that students be excused from regular classes during the coming week for special practice sessions. She did this even though there was a definite school policy to the contrary. She pleaded, cajoled, argued, and even cried in a vain attempt to change this policy. She left the office and was thoroughly convinced that the principal was unco-operative.

The problem of dealing with specialists is one of the most thought provoking and difficult areas in which the administrator must operate. In order to make wise decisions, he must have sufficient knowledge of these special areas to see where they fit in the total program. He must have the courage to act on this knowledge. A definite statement of the philosophy of the school, worked out by the whole staff, would provide a working guide to help the administrator make decisions in matters of this sort. Decisions concerning the teaching of special subjects need to be made by such administrators as principals or superintendents, depending on the size of the system. This type of administrator sees the educational program as a whole. He should also see it as it relates to the individual child. Decisions which affect the system as a whole should never be made by specialists but by general administrators.

Positive and Negative Decisions

Since the school administrator has many things to do, it is necessary for him to know when to make a decision and when not to make a decision. This calls for the ability to recognize such matters as the urgency of the situation, the origin of the problem, whether or not someone else could solve the problem better than he, and a host of other considerations. One of the most pertinent statements ever made in regard to this matter is credited to Barnard. In succinct language he states: [15]

The fine art of executive decision consists in not deciding questions that are not now pertinent, in not deciding prematurely, in not making decisions that cannot be made effective, and in not making decisions that others should make.

This is indeed the fine art! What Barnard is saying, among other things, is that administrators need to have a sense of timing in their decision-making. All of the work which goes into the making of a major decision can be wasted if it is announced at the wrong time. The old adage of striking while the iron is hot applies here.

The most important concern of the above statement lies in the admonition *not* to make a decision. We are well aware that ordinarily we think of decision-making as resulting in something being done. We see now that equally important is the idea that a decision may result in nothing being done. Decisions may, therefore, be classified into two major headings:

1. Positive—the decision to do something, to direct action, or to stop action.
2. Negative—the decision not to decide.

It is easy to see the value of positive decisions; but what is the value of negative decisions? When is it worthwhile to decide to do nothing? Consider the admonition not to make decisions which cannot be made effective. To do so would destroy the authority of the one making the decision. Many schools have found, for instance, that an order from the superintendent forbidding students to smoke on the school grounds could not be enforced. The effects of such an order are widespread in that other orders, that is, decisions by authorities, have been flaunted. The apparent solution involves not only the avoidance of such decisions on such activities but the necessity for group decision, which will be discussed later.

[15] Barnard, *op. cit.,* p. 194.

The admonition not to make decisions which others should make is basic to good morale in a school system. When the subordinates in a system cannot make decisions on matters of great concern to themselves, they feel no pride in their system, no responsibility for results, and, consequently, act in an automatic manner. They lose the drive to be creative, which is probably the most outstanding characteristic of a high morale faculty. Prudent delegation of the right to make decisions to teachers, supervisors, and principals is a liberating force in a school system. It is a liberating force for the administrator as well, since he should be free to make decisions regarding over-all policy, a matter on which no one is better equipped than he to make the decision. Decisions concerning instructional materials, audiovisual aids, classroom discipline, use of leisure time, subject matter, teaching techniques, curriculum construction can best be made at the various levels of a system by the people best qualified. There may be fear on the part of administrators that their staff members are not capable of making these decisions. But we should bear in mind that so long as they do not make decisions, they will never be able to. Skill in decision-making is difficult to acquire, but this skill can be developed by training and experience.

When Is a Decision Made?

In our discussion thus far, we have considered decisions as being of various types. First, we considered personal and organizational decisions, then positive and negative decisions. These have been considered from the point of view of the chief administrator in an organization. It is necessary to explore one additional facet before continuing with a further classification. We should be concerned with an answer to the question, When does an administrator make a decision? We know that executives are tremendously busy people and, as such, need some way of systematizing their work. They need to have a way of screening out that which they need not do from that which they must do. What, then, are the occasions for decision-making?

Barnard has divided the occasions for decision-making into three categories, depending on which of the three following sources they originate from: [16]

1. authoritative communication from superiors
2. cases referred for decision by subordinates
3. cases originating in the initiative of the executive concerned.

Each of these occasions requires a different type of decision. For purposes of brevity, we shall call the three types of decisions intermediary decisions, appellate decisions, and creative decisions, respectively.

[16] *Ibid.*, pp. 189-192.

Intermediary Decisions. These are very important decisions for the chief school administrator, probably more so for him than for any other type of executive in business or industry. The chief school administrator should be the executive officer of the board of education. A very large portion of his job is to execute the policies made by that board. This is a generally recognized function of good board of education procedure as evidenced by the Davies-Prestwood study.[17] They report that of 285 boards studied, 208 stated that the "superintendent executes board policies." In a study made by the American Association of School Administrators, it was reported that 77 per cent of the rural superintendents polled believed that they were firmly established as executive officers of the board, and 85 per cent of the city superintendents reported that they were fully established as executive officers.[18] There can be little doubt as to the position of the superintendent in relation to his board: he is generally accepted as the executive officer. As such, his position in the decision-making process is one of an intermediary. He receives the policy made by the board and then executes the policy. Depending on the size of the administrative staff and the nature of the policy, he either handles the affair himself or he delegates the authority to make the subsidiary decisions to others.

This sounds as though there could be no difficulty involved. Many complications do arise, however. Hunkins presents a case which illustrates the kind of difficulty in which an administrator can easily find himself.[19]

One of our buildings had been declared unsafe for school use. A new building had been erected to take its place. Before sidewalks could be completed the rainy season set in. The board decided that since the old building had already been in use six months after it was declared unsafe, it would not hurt to use it a few months longer and thus save the new building from damage from the mud.

But parents became anxious. They protested the delay in occupying the new building to me and some of the faculty. They said, "We voted bonds for the new building because you declared the old one unsafe; why jeopardize the lives of children any longer?" My reply was made too hurriedly and was prompted by a self-protective impulse. I said we only awaited the authorization of the board of education to move.

I was properly reminded, when the time came, by one of the board members that I had been disloyal to the board. I had not backed up the policy the board had adopted for protecting the building by explaining the reason for the delay.

There are several points in this case which stress the difficulty of the intermediary decision. The first is the obvious unpopularity of the board's policy. The superintendent had to bear the brunt of the community's opposition of this ruling; yet it was not entirely of his making. The superintend-

[17] Daniel R. Davies and Ellwood Prestwood, *Practical School Board Procedures* (New York, Chartwell House, 1951), p. 136.

[18] *The American School Superintendency: Thirtieth Yearbook of the American Association of School Administrators* (Washington, D. C., 1952), p. 115.

[19] Ralph V. Hunkins, *Superintendent and School Board* (Lincoln, University of Nebraska Press, 1949), pp. 75-76.

ent was still obligated to execute the order of the board and to interpret, in good faith, this ruling to the community. Being an executive officer is not always a popular post, but it is the very essence of the superintendency.

Another point to be considered is the extent to which the superintendent is involved in the policy of the board. Normally, he is consulted in the policy formulation in the first instance, and the board very often acts on his recommendation. He, therefore, is executing a policy which he was instrumental in formulating. This is all the more reason why he should not renege on the board, since it is a direct reflection on his own integrity.

In considering the above case, one additional point should be included. It should be noted that the board acted to set the value of the new building over against human values. The policy was to risk human lives to keep a new building from getting dirty. In a moral judgment of this sort the superintendent should indeed feel uncomfortable. If the superintendent is directed to execute a policy which he feels to be immoral, he should protest directly to the board during its meeting. He should not act counter to his governing board behind its back. His opposition should be straightforward.

Appellate Decisions. These are decisions on issues that are referred to the chief administrator for varied reasons. It may be that an individual in the school, charged with making a particular decision is incapable of arriving at a conclusion. A building principal, for instance, realizes that he cannot schedule the school band a sufficient number of periods a week. A supervisor cannot make progress with a teacher. Another type deals with instructions issued by the superintendent's office which are not understood by the staff and it becomes necessary to issue new instructions. This is a type of incompetency on the part of the administrator which requires him to make new decisions. Appellate cases also arise through novelty of conditions in the system. In rapidly growing districts, building principals are finding that large influxions of students at irregular times disturb the orderly processes of their schools. Numerous problems arise which require the superintendent to act, since new policy is needed under which the building principal can act. A more common type of appellate decision is required when there is conflict between two or more individuals and the matter is referred to the administrator. Superintendents are often called upon to settle conflicts like this between building principals and subject-matter supervisors. The supervisor feels that he can override the decisions of the building principal, and the building principal feels that he should be supreme in his building.

Let us examine a case which points up the difficulties that can arise in the handling of appellate decisions.

Mr. Richard Amason was the new seventh- and eighth-grade science teacher in Valleyville. He had moved down to Valleyville from Long Island, where he had to give up a high-paying teaching position because his wife did not like the climate. Mr. Amason was a veteran of ten years in the teaching profession, and he easily adjusted to his new position. He was offered and accepted the guidance job as well as coaching athletics after school. He seemed to be in good standing with the administration, especially with the principal, Miss Oxley.

Since Richard was the only man teacher in the school, except for the special shop and gym teachers who came twice a week, he spent much of his free time with the janitors in the janitors' room. There was a teachers' room in the building, but the other teachers, under the influence and urging of Miss Tomlinson, the English teacher, made it clear that they did not want his presence in the teachers' room. Miss Tomlinson was one of those autocratic teachers with a very bitter tongue and an overwhelming personality. She had two brothers who were in politics and quite influential in the local area. Years ago, when the school district was still under the influence of politicians, Miss Tomlinson got her appointment. She has been in and out of hot water several times because of her abusive language with the children and with the administration, but always seems to come out unscathed. Miss Oxley once told Mrs. Calhoun, the home-making teacher, that either Miss Tomlinson would have to go or she would, because she could not stand her much longer.

Richard and Miss Tomlinson never hit it off well together. Although they were on the same floor and their rooms near each other, they seldom had a pleasant word for each other. One day when Richard had one of Miss Tomlinson's homeroom boys out in the hall trying to discipline him, Miss Tomlinson came by, put her arms around the boy, and took him to her room.

The crisis came when she refused to let athletes out of her room at 3 P.M. for the interscholastic games. One day, Mr. Amason sent three different boys up to her room to get the boys out, but she refused to let them leave. He went up himself, but could not get them out. He pointed out to her that there was a definite school policy allowing children in interscholastic events to be dismissed at 3 P.M. so that they could arrive at their destinations on time. This did not have any effect on her.

One day Richard had a game with a distant school and it was important for him and his players to be on the 3:05 P.M. bus if they were to get to the game on time. Three of his best players were in Miss Tomlinson's room. She refused to let them go. Richard then called up the principal, Miss Oxley, at her home, because of illness, and explained the situation to her. He told her he wanted to turn Miss Tomlinson in to the superintendent and she told him to go right ahead. Two days later Miss Tomlinson received a letter from the superintendent, Mr. Jones, telling her that she has to let the ball players out, and if she didn't, he would bring up charges against her. She showed the letter to the other teachers with the remark that Richard Amason was a cry baby and had gone over the principal's head to squeal on a colleague. Some of them seemed impressed by her version and began to give Richard the cold shoulder. Miss Tomlinson further asserted that the three boys in question were all on the doubtful list of passers and needed their English more than their baseball. One more game remained to be played. On the day of the game none of the boys came out of Miss Tomlinson's room at 3 P.M. Mr. Amason became furious but couldn't report to the principal because she was still absent. Therefore, he called up Mr. Jones, the superintendent, who said he would take care of everything.

Richard was unable to influence Miss Tomlinson to act according to school policy, so he appealed to the principal. The principal, because of illness, and also probably because of the power of Miss Tomlinson in the community, asked that the appeal be referred to the superintendent. The superintendent acted, but Miss Tomlinson chose to ignore his ruling. This is not a common procedure, but, by the same token, it is not uncommon. The appellate decision of the superintendent was not put into effect because of the resistance of Miss Tomlinson. The superintendent must now find a way to make his appellate decision stick.

These appellate cases can best be controlled through careful development of rules and regulations that spell out administrative responsibilities without hampering the initiative of individuals. The diffusion of previous decisions to staff members allows them to act on the basis of precedence and so forms a basis of proven experience, although this was not the situation in the above case. Apparently, rulings from the superintendent concerning Miss Tomlinson had been ignored in the past also. The precedent was one which encouraged the ignoring of decisions rather than the following of them. The number of appellate cases is a measure of morale in that they reflect bickering and uncertainty among the staff. The fewer the number of appellate cases, the better the morale.

The handling of appellate cases is a true test of an administrator. He needs to determine which case he should handle and which he should let the participants handle. What Barnard has termed the fine art of decision-making seems to apply best to these cases.

Creative Decisions. These decisions lie in an area quite different from the two types mentioned above. The point of origin of the former decisions resides outside the person of the administrator. But creative decisions stem from the administrator himself. Very probably, it is in this classification of decisions that the administrator finds the opportunity to present a program, to originate change, to shape an organization, or to implement a philosophy. This type of decision-making is of that nature which distinguishes the truly creative administrator from the ordinary.

The assumption of this path of action by the administrator almost invariably results in criticism, in opposition by one group or another, and in far more difficulty than would ordinarily be encountered. What happens is that the administrator actually antagonizes many members of the faculty or the community by advocating change. Such advocacy indicates dissatisfaction with the *status in quo* or, in other words, with people. This stimulates an effort by these people to protect themselves, and so difficulty ensues.

An example will clarify this creative type of decision-making and also point up the issues involved.

Superintendent *B* was vitally interested in improving education in his community. He worked in a village of some 10,000 people within commuting distance of a large metropolitan area. The village had grown rapidly, mostly because of the immigration of people from the metropolitan area. The village had assumed the position of a prosperous middle-class community.

Superintendent *B* knew that a strong financial basis is necessary to build a good educational system. He investigated and found that the financial backing of each student in terms of true valuation of property was approximately $10,-000. Now, this was two thirds of the state average and indicated a weakness in the financial structure of the community. He reported his findings to the board of education and recommended that the board take the initiative in forming a citizens committee to discover ways and means of increasing the wealth of the community.

This is an illustration of action taken solely on the initiative of the superintendent. It was neither handed down from above nor appealed from the staff. He was actually the only one, as we shall see later, who was in a position, from a professional point of view, to originate such a suggestion and follow it through.

Some of the difficulties encountered as a result of this decision can be seen readily. Although the wealth available for school purposes was low, this was primarily due to choice. The people living in this community did not want industrial plants or other such sources of taxation in their community. They had chosen to live in this community because it lacked these things and was solely a residential area. Any attempt then to change the nature of the community would bring considerable opposition. The superintendent's original decision to take steps to improve the financial backing of the schools needed to be weighed against a set of values held by the community. The community had a choice between changing their environment by admitting industrial plants or by increasing the tax rate on the one source of taxable wealth, namely their homes. Whenever an administrator decides to originate a program of any sort he must weigh the consequences of the changes which he is attempting to bring about. This is one of the main reasons which cause school administrators to be very reticent about bringing change to their schools, since in weighing the consequences, he often finds that he must "go it alone." This he must do through personal choice, above and beyond the demands of the organization. The creative decision is the finest example of Barnard's *personal* decision. The ability and desire to make this kind of decision is a mark of an excellent educational leader.

GROUP DECISION

We have discussed, rather thoroughly, decision-making from the standpoint of the individual. We now need to investigate an area called *group decision*. For some time now, American educators have supported the principle that all who might be affected by a decision should share in making it. This principle has its basis in that somewhat nebulous concept known as "democratic administration." Recently, there has been a considerable amount of discussion as to the validity of this principle. Spalding, among others, raises some fundamental questions: [20]

It is frequently stated, as a theoretical principle, that all who might be affected by a decision should share in making it. This statement is so eminently plausible, particularly to anyone under the spell of this slogan of democratic administration, that it has been widely accepted and acted upon. Practice has created doubts about the soundness of the principle. These doubts arise first because the principle provides no operational procedure for selecting those who are to participate in making decisions nor in limiting their number. If it means anything operationally, it means that all who feel that they should take part should be allowed to do so, for failure to include them will clearly affect them. But what about those who are uniformed, who do not know that a decision is about to be made? How many of them would feel that they should participate if they knew what was going on? Who is to inform them? How many are to be informed? These questions have no present answer. It may be that they are not answerable.

John Miller, superintendent of schools in Great Neck, N. Y., in writing a critique of Spalding's lecture, adds fuel to the controversy. Referring to the above excerpt, Miller has this to say: [21]

Dr. Spalding's treatment of the subject of "Democratic Administration" bears reading and rereading. My personal feeling is that the words should be expunged from our pedagogical vocabulary. We know that school government or control is completely democratic in form, in that the people vote directly for board of education members or vote for the people who select board members and that, in many communities, people vote directly on the budget. What we in education have in mind when we talk about democratic administration is, I believe, the exercise of a democratic spirit, involving respect for the thinking, personalities, capabilities and responsibilities of others. We prate about having all affected by a decision share in making it. What we ought to be saying is, "Let him who has the responsibility for a decision take into account the thinking, personalities, capabilities and responsibilities of others."

The arguments for group participation in the decision-making process are equally vigorous. Wiles has this to say: [22]

The decision-making process is the most important phase of successful democratic leadership, because sharing decisions is the only control a democratic leader has. If he cannot get group members to participate in decision-making, help them to gain satisfaction from the process, and believe in the soundness of the decisions, he must resort to authoritarian procedures: he must either entice members of the group into behaving in the approved manner or else force them to do so.

[20] Willard B. Spalding, *The Superintendency of Public Schools—An Anxious Profession,* The Inglis Lecture (Cambridge, Mass., Harvard University Press, 1954), pp. 42-43.

[21] John L. Miller, "An Anxious Profession," *Nation's Schools,* Vol. 54, No. 4 (October, 1954), p. 116.

[22] Kimball Wiles, *Supervision for Better Schools,* 2d ed. (New York, Prentice-Hall, 1955), p. 173.

In a later section, it is interesting to note that Wiles modifies this view. In discussing the topic "The administration shares the decisions within its authority," he says: [23]

Any decision within the authority of the official leader may be shared, but care should be exercised to distinguish between those decisions that the official leader can make and those that are made by a higher authority, such as the board of education. Failure to make the boundaries of authority clear may cause frustration and may lead the group to reject further participation in decision-making.

If there are certain decisions within the authority of the official leader that he wishes to retain for himself, he should make these clear to the staff with which he works. Such action will be more acceptable than pretending to share all decisions and then vetoing decisions in areas in which the leader feels the staff to be incompetent.

This second statement draws in the lines somewhat. It causes us to raise additional questions. What decisions should the staff participate in making? Should the entire staff participate in making all decisions? What about the staff which has studied a problem for two years: should a newly appointed teacher, who presumably has not studied the problem, have as full a say as the others in the final decision? Is there a difference between being consulted on a question and sharing in decision-making? And another point, What does the research in group decision have to say about this subject?

Research in Group Decision

The research studies that have been quoted most widely to substantiate the contention that groups should be involved in decision-making are three: one by Levine and Butler [24] and two by Lewin.[25] In analyzing these studies we find they deal with problems that differ somewhat from those encountered in making decisions in school administration. All three are more concerned with changing the attitudes of individuals who were meeting together than with reaching a decision in an organized, formal group. In the Levine-Butler study, the purpose was to change the attitude of factory supervisors as they rated workmen. In the Lewin studies, an attempt was made to get housewives to serve beef hearts, sweetbreads, and kidneys in one case, and, in the other, to get new mothers to feed their babies cod liver oil and orange juice. In none of the studies were the groups free to make a decision; the decision had been made before the groups met. The purpose was to get the people in the groups to agree to a prearranged decision. The conclusion reached in each of these studies

[23] *Ibid.*, p. 339.

[24] Levine and Butler, *loc. cit.*, pp. 29-33.

[25] Kurt Lewin, "Studies in Group Decision," in *Group Dynamics*, ed. Dorwin Cartwright and Alvin Zander (Evanston, Ill., Row, Peterson, 1953), pp. 287-301.

is that it is easier to change an individual's attitude by working with him in a discussion group than by lecturing to him either individually or in a group. It would seem, then, that these studies do not constitute evidence to support the argument for faculty participation in decision-making. This criticism is seconded by Foote and Hart: [26]

A great deal could be said about the process of discussion *which culminates in a group decision* and thereby commits participants to some responsible and important kind of action. The matter needs a great deal more study. Much of the literature produced to date by social psychologists deals with highly formal discussion under the control of some so-called leader. No really binding decision is reached; even if there seems to be a decision, it is often fictitious, academic, unimportant. The kind of discussion and decision which launch some major social action—let us take the 1952 union-management negotiations in the steel industry as a clear-cut example—go on under drastically different circumstances. The leaders are genuine representatives of opposing factions, with diagonally opposed notions of what ought to be done. What passes as negotiation is mingled with threat, promise, flattery, browbeating, rhetoric, and the exertion of all kinds of economic, social and political power. This spectacle is not unique; discussion pure and undefiled by the more direct and effective means of exerting influence upon opinion hardly exists outside text books on public speaking and group dynamics.

We have established the fact that the validity of group decision has been questioned and that current research in group decision does not apply to the school situation. Does this mean that there should be no faculty participation in decision-making? Does it mean that the administrator should make all the decisions without consulting anyone? Clearly, in view of our earlier conclusions regarding groups, it does not. Our next step, then, is to determine to what extent decision-making in the schools should be shared.

Sharing Decision-making

The answer to the above set of questions might well reside in an analysis of the authority structure of the school. As Dubin points out, "A level of authority is a level of the organization at which relevant decisions are made." [27] If decisions are made by the faculty, then the level of authority has been set at the faculty level. This means that authority has been delegated to the faculty to make these decisions. It must be made very clear that if the superintendent has the authority to make a particular decision and he lets the faculty make the decision, then he is delegating his authority to the faculty. In this sense, sharing decision-making is delegation of

[26] Nelson N. Foote and Clyde W. Hart, "Public Opinion and Collective Behavior," in *Group Relations at the Crossroads*, ed. M. A. Sherif and M. O. Wilson (New York, Harper, 1953), pp. 314-315.

[27] Robert Dubin, ed., *Human Relations in Administration* (New York, Prentice-Hall, 1951), p. 223.

authority. There are, however, certain decisions that the superintendent should make which should not be made by the faculty—the decision to discharge a teacher, for instance. By the same reasoning, there are decisions that a building principal should make which should not be made by the faculty. On the other hand, there are certain decisions that should be made by the faculty and not by an administrator—the selection of textbooks, for example. Now, we are not talking about the process of decision-making; we are talking about the *actual making of the decision.* In each case, the person or group making the decision should *consult* with others. But the actual making of the decision must reside in one place or the other, with the administrator or with the group.

If it were possible to dichotomize the areas in which the administrator should make decisions and those in which the faculty should make decisions, we would have our problem solved. There are many areas in which the administrator has the authority to make decisions, and the authority to make these decisions should not be delegated. But there are other areas which involve future behavior of the faculty, and in these areas, unilateral decision-making by the administrator is foolish. There is an old story which illustrates the point:

A new principal was talking to his faculty about the future curriculum of the school. In the course of his talk, he expounded many very modern ideas and ended by saying, "From now on we will have Progressive Education in this school." The next morning one of the grade teachers decided she would make the switch. She asked the students what they wanted to do. Some said study birds, others said animals, one wanted to go for a walk, another sing; but, finally, one said, "Study Indians." The teacher thereupon pulled out her Indian unit, which she had been using for years, and taught it!

This story is, of course, a caricature, but it does illustrate the point. The research in group decision deals exactly with this sort of situation. It says that an individual's behavior will be changed if he participates in and approves of the decision being made. Decisions which are going to affect the professional behavior of teachers should be made at the faculty level. If the teacher's behavior is to be changed, they cannot be made anywhere else. This is, it seems to us, what Wiles is stressing when he quotes a principal as saying: [28]

I have a vote and an important one, but only one. I suggest. I recommend. I try to persuade. I vigorously defend. But if my faculty doesn't understand, doesn't believe in, doesn't agree with my ideas, regardless of merit, my ideas haven't much chance of being carried out effectively—and so I wait. I continue to work vigorously for those things which I believe, those things which seem to me to be best for the young people with whom I work.

In areas which do not affect the professional behavior (broadly interpreted) of teachers, the administrator should consult with those people

[28] Wiles, *op. cit.*, p. 176.

who have information which will be of help; but he must make the decision himself, regardless of the attitude of the faculty. There are times when he can and should use the veto. This should be clearly understood, and the areas in which the administrator assumes authority to make decisions should be familiar to all of the staff.

In those areas in which the administrator makes the final decision, he should still consult with others, whether they are teachers, specialists, laymen, board members, or custodians. Tannenbaum and Massarik, in an excellent article on decision-making, clarify this approach. They point out that the actual making of a decision involves three steps: (1) being aware of as many of the alternatives as possible; (2) defining alternatives in terms of consequences; and (3) making the decision.[29] They then state: "In enterprises, managerial subordinates, as subordinates, can participate in the first two steps of the managerial decision-making process. They cannot participate in the third step." [30]

Participation in the first two steps requires that the administrator consult with everyone who has relevant information and will be concerned with the results of the decision. Tannenbaum and Massarik indicate that this kind of participation in decision-making results in improved staff morale, less turnover, a greater readiness to accept change, greater ease in the management of subordinates, and an improved quality of managerial decisions.

SUMMARY

In this chapter, we indicated that there is general agreement that the decision-making process consists of approximately six steps. The six steps constitute a somewhat mechanical approach to decision-making, and several individuals using the same steps could very well make several different decisions because of differences in their perception and interpretation of words, motives, and cultural background, among other variables.

All decision-makers operate within a set of limits. This is the factor which determines how decisions are made as well as when they are made. Limits are set in organizations so that decisions will be made more rationally.

In our discussion of decisions made by individuals, we categorized decisions as personal and organizational, positive and negative. We also specified that there are three types of decisions: intermediary, appellate, and creative. We also discussed Barnard's "art of decision making."

Group decision-making was investigated and it was pointed out that the available research in group decision was not relevant to the making

[29] Robert Tannenbaum and Fred Massarik, "Sharing Decision-Making with Subordinates," in Dubin, *op. cit.*, pp. 223-228.
[30] *Ibid.*, p. 224.

of decisions in a formal organization. Decision-making is related to the level of authority in a school, and decisions should be made at that level at which authority resides. The faculty should have authority in those matters that directly influence their professional behavior. The authority of the administrator is that which is delegated to him by the board of education. In all cases, the person or persons making the decision should consult with those who have relevant information and will be affected by the consequences of the decision.

EXERCISES

1. Write down the last major decision which you made. What was the process which you went through to arrive at the decision? How does it compare with the suggested six steps?

2. What limits are placed upon the decision-making process in your school? Do they aid you in making decisions?

3. Draw a diagram of the lines of authority in your school system. Is the line of authority always clearly understood by all? How could your system improve this situation?

4. How do you distinguish between *personal* and *organizational* decisions in your school system?

5. Write a brief case illustrating intermediary decisions, appellate decisions, and creative decisions.

6. When did you last make a creative decision? Describe it in detail. What were the results?

7. What sort of decisions does the faculty in your school make? Is this consistent with the material in this chapter?

8. How are decisions regarding the teaching of "special" subjects made in your school system? What is the basis for this kind of procedure?

9. Has your school system a set of written policies indicating *who* is to make decisions, *what* decisions they are to make, and *how* they are to make them?

10. What does "democratic administration" mean to you?

SELECTED BIBLIOGRAPHY

BARNARD, Chester I., "The Environment of Decision," *The Function of the Executive* (Cambridge, Mass., Harvard University Press, 1938), pp. 185-199.

COUNTS, George S., *Decision Making and American Values in School Administration* (New York, Teachers College Bureau of Publications, 1954).

DAVIES, Daniel R., and HERROLD, Kenneth F., *Problem Solving for the Executive* (New London, Conn., Arthur C. Croft, 1954), 45 pp.

DUBIN, Robert, "Decision-making," *Human Relations in Administration* (New York, Prentice-Hall, 1951), pp. 188-228.

FOOTE, Nelson N., and HART, Clyde W., "Public Opinion and Collective Behavior," in *Group Relations at the Crossroads*, ed. M. A. Sherif and M. O. Wilson (New York, Harper, 1953), pp. 308-331.

GRIFFITHS, Daniel E., and WILEY, William T., *The Administrator and Group Dynamics* (Albany, N. Y., Capital Area School Development Association, 1953), 24 pp.

JOHNS, Ray, "Getting Decisions Made," *Executive Responsibility* (New York, Association Press, 1954), pp. 172-181.

LEVINE, Jacob, and BUTLER, John, "Lecture *vs.* Group Decision in Changing Behavior," *Journal of Applied Psychology*, Vol. 36, No. 1 (February, 1952), pp. 29-33.

LEWIN, Kurt, "Studies in Group Decision," in *Group Dynamics*, ed. Dorwin Cartwright, and Alvin Zander (Evanston, Ill., Row, Peterson, 1953), pp. 287-301.

MILLER, John L., "An Anxious Profession," *Nation's Schools*, Vol. 54, No. 4 (October, 1954), pp. 114-116.

SPALDING, Willard B., *The Superintendency of Public Schools—An Anxious Profession*, The Inglis Lecture (Cambridge, Mass., Harvard University Press, 1954).

WAGNER, R. H., and ARNOLD, C. C., *Handbook of Group Discussion* (Boston, Houghton Mifflin, 1950).

WILES, Kimball, "How Should Decisions Be Reached?" *Supervision for Better Schools*, 2d ed. (New York, Prentice-Hall, 1955), pp. 173-180.

CHAPTER **11**

Human Relations Approach
to Leadership

With this chapter we complete our examination of the content of human relations most pertinent to school administration. As the culminating point of this examination, we now bring our findings to bear upon a consideration of the school administrator as leader of a *formal* organization in a democratic society.

Our culture has shown a tremendous interest in leadership in the past twenty years. One recent bibliography, a selected one at that, contains 421 titles related to leadership and executive development.[1] When we realize that some of the works cited are reviews of as many as 124 other studies, we can begin to appreciate the enormous activity in this field. Obviously the school administrator cannot master this vast amount of information. He would not be wise even to try; the conflicting nature of many of the reports would only confuse him. Much of the research on leadership is being carried out under laboratory conditions. Some of the studies are concerned with informal structures; others with formal structures. A portion of the work is being done in real situations in business, industry, military organizations, and the public schools. In this chapter, we shall refer to as much of the theoretical work as is applicable to our study of the school administrator as an educational leader. But we shall approach the subject primarily through three basic considerations: the concept of headship, a definition of school leadership, and leadership behavior.

Elsewhere in the book, notably the chapters on the faculty meeting and group dynamics techniques, we consider leadership only as it relates to the discussion, or *informal,* group. In those chapters, we note that what is called group decision in the informal group differs substantially from group decision in an institution like the public school. A similar distinction exists between the leader of an informal group and the school administrator. They should not be discussed in the same terms. Much more relevant to our study of formal leadership are the three chapters on power,

---

[1] *Selected, Annotated Bibliography on Leadership and Executive Development,* prepublication edition (Officer Education Research Laboratory, Air Research and Development Command, Maxwell Air Force Base, Ala., 1955).

authority, and decision-making. Dubin, for example, stresses the strong relationship of these three elements to formal leadership as follows: [2]

Order in society is grounded in power. The organizations of society institutionalize power and are the means for carrying out the ordered and regular daily activities of society. Within organizations, the activities of the members and functionaries must be directed in systems of co-operation and co-ordination. These co-ordinating functions are grounded in authority—the expectation that direction will be followed. Involved in co-ordination and the exercise of authority is organization decision-making by the authority holder.

These words should have great meaning for us. We have examined, throughout the book, ways and means of making democratic leadership possible. It can be seen from the above quotation that there are some basic dilemmas for democratic leadership that arise from the nature of formal organizations. In view of the legal structure of education, with authority placed directly in the hands of certain individuals it can readily be seen that given certain legal power, administrators are in a position to exert other methods of control over teachers. Dubin points out that a change in authority comes about only through a change in power. In our chapter on power, we indicated several ways in which power had moved from the administrator to the teachers and thus brought democratic administration in the schools closer to realization. In connection with this, Dubin has made a statement which should not be overlooked: [3]

There has grown up around the notion of "human relations" the idea that it is either some magical way to build democracy into organizations, or that it makes people willing subjects of manipulation. These are shallow and worthless ways to view the meaning of a "human relations outlook." The significant orientation to a human relations approach is to seek an understanding of how people behave *in* organizations. Members of an organization understand authority and leadership and their functions. The problem is not to destroy authority or get rid of leadership. That would inevitably destroy the organization itself. The real problem is to make leadership and the exercise of authority operate according to the accepted values and beliefs of our society.

This states our task in this chapter, which is to define leadership in the public schools in terms of the accepted democratic values and beliefs of our society. To do so, we shall examine several concepts of leadership.

WHAT IS LEADERSHIP?

Shartle has given this matter considerable study and has come up with several definitions of leaders in different kinds of situations.[4] He points out that a leader can be:

[2] Robert Dubin, ed. *Human Relations in Administration* (New York, Prentice-Hall, 1951), p. 229.

[3] *Ibid.*, p. 230.

[4] Carroll L. Shartle, "Studies of Leadership by Interdisciplinary Methods," in *Leadership in American Education,* ed. Alonzo G. Grace (Chicago, University of Chicago Press, 1950), p. 32.

1. An individual who exercises positive influence acts on others.
2. An individual who exercises more or more important positive influence acts than any other member of the group or organization he is in.
3. An individual elected by a group as leader.
4. An individual who exercises most influence in goal setting or goal achievement of the group or organization.
5. An individual in a given office or position of apparently high influence potential.

Each of these definitions is important to a discussion of leadership in an educational context. We can start with the last definition. Here we have defined the superintendent of schools or the principal or the supervisor. Here we also have the teacher, since he is in a position of high influence potential in relation to student and parent. We can see that the staff of any school system also contains other leaders that fit into the first three definitions. Although the principal, for instance, is the appointed head of the school, the staff may well have a member who exercises more control over the teachers than does the principal. In faculty meetings, the ideas of this individual have more weight than the principal. He is also sought out by the teachers when they want advice. He really exercises "important positive influence acts" on the teachers because they want him to. Let us examine the case of Edmund Watts for the kind of leadership being exercised and contrast this with the behavior of the formal leader. Note the reaction of the teachers to both administrators and bear in mind that this takes place in a school system in which the authority is definitely fixed.

James Hall, guidance director and vice-principal at Sycamore Heights Central School, sat in his office and pondered his position. He wished that there was wiser counsel available upon which he could call. One thing seemed certain—something had to be done!

Hall has been in the system for several years, starting as a classroom teacher and eventually becoming guidance teacher and vice-principal. His work in the community and in the school had given him a good deal of leadership opportunity, and both faculty and townsfolk regarded Hall favorably. He had recently married one of the teachers, and people assumed that he would stay in Sycamore Heights as vice-principal until the supervising principal, Edmund Watts, changed jobs. Although Watts had been in the community longer than Hall, few expected him to remain permanently; but practically everyone expected Hall to stay. Watts just didn't seem to "fit in" with the community. Not that there was much open antagonism, but rather, a lack of open acceptance.

The present problem facing Hall arose from the nature of Watts's philosophy. Watts had strong *laissez-faire* tendencies in his makeup and evidenced great reluctance to enforce school regulations among either faculty or students. Consequently, both groups were taking advantage of Watts, and morale was rapidly deteriorating. Watts seemed unaware of the situation, spending almost every day in his office and little time about the building.

Because Hall had "risen from the ranks," he enjoyed closer relations with the faculty than Watts and, as a result of teacher confidences, was constantly aware of the increasing difficulties. Just this morning a teacher had come into his office.

Teacher: "Can I see you for a minute, Jim?"

Hall: "Sure, have a chair!"

Teacher: "Do you know if Wattsie spoke to the night janitors about leaving the aquarium in my room alone?"

Hall: "I don't know. In fact, I didn't even know you had trouble with them."

Teacher: "Trouble! I should say so. This is the fourth time this year that I complained about it. They fool with the water inlet and the temperature controls. Each time they do, I lose some valuable fish."

Hall: "Maybe he hasn't had a chance to see them yet."

Teacher: "I think he's afraid to speak to them about it, just the same as he's afraid to speak to them about taking milk from the cafeteria for their lunches. The cafeteria is short each month because of them, and the board has had the manager on the carpet about it. Who knows what else they've been taking."

Hall: "I'll speak to him about it and maybe we'll get this thing straightened out."

Teacher: "You know better than that, Jim. He won't do anything about it. I guess I just came in to blow off steam. I wish he'd get a better job so that you would take over. Maybe, he'll drop dead! Wouldn't be a bad idea, if you ask me. Well, I'll see you later."

Hall: "Be good now."

After the teacher had gone, Hall reviewed the conversation. It was the sixth such complaint from a teacher that week. All of them had shown impatience with Watts's failure to take action. Hall knew from his own experience that the complaints were usually justified. He had had similarly unsatisfying encounters. However, he doubted that the principal was afraid. He believed that by nature Watts was infinitely more philosophical than executive and shied away from unpleasant personal contacts.

That night at supper Hall and his wife had the following conversation:

Mrs. H.: "You missed a coffee party third period today."

Hall: "I was pretty busy all morning. What happened?"

Mrs. H.: "The four new teachers from Taylor Teachers College got together and appointed student monitors for their classes and came down to the faculty room for a coffee 'Klatch.' They stayed almost all period."

Hall: "I wonder if they are aware of the school rule against leaving classes without faculty supervision."

Mrs. H.: "They know all right, but figured that since Mr. Watts has only been on the top floor for scheduled observations, he probably wouldn't even know."

Hall: "I thought they were going to be real good teachers, too."

Mrs. H.: "They probably would if things weren't so lax. It's so bad now that the math teacher who has first period free isn't even going to come to school until 9:45. You ought to do something about it."

Hall: "That's just too much. I will do something about it."

But next morning Jim Hall could not determine what to do about it. If only there was some way to get Watts to exercise his authority without seeming to be undermining him, criticizing him, or "squealing" on the faculty. What to do?

There are several aspects of this case which call for comment. First of all, although Edmund Watts is the designated leader of the school system (in this school he is called a supervising principal), the teachers do not actually consider him to be the real leader. We note, though, that they still feel they must work *through* him. The teacher whose fish are dying because Watts won't speak to the janitor is a case in point. The teacher knows where the authority lies but at the same time seeks advice and help from the vice-principal. He is seeking to influence Watts in an indirect manner. Most of his behavior toward Watts is the same as it would be toward any person in authority over him. Jim Hall's behavior is similar. He will not go over Watts's head but prefers to work with him if at all possible. The attitude of the community is interesting also. They have become used to nomadic school administrators who stay just long enough to get a better job. Since Watts has had short tenure and has not lived long in the community, he has not made a place for himself in the community power structure. On the other hand, Hall, to some extent, has done this. He is expected to head the school when Watts moves on.

The foregoing case serves to illustrate the first of our three basic considerations: the concept of headship.

Headship

This concept has been examined at some length by Gibb, who holds that a principal like Mr. Watts is filling a headship position.[5] This situation occurs when a formal position is filled by a person who is not, and possibly never was, qualified to hold the job. He is somewhat of a figurehead. He holds the formal title but little else.

It is difficult to say just how many headships there are in the American public schools; but whenever a formal organization of this type is established, there are bound to be many. In fact, all administrative positions in the schools could be considered headships, for the original grant of authority is not to the person but to the position. The concept of headship, then, is one which we cannot disregard. However, if we think in terms of democratic leadership, we must go beyond this concept and examine those definitions that take into account the relationship of the leader to others.

Leadership in Relation to Others

Among the definitions to be considered, we should include that of Seeman, who concisely stated that leadership should be construed as "acts by persons which influence other persons in a shared direction." [6] Although this is a very brief definition, it is an excellent one. The appointed democratic leader as well as the informal leaders can be gathered in under this definition. James Hall, in many respects, could be described by this kind of statement. It is most appropriate, however, for those situations which

[5] Cecil A. Gibb, "The Principles and Traits of Leadership," *Journal of Abnormal and Social Psychology*, Vol. 42 (July, 1947), pp. 267-284.

[6] Melvin Seeman, "Some Status Correlates of Leadership," in *Leadership in American Education*, ed. Alonzo G. Grace (Chicago, University of Chicago Press, 1950), p. 43.

are described as "leaderless." In this sort of situation, a leaderless group of people is faced with a problem. The person who emerges to help the group solve the problem is generally considered to be the leader. Situations such as this are typical in an experimental framework, but they rarely occur in school work. There is invariably a member of every school group with considerably more status than other members of the group. This member is usually looked to for help in solving whatever problem faces the group. It may be, in fact, usually it is the case, that if this status member does not have the technical skill to help a group move in the direction in which it wants to go, he enlists the aid of the most skilled member of the group. It is somewhat questionable whether this skilled individual actually leads the group. In experimental situations, the skilled individual is considered to be the leader and the status member just a follower. Consider the case of a committee appointed in a high school to study building needs. The status member is a department chairman who is not familiar with techniques for determining the number of classrooms needed for a certain number of high school students. A member of the committee is a young man studying school administration on a part-time basis who is familiar with such devices as the Castoldi Nomogram,[7] a method of determining the number of classrooms needed for a given number of secondary school students. Now the point is: Who is the leader of the group? Is it the status member who allows the group to use the skills of the young teacher? Or is it the young teacher who can get the group where it wants to go? It would seem that the actual leadership is still with the status member, even though experimentalists in leadership would tend to disagree. The leadership would seem to reside in the individual to whom the group looks at times of *decision,* and the group members would not then look to the technician who had helped them toward a solution of their problems. Very probably leadership does not shift so much and so rapidly as many workers in leadership would have us believe.

The definition of Norton would tend to substantiate the conclusion arrived at above. He states: "Leadership means working with and through individuals. . . . Educational leadership finds expression through the personality of individuals. Hence, the necessity for the continuous growth in service of subordinates as well as of the leader." [8]

The point which becomes abundantly clear is that the leader need not necessarily have the immediate skill needed to aid the group at each particular movement of crisis. His job is to work toward the goal, utilizing the abilities of all members of the group. The group will advance more efficiently if the group members are continually growing and improving.

---

[7] *The Castoldi Nomogram* (Cambridge, Mass., New England School Development Council, 1954).

[8] John K. Norton, "Functional Philosophy of Education Is the Administrator's Compass," *Nation's Schools,* Vol. 12 (October, 1933), pp. 11-13.

A safeguard should be mentioned here. The leader could be construed to be a behind-the-scenes manipulator in this definition. It is necessary to point out that leadership means working with and through individuals toward a *shared* goal. This co-operative definition of the goal toward which a group moves is the safeguard the group should demand. Without it, the group is being manipulated.

The National Conference of Professors of Educational Administration early turned their work toward administrative leadership. One of their first publications was devoted to an analysis of the factors which go to make up a good definition of leadership. It stated: [9]

> The term leadership describes a relation between persons. It refers to inter-play among these persons. This relation, this interplay, results in one person becoming a leader—for a time, or for good, and other persons becoming fol-lowers. In short, one person affects another person or a group of persons in such a way that common direction is given to their efforts by this one person.

This common direction refers to much the same sort of thing as the concept of shared goals above. This is refined by considering three ideals which must be held in common by the group and its leaders. These ideals are: [10]

1. The dignity and worth of the individual.
2. Reliance upon the method of intelligence.
3. Reliance on the co-operative use of intelligence in the solution of prob-lems common to the group.

Kenan gives us a definition much like those we have been considering, but he adds another concept to the picture: "Leadership is a dynamic group relationship which motivates and directs a group toward a given goal and which is conditioned by the leader, the people led, and the situa-tion which surrounds them both." [11] Thus he adds the situation in which both the leader and the lead are immersed. But he does not specify the sit-uation, and the definition would hold for any type of environment. It would be as equally valid in an autocratic school as it would be in a democratic school. Although this has its merits in the study of leadership, it is not an advantage in evaluating the worth of leadership in a democratic society.

A definition which has received considerable attention of late is that of Jennings. She states: [12]

[9] Daniel Davies, ed., *Educational Leaders—Their Function and Preparation: A Report of the Second Work Conference of the National Conference of Professors of Educational Administration* (New York, Teachers College Bureau of Publications, 1948), p. 5.

[10] *Ibid.*, pp. 5-6.

[11] Thomas A. Kenan, "A Method of Investigating Executive Leadership" (Unpub-lished doctoral dissertation, Ohio State University, 1948), p. 12.

[12] Helen H. Jennings, "Leadership—A Dynamic Redefinition," *Journal of Educa-tional Sociology*, Vol. 17 (March, 1944), pp. 431-433.

Leadership thus appears as a manner of interacting with others, a social process of interaction involving behavior by and toward the individual "lifted" to the leader role by other individuals. The many particularized "styles" of leadership found in a community reflect not alone the different capacities of the individual leaders but the widely different needs of the population which require various representation.

Emphasis is placed in this definition not so much on the capacity of the person elevated to the leadership role as on the needs of the group. In terms of the old analgram, "Does the times make the man, or the man make the times," somewhat more emphasis is here placed on the times making the man. In any particular group, the leadership will be determined by the needs of the group as defined by its members. The person most capable, in the eyes of the members, will be elevated to leadership and will move the group in the direction of the gratification of its needs.

Some comment should be made on the process of defining group needs. It would seem that in this process of definition of needs the group also needs good leadership, since this very definition will determine later leadership and the direction in which the group will move. This is a role which the status leader could very well fill. The principal or superintendent, in outlining the limits of operation for the group,[13] sets about to determine the needs of the group. If the group accepts these limits and functions within them, it will seek leadership to move it in the direction necessary to accomplish the mission of the group. Difficulty is encountered in educational situations when the group approaches the "leaderless" group of the experimentalist. This happens when the person occupying the headship position offers no direction to his group. He does not help his group to clarify their aims, to set their sights, or to seek common goals. He may be so insecure in his appointed leadership role that he fears meeting with his group. He is afraid that others in the group will take over the leadership role if he attempts to lead his group actively. Just as "nature abhors a vacuum," so, too, do groups abhor a leadership vacuum. The needs of a group will be defined in some manner, however unsatisfactorily, and the group will act with leadership of some sort. In terms of institutionalized behavior, this is "bootlegged" leadership, and its direction is most unpredictable and can be most disastrous to the morale of a school system.

Much the same sort of definition as was presented by Jennings is presented by Stogdill. He states concerning leadership: "It appears ... to be a working relationship among members of a group, in which the leader acquires status through active participation and demonstration of his capacity for carrying co-operative tasks through to completion."[14]

---

[13] See above, Ch. 10.
[14] Ralph M. Stogdill, "Personal Factors Associated with Leadership: A Survey of the Literature," *Journal of Psychology*, Vol. 25 (1948), pp. 35-71.

Mackenzie and Corey have shed much light on the process of educational leadership in their book, *Instructional Leadership*. In their first chapter, "Our Conception of Leadership," they discuss at length a working definition of educational leadership. Among other things they say: "Our conception of leadership can probably best be understood if leadership is viewed as a natural accompaniment of the goal-seeking behavior of human beings." [15] They continue: "The key to our conception of leadership lies in an understanding of the process of giving and receiving help in order to maintain an existing condition against threat, to identify new goals, or to attain goals that are known and defined." [16] Going further, they then state: [17]

we believe it helpful (1) not to equate leadership with any appointive, elective, or hereditary position and (2) to recognize that every individual probably has control of some means someone else wants to use and is able to a certain extent, through study and practice, to increase this control. The holding of an official leadership position is not necessary for the control of means.

These observations led them to formulate the following definition of leadership: [18]

"A recognized leader" is a person who is seen by individuals or groups as helping or being able to help provide the means they desire to use to identify or attain their goals.
"Recognized leadership" is a name for those activities that are seen by individuals or groups as helping or potentially helping to provide the means they desire to use to identify or attain their goals.

This may be said to be a good definition with one exception. It is somewhat difficult to understand the earlier statement: "an official leadership position is not necessary for the control of means." We feel that any definition of leadership in an institution such as the public schools must, of necessity, include consideration of the headship. The appointed leader cannot be ignored if there is to be such a thing as attainment of goals within the framework of an institution. Although it is true that every person is a potential leader in that he can aid the group at some time or other to attain its goal, leadership in an established institution must have a broader frame of reference. Leadership should be construed as that which aids in the attainment of the broad goals of education, which would then include within itself the co-ordination of all of those who aid in attaining subgoals. The concept of every man a leader and of constantly shifting leadership within a group is true but not helpful. A definition of

[15] Gordon N. Mackenzie, Stephen M. Corey, and others, *Instructional Leadership* (New York, Teachers College Bureau of Publications, 1954), p. 4.
[16] *Ibid.,* pp. 4-5.
[17] *Ibid.,* p. 9.
[18] *Ibid.,* p. 10.

leadership should encompass all of these lesser leaders who are actually *good followers.*

Where are we in our search for a definition of democratic leadership? After surveying the field, the possibility of a composite definition should be considered, keeping in mind that this is a definition with a single purpose. We can formulate this definition in terms of the superintendent or chief school officer and then define other leadership roles in education in terms of it: [19]

A leader, as applied to the school superintendency, is a person who occupies a position of headship; whose acts influence other persons in a shared direction within the framework of democratic principles; and whose status is dependent upon the degree and worth of his active participation and demonstration of his capacity for carrying co-operative tasks to a successful completion, as evaluated by the community through its official representatives.

Although this is a definition of a formal leader, it does not exclude from consideration the informal leader. The point is, the informal leader is actually the one defined by Mackenzie and Corey, and, if a school system is to function as a system, these informal leaders must have their activities co-ordinated with the goals of the system. Administrative leadership is concerned with the co-ordination or co-operation of the various informal leaders so as to achieve the over-all goals of the organization.[20]

LEADERSHIP BEHAVIOR

We have examined various attempts to define the leadership of school administrators in the American culture. Probably none of us is completely satisfied with the definition at which we finally arrived. It is somewhat cumbersome, yet it does include most of the facets of leadership about which we are concerned. We now raise the question, How does the successful school administrator behave in his leadership position? Is it possible to identify a set or sets of descriptions of behavior so that we can observe the superintendent as a leader?

There have been several studies of leadership behavior in recent years. Sternloff made a study of the effective behavior of administrators, using Flanagan's critical-incident technique.[21] All school board members and school administrators in Wisconsin were asked to participate. Of these, 42 per cent cf the administrators and 14 per cent of the board members reported incidents. These incidents were analyzed so as to produce

[19] Daniel E. Griffiths, "An Evaluation of the Leadership of the School Superintendent" (Unpublished Ph.D. dissertation, Yale University, 1952), p. 45. A digest of this study was published by the CPEA-MAR Center of Teachers College, Columbia University.

[20] Dubin, *op. cit.*, pp. 238-240.

[21] Robert Elmer Sternloff, "The Critical Requirements for School Administrators Based upon an Analysis of Critical Incidents" (Unpublished Ph.D. dissertation, University of Wisconsin, 1953).

a list of twenty-seven "basic general behaviors of the effective school administrator."

The author made a study of the administrative behavior of successful and unsuccessful school superintendents in Connecticut and New York.[22] He distributed checklists to the teachers of superintendents who had previously been rated as "successful" or "unsuccessful" by a group of judges. The source of the items on the checklist was Jennings' study of the behavior characteristics of leaders and nonleaders.[23] From thirty-nine school systems 1545 check lists were returned. Differences were established by means of Fisher's "t" test.

Bills and Hopper also reported an extensive study of "successful" school administrators in the state of Kentucky.[24] Through the use of numerous psychological tests, Q-sort measures, and recorded interviews, they were able to describe the behavior of successful school administrators.

Another study was made by the Ohio Cooperative Program in Educational Administration Center to "identify the factors related to leadership behavior in the educational administrative situation." [25]

Both Griffiths and Ovsiew conducted studies in the area of administrative practices. Griffiths attempted to answer the question: What does the successful superintendent *do* that the unsuccessful superintendent does not do? [26] Ovsiew worked with administrative practices gathered from schools systems in the Metropolitan School Study Council. By use of the jury method, he isolated some ninety-seven administrative practices which he called "emerging." [27] Both of these studies describe the things that school administrators who meet our definition of successful leaders do. They are the extensionalization of the behavior of the administrator. They are the acts by which the administrator *does* his job.

Our technique for describing the administrator's behavior will be to use categories drawn from the above-mentioned studies and from some descriptions of leaders in business and industry.

The School Administrator As an Initiator

Griffiths found that the two groups of superintendents, successful and unsuccessful, differed most significantly in this area which was called the

---

[22] Daniel E. Griffiths, "Administrative Behavior and Personality of 'Successful' School Superintendents," paper read at a meeting of the American Educational Research Association, Cleveland, Ohio, April 4, 1955.

[23] Helen H. Jennings, *Leadership and Isolation,* 2d ed. (New York, Longmans, Green, 1950), pp. 145-150.

[24] Robert L. Hopper and Robert E. Bills, "What's a Good Administrator Made Of?" *The School Executive* (March, 1955), pp. 93-95.

[25] "CPEA in Ohio," *The School Executive* (June, 1955), pp. 71-83.

[26] *Op. cit.*

[27] Leon Ovsiew, *Emerging Practices in School Administration* (New York, Teachers College Bureau of Publications, 1953).

area of initiative. Teachers' ratings indicated they placed most stress on three items of the checklist which was used:

1. He displays initiative.
2. He presents well-organized plans.
3. He is a very hard worker.

The leadership behavior of the administrator as an initiator is typified by the man who is hard working and self-driving, who presents well-organized plans to his faculty. This is the kind of behavior teachers think of when they picture the successful superintendent.

Stenloff found many of the same behavior characteristics. In fact, five of the twenty-seven basic general behaviors of the effective school administrator fall into the initiator category. With the number that precedes each item indicating its rank order, these behaviors are: [28]

2. Provides pertinent information concerning school problems and suspends judgment until pertinent facts have been examined.
9. Organizes citizen or parent advisory groups and co-operates with them in study and solution of school problems.
10. Willingly devotes extra time to important school affairs.
12. Courageously demands that recommendations he considers necessary for the welfare of the school be accepted and holds to these recommendations in the face of unjust pressures and influences, in spite of jeopardy to his personal position.
15. Organizes the schools to offer community services and provides for community use of school facilities.
24. Initiates action promptly in cases of emergency.

Hopper and Bills report that the persons whom they consider to be ideal administrators—that is, the broad personality type categorized as those who "accept their own worth and believe that other people are equally or more accepting of their worth," can present well-organized plans. They point out that this type of administrator can perceive details in their proper perspective and organize them into meaningful plans and programs.

This concept of the successful administrator being a hard worker and displaying initiative is commonly accepted as an indication of a successful leader in other fields. Kettering makes this statement about industrial executives: [29]

I often tell my people that I don't want any fellow who has a job working for me; what I want is a fellow whom the job has. I want the job to get the fellow and not the fellow to get the job. And I want the job to get hold of this man so hard no matter where he is, the job has him for keeps. I want that job

---

[28] As reported in William W. Savage and Harlan D. Beem, "The Effective Administrator," *Administrator's Notebook*, Midwest Administration Center, University of Chicago, Vol. 2, No. 2 (October, 1953).

[29] Charles F. Kettering, "A Man and a Job," *Coronet* (September, 1949), p. 72. Copyright, 1949, by Esquire, Inc.

to have him in his clutches when he goes to bed at night, and in the morning I want that same job to be sitting at the foot of his bed telling him it's time to get up and go to work. And when a job gets a fellow that way, he's sure to amount to something.

Chris Argyris, in his fascinating case study of a top industrial executive, quotes him as saying: [30]

The primary job in life is to get your job done. I just can't see how some of the fellows in this plant expect to get ahead if they don't work hard in their job. Now you take two people with equal ability. One guy is interested in his job, whatever it is. The other guy is interested in his job, but also in his golf, basketball, or whatever you want to make it. The guys want to put their effort into where their interests lie. The man who's putting his interest in his job is going to get ahead, and the other fellow is going to stay where he is. He may go ahead in other fields, he may become a star bowler, but he may also be pushing a wheelbarrow in the plant somewhere. I can't figure these guys out who spend all their spare time in sports or something like that.

The tremendous drive pictured for these successful leaders should certainly frighten those who believe in the forty-hour week! These studies of top leaders, then, give us a picture of his behavior in terms of hard work, great initiative which culminates in well-prepared plans and programs. This is the first aspect of leader behavior in a formal organization.

The School Administrator As an Improver

The next cluster of items which Griffiths isolated included these two:

1. He provides opportunities for teachers to improve professionally.
2. He encourages his teachers to do better work.

We have in the description of this type of behavior the school administrator as an *improver* of the people with whom he works. He is a person so secure himself that he wants the people surrounding him to be just as good as possible. He wants them to do the finest job possible and provides encouragement and opportunities for them to improve.

Sternloff found that the following were critical incidents which came under this category: [31]

4. Utilizes consultants and specialists outside the school and co-operates with them in solving educational problems.
11. Thoroughly understands the important requirements of jobs under his supervision, selects, and assigns persons according to the requirements, and promotes growth of personnel.
21. Provides counseling and other guidance services for school personnel.

One school superintendent, who had just moved into a city superintendency, recognized the need for the teachers to improve professionally.

[30] Chris Argyris, *Executive Leadership* (New York, Harper, 1953), p. 27.
[31] Savage and Beems, *loc. cit.*

There had been little encouragement of teachers to do in-service work; nor had any opportunities to do so been made available to them. This superintendent gave leadership to the plan described below.

A somewhat unique adaptation of the workshop idea of in-service education has been carried on for several years in one city. This city school system operates a four-week summer workshop for elementary school teachers. Attendance at this workshop is voluntary, in accord with what is considered to be best practice. A director from the school system is appointed and he, in co-operation with the teachers, works out the program. Consultants have been obtained from book companies, state department of education, nearby colleges, and from the local staff. The content of the first workshop was concerned with improving classroom instruction, and to do this a demonstration teaching school was set up. Four groups of elementary school pupils were recruited to act as the student body of the experimental school. Subsequent summer programs dealt with such programs as remedial reading, visual aids, and elementary science. Desire on the part of the teacher to receive college credit for this workshop has decreased over the years and now there is none. The cost per workshop has averaged between $400 and $450 for the entire summer. This cost has been borne by the board of education.

The School Administrator As a Recognizer

This category embraces the following items:

1. He recognizes and encourages initiative.
2. He has insight into the problems of others.
3. He sees the potentialities in individuals.

It is apparent from the nature of these items that teachers see the successful school administrator as one who has keen perceptions of what happens around him. He can see individuals exercising initiative and has the internal security necessary to encourage them. He has insight in the problems of other people both in the system and outside. In particular, he has and exercises the ability to understand the problems of faculty members. He can see potentialities in individuals, and, by acting upon these, he builds a better team. He knows his faculty and can make use of the abilities of each staff member.

This behavior of a *recognizer* has had little attention. Indeed, we need to look to such writings as Woodrow Wilson's *Leaders of Men* for a discussion of certain aspects of this type of behavior. Wilson identified *sympathy* as the first requisite of leadership, but he equated sympathy with *insight*. He stated: "Successful leadership is a product of sympathy, not antagonism." By this he meant that the leader must be able to understand the feelings, attitudes, and problems of the people he would lead. In developing this point Wilson wrote: [32]

[32] Quoted in T. H. Vail Motter, "Sympathy, Insight, Interpretation," *The New York Times Magazine* (October 19, 1952), p. 34, from Woodrow Wilson, *Leaders of Men,* edited, with introduction and notes, by T. H. Vail Motter (Princeton, N. J., Princeton University Press, 1952).

Leadership, for the statesman, is interpretation. He must read the common thought: he must test and calculate very circumspectly the preparation of the nation for the next move in the progress of politics. . . . The ear of the leader must ring with the voices of the people. He cannot be of the school of prophets; he must be of the number of those who studiously serve the slow-paced daily need.

The successful school administrator needs this ability. He needs to have that insight into people, their problems, and their thinking, so that he can make decisions that will truly be in accord with the public interest and with the faculty.

The other aspect of the recognizer category deals with seeing the potentialities in others. The public schools have done too little with this concept. How many superintendents are on the lookout for top-notch administrative possibilities in their faculties? How many choose those with executive talents, give them special tasks to develop their capacities so that they may become good administrators? The answer is not too many.

The late Harry Linton devised a plan for the development of school administrators in the public schools of Schenectady, N. Y. The plan may be described as follows:

One city school system has worked out a procedure for discovering and developing administrative talent. When a principal feels that a person in his school is of sufficient leadership caliber he reports this fact to the central office. This person is then relieved of part of his teaching load and is given some administrative tasks to perform. He may be assigned to the principal's office for a few hours to handle such routine duties as attendance or textbooks or he may be assigned to the central office or he may be given a special assignment elsewhere in the system. While doing this work he is requested to start his graduate studies in school administration (if he has not done this already). If his work is satisfactory, he is usually given a temporary assignment in a full-time administrative position. During this time he sits in on central staff and administrative and supervisory staff meetings, many of which are training courses in leadership, group dynamics, and technical subjects. Successful completion of this temporary assignment usually is followed by a permanent assignment. The advantages are clear in that the embryo administrator is observed to be a leadership prospect, is given temporary assignments where his work can be closely supervised, training can be given where needed, and the administrator can be appointed with very little risk as to his future effectiveness.

The School Administrator As a Helper

The *helper* cluster categorizes the administrator as follows:

1. He is solicitous concerning his new teachers.
2. He is always ready to help others solve their problems.

This indicates that teachers see the successful school superintendent as a person who stands ready to help them both professionally and personally.

Sternloff identified two kinds of administrative behavior under the heading of helper: [33]

8. Shows a sincere interest in the welfare of school personnel.
18. Safeguards the health of school personnel and provides for their personal safety.

Hopper and Bills get at this concept of the school administrator as a helper when they say: [34]

Successful administrators continue to create permissive, accepting, understanding, threat-free environments in which people can grow. They continue to make available material and services which the community and the professional staff believe to be important.

Jenkins considers this helping relationship from the standpoint of the faculty by raising the question: When people are really helpful to us, what do they do? His answer indicates that the good helper acted on a set of principles: [35]

1. He made it clear to us that he was not "taking over" the problem. It was still our problem—we had the responsibility for it, and we had to do our own thinking about it. Maybe we resented a little his not giving us an immediate solution, but *he helped us to see that he couldn't solve our problem for us.*
2. He indicated in many ways that we were neither "stupid" or "unusual" because we had a problem. We didn't feel branded as failures. *He accepted our problem as a matter of course.*
3. He helped us see the values of working on the problem. He pointed out that it would be very much worth our while to seek the best answer to the problem, and *he made us feel encouraged about it.*
4. He seemed to be aware of some reasons why we were having the difficulty, but he didn't tell us what was "wrong" with us. *He helped us to find a positive approach to the problem and to discover our own confusion in thinking.*
5. He asked us valuable questions about the nature of the problem, why it occurred, and what symptoms of it were evident. *He helped us to see the need for diagnosing the problem* before thinking about solutions to it.
6. As we talked further *he helped us to set up some criteria for testing our ideas about solutions.* We found it much easier to determine which ideas were likely to be fruitful.

The successful school superintendent realizes that helping another person is a complex sort of activity. He knows that "helping" and "imposing" are *not* synonymous. He realizes that by helping in the sense that Jenkins describes above, he can improve the way in which the school functions in the community.

[33] Savage and Beems, *loc. cit.*
[34] *Loc. cit.*, p. 95.
[35] David H. Jenkins, "The Helping Relationship in Education," *University of Michigan School of Education Bulletin,* Vol. 22, No. 5 (February, 1951), pp. 65-66.

We noted in the chapter on morale, that lack of orientation of first-year teachers contributed to low morale. Ovsiew indicated that superintendents in the metropolitan New York area were exercising leadership in establishing an orientation program in their systems. He found the three following practices being used: [36]

The Workshop

A special two- or three-day induction program for new teachers is held before the opening of school. These meetings feature lunches, teas, dinners, tours of the community, all at the expense of the board. Orientation programs are scheduled in curriculum, resources, and special services, rules of the system, and for the introduction of new teachers to all of the administrative staff and board of education members. Some time is allowed for special individual meetings with the superintendent and for the principal.

The Welcoming Committee

A local teachers association subcommittee makes special plans for welcoming new teachers, socially and professionally. This committee helps teachers find living quarters, provides a "buddy" or special teacher counselor, presents new teachers with a handbook or portfolio which tells a great deal about the school and the community and provides sample forms used in the schools as well as a public library card, a timetable, and a list of community organizations.

Social Affairs

"Breaking bread" is always an excellent way to make a friendly start:
   a. The PTA gives a supper at which the new teachers are guests of honor. Also, a series of teas is given by the "class mothers" of each new teacher's class.
   b. The superintendent and his wife are hosts at an informal picnic for new teachers which members of the board also attend.
   c. The PTA and several community organizations combine to sponsor a dinner party for new teachers. After the dinner an informal social to which citizens are invited serves to help new teachers meet the people they will need to know.
   d. The board of education is the host at an informal party for new teachers.

Administrative behavior of this sort is not unusual, and the number of workshops and other ways of orienting new teachers is on the increase. As yet there is no study which indicates the number of these practices. In all probability this concern for the beginning teacher is another product of the teacher shortage. For that matter, the teacher shortage is one of the causes of the emphasis on human relations in the field of education.

The School Administrator As an Effective Speaker

There is general agreement in the literature on this behavior. The successful school administrator is apparently one who can speak effectively in public. In Griffiths' study this item was the second most significant difference found between successful and unsuccessful superintendents. It

[36] Ovsiew, *op. cit.*, pp. 57-58.

is, at least in part, through the medium of public speaking that the school administrator interprets the schools to the public. As he speaks to the organized groups in the community, he pictures for them what the schools are, what they are doing, where they are going, and what they need. If he cannot do this in a clear and lucid manner, public opinion of the schools will be unfavorable. We recently discussed this matter with a political leader of a medium-sized city. The city had just recently had a new superintendent. In asking for his reaction, this political leader said: "Well, I don't know too much about him, but I have heard him speak at several of the service clubs. He does a good job of speaking and I think our schools are in good hands now."

It is surprising how little attention has been paid to the administrator's ability to give a good talk. Our graduate schools have not been concerned at all with this extremely important aspect of administrative behavior. Considering the fact that it is relatively easy to learn how to give a good speech, it is unfortunate that more emphasis is not given to this point. We cannot recommend too strongly to administrators and prospective administrators that they make every effort possible to improve their speech. We also recommend to the graduate schools that they make use of the speech clinics in their institutions.

The School Administrator As a Co-ordinator

This is another type of behavior on which there is very general agreement. In fact, there is no disagreement whatsoever. We need, however, to spell out this kind of behavior, since there is more implied than the co-ordination of others. As Davies and Herrold point out under this heading, the administrator can be more effective if he knows himself: [37]

He should know the areas in which he is strong, weak, or average. . . . He should know his own mannerisms, prejudices, and attitudes which are likely to please or irritate others, and he should distinguish what kinds of people are susceptible to each. He should know his own needs, so far as they are conscious, and his own motivations. He should be able to allow for his own changing physical states and emotional levels. Knowing these things will give him more rational control over his own behavior and enable him to predict the reactions of himself and others.

Others have referred to this very necessary aspect of administrative behavior as insight into oneself. Perhaps the old saying that one must know himself before he can know others is very true.

The second aspect of the school administrator as a co-ordinator is concerned with the co-ordination of all of the human resources in the school

[37] Daniel R. Davies and Kenneth F. Herrold, *Leadership in Action* (New London, Conn., Arthur C. Croft, 1954), p. 43.

and community so that both may improve. Sternloff found that effective co-ordination meant that the administrator: [38]

5. Encourages all persons who will be affected to participate in policy development and stimulates co-operative planning.
27. Utilizes parents and co-operates with them to solve pupil problems satisfactorily.

In discussing the top executive, Wald and Doty conclude: [39]

He is interested in people—particularly in selling them on the idea of funda-mental co-operation. He is interested in the written and spoken word as a means of communicating his ideas. He is not preoccupied with the technical phases of his work, but rather with promoting harmonious human relations.

The behavior of the successful administrator is such that he encourages co-operation on the part of all concerned. He co-ordinates their efforts so that each will be able to contribute to the purposes and functions of the organization. This means that, on occasion, he is a good follower. He allows and encourages others to lead when they can do a better job of it than he can.

Although acting as a co-ordinator, the school administrator does not need to keep his finger in everything and his thumb on everything. The administrator co-ordinates through a process of "loose" supervision in that although he knows what is going on, he does not constantly impose his will on those around him.

The School Administrator As a Social Man

This type of behavior categorizes those acts which are the *sine qua non* of the school administrator. This category Griffiths found to include such descriptive statements as:

1. He is very dependable. (Does not go back on his word.)
2. He is consistent in his disposition. (Does not fly off the handle.)
3. He is courteous and friendly.

Griffiths found no significant difference between successful and unsuc-cessful administrators on these three items. In addition, teachers rated their superintendents uniformly high in these behaviors. This should be interpreted to mean that this was common behavior on the part of the administrators studied. This type of behavior on the part of a responsible administrator undergirds all of his behavior. If he has all of the other attributes of a good administrator and cannot be trusted, then all of his desirable behavior is of no avail.

[38] Savage and Beems, *loc. cit.*
[39] Robert M. Wald and Roy A. Doty, "The Top Executive—A Firsthand Profile," *Harvard Business Review,* Vol. 32, No. 4 (July-August, 1954), p. 53.

SUMMARY

In this chapter we discussed the formal leadership of American public schools. There is much confusion existing in the discussions of leadership, primarily because of the failure to distinguish between formal and informal leadership. We discussed the difficulties which exist for the practice of democratic leadership in the formal structure of the public schools. We faced the problem that is central to the leadership of the public schools, namely, to make leadership and the exercise of authority function according to the accepted values and beliefs of our society.

In attempting to define leadership in a formal organization, we noted the difference between *headship* and *leadership*. Since all administrators in formal organizations are basically headships, we must acknowledge this and work with the concept. We arrived at a definition of democratic leadership through a composite of other definitions.

With this definition of democratic leadership established, we discussed the kind of behavior which successful administrators exhibit in the performance of their duties. The school administrator was discussed as an initiator, an improver, a recognizer, a helper, an effective public speaker, a co-ordinator, and as a social man. It should not be construed from this list of characteristic behaviors that there are no other effective behaviors or that every successful school administrator behaves in these ways all of the time. This list averages out individual differences and contains those behaviors which have been reported by several observers of many administrators.

EXERCISES

1. What is the major difference between formal and informal leaders in terms of influencing the behavior of others?

2. Illustrate by reference to school situations the difference between a superintendent who fills a headship position and one who is a functional leader of the school system.

3. How would you resolve the problem which Jim Hall faces in the case of Edmund Watts?

4. Think through your past few days as an administrator. How many of your activities can you categorize under each of the behaviors listed in the summary.

5. Work out a simple device which you can use to check the effectiveness of your leadership.

6. Do you attempt to lead the board of education in the same way that you attempt to lead your faculty? If not, why not? Does this suggest anything for a theory of leadership?

7. What are some of the dilemmas of democratic leadership?

8. "Democratic leadership consists of a number of skills that can be learned." Evaluate this statement.

9. What is "the human relations approach" to school administration?

10. Think of the best educational leader you know or have ever met. Write a statement describing why you think he is the best leader.

SELECTED BIBLIOGRAPHY

ARGYRIS, Chris, *Executive Leadership* (New York, Harper, 1953).

CAMPBELL, Clyde, ed., *Practical Applications of Democratic Administration* (New York, Harper, 1952).

DAVIES, Daniel R., and HERROLD, Kenneth F., *Leadership and Morale* (New London, Conn., Arthur C. Croft, 1955).

————, *Leadership in Action* (New London, Conn., Arthur C. Croft, 1954).

DUBIN, Robert, ed., *Human Relations in Administration* (New York, Prentice-Hall, 1951), pp. 229-253.

GIBB, Cecil A., "The Principles and Traits of Leadership," *Journal of Abnormal and Social Psychology,* Vol. 42 (July, 1947), pp. 267-284.

GOULDNER, Alvin W., ed., *Studies in Leadership* (New York, Harper, 1950).

GUILFORD, Joan S., "Temperament Traits of Executives and Supervisors Measured by the Guilford Personality Inventories," *Journal of Applied Psychology,* Vol. 36, No. 4 (August, 1952), pp. 228-233.

HOPPER, Robert L., and BILLS, Robert E., "What's a Good Administrator Made Of?" *The School Executive* (March, 1955), pp. 93-95.

JENKINS, David H., "The Helping Relationship in Education," *University of Michigan School of Education Bulletin,* Vol. 22, No. 5 (February, 1951), pp. 65-68.

JENNINGS, Helen Hall, *Leadership and Isolation,* 2d ed. (New York, Longmans, Green, 1950).

JOHNS, Ray, *Executive Responsibility* (New York, Association Press, 1954).

MACKENZIE, Gordon N., COREY, Stephen M., and others, *Instructional Leadership* (New York, Teachers College Bureau of Publications, 1954).

MORRIS, Richard T., and SEEMAN, Melvin, "The Problem of Leadership: An Interdisciplinary Approach," *American Journal of Sociology,* Vol. 56, No. 2 (1950), pp. 149-155.

PASSOW, A. Harry, "Conception of Educational Leadership," *Teachers College Record,* Vol. 54, No. 6 (March, 1953), pp. 324-331.

SAVAGE, William W., and BEEM, Harlan D., "The Effective Administrator," *Administrator's Notebook,* Midwest Administration Center, University of Chicago, Vol. 2, No. 2 (October, 1953).

SHARTLE, Carroll L., "Studies of Leadership by Interdisciplinary Methods," in *Leadership in American Education,* ed. Alonzo G. Grace (Chicago, University of Chicago Press, 1950).

STOGDILL, Ralph M., "Personal Factors Associated with Leadership: A Survey of the Literature," *Journal of Psychology,* Vol. 25 (1948), pp. 35-71.

URIS, Auren, *How To Be a Successful Leader* (New York, McGraw-Hill, 1953).

WALD, Robert M., and DOTY, Roy A., "The Top Executive—A Firsthand Profile," *Harvard Business Review,* Vol. 32, No. 4 (July-August, 1954), pp. 45-54.

PART TWO

Some Problem Areas

CHAPTER **12**

The Faculty Meeting

Someone has characterized education as "doing better those things we always do." Without discussing the merits of the particular educational philosophy, we can subscribe to it in reference to one aspect of the school administrator's responsibilities. This has to do with what are generically called faculty meetings. We will use the term broadly to include staff meetings, teachers' meetings, departmental meetings, and the like.

Faculty meetings need to be improved. The literature on the subject is characterized by this conclusion, and the author's experience and talks with both teachers and administrators further support it. The question of improving faculty meetings, then, is the one that we propose to answer in this chapter. In order to do so, however, we must first recognize the weaknesses that prevail.

WEAKNESSES IN FACULTY MEETINGS

Although available research on faculty meetings is limited, that which we do have is extremely helpful. A survey by Cook and Full reveals many of the things which teachers find to be wrong. The study established five standards for faculty meetings and questioned the teaching staffs of 240 schools concerning their achievement of these standards. The standards, together with the shortcomings reported by the teachers, are as follows, and it might be worthwhile for us to check our own meetings against this list: [1]

1. Faculty meetings must be concerned with teachers' professional needs and must be focused on educational problems growing out of the immediate school environment.

Slightly more than three quarters of the 240 schools reported that teachers were allowed *no* say in what problems would be studied. Only 14 per cent of the schools indicated that this criterion was met. This might be considered the prime reason for poor faculty meetings—the teachers are not meeting to work out *their own problems.*

2. Faculty meetings must be concerned with problems having broad educational import.

[1] K. A. Cook and Harold Full, "Is the School Faculty Meeting Significant in Promoting Professional Growth?" *School Review,* Vol. 56 (November, 1948), pp. 519–524.

Less than 8 per cent of the schools reported that their meetings were concerned with significant educational problems. We noted in our work on motivation that a person must consider that his work is significant or he will lose his self-respect. The way to begin to improve faculty meetings is to make certain that the problems discussed are considered significant by the *faculty*. They may appear piddling to the administrator, but that is not important. He should start where the faculty is, and the meetings should be based upon *its* problems. Then from this base, the faculty can move forward to a study of more significant problems.

3. Faculty meetings must be well planned, and teachers should participate in the planning.

The returns on this standard are as alarming as the preceding ones. Teachers reported that it was customary in one fifth of the schools for them to be notified of meetings *the day they were to be held.* In 43 per cent of the schools, teachers were notified a day ahead of time.

As to actual planning, only 10 per cent of the schools reported using cooperative planning; in 58 per cent of the schools, the principal did all of the planning. They also reported that in 65 per cent of the meetings, the principal presided and directed the discussion.

4. Teachers must prepare for faculty meetings.

Relative to this criterion, 63 per cent of the teachers reported spending less than thirty minutes preparing for faculty meetings, and more than half of them spent *no time at all.*

5. Informal participation should characterize the discussion in faculty meetings.

This was the one criterion which seemed most generally achieved. Sixty-one per cent of the schools indicated that the informal discussion method was used. However, favorable as this is, it is offset by that fact that one fifth of the schools reported little participation on the part of teachers.

In summary, Cook and Full found that teachers lacked a say in what problems would be discussed in faculty meetings; that it was extremely rare to have a problem of educational significance to teachers discussed; that teachers received little or no notice of meetings to be held; and that they had little part in the planning or leading of faculty meetings. From these data it must be concluded that the tremendous constructive potential inherent in faculty meetings is not being tapped at present. The statement by Heywood summarizes a rather generally held position regarding faculty meetings: [2]

Textbooks in educational administration stress the value of meetings of teachers and administrators; but teachers often express the opinion that faculty meetings are of little value either in self-improvement or in school improvement. Many teachers resent being asked to attend meetings at all.

Since faculty meetings are undoubtedly a great resource for the improvement of instruction, let us investigate some of the ways in which faculty meetings can be improved.

[2] Stanley J. Heywood, "What's Wrong with Faculty Meetings?" *Administrator's Notebook*, Midwest Administration Center, University of Chicago, Vol. 1, No. 5 (December, 1952).

PREPARATION FOR FACULTY MEETINGS

We note, from the Cook and Full study, that the preparation for faculty meetings is one of the weakest areas. Evidence of this was presented from both the point of view of the administrator and that of the teachers. Administrators did not have clearly in mind the purposes of the meetings, did not announce the meetings in advance, and did not plan the process of the meetings. On the other hand, no doubt as a result of poor administrator planning, teachers devoted practically no time to preparation for their role in faculty meetings. In discussing how to prepare for a faculty meeting, our preliminary concern is to determine *why* a meeting is to be held and *what* that meeting is to cover.

Why Meetings Are Held

There is, of course, always the question of whether or not there should be a meeting, to which Davies and Herrold provide the following succinct answer. They state there should *not* be a faculty meeting: [3]

Unless a meeting of a group is the best way to satisfy a need, solve a problem, or meet a situation.

Unless there is time to plan and prepare for a productive meeting.

Unless appropriate time and place can be arranged.

Unless a time can be set when members can be reasonably free from tensions, pressures, and conflicting demands.

Unless the group members can be and have been properly briefed in advance for the work of the meeting.

Unless the problem and the related evidence can be communicated to the members with enough time left for adequate discussion.

Unless those who are involved in the consequences of the meeting can be present and share in making the decisions.

There should be a meeting:

If a group has common problems and concerns that a meeting can deal with.

If group members are going to be involved in the consequences of the decisions which have to be made.

If group morale and communication are slipping.

If the group wants to meet.

These criteria not only answer the question; they establish a set of human relations concepts that are guidelines to all aspects of the faculty meeting as well as to personal relations of the administrator with his staff. If an administrator respects the members of his faculty as human beings, he will not be cavalier in his scheduling of faculty meetings. The number

[3] Daniel R. Davies and Kenneth F. Herrold, *Make Your Staff Meetings Count!* (New London, Conn., Arthur C. Croft, 1954), pp. 27-28.

of man-hours per week lost in useless and poorly planned faculty meetings is staggering.

Although the above list includes some of the reasons for holding meetings, other literature on the subject offers more specific purposes with which we should familiarize ourselves.

Specific Purposes of Faculty Meetings

To facilitate our discussion we can say, somewhat arbitrarily, that the purposes of faculty meetings fall under three headings:

1. Orientation.
2. In-service growth.
3. Administrative.

Orientation meetings would cover those that serve to introduce the new teachers to the system, the building, or the department. Good practice seems to indicate that they should be conducted as a series extending well into the school year.[4] In-service growth can be achieved through skillfully planned and carefully executed staff meetings. Good faculty meetings probably do more than any other medium to improve education in a school system. Administrative meetings are for the purpose of carrying on the business of the school. There are better ways of making announcements, but they may be made at a meeting. Opinions can be obtained for making policy, and teachers can participate in decision-making on school problems.

Orientation Meetings. Faculty meetings should always be held at the beginning of each school year to "get off on the right foot." This is the time for teachers to renew their friendships of past years; the time for veteran teachers to meet new teachers; for new teachers to learn the "ropes," the school regulations, by-laws, and directives; for building a concept of team play. Many schools now schedule these meetings for several days prior to the opening of school. It is obvious from the purposes cited that the meeting must be longer than the traditional one-hour meeting prior to the beginning of classes. A trend toward teacher workshops of from three to five days' duration before the opening of school has been observed in leading school systems. Such meetings make available the time, at least, to accomplish these purposes.

Many schools have meetings for new teachers scheduled from September through December, which have proved to be quite valuable.[5] Each

---

[4] Daniel E. Griffiths, "An Evaluation of the Leadership of the School Superintendent" (Unpublished Ph.D. dissertation, Yale University, 1952). A digest of this study was published by the CPEA-MAR Center of Teachers College, Columbia University.

[5] For descriptions of these practices, see *The New Teacher* (New York, Metropolitan School Study Council, 1950), and W. J. B. Truitt, "Orienting New Teachers," *The School Executive*, Vol. 73, No. 12 (August, 1954), pp. 58-59.

meeting has as its purpose the presentation of a different part of school life. At one meeting, the dental hygienist tells of her work; at another meeting the curriculum co-ordinator will discuss curricular policy; and so on.

Meetings for In-service Growth. A basic purpose of faculty meetings is the improvement of the teaching staff. A well-planned series of faculty meetings can do much to further this objective. The detailed case study at the end of this chapter tells the story of how one school system planned and executed a series of faculty meetings in which they tackled a vital problem. In the process of seeking the solution, the whole staff was up-graded.

Another school system held a series of faculty meetings planned as a "round-robin" set of demonstration teaching situations. The teachers in one department would teach demonstration classes and be observed by the other teachers in the school. After the pupils had been dismissed, the host teacher would discuss his aims, purposes, and classroom techniques. This would be followed by a general discussion. The benefits claimed for this procedure are that the teachers could [6]

1. Borrow techniques from one another.
2. Understand the real situation of the class and be more apt to criticize one another without bias.
3. Break down tensions and secrecy.

Another series of meetings pointed directly at the improvement of one particular skill was instituted by the school faculty which set out to learn how to teach creative writing more effectively. Twenty-four meetings were held with an observable improvement in the creative writing of the students.[7]

The small high school faculty which used its meetings to gain competence in guidance illustrates another specific purpose. This faculty held case conferences and used role-playing as a technique to broaden its understanding of pupil problems and behavior.[8]

These have been a few examples of how faculties have used their meetings as ways of improving themselves. Later we shall consider how to plan and carry out faculty meetings so that the purposes of in-service growth can be accomplished.

Administrative Meetings. There are many meetings and portions of meetings each year which are devoted to the business of running the school. In some schools the problems related to running the school are

[6] Rebecca Hellerstein, "Eye-opener Faculty Meetings," *Clearing House,* Vol. 22 (November, 1947), p. 154.

[7] Ona Belle Demaree, "Faculty Meetings Can Be Productive," *National Elementary Principals Journal,* Vol. 32 (September, 1952), pp. 67-73.

[8] Glyn Morris, "The Faculty Meeting As a Guidance Resource in Small Rural Schools," *Education,* Vol. 74 (April, 1954), pp. 501-506.

handled exclusively by the superintendent. For the sake of convenience, we have termed this kind of school administration, *autocratic*. We have established, to a degree, the concept that morale and production would be higher if the staff were allowed to participate in arriving at decisions on matters which affect them. To many people this is so fundamental that they need no proof; but research evidence demonstrates that the democratic way is a reasonable basis on which to operate.

Yauch points out the kind of administrative responsibilities in which teachers can reasonably be expected to have a voice: [9]

Examples of specific administrative responsibilities which teachers may determine are such matters as the behavior of children at times when they are not directly under the supervision of a single teacher. What shall the teachers do with children on rainy days; what shall be their method of controlling conduct on the playground at noontime; what doors shall they use in entering and leaving the building? These are questions that can best be answered by the staff in conference. Then, too, there is the matter of class schedules for the use of special rooms and equipment. During the winter months the gymnasium must be scheduled in such a way that all teachers have an equitable amount of time for its use; the motion-picture projector must be scheduled so that all teachers may have a maximum amount of time for it. Textbooks need to be distributed so that teachers will have the books when they need them. All these practical matters are ones on which it has been found profitable to invite teacher planning and participation.

It may be necessary to structure the meeting so that the group can be "forced" to come to a decision on the matter at hand. This does not mean that the meeting is "rigged" and that the faculty will come up with the administrator's answer. Rather, it means that the faculty meeting be so structured as to require the group to make its own decision. At present, many meetings are so set up that it is impossible to come to any decision at all; the group wastes time and fails to agree. Ways of improving these meetings will be discussed. Perhaps Robert's *Rules of Order* should be applied, or a plan such as the one outlined below should be used.

It should be noted that there are certain instances which do not fall precisely under one of the categories we have specified but involve all three. The participation of the faculty in the making of school policy is one of these. There is, first, an orientation to the problem concerning which policy is to be made; then a period of self-education, during which time the faculty learns as much as it can about all phases of the problem; and, finally, there is the administrative matter of recommending a specific policy. In such cases, the administrative meeting serves as the capstone for a series of meetings, during which a policy has been hammered out.

[9] Wilbur A. Yauch, *Improving Human Relations in School Administration* (New York, Harper, 1949), p. 75.

FACULTY PARTICIPATION IN PLANNING

Two of the five criteria set by Cook and Full concerned preparation:

1. Faculty meetings must be well planned, and teachers should participate in the planning.
2. Teachers must prepare for faculty meetings.

Their findings indicated that planning and preparation were two things commonly lacking in the usual faculty meeting.

There is no good reason for having a faculty meeting if adequate preparation is not made. There is no conceivable excuse for the multitude of wasted hours spent by frustrated faculties all over the country. If looked at in terms of wasted money, the loss is awesome. For instance, in the average New York State public school with a faculty of thirty which holds ten two-hour meetings per year the loss in teacher-days of pay is $2500. Multiply this by the thousands of schools of this size in the country and the loss becomes astronomical.

Although the particular kind of planning to be done for a meeting depends on the type of faculty meeting to be held (orientation, in-service growth, or administrative), there are several planning steps common to all. These steps are general in nature and can be expanded, depending on the content of the meeting:

1. The faculty should participate in an active fashion in the planning of each faculty meeting.[10]

The evidence, in the form of testimonials from the educational literature, indicates that in the experience of most school administrators, interest and achievement has improved when the faculty helps to plan meetings.

2. Faculty members who do the planning should be chosen by the faculty.

This eliminates one source of insecurity on the part of the staff. Planning of faculty meetings might be the special job of a faculty council or the job of a special committee. In either case, the faculty should choose the people who will plan the meeting for them. It is reasonable, but not imperative, that the membership of this planning group be changed in a relatively frequent and orderly manner. Members should stay on the committee long enough to gain competence and to give meetings a needed continuity. There is no hard and fast rule, but members should not serve

[10] This point of view is best expressed in F. L. Pond, "How Can Faculty Meetings Become More Effective Professional Experiences?" *National Association of Secondary School Principals Bulletin,* Vol. 36 (March, 1952), pp. 216-225.

so long that they feel they are being imposed upon or so long that the faculty feels it is being by-passed.

    3. Planning should take place around the problems of the faculty.

Whatever the purpose of the meeting, the problems discussed *must* be the problems which the staff recognizes and accepts. It maybe that the problems will seem trivial to the administrator; but unless he does start with the problems of the staff, the staff will never get to the bigger over-all problems. An example of this is found in the case which follows this chapter. Here, a faculty recognized that several things needed study: Why did Johnny get promoted to the third grade? What do I do in a parent-teacher interview? Why can't we have a different report card? The supervising principal wanted a promotion policy for the whole system, but it was necessary for the individual problems of the teachers to be discussed first so that the staff could see how all of these things fitted together.

    4. The planning committee should prepare an agendum for each meeting which should be distributed to all staff members at least two days before the meeting.

This is one of the most neglected aspects of the planning for faculty meetings. Teachers arrive at meetings wondering why it has been called, what they will be required to do, and the like. They are *cold*, from all points of view, to the whole proceeding. The agendum should contain the items to be taken up, if it is an administrative meeting, with a brief explanation of each item. If it is an orientation or in-service meeting, the agendum should be more comprehensive and should be distributed to the teachers much earlier. It should contain the items to be discussed, but, in addition, it should have resource materials to be read and studied so that the faculty members are prepared to discuss the topic in an informed manner. It should be pointed out that the agendum should not be presented as a completed fact. The first order of business should be the revision of the agendum so that the faculty members can add, delete, or change the order of business. The teachers will not make radical changes in the agendum, but the knowledge that they can change it if they wish will make them feel more secure.

    5. Provide resources for the faculty meeting.

The planning committee has as its responsibility the marshaling of all resources possible for the successful completion of the meeting. They should provide, for example, appropriate charts, graphs, films, slides, periodicals, and consultants.

    6. Provide for a written record of the meeting.

In order to preserve the work that is accomplished at each meeting, a record should be kept. It is not necessary to make a running record, but it is imperative that the material which will help the group to solve its problems be recorded. In administrative meetings, the motions and votes, as well as the issues of the discussion should be recorded in writing. All such records should be abstracted and sent to each faculty member shortly after the meeting and certainly prior to the next meeting.

The Time Element

There is still a considerable amount of controversy about the time element in faculty meetings. There are those who say that a faculty meeting can be held at practically any time: before school; during school hours, with students monitoring the classrooms; during lunch hour, after school, at dinnertime, and after dinner—in fact, any old time.[11] Others, in discussing how long the meetings should be, give figures ranging from forty minutes to two hours, with most indicating an hour as optimum. There is also some indication that meetings should be held frequently; but then others say they should be well spaced to avoid "meeting fatigue."

In the face of all this conflicting opinion, it must first be stated that there is little or no research in the area of the time element; that is to say, no controlled research. Although administrators have tried various time arrangements and have hit upon some which seem to be more workable than others, it is extremely difficult to make valid generalizations. Those made in this book are based upon research in group dynamics and a survey of the literature that does exist.

First of all, if the meeting is actually one at which work is to be done and the staff is to reach a decision, it must be scheduled for more than an hour. Studies in this area indicates that rarely does a group get much done in less than an hour.[12] If the staff actually is participating in the meeting, two hours is not too long. Elsbree and Reutter recommend two hours as the optimum time for meetings, and this is in agreement with both experience and recent literature.[13] The group has time to have refreshments, socialize, warm up, go to work, and come to grips with the problem. The emphasis here is on group *participation*. If the faculty is expected to just sit and listen to something in which it is not interested, then any time is too long. Two hours is an optimum time for a well-planned meeting in

[11] Yauch, *op. cit.*, pp. 67-70.
[12] Davies and Herrold, *op. cit.*, p. 28; M. W. Barnes, "How to Have a Good Faculty Meeting: Suggestions and Reactions by Teachers and Principals," *National Education Association Journal*, Vol. 42 (January, 1953), pp. 39-41.
[13] Willard S. Elsbree and E. Edmund Reutter, Jr., *Staff Personnel in the Public Schools* (New York, Prentice-Hall, 1954), p. 228.

which the faculty participates in solving a problem that it recognizes as its own.

There is but one time for a two-hour faculty meeting, and that is after school. There is a growing practice to dismiss school early on the day of a faculty meeting so that teachers do not have to work two hours or more beyond their regular work day. This practice of early dismissal varies: some schools dismiss an hour early and have the teachers give up an hour of their time; [14] other schools dismiss classes for half a day and hold the meeting entirely on school time. The latter practice is common in the central schools of New York State. Here six half-day supervisory meetings per year are mandated by law, and the district superintendents schedule faculty meetings for in-service training on these half days. When the half day is available, meetings longer than two hours can be planned safely.

Another important time element is frequency of meetings. If the school year is proceeding without unusual incidents, one general meeting a month will suffice, with department and committee meetings interspersed.[15] The objection is sometimes raised, Why hold a meeting a month if there is nothing to discuss? The point is that in an alert school there are always problems. There is never enough time to discuss them all fully. One well-planned faculty meeting a month should never be too many. If the school is in the throes of rapid change, the faculty will need the security of even more meetings than this.[16] These meetings should be informative and should help the staff to face up to the changes and to plan together.

It should go without saying that the meetings should start on time and end on time. Very frequent meetings should not be scheduled without good cause, such as rapid change in the school, community difficulty, and the like. Meetings should not be scheduled close to holidays or on Friday afternoons. Keep emergency meetings (those called on short notice) to an absolute minimum.

The Meeting Place

"Good staff meetings occur only in a favorable climate." [17] The place in which a meeting is held does not create the favorable climate so necessary to a good meeting, but it is certainly a contributing factor. Lack of a suitable meeting place can spoil much of the good climate that exists. To this extent it is a limiting factor.

[14] W. R. Cleminson, "How Can Faculty Meetings Be Made Professional?" *National Association of Secondary School Principals Bulletin*, Vol. 36 (April, 1952), pp. 37-44.
[15] *Ibid.*
[16] Alex Bavelas, "Some Problems of Organizational Change," *Journal of Social Issues*, Vol. 4, No. 3 (Summer, 1948), pp. 48-52.
[17] Barnes, *op. cit.*, p. 39.

There seems to be general agreement on the matter of a meeting place. The room should be large enough to hold all of the participants comfortably but not so large that the group is lost. If at all possible, the staff members should sit around tables so that they might see each other and also be able to use whatever pertinent materials are supplied them. This sitting around together increases the group sense of working together; it helps dispel the feeling of isolation which arises when people sit so that they cannot all see each other. Rooms with furniture fastened to the floor should be avoided if possible. In addition to pleasant surroundings, the room should be equipped with a chalkboard and all that goes with it. It is also a good idea to have available a bulletin board, a projector and screen, and other such visual aids. Remember, a faculty meeting room is a workroom. It should be equipped so that the faculty can work out its problems together.

Organization of the Faculty Meeting

Although, in general, the organization of the faculty meeting will depend on the purpose of the meeting, there are some generalizations which can be made. There are a great many ways of organizing a meeting, all of which call for preparation. The planning committee must select the techniques best suited to achieve the purpose of the meeting. In making this selection, however, there are certain procedural considerations the committee should bear in mind. In all cases where the faculty is expected to reach a decision or consensus, either in a business or an in-service training meeting, it will be necessary to:

1. Communicate the problem.
2. Allow for clarification.
3. Allow for discussion.
4. Make provision for consensus.

The structure of the meeting should be planned to provide the *best* way by which the above steps can be accomplished. The meeting can use any number of techniques or procedures, such as:

1. A speech.
2. A panel.
3. A demonstration.
4. Role-playing.
5. A film, filmstrip, or other audiovisual aid.
6. Some one of the above with a consultant.

The practice most recommended is to have the faculty meet together as a body, then to break up the total group into smaller units no larger than from twelve to fifteen members, and then to bring the whole group together again for a final session. Diagrammatically, the faculty meeting would look like this:

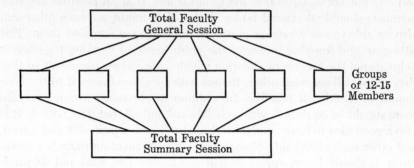

This sort of arrangement has several advantages:

1. It provides for unity in that presentation and consensus are arrived at by the entire group.
2. It provides an opportunity for *every* person to be an active, verbal participant. It is very rare for a person to attend a meeting of this sort and not talk.
3. The "moving around" has value in itself in that individuals get "stirred up" and revitalized by moving. More people are in informal situations, i.e., moving to a room for a small meeting or rearranging chairs for buzz sessions.
4. Meetings which use this technique can be scheduled for longer periods of time since individuals do not get bored when they move around and when they are made responsible for the success of the meeting as they are in the smaller meetings.

The Role of the Administrator

The educational literature concurs in its opinion that ideally the school administrator should assume the role of a *resource* person in the faculty meeting, providing the group with as much information as may be needed to help it reach a decision. It also agrees that teachers should chair the meetings and act as discussion leaders. Wiles offers some very sensible advice on this score when he points out that the official leader of the group may be the only person skilled in group discussion techniques and so qualified to assume the leadership role.[18] Wiles also points out that it is the responsibility of the official leader to develop discussion skills among the teachers so that they become effective leaders. Modern leadership theory also emphasizes the fact that the individual who will actually lead a group is the one who is best qualified. Therefore, the school administrator should select for discussion leaders those who are best qualified;

[18] Kimball Wiles, *Supervision for Better Schools,* 2d. ed. (New York, Prentice-Hall, 1955), p. 157.

otherwise, he may find the meeting being led from the floor! However, if he himself is best qualified to lead the meeting, he should do so.

The Consultant

More and more school systems are making use of consultants to work with faculties. This is basically a very sound practice and reflects a sincere desire for the most expert of advice in seeking a solution to the problem at hand. Several suggestions can be made which will help the consultant to do a better job and the school system to get the most benefit from the consultant. Savage makes nine suggestions for more effective use of consultants.[19]

1. Be certain you and your staff are ready for a consultant's help before you seek it.
2. Seek the assistance of a consultant qualified to help you with your problem.
3. Ask for the consultant's services in advance of the time that you need them.
4. Give the consultant specific information about your situation and needs.
5. Specify the kind of help that you want the consultant to give.
6. In planning with the consultant, give him information about the activities you believe should be carried out during his visit.
7. Set aside sufficient time for the consultant's visit.
8. Evaluate the consultative services that you receive.
9. Move forward after the consultant leaves.

This is a comprehensive and precise listing of steps to be taken concerning consultants; but when they apply to faculty meetings, some of the above points need emphasis. First of all, the administrator should know the problem well enough and should make a thorough enough inquiry into the qualifications of consultants to be able to select *one* consultant to do the job. Probably the least effective method of getting a consultant is to ask the state department of education or a college for *any* consultant in a certain field. *Get the consultant who can do your particular job.* A second criterion in the case of faculty meetings is the personality of the consultant. In a faculty meeting situation, the consultant not only needs to know how to overcome a specific problem but how to bring a group to the point where it can solve the problem. In considering the personality of the consultant, it is important to keep in mind the kind of a job the consultant is expected to do. The administrator should ask himself these questions:

1. Is this to be a "one shot" meeting?
2. Is this to be a series of meetings, all using the same consultant?

[19] William W. Savage, "Making the Most of the Consultant," *Administrator's Note book*, Midwest Administration Center, University of Chicago, Vol. 1, No. 3 (October 1953).

3. Is this·to be the kick-off meeting of a year-long study in which various consultants are to be used?

These should serve as guides to the kind of consultant he seeks. Some consultants have the knack of being inspirational, others of helping teachers to produce over a long period of time. Thirdly, the consultant needs very specific instructions as to what is expected of him. This is probably the point most overlooked in dealing with consultants. *Tell him very specifically what you and your faculty expect of him.* Finally, make provisions for a follow-up visit from the consultant. No consultant will do all that is needed in one meeting.

SPECIAL PROBLEMS

There are numerous special problems which recur in the course of a series of faculty meetings. These problems concern difficulties encountered in reaching a decision in conflict situations, as well as the more usual procedural difficulties. Some suggestions can be made to help alleviate these problems.

Conflict Situations

There are in education a vast number of emotional issues. In fact, practically any issue which requires some person to change a procedure or practice is apt to be approached more on an emotional basis than on any other. When dealing with these issues in a faculty meeting, it is often impossible to get the group to come to a decision supported by a substantial majority. Many violent differences of opinion are caused by ignorance on the part of individuals or groups. An example of this is the only too common case of the secondary school teachers blaming the elementary school teachers for not teaching children to read properly. A better understanding of the elementary school program on the part of secondary teachers would minimize this criticism. Similarly, the tensions arising in a faculty meeting can be reduced if the conflicting parties can be made to understand each other's point of view.

Lee proposes a procedure which has been tried successfully in a business situation.[20] Similar methods have been used in faculty groups, but Lee's approach has a rationale based upon general semantics and is developed in greater detail than are other plans.

The plan which Lee suggests is to be put into effect when a group has reached an impasse and the conflict is marked. This situation is evident when one faction ceases to listen to the other and each faction merely

[20] Irving J. Lee, "Procedure for 'Coercing' Agreement," *Harvard Business Review* (January-February, 1954), pp. 39-45.

repeats its own position. At this point, it is up to the chairman to raise a *question of privilege for the group,* so that until further notice, all talking which expresses a difference of opinion is out of order. Any proponent of the view which caused the controversy then is allowed to state his opinion without any refutation or argument. The opposition then is permitted to raise three kinds of questions.

The first kind are called *questions for clarification.* The opposition may ask, "Did you say...?" "Do you mean...?" "What did you mean when you said...?" Note that this procedure endeavors to clarify for the listener what the speaker means. It is an attempt to forestall argument until the listener has a clear picture of what the proponent has in mind. It also tends to lessen the possibility of private interpretations being injected into the meeting. The reasoning behind this approach is derived from Korzybski's analysis of a "semantically disturbed man": [21]

When he hears something he does not like, he does not ask "what do you mean?" but, under the semantic pressure of identification, he ascribes his own meanings to the other fellow's words.... Upon hearing anything strange, his semantic reaction is underlayed and may appear as, "I disagree with you" or "I don't believe you," etc. There is no reason to be dramatic about any unwelcome statement. One needs definitions and interpretations of such statements, which probably are correct from the speaker's point of view, if we grant him his informations, his undefined terms, the structure of his language and premises which build up his semantic reactions.

We must grant that many factions in conflict fit the description of Korzybski's "semantically disturbed man." If the situation can be controlled so that individuals in the group undergo the self-discipline necessary to raise questions to *clarify* the statements of their opponents, they will be behaving in a more semantically sane manner.

Once the speaker's frame of reference has been clarified, members of the group may ask for *information concerning the uniqueness of particular characteristics of the condition or proposal* under consideration. The question which is raised is this, "In what way is this proposal different from other proposals we have heard?"

The third kind of questioning permitted involves *information concerning the means of investigating the speaker's assumptions or predictions.* What the questioner is getting at here is some way in which the speaker's inferences can be checked in a nonverbal manner. The question could very well be: "Can you tell us of any way of testing your assumptions or predictions?"

It can be seen that this procedure takes time. In fact, in one case, the presentation of one side and the questioning of it took a whole afternoon. But if the group is in *basic disagreement,* all decisions which the group

[21] Alfred Korzybski, *Science and Sanity,* 2d ed. (Lakewood, Conn., Institute of General Semantics, 1941), p. 418.

attempts to make will be affected. Time spent eliminating conflict at this stage means time saved later. Then too, once this process has been learned, it will affect the behavior of group members and they will tend to use it as a part of their ordinary approach to conflict situations.

There are other values in this approach to conflict situations which became evident to Lee as he worked with his business group. The first was the recognition by group members that they could get a hearing for their ideas. They could present an idea, have it clarified, examined, and understood before it was "jumped on" by other members. It was also noticed that individuals were more willing to give up a pet idea after being submitted to this type of questioning than they were previously. The second value concerned the reduction of tension in the group. Observation previous to the introduction of this plan led one to believe that "a motion seemed to be an invitation to combat." [22] Following introduction of the plan, it was noted that the energy used for argument now went into the questioning process. Although many question sessions were tense, they were not as tense as previously. It was observed that people were more occupied fighting problems, not people. The third value was increased co-operation on the part of the group members. This plan is in essence a guarantee against unfairness, so that one big reason for a lack of co-operation was removed.

When putting this plan into action:

1. The group should be thoroughly prepared for its use. A meeting or two should be devoted to the plan, its purpose, and its procedures.
2. The chairman should use the plan *only* for major conflicts.
3. The chairman should not compromise by permitting some arguments and refutation. These should be ruled out immediately and conclusively.
4. The chairman should be prepared to spend some time in using the plan. He should not become impatient.

Procedural Difficulties

There are several common problems that plague faculty meetings. These concern such procedures as getting the meeting underway, building the agenda, keeping things moving, and closing the meeting. Most of the difficulties arise when the planning and organization that we discussed above have been neglected. There are, however, some ways of handling these procedures during the course of the meeting so as to avoid, or at least reduce, such difficulties.

Beginning the Meeting. The common fault in beginning meetings occurs when the leader indicates that the meeting is called because "they" want it, "they" being a somewhat nebulous reference to the administration. "They want us to raise some questions"; "they want us to discuss a topic."

[22] Lee, *op. cit.*

He should, instead, refer to the needs of the people in the group and relate the purpose of the meeting to these needs. If he cannot do this, he should consider seriously the reason for holding the meeting at all. A short, provocative statement to this effect should be sufficient to get the group underway.

Building the Agendum. Although many administrators have an agendum for each faculty meeting, they usually adhere to it too rigorously. It was pointed out above that the agendum should be built by a planning committee and should be distributed to the faculty at least two days prior to the meeting. This agendum should be a *flexible* one however, and should be revised at the beginning of each meeting. The following questions should be raised: "Are the items of the agendum in the desired order?" "Are all of the important matters for discussion on the agendum?" "Do you feel the matters on the agendum should be discussed?" The group should act then to consider the revisions it desires. The method adopted might very well be parliamentary procedure, with the group voting on each change.

Keeping Things Moving. Every once in a while a faculty meeting "bogs down." The discussion comes to a halt, and it would seem that the group has gone as far as it can with the topic. At this point, the group recorder should be asked to summarize the discussion on the particular issue under discussion. This should cause the group either to see the issue more clearly and raise new questions, thereby continuing the discussion, or to move on to another topic.

Although the foregoing technique is recommended, a sensitive discussion leader should ask himself why these lapses in the discussion occur. He should seek the causes for the group's apathy. It may be that the group does not feel that this is a problem for its consideration. The teachers may feel that it falls within the realm of someone else's authority or that they can do nothing about it. In some cases, they may have been brought into a meeting to discuss a question of interest only to the principal or planning committee. There is also the possibility that the physical conditions are uncomfortable and therefore distracting. The falling off of group interest is a symptom and should be treated as such. Look for the cause!

Closing the Meeting. Many faculty meetings move along quickly to the time agreed upon for adjournment and then the leader must stop the meeting. This leaves the group wondering just what it has accomplished. The group leader needs to plan ahead so that there will be time for evaluation. In a reasonably small group this should take from five to ten minutes. A careful eye on the clock by the group leader will enable him to pace the meeting so that it comes to an orderly and planned conclusion.

EVALUATION

In order to improve faculty meetings it is necessary to evaluate constantly and to act on the results of the evaluations. Different sorts of meetings call for different sorts of evaluating procedures. In very small groups a simple, short procedure would suffice. A committee might take five minutes before adjourning to answer the question, How did we do today? Larger groups might do the same thing but, in this case, a more valid evaluation might be arrived at if a written reaction sheet were used. The written sheet has several advantages over the oral critique:

1. It is secret and people are more apt to give their real reactions.
2. It tends to be more easily handled. Answers can be tallied, and comparisons can be made.
3. It is more inclusive in two ways: everyone gives an evaluation and reacts to all phases of the meeting.

The reaction sheet should be simple, preferably one sheet in length, and contain open-ended as well as objective questions. The reaction form included in this chapter is one which has been used widely by both the New York State Teachers Association and the Capital Area School Development Association. Note that the form calls for an over-all rating on a five-point scale. This forces the participant to think in terms of the meeting as a whole. Then he is asked to consider the meeting by parts in terms of what he "liked" and "disliked" about the meeting. The participant is then asked to suggest ways of improving the meetings. This can be of great value to a school system planning a series of meetings. One will usually find the same suggestions running through the evaluation blanks. The last question, "What did you think this group was trying to do?" has an especial value. The answers to this question can furnish leads to how well the purpose of the meeting has been understood and achieved. After all, this is the most important aspect for the evaluator. The meeting has been called to realize a particular purpose, and if the group has missed this purpose, the meeting has been to little avail. In order to give every possible opportunity to each participant to express himself about the meeting, the "Other comments" item is included. One should not be surprised by what is included here!

Each time an evaluative process is used, there should be a report back to the group concerning the results. There should also be a statement concerning what has been done to implement the suggestions and criticisms. If a particular criticism cannot be met, the group should be told so frankly and honestly. If criticisms can be met, they, too, should be reported. Meeting criticism in a forthright manner will increase morale and will stimulate more valid evaluations on the part of the participants.

Finally, there is considerable value in using a group observer. This member has as his mission the job of reporting to the group on its procedure.[23] Although the observer does not comment on the content of the discussion, he does indicate what the group has been doing. He describes to the group what he has seen it do. For instance, he might observe, "You took eleven minutes to get warmed up" or "Of the twelve people in the group, four talked" or "One person talked half of the total time." These observations are not evaluations in themselves but give the group a basis on which it can evaluate itself.

AN IN-SERVICE EDUCATION PROGRAM

Dr. Dan Green was in his office at State College early in September when his phone rang. It was Jack Deming, supervising principal at the Casmier Central School. Jack had an idea, and he wanted to know if he could get some help on his proposal.

"I want to have a top-notch series of workshops this year. The Teachers Association wants to work on the pupil-promotion policy we have, and they want to improve it. We want to have credit granted by State College and also want some good consultants. We have the money and are ready to go. What do you think?"

"Fine idea. I'll draw up some tentative plans, talk with the powers here, and then come out and meet with your committee and get going."

Green got going. He sketched out a series of workshop sessions, indicating tentative topics, consultants, and organization of sessions. Although State College had not sponsored such a series of workshop sessions before, the idea was well received. It was decided that three hours' credit could be granted for a workshop of ten sessions of two-and-a-half-hours each.

Green traveled out to Casmier Central and met with the planning committee. The purpose of the series was worked over and clarified. Emphasis was to be placed on the development of an effective pupil-promotion program by relating emerging concepts of child growth to this very practical school problem. It should be pointed out that Casmier had a promotion policy which was generally understood to have been adopted by the administration. The problem, however, was that the teachers did not generally agree with the policy. In some cases, they did not know what the policy was; and in others, either they did not agree with it or they felt the community did not, so they promoted pupils on their own individual policies. This created poor morale, since each teacher was suspicious of the standards of the neighboring teacher. There was also a tremendous rift between elementary and secondary school teachers with regard to promotion policy. Within these two groups there was a difference of opinion between the primary and intermediate grades and between the junior and senior high schools.

The Casmier Central School was located in a small manufacturing town. The centralization included many small rural communities surrounding the town, so the school population of 1200 was equally divided between town and farm children. Casmier had a staff of sixty teachers, a supervising principal, high school principal, and an elementary superviser. Jack Deming was generally recognized as an educational leader in his section of the state and enjoyed excellent relations in his community. The staff was somewhat younger than the usual school staff and could be considered somewhat above average in ability.

[23] See above, pp. 172-173.

The first workshop was a problem census conducted by an outstanding consultant. He opened the workshop with a discussion of six commonly held concepts of pupil promotion. The teachers then divided into four discussion groups according to the grades they taught: primary, intermediate, junior high, and senior high. Discussion leaders and group recorders had been selected for each of four groups, and instructions had been prepared for each. The groups each raised all of the questions which they thought pertinent. After an hour of discussion, the teachers met again in general session to hear the recorders give the gist of the discussion in their groups. This was conducted as a panel with the consultant as chairman.

Following the workshop, Dr. Green classified the questions according to seven different categories: philosophical bases, psychological bases, curricular implications, evaluation of pupil growth, public relations, administration, and research.

The next workshop had as its theme the philosophical bases of pupil promotion. Following this workshop, the teachers in each group prepared statements of the philosophy that they would like to see adopted. These four statements were then worked on by the planning committee, rewritten, and submitted to the faculty for approval. This final statement served as the basis for other work.

The workshops continued using as a pattern the organization of a general session, group discussions, and then a return to the general session. There was one deviation from the pattern when one consultant presented a film strip on core curriculum. She talked to the whole group, and a large group discussion was held. Alternate workshops were formally evaluated by the use of a simple evaluation blank.[24] This blank called for an evaluation on a five-point scale and included questions on what the teachers liked and disliked about the workshop, as well as what the meeting was trying to accomplish and how the workshops could be improved. These were reviewed and tabulated after each meeting, and an attempt made to remedy the difficulties reported.

One of the comments frequently received at the beginning of the workshops concerned the *time* of the meeting. School was dismissed early on the day of the workshop, and the teachers went to one of the elementary schools where the workshop opened at 2.30 P.M. The schedule consisted of a general session of about forty minutes duration, a coffee break of about ten minutes, discussion groups for sixty minutes, and a thirty-minute round-up. The teachers felt this was too long a stretch following a working day. It was explained by the administration that it would be possible only occasionally to dismiss school earlier. This was done twice. School was dismissed at noon, luncheon was served to the teachers, and the workshop started at one o'clock and ran until five o'clock. This arrangement seemed more satisfactory in that it was less tiring and also provided a longer period of time to be spent on the work at hand. There were still some comments concerning the time at the end of the year, however.

Supplemental Activities

The theme of the workshop carried over into several areas of the teachers' activities during the year. Some of the regular faculty meetings were devoted to a discussion of the workshops. Materials distributed at the workshop were read and discussed in the faculty meetings.

One of the PTA meetings was devoted to concepts of promotion. The consultant who worked in the afternoon meeting stayed over and worked with the

24 See model on p. 278.

PTA. The following September, the first PTA meeting of the year was devoted to a discussion of the report on promotion policy drawn up by the workshop.

Although an attempt was made to have community representatives at the faculty workshops, only a very few citizens came. The PTA meetings proved to be a much better way of getting new ideas about pupil promotion across to the public.

Materials and References

The availability of resource materials was one of the major problems in a large workshop which was so far from the home college. This was solved in two ways. First of all, books which were recommended by the director or the consultants were purchased by the Casmier Central School and placed in the professional library. Secondly, many materials were duplicated and distributed to all teachers. These were used in many ways. Some were used as follow-up reading, others were designed to be read and followed during the workshop, and still others were read prior to the workshop. It seemed that the use of duplicated materials was the most satisfactory solution.

Preparation of the Promotion Policy Statement

Since the purpose of the workshops was to prepare a statement of promotion policy which would be satisfactory and agreeable to all or most of the staff, work was begun on the statement itself in the ninth meeting. At this meeting, the teachers met in their individual groups with a consultant in each group. They had copies of the questions that they had raised at the beginning of the workshop during the problem census. They prepared answers for each question based upon the statements of consultants used during the year, materials read, the results of numerous discussions, and their own experiences. These answers were all recorded, and care was taken to arrive at a consensus.

The director of the workshop then took the several sets of answers and collated them. There was, of course, some disagreement as to basic policy, but far more with regard to ways of implementing the policy. All in all, however, the faculty members were much closer together than they had been in September. The variation seemed to be much less pronounced.

The collated report on proposed policy was then presented to the whole faculty at the last workshop of the year. Each teacher was given a copy, and the whole group read the report together. There was much discussion, and a consensus was arrived at on all points. It meant some compromising, but this occurred without undue difficulty.

The final report was then prepared which could be said to be one that was acceptable to practically all teachers in its entirety.

Final Evaluation

As a final evaluating device, each teacher was asked to prepare a short paper on what the workshop had meant for his work. These statements were supposed to be only two pages long, but some felt inspired to write as much as twelve pages. In general, the papers were quite enthusiastic about the workshop. Some of the recurring comments were concerned with the following ideas:

1. It is reassuring to have a policy because previously the teacher who got a problem child didn't know why he was promoted.

2. The process of the workshops was valuable (sitting down and talking things over).
3. Teachers in general liked the recommended system of marking both in relation to the child's ability and in relation to achievement standards.

Problems were also brought up. For example, one teacher had tried using sociograms and found that in her grade, the seventh, a different picture was presented each time, and she didn't know how to use the results. Several comments indicated that a need was felt for the group to "reach a decision." Regret was expressed that the year ended without an "official promotion policy." There were several indications that the quest for certainty is still strong among teachers.

Some comments from participants were:

Jack Deming: "The writer is rather proud of the workshop as it developed. Our sincere thanks go out to State College for its help which was beyond the normal call of duty."

Elementary Supervisor: "From my standpoint as an administrator in the elementary school, I felt that the greatest benefit that I have derived is a crystallization of my own ideas in line with the expression of the majority of our teachers."

Teacher: "In general I found much which was applicable to my own department. I found the discussions thought provoking. I think our professional understanding was raised by this series of workshops. I think it will give us better goals to shoot for."

A composite rating of the reaction to the workshop series was obtained by weighing each response, that is, Poor—1, Fair—2, and so forth. These were averaged, and the rating was 3.6. This numerical rating has less value than the written criticisms in terms of improving future workshops, although it does give an over-all rating which is of interest.

PARTICIPANT'S EVALUATION BLANK

1. How do you rate this workshop? Please underline one of the words below.

    Poor   Fair   All Right   Good   Excellent

2. What did you especially like about the workshop?

3. What did you dislike?

4. How would you improve the workshop?

5. What did you think this group was trying to do?

6. Other comments:

You need not sign your name

EXERCISES

1. Using the data in the chapter, construct a checklist against which you can evaluate your faculty meetings.
2. If the teachers in your school resent attending faculty meetings, work out a plan of activities and experiences which will make faculty meetings more interesting and worthwhile.
3. How can you move administrative details out of your faculty meetings and so save time for really valuable experiences?
4. When should Roberts' *Rules* be used?
5. Is it necessary to have the faculty reach unanimous agreement when discussing policy formation? Give the pros and cons.
6. Evaluate your faculty meeting room in light of the suggestions made in the text. Could you find a room better suited for meetings?
7. How can the principal decide whether he should preside at faculty meetings?
8. Outline the way in which you can make best use of a consultant for your next faculty meeting.
9. What are the criteria one should use in evaluating a faculty meeting?
10. How can an observer be of value to a faculty meeting?

SELECTED BIBLIOGRAPHY

BARNES, M. W., "How to Have a Good Faculty Meeting: Suggestions and Reactions by Teachers and Principals," *National Education Association Journal,* Vol. 42 (January, 1953), pp. 39-41.

CLEMINSON, W. R., "How Can Faculty Meetings Be Made Professional?" *National Association of Secondary School Principals Bulletin,* Vol. 36 (April, 1952), pp. 37-44.

COOK, K. A., and FULL, Harold, "Is the School Faculty Meeting Significant in Promoting Professional Growth?" *School Review,* Vol. 56 (November, 1948), pp. 519–524.

DAVIES, Daniel R., and HERROLD, Kenneth F., *Make Your Staff Meetings Count!* (New London, Conn., Arthur C. Croft, 1954).

DEMAREE, Ona Belle, "Faculty Meetings Can Be Productive," *National Elementary Principals Journal,* Vol. 32 (September, 1952), pp. 67-73.

ELSBREE, Willard S., and REUTTER, E. Edmund, Jr., *Staff Personnel in the Public Schools* (New York, Prentice-Hall, 1954), pp. 226-235.

HELLERSTEIN, Rebecca, "Eye-opener Faculty Meetings," *Clearing House,* Vol. 22 (November, 1947), p. 154.

HEYWOOD, Stanley J., "What's Wrong with Faculty Meetings?" *Administrator's Notebook,* Midwest Administration Center, University of Chicago, Vol. 1, No. 5 (December, 1952).

JAMES, Edward W., and WEBER, Robert A., *School Consultants: Roles Assumed and Techniques Employed,* Southwestern Cooperative Program in Educational Administration (Austin, University of Texas, 1954).

LEE, Irving J., "Procedure for 'Coercing' Agreement," *Harvard Business Review,* (January-February, 1954), pp. 39-45.

MORRIS, Glyn, "The Faculty Meeting As a Guidance Resource in Small Rural Schools," *Education,* Vol. 74 (April, 1954), pp. 501-506.

POND, F. L., "How Can Faculty Meetings Become More Effective Professional Experiences?" *National Association of Secondary School Principals Bulletin,* Vol. 36 (March, 1952), pp. 216-225.

SAVAGE, William W., "Making the Most of the Consultant," *Administrator's Notebook,* Midwest Administration Center, University of Chicago, Vol. 1, No. 3 (October, 1953).

The New Teacher (New York, Metropolitan School Study Council, 1950).

TRUITT, W. J. B., "Orienting New Teachers," *The School Executive,* Vol. 73, No. 12 (August, 1954), pp. 58-59.

WILES, Kimball, *Supervision for Better Schools,* 2d ed. (New York, Prentice-Hall, 1955), pp. 181-210.

YAUCH, Wilbur A., *Improving Human Relations in School Administration* (New York, Harper, 1949), pp. 65-83.

CHAPTER 13

Working with Specialists

One of the newest problems in the educational field is that of working with the specialists, who, in increasing numbers, are being assigned to the central staffs of the public schools. In view of the limited scrutiny it has received from educators so far, the problem is not one that can be discussed authoritatively. Nevertheless, the administrative time and attention that school specialists have come to require renders them a topic for discussion in this part of our study.

The problems that the management of specialists involves have long been recognized in business and industry, and some concepts of use to us have been formulated by research in these fields. In discussing this problem area within the educational framework, we shall not attempt to provide a complete list of those people on the school staff who are called "special" teachers or administrators. Neither shall we concern ourselves with the co-curricular versus extracurricular battle. Rather, our first consideration will be to arrive at a general definition of the school specialist. Having established this, we shall then be in a position to raise some questions and pose some hypotheses concerning the nature of the specialist problem, the shortcomings of specialization, and approaches to the solution of the problem.

DEFINITION OF THE SCHOOL SPECIALIST

To a certain extent, all teachers are specialists in that they all possess certain basic skills and competencies in their particular subjects. A distinction between the regular classroom teacher and the specialist, such as the curriculum co-ordinator, the guidance director, or the teacher of music or art, then, might provide a good approach to the definition we seek.

Inasmuch as the school administrator usually has been a classroom teacher prior to his appointment, he may be assumed to possess many of the skills of the regular teachers of his staff. Naturally, if he has taught social studies, for example, he cannot have as full a knowledge of English as does the teacher of that subject. Certainly, each teacher is expected to have developed greater specific knowledge than has the administrator. What the administrator does have, however, is a knowledge of the problems that are apt to come up in the course of regular classroom teaching. Therefore the policies, decisions, and facilities required by the classroom teacher are, in the main, familiar to him.

On the other hand, the specialist is one who possesses certain skills and knowledge that are not possessed by the administrator or, for that matter, by anyone else in the school except a like specialist. This basic distinction, then, becomes our definition. The specialist is a person who knows far more than the administrator about some particular aspect of the school situation. Accordingly, any conclusions we draw in the following discussion of the specialist problem may be applied to all those who fall under this definition. It should be noted, however, that this definition does not include the visiting consultant, who was discussed in Chapter 12.[1] Here, we are concerned only with specialists who are members of the school staff, primarily because the available data are limited to this group, and seem to have some skill not possessed by others, even though the skill is somewhat rudimentary in nature. Specialization is a product of our times, and there is little likelihood that it will be abandoned or eliminated, as many would like. The problem for us to consider is not how to do away with the specialist but how to work with him on the administrative level.

Increased Number of Specialists

In the years since World War II, specialists have been added to the staffs of schools in very large numbers. Although no one has an exact figure for the country as a whole, some indication of the magnitude of the trend can be gained from a study just completed in New York State. In this state it was determined that there had been a 100 per cent increase in the group known as supervisors (including curriculum co-ordinators, elementary supervisors, and subject-matter supervisors) during the period, 1948-1955, and an increase of 200 per cent in school business administrators during the period 1951-1955. Even if the figures for the rest of the country are only, say, half as large, there is a tremendous trend underway.

Importance of Specialists

It is not too difficult to account for the trend toward specialists. As the curricular offerings of the public schools have increased there has appeared the need for more people with special skills and abilities. The expansion of school districts, due both to redistricting and to increased birth rate, has brought about a corrresponding increase in supervisory personnel and administrators to whom the chief school administrator can delegate certain functions. Moreover, increased knowledge and skill in the content of the curriculum has made it necessary to add specialists who

---

[1] See above, pp. 269-270.

are familiar with these gains. Advances in the teaching of reading are a good example of this. Finally, the acquisition of these subject specialists has created the need for curriculum specialists who are able to see the curricular program as a whole.

School administration cannot be expected to improve unless it does add specialists to the staff. We cannot expect the school administrator to perform as an educational leader and still handle all of the complex administrative responsibilities of a modern school. As a line officer, he should be a generalist. It is his function to perceive the total educational experience of each child and to act in the best interests of the child. In this respect, the administrator can make his greatest contribution to education through the acquisition of a competent school staff which functions as a team. Although he should not have line responsibilities over teachers, the specialist does have a key role to play on that team.[2] However, the relatively new and heavy addition of specialists to school staffs has caused certain administrative problems which were present to a small degree in the past to become acute. These problems and some suggestions for their solutions will be our concern in the remaining sections of this chapter.

The Problems

The problems that the administrator faces in working with specialists are of two varieties: (1) those involved in the *services* that the specialists bring to the school, and (2) those involved in the *limitations* of the specialists themselves. In one of the few discussions of this topic in the literature of educational administration, Shane and Yauch point up both aspects: [3]

The increase in special fields and services has multiplied both duties and responsibilities of principals and superintendents. Some of the problems of leadership are related to scheduling pupils' time, evaluating a program in terms of which his own preparation is meager, and the apparent inability of some special subject teachers to see their field as a component of a total program of school living.

Services. One of the problems caused by increased services concerns the scheduling of these services. For example, driver training requires that a small number of students be scheduled for a period of time less than a semester. Although this is not an insurmountable problem, it differs from the ordinary.

The fact that the school day has a finite length, poses a somewhat greater difficulty. As services are added, something must be deleted. The

---

[2] For a discussion of the place of the specialist in the school organization, see Chapter 15.

[3] Harold G. Shane and Wilbur A. Yauch, *Creative School Administration* (New York, Holt, 1954), p. 364.

problem of what to drop is an extremely difficult one. One solution is to lengthen the school day, but this only puts off the day of final reckoning since special services will continue to be added.

The most difficult problem that confronts the administrator, however, is the evaluation of a program in which he has little competence. How can he know, for instance, how effective the driver-training program or the program of the dental hygienist is? The administrator cannot be expected to be thoroughly competent in these fields, yet he does have the responsibility for seeing that they are effective programs.

Limitations of the Specialist. Roethlisberger has reminded us that when we speak of specialists we are talking about human beings who are responding, in their way, to a situation. We should keep this in mind, because the problem is primarily a human not a technical problem.

Thorstein Veblen has suggested that the specialist is characterized by "trained incapacity"; that is, although he is expert in one area, he is, of necessity, inexpert in other areas. As Dubin puts it: [4]

> The intensity of his training in one area means training in other areas is usually neglected. The intensity of concentration upon the problems of one area means that consideration of surrounding areas is often limited to the "all other things being equal" approach. To the administrator or executive who co-ordinates the work of different kinds of specialists, all other things are not equal. They must be considered as important variables in a total situation.

The chief limitation of the specialist is his inability to see his own field of endeavor in proper perspective. He fails to understand that his is just one of many specializations in the total school curriculum. The school administrator must see the total picture, he must consider the demands of all specialists in relation to the needs of the child.

Despite this limitation, the specialist has an advantage over most people because they have little knowledge in his area. Furthermore, he sometimes attempts to maintain this advantage in various ways. First of all, he tends to keep much of his knowledge secret. He does not freely and easily give of his knowledge because if he did, he would no longer maintain an advantage over us. Moore and Tumin indicate the means whereby this differential of knowledge is maintained: "A common device is that of specialized and possibly esoteric vocabulary, or the use of instruments and techniques not intrinsically required for the solution but seemingly so." [5]

At this point, it becomes evident that our description of the characteristics of the specialist holds true for many but is not true for others. Many specialists have been able to overcome the deficiency in training which

[4] Robert Dubin, ed., *Human Relations in Administration* (New York, Prentice-Hall, 1951), p. 114.

[5] Wilbur E. Moore and Melvin M. Tumin, "Some Social Functions of Ignorance," *American Sociological Review*, Vol. 17 (December, 1949), p. 789.

has caused them to see only one segment of the total program. This gives us a lead to the solution of the specialist problem which will be discussed later in this chapter.

Another limitation that has been observed is the tendency of many specialists to identify with other specialists and to ignore the arguments of nonspecialists. The director of health and physical education, for instance, is much more apt to heed the recommendation of his state association in matters of teaching physical education than the recommendation of the curriculum co-ordinator in his school system.

Specialists also are apt to confuse the importance of their knowledge with the significance of what they recommend. For example, the art teacher may consider the superintendent to be standing in his way when a recommendation he has made is not acted upon favorably.

A final limitation to be mentioned is the specialist's aversion to new ideas, particularly if these ideas come from outside the specialist group. The English teacher, for instance, who has ideas as to how mathematics should be taught will not get a very sympathetic hearing from the math people.[6]

SOLVING THE SPECIALIST PROBLEM

We have indicated the value of specialists to school systems and discussed some of the problems which come about by acquiring specialists in increasing numbers. The value of specialists is so great that we should not be overly concerned with their limitations. After all, we have enumerated throughout this book the many limitations of school administrators. One objective should be to alleviate the limitations of both so that we can attain a better educational system.

In searching for solutions to the specialist's problems, we might well start with Roethlisberger who discusses these problems from the point of view of industry.[7]

However, when the administrator has to conceive of his organization as a functioning whole and has to assess the contributions of each specialist group to it and make decisions in accordance with his size-up of the total situation, he is up against a concrete situation involving the interactions of people. And for this purpose what skills does he use? In terms of what data does he act? In what frame of reference is his thought set? If all the specialist skills are not the skill of the administrator, if all these partial controls of different specialist groups do not add up to the final control exercised by the administrator, then what is

[6] For further reading on the limitations of specialists, see Harold J. Laski, "The Limitations of the Expert," *Harper's Magazine*, Vol. 162 (December, 1930), pp. 102-106; Robert K. Merton, "The Machine, the Worker, and the Engineer," *Science*, Vol. 105 (January 24, 1947), pp. 79-81; and Dubin, *op. cit.*, pp. 113-138.

[7] F. J. Roethlisberger, *Management and Morale* (Cambridge, Mass., Harvard University Press, 1941), pp. 157-158. Copyright, 1941, by the President and Fellows of Harvard College.

the administrative skill? What is that part of the situation which may be ignored or inaccurately stated by the limitations of a specialist logic, which must be understood and taken into account by the administrator if the control exercised is to be adequate?

It is obvious that the points made by Roethlisberger are of importance to school administrators since their primary responsibility is to see the situation as a whole. They must see each specialist contributing to the whole. The most important lead to the solution of our problem lies in this direction.

Co-operative Approach

The acquisition of more and more specialists in the schools has increased the demand for more time and money for each specialized area. The music teacher wants more time for orchestral practice, more money for instruments. The psychologist wants more time for interviews and tests. The coaches want more time for practice, more money for equipment. Shane and McSwain note a study which shows that "enrichment" activities may constitute at least half the school time of first- and second-grade students.[8] Our concern here is not whether or not this should be but that the situation does create the administrative problem of deciding how much time and money should be devoted to each area.

A suggested procedure toward the handling of this problem is one which utilizes the co-operative approach. This was tried by one high school principal with very good results. The high school, which had a school week of twenty-five fifty-minute periods, was in the midst of a complete revision of its course of study. Each area was demanding more time for itself. The principal called a faculty meeting and asked the teachers in each area to get together and note on a card the number of periods per week which they thought to be the optimum for the students. The English teachers, for example, were to write the number of periods of English which would be optimum for each student. After each area had designated the number of optimum periods, the principal gathered up the cards and then wrote the area name and the requested periods on the blackboard. The total number of periods was 72. The effect was immediate. At this point, the specialists saw their demands in relation to the other demands and to the total curriculum. The principal got much more co-operation during the remainder of the study.

The essence of the co-operative approach to this type of problem is that each specialist is forced to see himself in relation to other specialists and to the regular teachers. He also sees the problem of the school administrator, who must view the school system as a totality.

[8] Harold G. Shane and E. T. McSwain, *Evaluation and the Elementary Curriculum* (New York, Henry Holt, 1951), p. 268.

Modifying Perception

The most important step toward an improved working relationship with the specialist, we believe, involves a modification of his basic weakness— a lack of perspective. The school administrator should institute a program of intravisitations, in which various specialists are made aware of other aspects of the school program.[9] This should be done in a realistic manner, and the people involved should not merely observe other situations. For example, the music consultant and the elementary school teacher might exchange jobs for a day or two. In this way, each would gain a better understanding of the other's work and problems, and the consultant then would be more likely to see that music is but one part of the total program.

This procedure is also recommended for high school and elementary school teachers, although they do not fall under our definition of specialist. Neither has a clear picture of what the other is doing. Since the high school teacher normally has a much narrower area of responsibility than does the elementary teacher, his perspective would be broadened greatly by this experience.

The end result of this procedure would be a faculty which perceives the roles of all its members in a much more realistic fashion. The teachers would begin to see themselves and others in relation to the total situation. Some school administrators have found it worthwhile to have all of their teachers take a bus ride around the district in which they teach, which many of them have never even seen. Such a trip accomplishes the rudimentary task of having all of the teachers see the district together. It is another common experience that helps them to broaden their common perceptions.

Evaluating Requests

In the two procedures recommended above we have tried to broaden the perspective of specialists. There are, however, many situations in which neither of the above procedures is effective. Both are essentially educational, and their full results are long range in nature. The problem of the many requests of the specialist still remains. What does the school administrator do when the specialist wants to change a method of teaching that is accepted generally as school policy? Should the administrator, for instance, change the method of teaching reading upon the assurance of the reading consultant that this new way is *the* way? Or should he add another period for the teaching of health because the state group in this

---

[9] For descriptions of this practice, see H. S. Bech, "New Perspective When Special and Regular Teachers Change Places," *Exceptional Child*, Vol. 20 (January, 1954), pp. 162-163), and Daniel E. Griffiths, "Off on the Right Foot," *New York State Education* (October, 1952), p. 52.

area insists that it is imperative? Requests of this sort, of course, are not restricted to these two groups and are legion.

The administrator should use a systemized approach in handling such requests. He should not deal with them one by one. Most of the requests will concern requests for more pupil time. The systematized approach to these problems should be based upon the thesis that the content of the curriculum is the responsibility of the total faculty. Any requests for additional time should be referred to the faculty or its representatives. This accomplishes several things:

1. It slows down the request for rapid changes. Often a request can be seen more clearly and objectively after a lapse of time. It sometimes happens that even the person who made the request changes his mind.
2. Giving one area more time means another area has less time. The people being deprived of time should have an opportunity to be heard.
3. Placing responsibility for curriculum change in the hands of the faculty increases the chances that the faculty will act more reasonably.

Requests which should not be referred to the faculty need to be handled in the manner described in Chapter 10. The administrator needs to involve the specialist in the process so that he will be more apt to accept the decision. The administrator needs also to make the decision with regard to the effect it will have on the total situation.

Other procedures which should be used include checking the specialists' recommendations against the recommendations of other specialists working in the same field. Specialists may vary in their recommendations, so the administrator needs to consult more than one. If the curriculum coordinator recommends a basic change in the curriculum, his recommendation should be validated by discussing the matter with consultants from the state education department and universities. Major changes should be based upon a consensus of thought of many specialists.

The administrator also needs to apply the criterion of consistency to the specialists' recommendation. He needs to ask himself if today's recommendation is consistent with yesterday's.

SUMMARY

In this chapter we have dealt with the problem of working with specialists. In Chapter 1, we stated that conceptual skill was the highest skill of the good administrator. His skill in integrating the specialists into the school system and, at the same time, considering to the fullest extent possible the human values involved is the crux of this problem.

It was demonstrated that there is now a great influx of specialists into the schools. This has been brought about by an increase in the size of school districts, a greater complexity of the curriculum, and an increase in the knowledge and skills in subject areas. Problems are created in terms of the administration of added services and the limitations of specialists.

Three general approaches to the solution of this problem were recommended. The co-operative approach to specialists' requests for time, money, and facilities was placed first on the list. Through co-operative study the problem can be alleviated. The second approach involved changing the perceptions of specialists, and the third dealt with criteria for administrative evaluation of the specialists' requests.

EXERCISES

1. Whom do you consider to be specialists in your school system?
2. List the problems you have encountered as you have worked with specialists. How did you attempt to solve these problems?
3. Do you have more problems with one particular specialist? Why is this so? Can you list the reasons for these problems?
4. The number of specialists in our schools will most probably increase greatly in the next few years. What revision in your school organization would help to alleviate specialist problems?
5. Why is the concept of the "autonomous" principal advocated in our discussion of specialists?
6. Have you observed in your specialists the reputed weaknesses that were discussed in this chapter? Can you account for those which you cannot observe?
7. Can you suggest any other methods of increasing the perspective of specialists?
8. Do you agree with the statement, "Every administrator should first be a specialist?" What difficulties are encountered if this is put into effect?

SELECTED BIBLIOGRAPHY

BECH, H. S., "New Perspective When Special and Regular Teachers Change Places," *Exceptional Child,* Vol. 20 (January, 1954), pp. 162-163.

DUBIN, Robert, ed., "Specialists," *Human Relations in Administration* (New York, Prentice-Hall, 1951), pp. 113-138.

GRIFFITHS, Daniel E., "Off on the Right Foot," *New York State Education* (October, 1952), p. 52.

LASKI, Harold J., "The Limitations of the Expert," *Harper's Magazine,* Vol. 162 (December, 1930), pp. 102-106.

MOORE, Wilbur E. and TUMIN, Melvin M., "Some Social Functions of Ignorance," *American Sociological Review,* Vol. 17 (December, 1949), pp. 788-789.

ROETHLISBERGER, F. J., "Concerning People Who Deal with Cooperative Phenomena," *Management and Morale* (Cambridge, Mass., Harvard University Press, 1941), pp. 137-159.

SHANE, Harold G. and YAUCH, Wilbur A., *Creative School Administration* (New York, Holt, 1954), pp. 361-392.

CHAPTER **14**

Working with the Community

It is almost a truism to state that the community has become increasingly important to the school administrator. This is true, not only because of the growing popularity of what is called the "community school" but because of the greater public interest in school affairs. Not all of this interest is benevolent; a great deal of it has to do with cutting costs. Communities have found that the school tax is just about the only tax over which its members can exercise control, particularly in independent school districts. As a consequence, they have set out to keep school taxes as low as possible. On the other hand, there is a movement on the part of those sincerely interested in the improvement of education. This group is very large and numbers among its constituents parents, professional people, businessmen, and industrialists. They view the teacher and classroom shortage as a serious threat to the future of our country, and they want to solve the problem.

In this chapter we will discuss ways in which the administrator can *learn* about his community and ways in which he can *work* with his community. In order to work intelligently with the community, the administrator must know a great deal about it, for his knowledge will condition the methods that he uses. No one method or procedure will suffice for all types of communities. This point has been developed by at least two sociologists, who point out, for example, that methods developed in small communities do not work when applied to large communities. Johnson states: [1]

Poston and other educators have demonstrated the amazing vitality of the community development method in small towns. These towns have also been isolated ones, usually culturally starved and desperately in need of regeneration. The cities present an altogether different kind of situation and it is imperative to keep that fact in mind. An attempt to apply to city based adult education programs the techniques developed in and for the small towns, would, I believe, be a calamity.... Cities cannot be treated as a collection of small towns. The social structure of an Akron, Ohio, is infinitely more complicated than that of a small town. An overriding need of cities is not to stimulate people to take action

[1] Eugene I. Johnson, "Comments," *Adult Education*, Vol. 4, No. 6 (September, 1954), pp. 196-197.

on their own, but to close the gap between the planning of the agencies and organizations of a city and the thinking of the people in the city.

Solon Kimball has also indicated that the group discussion technique, which works so well with middle- and upper-class people, does not work at all with lower-class people.[2] In the lower classes, there is little sympathy with the concept of "talking over" problems. They feel that if something is wrong, it's wrong, and it should be remedied. We see two-valued thinking in this group.

We should keep in mind when working with the community, just as with working with the faculty or any other group, that it is necessary to have accurate perception. One must *know* the group he is to work with. This means that the school administrator should know the *facts* about his community, as well as the feelings and opinions of the community. Determining the power structure of the community has been discussed in Chapter 5. Aside from the observations which any alert school administrator makes constantly, there are two methods of "learning" the community: the first is the national census, and the second is the public-opinion survey.

CENSUS REPORTS

There are certain facts which a school administrator must have if he is to know the community. Under ordinary circumstances, the reports compiled by the U. S. Bureau of the Census constitute the best source of facts about the community. There are some difficulties to be encountered in using census data, and these must be taken into account in any study that is made. The bulk of the census data is collected once every ten years. This means that as the administrator approaches the end of each ten-year period (ending in zero), he has "old" data. In some areas, the census data are kept up to date and can be verified easily. A more serious difficulty is that census data are reported by municipalities and not by school districts. This can be offset by an intelligent evaluation of the material, however. With all their shortcomings, census data still provide the best information available to most school administrators. Ordinarily, the only time the administrator will have better information is when a comprehensive local survey is made by a professional group.

What kinds of information are available to the school administrator through these census reports? The information which is probably most helpful is found in a set of bulletins, one for each state, published by the U. S. Bureau of the Census.[3] By consulting the bulletin for his particular

[2] Solon Kimball, "Anthropology and Communication," *Teachers College Record,* Vol. 57, No. 2 (November, 1955), p. 70.

[3] U. S. Bureau of the Census, *Census of Population, 1950: Characteristics of the Population* (Washington, D. C., 1953), Vol. 2.

state, the administrator can determine such population characteristics of his community as color by sex, race by sex, age by color and sex, citizenship and nativity of the population twenty-one years old and over, years of school completed by persons twenty-five years old and over by color and sex, marital status by color, married couples, families, households, institutional population, and country of birth of foreign-born population. There are also such economic statistics as employment status by color and sex, labor force and gainful workers by color and sex, income of families and unrelated individuals.

Volume 2 of the census reports data for communities of a population of 2500 and over. However, data on smaller communities have been gathered and are available upon request from the Director, Bureau of the Census, Washington 25, D. C.

PUBLIC-OPINION SURVEY

One of the areas about which the public schools have been most backward is that of measuring public opinion. Educational literature contains few studies which have been undertaken to determine just what the public is thinking and what it wants from its public schools. Too often we are apt to listen to the small vocal groups instead of making a greater effort to determine just what all of the people think and want. The techniques for polling public opinion have been known for some time. Certainly in education we should begin to use them.

Once we begin to think about it, the values of plumbing community opinion become obvious. In the first place, public-opinion polls give us information concerning the *climate* in which the schools are being operated. At the present time, for instance, just how disturbed are the people in a community over the modern methods of teaching reading? Do they really want to go back to the phonetic method? A school administrator would know better what to do if he had this information. The second value is that once the administrator knows the opinions of his community, he can begin to *communicate* with the community in an intelligent manner. If the community is seriously disturbed about the teaching of reading, the administrator would then need to go about the process of "teaching" the entire community. He would need to discuss, through various media, the method being used in the schools, its advantages and disadvantages, and the results which have been obtained. This leads to the third value. With a knowledge of the community and the results of communicating with it, the administrator can *plan for action*. He knows whether or not it is the right time to start a new program in reading or to try for a favorable vote on a bond issue.

Determining Factors of the Public-opinion Survey

McCormick has summarized the factors that determine the success of a public-opinion poll as follows: [4]

1. The size of the sample.
2. The structure of the cross section.
3. The questions asked.
4. The timing of the survey.

Each of these factors is important, and by setting up his poll so as to account for each, the school administrator can make a surprisingly accurate estimate of the opinion in his community with relatively little effort. Public-opinion polling is not a mysterious practice. There are a few simple principles to be observed, and these can be mastered with little difficulty.

Size of the Sample. In determining the opinion of a community it is not necessary to talk to everyone. The task is to talk to or send questionnaires to a certain few people. This set of people is called a *sample*. The sample should be large enough and representative enough so that the opinion of the sample will be the same as the opinion of the total group. Hedlund has compiled a table which gives the range of error, division of opinion, and the size of sample necessary.[5]

Size of Sample Necessary to Predict Opinion for Various Ranges of Accuracy and Division of Opinion

	DIVISION OF OPINION		
RANGE OF ERROR	*80%-20%*	*65%-35%*	*50%-50%*
1%	6147	8740	9604
5%	246	350	385
10%	62	88	97

The range of error commonly accepted by social scientists is 5 per cent, so we can use the figures appearing opposite it. If the issue being investigated were particularly controversial, we would assume the population opinion to be split 50-50. In this case, we should sample 385 people in the community. (This is regardless of the size of the community.) If the issue were not so controversial, a smaller number would suffice; but in order to be safe, we should use 385. It should be noted that smaller samples have been used, but there is great difficulty in convincing the layman that a small sample is accurate. The layman still remembers the failure of the Literary Digest Poll and the failure of practically all polls in the 1948 presidential election. The size of the sample should be such that it would be acceptable to the community.

[4] Felix J. McCormick, "The Measurement of Public Understanding of Education" (Unpublished Ed.D. project, Teachers College, Columbia University, 1949), pp. 29-30.
[5] Paul A. Hedlund, "Measuring Public Opinion on School Issues" (Unpublished Ed.D. project, Teachers College, Columbia University, 1947), p. 23.

Structure of the Sample. Of even more importance than the size of the sample is its *structure.* Adding to the size of the sample may only compound the errors involved. Who is in the sample is of extreme importance. Hedlund has this to say about the structure of a sample: [6]

If the population were homogeneous, all that would need to be done is to select the sample at random, but populations to be sampled are usually heterogeneous, that is, composed of dissimilar elements not uniformly distributed in the population. To select a representative sample for such a population, use is made of the *controlled* or *stratified* sample. Certain important determinants of opinion, such as economic status, age, and sex are set up as controls, and the sample is selected so it reaches each important group in the population in the proper proportions. For example, if 53 per cent of the population are men, 53 per cent of the sample should be men, and if 17 per cent of the population are over 60 years of age, 17 per cent of the sample should be of this age, and so on. Small variations from these proportions need not, however, be of concern to the poll taken, for these *sampling* errors will be made in drawing any sample and are simply due to the operation of laws of chance.

The factors to be taken into account when stratifying the sample are those of sex, economic status, place of residence, urban or non-urban, age, political affiliation, educational level, religion, color, and place of birth. If we were to have a perfectly stratified sample, it would be stratified for all of these factors. The stratification of a sample for even two or three factors is difficult; stratification for all of the above factors would be an almost insurmountable task.

There are ways of selecting a sample to achieve accurate results without all of the difficult work usually required. McCormick worked out five solutions to this problem. We will discuss those two which he found to give the best sample. Ross describes McCormick's procedures as follows: [7]

Method D—Eighth-Grade Pupils as Interviewers

A major purpose ... was the development of the most simple method possible. Therefore, the pupils used in this method received practically no instructions. A one-page instruction sheet, describing some of the problems of polling was sent to each eighth-grade teacher (in the Junior High School). Each teacher was requested to:

1. Select two boys and two girls to serve as interviewers.
2. Select them so that no two live in the same elementary school district (or section of the same elementary school district).
3. Select them so that one comes from an economically poor home, two from average homes, and one from a better-than-average home.
4. Do not select anyone if his parents have previously filled in the questionnaire.
5. Give each interviewer two envelopes containing the covering letter and the polls.

[6] *Ibid.,* p. 22.

[7] Donald H. Ross and others, *Administration for Adaptability: Public Understanding of Schools and Their Power* (New York, Metropolitan School Study Council, 1951), Vol. 1, pp. 111-112.

6. Instruct the interviewers as follows:

Boys—(*a*) Obtain one interview from your mother.

(*b*) Obtain the other interview from a male neighbor who is either under 30 years of age or over 50 years of age and who has no children in public school.

(Girls—Reverse of above as to sex of two types of respondents.)

The polls were returned to the classroom teacher and turned over to the principal, who forwarded them to the central administration building.

Method *E* was precisely the same except that fifth- and sixth-grade students were used. In both cases, samples were produced that accurately and reliably measured the understanding of education in the community. This method is simple and foolproof in that the student merely hands the poll to the adult and waits for it to be completed. Some schools using this technique have achieved 100 per cent returns. The number of students (the above called for four from each classroom) depends on the number of sections of the grade being used for interviewing. McCormick states that no credence at all should be placed in less than 100 interviews. Of course, if statistically reliable results are desired, there should be 385 interviews.

Questions Asked. One of the great difficulties of constructing a public-opinion poll involves the wording of the questions to be asked. Since the professional educator is accustomed to talking with other professionals and often uses technical terms, he has considerable difficulty in communicating with lay people. Reference to Chapter 4 should help to clarify this problem; but the following generally accepted guides should also be noted:

1. Keep the questionnaire short. Ask about ten questions. If you want more information, repeat the procedure at a later time.
2. Use simple language. Do not use technical terms. Try the questions on the students to see if they understand what you are saying.
3. Ask questions of opinion, not fact. Leave personalities out of the questions.
4. Ask short questions which can be answered objectively. Word questions so that the respondent can answer "Yes" or "No," "Pleased" or "Displeased." Multiple-choice questions may also be asked so that the respondent can answer clearly and precisely.
5. Ask unbiased questions. Leave out all "colored" words or, in the language of Chapter 4, words with intensional meanings.
6. There are times when it is useful to ask open-ended questions in which a person is asked to answer in his own words. Although the answers to questions of this sort are very revealing, they are sometimes difficult to analyze. The illustration on the next page [8] is an example of a good question with the answers analyzed in excellent form.

Before the questions are used in a poll they should be tried out on several people. There are very few first versions that do not require rephras-

[8] Taken from Rhetta M. Arter, *Living in Chelsea* (New York, The Center for Human Relations Studies, New York University, 1954), p. 25.

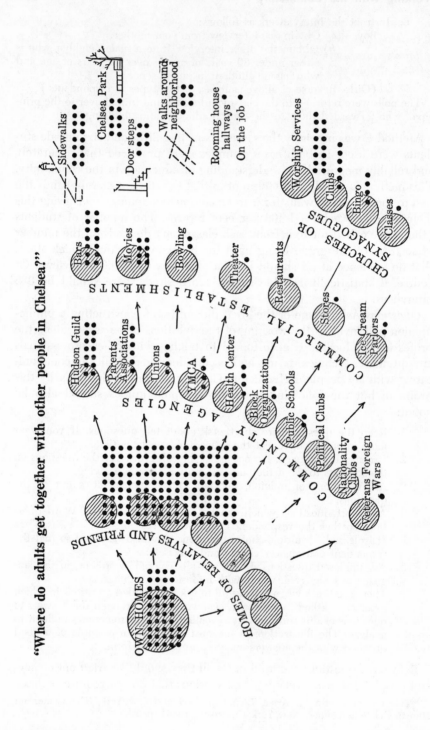

"Where do adults get together with other people in Chelsea?"

OWN HOMES

HOMES OF RELATIVES AND FRIENDS

COMMUNITY AGENCIES

Hudson Guild
Parents Associations
Unions
YMCA
Health Center
Block Organization
Public Schools
Political Clubs
Nationality Clubs
Veterans Foreign Wars

COMMERCIAL ESTABLISHMENTS

Bars
Movies
Bowling
Theater
Restaurants
Stores
Ice-Cream Parlors

CHURCHES OR SYNAGOGUES

Worship Services
Clubs
Bingo
Classes

Sidewalks
Chelsea Park
Door steps
Walks around neighborhood
Rooming house hallways
On the job

ing, and each question should be given several writings and trials to determine the clearest wording.

Timing. An important factor sometimes overlooked in conducting a public-opinion poll is timing. Ross makes four observations regarding this point: [9]

1. Opinions change, and allowance must always be made in predicting human action at a date later than that on which the survey was made.
2. Well-publicized single events may cause a temporary skewing of opinion.
3. Chronological proximity of certain extraneous experiences for a large part of the sample in common may cause some transfer to educational opinion (e.g., it would be unwise to conduct a poll on new school buildings on April 16).
4. The timing of the poll may determine the number of usable responses. A failure to obtain responses from any sizable portion of the sample would prejudice its statistical reliability.

We have been considering ways by which the administrator can learn his community. Through the census he can learn the facts about his community. By using polling techniques, he can learn the opinions and attitudes of the community. He should always be alert to what is going on about him so that he can sense the tenor of the community. Many feel that this "sensing" is enough to do, but it is not. The number of acquaintances that any administrator has constitutes too small a sample for him to be certain that it reflects accurately what the community thinks and feels. With a background of community knowledge built upon the foregoing sources and techniques, the administrator's next consideration is how to work with his community.

The school administrator works with the community just as any enlightened citizen would; that is, he is a member of various groups of particular interest to him, and, through these groups, he works to improve the community. He also participates in various meetings of the community, votes his mind on all issues, and, in general, is a good citizen. The school administrator, however, has a responsibility above and beyond this. He needs to work closely with the community on all matters relating to the school. *This is a primary responsibility,* and "matters relating to the school" should be interpreted very broadly. If, for instance, a community is losing its industries, this should not be interpreted as a nonschool problem, for it will have a direct effect upon the quality of education that the community will have. In all matters affecting the schools, the administrator should assume a leadership role. One of the most effective methods of working with the community is through the use of citizen committees.

[9] Ross, *op. cit.,* p. 88.

THE CITIZEN COMMITTEE

As we trace the growth of citizen committees in the literature we find very few studies that question their validity. There are some which challenge the *functions* of these committees, but none seems to be vigorously opposed to their existence. Davies and Herrold review the reasons for the formation of citizen groups. They point out that: [10]

1. *Some committees are started because "it's the style."* . . . Occasionally a school administrator launches a citizen committee in an attempt to make a good impression on high status groups in the community, or on the graduate department where he is seeking an advanced degree, or to please a state education department which has its eye on him. . . .

2. *Some committees are started because it is the "clever" thing to do—* because they may serve to strengthen policies or decisions already made. . . .

3. *Some committees are set up to grind a personal ax.* . . . Regardless of who tries this type of artificial motivation—college professors, prejudiced pressure groups, or persons trying to work out their own individual frustrations and disappointments—this method of getting citizen committees started is not good. . . .

4. *Some committees are intended to upset the* STATUS QUO. This kind of committee is usually started *outside* the school organization by a group of citizens interested in what, according to their own definition, they call *school improvement.* . . .

5. *Some committees are to marshal intelligent support against attacks.* Well-organized citizen committees can provide support for school administration in times of crises. Without such backing to counteract sudden and irrational attacks, especially in these times, any school administrator is vulnerable. . . .

6. *Some committees are organized to help harness the power of education for improvement of both school and community.* Most administrators and boards today honestly attempt to see that the committee is genuinely a citizen committee and not a pawn of the board, the school administration, or some pressure group.

To this list we might add the observation that a large number of school districts do not see the value of citizen committees until *after* the district has lost a bond issue or has had some other setback. In other words, any number of districts have been *forced* into the formation of these committees. Fortunately, once the committee has been formed, the experience is usually a mutually satisfactory one, and the practice is continued.

It can be seen from the above that the reasons for which committees have been formed range from very selfish to the most democratic and constructive. Unfortunately, most of the reasons indicate that boards and administrators in some cases are attempting to manipulate the public.

[10] Daniel R. Davies and Kenneth F. Herrold, *Citizens Committees* (New London, Conn., Arthur C. Croft, 1954), pp. 19-20.

Needless to say, committees should be formed only as an honest effort to involve more and more citizens in the policy-making functions of the schools.

Functions of the Citizen Committee

What is the function of the citizen committee? How can it help education? Lund made a national survey of citizen committees and received the following comments from school superintendents about what the committees of their communities had accomplished: [11]

These groups supplied the leadership in planning educational policies and programs for our school district.

The pressing school building problem and lack of funds to meet the pending crisis was minutely studied by a lay group. They saw the great need of such a building program and successfully campaigned in its behalf.

For several years past parent committees have assisted in the preparation and evaluation of report cards.

The members of the committee take information back to their respective groups.

Our lay group in conjunction with the teachers and board of education worked together for two years developing a new salary schedule for teachers.

The group studied the educational needs and unmet needs of our school, as a consequence we gained many changes which were hither-to denied us.

To these may be added the fact that the committee enables the school administrator to keep in close contact with community thinking. If it is organized to represent various strata, it also functions as a channel of communication between him and the community,[12] though there is considerable doubt that this is often the case. Regardless of what objective the committee is set up to accomplish, the basic value is that which Rogers points out: [13]

The ideal of democratic deliberation is an intelligent and uncoerced consensus concerning what should be done. It is this full utilization of human resources in the guidance of communication that justifies the democratic faith that democratic co-operation leads to policies and programs which are more relevant to existing conditions, more sensitive to all human values, more generally satisfying to man concerned, and more enduring than policies and programs based on any other mode of social co-operation.

[11] John Lund, *Educational Leadership in Action: A Study of Current Patterns of Participation by Citizens, Staff, and Youth in Policy and Program Development* (Washington, D. C., U. S. Department of Health, Welfare, and Education, Office of Education, 1949), p. 2.

[12] John H. Hull, "Functioning Patterns of Lay Advisory Committee Organization," *American School Board Journal,* Vol. 119 (December, 1949), p. 28.

[13] Virgil Rogers, "Democratic School Administration," *Education Digest,* Vol. 10 (July, 1945). Reprinted by permission of the National Society of College Teachers of Education.

Standing vs. Temporary Committee

Once it is decided to have a citizen committee, the major issue to be resolved is whether it is to be a standing or temporary committee. At the present time there is agitation for both.[14] On the one hand, it is argued that the community should have the benefit of a standing committee, one which meets periodically to consider those problems which face the school system. Its members would be appointed or elected so as to provide for continuous representation. On the other hand, there are those who argue for a temporary committee appointed to study a particular problem and disbanded after its report has been concluded. It must be stated that there is little or no evidence to indicate which is the better type. Each community must make its own decision. One danger of the standing committee should be pointed out: it could grow to challenge the right of the board of education to make decisions which differ from those it advocates. This would appear to be a strong argument in favor of the temporary committee.

Formation of the Citizen Committee

Problems in this area include: Who should appoint the members of a citizen committee? Who should be a member of a citizen committee? Here, again, we come to an impasse as far as clear and unequivocal directions in answering our questions. Toy summarizes the experience of the country in this manner: [15]

We know of successful groups [citizen committees] appointed by school superintendents. Others equally successful have had their members appointed by school boards, by individual layman, by city governments, by civic associations, and by special nominating committees, which in turn had been appointed by any of the foregoing. The question of what method works best for any given community involves the purpose, length of term, and community.

In spite of this wide variation in practice, the literature seems to indicate a definite trend toward two general types of citizen committees. The first, and most favored, is the committee formed at the invitation of the board of education.[16] Both Lund and Hull report that most citizen committees are formed in this way. Either the board writes to organizations in the community and requests them to send a member to the first meeting of the citizen committee or it selects members regardless of the organizations to which they belong. Although the method in which the board

---

[14] Angelo Giaudrone, *Lay Advisory Committees* (Washington, D. C., American Association of School Administrators, 1951).

[15] Henry Toy, Jr., "Local Citizens Committees," *Nation's Schools*, Vol. 46 (July, 1950), p. 26.

[16] J. H. Hull, "How to Organize Lay Advisory Committees," *School Executive*, Vol. 70 (December, 1950), p. 49.

asks organizations to send representatives is favored, there are many serious obstacles to this plan, the chief of which is that the organizations may not send their best people.

The second general type of committee is the independent citizen committee. Its members may be elected or appointed, but its chief distinction is that it is completely separate from the board of education. Many groups around the country which purport to be independent citizen committees have presented the greatest blocks to good education. If, however, its membership is open to the public and it works in good faith with the board of education, the independent citizen committee can contribute a good deal toward educational progress. The record of the committee of Great Neck, N. Y., for example, is outstanding. The administration and board of education should strive to maintain the best liaison possible with groups of this type, for they provide a real challenge to school leadership.

From the above discussion it is obvious that the only way in which the question of who should be selected to be a member has any relevance is if the board and/or the administration selects the membership of the citizen committee. We agree with Hull when he says that the only agent qualified to issue the invitation to organize a lay committee is the board of education.[17] This method is to be preferred by far. The chief advantages are:

1. The board is able to invite those who can make the most significant contributions. It does not have to take potluck on the membership.
2. The board can select so that the committee represents various social, economic, and educational strata as well as various organized groups.
3. The board can select members of the power structure of the community so that the results of the committee's deliberations will carry some weight.
4. The board can establish procedures of operation and assure greater liaison if it organizes the committee on an invitation basis.
5. The board is assured of a more co-operative group since the members will not feel that they are present as representatives of various groups of the community.

There is some question as to the number of citizens who should serve on the committee. If the committee is to work as a unit, there should not be more than fifteen members. If the citizen committee is a large one which will operate as several working committees, each subgroup should not exceed fifteen members.

Procedures

The way of working with citizen committees should not vary appreciably from good committee procedures as described in preceding chapters.

[17] *Ibid.*

There is, however, one major difference between citizen committees and faculty or other types of professional groups which needs comment. One of the fallacies of the citizen committee movement is the notion that if we call a group of intelligent citizens together, they can solve our educational problems for us. Acting upon this assumption, school boards and administrators have presented citizen groups with the problem and expected a quick solution. They have very often been amazed at the lack of understanding which citizens have of educational problems. Those who have worked successfully with citizen committees have provided both information and consultants so that citizens had the facts on which to work. It is a serious error to try to work with citizen groups without thoroughly briefing them on the nature of the problem and the relevant research and other data that are available. Citizen committees are not miracle committees. They are composed of intelligent lay people, who, once they acquire an appropriate background, can make decisions that are wise.

SUMMARY

The school administrator's relations with the community encompasses two major aspects. The first is concerned with *learning* the community, the second is concerned with *working* with the community. We reviewed two methods of learning the community, starting with the United States census. The census can be used to ascertain the "facts" of the community. As was pointed out, people in the different social, economic, and educational strata (among the several other strata) of the community think differently about the schools. Indeed, as Mead has said, the basic function of the school is dependent upon the kind of people who live in the community.[18] Knowing the facts of the community, the school administrator needs to understand how the community feels about the school and educational issues. We then considered the opinion poll. We discussed in some detail the factors which determine the success of a poll: *a*) the size of the sample, *b*) the structure of the cross section, *c*) the questions asked, *d*) the timing of the survey. We indicated McCormick's method of polling using school children. This is a reliable procedure which can be used in any school community except when the issue is very controversial. Although the method would probably work even then, the opposition would be likely to criticize the use of school children.

In discussing the citizen committee as a method of working with the community, we pointed out the lack of definitive studies on which to make decisions on the issues at stake. Citizen committees should be formed only as honest attempts on the part of school people to harness the power of the community to improve the school and community. We took the posi-

[18] Margaret Mead, *The School in American Culture,* The Inglis Lecture (Cambridge, Mass., Harvard University Press, 1951), *passim.*

tion that the board of education should appoint members to a citizen committee to study a particular problem. Upon completion of the study the committee should be disbanded. It should be pointed out, however, that almost every conceivable plan has been tried and has worked in some place or other. The success of the citizen committee is dependent more upon spirit than upon form. If both the citizens and school people approach each other with the sincere hope of improving education, and if the school people can exercise sufficient skill, the endeavor will be a success. It was pointed out, finally, that the educators should not expect too much from lay people. The lay people should be given facts, data, consultants, and as many other aids as possible to help them arrive at solutions to the problem on which they are working.

EXERCISES

1. Use the United States census reports to look up your community and determine as many facts as possible.
2. Interpret the facts learned in question 1 and indicate how the interpretation can help you to be a better administrator.
3. Set up an opinion poll using McCormick's method. Try to determine how the community feels about the leading educational issues of the times.
4. How would you determine membership of a citizen committee in your school community?
5. What advantages would accrue to your school district from the activities of a citizen committee at the present time?
6. What are the advantages and disadvantages of an independent citizen committee?
7. What are the advantages and disadvantages of a citizen committee appointed by the board of education?
8. What are some of the special problems of working with citizen committees not present in professional committees?
9. Discuss the four factors which determine the success of an opinion poll.
10. What are the criteria for the wording of a good poll question?

SELECTED BIBLIOGRAPHY

ARTER, Rhetta M., *Living in Chelsea* (New York, The Center For Human Relations Studies, New York University, 1954), 43 pp.

CAMPBELL, Clyde M., "Illinois Set Up Advisory Boards," *School Executive,* Vol. 65 (May, 1946), pp. 52-53.

CAMPBELL, Roald F., and RAMSEYER, John A., *The Dynamics of School-Community Relationships* (New York, Allyn and Bacon, 1955).

DAVIES, Daniel R., and HERROLD, Kenneth F., *Citizens Committees* (New London, Conn., Arthur C. Croft, 1954), 48 pp.

FISK, Robert F., *Public Understanding of What Good Schools Can Do* (New York, Teachers College Bureau of Publications, 1944), 86 pp.

GIAUDRONE, Angelo, *Lay Advisory Committees* (Washington, D. C., American Association of School Administrators. 1951), 27 pp.

GRIEDER, Calvin, "Citizen's Advisory Committees—Have They a Rightful Place?" *Nation's Schools*, Vol. 28 (September, 1941), pp. 29-30.

HANSON, Earl H., "Should Non-elected Lay Groups Organize about School Boards?" *American School Board Journal*, Vol. 109 (October, 1944), pp. 23-24.

HULL, J. H., "Functioning Patterns of Lay Advisory Committee Organization," *American School Board Journal*, Vol. 119 (December, 1949), p. 28.

————, "How Big Shall the Educational Advisory Committee Be?" *American School Board Journal*, Vol. 120 (April, 1950), p. 53.

————, "How to Organize Lay Advisory Committees," *School Executive*, Vol. 70 (December, 1950), p. 49.

————, "Lay Advisory Committee Membership," *American School Board Journal*, Vol. 120 (February, 1950), p. 26.

————, "Organization Meetings for Lay Advisory Committees," *American School Board Journal*, Vol. 120 (May, 1950), p. 59.

————, "Some Principles of Lay Advisory Committee Organization," *American School Board Journal*, Vol. 119 (September, 1949), pp. 30-31.

————, "The Torrane Plan for Lay Participation," *American School Board Journal*, Vol. 118 (February, 1948), pp. 32-33.

LUND, John, *Educational Leadership in Action: A Study of Current Patterns of Participation by Citizens, Staff, and Youth in Policy and Program Development* (Washington, D. C., U. S. Department of Health, Welfare and Education, Office of Education, 1949), 15 pp.

OGDEN, Jean, and OGDEN, Jess, *Small Communities in Action: Stories of Citizens Programs at Work* (New York, Harper, 1946).

ROSS, Donald H., and others, *Administration for Adaptability: Public Understanding of Schools and Their Power* (New York, Metropolitan School Study Council, 1951), Vol. 1.

TOY, Henry Jr., "Local Citizens Committees," *Nation's Schools*, Vol. 46 (July, 1950), pp. 26-28.

CHAPTER 15

Organization for Human Relations

It is the thesis of this chapter that improving the formal organization of the personnel is a major step toward optimum achievement in a school system. This improvement can best be realized by the implementation of the human relations concepts and techniques that we discussed in Part 1. The school is a social institution, and, as Drucker has said, "An institution is like a tune; it is not constituted by individual sounds but by the relations between them." [1] It follows, then, that it is much more important to have good people who can work well together in an organization than to have an organizational plan which looks fine only in a line and staff diagram. In fact, that system which has good people working well together with the world's worst organizational plan will be more successful than the system which has the world's best organizational plan and people who work poorly together. However, the best system is that which has good personnel working well together within the framework of the best possible organizational plan.

Our approach to this problem will be, first, to discuss the line and staff concept under which virtually all schools operate today and, second, to suggest six guides to good administrative staffing. [2] Finally, we shall present the case study of one school system which has based its organization on these guides.

LINE AND STAFF

Practically every school system in the United States is organized on a line and staff pattern. We say "practically" because there has been a great deal of criticism concerning the line and staff organization, and it is possible that some school has devised an organizational pattern which is not line and staff oriented. No such organization has yet been reported in the literature. What is this line and staff organization which is so adversely criticized yet which continues to survive 100 per cent?

[1] Peter F. Drucker, *Concept of the Corporation* (New York, John Day, 1946), p. 26.
[2] The study upon which this chapter is based was made under the direction of Richard Wynn of Teachers College, Columbia University, and was undertaken as a project of the Cooperative Development of Public School Administration in New York State.

When we use the term *line* and the term *staff,* we are referring to kinds of administrative officers. Line officers are those people to whom the board of education has delegated power. This power is revealed through certain manifestations of authority. The superintendent of schools is a line officer; so, too, is the building principal. As a line officer, the superintendent selects certain candidates and recommends that they be hired. At other times, he recommends that they be promoted or given salary raises or granted a sabbatical leave or given permission to purchase equipment. Officers who can make these decisions are line officers. A line officer is also a "generalist," with competence in many areas, as contrasted with the specialist, who is expert in one area.

On the other hand, there are those who are called staff officers. Consultants, helping teachers, and, sometimes, assistant superintendents are staff officers. These staff officers have *special* skills or talents. A consultant in reading is a specialist in this area. A helping teacher might be a specialist in the teaching of elementary school students. A staff officer is a specialist in a particular area whose job it is to give advice, when it is requested, to teachers and line officials. Although this definition applies generally, we can go further in our discussion and point out that there are two types of staff officers: *general staff* and *auxiliary service staff.* The general staff officer is a generalist who provides line officers with information on which decisions can be made and serves a co-ordinating function, thereby often exercising line authority. He exercises authority, however, only when it is delegated to him by a superior. A deputy superintendent who is given special assignments illustrates the general staff officer. The auxiliary service staff personnel are specialists who supply expert assistance when it is requested but have no authority except that which is derived from their specialized knowledge. Reading consultants and the like are auxiliary service staff.

Now, any school system, as long as it is an *organized social institution,* is going to have need of line officers and staff officers as defined above. If it does not have them, then it is not an institution. We have pointed out in the chapters on power and authority that power is the cement which binds a social organization together. The problem is not to destroy power and authority but to use them in a manner acceptable in a democratic society. If we abolished authority in school systems, then we would not have school *systems;* we would have an individual tutorial system. Of course, if the parent paid the tutor, we would start our lines of authority all over again!

A realistic approach to the problem is one which would seek to organize as democratically as possible, recognizing that the line and staff concept is inevitable. This is not as difficult as many would have us believe it to be. Lines of authority change when power shifts from group to group. It has been pointed out that there has been a gradual shift of power from administrators to teachers.[3] This trend will no doubt continue. With this shift of power an actuality it is much easier to speak realistically of changing the structure of the schools. Teachers who hold no power cannot function effectively in a committee with administrators. You cannot make teachers and administrators peers by fiat. However, social conditions within the past generation have done what fiat could never do. Let's note again what Dubin has to say about authority in social organizations: [4]

members of an organization understand authority and leadership and their functions. The problem is not to destroy authority or get rid of leadership. That would inevitably destroy the organization itself. The real problem is to make leadership and the exercise of authority operate according to the accepted values and beliefs of our society.

Let us note that what we have been talking about is called the *formal organization* of a school system. There also exists in every school system what is known as an *informal organization,* but this will be discussed in the following chapter.

GUIDELINES FOR ADMINISTRATIVE STAFFING

Content

A study of administrative staffing sponsored by the Cooperative Development of Public School Administration in New York has recently been completed. This study attempted to determine modern concepts of administrative staffing by examining the literature of school administration, business, industry, and the armed services. In addition, "best practice" in administrative staffing was examined by studying the administrative structure of eleven school systems in New York, New Jersey, and Pennsylvania which had been selected as superior examples by a jury of judges. As an outcome of this study six guidelines to administrative staffing were formulated which would provide a staff structure that recognizes authority at the same time that it recognizes the need for individual freedom on the part of the teacher. It is felt that these guidelines would provide for a structure consistent with the theory of human relations as developed in Part 1 of this text. Let us examine the guidelines: [5]

Guideline 1
   The purpose of organization is to clarify and distribute tasks, power, and responsibility among individuals and groups in an orderly manner consistent with the purposes of the enterprise.

[3] See Ch. 5, pp. 115-118.
[4] Robert Dubin, ed., *Human Relations in Administration* (New York, Prentice-Hall, 1951), p. 230.
[5] *Modern Practices and Concepts of Staffing Schools* (Albany, N. Y., Cooperative Development of Public School Administration, 1955).

This guideline centers attention on work assignment rather than the individual. If tasks, power, and responsibility are to be distributed among personnel in an orderly manner, some logical analysis and description of the tasks to be performed must be made. This study has revealed that too many school systems operate without any well-defined and orderly distribution of tasks, authority, and responsibility, and that many more have tended to perpetuate a staff that has grown up around the personal interests and special capabilities of individual staff members without adequate regard for the total job to be done.

This suggests that it is most helpful to think of administrative organization in terms of the purposes to be served. Thus one comes to recognize that there is no intrinsic value in, let us say, the "director of audiovisual services" as a position but only as that position relates to the total effectiveness of the educational enterprise. Thus, people and positions become the means, and purpose becomes the end of organization. All administrative functions are important only to the extent that they contribute toward the improvement of educational opportunity for children.

Guideline 2
> *The role of the central staff should be one of leadership, stimulation, coordination, and service instead of one of inspection and command.*

This concept assumes that teachers are responsible, dependable, mature colleagues of the administrators, important in their own right and not menial subordinates who must be closely controlled and autocratically managed. With this de-emphasis upon the inspectorial role of the administrator, one might well question the worth of the span of control theory in administration which held that an administrator could not operate efficiently if he had more than a small number (frequently thought of as six) of persons reporting directly to him. With the group approach to administrative operation, the administrator might work very effectively with larger numbers of subordinates.

Guideline 3
> *The administrative functions should be organized to provide the machinery for democratic operation.*

The school system should be organized to encourage the creativity and self-expression of all concerned: teachers, parents, and pupils. For example, it is clear that decisions should be made as close to the source of effective action as possible. This suggests a decentralization of decision-making in many areas. It suggests that people must be free not only to talk about needs and issues but also to act and to accept responsibility for their actions.

Guideline 4
> *The administrative staff should be organized to provide individual persons on a staff and individual units in a school system with as much freedom for individual initiative as is consistent with efficient operation and prudential controls.*

The hampering effect on human enterprise of complex procedures, strict chains of command, and many control devices is well known to any veteran of military service. Conversely, the simplicity of the administrative organization in small school systems is well known to many teachers and administrators who have enjoyed the direct, informal contacts that are possible within small organizations. While recognizing the need for some system-wide unity of policy and program, individuals and individual units should be allowed to make adaptations to differing needs within the broad framework of policy.

Guideline 5

> *The organization should be under unit control, and all major administrative officers should be trained professional educators.*

In the unit type of organization, one individual, the superintendent of schools, administers in person or directs the administration of the whole organization. All employees are subordinate to this single officer. In dual or multiple organization, certain functions, very often the business function, are administered by one or more persons who are co-ordinate with the superintendent and responsible to the board of education. Unit control is well established in theory and is practiced by 90 per cent of the schools in the country. Because of the concept of two co-ordinate persons attempting to head an organization is so wrong in educational administration, as it is in all human enterprise, CDPSA is unalterably opposed to dual or multiple organization.

The second aspect of the guideline applies chiefly to the business management official who may not be professionally trained in education. It is the opinion of CDPSA that all personnel serving an administrative, supervisory, or teaching function should have a background of training in education.

Guideline 6

> *The administrative organization, by its very structure, should provide for the continuous and co-operative evaluation and redirection of the organization from the standpoint of adequacy (the degree to which goals are reached) and efficiency (the degree to which goals are reached relative to the available resources).*

Any organization needs to make a continuous evaluation of itself in order to keep "on target." The researchers working with this study found numerous cases where school organizations have expanded in an undirected fashion and have perpetuated obsolete organization without reference to needs. This evaluation should be a co-operative assessment of the organization to avoid the natural bias the incumbents might exhibit toward the *status quo*. This evaluation should focus not only upon the adequacy of the organization but also upon the efficient use of human and material resources.

Function

What is accomplished by this set of guidelines? First of all, these guides to administrative staffing indicate that *recognition of authority is different from imposition of authority*. A staff organized according to these guides will provide for "normal" authority which will always be present, yet it protects the teacher from imposition by a large number of line officers. Second, *line officers are kept at a minimum and staff officers at a maximum*. As we will see, there is only *one* level of authority between the teacher and the superintendent. Third, decisions can be made *on the spot* by the responsible individual, be he teacher or administrator. Fourth, all specialists are used on an "on call" basis, recognizing that the imposition of help on an authoritarian basis will not bring change in the teacher. Fifth, the entire set of guides is based upon the concept of "team play" rather than "passing the word down," on co-operation rather than domination. Sixth, the democratic values of the worth of the individual and the dignity of man form the frame of reference for the operation of the school system.

What would the administrative staff of a school system be like if it were organized according to the above guidelines? Realizing full well that any set of guides will be modified by local conditions, we would have to know something about a community before a staff could be organized. It would be necessary to take into account the wealth of the community, community characteristics, education aspirations, and the like. With this in mind, we shall now consider in detail the organizational plan adopted by the Ridgeway school system and describe its staff.

RIDGEWAY

Ridgeway is what the sociologists would call a well-integrated community. This means that the stresses and strains which result from an influx of new dwellers do not exist. There has been little room for expansion, so that very few people have moved in. The citizens have worked out methods whereby changes can be taken in stride. It now has a population of 25,000, and since there has been no general influx, this is a relatively stable figure. There are only 4200 pupils in the public schools, and very few children of the community attend parochial or private schools. Ridgeway is considered to be a favored community economically, and over $450 is spent per student, exclusive of what is spent for debt service and capital outlay. The economy is considered to be well balanced since there are many small industries, shops, and businesses. It has a larger proportion of professional people than is normally found in the average small city, which is due partly to the proximity of Ridgeway to Metropolis. A large percentage of Ridgeway students go to college, and the community takes great pride in its schools. Ridgeway is very small for a city of its population, having an area of only six square miles. Consequently, little money must be spent for transportation, thereby leaving a greater proportion to be spent on the educational program.

The Ridgeway school system is comprised of six elementary schools, one junior high school, and one senior high school. The professional staff numbers 247, a ratio of seventeen students to one professional staff member. At the present time, about 7 per cent of the budget is spent on administrative services. A number of years ago the schools were surveyed by a university team, and most of the recommendations made by this group have been put into effect. The present superintendent has been in his position for six years.

Central Administrative Staff

The central administrative staff is composed of the superintendent of education; two assistant superintendents, one in charge of funds and facilities, the other in charge of educational opportunity; and a co-ordinator of research. These people would all be called general staff officers, with the exception of the superintendent, in terms of the definition we arrived at earlier. Their function in the system is definitely one of service. They are "on call" to principals and teachers. The assistant superintendent for funds and facilities, for example, is "on call" for purposes of aiding principals and teachers in matters relating to business affairs.

The central staff, together with the principals, is organized into what is called the *administrative cabinet*. This cabinet meets every two weeks on schedule and whenever else *any* member of the council feels it to be necessary. The fact that this latter condition prevails indicates that each member has high status in the council and that it is not the pawn of the superintendent. The council works on each major policy change and is consulted on all major decisions that the superintendent must make. This means that the superintendent shares his decision-making but does not delegate *his* decision-making power.[6] In addition to decision-sharing, the cabinet serves a valuable purpose in the co-ordination of programs and intercommunication among administrative personnel. Other staff members, including teachers are invited to attend council meetings when matters on which they are expert are to be discussed. As we will see, the principal is a key person in this type of organization, and it is necessary for all building principals to work closely together in order that educational policies and programs be co-ordinated. At the same time, the assistant superintendent for educational opportunity can integrate his service specialists with the total program. With specialists "on call," the assistant superintendent must "sell" the changes which the specialists feel to be necessary in teaching methods and in the program. The cabinet meeting can serve many indispensable functions.

Division of Educational Opportunity

This division is headed by the assistant superintendent in charge of educational opportunity. Three co-ordinators are directly responsible to him: the co-ordinator of instructional services, the co-ordinator of pupil personnel services, and the co-ordinator of adult education and community relations. These co-ordinators are responsible for the activities of the several consultants and specialists in their particular areas. The line responsibility of the consultants and specialists is to the assistant superintendent, but while in a building, they work under the direction of the building principal. Because of this, they are truly "on call" and must work *co-operatively* with the classroom teachers. Many schools want their consultants to work co-operatively with teachers yet place them in positions of line authority. This is contrary to the guidelines developed above and to the theory of human behavior in organizations as developed in Part 1.

[6] See Chapter 10.

There is another obvious advantage to this plan of co-operative organization. The consultant or specialist in a particular area is apt to see the student only in terms of his speciality. The art consultant, for instance, perceives the student in terms of art experiences. If each consultant were allowed to impose his own program directly upon the classroom teacher, the resulting program would reflect the power of the consultant rather than the needs of the child. Under Ridgeway's approach, the building principal is responsible for the total educational experience of the student, and he can bring to bear upon the needs of the student the particular expert help which is most appropriate. The various specialists work through the co-ordination and direction of the building principal.

Another example of the use of the consultant demonstrates the value of this approach. The building principal is the person who visits classes to determine which teachers need help and what sort of help they need. When this has been established, he contacts the proper consultant and requests aid for the particular teacher. It should be noted that a teacher who perceives that he needs help can request it, but many times a teacher who needs help does not realize it. This type of organization recognizes the fact that administration and supervision cannot actually be separated.[7] It makes possible a workable method of combining these two functions in one person in such a way as not to damage either.

Division of Funds and Facilities

This division is headed by an assistant superintendent of status equal to that of the building principals and the assistant superintendent in charge of educational opportunity. Two persons, a director of buildings and grounds and a director of food services report directly to this assistant superintendent. They are responsible for the efficiency of the matrons, custodians, and cafeteria workers, although these report directly to the building principal where they are employed. The building principal is the one who makes recommendations to the superintendent concerning the hiring, discharging, transfer, etc., of these people. The line of authority for these workers is from the board to the superintendent to the principal to the worker. Should the principal conclude that a custodian is not performing his duties efficiently, he requests the director of buildings and grounds to instruct the custodian in the proper procedures.

Teachers Council

The Ridgeway Teachers Council is composed of two teachers from each building and one teacher from each subject division. The council meets

[7] William H. Burton and Leo J. Brueckner, *Supervision: A Social Process,* 3d ed. (New York, Appleton-Century-Crofts, 1955), p. 108.

Ridgeway City Schools

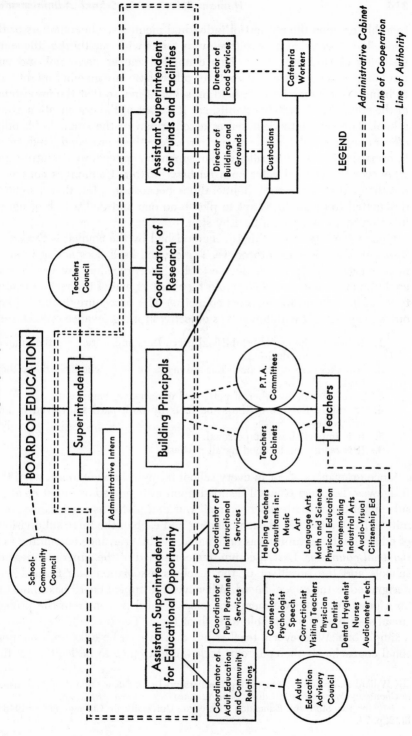

LEGEND

======= *Administrative Cabinet*

- - - - - - *Line of Cooperation*

———— *Line of Authority*

BOARD OF EDUCATION

School-Community Council

Superintendent

Administrative Intern

Teachers Council

Coordinator of Research

Assistant Superintendent for Funds and Facilities

Director of Buildings and Grounds

Director of Food Services

Custodians

Cafeteria Workers

Building Principals

P.T.A. Committees

Teachers Cabinets

Teachers

Assistant Superintendent for Educational Opportunity

Coordinator of Adult Education and Community Relations

Coordinator of Pupil Personnel Services

Coordinator of Instructional Services

Adult Education Advisory Council

Counselors
Psychologist
Speech Correctionist
Visiting Teachers
Physician
Dentist
Dental Hygienist
Nurses
Audiometer Tech

Helping Teachers Consultants in:
Music
Art
Language Arts
Math and Science
Physical Education
Homemaking
Industrial Arts
Audio-Visual
Citizenship Ed

monthly or upon the request of individual members. The members of the council are elected and serve three-year terms with one third of the council being elected each year. This council discusses personnel and curriculum problems as well as whatever other topic any member might wish to bring up. All meetings are held on school time, so that the importance of the council is definitely established. It is part of the organization of the school. The superintendent serves as chairman of the council. All other officers are elected for a one-year term. Meetings are conducted on an informal basis; however, rules of parliamentary procedure are introduced whenever the council votes on a *business* matter. Unanimous consent is not the goal of the group's deliberations because it is felt that a solution designated to please all is apt to please no one and that a lack of agreement on major issues is a healthy sign.

One of the interesting things accomplished by the council is the establishment of a grievance procedure. The council itself does not sit in judgment on grievances, but it does establish the procedure by which they could be ameliorated. (This should be noted as one of the recommended types of enterprises for teachers councils.) The procedure finally worked out is in agreement with Spalding's objectives for a grievance procedure: [8]

1. It insures the use of established precedents and so reduces the number of conflicting decisions.
2. It makes certain that decisions are made by those who have the authority to make them.
3. It reduces the number of petty and unnecessary complaints.
4. It insures the use of the same facts by both parties involved in any grievance.
5. It is impartial and impersonal.
6. It is readily understood by all parties.

Since grievances occur in every school it might be well to see what the Ridgeway Teachers Council decided upon as a procedure. First of all, a subcommittee of the teachers council was designated as a grievance committee. Next, a teacher in each building and each of the three subdivisions of education opportunity was designated by the grievance committee as a *personal counselor*. Last, a committee composed of the superintendent of schools and the president of the teachers association was formed and designated as the *appeal board*. Whenever the appeal board has to decide on a grievance, the two members select a third person from the professional staff who is acceptable to both of them. The procedure adopted is a simple one. Whenever a teacher has a grievance he talks with his personal counselor. If the counselor feels the grievance to be legitimate, the

[8] Willard B. Spalding, "Organizing the Personnel of a Democratic School System," in *Changing Conceptions in Educational Administration: Forty-fifth Yearbook*, National Society for the Study of Education (Chicago, University of Chicago Press, 1946), Pt. 2, p. 74.

two confer with the building principal or, in the case of special personnel, the assistant superintendent. This usually results in a satisfactory settlement. If the teacher and counselor still feel they have not received just treatment, they may appeal. The appeal is written, one copy going to the grievance committee, the other to the administrative council. These two groups then get together to resolve the issue. Final appeals are carried to the appeal board for final disposition. In the case of a grievance lodged against a teacher by an administrator, the first step described above is skipped, but otherwise the action proceeds as outlined.

It is odd that this procedure, similar to the one described ten years ago by Spalding, has never caught on in this country. The number of schools using a plan even vaguely resembling the one described is very small.

School-Community Council

A school community council was created several years ago and has proved to be an effective means of involving lay citizens in school and community problems. As in the teachers council, "ground rules" were set up so that citizens and school people understand the bounds within which they are to operate.

SUMMARY

We have established a set of six guides to administrative staffing and illustrated their use by a case study. The case study demonstrates the practicability of organizing a school system in accordance with the findings of research in human relations. We have employed what could properly be called the "human relations approach" to administrative staffing. Although the general concept of line and staff organization has been maintained, the disadvantages of the scheme have been minimized to the point where they do not constitute a major threat to democratic living.

EXERCISES

1. How does the organization of your school system compare with the one described in this chapter? Draw yours and describe briefly the responsibilities of each position.
2. What are the advantages of the "autonomous" principal?
3. What are the disadvantages of organizational patterns which made use of directors with authority over principals and teachers?
4. Does your school have a definite system for handling grievances? How are they handled?
5. Name all of the administrators in your system and indicate whether they are line, general staff, or auxiliary service staff.

SELECTED BIBLIOGRAPHY

ANDERSON, Walter A., and others, *Organization for Administration: Supervision and Guidance in the Garden City Public Schools* (New York, Center for Community and Field Studies, New York University, 1955).

BURTON, William H., and BRUECKNER, Leo J., *Supervision: A Social Process,* 3d ed. (New York, Appleton-Century-Crofts, 1955), pp. 91-126.

GRIFFITHS, Daniel, FISK, Robert, and HOLLOWAY, George, *Organization and Administration of Kenmore Secondary Schools* (Buffalo, N. Y., Western New York School Study Council, 1956).

HAGMAN, Harlan L., and SCHWARTZ, Alfred, "The Factor of Organization in Administration," *Administration in Profile for School Executives* (New York, Harper, 1955).

Modern Practices and Concepts of Staffing Schools (Albany, N. Y., Cooperative Development of Public School Administration, 1955).

SKOGSBURG, Alfred H., *Administrative Operational Patterns* (New York, Teachers College Bureau of Publications, 1950).

SPALDING, Willard B., "Organizing the Personnel of a Democratic School System," in *Changing Conceptions in Educational Administration: Forty-fifth Yearbook,* National Society for the Study of Education (Chicago, University of Chicago Press, 1946), Pt. 2, pp. 53-85.

CHAPTER 16

Informal Organization

In the preceding chapter, we discussed certain guidelines to the formal organization of a school system. Many people feel that once they understand the formal structure of an organization, they understand how things are done. The idea prevails that the man at the top of the organizational ladder is the one who pulls the strings and that each person has exactly as much authority and responsibility as is indicated by the line and staff chart. Also prevalent is the conviction that in order to "get something done," a person always has to work through the chain of command as it appears in the diagram.

As we think about this problem, however, we suddenly come up short and say, "Yes, sometimes it works like that, but very often it doesn't." And, as we consider further, we note that people do not always go through the chain of command. They sometimes work out ways of doing things in a manner that is not prescribed but seems to them to be much faster and more efficient. Moreover, some persons lower down in the chain of command seem to be able to get certain things done, when the individual who is authorized to do them cannot. We are aware, also, of the way news travels in the school system; it seldom requires an official announcement to have all the teachers know of certain important actions that will affect them.

Each of the situations we have just described is due to the activity of small groups or cliques. Every administrator will confirm the existence of these groups in his system. They are not formally organized; their membership fluctuates somewhat; and their power and prestige varies, depending on the strength of several factors. It has been observed that these informal groups can help or hinder morale and that they definitely influence the accomplishments of a school. Although there are times when the normal processes of education in a school system are slowed down by these informal groups, there are other times when these processes are accelerated by them. As administrators, then, we are concerned not only with the question of why this difference exists but how we can encourage these groups toward the more constructive end. The answers to both these considerations begin with an understanding of the structure of informal groups.

317

THE NATURE OF INFORMAL ORGANIZATION

Most of those who have attempted to define the term usually end up with a description rather than a hard and fast definition. Simon, for instance, has this to say: [1]

The term "informal organization" refers to interpersonal relations in the organization that affect decisions within it but either are omitted from the formal scheme or are not consistent with that scheme. It would probably be fair to say that no formal organization will operate efficiently without an accompanying informal organization. Every new organization must have its initial "shakedown cruise" before it will run smoothly; and each new organization member must establish informal relations with his colleagues before he becomes a significant part of the working organization.

Barnard talks about persons interacting with one another without any "specific conscious *joint* purpose." As a result the behavior, emotions, and thoughts of the persons involved are affected. Concerning these activities he says: [2]

informal organization is indefinite and rather structureless, and has no definite subdivision. It may be regarded as a shapeless mass of quite varied densities, the variation in density being a result of external factors affecting the closeness of people geographically or of formal purposes which bring them specially into contact for conscious joint accomplishments. These areas of special density I call informal organizations, as distinguished from societal or general organizations in its informal aspects. Thus there is an informal organization of a community, of a state. For our purposes, it is important that there are informal organizations related to formal organizations everywhere.

These two discussions stress the variability of informal structure. They point out that although it is extremely difficult to diagram the informal organization of a group, it is always present. Informal organization is present at two stages of the development of a formal organization. First, we always have some informal organization before we have a formal organization. In education, for instance, we had instruction given to the young by the adults of the tribe. As civilization progressed, individual families hired tutors for their children, and then the educative process was formalized by the formation of a system of schools and colleges. Informal organization precedes formal organization. Second, informal organization accompanies formal organization. When people are structured together, they will always seek other methods of working together. As they do, forms of behavior which differ from those of the formal organization are set up.

[1] Herbert A. Simon, *Administrative Behavior* (New York, Macmillan, 1950), pp. 148, 149.

[2] Chester I. Barnard, *The Function of the Executive* (Cambridge, Mass., Harvard University Press, 1938), p. 115. Copyright, 1938, by the President and Fellows of Harvard College.

These different forms are not firm and steady but vary as circumstances warrant. The data derived from the study of leadership that emerges from "leaderless" groups quite clearly indicate this relationship of varying behavior and situations.

THE FORMATION OF INFORMAL GROUPS

Research on the formation of informal groups in the public schools has not been extensive. In fact, the topic is rarely discussed in school administration texts. In view of this, and in order to simplify our approach, we shall present a case history illustrating the development of one such group and then discuss the factors which led the faculty to informal organization.

Hidden Valley School was a small public school quite isolated from the world. There were only two roads leading into the valley and the community was so small that all but two of the twelve teachers lived outside the valley. They traveled some twenty miles each way. The principal, Mr. Alexander, lived in the valley in a house owned by the school district. The school, although there were only 200 students, was organized into three departments: elementary, high school academic, and trades, each with a chairman and its own building. The avowed intent of Mr. Alexander was to rotate chairmen.

In 1948, seven new faculty members were employed at the Hidden Valley School. There were also four members of the past year's staff and Mr. Alexander, who had served as principal for two years. Mr. Casey of the print shop, Mrs. Barton, the eighth-grade teacher, and Mr. Martin, the English teacher, were appointed chairmen of the above-mentioned departments. They were very helpful to the new teachers and worked with them to the extent that all but one returned for the following year. Although they worked well with their teachers, the chairmen were quite outspoken in their criticism of the principal.

Mr. Alexander had come to Hidden Valley from Morriston, a small community some fifty miles away. It was generally understood that he had not been very satisfactory at Morriston and that the board had requested his resignation. He was a little touchy about this and explained to those around him that he was "just too progressive for that small town."

The faculty was in the habit of stopping off at the carpentry shop each noon after lunch and having informal "bull sessions" with each other. This exchange of information during lunch hour led to all the activity which follows.

The teachers found by comparing notes with each other that the supplies were being doled out by the principal, not as they arrived, but as he saw fit. Some teachers were in possession of most of their ordered equipment, but others had gotten little of the teaching supplies. By making an issue of some of the supplies, the teachers found that Mr. Alexander was in the habit of holding back a certain amount of equipment when it came in. When a teacher became irate over the lack of certain items, Mr. Alexander would appease him by going to his locker and giving the teacher the supplies he asked for.

At another noon session, the teachers found that some were being docked for days they had taken off, but that others were paid for days off. When questioned on sick-leave policy, the principal replied, "You are permitted ten days a year, *personal* sick leave only." Thereafter, the teachers who had personal difficulties or family illnesses which necessitated taking time off did not tell the true story to the principal but called in sick or had someone else do so for them.

During the winter months, several teachers had some close calls driving to school on slippery roads. One faculty member smashed his car beyond repair. The faculty recalled that the year previous, a teacher had been hospitalized because of a bad weather accident. The school was never closed on days when other public schools in the area were, and the staff wondered if they weren't entitled to a little consideration on this score.

The next year, 1949, one teacher left and two new teachers were hired, the second on recommendation of the faculty in order to cut class loads. At this time, new chairmen were appointed for each department and told at the faculty meeting that the position was strictly honorary and would be rotated each year, so that each teacher would be expected to take his or her turn as designated by the principal. The two teachers appointed as chairmen of the trade and elementary departments at that time will start their *eighth* consecutive year this fall.

The position of chairman entailed handling all communications through the one phone in his building and relaying messages to the other teachers in that building. In addition, each chairman was responsible for building cleanup and maintenance plus all grades (marking sheets), registers, and absentee lists. The chairmen made up their individual building rules and were responsible for seeing that they were carried out. Internal problems of hall passes, recess time, and supervision were generally settled in faculty meetings of the building personnel.

Because the rules were different in each building, there was a marked dissatisfaction among the students and some grumbling from the teachers.

The staff noticed that it seemed to be the principal's philosophy to let the new teachers, "sink or swim," by themselves with little or no help from the administration. A satisfactory job by a teacher meant that he had stayed for a year without quitting or being thrown out of his room by the students. Professional competence in teaching subject matter had very little to do with rehiring a teacher. Tenure was granted to all teachers who stayed for the probationary period. There was a tremendous amount of variation in the classroom procedures and disciplinary action.

In the meantime, faculty meetings were sporadic and of little value when they were held. Two or three "first-year" teachers would leave every term; some very bitter about the school and administration. The remaining nucleus of "old timers" worked hard to keep the school functioning.

Gradually these teachers gained confidence in themselves and did something about the situation which seemed to be quite drastic but which was felt to be necessary. They drew up a petition calling for seven administrative improvements and submitted it to the principal and to the board of education. All twelve teachers signed the paper, which read as follows:

> In order to consolidate our thinking on various problems for the benefit of Hidden Valley School and to raise the standards, morale, and welfare of the school personnel, as well as that of the students, the following administrative steps are hereby recommended:
>
> 1. SALARY: scale to be kept higher than other schools with equivalent positions in order to attract and keep desirable personnel. Schedule of years and salary to be included in a manual (See Item 7).
> 2. SICK LEAVE: to be interpreted more broadly to include family emergencies.
> 3. CONTRACTS: to be given to teachers prior to March 1. To be returned by March 15.

4. BAD WEATHER: closings to coincide with those of other public schools in order to prevent any possibility of accident due to impossible road conditions.
5. REQUISITIONS: turned in complete by May 30 should be filled and materials ready for use in September in order for teachers to be able to plan program well in advance of school opening.
6. FACULTY MEETINGS: to be held at regular intervals in order to clarify issues as they arise.
7. MANUAL: of regulations governing the school be published and distributed. Check made on interpretation and usage of the rules, regularly, by the principal by visits to the school buildings.

Mr. Alexander called a faculty meeting immediately after receiving his copy of the petition and began by berating the staff for going over his head and sending a copy of the petition to the board of education. Then he said that since nothing could be done without a crisis, he was glad to see that a crisis had been reached; now he felt that he could recommend some needed changes in school policy to the board. Mr. Alexander further stated that his position was favorable for most of the recommendations and that he was pleased to see such an aggressive group of teachers who were interested in raising the standards of the institution in which they worked. However, his hands were tied on most of these matters—they would be referred to the school board at their very next meeting.

The principal then dealt with the issues, one by one, as follows:
1. SALARY: He agreed that the teachers should all get more money for the type of work they were doing but commented that salary should not have been first item on the list because it would seem to the board members that the teachers were being unduly mercenary.
2. SICK LEAVE: This item was skipped entirely.
3. CONTRACTS: He promised earlier contracts.
4. BAD WEATHER DAYS: He pointed out that the students lived very near the school and therefore were always there, and that it was up to the teachers to get to school as best they could. "Get here anytime you can; if you're late, it won't matter."
5. REQUISITIONS: He claimed that these couldn't possibly be filled by September because money was allotted to the school monthly and purchases had to be made that way. (None of the teachers had ever heard of this before.)
6. FACULTY MEETINGS: He promised more regular meetings.
7. MANUAL: A committee was set up to gather information for a manual. As for the rest of the suggestion, Mr. Alexander said he did not believe in "snoopervision," and since they were all good teachers, a check visit was unnecessary.

In reading this case we can see how a typical informal structuring of the faculty started. The faculty formed the habit of meeting together in the carpentry shop during each noon hour. This provided a setting in which the needs of individuals could be expressed. As these needs were expressed, it was realized that certain of them, namely, supplies and sick leave, were common to the group. Further, the formal organization not only did not help to meet the needs of the group with regard to these items, but it actually created the problems relevant to these needs. As the group continued to talk together, other common needs became obvious, and the group began to wonder how it could act to meet its needs. We should note that if the teachers had felt that the formal structure of the school provided the necessary solutions to their problems, they would not have had the common interests around which to organize.

MOTIVATIONS OF INFORMAL GROUPS

The motivation of the members of informal groups within formal organizations are both personal and institutional. The personal motivation which exists is due to the needs which they have as persons. In the above case, the issues of salary, stormy weather, sick leave, and contracts would fall into this category. The issues relating to requisitions, faculty meetings, and the manual fall primarily into the second category. Of course, the two are not completely separate, and one should not attempt to place them into discrete groups. It should be noted, however, that although informal organizations are created to meet individual needs which are not being met by the formal organization, they also may be formed to improve the organization itself. In the above case, the teachers felt that they had a professional responsibility to improve what they thought was a very bad situation. The motivation of the group was not entirely selfish.

SUBVERSIVE INFLUENCE OF INFORMAL GROUPS

Although we have noted that informal groups organize to fill individual needs of the members and also to improve the organization, these goals are always in terms of the individual and not the formal organization. There are times when the informal organization is formed to oppose the authority of the organization. This is a symptom of poor morale and has been found in industry, where the informal group sometimes sets a production level for its members which is below the production level expected by the company. The informal group polices its decision by all measures, including the use of force and subterfuge. In the above case, for instance, the teachers decided to use the sick-leave provision as they interpreted it and lie, if necessary, to get the benefit that they considered rightfully theirs.

Informal groups in schools often subvert the purpose of the school. One example is the way in which the older teachers condition the new teachers. Generally, the older teachers take the new ones aside and indicate that the "theory" they learned in college is useless and that they ought not expect to initiate too many reforms. In other words, the veteran teachers act to make the new teachers conform to their pattern of working, and since the nature of education is evolving and experimental, this constitutes subversive activity.

INFORMAL ORGANIZATION AND
THE ADMINISTRATOR

What implications are there in our discussion of informal organizations for the practicing school administrator? Although most administrators are aware of the ways in which the formal pattern of organization of the school is contradicted, they generally do not realize the total effect of informal groups. It also seems that they are unaware of the reasons why these groups form and how they operate.

The administrator should realize that informal groups form because, from the point of view of individuals, there is something wrong, something inefficient in the system. In one situation in which he worked, the author found, for instance, that it was virtually impossible to obtain supplies and equipment through official channels. He discovered that there was an informal group, practically a social order, set up among the nonteaching employees of the school. They gave each other, very freely, of whatever each wanted. After this discovery, he had little difficulty in obtaining anything in this line because he worked through his secretary. The author reasoned that inasmuch as supplies and equipment were plentiful and no one was being deprived by this procedure, short-cutting the official channels was a proper thing to do. This is a common procedure in institutions.

The school administrator needs to evaluate each short-cut that is brought to his attention in terms of whether or not it is more effective than the procedure which is in the formal structure. Generally speaking, he will find that incorporating such short-cuts into the formal operating structure *decentralizes* authority. Many of the attempts of informal groups to change procedures are of the sort which will cut red tape and work across lines of authority.

The primary responsibility of the school administrator in handling this problem is to attempt to make the informal and formal structures congruent. To the extent that he is successful in recognizing informal groups which have constructive goals and incorporating their suggestions into the structure he will have a high morale school. When informal groups have a destructive or subversive goal, he should attempt to work with the group so that it redefines its goals. Its destructive goal may be due to poor communication and the inability of the administrator to define and interpret properly the goals of the school with the staff.

DEMOCRATIC IMPLICATIONS OF
INFORMAL GROUPS

One of the most significant aspects of our discussion of informal groups in formal organizations deals with the democratic nature of these groups.

As we have described the process by which informal groups came into being and grow, their democratic nature has become obvious. Here are groups which come to life because of common needs. They are leaderless, at first, and, as they develop, they go through a succession of leaders. The one who can help at a particular moment is the leader. As the group gains strength and validates its goals, the formal structure changes to admit the new concept, and the cycle starts again.

The climate of the school should be such that these groups will form but will also *test their goals*. The administrator should strive to establish a permissive atmosphere in which the informal group can thrive, but he also needs to diagnose the groups to determine whether or not they would destroy the parent organization. Hagman and Schwartz have a statement which summarizes this discussion particularly well: [3]

The administrator who frowns on the short cuts and unofficial activities by which personnel in the organization seem to secure some immediate objectives should be cautious about disturbing the kind of human relations in the organization which permits accomplishment outside the formal channels of operation. If the accomplishment is of a kind serving the general purposes of the organization and if the modification in process does not weaken the formal organization, the informal practice can add to the efficiency of the enterprise. Though the supervisory staff may be established to answer questions teachers may raise, many questions are better answered by fellow teachers in the school situation in which the question is raised and in terms of the particular conditions which prevail at the time of the question. When a teacher needs the special service of the school custodian, insistence upon requests being made to a custodial supervisory officer rather than to the custodian directly may prevent a need from being met. It is likely that in all schools the custodial staff performs many tasks not contemplated when the organizational charts were drawn and duties assigned.

There is much truth in the declaration that most organizations would be tied up in their own processes if it were not for the modification and irregularities of the informal organization which accompanies the formal organization.

SUMMARY

Informal organization precedes formal organization. It occurs when groups are formed to meet needs common to a set of individuals. Once the formal group comes into being, its structure gives rise to needs which it cannot meet. This causes informal groups to be formed. Informal organization is to be found in every organization. In fact it has been said: [4]

The formal organization cannot take into account the sentiments and values residing in the social organization by means of which individuals or groups of individuals are informally differentiated, ordered, and integrated.... Without

[3] Harlan L. Hagman and Alfred Schwartz, *Administration in Profile for School Executives* (New York, Harper, 1955), p. 92.

[4] F. S. Roethlisberger and William J. Dickson, *Management and the Worker* (Cambridge, Mass., Harvard University Press, 1941), pp. 560-562. Copyright, 1939, by the President and Fellows of Harvard College.

them, formal organization could not survive for long. Formal and informal organization are interdependent aspects of social interaction.

We find informal organization emerging most frequently in those organizations whose formal structure does not provide adequate opportunity for satisfying the need for recognition, interaction, and other common needs. In addition to personal needs, informal groups organize to perform the functions of the institution in a manner which they feel to be more efficient.

The democratic values that can accrue from informal groups in a school system should cause an administrator to work toward creating an environment in which such groups will thrive and, at the same time, work with the groups to define their goals in constructive directions.

EXERCISES

1. What kind of informal organization exists in your school system?
2. What were the needs around which the various groups were formed?
3. What is your attitude as an administrator concerning these informal groups?
4. Consider the demands of one particular informal group in your school system. Would the demands of this group strengthen or weaken the formal structure of the school if they were accepted? What kind of changes would be required? Why does the group demand what it does? Have you, as an administrator, aided them in defining these goals?
5. What is the informal structure of your community? What groups does it contain? What do they want?

SELECTED BIBLIOGRAPHY

BARNARD, Chester I., *The Functions of the Executive* (Cambridge, Mass., Harvard University Press, 1947), pp. 114-126.

DUBIN, Robert, ed., *Human Relations in Administration* (New York, Prentice-Hall, 1951), pp. 47-78.

HAGMAN, Harlan L., and SCHWARTZ, Alfred, *Administration in Profile for School Executives* (New York, Harper, 1955), pp. 74-106.

ROETHLISBERGER, F. J., *Management and Morale* (Cambridge, Mass., Harvard University Press, 1952), pp. 46-66.

———, and DICKMAN, William J., *Management and the Worker* (Cambridge, Mass., Harvard University Press, 1941).

WHYTE, William Foote, *Human Relations in the Restaurant Industry* (New York, McGraw-Hill, 1948).

CHAPTER 17

Working with the
Board of Education

The relationship between the board of education and the school staff, particularly the chief administrator, is generally considered to be pertinent to any discussion of human relations and school administration. Many of the specific actions of the board on matters of business affect the human relations of the school staff. This is true of board decisions concerning budget policies, purchasing procedures, records keeping, and the like. Although this chapter is primarily concerned with the relationship between the chief school administrator and the board of education, the frame of reference in which the subject is discussed indicates that the board is a vital element of the total educational enterprise.

Since we are writing for school administrators and not board members, it is necessary that certain limitations be imposed upon our discussion. We will not be overly concerned with the technicalities of board operation. These have been covered adequately in several recent texts which are listed in the selected bibliography for this chapter. Rather, we shall discuss the ways in which the administrator works with the board—the personal as well as the institutional relationships and the various official and unofficial functions of each. We shall consider the superintendent both as executive officer of the board and as leader of the board. Finally, we shall touch briefly on the conventional type of board organization and its consequences.

FUNCTIONS OF THE BOARD AND
THE SUPERINTENDENT

Invariably, it is stated that the function of the board is to *legislate* and the function of the superintendent is to *execute*. In other words, the board *establishes* policy and the superintendent *administers* the policy. This, however, though generally accepted, would seem to be an oversimplification of what is actually a rather complex relationship. A study undertaken by the author brought out one weakness in this simple delineation of responsibility. A modified "forced-choice" questionnaire was administered to school board chairmen in twenty-four selected school systems in two states. The superintendents in these systems had previously been rated as to their effectiveness. It was assumed that the boards in those systems whose superintendents were rated most successful would have delineated most clearly between policy making and administration. Instead, it was found that there was little difference in the way in which the board chairmen of the most successful and least successful superintendents reacted to the questions.[1] This was interpreted to mean that there was no real dichotomy of board and superintendent functions. As far as could be determined through a series of interviews of boards and superintendents in apparently the best operating situations, they worked as a team, with considerable overlap in functions.

There is some evidence to substantiate the above findings. Appleby noted that in actual practice policy formulation and administration are interrelated.[2] This interrelation comes about because the board needs to know certain facts which only the superintendent has before policy can be made wisely. Likewise, in order to administer policy, the superintendent needs to understand all ramifications of the policy, and he can do so only if he is in on the development of the policy from the outset. In actual practice, in good school situations, it has been found that the superintendent normally supplies the evidence on which the board makes the policy. The board, in turn, is interested in the administration of the policy and checks on it by asking the superintendent to make periodic reports. In this manner, the board exercises control over the administration of the school.

These studies postulate a somewhat different approach to the relationship between the board and the superintendent than is found normally in the textbooks. They indicate that there should exist only a general understanding as to the demarcation of duties between the board and the administrator. A sense of co-operation and co-ordination should be developed that permits a liberal exchange of ideas and views from which both the function of administration and the function of policy making can profit. The board should utilize the professional knowledge and experience of the administrator as a constant source of information and techniques. This is not to imply that the superintendent is always correct in his assumptions and decisions; but, for all policies under consideration, the administrator should act as a resource person and furnish the board with pertinent information. Nor does it suggest that the board rubber-stamp, that is, automatically accept, the recommendations of the superintendent. The board members must weigh his evidence against their own experience,

---

[1] Daniel E. Griffiths, "An Evaluation of the Leadership of the School Superintendent" (Unpublished Ph.D., dissertation, Yale University, 1952).

[2] Paul H. Appleby, *Policy and Administration* (University, Ala., University of Alabama Press, 1949).

their knowledge of what the community wants, and they also must apply the measures of consistency that laymen working with a specialist should apply.[3] Thus, the relationship between the board and the administrator can probably best be described as one of *teamwork*. One cannot function effectively without the other. Good policies cannot be made without the help of the superintendent, and good administration is impossible without the support and encouragement of the board.

THE SUPERINTENDENT AS EXECUTIVE OFFICER

Most superintendents in the country consider themselves to be executive officers of the board of education. A study by the American Association of School Administrators indicates this to be true of 85 per cent of the city superintendents and 77 per cent of the rural superintendents.[4] The report made it quite clear, however, that there was much confusion about the meaning of the term *executive officer*. There is a tremendous range in the way in which superintendents actually function as executive officers. One extreme of this range can best be illustrated by the following situation.

We were sitting in a superintendent's office talking with him during a Christmas vacation when a knock came at the door. There stood a mechanic, who asked, "Where's the fire extinguisher that needs fixing?" The superintendent, obviously at sea, asked a couple of questions, and finally the mechanic said, "Well, Mr. Brown is a member of the board and he told me to come and fix the extinguisher. I should think you would at least know where it is!"

In this case, Mr. Brown was chairman of the standing committee on building maintenance, and he "administered" that area without consulting the superintendent. As can be seen, he inspected the buildings, made arrangements for repairs, and submitted the bills. Some board members go a step further and actually make the repairs themselves!

A second example shows even more clearly the superintendent's failure to function as executive officer of his board:

During a particularly heavy rainstorm a walk had washed out in the play area of the Downs Central School. The washout made the walk dangerous to use, but the damage was of such a nature that it could have been repaired in a very short time at a cost of about $25.00. The supervising principal called the board member in charge of grounds but was unable to reach him. Since he could not have it repaired on his own, he had to stop all outdoor physical education activities for the day.

In both cases the superintendent considered himself the executive officer of the board. Actually, neither could spend $25 without the permission

[3] See above, Ch. 13.
[4] *The American School Superintendent: Thirtieth Yearbook* (Washington, D. C., American Association of School Administrators, 1952), p. 115.

of at least one member of the board, and sometimes, without the vote of the whole board.

At the other extreme of the range, there is the superintendent whose authority is almost supreme. The board rubber-stamps all his decisions. In one community the superintendent even selects the board members and merely submits their names to the mayor for official appointment. These superintendents are functioning as executive officers of their boards, of course. But here the function becomes autocratic, not co-operative. And in such cases, usually, the entire school operation reflects this kind of administrative behavior.

The concept of the executive officer is quite clear in the literature, although it is not clear in practice. The American Association of School Administrators has presented a picture of the superintendent as executive officer of the board in a situation in which the spirit of teamwork is high. In relation to the general purposes of the school they say: [5]

Board: Legislates and establishes general policies, such as the scope of the educational offerings to be maintained, from nursery school to junior college; sets length of school year and vacations; decides extent of expenditures to be made for education; decides upon holidays to be provided; uses effort to secure state legislation to meet local needs; employs a professional school executive to administer the schools and evaluates and appraises his services.

Superintendent: Assumes immediate charge of the entire school system, as the board's chief executive officer in large school systems and often as its only executive officer in smaller school systems; co-ordinates the work of all administrative departments, preferably as a superior officer under whom business and other executives in the system serve; executes the policies of the board or assumes responsibility for seeing that they are executed and recommends policies for the board to consider in improving the system and its educational service to the pupils and the community.

Why is it that this obviously clear and logical definition of the executive functions of the superintendent is not generally accepted by board members, particularly in small school districts? Hunkins is probably quite correct when he says: [6]

In the larger communities the members of the boards of education are likely to have had more opportunity for experience in the delegation of executive duties than those in smaller communities. The urban board may be composed of members who are directors of banks, foremen in factories, managers of corporations, or others with daily practice in delegating duties. The successful delegation of duties may, in fact, be the very basis for their success in daily life.

When such people are elected to a board of education it strikes them at once that the wise thing to do is to refer managerial responsibility quite completely to those trained for the specialized work. Such men have neither the time nor the inclination for executive detail outside their own realm of training. They are

[5] *School Boards in Action: Twenty-fourth Yearbook* (Washington, D. C., American Association of School Administrators, 1946), p. 49.

[6] Ralph V. Hunkins, *Superintendent and School Board* (Lincoln, Neb., University of Nebraska Press, 1949), pp. 12-13.

used to formulating policies and assigning the execution of them to others. They carry this principle naturally into their actions and reactions as board members.

In contrast, the characteristics of the typical small community board member is apt to be strikingly different. Such a board member may be the proprietor of a small business responsible for the direction of a few or even no employees, a doctor who is his own bookkeeper, a lawyer who does his own typewriting, a farmer who does possibly all of his own work, or a housewife unaccustomed even to directing servants.

With such a background of daily experience it is not difficult to conceive the attitude that these smaller-community leaders will take toward their responsibilities if they find themselves on a board of education. They are used to doing things directly and personally, without delegating much, if any, work to others. To them the implication of their responsibilities as board members is plain. They have been elected by the people to run the schools. The job looms as a personal obligation—just as their daily work is an obligation to roll up their sleeves and wade in. Soap, pencils, paper, and desks need to be bought. Teachers need to be employed. So they proceed to purchase the supplies and to interview applicants for the teaching vacancies that exist. They proceed to get these things done in the best way they know.

A complaint from a school patron to one of these board members constitutes, in his mind, a personal assignment to look into the matter and make an adjustment. It just does not naturally occur to such board members that it would be better and simpler and easier for them to delegate such responsibilities to the superintendent of schools.

It is this situation that makes the small-town school superintendency a difficult position to fill satisfactorily. Proper working conditions in connection with the division of responsibilities for the administration of the schools, by the nature of the situation, are difficult to establish and to maintain. It is under such a burden that the typical inexperienced and untried school superintendent is destined to begin his career.

This states very clearly the way in which the human factors clash with the theory of school administration. It is also evident that much of the theory of school administration is drawn from experiences with urban or suburban schools. These schools become known as "pilot" schools, and their practices are urged upon other schools. It is obvious from both Hunkin's explanation and an examination of other studies on the subject that the accepted definition of executive officer of the board came about because of the type of school board members which these urban and suburban school districts had. There is no doubt, either, that when boards have efficient, well-trained superintendents, this relationship works much better than when the superintendent plays a more menial role. Unquestionably a superintendent should always strive to establish this relationship between himself and the board.

As was implied above, there are two major obstacles to the establishment of the superintendent as executive officer of the board in smaller communities. The first has to do with board members, and the second with superintendents. First, the way of life of the board member militates against his working on a policy-making level. Inasmuch as he *does* everything in his own enterprise, he cannot see why the job of board member should be any different. His background conditions his perception of the present situation, namely, the board-superintendent relationship. With this conditioned perception of his role, he can see no necessity for an executive officer. The second point is that superintendents usually begin their careers in small communities. They come into the position with no administrative background and, generally, with inadequate training. They are not equipped either professionally or emotionally to become the executive officer of the board. Furthermore, they stay just long enough to learn the job, get a better one, and then they are gone. With nomadic school administrators, there is little chance to develop the relationship which exists in larger communities, where the board members are of the professional and managerial group and the superintendent is highly skilled, selected, and has long tenure of office. What actually happens is that the board members develop a degree of skill as administrators and provide the small school district with whatever stability it does have.

The concept of the executive officer of the board of education must be viewed as a flexible guide. It is a highly desirable goal to attain when both board members and superintendent are fitted by background and training to accept these roles. For the present, however, those communities lacking the necessary prerequisites will have to be content with something else.

As a superintendent moves into a new situation, he should analyze those characteristics of the board members that will determine how much of an executive officer he can become. He should also work from the outset to convince the board that he is competent. The burden of proof is always on the superintendent. If he proceeds with discretion, he can establish rapport with the board and evolve his executive responsibilities and duties. A sound relationship between the board and the superintendent is a highly personal sort of thing and is not attained by fiat or by previous rules and regulations.

THE SUPERINTENDENT AS BOARD LEADER

We have discussed at some length the concept of the superintendent as a leader of the school staff. We learned that he exercises authority and has his leadership position firmly established in legal terms. We also demonstrated that it was necessary for him to establish himself as the chosen leader of his staff. In working with the board of education, the superintendent is in quite a different position. All his power and authority derives from the board. The board of education is the superior in the situation, not the superintendent. How then does the superintendent "lead" the board of education?

Being realistic about this problem of the superintendent as the leader of the board of education, we know very well that many superintendents exercise no leadership at all. They have not been able to determine ways and means by which to influence their boards. Many have tried *direct* methods —that is, they have "told" the board what they wanted—and having been rebuked, have stopped all efforts. A direct and open approach often appears to the board member to be a frontal attack on his authority, which he immediately moves to resist. In Chapter 6, however, we found that another method of influencing institutional superiors is *indirection*.

Indirect Approach

If, by a process of education, the board can be made to see that the superintendent's position on an issue is valid, it will be much more likely to adopt his suggestions. In Hunkins' very practical and valuable book there is a case describing this method of exerting leadership.[7]

A certain superintendent was convinced that a junior high school should be established in the community. The board of education, he had reason to know, was opposed to the junior high school idea. The superintendent was new on the job, so he waited several months before he even mentioned junior high school. During those months he was building up an effective relationship with the board, or trying to.

Eventually the time came when the superintendent found an opportunity to mention the spread of junior high schools in this country. In fact, several opportunities to mention the matter informally came along, after board meetings and at other times when the board was not in business session. The superintendent took occasion to present board members with some articles about junior high schools. Some of these were read by the more conscientious members. In reporting on his attendance at educational conventions, the superintendent had further opportunity to mention junior high schools by referring to addresses about their advantages.

Finally the time came to make a recommendation about a junior high school. But the superintendent's first recommendation was not that a junior high school be decided upon. Rather, he recommended that the board give careful consideration to the advantages of junior high schools. With this recommendation the superintendent presented data on the growth of the junior high school movement and a summary of the arguments for such an organization.

This approach led in time to the appointment of a committee of board members to study more deeply the issues and to present a recommendation. By this act of appointing a committee the board made the issue their issue. Before that the matter was wholly in the hands of the superintendent—or rather in the mind of the superintendent. The committee in the end recommended the establishment of a local junior high school and the board accepted the recommendation.

We may summarize the procedure used by the superintendent in *leading* the board to its final decision as follows:

1. He was firmly convinced, on the basis of his knowledge of education, that a junior high school was needed.

[7] *Ibid.*, pp. 32-33.

2. He adopted an indirect approach and did not openly try to impose his will.
3. He did not hurry.
4. He dropped remarks concerning the advantages of the junior high school.
5. He distributed articles on the advantages of junior high schools.
6. He never directly recommended a junior high school, recommending only that it be studied.
7. He got the board to think of this as their solution.

This indirect approach may be considered theoretically sound because sociologists and group dynamics people find it to be the method by which subordinates most frequently influence superiors. The fact that many superintendents have used it successfully would tend to support it from a practical point of view. Nevertheless, there are some who question the ethics of this procedure. It is important for us, therefore, to understand exactly how indirection differs from manipulation.

In Chapter 5, we discussed those methods of exerting power which are acceptable in a democratic society and concluded that manipulation was *not* one of them. Although the superintendent in the above case used indirect methods to influence his board, he made explicit, from the beginning, where his sympathies lay and what he thought was the best plan. There was never any question as to his views concerning junior high schools.

In terms of ethics, the superintendent who uses indirect methods of leading the board behaves ethically so long as he makes explicit his feelings in the matter. If he is aboveboard and honest, he is not guilty of manipulation. He would be manipulating the board if he led them to think he favored one plan while rigging the situation to get the board to believe in another. In other words, if the superintendent in our illustration had led the board to think he agreed with their original position on junior high schools while he dropped hints, provided articles, and the like, then he would have been guilty of manipulation. Since this was not the case, the superintendent was on sound ethical grounds as defined in our democratic society.

Having established the validity of indirection, we well may wonder if the superintendent must always use this time-consuming approach. The answer, of course, is no, and the conditions under which the direct method is feasible merit our attention.

Direct Approach

The ability to use the direct approach does not come quickly or without considerable interaction. The superintendent should always use an indirect approach on major issues when he is new to the position. A feeling of confidence on the part of the board must be established and nurtured until it gives rise to something akin to what Burton calls "the authority of the situation." [8] As the superintendent works with the board over a period of years, the board comes to realize his strengths. It realizes that he has ability in certain areas and can be trusted to accept more and more responsibility. He develops power and authority quite separate from that which the board has granted him. Thus, when a situation arises and the board knows that the superintendent is competent to handle the issue without its interference, it is inclined to let him do so. This attitude carries over into other affairs in which the board has authority, and the superintendent finds that the board expects direct statements from him on these matters. His professional authority is recognized as equal to their legal authority and they can then act together as equals. When the superintendent has attained this relationship with his board, he no longer needs to use the indirect approach on all issues.

Orientation of New Board Members

One of the most profitable areas of board leadership to the superintendent is in the matter of orientation of new board members. Board membership is a rather complicated job which takes much time and effort to master. The superintendent is in a position to suggest to present board members that they inaugurate a program of orientation for the new members. The superintendent has a great deal at stake in such a program. Many men are elected to the board of education for the purpose of accomplishing particular objectives. They represent pressure groups or are elected on a "reform" basis. Others accept the job in good faith, but know nothing at all of the duties and responsibilities of their position. The superintendent is the school official who has to overcome the obstacles created by a poor board of education, so it is profitable for him to do what he can to teach the new board member his job as soon as possible.

A program of orientation can begin when candidates declare that they intend to seek election to the board. At this time, the board should send to each candidate a few selected articles or books which describe the job of the school board member. Possibly the best book at the present time is *The Challenge of School Board Membership* by Daniel R. Davies and Fred W. Hosler.[9] This little book is written in a very readable style which appeals to board members and includes a discussion of the importance of the job, what the job entails, what good schools are like, and many other topics of major interest to a new board member. It could be read easily in one evening and would help to set the stage for later work.

All candidates should be invited to a board meeting so that they may see how the business of the school district is transacted. Those who are

---

[8] William H. Burton and Leo J. Brueckner, *Supervision: A Social Process*, 3d ed. (New York, Appleton-Century-Crofts, 1955), pp. 111-112.

[9] New York, Chartwell House, 1949.

elected will then understand better how the board operates, and this will cut down the time it takes for them to function as effective board members.

Once the election is over, it is desirable for the board and superintendent to welcome the new member. This might be done by means of a congratulatory message, but a personal welcome is preferable. Some boards make certain that there is a lengthy write-up in the newspaper announcing the winner of the election and presenting the new board member's qualifications to the public. Other communities present a certificate of merit to the new board member at a high school assembly. This certificate attests to the fact that the holder is a member of the board and therefore entitled to certain rights and privileges, such as complimentary admission to school games, dramatics, and the like.

New board members should be taken on a tour of the school buildings, preferably with the board chairman and the superintendent as guides. He should be made thoroughly familiar with the plant. He should meet the principals and the teachers. Knowing the system, both personnel and material, he will be in a better position to make decisions at a later time.

The new member should be presented with certain materials which he can study at his leisure. A recent publication for the new school board member carried the list which is reprinted below. Not all of this material should be given to the board member at one time. The list should be used as a reference, from which the superintendent chooses that material which is most appropriate to the problem at hand.[10]

1. A copy of the rules and regulations of the board—this should include a number of pertinent data in addition to the usual information such as powers and duties of the administrator. Some of these things would be:
   a. History of the school system.
   b. Organization of the school system.
   c. Past and present policies of the board.
   d. Insurance program.
   e. Rental arrangements.
2. A handbook on school law—a must in all board members' libraries. A very fine one was published for New York school board members by the New York State School Boards Association.
3. A review of the board's minutes of the past five years—through this medium the member-elect might gain better insight into the workings of the board of education.
4. A faculty and student handbook—this is a good way by which the member-elect may become better acquainted with the life of both the staff and the student body. All too often this phase of an orientation program is neglected with the result that there is a big gap in the knowledge of the board member with respect to his school. Through this media he will learn of the various faculty standing committees and of the various projects of the staff. The faculty handbook should present a working schedule for the day so the board member

[10] Daniel E. Griffiths and William T. Wiley, *A Handbook for the New School Board Member* (Albany, N. Y., Capital Area School Development Association, 1952).

may be able to understand problems relating to the individual schools. The faculty handbook should include such things as:

    a. In-service training program.
    b. Staff meeting calendar.
    c. Salary schedule.
    d. Rules and regulations.

The student handbook affords the board member the opportunity to gain an insight into the life and mores of the student body.

5. A report on recent surveys of the school system—it should be safe to assume that the new board member knows little or nothing of the whole educative scheme. Complete and up-to-date studies and surveys of all aspects of the school system should be a goal of all boards and administrators. There have been many instruments developed which will make school surveys valid and reliable. Probably the best known survey instrument is the *Evaluative Criteria* published by the Co-operative Study of Secondary School Standards. These surveys should be written so that the laymen may readily comprehend them. These studies should run the gamut of the educational program from current maintenance practices to improvement of the curriculum.

6. A financial report of the past five years—within a financial report many policies and procedures may be set forth which might otherwise be neglected. This will provide the background for intelligent financial planning.

7. A folder on the past reports of the administrator—it is through reading these reports that many questions of the member-elect are answered. It also serves as a basis upon which an intelligent discussion may be carried on between the administrator and the member-elect. In too many instances, boards of education suffer because the new members have no idea or conception of why and how the school is administered.

8. A copy of the bus routes—the member-elect may better be able to visualize the problems entailed in transportation if he sees the maps and distances involved.

9. A folder of the recent educational periodicals—it is only with a sound background in the various philosophies of curriculum that a board member can do an accurate and complete job. It is not expected or hoped that the member-elect should become an expert in the field of curriculum, but he should cultivate at least a working knowledge of the basic fundamentals so that he might carry on intelligent discussions when this topic comes up for consideration before the board.

10. A statement of the long-range educational plans—such a folder is necessary to the understanding of the long-range building program among other things. It is not only necessary to make other long-range plans such as bond issues known, but also to be cognizant of these factors so that present plans may be constructed accordingly.

11. A subscription to the following magazines:

    a. *American School Board Journal*—a fine periodical which presents reports on the leading issues in national education written in a layman's vocabulary.
    b. *The Nation's Schools*—a monthly magazine which covers national items of interest having to do with classroom problems, issues, trends, and practices.
    c. *The School Executive*—a monthly magazine written from the viewpoint of the school administrator. It enables the board member to see the problems which confront the administrator.

12. A copy of each of the following books:
    a. *The Challenge of School Board Membership* by Daniel R. Davies and Fred W. Hosler—A down-to-earth discussion of the various subjects with which board members are concerned when determining policy.
    b. *Practical School Board Procedures* by Daniel R. Davies and Elwood L. Prestwood—A report of a study which determined those practices used by many fine boards of education.

School Board Institutes

Many a superintendent who has not been able to make his point with his board has found his point made at a school board institute. These institutes have become very popular lately. Usually a college or university sponsors the institute. Boards are invited to attend, along with their administrators. They usually pay a small fee to defray expenses. At the institute the boards get a chance to hear experts discuss problems vital to the boards. They also get a chance to talk to other board members who have experienced similar problems. This is one of the finest methods of helping board members to grow in their jobs.

State organizations of school boards have done a great deal to help members. They have co-sponsored institutes in some states, issued bulletins and periodicals, and, in general, increased the prestige of board membership in the whole country. A superintendent should encourage his board to belong to its state organization.

Written Policies

The leadership of the superintendent can be reflected in another way that is not quite so obvious. He can encourage the board to adopt a set of written policies. Although every board has a more or less well-understood set of policies, failure to have them in a written form has been the cause of poor human relations and inefficient board action. Committing policies to writing gives the superintendent a guide by which he may act. He is more likely to really be the executive officer of the board if there are written policies, since both he and the board would be more secure in allowing him to act more independently. A set of policies also gives the teachers greater security, since it specifies those areas in which they are free to act. In general, it can be said that boards which operate under written policy are more effective than those which do not.[11] Many state school board associations have published guides for the preparation of written rules and regulations. Each board should use the guide for its particular state because of differences in state laws. In New York State a

[11] Richard E. Whalen, Jr., "Effectiveness of Elected and Appointed Board Members" (Unpublished doctoral dissertation, Indiana University, 1953).

particularly fine guide has been written by John W. Polley and Donald H. Ross.[12]

The Superintendent at Board Meetings

A very important aspect of leadership concerns the superintendent's relations with the board during its meetings. The particulars of the role of the superintendent in the board meeting are very interesting and as yet have not been subjected to definitive study. The superintendent is not the chairman of this meeting; nor is he even a voting member. In many districts he is often the secretary or the clerk of the meeting. In terms of our analysis of group structure, the superintendent most closely approximates a consultant. Yet he is more than a consultant, since he has been granted much authority and is responsible for the administration of the total school system. There is another marked difference between the superintendent and a consultant; he must administer the decisions made at these board meetings, whether he approves of them or not.

Even though the superintendent faces a number of role conflicts at the board meeting, this is the place where he can most effectively exercise board leadership. The success of his leadership, however, depends on how skilled he is in evaluating people and situations. First, the superintendent should know when to talk and when to listen. This he learns through a process of analyzing the behavior and attitudes of each board member. Second, he should develop a sense of timing so that he knows when a bit of evidence or an opinion will best be received. Third, he needs to know the kind of evidence that each board member will accept. Fourth, he needs to know why each member of the board is serving as a member—his purposes and his needs. When the superintendent knows the members of his board this well, he can work with them very effectively.

Hunkins has summarized the functions of the superintendent in board meetings as follows: [13]

The superintendent as rightly the board's executive must attend the board meetings. Where that has not been the custom the superintendent by well directed arguments and by insistence if necessary must gain admission to the meetings.

By the effectiveness with which he operates at board meetings, the superintendent must demonstrate his indispensability there.

Since in the meeting is the only place the board members have any power legally and since they are likely to be busy people, the business to be handled should be reserved in so far as possible for the official meetings.

The superintendent should use his influence to have the meetings handled as efficiently as possible. There should be an adopted and workable order of busi-

---

[12] John W. Polley and Donald H. Ross, *Statement of Policies: A Handbook for School Boards* (Albany, N. Y., New York State School Boards Association, 1953).

[13] Hunkins, *op. cit.*, pp. 44-45.

ness with copies in front of all members. The meetings should start on time and move with reasonable celerity.

The superintendent should prepare thoroughly for all business he expects to bring before the board. He should have the facts and the arguments well in hand and be prepared, if possible, to meet contingencies that might arise in the way of opposition.

One of the superintendent's chief functions at board meetings is to present reports on the progress of the schools. Some of such reports may be in writing but more often in a smaller school system they will be given orally. They should cover the vital educational procedures of the school and be presented in a way to reach the understanding and enlist the interest of lay board members.

Decisions on major matters must not be expected by the superintendent on their first presentation. There must be time for board members to ponder and grow used to new ideas especially if serious changes in procedure are involved or major financial outlay is entailed.

Best results are obtained in connection with large undertakings if the board moves gradually into the position of sponsorship on their own part.

In presenting material to the board graphic methods are often helpful—tables, charts, diagrams.

The superintendent should serve as a source of information on the educational features and also the business aspects of the various policies and issues deliberated upon by the board. In many cases he will be assigned the task of finding the needed information and reporting upon it at a subsequent meeting.

The superintendent should conduct himself in a way at meetings to encourage participation in the discussions on the part of all the members, to the end that the decisions will represent the collective wisdom of the group.

The meeting should be pleasant for all with a little time for sociability and jokes, some candy during the meetings, and possibly more refreshments some place after the meeting. The superintendent is the key.

THE AGENDA

There is very little question as to whether or not there should be agenda prepared prior to the meeting. The only argument against these is that they tend to restrict the business that the board should cover. This objection is easily overcome, though, by keeping the agenda flexible and making a consideration of the content the first order of business. All board members should be entitled to have any subject placed upon the agenda and also to change the order of the agenda.

In most systems the agenda is prepared by the superintendent, with the advice of the board chairman. This is probably the best procedure; but the superintendent should make certain that a copy of the agenda is sent to each board member at least two days prior to the meeting. A copy should also be sent to the press. Reports, data, or other evidence that will help the board member to formulate an opinion on each issue should accompany the agenda.

It should be mentioned that the order of business is an important way of influencing the board. Some superintendents place a particularly controversial matter last in the hope that the board will never get to it. One superintendent started doing this a year ago, and the matter he sought to avoid has not yet come up! On the other hand, those issues which the superintendent considers most important should be placed first. In practice, however, the board should always reserve the right to change the order of business.

THE MEETING PLACE

The meeting place of the board is just as important as is the meeting place of any other group. This has been discussed in Chapter 12. The members need to be seated comfortably, preferably around a table or set of tables in a square or hexagonal form. They need to be able to see and hear each other without strain. The room should, of course, be well lighted and properly heated and ventilated. There should be facilities for making coffee and serving refreshments.

ORGANIZATION OF BOARDS

For years the literature of school administration has urged that boards of education organize as a committee of the whole; yet a vast majority of the boards in the country organize as a group of standing committees. There are transportation committees, teachers committees, grounds committees, insurance committees, and so on. These committees probably are popular because of the reasons advanced by Hunkins, which we quoted earlier.[14] Many board members are used to *doing* things, and so it seems advisable to organize into committees to do specific things. As one superintendent put it, "It makes them feel happy that way!"

From a human relations point of view, the multiple standing committee organization is anything but desirable. First of all, it results in inefficient board action. One of two procedures usually is followed. In the one, the standing committee first considers, say, a problem in insurance and reports to the whole board. The whole board then considers the whole problem over again before making a decision, thereby wasting much time and energy. In the other, the standing committee considers the problem and comes to a conclusion. Upon presenting the conclusion to the whole board, the decision is rubber-stamped. In this case, the board is acting improperly since each member was elected to the board to represent the whole community on every matter to come before the board.

Standing committees are apt to overstep the purposes for which they were created. This is inevitable since standing committees are generally administrative in nature. So we have two groups, one lay, the other professional, attempting to administer the same function. This results in dividing the loyalties of the staff and causes confusion. Dual systems of

14 See above, pp. 329-330.

administration can never work because no one person can be held accountable. When control is lost there is no organization.

There appears to be no good reason for the establishment of standing committees. A board should be organized as a committee of the whole. Whenever the board is faced by a problem which needs special study, a committee should be appointed to do the particular job with the understanding that it will be disbanded when it has reported its findings. Committees of this sort are less apt to become administrative in function.

SUMMARY

The desired relationship between the board of education and the superintendent of schools is one of co-operation and mutual understanding. The board and the administrator should become a smoothly working team. Under this concept, it is not quite so necessary to delineate clearly between the legislative power of the board and the administrative function of the superintendent. Policy making and policy administration are interrelated and can be dichotomized in an arbitrary manner at best.

Although the superintendent should be the executive officer of the board of education and most superintendents feel that they are, there is a tremendous range in executive duties. The problem is twofold: on the one hand, we have board members who are not used to delegating authority in their own work, and, on the other, we have administrators who have no administrative experience or training. The superintendent will become an executive officer to the degree that he can overcome these two conditions.

The superintendent should adopt a policy of working to influence or lead the board of education through indirection. He should not force his views upon the board. He needs to supply information, opinion, and evidence, until the board finally adopts his position as its own. When this happens the board will move ahead with great energy and vigor. To insure that his use of indirection is ethically sound the superintendent should always make explicit his position on the issue. Once the board has come to recognize him as a man of ability, the superintendent can use a more direct approach.

The superintendent exercises his leadership most directly as he helps the board members to grow in their jobs. He develops a program of orientation for new board members and devises ways in which veteran members can learn more about the job. His peculiar role at board meetings, although difficult, gives him opportunities to lead the board to wise decisions.

EXERCISES

1. Prepare a program for the orientation of new school board members in your school district. What phases of this program would you stress? Why?

2. Outline a procedure which a superintendent could use with a board member who was elected through the activities of a pressure group.

3. Use the book, *Practical School Board Procedures* by Davies and Prestwood to develop a checklist of desirable procedures for your board of education.

4. Discuss the relative values of the direct and the indirect methods of influencing a board in relation to a specific controversial issue now confronting your board.

5. Assuming that your board is organized with standing committees, what procedure should you use to have the board organize as a committee of the whole?

SELECTED BIBLIOGRAPHY

DAVIES, Daniel R., and HERROLD, Kenneth F., *When Your School Board Meets* (New London, Conn., Arthur C. Crofts, 1955).

————, and HOSLER, Fred W., *The Challenge of School Board Membership* (New York, Chartwell House, 1951).

————, and PRESTWOOD, Elwood, *Practical School Board Procedures* (New York, Chartwell House, 1951).

GRIFFITHS, Daniel E., and WILEY, William T., *A Handbook for the New School Board Member* (Albany, N. Y., Capital School Development Association, 1952).

HUNKINS, Ralph V., *Superintendent and School Board* (Lincoln, Neb., University of Nebraska Press, 1949).

MESSICK, John D., *The Discretionary Powers of School Boards* (Durham, N. C., Duke University Press, 1949).

REEVES, Charles Everand, *School Boards: Their Status, Functions, and Activities* (New York, Prentice-Hall, 1954).

School Boards in Action: Twenty-fourth Yearbook (Washington, D. C., American Association of School Administrators, 1946).

School Board–Superintendent Relationships: Thirty-fourth Yearbook (Washington, D. C., American Association of School Administrators, 1956).

SMITH, Max S., and SMITTLE, W. Ray., *The Board of Education and Educational Policy Development* (Ann Arbor, Mich., Edwards Brothers, 1954).

PART THREE

Case Studies

Administrative Relations with Pupils

SLACKS FOR SALLY

It was shortly after the opening of school toward the end of the second week of the new school year, and the usual postdismissal traffic in the school office had about subsided. Principal Nixon was just returning from the busloading area and, as he entered the office, was greeted by Mrs. Katherine Conger, the new homemaking teacher.

Mrs. Conger: "Hello, Mr. Nixon, are you busy?"

Mr. Nixon: "Sure, Katherine, always busy this time of the year, but never too busy to talk with a teacher. Come in." Mr. Nixon motioned Mrs. Conger into his own office, to which the door was seldom closed. "Have a chair? How are things going in the homemaking department?"

Mrs. Conger: "Oh, quite well. I have some very nice girls. That was what I wanted to see you about. Perhaps I should have come to you before I did this, but anyway I have a little disciplining problem which you should know about. I dismissed five girls from the homemaking class today for wearing dungarees."

Mr. Nixon: "That sounds interesting. Go ahead."

Katherine: "Well, they didn't like it very much. But they were just trying to test me out. You see I told all of my homemaking girls yesterday that one of my regulations was that there were to be no slacks or dungarees worn in the homemaking classes. So today, in walked five girls with dungarees."

Mr. Nixon: "What were the girls' reactions in class when you told them not to wear these clothes?"

Katherine: "Well, most of them seemed to go along with the idea, except these freshmen girls. We talked about it in class and I told them the reasons why I felt they should not wear them. An important part of their course is to learn good grooming and this means, partly, wearing appropriate clothes for various occasions. We agreed that there was a place for dungarees for girls, such as helping with chores at home or working in the garden and like that. I don't feel the girls should wear them to school, particularly when they are studying things that have to do with the right selections of clothing. And that goes for slacks too."

345

Mr. Nixon: "I see. It may work out all right and then again it might be pretty hard to enforce."

Katherine: "I suppose I should have talked with you about it first; I hope I haven't started something that will mean embarrassment. But where I taught before, we had this sort of rule."

Mr. Nixon: "Well, the truth of the matter is that we have had no school policy about the clothing children shall wear so far as I know. But I have felt in noticing some of the girls now and then that something ought to be done! Up to now, if there was some girl who looked particularly sloppy, I have tried to have the nurse or girls' physical education or some other woman teacher work on the girl. Of course the other homemaking teachers have tried to discourage it also."

Mr. Nixon paused for a moment. He felt quite fortunate in having Katherine on the staff, partly because she had had three years experience, and also because he knew quite a bit about her fine family background and the character of the girl as a former pupil of the school. Furthermore, he had secured her at a very modest salary because she had recently married a young man of the community. So he continued, "I don't want to discourage you, Katherine; it may be a very good idea. I can certainly go along with you one hundred per cent on the dungarees, although I am not quite so sure on the slacks. Slacks can look quite dressy when they are cleaned and pressed. Some of the parents might put up a kick. But—we'll see what happens."

Katherine: "Thank you, Mr. Nixon. I'm sure the girls won't cause any trouble, once they see that I mean business. And I expect to give them some praise when they come to class looking as they should."

Mr. Nixon: "O.K., keep me posted on any developments."

The next day, the recalcitrant girls came to school looking like magazine ads. Mrs. Conger made a point to tell them how well they looked.

Repercussions from parents expected by Principal Nixon did not develop. The father of one of the five girls inquired about the matter indirectly through the PTA president.

Later in the year, toward the end of the winter, resistance to the regulation was made by one of the senior girls taking the Homemaking 3 course. This girl, Sally Campbell, was somewhat older than her classmates. The parents were fairly well-to-do and had lavished considerable material things upon her. She frequently wore rather expensive looking clothes. She came to the office one day to see Principal Nixon, wearing a nice looking pair of grey slacks.

Sally: "Mr. Nixon, may I see you?"

Mr. Nixon: "Certainly, Sally. Come in and have a chair. What cooks?"

Sally: "We-e-ll, it's like this; I have a little gripe. Mrs. Conger sent me out of class today to the library because I came to class with these slacks on. Frankly, I don't think that's right."

Mr. Nixon: "I see. Did you know that Mrs. Conger does not wish her girls to wear slacks or dungarees to school?"

Sally: "Well, she said something about it last fall. I never would think of wearing dungarees to school, but slacks—well, I just can't see where there's any reason to make such a rule."

Mr. Nixon: "Mrs. Conger and I talked over this regulation last fall and I assured her that she could go ahead with it. I see no reason why all the girls should not co-operate with her. After all, it doesn't mean any hardship to you, does it?"

Sally: "Well, I suppose not."

Mr. Nixon: "You think it over and see if it isn't better to go along with Mrs. Conger."

Sally left the office. However, she was back again the next day with the same story. This time she made a point that her father was going to insist on her being allowed to wear the slacks and that she should be permitted to remain in the class. Mr. Nixon closed the conversation, saying, "I cannot give you permission to re-enter the class against Mrs. Conger's wishes, and I cannot make you any promises of any kind. However, I'll consider the matter more thoroughly and see if I can come up with something."

There was a board meeting scheduled for Friday of that week, and Mr. Nixon decided to see what the members and the district superintendent might have to say regarding the matter.

That same evening while eating his supper, Mr. Nixon had a telephone call from Sally's father. He was courteous but obviously very determined to force an issue of the affair. He asked the unanswerable question that Mr. Nixon had expected would eventually come up: "Why doesn't the rule apply to all the girls and not just those in Mrs. Conger's classes?"

At the board meeting when Mr. Nixon recited the case, he asked for opinions of the members. Although there were some differences, in general the members felt that any general regulation in such a matter would be unwise and that the principal and teacher should adjust the situation as best they could.

Mr. Nixon decided to see Katherine before school opened on Monday and try to figure out a compromise which would not result in her losing face before the pupils and also would not result in his letting her down.

PETER SHACKLETON[1]

The disciplinary committee, consisting of the headmaster, dean of students, and five members of the faculty, had convened on Monday afternoon, April 24, to consider the case of Peter Shackleton, a member of the class of 1951 in his third (11th grade) year at the school. The committee

[1] Copyright, 1951, by the President and Fellows of Harvard College. Reprinted by permission of the Harvard Graduate School of Education.

had been summoned by the headmaster because of a report turned in early Monday morning by Shackleton's housemaster, Mr. Dunning. The report ran as follows:

When I checked on Sunday morning the sign-in list of boys in my dormitory who had attended the Saturday night movies, I noticed the following irregularity. Shackleton's name and time of return, 10:23 P.M., had been "sandwiched" in between the names and times of two boys—roommates—who invariably return from the movies and sign in together. Furthermore, the reported time of return of the second boy had obviously been tampered with and changed to a time— 10:25—five minutes later than that of his roommate. Both boys have categorically stated to me this morning—Sunday—that they returned together, signed in together as they usually do, with no other boy intervening, and posted identical times of 10:20. I then conferred with Shackleton, who said that he had forgotten to sign in until ten minutes or so after the entire group had returned from the movies. Rather than sign in at the end of the list, he had chosen to put his name where, in his opinion, it belonged on the basis of his best recollection of the time of his return. He had no explanation to offer as to the tampering with the second boy's time. When asked if he had returned from the movies with any individual students who could testify to the fact and approximate time of his return, he gave me the names of Blanchard and Pemberton, both members of his class residing in nearby dormitories. I then dismissed him until further notice. Telephone calls to Blanchard's and Pemberton's housemasters revealed the fact that both boys had been given special permission to stay out half an hour after the movies were over in order to escort Blanchard's sister and her roommate to the Inn where the girls had left their car. Blanchard had signed in at 10:44, Pemberton at 10:46. I recalled Shackleton and presented him with these facts. He readily admitted that he had met the girls during the afternoon, had sat with them and their escorts at the school movies, and had subsequently decided to "take a chance" on signing in at the dormitory after the girls had left in the hope that he could "get away with it." I pointed out to him, in view of the fact that he was already on academic probation, the seriousness of what he had done—an intentionally false sign-in and an open falsehood to his housemaster, not to mention the possible result of altering another boy's posted return. I also told him that as I had no choice in the matter, the episode would be reported to the dean Monday morning.

(s) Benjamin Dunning
Sunday, April 23

Mr. Dunning had been asked to attend the disciplinary committee's meeting as Shackleton's housemaster and faculty adviser. He declared that, so far as observance of school and dormitory rules was concerned, Shackleton had given him no trouble during the course of the year. His academic record had been very poor throughout both fall and winter terms; three of his teachers had reported a generally poor effort and unsatisfactory attitude in the classroom, with the result that Shackleton had been placed on academic probation just prior to the Easter vacation. Mr. Dunning further stated that he suspected Shackleton of repeated smoking behind the locked door of his room, but he had no definite proof other than an occasional aroma of smoke and a somewhat guilty attitude on the part of the boy. Shackleton and his roommate—a quiet, studious boy who did very well in his studies—kept themselves quite apart from the other students in their class and took little share in dormitory activities. Mr. Dunning commented that Shackleton had little awareness of community obligations and responsibilities, that he mixed with the other boys only when it was to his advantage to do so, and that his conversations with Mr. Dunning in the past had been almost exclusively confined to Shackleton's own personal experiences and spheres of interest. As there were no further requests for information, Mr. Dunning left the committee to their deliberations.

The dean then took up Shackleton's official folder, containing all official correspondence between the boy's family and the school, admission data and test scores, academic reports for the previous two years, housemaster memoranda for the current year. Reading selections from the folder, the dean was able to present to the committee a reasonably objective picture of Shackleton and his relationship with the school over a period of two-and-one-half years. Several facts immediately stood out significantly: Shackleton had a good mind that he never used to anything approaching capacity; his teachers, for the greater part, had found him an able performer when he was interested, but otherwise a passive and indifferent student who frequently sought to cut corners; he had a number of acquaintances but very few friends; the oldest child in a well-to-do family, he had a very generous spending allowance; and, finally, he gave the impression of being precociously sophisticated and versed in the ways of the world. In conclusion, the dean stated that he had interviewed Shackleton that morning and that the boy had readily admitted to the details of Mr. Dunning's report but had been unable to explain an act that he knew was contrary to the regular procedure of the school.

On the basis of Mr. Dunning's remarks to the committee and of the dean's observations from the folder, a lengthy discussion ensued. It was observed at the outset that extenuating circumstances in any boy's favor must necessarily be of considerable weight to justify that boy's retention in the school when he is already in a probationary status and subsequently violates an important rule of conduct. Were there such extenuating circumstances in Shackleton's favor? To several members of the committee none appeared to exist. On the other hand, while Shackleton's academic record up to date was certainly far from satisfactory, it was plain that he had never before run afoul of the rules and regulations, major or minor, and that his difficulties at the present time were largely caused by an almost total absence of proper academic and social motivation, which arose, it seemed, from a basically unformed and undisciplined character. It was on these grounds, then, that the discussion continued for an hour or so until the headmaster, feeling that the case had been thoroughly probed and explored and that there was little likelihood of fresh and significant evidence, called for a vote from the committee—should Shackleton be retained in the school or not? The vote split the committee down the middle, three to three, and the headmaster found himself confronted with the ultimate responsibility and the final word. After stating to the committee his intention of reweighing the immediate evidence upon Shackleton's recent offense as well as reading *in toto* the background material in the boy's folder, the headmaster adjourned the meeting until the following morning. He then proceeded to examine the contents of the file, beginning with the parents' confidential memorandum that had been written just prior to Shackleton's first year at the school. The following excerpts seemed to be of particular significance:

Social Characteristics

"Popularity good (makes a good impression with older people). Excellent ability to mix *when he is interested.* Interest in others only fair. Is self-centered. No shyness."

Scholarship

"Is a fair student—has never been up against sufficient competition to have to really exert himself."

Special Needs

"Needs to learn consideration for others, and to realize that he must give as well as take. Has matured rapidly and has been in great demand with boys and girls two and three years older. This has tended to make him overly self-confident—to the point of cockiness. He is interested in himself predominantly and so long as things are going along to suit him, is happy and genial. He does not ever sacrifice any of his own pleasures agreeably. He has been spoiled since he was a little boy—by older people, rather than his parents. He needs to learn that he cannot go on forever doing things to suit himself regardless of others. He is devoted to his father and his younger brother. He also adores his youngest sister. He is inclined to scorn his twelve-year old sister, who adores him. He criticizes her constantly—never attempts to build her up, or help her in any way. I feel that Pete is going through a difficult phase which boarding school will correct. I am prepared for him to be miserable until he adjusts himself. His potentialities are so great that once he gets over his present mixed-up frame of mind, I feel that he will be a credit to his parents and the school ..."

During his first year at the school, Shackleton lived in a large dormitory of about forty-five boys. In charge were two married masters and one bachelor, together with three senior proctors. These younger boys, unlike the rest of the school, had their own dining hall, recreation rooms, and athletic activities. They were carefully supervised in an atmosphere that was as friendly, congenial, and homelike as the resident masters could make it. Shackleton's academic record was undistinguished throughout the year, and the following June found him ranked 82d in a class of 110 with a weighted average of 65. Quantitative and verbal aptitude test scores placed him in the upper half of his class, and his I.Q. was 124. On November 18, he had been placed on academic restriction; the restriction was continued in February and removed just before the Easter vacation. His senior housemaster reported on him at the end of the year as follows:

As a Citizen

"The country-club type. Blase with some false modesty. Mature acting and appearing."

As a Student

"Capable of much better work than he is producing. One teacher calls him 'elegant idler.' Soft and sloppy in his thinking. Needs mental discipline. Should be practically an honor student."

Contribution to School

"I am afraid, if any, his contribution will be mostly social. He has beautiful manners and a fund of chitchat when he chooses to exert himself. For the most part he is pleasant and charming."

In his second year Shackleton was assigned to a master's house with five other boys. Here he had considerably more freedom than he had enjoyed the year before; he ate his meals in his class hall in the school commons, did not have the close supervision of the previous year so far as his studies were concerned, and was granted certain new privileges in keeping with his rise in status. His academic performance during the year was almost an exact replica of his record for the first year. On February 10, he was placed on academic restriction. On March 11, he was voted on probation, from which he was removed on May 4. In June, he ranked 120 in a class of 155 with an average, again, of 65. Aptitude test scores placed him in the middle of his class; his I.Q. was 122. His housemaster's comments at the end of the year closely resembled those of the previous year:

As a Citizen

"Shackleton is interested in Mr. Shackleton. I find that he has some trouble with making friends because of his desire to talk about himself all the time. He can put forth very good manners and conduct when he has to."

As a Student

"I marvel at the marks he gets with the amount of work he does. He is not the most industrious boy in the school. Loves to waste time going downtown and playing victrolas."

Contribution to School

"None."

In September, 1949, Shackleton and his roommate, the only close friend he had made during two years at the school, moved into a large brick dormitory in a quadrangle that housed the entire class. Here he lived in immediate proximity to sixteen other boys of his own age, under the supervision of Mr. Benjamin Dunning, housemaster. He was now an upperclassman, with certain privileges and responsibilities that went with his age and class. He was not required to report personally to his housemaster when he returned during evening study hours from the library or on Saturday nights when he came back from the movies or recreation hall. He and his roommate shared a study, with two adjoining bedrooms. They took little part in dormitory life and were invariably found in their own rooms when Mr. Dunning made his rounds. The headmaster read with considerable interest the comments made by Mr. Dunning in the latter's fall term report to Shackleton's family.

"I may as well state frankly at the outset that this is not a favorable report in any way, shape, or manner. Of the thirty-one failure or low-pass teacher reports in Peter's file, covering two years and one term, thirty spoke unfavorably of his effort and attitude in the classroom.

"I find him exceedingly self-centered, glib, inconsiderate of others, oblivious of things and people that do not concern his own interests, courteous, charming, and endowed with latent possibilities that evidently nothing and nobody, myself included, have been able to arouse or develop. And I am convinced that the possibilities are there.

"If I were to venture a glimpse into Peter's future, I would say that he was riding for one big, magnificent fall. How to avoid it?"

At the end of the winter term, which was Shackleton's most recent rating period, he stood 129th in a class of 217 with an average of 67. Although he failed no courses at this time, he was once more voted on probation because of three extremely unsatisfactory teacher reports covering the period of the winter term. This, then, was Shackleton's status in the school on Monday, April 24.

During the assembly period Tuesday morning the headmaster reconvened the disciplinary committee and announced to them his decision.

He gave a detailed account of Shackleton's career in the school and presented his reasons for his action.

DOREEN [2]

Interpretation of Test Record

Doreen's test performances over a period of four years indicate that in general mental ability, reading comprehension, and mathematics, she was well down in the lower third of her age and grade groups. Her scores on vocabulary and speed of reading tests varied from the lower to the middle third of her group. On the Minnesota Paper Form Board Test, her scores varied from the middle to the upper third. Her best test performance seemed to be in nonverbal material. Six mental tests administered over a period of four years indicate that her true I.Q. score was probably not above 95; and with the substantiating evidence from reading, languages, and mathematics test scores, it is evident that Doreen achieved less-than-average academic attainments for pupils of her age and grade.

School Record

English—Grade 8: She didn't like English, because she "didn't like to read and couldn't keep up a conversation." Mark, *C*. Grade 9: Her English teacher stated that her effort was good but that she used poor judgment in her work; oral English teacher stated that she spoke too rapidly and indistinctly and that her grammar and enunciation were "atrocious." Mark, *C*. Grade 10: English teacher reported that frequent absences handicapped her work. Mark, *C*.

Mathematics—Grades 8, 9: Her performance in arithmetic was below average, as her test scores would indicate. Mark, *C*.

Business—During her first year in high school, she took a business course but had considerable difficulty in typing and bookkeeping. Grade 10: Teachers stated she had neither interest nor aptitude in business subjects; absence also accounted for her failures. Mark, *F*. Grade 11: Teacher reported that no effort was made; nor was any work done in business organization. Mark, *F*.

Arts—Grade 8: She liked to sketch faces and figures. She said, "Drawing comes easy to me." Mark, *B*. Grade 9: She stated that music was her favorite subject because it came nearest to theater work. Mark, *A*. Grade 10: Home-management teacher reported that her work was poor because

[2] From John W. M. Rothney and Bert A. Roens, *Guidance of American Youth* (Cambridge, Mass., Harvard University Press, 1950), pp. 40-47. Copyright, 1950, by the President and Fellows of Harvard College. Reprinted by permission of the publishers.

she was absent from school frequently, and, as a result, was constantly behind the class. Mark, *C.* Music teacher reported low marks were the result of absence, despite the fact that she was a hard worker. Mark, *C.*

Social Studies—Grade 9: She said she "didn't care for history and didn't like the teacher." Mark, *C.* Grade 10: History teacher reported that she was capable of good work if she were not absent so frequently. Mark, *C.* Teacher of problems of democracy reported that her frequent absences made it necessary for her to work very hard to pass. Mark, *C.*

Family Data

Doreen was the youngest of four children of American-born parents. Her father was a salesman and two of her brothers were office workers. Her elder sister had been very successful in recent theatrical appearances. Her mother, prior to her marriage, had made several successful appearances in New England theaters. The father had been a member of a theatrical group for a number of years and was very much interested in the stage. From the time Doreen and her older sister entered school, their mother had spent a good deal of time teaching them to perform publicly. Doreen's family life was centered around the theater. The parents attended church regularly, but the children attended only occasionally.

Health Data

Doreen was in good health according to the school medical examinations and parents' comments. At the age of fourteen, she contracted rheumatism in her legs and neuritis in her arms. They caused considerable pain, and she was absent from school a total of thirty-one days because of this difficulty. Her physician was hopeful that the treatment for the rheumatism and neuritis would take permanent effect.

Occupational Experience

Doreen had been an entertainer at a number of parties, dances, clubs, and other social events, but she had never received any remuneration. She had done occasional broadcasting with her sister over a local station.

Vocational Choice

Doreen had only one vocational choice during the whole period of counseling. She was determined to become an actress. She stated that something within her prompted her toward this choice, and her sister's success had been a strong motivating factor.

Counseling

Doreen was first interviewed by the counselor during the fall of her eighth year in school. At the time, she was a small, unattractive, plump brunette who spoke so rapidly that words poured out in a jumble; and conversation was limited to her own activities and her theatrical career. She was proud of the fact that she could learn parts of plays even though she could not read them very well. She told of her sister's success at great length and repeated many times the desire to be like her. While she talked of her sister, the counselor observed some signs of envy and jealousy. Doreen was reluctant to discuss school, except to say that she disliked it and was determined to leave school just as soon as she was sixteen years old. She disliked her teachers, and they in turn disliked her.

In subsequent interviews with Doreen's teachers, it was learned that her difficulty was caused by persistent whispering, the fact that she had made it very clear to her teachers that she was not interested in any kind of school work, and that she was merely "marking time" until she could withdraw from school. During the next two years, the counselor attempted to change Doreen's attitude toward school by pointing out that as long as she had to remain there, she could make things pleasant for herself by pleasing her teachers. Her whispering habit did not decrease, but she became more willing to co-operate with teachers and counselor. She did so, she said, only on condition that they would recognize her plan to leave school at the age of sixteen.

Despite efforts by teachers and counselor, Doreen's unhappiness in school increased throughout the eleventh grade. The counselor finally learned that she was very much disturbed because she thought the other pupils did not appreciate her talent as much as she thought they should. It seemed that Doreen, in compensation for her lack of success in school work, boasted of her ability as an actress, and some of her classmates expressed doubts as to the veracity of her statements, even to the point of teasing and ridicule. The counselor was able to correct this situation in part by explaining the response that boasting evokes from certain people.

In several interviews with her near the end of her junior year, the counselor realized that she was serious about her plan to run away from home and go to New York, where she was sure she could become a successful actress. He spent considerable time in an attempt to convince her of the difficulties involved in such a venture. She had worked out a detailed plan for running away, but as rapport was developed and as she recognized the sincerity of the counselor's appreciation of her ability and ambition, he secured a promise from her that she would notify him before attempting any such escapade. He did not know whether he ought to notify her parents about her plans to go to New York and take the chance of losing rapport with Doreen by violating her confidence, or whether he ought to attempt to handle the problem himself.

ANGELO

As a member of the freshman football team, Angelo came along fast and by the end of the season was one of the scrappiest and best players on the squad. He quit school when he became sixteen later on in the year to work in his father's store. The following fall he decided to re-enter school, and Harold Keene, the principal, allowed him to do this after talking with him at length about the decision. Angelo had been somewhat of a discipline problem in the past, but Mr. Keene felt he had potentialities he hadn't shown and was convinced that Angelo intended to be a good citizen and would profit from further schooling. He knew Angelo planned to play freshman football again and also knew he would be a good player and perhaps gain recognition that would be helpful to him. Bruce Bradford, the freshman coach, told Angelo he would be glad to have him play again, that he had a lot to offer the team, but that he was in a rather unusual position and would be expected to stay out of trouble in school. Angelo assured him that he wanted to play very badly and would be careful to do nothing that might get him removed from the squad. He started school the following Monday as a ninth-grader, a week late.

Bradford was particularly happy at the idea of having Angelo on the squad again for two reasons. He felt as Mr. Keene did that Angelo had many capabilities and that football would help him, but he also had visions of Angelo, a hard, fast runner and left-handed passer fitting beautifully into the wing back slot in the single wing formation he was inaugurating that year.

Practice moved along for three weeks and Angelo looked good, both in his position and as a self-appointed and accepted leader in various conditioning drills and as general spirit-keeper-upper. Then, one day during practice William Hess, the head coach and physical education director, came up to Bradford during practice.

"Hi, Bruce."

"Hello, Bill, what's up?"

"Angelo was caught smoking. Do you want the privilege of kicking him off the team or do you want me to?"

The response was rather slow in coming.

"You seem to have the facts, Bill, I guess you'd better do it."

Bradford went on with practice and told Angelo Mr. Hess wanted to see him. After a short talk, Angelo went into the building. When he came out, he was dressed in street clothes and looked very dejected. He told his coach what had happened and Bradford immediately asked him if he wanted to help coach the backfield. He said, "Yes," and Bradford asked him to report in street clothes each day after the conditioning exercises were over.

About a week later, Bradford received a note asking him to report to Mr. Keene.

"Bruce, I want to talk with you about Angelo. He has been coming in once a week to tell me how things are going. Today he told me Bill kicked him off the team for smoking. I've talked with Bill and told him just what I'm telling you. You're coach of that squad, Bruce, and if anyone kicks a squad member off, it's going to be you. I'm not telling you you should keep Angelo on, I just want it to be your decision. Angelo told me he wasn't smoking, but was holding a cigarette in each hand for a couple of fellows who were going in to look over a dance in the gym. I believe him. Think it over, look into it further, and let me know what you decide."

Bradford decided to talk to Hess first.

"Certainly football would be good for Angelo, Bruce, but what can you do? One of the janitors saw him smoking and he bragged to Mr. Robinson in science class that he smoked. You certainly can't leave him on the squad when the other boys know this."

Before practice the next day, Angelo said, "I wasn't smoking. I was holding two cigarettes for Bill and John while they looked in on the dance."

"That wasn't using very good judgment, Angie, and neither was bragging to Mr. Robinson that you smoke."

"I meant I have smoked. I gave it up when football started. I know it affects my wind. He doesn't like me for the same reason Mr. Hess doesn't. I talked up to him a couple of times."

"I'm going to bat for you, Angelo. I can't promise anything, but I want to know first you're not pulling the wool over my eyes."

"I'm not, coach, believe me."

"I do, Angie."

Upon being questioned specifically, the janitor admitted he hadn't actually seen Angelo smoking.

Bradford then interviewed three members of the varsity squad that Hess coached, asking them without giving names to estimate the number of people on the varsity squad that were smoking. The numbers varied, but they all knew some who were smoking. One boy apparently was smoking quite heavily.

When approached with this information, Hess replied, "Sure, I know some of the boys are smoking, but I haven't caught them yet. As soon as I do, they are off the squad—I don't care who they are."

Mr. Robinson couldn't remember the exact wording of Angelo's statement but added the information that the day Angelo was kicked off he saw him lighting up a cigarette as he rode off alone on his bicycle.

Having gathered what information he could, Bradford decided to make his decision that night and tell Harold Keene about it in the morning.

FRITZ KLOSTER

New plastic-topped desks had been placed in Room 202, and the students had been asked by the teacher to make every effort to keep them unmarred. On the third day after the desks had been placed in the room, the teacher noted that a large swastika had been carved through the thick plastic top of one desk—evidently with a sharp instrument. The teacher noted the names of the six pupils who sat in this seat and reported the matter to the principal. A large pocket knife was found opened within the desk and also presented to the principal.

Principal Walters knew the owner of the knife upon seeing it. The knife had reached the office following a previous wrongdoing. When the teacher reported that Fritz Kloster was one of the six pupils sitting in this seat, it confirmed his belief that Fritz must be responsible.

During the interview which followed, Fritz readily admitted that it was his knife and asked, "Where did ya find it?" However, he vigorously denied that he knew anything about the desk carving.

Only a week later, a boy reported to the football coach that $4.75 had been taken from his wallet during football practice. The coach, who drives the players home in a school bus, was shocked when he heard the following conversation taking place between Fritz and another boy as they rode homeward:

"Where did you get that hatchet, Fritz?"

"Bought it down at Higgins Hardware."

"How much?"

"Four seventy-five."

The coach explained that Fritz frequently dressed quickly in order to run downtown for a few minutes before the other boys were ready to board the bus. He evidently had purchased the hatchet at that time.

Interpretation of Test Record

Standardized tests show that Fritz always ranks from one to two school years above average. His I.Q. has been recorded as 113.

Achievement in Tool Subjects

Teacher reports indicate that he has been average or above average at each grade level with the usual added comment that he is a good reader. He has failed only one course—English—and that was because of a complete lack of interest.

Mental Ability and Effort

All teachers reported him above average in ability. Effort was average or fair. Several commented that he was very careless and had to be continually reminded in order to get work done. He does excellent work in subjects that he feels he needs. However, if he feels that the subjects are "just a waste of time," he lays down on the job and only does enough work to pass.

Interests

Fritz had an early interest in farming which has now disappeared. Beyond an expected interest in hunting and athletics, he is most attracted to mechanics and reading. He has become one of the school's most proficient library users and reads most types of books, including some of the most difficult novels found in the library.

Family Data

Fritz's mother died at about the time he entered school and his father remarried. He disliked his stepmother, from earliest comments, and felt that she took his father away from him. He has a sister who is seven years older. They are quite close to each other. The sister was never a problem in school or at home, but shared Fritz's dislike for the stepmother. Upon graduation from high school, she left home to work elsewhere and apparently seldom returns.

Principal Walters characterizes both Mr. and Mrs. Kloster as "wonderful, hard-working people." He adds that Mr. Kloster is rather easygoing by nature and not much of a disciplinarian. Mrs. Kloster never has had any children of her own and found Fritz and his sister to be a little out of hand. Because she enforced good manners and handled the disciplinary matters, the children did not like her.

As time passed and the father backed the stepmother in her decisions, Fritz lost his respect for his father, also. Now he says, "We fight all the time and can't get along together."

Vocational Choice

Fritz is determined that he will attend a technical school with which he has already communicated and study diesel engineering. He seems very set in his choice and takes a "don't-care" attitude toward any subjects or phases of subjects which he feels will not directly help him in fulfilling this purpose.

Social Conduct

If ever a boy walked with the proverbial chip on his shoulder, it is Fritz. He takes a rather arrogant attitude toward the world in general and his school life in particular. He has a rather cold shell about him which is difficult to pierce, particularly if the conversation is centered upon his misconduct.

His classmates are never genuinely friendly with him. He invariably stands by himself. At times he becomes very generous with his friendship and forces himself upon would-be friends. Frequently this is all forgotten within a space of hours, and the old relationship between Fritz and society holds sway.

As a pupil, Fritz is loud and rude. He is one of those pupils who is constantly being summoned to the principal's office regarding one matter or another. His second-grade teacher wrote in his guidance folder: "Belligerent—egotistical—any wrong doing on his part is always unintentional—rationalizes for his own benefit—unpopular—talks incessantly—cannot take criticism." Other grade teachers have only re-echoed these notes with the passing of time.

During the sixth grade, Fritz twice ran away from home. The first time he was accompanied by another boy, but was soon found and returned home. Somewhat later he again disappeared. Police, neighbors, and school officials searched for several days without finding him. Finally he was discovered in an old barn. The boy who had previously accompanied him had been carrying food to him nights.

Both of his parents felt that they had gone as far as they could with Fritz. They sent him to a boys' military school in a neighboring state where he remained for a year and one half. He did better than average work and proved to be no problem. At the end of this period, his father decided to send him to public school both because his help was needed on the farm and because of the prohibitive cost of sending him to the military school.

Since his return, Fritz appears to have picked up where he left off.

Counseling

In interviews with the guidance counselor, Fritz refuses to go beyond perfunctory remarks until assured that what he says will be "kept private," as he says. He then speaks very strongly against the manner in which his parents treat him. He also speaks strongly against the required subjects that the school offers.

Interviews reveal that Fritz feels perfectly justified in acting as he does in school and can see no reason for changing his attitude or his conduct.

One of the faculty members summed the problem up by saying, "Fritz has a good head on his shoulders and knows how to use it. The pity of it is that he doesn't think that anyone in this school is smart enough to teach him anything. When he goes to college or gets a job, he's going to realize how much he has missed that he could have learned right here in high school."

Mr. Walters feels that the problem goes even further. Not only does he feel that Fritz is missing out on school, but he feels that the boy will be a definite problem for society once he leaves school unless something constructive is done. For ten years his school has failed to do anything to help Fritz with his problems. When will they begin?

The principal has circulated requests for help among faculty members. Is there help for a boy like Fritz? The problem is to find a solution or at least an aid before it is too late.

JOEY'S TWO FRONT TEETH

The final chord of "Cape Cod Chantey" had hardly issued from the concert grand in the Medville Central School auditorium when the air was filled with the vociferous voices of nearly one hundred squirming fifth- and sixth-graders.

Mrs. Haas, the music teacher, clapped her hands for silence, then briefly explained the plans for the next rehearsal and the usual instructions for leaving the auditorium. The floor of Medville's auditorium is of the sloping type commonly found in moving-picture theaters.

Stealing a glance at the clock as she kept a weather eye on her charges, Mrs. Haas directed the children to walk up the aisle by twos, the back row to leave first. She, herself, walked beside the leaders in order to reach a pinnacle position at the rear of the room and watch the entire operation of filing out.

Before she reached her destination, it happened! Ted Mahon, who was standing about forty feet down the sloping aisle from his teacher, noted that Mrs. Haas had turned her back on the situation. He gave his partner, Joey deSelvo, a playful shove which caught Joey off balance and sent him sprawling into the seats with a crash that sent the music teacher rushing to the scene. The damage was done, however. Joey was holding his hand over his face and trying to act very brave about the whole thing as he picked himself up from the seats on which he had fallen. Nevertheless, he was in evident pain.

At Mrs. Haas's demand, Joey removed his hand from his face and the seriousness of the accident was revealed. Joey's two front teeth had been cleanly knocked out, and he was holding them in his hand.

Quieting the shocked children as best she could, gaining the assistance of a passing teacher, and pulling Joey along behind her almost at the same time, Mrs. Haas headed for the nurse's office.

The nurse immediately swung into action. She cleaned some of the blood from the face of the victim, surveyed the damage, then telephoned the village dentist and made arrangements to have Joey sent at once for careful examination.

Dr. Garry shook his head and confirmed the fact that Joey could never again have his own front teeth.

School had hardly gotten underway the following September when rumors that a lawsuit was being filed reached Mrs. Haas's ears. This information would naturally have a disturbing effect upon anyone in Mrs. Haas's position, but in her particular case it was the proverbial straw that broke the camel's back.

Helen Haas was a conscientious young teacher with successful experience in several schools who had given up teaching and moved to Medville shortly after marrying a widower-father of four children. Subsequently, she gave birth to her first child, and the family was a burdensome, but happy one. Two years after the birth of her child, her husband suffered a shock and was forced to remain in bed.

Mrs. Haas attempted to balance the loss of income by a rigid system of economy, but it soon became apparent that some other source of income must be found. She applied for, and was elected to, a job in Medville Central School as a teacher of vocal music. Her principal described her as being, "workmanlike, conscientious, and sincere, but hardly colorful." Her job meant a great deal to her, for it was the sole source of income to feed the seven mouths of the family.

Upon hearing that she might be involved in a court suit, she sought out her principal, Mr. Jackson, and broke down completely in his office. She said that she was in her final year before gaining tenure rights and now, with security so close for her and her family, she was going to lose her job. The principal tried to soothe her, but made no statement regarding the security of her position.

A few days later, she again visited his office. She knew definitely that a lawsuit was being drawn up, she said, and she wanted to resign and seek employment elsewhere rather than go through with the ordeal of the trial. She had enough trouble caring for her sick husband and her family without bringing a lawsuit into the picture.

Mr. Jackson reminded her that the case would undoubtedly proceed regardless of whether she resigned and again gave her reassurances that everything would work out all right.

Fully realizing her difficulties, he asked her to meet with the board of education, the district superintendent, and himself. It was explained to her at this meeting that the decision of the court in this matter would have no effect upon whether she were granted tenure or not. Her application for tenure would be reviewed as though she had never been involved in the incident. Grasping for straws, she pleaded with them to grant her tenure immediately, if such were the case. They explained to her that this would set a precedent that might be painful to the board later on and they could not take this action. She seemed somewhat cheered by the meeting.

Don Bigby, a vigorous young trial lawyer who had practiced in Medville for a number of years, had dueled with the board of education of the Central School on a number of occasions. Although the tiffs had been minor in importance, he usually won them and so gained a reputation.

Nicholas deSelvo, father of Joey, thought of Bigby immediately and sought him out as being one likely to win his lawsuit. By late summer, the elder deSelvo had presented his case to Bigby and the two agreed to sue in the amount of $7500. Five thousand dollars was asked for damages, and $2500 for medical expenses.

Six months after young Ted Mahon had made his momentous shove, the supreme court convened in Seneca, a village only four miles removed from Medville. Since the opening of school, conflicting stories had been circulating concerning the approaching trial, and, by the time court opened shortly before the holidays, the citizenry of Medville and Seneca was agog with excitement over the outcome.

Bigby, in the usual cautious manner of a jurist, had issued a subpoena for everyone even remotely concerned with the case. As counsel for the plaintiff (Mr. deSelvo), he was suing Mrs. Haas, Mr. Jackson, and the board of education. Direct suits upon Mrs. Haas and her principal were subsequently dropped, and the case entered court charging the board of education with negligence in not providing proper supervision for the period in which the accident occurred.

Representing the board of education as defense counsel was Brooks Silliman, a lawyer for the insurance firm in the state capital with which the Central School held policies.

In the course of presenting his plea, Bigby called upon Mrs. Haas, the school nurse, Mr. Jackson, and the district superintendent. All were cross-examined by Mr. Silliman.

"Any teacher in charge of such a group," Mr. Bigby maintained, "should have stationed himself either at the front or rear of the auditorium looking at the entire group. Because this teacher was not in a position to watch the entire group, this unfortunate accident occurred."

"Mrs. Haas was attempting to reach such a position," Mr. Silliman replied, "but because of the nature of the class and the large number of pupils assigned to her that period, could not reach the position before the pupils left their seats. This accident was unavoidable."

"If there were too many pupils for her to successfully manage," retorted Mr. Bigby, "then it is clearly the fault of the board of education for not providing an adequate number of teachers, and they are guilty, as charged, with negligence in not providing adequate supervision."

Mr. Silliman brought his position to rest by maintaining, "An incident of this nature would have occurred regardless of the supervision provided. This boy (Joey) was the victim of boyhood fooling that backfired and this is a chance that parents must take in sending their children to school. No school can provide protection against incidents such as this. They occur so quickly that no amount of supervision can prevent them."

On this note, the judge's gavel pronounced the end of the first day's session, and the litigation shifted to the barbershops, drugstores, and taverns of Medville and Seneca until the following morning.

Administrative Relations
with Teachers

JULIA BROCKTON[1]

Miss Julia Brockton had been teaching in the Mitchell school system for twenty years. Prior to her transfer to Maple Street she had spent eighteen years teaching the first grade in a school in a poor section of the town. Several earlier requests for transfers to other schools had not been granted. When the new Maple Street Elementary School was built she again requested a change. Because of her long tenure in the system the request was granted.

The Maple Street School served an entirely different type of clientele. It was in a strictly residential area of upper-middle-class homes. The school was well equipped and the classes were small. The PTA was very active and very helpful in its co-operation with school authorities.

In addition to Miss Brockton, two other teachers formerly employed in the Mitchell school system were assigned to the Maple Street School when it was opened. The rest of the staff, consisting of five teachers and a principal, were new to the Mitchell system but had had some experience teaching in other cities.

Mr. Robert Fenton came to Mitchell from Marine City where he had been teaching principal in a small elementary building for five years. He was about thirty years of age. In the Mitchell system, elementary schools with fewer than twelve teachers were assigned a half-time principal. In accordance with this policy, Mr. Fenton spent his forenoons at the Wilson School, and his afternoons at the Maple Street School, with administrative responsibility for both.

Miss Brockton lived with an elderly uncle who was crippled. Their only source of income was her salary. She was a very effective teacher but participated in no community activities of any kind and had a very limited social life. She took little interest in anything about the school outside of

[1] Prepared in the Department of Education, Ohio University, by H. E. Benz and Helen L. Woods. Copyright, 1955, by the Ohio University Press. Reprinted by permission of the publishers.

her own room. Her attendance at PTA meetings was erratic, and she refused to remain after school for meetings of any kind. Teachers' meetings were held every Wednesday noon. The teachers were asked to give up ten minutes of their lunch hour, and the children returned to school half an hour late so the meetings could last forty minutes. Miss Brockton refused to come in ten minutes early and always walked into the meeting exactly ten minutes late. When questioned by Mr. Fenton, she replied that "they" had no right to ask her to give up ten minutes of her time. She said it was different with the other teachers; but because of having to care for her uncle when she was at home, she needed every spare minute. Mr. Fenton realized that she did have a difficult life, so he didn't press the issue.

The teachers in the building had formed the habit of getting together for coffee during the recess period every morning. This was possible because the playground was large and protected from the streets. The teachers would take turns, with two of them staying outside with the children while the others had coffee. This seemed to work out very well. Mr. Fenton was not aware of this custom because he was in the building only in the afternoon. Miss Brockton enjoyed this arrangement as much as the rest of the teachers.

One day, during the second year of operation of the Maple Street School, while the teachers were having their little gathering, the subject of the next teachers' meeting was brought up. Miss Jones, one of the new teachers and a much younger person than Miss Brockton, remarked she didn't think it was fair for Miss Brockton always to come late to the teachers' meetings. Miss Brockton explained that she did not feel any responsibility for allowing the meetings to intrude on her noon hour and explained why she always came late. The two older teachers sympathized with her and said they understood. Miss Jones and several of the others were determined to press the issue, so they brought up the subject of Miss Brockton not taking part in any of the teacher's committees. Miss Brockton said that "they had no right" to ask her to do any extra work, since she had been working in that system for twenty years. The five new teachers expressed strong dissent from this point of view, and the group broke up with noticeable feelings of resentment on the part of everyone.

Soon after this episode occurred, Mr. Fenton became aware that something was happening to the morale of his teaching staff. The next month was characterized by much expression of ill feeling among the teachers. Miss Brockton and Miss Jones seemed to be continually finding fault with each other. Mr. Fenton knew about the ill feeling, especially as it affected these two, but he didn't know what to do about it. The difference in the ages and the recency of the training of the two women seemed to make a great difference in the way they thought things should be done. Mr. Fenton was quite worried because he didn't want to lose Miss Jones, and he didn't like to see Miss Brockton become increasingly unhappy. He knew that because of her home conditions Miss Brockton wouldn't leave, but he wasn't so sure about Miss Jones. Eventually Miss Brockton stopped coming to the coffee gathering and stayed in her room during the intermission period. Miss Jones showed increasing evidence of resentment and disapproval of Miss Brockton.

A few weeks later, Miss Jones learned of another of Miss Brockton's actions which further excited her. She learned that Miss Brockton was allowing the children in her room to enter the school building early at noon through a side door next to her room. This was against the school policy. Miss Jones decided to tell Mr. Fenton about the matter. Soon after the report, Mr. Fenton went to Miss Brockton and told her that she was not to allow the children to come in early. He also reminded her that other teachers were complaining about her and that she would have to become more active on committees and come to meetings on time. Miss Brockton became very angry and expressed her hostility toward Miss Jones in strong language, finally expressing the opinion that what Miss Jones was doing was much worse than avoiding work. Miss Brockton then told about the coffee gatherings. This recital surprised Mr. Fenton, for he had not known about these.

Mr. Fenton now realized that he didn't know much about what went on in his school and wondered what to do next. He felt that because of the shortage of good teachers he did not dare to run the risk of losing either of these two women. He also knew that if some kind of harmony were not restored his staff faced progressive demoralization.

NANCY McCRARY[2]

Nancy McCrary was a vivacious young teacher who had been in Wilkinsburg Schools five years. Preceding this, she had taught one year in a small rural high school near Elkhart, Indiana. Her aged father and invalid mother, who lived in Elkhart, depended completely upon her for financial support.

She was a graduate of Elkhart High School and the University of Indiana. She was now spending her summers at the latter institution working toward her master's degree. Her major field on the undergraduate level had been English, while her minor field had been stenography. On the graduate level, all of her work had been in the departments of English and education. Often, she mentioned to her friends her desire to be on the administrative staff of a high school or small college; however, all her experience at Wilkinsburg High School had been in teaching typing and

[2] Prepared in the Department of Education, Ohio University, by H. E. Benz and Jacob H. See. Copyright, 1955, by the Ohio University Press. Reprinted by permission of the publishers.

shorthand. Although these subjects lay in Miss McCrary's minor field, her students had been able to compete satisfactorily with students from other local high schools for stenographic positions.

Miss McCrary and her roommate, Martha Everett, lived in furnished rooms near the high school. Miss Everett had come to Wilkinsburg the same year that Miss McCrary had. Both had attended the same high school and university. Miss Everett's fields were English and history. Her parents also lived in Elkhart, where her father worked as a dispatcher for the C. & O. Railway.

Both teachers had often voiced their intentions of remaining in the profession, and both seemed to have a genuine interest in newer and better methods of teaching. Miss Everett had won the confidence of the pupils and the community by her ability to present subject matter to her classes in an interesting way. Several of her students had placed high in district scholarship tests in English, and two years ago one had been fourth in the state. Miss Everett was not the jovial type that Miss McCrary was. She was thought of by the community as a typical "schoolmarm."

The girls' friends at Wilkinsburg consisted mainly of people their age and younger. However, they had become closely acquainted with a few of the other teachers' families. Of the latter, perhaps the Walton's were most intimate. Mr. and Mrs. Walton were life-long residents of Wilkinsburg. Mr. Robert Walton had been a teacher for the Wilkinsburg School for seventeen years. During the past four years, he had acted as coach. He was a graduate of Cotsworth College and a teacher of history and industrial arts. His brother was a member of the local board of education. Coach Walton had become very popular during the past few years by coaching winning basketball teams for three consecutive years. No other school had ever won the county crown three times in succession. In addition, Wilkinsburg had won two district championships. Miss McCrary and Miss Everett were frequent visitors at the Walton home. Often the four dined out or took Sunday rides together.

Miss McCrary had been in charge of the school's cheerleaders for two years. To compensate for this duty, she had not been given a home-room assignment.

By state law, any teacher possessing a professional certificate is entitled to a continuing contract after teaching five consecutive years in one school district, if the district has an enrollment of 800 or more. This law further stipulates that such contracts may be awarded at the end of the third year or may be postponed one period after five years' service. At the termination of one limited contract of one or two years beyond the five-year period, a teacher must be given continuing status or must be dismissed. Wilkinsburg had been giving such continuing contracts at the end of five years' service. The school district had an enrollment of 1066, with a staff of thirty-five full-time teachers, a supervising principal, and an assistant principal. Twenty of the thirty-seven teachers held continuing contracts. Miss McCrary and Miss Everett were anticipating continuing contracts this year, when their five-year periods ended.

The school's supervising principal, M. R. Fairchild, had returned to his post in September, 1946, after a leave of absence for three years in the naval service. During his absence, a former teacher, Warren Corey had taken charge. When Mr. Fairchild returned, Mr. Corey had resigned from school work to enter the advertising business. Principal Fairchild had received numerous unfavorable comments about the situation which existed in the administration and faculty during his absence but had ignored them. Complaints against Miss McCrary were numerous. She had taught for him for one year preceding his naval service, and her work had been satisfactory; but since his return, he had observed certain things that caused him concern.

On the opening day of school, he had overheard bits of a conversation on the playground between Miss McCrary and a senior girl:

Student: "Hi, Mac!"

Miss McCrary: "Why hello, Marj. Are you glad to be getting back to school?"

Student: "Yeh, and I guess I'll be with you two periods each day this year. It's sure nice to have someone who understands you and can teach you without making you slave."

Throughout the year the students called Miss McCrary by the nickname "Mac." She did not seem to resent it. Mr. Fairchild also observed that during the time before and after school and at noon, Miss McCrary's typing room was a favorite place for students to loaf. She seemed to be on fairly intimate terms with them.

That the students often took their troubles to Miss McCrary, he was certain. Several times during the year she had come to him requesting special permissions for school parties. These permissions were usually for dancing, a practice that was normally taboo at Wilkinsburg school functions. On one occasion she was known to have sympathized with a senior girl who was failing a government class to such an extent that the government teacher accused Miss McCrary of being meddlesome.

When new school regulations were proposed at teachers' meetings, Miss McCrary was frequently pessimistic about their enforceability. She was not very co-operative about enforcing some regulations which she termed useless. Among these was one requiring a written excuse for anyone who came late to class. Another was the rule requiring all students who traveled about the building during actual class time to carry a "pass" indicating destination, place from which the student was excused, and the excusing teacher's signature.

Worse than all these was her laxity in checking the class roll. Principal Fairchild questioned her several times concerning her failure to check those absent from her six classes and report their names to the office. Usually she pleaded forgetfulness. Once she stated that she had left her roll book at her apartment.

During an actual supervision visit in Miss McCrary's shorthand class, Mr. Fairchild noticed a tardiness in beginning the class. The delay was caused by a discussion among the students and Miss McCrary concerning new costumes for the cheerleaders.

On checking over the first-semester grade reports, Principal Fairchild had found that the marks assigned to various students by Miss McCrary were almost without exception higher than those assigned to the same students by other teachers in other classes.

When the government teacher, who was also a twelfth-grade home room adviser, approached Miss McCrary on the subject of unduly high marks, the latter responded with the suggestion that some teachers were jealous because she could get students to earn high marks easily. This the government teacher had reported to Principal Fairchild.

The climax came one warm afternoon in early March when Mr. Gates, president of the local board of education and also county attendance officer for four townships, was directing some shrub planting on the school lawn.

During the interval between the fifth and sixth periods, Mr. Gates had seen a boy and girl go out the side door of the building, cross the street, and enter a restaurant. Mr. Gates, who recognized the two students, had come straight to Principal Fairchild's office with the information. Mr. Fairchild made a check and found that these two students belonged in Miss McCrary's class. He also noted that she had not reported their absence from class. Mr. Gates seemed somewhat upset about the matter and suggested that it be straightened out immediately. With that suggestion, he left the principal's office. Mr. Fairchild then summoned Miss McCrary and gave her the entire account, including the source of his information.

This infuriated Miss McCrary to the extent that she made some uncomplimentary remarks about Mr. Gates as an attendance officer and further stated that he should have questioned the two students as soon as he was aware of their intentions. Mr. Gates had, meanwhile, returned to the reception room outside the office and had heard her remarks.

As Miss McCrary left the office, she saw Mr. Gates and knew that he must have overheard her remarks. She returned to her class. Mr. Gates and Mr. Fairchild decided to let things stand as they were. The truant students were taken care of the next day by Principal Fairchild himself.

Miss McCrary began to worry about the effect of this incident on her receiving a continuing contract. That evening she and Miss Everett visited Coach Walton and his wife. The four then visited Coach Walton's brother who was a board member. William Walton had seldom lined up with Mr.

Gates on controversial issues at previous board meetings, and, upon hearing of this episode, promised that it would not affect the granting of the continuing contracts.

When the question of notifications to teachers for the coming year was brought before the board in late March, 1946, Principal Fairchild was asked for recommendations. He advised the board that inasmuch as new teachers would be difficult to obtain, the entire present staff should be rehired.

Later in the meeting, the subject of continuing-contract status came up. Gates, president of the board, stated that he felt the board should be reluctant in granting continuing contracts, for more than half the staff were "permanent teachers" and some provision should be made for young people of the district who entered the teaching profession and wished to locate near home. Another member asked when the notifications of contracts had to be sent out by the board. Principal Fairchild answered that notification of dismissal had to be sent before March 31, but notification of continuing contract had an April 30 deadline.

He also informed the board that Miss McCrary and Miss Everett had completed five years and that they had requested him to put their cases before the board for consideration. Mr. Walton stated that inasmuch as no dismissals were to be made, the contracts could well be considered at this meeting. He, therefore, made the motion that continuing contracts be granted to Miss McCrary and Miss Everett. There was no second to the motion. After much discussion, a motion was made and passed (4–1) to postpone consideration until the regular April meeting.

Following the March meeting, Mr. Walton resigned from the board in protest. A successor was appointed, and, at the April meeting, both Miss McCrary and Miss Everett were given two-year limited contracts instead of continuing contracts.

That evening, after the close of the meeting, Principal Fairchild thought over the occurrences. He knew the value of a teacher such as Miss Everett. He was nearly certain that she would not remain if Miss McCrary did not. He also realized that the two-year period for which they had been rehired would merely be sufficient time for teachers to become more plentiful and for the board to find a replacement for Miss McCrary. He was positive that this was the intention of the board. He pondered as to what could be done.

MR. GOODYEAR

Mr. Goodyear came to Ruskinville in September, 1951, eager to carry out his new responsibilities as teacher of ninth-grade social studies to the best of his ability. He was thirty years old, unmarried, of a stocky build, and very much interested in the profession. He had taught in a nearby central school for two years on the junior high level.

Soon after the school year had begun, Mr. Goodyear was greatly disturbed by the lack of discipline within the school. He was particularly irritated by the conduct of the students in study hall to which he was assigned during the last period of the day. In order to stop some of the confusion, he began to put into effect some study-hall regulations of his own. The students, at first, were violently opposed to these regulations, but later found them rather humorous, as did several members of the faculty who assumed a certain "tongue-in-cheek" attitude toward him.

In the meantime, several comments were forthcoming from the students regarding the activities in the last-period study hall. One senior girl, who had recently been transferred into the study hall, had this to relate to one of her teachers, "I wouldn't have missed it for the world. It's as good as a show. He demands perfect silence, then leaves the room. Soon we see him peeking through the window of the door and taking the names of those who are talking. Then he re-enters and puts those students on detention."

One boy said, "I sit with a group of boys in the front of the large study hall. Soon I begin to whistle. Goodyear, whose desk is located in the back of the room, hustles to the front demanding who the culprit is. Then someone in the back begins to whistle, and the merry-go-round begins. Gee! It sure is a circus."

Then the students became more vicious. When Mr. Goodyear was absent from his classroom, they would cover his blackboard with obscene names or throw his books out of the third-story window into the snow. When he was teaching, they would pay very little attention to anything he had to say.

Mr. Goodyear began wearing a path between his classroom and the vice-principal's office, reporting first this and then, that. He placed numerous students on detention each day to punish them. Soon the vice-principal suggested that he not place so many students on detention.

Early in the school year, Mr. Goodyear began a policy of taking students on trips to various points of interest throughout the state. These activities were provided on his own free time and at his own expense. He prepared very faithfully and appeared to be very conscientious regarding his subject matter and classroom work.

Goodyear was definitely disillusioned with his new position. He wanted to be liked, and he was disappointed when the freshmen never invited him to any of their functions.

One teacher frequently remarked that his personality flaw was a lack of a sense of humor.

The situation remained the same until one day in March. Two students had broken a rule, and Mr. Goodyear had quickly placed them on detention. The boys told him that they would not appear as they had an intramural game at that time. During the noon hour, Mr. Goodyear discovered that the boys had not put in an appearance. He went immediately to the gymnasium and escorted the boys to the detention hall. Mr. Hayden, the coach, was very upset because his game had been interrupted and two of the best players on the freshman squad had been whisked away. The freshmen were terribly upset and even more so when they lost the game.

The coach reported the incident to the principal, Mr. Cross, who was very interested in school athletics. Mr. Goodyear was called to the office and very quickly told that athletics were more important than detention. Indignant and confused, Mr. Goodyear returned to his classes to suffer the abuse of the freshmen for the remainder of the afternoon.

A number of teachers began to sympathize with Goodyear's plight— possibly seeing themselves in the same situation. A slight feeling of resentment came to the fore among the teachers toward the coach and the principal.

Contract time approached. Mr. Cross, who had frequently remarked during his ten-year stay at Ruskinville, "I've never made a mistake in hiring a teacher," was faced with the decision of whether or not to recommend Mr. Goodyear for another year.

In the meantime things had quieted down considerably and no additional problems had arisen.

VALLEY ELEMENTARY SCHOOL[3]

Mr. Arthur Metcalf, the newly hired principal of the Valley Elementary School, walked briskly up the steps of the red brick school building. It was the last week in August and he had a lot of plans to make preparatory to the opening of school the following week. Hurriedly, he entered the building and proceeded upstairs to his office, stopping only long enough to glance at a few new items of playground equipment which had arrived the day before.

Once in his office, he immediately began to write several paragraphs which he added to the bulletin he was preparing for distribution on the first day of school. He was so involved in his work that he failed to hear the footsteps of the man who was approaching the office.

"This room looks familiar," said the man as he entered the office. "I'm Charles Burns, the former principal. I was passing through town and thought I would stop and pick up a few of my books which I forgot when I left the school last spring."

"How do you do, Mr. Burns," said the startled Mr. Metcalf. "I believe you'll find your books right here in this bookcase. This is the opportunity for which I have been waiting. Maybe you can tell me a few things about the school that might help me to adjust a little faster to the new situation.

[3] Prepared in the Department of Education, Ohio University, by H. E. Benz and Kenneth L. Cleland. Copyright, 1955, by the Ohio University Press. Reprinted by permission of the publishers.

Perhaps it would be a good idea for you to give me a little character sketch of the people I'll be working with this year."

"I'll be glad to give you some information, Mr. Metcalf, but I'm afraid my opinion will be slightly prejudiced. You see, I was the principal here in name only. Because of the aggressiveness of the staff, I had little actual authority. Each teacher in this school is a self-appointed administrator, running his part of the school as he deems necessary. Due to these circumstances, unified school policy and co-operation are nonexistent.

"You will receive very little help from the superintendents. Mr. Bartlett the county superintendent, visits the school perhaps twice a year—if he happens to be around this way. These visits usually last about an hour. Mr. Rose, the district superintendent who is also the principal of the local consolidated high school, has time only to mail out the schedules for the current school term. The total responsibility of administration is in your hands."

"That gives me a good picture of that side of the situation. The problem of the aggressiveness of the teachers, which you mentioned, interests me. Although I have been away for four years, I've lived in this community quite a long time and have a speaking acquaintance with all of the teachers, but I know none of them intimately. Some information about their professional abilities would be a great help," suggested Mr. Metcalf.

"The first-grade teacher is Miss Adams," continued Mr. Burns. "Her principal professional asset is her twenty-four years of experience. She is very independent. You will find out sooner or later that she seldom arrives at school on time.

"Mrs. Blair of the second grade has had seven years of experience, has twenty-one college credits and a temporary certificate. She is the mother of two grown sons. She taught here from 1928 to 1930, then quit to get married. Five years ago her husband died, and she resumed teaching.

"The third- and fourth-grade teacher is Mrs. Noland. She has a Bachelor of Science degree and four years of experience. She is divorced and her out-of-school life has been criticized by the community.

"Mrs. Perry is the teacher of the fifth and sixth grades. She also has two grown sons who, naturally, are the center of her life and activities. She has had fourteen years of teaching experience. Her instructional methods leave little to the child's imagination, for she covers the textbooks thoroughly. She considers herself an expert disciplinarian. Her husband enjoys a high social position in the community, mainly because of his political activities. Mrs. Perry is more aggressive in assuming the position of a self-appointed principal than are the other teachers.

"There you are, Mr. Metcalf, but don't let me discourage you. Perhaps you will find an entirely changed staff. You've no doubt faced situations such as this before."

"No, I haven't," confessed Mr. Metcalf. "That is why I was anxious to get this information. My experience consists of four years in the army, including both domestic and foreign duty."

"That experience should serve you well on this job. I hope everything goes well, Mr. Metcalf. Good luck!" Mr. Burns took his books under his arms and departed, leaving Mr. Metcalf in deep thought about the problems of the coming year.

In an effort to gain encouragement and reassurance, Mr. Metcalf contacted Mr. Rose on the telephone. The busy Mr. Rose had little to say. The only enlightenment from this superintendent was the suggestion that Mr. Metcalf immediately let all his teachers know who was to be "boss."

Discouraged, Mr. Metcalf turned from the telephone muttering to himself, "So this is the introduction to my new job for the coming year."

The first day of school found Mr. Metcalf full of renewed confidence and enthusiasm for his job. The schedule called for a half-day session, so the afternoon was devoted to a staff meeting. Renewing acquaintances and comparing summer experiences occupied most of the time of the meeting. Mr. Metcalf did not issue his declaration as he had been advised to do but stated humbly that he wished for the co-operation and support of the members of the staff in helping him carry out a successful school program during the coming term. There were no remarks forthcoming from his plea.

The first two weeks of school passed smoothly. Mr. Metcalf was delighted and eagerly continued his efforts to secure co-operation. However, on Monday of the third week trouble started.

On the day in question, Mr. Metcalf, as usual, arrived at school before the teachers did. As soon as he arrived, he observed the aftermath of a Sunday evening watermelon party which had been held on the school grounds. The persons involved had gained entrance to the building and had left the unwanted portions of the melons on the gymnasium floor. Mr. Metcalf was shocked at the ugly sight and determined to seek out the offenders and punish them.

"Billy," he called to the boy who was standing beside the drinking fountain, "did you have a nice time at the party last night?"

Billy gulped, "Yes, sir," and soon told the story of last night's party. Mr. Metcalf learned that the guilty pupils were representative of all rooms in the building. He called them together in his office.

"Boys and girls, I realize that you like to have parties; but when you see the unattractive condition of your rooms this morning, what do you think of the fun you had last night?"

"It looks terrible, Mr. Metcalf, and we're sorry." The apology came from a little third-grader. It was followed by similar statements from most of the others in the group. One of the sixth-graders suggested that they all get busy and clean up the mess. The others eagerly volunteered to help, and all eyes turned toward Mr. Metcalf, awaiting his approval. As this was the first offense of the year for the pupils and they seemed to be genuinely sorry for their misbehavior, Mr. Metcalf gave his approval. The larger pupils went in search of brooms, while the others began to pick up the melon rinds.

This action was completed without the knowledge of any of the teachers. They heard it from the pupils in their rooms when they inquired about the whereabouts of the missing children. At once, several of them engaged in severe criticism of the principal. These teachers felt that they should have participated in determining the method of punishment.

Mr. Metcalf called a staff meeting for the hour immediately following the close of school, and his action was at once criticized by all the staff. At the meeting, he attempted to justify his handling of the party episode, but with scant success. Each teacher was given an opportunity to state just how she would have handled the situation.

Mrs. Perry contributed her suggestion. "The children should have been made to apologize to each teacher and been denied the opportunity of participating in playground activities for a week. I guess they would remember that the next time they wanted to have a party on the school grounds," she declared.

Mrs. Noland agreed with Mrs. Perry.

Miss Blair said she thought the older pupils should be given extra work and that she could handle the punishment of her second graders in her own way.

Miss Adams had still a different solution. It also was different from the principal's action.

Finally, Mrs. Perry said bitterly, "You are the principal so run the school as you please." With this remark, she gathered up her coat and hat and walked out, followed by the other teachers.

From then on, the principal tried to use the method suggested by the district superintendent, by being the "boss." He dictated instructions to the teachers the remainder of the year. Few of these orders were executed. The teachers made their own regulations concerning the playground, which were contrary to the general scheme which had been prepared by the principal. The teachers themselves were not in accord with each other and constantly disagreed on minor details.

Mr. Metcalf, sensing his weaknesses, told the school board that he was resigning in May. He gave as his reason that he wished to go to school. The following September, he enrolled in a southern university to work for his master's degree.

RUTH HEPBURN

Ruth Hepburn, a recent graduate of Herbert, accepted the position of teaching eleventh- and twelfth-grade English at Blissville High School. One of her duties as a teacher of senior English was to direct the senior play and the junior play. Her experience in this particular field of English teaching was extremely limited.

Ruth's predecessor, Nora Bruce, had married and settled in the community. When she became pregnant, she had decided to give up her career and devote her time and efforts to her family. Nora had been a successful teacher, and many on the staff and in the community had expressed their regrets when she retired. One of her greatest assets had been her tremendous ability in the field of dramatics.

When Ruth came to Blissville, Nora called and offered to give to the new teacher all the assistance that she could to help her to adjust herself to her new job. Nora made one remark that somewhat puzzled Ruth, "Watch Baxter; he may give you trouble."

Ruth met Oliver Baxter on the first day of school. She discovered that Oliver was the high school art teacher and had been teaching at Blissville for seven years. Not only was he considered an excellent art teacher, but he was also very interested in dramatics. He told her that he had always done the sets and scenery for Nora's plays, and would be glad to co-operate with her in any way. Ruth was very pleased, because her knowledge of designing and constructing sets was practically nil.

Ruth found her new job both interesting and enjoyable. Her only difficulty was a slight discipline problem with one of her junior, or eleventh-grade, English classes, but it appeared to be nothing serious. She felt that she had made a good beginning.

In November, Ruth began making preparations for the senior play. She found the senior class a very co-operative and willing group. When rehearsals had gotten under way, she always found Oliver standing by. On several occasions, Oliver had offered his advice and frequently had informed her how Nora had handled certain situations. Ruth welcomed the advice at first but gradually was becoming annoyed at the continual, "Nora did it this way" or "Nora had better results with this technique," etc. After two or three weeks of this kibitzing, Ruth calmly told Oliver, "I'm not Nora." He took the hint, did the scenery, and sat back.

The play went off very well, and several people, including members of the faculty and of the community, commented that the play was one of the best that Blissville High had yet put on. Nora congratulated Ruth on her success, and Oliver offered no comments.

The junior play went into rehearsal in March. Ruth immediately ran into difficulty because she did not cast one of the "shining lights" in the class in one of the top roles. At rehearsals, she found little co-operation, and the play progressed very slowly. She was definitely discouraged.

In the meantime, one eleventh-grade student remarked to another teacher, "Oliver (All the students called him by his first name because he had grown up in the community and was the mayor's son.) said that Miss Hepburn was going to ruin the junior play. He said that she doesn't know anything about dramatics and that the only reason the senior play was any good was because he gave her advice."

Once again Oliver began attending rehearsals and adding suggestions. One evening Ruth became very irritated, and as soon as the rehearsal was completed, she told him that she was through with the play and that he could direct it.

The whispering campaign began. Oliver commented to several teachers that Ruth ought to be dismissed, that she should, at least, be denied another year in the system. He directed his remarks not only to members of the staff but to the students as well, with the result that Ruth's eleventh-grade English classes were a torturous experience each day.

The junior play was just a so-so production, but several members of the community felt that Oliver had done a good job, considering the circumstances under which he had agreed to do it.

In the meantime, Ruth refused to speak to Oliver, and many of the younger faculty members were highly indignant at his behavior. The older ones apparently had become accustomed to it, but they did not sanction it.

After the play had been put on, the tension on the third floor of the school relaxed somewhat. The majority of the eleventh-grade students calmed down—the seniors were in Ruth's corner all during the match. Things remained so for the remainder of the year.

Oliver had made it apparent that he intended to direct the senior and junior plays the following year. Ruth felt that she was neglecting her duties but was hesitant to voice her desire to take over the helm, although she had been urged to do so by several teachers.

The principal, Mr. Casey, was made aware of the situation, but he was puzzled as to what path to follow. He wanted to maintain friendly relations among his faculty members. He did not want to dismiss Miss Hepburn, because he recognized her abilities as a teacher and a person. He wondered just what he should do.

HARRY JONES

Harry Jones upon graduation from a liberal arts college was interested in literature, had a decent background in it, and had resolved to teach English in high school. His grades were well above average. He had just missed Phi Beta Kappa and had been interested in teaching from his first year in college. He had directed his course of study in college toward that end.

The college did not offer any practice teaching program, so Harry went in September, 1929, to a job in Texville, aglow with idealistic notions that beauty and truth from the books of the masters would save the world. And he was going to be a part of the rescue.

His interview with the superintendent, Harry Frank, which was arranged not by the teachers' agency with which he was registered but by a member of the state department, was disappointing in one respect. Although the first meeting resulted in the signing of a contract, Mr. Frank suggested that instead of $1400, the usual pay for a beginning teacher, he would be happy to give Mr. Jones $1500, out of which he could pay the agency its fee.

"I know you were not informed by the agency of this opening, but Mr. Filbert, who runs the agency, is a good friend of mine, through whom I get many of my teachers. So I'm giving you enough salary to pay the agency its usual fee."

This first interview with Mr. Frank was the last formal meeting Harry had with him until midterm. Occasionally Mr. Frank met Harry in the halls, and, occasionally, once a month perhaps, the principal, a Miss Hacker, held a brief faculty meeting.

There were four members of the English department, of which one was chairman. Once there was a meeting of that department. On that occasion, Mr. White, the head of the department, showed the other teachers an Elizabethan theater which he said was once made by one of his pupils and which he presented whenever a visitor came to his class. It was something concrete to impress the caller, and his students were prepared to answer questions about Shakespeare when called upon. And he made one other comment, "All high school students should write at least one composition a week and cover the work outlined in the texts by the end of the year."

Harry had a home room, five classes in English (four preparations), and a study hall. He didn't live in Texville but preferred to commute to a town twenty miles away where he lived with his mother and younger sister. There were other reasons for commuting. Texville (population 7500) was a factory town with a main street and a few old residences. Most of the foreign element worked in the large factory which supported the town. The odors from that industry—paper making can create especially disagreeable odors—the poor opportunities for diversion, the influence of prohibition on the town all recommended the drive home to a city of 130,000 population.

Yes, Texville with its population, its management group, shopkeepers, and factory hands was a divided city, rich in graft, with no one getting into serious trouble because, though divided in spirit, all were dependent economically.

At the end of the first four months Harry reported to the superintendent, even though he knew Mr. Frank preferred to play golf in season and talk golf out of season to talking of professional matters with a teacher. His office was in the same building, Miss Hacker was old and forbidding, and Mr. Frank had hired Harry, so Harry poured out his soul to an equally bewildered superintendent who three months before would have been playing golf on school time.

"Mr. Frank," he began, "I'm a failure, and you should know it by now. I've tried and tried, only to know that I'm your worst teacher. In fairness to the students in my classes you should fire me."

"Well now," countered the superintendent, "I know a lot more about you and your teaching than you think. The students like you, the parents have good reports for you, and you don't have any discipline cases. I haven't visited your classes, nor has Miss Hacker, but I'm aware of what goes on. I keep my ear to the ground, and I think you're one of my best teachers."

"But Mr. Frank," fumbled Harry, "I just can't find time to do all I should. Right now I'm supposed to teach a play by Shakespeare that I've never read before, correct five sets of themes, read a few hundred pages in *Ivanhoe,* prepare myself for teaching a collection of poetry in the anthology—and—well that's the way it's been all year. I just can't keep the pace. You see every kid I have should write a lot to pass the final examinations; they're weak in both speech and writing, 50 per cent talk Italian at home exclusively—and—well, I have come to you to say that if you can find some one to replace a teacher that's just marking time, you'd better. I'm ready to resign at your convenience."

"Why my good boy, that's absurd. You're doing fine. You're just low in spirits. It's a case of early spring fever. I do have, however, two books I'd like to have you read that may help, one in psychology and the other in method. I think they'll help you a lot. Now you just trot back to class and stop fussing."

The superintendent reported the interview to Miss Hacker, a teacher up from the ranks, principal for twenty years, soon to retire. A week later, she entered Harry's classroom, listened briefly to a recitation, and, during the change in classes, advised Harry further.

"If you have any problems, Mr. Jones, you bring them to me. You've done beautifully so far this year, and if I can help you further be sure to call on me. I understand from Mr. Frank you're a little dispirited. You'll get over that, I'm sure. And remember, we think you're doing just fine."

Harry knew better, but he struggled on almost to the breaking point. When he sat down to read the texts, he thought of the compositions; and when he sat with the compositions, he thought of the texts he should be reading. And when spring really did come, he decided to quit. He knew it was a "dirty trick" to just "up and leave," but the superintendent had been warned in advance. He knew, too, that noon when he walked toward the superintendent's home that if this were the script for a play, he wouldn't find the superintendent in. Well, he wasn't in, and that night he met an old friend, also a teacher but one of several more years' experience.

She advised that whatever Harry do he should "stick it out." "You'll be ruined for any job if you leave now," she warned. "Just hold on and snap out of your mood."

Well, Harry didn't snap out of his mood, but he did "stick it out." Contracts came out soon after, and Harry returned his unsigned.

The year ended in an ulcerated tooth which resulted in his only days of absence. A satisfactory number of his students passed the final examination, and Harry was offered, that summer, a job with a newspaper in his hometown writing "obits," as the depression closed in.

MEADE ROWLAND

Meade Rowland, a man of thirty, had taught physical education at the Township Central School for five years. He was a local boy with a wife and a son of seven who lived with his grandparents. He was well known throughout the community for his carefree way of living. He had a pleasing personality and a good number of friends. Two of his best friends, were on the board of education.

Rowland constantly boasted about getting his pay for doing nothing. Whenever he found a teacher doing work, he would say, "Why be so foolish; you won't get any more money, so why not be like me! Get smart." He had made this statement in one form or another to every teacher in the school. The teachers paid little attention to him.

By the middle of November of his fifth year, shortly after the basketball season started, he began leaving his gym classes unsupervised to take care of preparations for the games. He was very careful to do this when Mr. Bolton, the supervising principal, was out of the building. Because of a new building program, Mr. Bolton was out of the building a great deal that fall.

The gym classes soon got out of control and were causing disturbances in the lower halls. Finally Mrs. Olin, a sixth-grade teacher, went to Rowland:

Mrs. Olin: "I think this thing has gone far enough. Your students are running around the halls knocking on doors and disturbing classes. Now I think something should be done."

Rowland: "Now sister, take it easy you'll live longer. You take care of your business and I'll take care of mine."

Mrs. Olin: "We'll see whose business it is. You know, I know a couple of the board members pretty well too."

That night after school Mrs. Olin, who had taught in the school for eighteen years, got a group of the older teachers together to discuss the problem. The result of the meeting was that Mrs. Olin was to discuss the problem with Mr. Bolton the next day. The next morning Mrs. Olin went to see Mr. Bolton in his office:

Mrs. Olin: "Could I see you for a conference this morning during my free period at 10:45?"

Mr. Bolton: "I'm terribly busy with this new building and shouldn't take the time. Is it very important?"

Mrs. Olin: "For the good of this school it's extremely important. It's about Mr. Rowland."

Mr. Bolton: "Oh I see! Well, I suppose I can make time. You come right down at 10:45, and we'll discuss it for a few minutes."

Mrs. Olin: "The teachers feel that you should know what's going on when you aren't here. I'll be down right at 10:45. I think the board should know about this also because they are interested. I know two board members very well, and ..."

Mr. Bolton: "All right, Mrs. Olin, we'll discuss it at 10:45."

When Mrs. Olin left, Mr. Bolton began turning the problem over in his mind. He had already heard about Rowland from a board member, and several parents had called him on the phone to complain. He had spoken with Rowland on two occasions but without success. Rowland would be one of the teachers up for tenure this year. The board would be discussing teachers soon, and he didn't want to divide the board on the Rowland issue. In his own mind, he wanted to keep Rowland mainly because he produced winning teams. He further knew that Mrs. Olin, once aroused, would push the issue until something was done. He reflected further: how should I handle Mrs. Olin at 10:45? What can I say to Rowland? What do I do if Mrs. Olin goes to the board?

ANNA ROBERTSON

Anna Robertson had taught in the Overdale Central School for twelve years. She previously had taught six years in Vermont and two years on Long Island. Her duties at Overdale Central included five classes of commercial subjects, one study hall, and social advisor for the senior class. She had married two years after coming to Overdale and made every effort to let the faculty know that she did not lead a happily married life. She complained constantly about her husband and how hard she had to work at home.

She always had some personal problem with a teacher, the principal, or a student. During her twelfth year at Overdale, things seemed to be much worse. The supervising principal, Albert Bronner, had appointed a committee to work on a salary schedule to be presented to the board, but Anna was not placed on this committee. Immediately after the faculty meeting, at which the committee was appointed, was over she went into Miss Gardner's room to complain:

Anna Robertson: "Well, I see you managed to get on that committee. It's obvious you stand in good at the office. I've done a good job here for twelve years and had experience before that—so what does he do but put a first-year teacher on the committee."

Miss Gardner: "I'm sorry you feel that way about it. Perhaps if you went to Mr. Bronner and told him you would like to serve on the committee he would put you on it. As nearly as I can tell, he tried to have each group represented on the committee. I represent the new teachers, Mrs. Dodge represents the ones with more experience, Mr. Thorsen the high school group, and Miss Burdick the elementary teachers, etc. Do you see what I mean?"

Anna Robertson: "That's a poor way of doing it. Teachers with experience know what's needed. I have had twenty years of experience, and there are teachers here with five years' experience who make more than I do. I'll resign if they don't give me $500 more this year. I need the money. I have a house to keep going. You are single and make plenty to live on."

Miss Gardner: "I don't feel that we should discuss this any further Anna, it will just go toward bad feelings and I don't want that; we all have to work together."

That evening at home Anna talked throughout the evening to her husband about the school, faculty, and administration. Next morning, she began again when she saw Mrs. Dodge walk into her room.

Anna Robertson: "What do you think about Bronner putting Gardner on the committee?"

Mrs. Dodge: "I hadn't thought anything about it. Why, should I?"

Anna Robertson: "You know this is her first year here and he'll be able to get his own way with her on the committee. Besides he picked those who agree with him all the time. You are the only one on the committee he can't push around."

Mrs. Dodge: "Now that you mention it I think more older teachers should be on the committee. I believe I'll speak to Bronner and ask him to make more additions of older teachers to the committee."

Anna Robertson: "If you get a chance remind him of my experience. I should be on that committee with all my service to this school. I told my husband last night that if I didn't get $500 more next year they can get a new commercial teacher. I wouldn't have any trouble at all getting another job with my experience. You can tell Bronner that too, I don't care what he knows."

Mrs. Dodge saw Mr. Bronner during the noon hour and mentioned to him that perhaps it would be better to add one or two of the older teachers to the committee. She explained that since there was such a wide gap between experience and step number, perhaps the older teachers would feel better about having more representation. Mrs. Dodge also indicated that Anna Robertson would like to be on the committee. Mr. Bronner indicated that he had spent considerable time in studying who should be on the committee and was convinced that the best possible group had been chosen. He further stated that he definitely did not want Mrs. Robertson on the committee.

The committee met the next Monday after school to make preliminary plans for organization. Mrs. Dodge was elected chairman, and it was decided to have a general faculty meeting to get ideas from the other members of the faculty. This meeting was held on Thursday of the same week. Mr. Bronner made it a point not to be present in order that the teachers might express their views freely. They did!

Before the meeting was over, however, Anna Robertson had made it a very unpleasant affair, stating that the only reason that particular committee had been appointed was that they worked hand-in-glove with Bronner and he would run the whole show and they would approve anything he wanted to do. Two other teachers who had had a personal dislike for Mr. Thorsen (over his popularity with pupils and teachers) agreed with Anna. The meeting ended in complete turmoil.

Next morning, the committee reported to Mr. Bronner before school started and asked if they might resign. He asked what the difficulty was, and Mrs. Dodge gave a summary of the meeting the afternoon before.

Mr. Bronner was very displeased and told the committee he would think about the matter throughout the day and they would meet in his office after school to discuss it further. The teachers returned to their classes, and Mr. Bronner sat looking out of the window in an effort to control his temper. He had worked hard to get the board to agree to have a committee of teachers work on salaries and now, finally, when they did agree, this had to happen. What was he going to do about Anna Robertson?

JOHN DALTON

Newton Central School had been the subject of many heated arguments, not only in Newton itself but many of the surrounding towns. It was a rather small central school with an enrollment of about 900 students—grades K through 12. Most arguments centered around the acting principal, Thomas Cantwell, who, after acting as principal for six years, was asked to resign. He refused to resign and carried his case to the state education department when his board voted 3-2 not to hire him for the following year.

After a somewhat tedious battle that proceeded for six months, Mr. Cantwell was reinstated as principal, and three members of the board of education resigned. While he was battling the board, Mr. Carlton, a high school science teacher, acted as principal. When the former principal came back, he found things had changed for the worse—the morale of the faculty was very poor. Mrs. Getty, the high school English teacher, gave her opinion one day in the teachers room, "It's deplorable—half the faculty wants Mr. Cantwell to leave and does not hesitate to make known its feelings, while the other half, knowing what a fine man he is and the horrible deal the board gave him, wants him to stay."

On November 1, Mr. Cantwell asked the board to accept his resignation, and, although there was a lengthy discussion among the board members, they voted to accept his resignation. Mr. Carlton again assumed the responsibilities of principal and remained in the position until the first of February, when a new principal with fifteen years' experience was elected by the board of education.

During all the business of firing and hiring principals, John Dalton, the physical education teacher and coach, had brought to Newton winning basketball teams; and when games were played to capacity crowds, little thought was given to the former principal or the new administrator, Robert Newbrand. Dalton's well-coached teams were the talk of the town in Newton, and coaches who played his team respected his ability as a coach. The student body as well as a large majority of the townspeople were justifiably proud of "Big John" because of his impressive victories, especially against larger schools. He had been heard to speak against the former principal, Mr. Cantwell, while he was still the school's administrator although it was among friends. He never made any statements for the record against Mr. Cantwell, as had some of the other teachers when the principal had his legal fight with the board of education. He was never friendly with Cantwell, but the principal always felt that it wasn't personal.

The coach did show partiality against the principal's son, Bob, by not using him too much throughout the season, even though many coaches agreed that young Bob Cantwell was one of the better players at Newton. But then, the former principal felt that Mr. Dalton was coaching the team and knew the boys better than he.

When John Dalton was up for tenure, Mr. Cantwell considered the fact that although there was no great love lost between him and the coach, Dalton was winning games for the school. He felt that Dalton's methods were not the best but did not give this too much consideration in deciding to recommend him for tenure. His judgment to give him tenure was somewhat influenced (even though to a very small extent) by the fact that he had started to have trouble with the board and the coach had very good personal friends that served on the local board who were also avid basketball fans.

When Mr. Newbrand took over the reins in February, Big John had an eleven-game winning streak going. The new principal had been privately informed by a board member that John Dalton was a very important member of the faculty and was very influential among the teachers. The principal assumed it was because of his string of victories and decided to drive up to Potterville to see Newton play its archrival who also had an impressive record.

The game was very enjoyable to watch, especially for Mr. Newbrand, who had formerly been a coach himself. Although it was a very closely contested game, the principal was rather surprised to see his coach continually complain to the officials and loudly berate his players when they made mistakes. The final score showed Potterville the victor by a score of 65 to 64 after two overtimes.

About half an hour after the end of the game, Mr. Carlton, who was a close friend of Dalton's and who always traveled with the team, went to him team's locker room to find that the Newton boys had pulled several pipes away from the walls, breaking two pipe joints, with a resultant spray of water drenching the locker room. He notified the home coach and mentioned that he did not know how it happened and then left.

Three days later, Mr. Newbrand received a letter from the Potterville principal explaining what had happened on the night of the game and stating that he knew Mr. Newbrand would not condone such action by his student body. Enclosed was a bill for $16.00 to pay for the damages.

Mr. Newbrand called John Dalton into his office and handed him the letter, "Did you know anything about this John?"

"Well, Dick Carlton and I went hunting Saturday and he mentioned it to me but I think they're padding the bill."

"Did you see the damage done by our boys before you left?"

"No I didn't," replied Mr. Dalton. "As soon as the game was over I went to the officials dressing room, and one of the managers brought my coat upstairs. Did you ever see such poor officiating in all your life? Why on one play—"

"Before you discuss the officiating," interrupted the principal, "do you know who broke the pipes at Potterville?"

"No sir, I don't."

"Will you please see the boys at the end of this period and find out who is responsible for the damage?"

John Dalton had the school secretary ask the members of the varsity basketball squad to meet in the gym for a few minutes at the end of the period and then went down and waited for them to appear. When they were all assembled on one section of the bleachers, the coach told them about the letter from Potterville and advised the boys who caused the damage to report to Mr. Newbrand before school was out. He then left the boys without any further discussion of the case.

The boys, left alone, started to discuss the extent of punishment that would befall the three boys who had broken the shower pipe. Tom Smith, the star and league scoring leader, felt that even if he hadn't done it all alone, he would have more of a chance getting off the "hook" than the other boys, so he decided to go to the principal's office and take the "rap."

Tom went straight to the principal's office without seeing the coach, as he felt that the new principal would be lenient and excuse him for his behavior Friday night. Mr. Newbrand asked him to sit down. As soon as he was seated, he stood right up again and said, "Sir, I broke the water pipe in Potterville, and I'm sorry I did it."

"There is no excuse for wanton destruction of people's property especially when you are a guest."

"Yes sir," quickly replied Tom, "I realize that now but I guess after the game I was mad and didn't think what I was doing. I apologize, Mr. Newbrand. It will never happen again. I'm sorry."

"I'm sorry, too, Tom—sorry that I have to restrict you from Friday's game for your uncalled-for actions."

"But sir," pleaded the boy, "we have to win this one coming up, and coach will have to have his squad at full strength."

"I would like to see coach win the next one, too, Tom; but I cannot condone your actions—our primary aim here is to have a respectable school and a courteous student body. That is all, Tom. You may go now."

Tom Smith found the coach in the gym office and told him what had happened with Mr. Newbrand.

"Well, I'll see about this," stormed Mr. Dalton, and he walked out of his office and up to see the principal.

"Mr. Newbrand, Tom has just informed me that you forbid him to play this Friday."

"Yes, Coach, I think it's the only thing to do to get some of these students to realize that they represent Newton High School and act like gentlemen when they are guests at another school."

"I think Tom has learned his lesson, sir, and I have to have him for this next game. He probably lost his head after losing that tight one at Potterville and didn't realize what he was doing."

"I'm sorry, Coach, but I must insist that he be benched for this Friday's game."

"Is that final?" asked the Coach.

"I'm afraid it is!"

Mr. Dalton became noticeably upset and started to speak several times when finally, he said with cold anger, "If Smith doesn't play Friday, I will tender my resignation."

ROBERT RINGROSE

With the approach of the March, 1949, meeting of the board of education at Simpson Central School, Principal Ned Donaldson was at work preparing to make recommendations for teacher appointments. Several of the staff would be eligible for tenure consideration, including Robert Ringrose, the music teacher. The matter of a decision on whether to recommend Ringrose for tenure was a perplexing problem for Principal Donaldson.

This was Donaldson's second year as principal, and Ringrose's third as teacher, Donaldson having been science teacher in the school prior to his appointment as principal. Both men were of about the same age, their early forties. During Ringrose's first year, the year 1946-1947, both men had worked together on a committee of the local teachers' association, which had been formed to make some requests to the board of education relative to salary adjustments.

Robert Ringrose and Ned Donaldson were opposites in behavior patterns. Robert was a self-assured, aggressive individual, possessing a temper which frequently got the better of him and a caustic tongue. Ned was the modest type, possessed of insufficient self-confidence, sensitive to the feelings of other people, and often overly cautious in trying to see all the viewpoints of a problem before coming to a decision. The last-mentioned characteristic had led some persons, including Robert, to regard him as indecisive.

Robert's work as a teacher of music appeared to be satisfactory so far as Ned's limited observations during his first year as principal was concerned. Since there was only the one music teacher, Robert was obliged to teach both the grade vocal music and the instrumental work. Each grade room was visited twice a week, and the remaining time was given to the teaching of group instrumental lessons and to rehearsals of the concert and junior bands. This schedule allowed for scarcely any free periods during the week; hence Robert attended to the various administrative details of the music department after school hours.

During the two years prior to Robert's employment, the school had had two very incompetent female music instructors, following upon a well-liked and successful teacher. Under the two poor teachers, discipline and accomplishment had deteriorated to a low level in the instrumental work, and the band was practically at a standstill. When the board president and the former principal had interviewed Robert for the position, they had emphasized the point that they wanted someone who could build the band back to a respectable organization and discipline the pupils. Robert had assured them in positive tones that he could fill the bill.

It was not long after his first year as principal was underway that Ned became aware of friction between some of the teachers (particularly upper elementary) and Robert. The particular cause seemed to be the operation of a rotating instrument schedule, an innovation of the previous year. At Robert's request, the former principal had permitted a trial of the rotating schedule. This schedule was so arranged that a given instrumental group, for example, trumpet beginners, met once each week during one of the regular class periods of the day. The time of this group lesson changed each week, until it had rotated through all the five or six class periods which could be used. This meant that the pupil in any instrument group would miss his English class once in four or five weeks in order to have his instrument lesson; and the same was true of his other classes. Principal Donaldson had decided, after discussing the matter with Robert, to continue with this plan. On Monday of each week, the week's schedule with pupils' names was posted in all of the home rooms.

The teachers who objected to this plan did so on the grounds that it was difficult to keep track of the youngsters and that it always happened that someone was absent from a class when new work was being presented. Occasionally, a teacher would withhold a pupil from his instrument lesson, and this invariably led to words and hard feelings between Robert and the teacher.

The teachers of the elementary grades also brought to the attention of Principal Donaldson that Robert was not always prompt in meeting the grade vocal groups. When Ned brought this to Robert's attention, his explanation was that the schedule was so tight that delays were occasionally unavoidable. He added that the teachers were probably sore because they could not have as much free time for themselves when he was late.

As time went along and Robert continued into his third year, it became increasingly evident that a considerable number of the faculty developed a strong dislike for him. One incident which caused a considerable consternation among the faculty occurred between Robert and the third-grade teacher. One of Robert's three sons was in the third grade. One day, while Robert was passing through the corridor, he noticed his son standing outside the door of his room and learned that he was being disciplined. Since it was lunch time for that grade, the teacher and the rest of the grade were in the cafeteria. The teacher fully intended that the boy should eat his lunch later while the rest of the grade were on the playground. However, Robert assumed that his son was being denied his lunch and without further investigation went to the cafeteria and loudly berated the third-grade teacher in the hearing of all present. Although conferences with Principal Donaldson resulted in an apology, relations were now more strained than previously.

In Robert's work with the band, there had been steady progress until, in the third year, the organization succeeded in obtaining a "B" rating in a medium class of schools at the state music festival. Two or three concerts were given during the year which could definitely be called successful in terms of what had taken place in the two previous years. Instrumental lessons had been extended to the fourth grade on the basis of musical aptitude tests, which Robert had given. He also organized a junior band in the second semester of his second and third years.

In the business end of the music department, Robert had made considerable progress. He set up a filing system for the music and record-keeping details, inventoried equipment, arranged an instrument rental system, and put the music association's financial accounting in order. In short, he had brought order out of chaos.

As Principal Donaldson recalled these and various other incidents and details of Robert's career in the school, he also remembered the laborious sessions that he and Robert had had in the office over matters of policy relating to the music department. He also recalled that Robert had frequently been quite outspoken in criticism of other administrative policies which did not directly concern him.

Principal Donaldson also remembered that Mrs. Ringrose had been employed that year as a second-grade teacher and was doing quite an acceptable job. Refusal to recommend Robert for his job would undoubtedly mean the loss of Mrs. Ringrose at a time when elementary teachers were hard to obtain.

GUM CHEWING AT RIVERDALE

Miss Sweeney, an English teacher in Riverdale High School for the past twenty-five years, was confronted with a problem in the opening semester of school, which, now at the beginning of the second semester, was causing confusion throughout the entire school.

In September, Miss Sweeney had been very irritated by gum chewing in her classes and had laid down the rule, in no uncertain terms, that there would be absolutely no gum chewing in any of her classes. She made several satirical remarks about the habit and said she would not tolerate it. As weeks went on, it was apparent to her the students were doing it mainly to annoy her and to take a few minutes off each class for a march to the basket, row by row.

Miss Sweeney then took it upon herself to lay down the rule on no gum chewing in her third-period study hall. There was no general school rule on gum chewing, but she made an issue of it anytime and everywhere she met students chewing.

Several of the younger teachers had informed her, when she brought up the subject one day in the faculty room, that they thought it best for her to forget the whole matter, or at least to "soft-pedal" it, and that gradually it would die out. They had discovered that if you made little of an incident, it would not grow to huge proportions.

Miss Sweeney resented the friendly advice and reminded them that she had been at Riverdale High School a little longer than they and that having more experience, she knew how to deal with such situations.

The next incident occurred when Miss Sweeney, on her way to lunch, stopped a group of students in the corridor and made them throw away their gum. The students were angry and immediately went upstairs to the principal's office and complained of the incident, stating it was their lunch hour, and furthermore, they were not Miss Sweeney's students in English, and they felt they could do what they wanted during lunch period.

For several days Mr. Bolt pondered on the problem as to just what action to take. In the meantime, Brotherhood Week approached. Miss Sweeney had charge of a school assembly program to which parents and friends were invited. The program was carefully planned and went off fairly well, except that the students had decided ahead of time to get even with Miss Sweeney and so have each speaker or singer appear on the stage chewing gum.

Reactions came from the parents, visitors, and the press, but not from the faculty. Three parents visited Mr. Bolt after the program to voice their opinion against the gum chewing. Mr. Bolt, who had left the auditorium after introducing the class chairman of the program, was quite surprised and made little or no comment. The local newspaper, in writing up the incident, called attention to the excellent Brotherhood program which was marred only by mouthfuls of gum.

Mr. Bolt realized that the time for some kind of action had arrived. He must make a decision on how to handle the gum chewing.

Administrative Relations with the Board of Education

ANDREW NORWOOD[1]

The teachers at Gainville High School in New York State, looked forward to the opening of the 1946 school year with considerable anticipation. During the month of August, they contacted one another, hoping to learn something about the newly appointed principal, Andrew Norwood. The Gainville Evening Herald had published a little information, but no one had met him or had any additional information about him. The article in the paper stated that Mr. Norwood was a graduate of Illinois State University, where he had also received his master's degree in education. During the war he had been director of public relations in a chemical plant in Northtown, N. Y. Before the war, he had spent thirteen years teaching in Jayville, N. Y. This was to be his first position as a high school administrator. Mr. Norwood was thirty-eight years of age, married, and had a seven-year-old son.

School opened the Tuesday after Labor Day without any of the teachers having seen Mr. Norwood. Much to their surprise, the first day was well planned and executed. Scheduling ran smoothly with a minimum of conflicts, books were issued with little confusion, and the students were sent home at 11 o'clock. A teachers' meeting followed, during which Mr. Norwood spoke briefly, commending the teachers on their successful start that morning, and asking them for their continued co-operation throughout the year. Informal conversation with the new principal followed the meeting, and teachers commented to each other that Mr. Norwood showed promise of being an excellent leader.

The next morning classes met for the first time, but things did not run as smoothly as had been anticipated. During two periods, the study hall could not handle all of the students scheduled for it. At other times, only a few students were in the study hall. The situation became so bad that

[1] Prepared in the Department of Education, Ohio University, by H. E. Benz and Walter H. Herriott. Copyright, 1955, by the Ohio University Press. Reprinted by permission of the publishers.

Mr. Norwood sent the students home and called another teachers' meeting. The schedule was revised so that it was workable but not entirely satisfactory. At the close of this meeting, Mrs. Blair, an English teacher, approached Mr. Norwood.

Mrs. Blair: "Other New York state schools have been increasing the salaries of their teachers, and we have been wondering when the board is going to take some action to increase ours. Will you speak to them about it?"

Mr. Norwood: "That's the trouble with teachers; they want salary increases when the school has more need for the money than they have."

Mrs. Blair: "Then you don't think we need an increased salary?"

Mr. Norwood: "Not exactly that. I'll mention it to the board, but they have to pay so much for improvements and administration that they can't afford to increase the teachers' salaries right now."

Mr. Donaldson, the president of the board of education, was a man in his early seventies. He was generally regarded by the townspeople as a narrow-minded religious fanatic, but he had done much in a material way for the schools, and probably had been elected to the board for that reason. Having completed only the first four grades, he was limited in his cultural outlook. In his youth he had been rowdy; later he settled down, married well, and now delighted in running the schools.

During the first board meeting the following conversation occurred:

Mr. Donaldson: "Mr. Malone, the music teacher, informs me that you are not co-operating with him."

Mr. Norwood: "In what way have I failed to co-operate?"

Mr. Donaldson: "You are telling him what to do and how to do it. Besides that, I hear that he has to hold band practice at noon."

Mr. Norwood: "Noon is the only possible time for band. In regard to the other, I think he needs some help. After all, my band in Jayville won the state championship, so I know what he lacks."

Mr. Donaldson: "Just remember you're new here, and we will not tolerate lack of co-operation."

Mr. Norwood: "How about you minding your own business. I was hired to administer the high school, and I shall continue to do so to the best of my ability."

Things were quiet for several weeks. Then one day Mr. Norwood struck a neighbor's child for tripping his small son. News of this incident spread throughout the community, and soon school children began calling him such names as "Big Bully" and "Old Meanie."

Soon after this, he slapped the faces of two boys for shoving other students during the exchange of classes. The parents of the boys went to the board. A special meeting was called, at which, Mr. Norwood, the two boys, and the boys' parents were asked to appear. Mr. Norwood called the county superintendent and asked him to come to the meeting.

The conversation at this meeting was not recorded, but the procedure was as follows. Both boys were permitted to tell their stories, during which the parents and board members interrupted with comments, questions, and elaborations. Mr. Norwood remained silent and composed during this procedure. At the end he asked for suggestions as to the type of disciplinary action they would recommend. To this the board responded by ruling out corporal punishment, except in extreme cases, and had two paddles made to meet with their approval. The parents made no suggestions. After this incident, students boasted that the board was on their side.

This occurrence soon proved to have an effect on the life of the school. Absence and truancy increased; school property was defaced and, in some instances, destroyed; teachers could hardly maintain enough discipline to hold classes; and several women teachers threatened to resign.

Late one Friday afternoon, Mr. Norwood walked into the chemistry laboratory to talk with Mr. Briggs, the young science teacher, who seemed to be the only teacher in the school who had no trouble with discipline at this time. Mr. Briggs was a disabled veteran, a quiet person, well-liked by the students, who never seemed to question his authority. With this in mind Mr. Norwood opened the conversation.

Mr. Norwood: "The disciplinary problem in this school is beyond my control. When I was a teacher, I had no trouble with discipline because my students respected me and knew I was the "boss"; but what can I do here as an administrator when I don't even have the board of education behind me? I'm seriously considering resigning."

Mr. Briggs: "You may be down, but don't go out without a fight."

Mr. Norwood: "But what can I do when the board tries to beat me at every turn? There isn't an intelligent, educated person on that board with any interest in improving the school system, and it is headed by an old goat who never got beyond the fourth grade. I don't know what's wrong with the parents in this town—whether they don't vote intelligently for board members or whether they don't vote at all."

Mr. Briggs: "I'll admit you have a problem. Mr. Donaldson is impossible to get along with unless you're on his side, and what intelligent administrator could be? You might try polishing the apple a bit by visiting his church."

Mr. Norwood: "I refuse to do that."

Mr. Briggs: "Then why don't you tell the board the results of their action? I'll go along and support your statement."

Mr. Norwood: "No, I don't want to drag you into this. I guess the only thing for me to do is lay down the law to the students and see that it's enforced, then hope that the board will back me up in whatever I do."

After Christmas vacation Mr. Norwood announced that privileges would be denied those students whose behavior warranted such action. Several days later he announced that certain students would not be allowed to attend the next home basketball game because of their behavior. The night of the game they came anyway. On seeing Mr. Norwood standing at the door, they left. Soon they returned with Mr. Donaldson.

Mr. Donaldson: "You can't stop these students from attending the game. This is a public affair."

Mr. Norwood: "They know that they are being disciplined, and you know that I have authority to keep undesirable characters out."

Mr. Archer, the history teacher, was selling tickets. It was at this point that Mr. Donaldson attempted to draw him into the argument.

Mr. Donaldson: "Mr. Archer! Sell these students tickets!"

Mr. Norwood: "Don't you dare!"

Mr. Archer: "Gentlemen, why don't you go to the office to discuss this matter. Don't make a scene here in public."

Mr. Donaldson: (Pointing his finger at Mr. Archer.) "This man Norwood has ruined this school hasn't he, Mr. Archer?"

Mr. Norwood: "Tell the damn fool who has caused all the trouble."

Mr. Archer: "Gentlemen, I am only selling tickets and want no part in the argument."

Mr. Donaldson: "Don't you swear at me!"

Mr. Norwood: "It's about time somebody swore at you."

With this Mr. Norwood went home. The students went in to see the game without paying since Mr. Archer refused to sell them tickets.

The next day Mr. Norwood submitted his resignation to the board and county superintendent. With his resignation he recommended that Mr. Briggs be appointed principal.

That evening Mr. Briggs was called to a special meeting of the board and asked to take the principal's position. Mr. Briggs hesitated. If he accepted the position he would be the seventh principal in six years.

A PRINCIPAL FOR THE MONTGOMERY SCHOOL[2]

Dr. Jim Peters, superintendent of schools in Oakville, ran his fingers through his greying hair, looked over the top of his feet propped up on his desk, and said to his friend, "Tom, I've a problem on my hands—and I don't know the answer. Our new twenty-five room, six-year high school in the Montgomery district will be ready this fall. It's a good school, in a good, fast-growing middle-class residential district. You'd be amazed how

[2] Copyright, 1951, by the President and Fellows of Harvard College. Reprinted by permission of the Harvard Graduate School of Education.

that section out in the west end has grown. New industrial plants during the war years not only brought a great many new people to Oakville, but the higher wages then and since have meant that many people have been able to move out of the more run-down sections of the city and build themselves modern homes out there. My wife was saying the other day that while there is a lot of charm to the big old frame houses on our elm-lined streets, yet that spic-and-span fast-growing Montgomery district also has an appealing air of being well kept and on its way.

"Anyway, my problem is that I have to recommend a principal for the new Montgomery School."

"That shouldn't be too difficult," said Tom Hughes, longtime friend of Dr. Peters and a superintendent himself in a neighboring state. "The position is a bit of a plum, isn't it? . . . New, modern building . . . One of the largest schools in Oakville . . . Chance to grow up with the Montgomery district . . . Top salary, I suppose . . ."

"Yes, the salary isn't too bad—although school salaries in Oakville generally are not what they should be. It's not easy to push teachers' salaries very high when the general wage level in the city as a whole is lower than that in many other cities of similar size. But we have been swamped with applications for the new principalship.

"There are some likely-looking candidates, Tom: a couple of them with outstanding records behind them. One man especially impresses me. You probably know him—Smith, from your state department. He came over to see me the other day. He's young and personable and ambitious, with an amazing record behind him for a thirty-five-year-old."

"Yes, I know Smith. He taught for me for a while before Townsend snapped him up as high school principal. The state department took him away from Townsend a couple of years ago as an assistant in instructional supervision. He has done well there, too, from what I hear."

"Yes, his application is highly recommended by your assistant commissioner, among others. The boy seems to have experience, gets along well with people, gets things done. He taught on the summer faculty at Curry College last year. And he is really keen on doing one of those community jobs in the Montgomery School."

Hughes looked quizzical. "Doesn't sound as if you would have too much trouble recommending Smith for the principalship!"

"Perhaps not. But it's a delicate situation here in Oakville. The city is devilishly conservative: almost ingrown, you might say. We have had the same five-man school committee for fourteen years, for example, in re-election mostly by acclamation. Good board, too, for that matter. But Smith has a big strike against him from the first: he's from out-of-state. It was only the teacher shortage during the war that brought the school board around to appointing any but local people as teachers. There has never been any policy spelled out in writing on the matter, but the teacher selection subcommittee of the board still picks the local applicants first and turns to outsiders only when the local list is exhausted. By state law, selections have to be made from names recommended by me; but for years and years—since long before my time—it has been customary for the superintendent to submit two lists to the subcommittee: a local list and 'others.' "

"And you still do it that way?"

"Well, yes. . . . And in theory it's probably nothing to be proud of. But in each of my seven years as superintendent we have needed so many new teachers that we have been able to pick the cream of the crop of outsiders as well as the local people anyway. In fact, the whole thing has worked out rather well without antagonizing anybody."

"But the new principalship is somewhat different?"

"Yes it is. Old Man Hamilton expects to get it. You may know him. He's a great conference hound, even though he never contributes anything to a conference or takes any new ideas away from it with him either! He's a Kiwanian, and an official in the Congregational church. He comes of one of the older families in this area; he has a brother-in-law on the board, an older brother is the district court judge, and his best friend is the editor of the *Examiner*. He's been principal of Central Junior High for fifteen years or so . . . A.B. degree in 1911, due for retirement in four years. He looks to Montgomery School as a just reward for thirty-eight years of service: a sort of comfortable, well-paid, 'prestigeful' post from which to retire."

"How effective is he at Central?"

"He gets by down there. His returns always reach us on time, and his building maintenance costs are low. Never any serious accident or discipline problems to plague me with. Not much ever happens down there, though, other than the traditional day-by-day type of thing. Not much imagination. Our little survey three years ago showed Central with the highest percentage of drop-outs in the city, and the high schools often complain about the students they get from Central. But Hammy points out that his school is on the wrong side of the tracks, and he probably has something there. That may also account for more teachers asking to be transferred out of Central than any other school."

"What would the public think of his appointment?"

"Well, if they thought about it much at all, they would mostly approve, I suppose. He is a solid local citizen, a pillar of the church. Promotion to a large new school, in a much more desirable area, would fit the community pattern to a T."

"When you say the people would approve, do you include those whose children presently attend his school—or the graduates from his school?"

"Well, I don't know. They wouldn't be a very influential group anyway. But you're quite right in wondering whether those who will make the decision really know anything about Hammy's work as an educator. They just think of him as a good fellow: not an outstanding person, of course, but then school men are not supposed to be outstanding.

"Hammy has applied for the job, and everybody knows it. Our school regulations require that the school committee as a whole consider appointments to principalships. By custom (which weighs heavily in this old town) this means that the superintendent selects the two or three best applications and presents them to the committee in order of preference, stating reasons for his choice. But most of the time it is all prearranged, since the superintendent makes his recommendations—again by custom— by agreement with the three-man teacher selection subcommittee."

"What does that subcommittee think of Hamilton?"

"We played golf yesterday. I thought I'd put them in a good mood by beating me hands down! Of course, it turned out to be a poor day, but we started out anyway. Rain turned us back at the seventh. It was only my second time out this year, and the old Marlborough course was in mighty good shape. I was playing with Art Goodier, and he was fit to be tied. Lost two balls off the tee on that wicked dog's leg on the 3rd hole. That made him so mad he sliced another into the lake on the 4th ..."

"What did the committee think of Hamilton, though?"

"Oh, yes, Hamilton. Well, they weren't much interested in the problem —or, rather, they saw no problem at all. They just take it for granted from the beginning that Hammy is the man. The chairman of the board broached the matter before I did, in fact, by asking, 'Well, with Hammy at the Montgomery School, who should we put in his old job at Central?'

"Not to be too pointed, I said that many first-rate men had applied for the Montgomery School and that although Hammy would be a logical choice, there were others whom we might consider too: younger men, also of proven ability, with energy and imagination to enable them to do a bang-up job in the new school and new community.

" 'Jim,' the chairman said, 'that doesn't sound like you at all. Everybody in Oakville expects Hammy to get the job. After all, he's earned it! He has stayed here and done a good job all these years—nobody has found fault with it. And he hasn't run off to whatever city would pay him a little more money, either!'

"That last was something of a crack at me, Tom. I started out here, as you know, but moved from Union High to a larger principalship in Thurston. After that 'crime,' added to my chasing after a higher degree, it was only the illness of the assistant superintendent and the fact that I had kept my home here in Oakville that won me a 4-1 appointment as superintendent when Mr. Hatch died.

"Anyway, we left it that the subcommittee would try to drop in here at four-thirty today to look over the dossiers on Hamilton and Smith and another local man I have thrown in for effect. I really don't know how hard to fight for Smith. I firmly believe he is the better man for the Montgomery School, both from the point of view of the community and of the children who will attend the school.

"But maybe that would be asking too much all at once, making too sharp a break with custom here in tradition-bound Oakville. Maybe I am just getting to feel a bit guilty about letting things drift along as long as I have. I suppose changes have to take place gradually. Probably I should have started in years ago."

PRINCIPAL BLACK

It was December 9, and Central School had begun to buzz with that peculiar activity that permeates schools before Christmas. Principal Black had no way of knowing that in a few hours he and his school would explode into headlines, become a *cause célèbre*.

The first intimation of the maelstrom that was brewing came that evening after supper. The telephone rang and Mr. Black answered it. "Mr. Black, I am a reporter representing the *Journal*. Would you like to make a statement concerning the Henderson story?" For an instant the question had no meaning for Mr. Black but, even as he said, "I'm sorry I don't understand," he remembered the Henderson girl in slacks and Mrs. Henderson's telephone call. It was one of those nuisance problems handled almost casually by principals daily. The rules were clear, there was no doubt about the school policy on the matter, and there was well-established precedent for the principal's action.

Later Mr. Black described the incident to the school attorney as follows:

On December 9, Alice Henderson appeared in the classroom dressed in slacks. The teacher, in keeping with the policy of the school, reminded her that the girls are to wear dresses or skirts and blouses in the regular classrooms. Alice refused to do so, saying that her mother made her wear slacks. She admitted that she was aware of the school policy. I asked her if she had a skirt or dress with her and she said no. Since she lives only a few houses (six) from the school, I asked her if she would run home and change. She offered no objection. A few minutes later, her mother called me on the telephone and informed me that she had told her daughter to wear slacks to school and that she would not send her back unless she could wear them to her regular classes. I attempted to explain the situation from our standpoint but without success.

In view of the fact that conflicts with this particular parent had been common in the past and had finally been settled by more than reasonable co-operation on the part of the school, I did not take this defiance too seriously and was of the opinion that this too would straighten itself out within a few days. We, of course, made no public issue of the matter any more than we would any infraction of school regulations.

Mr. Black had reason to believe that he had acted correctly in this matter. He had been principal of Central School for fourteen years, and most of his teaching staff had had long service in the school. Both he and his staff knew the policies of the school well and understood the people of Centralville thoroughly.

Centralville was a small rural community. It was rather isolated. It had one railroad connecting it with the nearest large city fifty miles away. There were no main highways leading into this small village. Almost all of the 2000 inhabitants of Centralville had been born and raised there. Mr. Henderson's family was one of the few families which had recently moved into the community. They came from New York City. Most of the people were farmers or storekeepers. There was just one small factory in the community. It had expanded slightly because of government contracts. Mr. Henderson worked in this factory. There was little or no economic or social class difference in Centralville. The president of the board of education was the local stationmaster. The people were proud of their school and prouder of its reputation for having such well-behaved students. As Mr. Black explained, the community was "conservative, somewhat narrow one might say."

The principal felt that he had done what the community wanted him to do, that is, enforce the regulations which it felt were necessary in order to "instill in our young people a healthy respect for discipline and authority."

However, Mr. Henderson was not yet a member of the community. He did not react like a member of that community. When his wife told him of the slacks incident, he did an unheard of thing in Centralville, he called a newspaper in a nearby town and told them that his daughter was put out of school for wearing slacks. He pointed out that because of the cold weather it was necessary that his daughter wear warm clothes and that regardless of weather, neither the principal nor the board of education had a right to dictate what his children should wear.

In a written statement, Mr. Black told what happened next:

On the following Monday morning the father appeared at school with his daughter in her slacks, together with two newspaper reporters and a news cameraman. The usual orderly routine of the opening of school was quite completely disrupted, as one can well imagine. We invited the father and the girl into my office for a conference but refused admittance to the newsmen. My office secretary and our elementary supervisor were also present. The father belligerently demanded that his daughter be admitted to school and to her regular classes wearing the slacks. Again I attempted to explain our viewpoint and earnestly solicited his co-operation. He refused to consider the matter sensibly and made some remark concerning the fact that "we are not living in Russia." Whereupon the youngster chimed in, "Yes, we are living in a free country, and you have no right to make rules and regulations. We have a right to do as we please." Again, I attempted to clarify the issue but with no success. The father then asked if his daughter was going to be readmitted to school or not. In reply, I pointed out that since there was no regulation prohibiting the wearing of slacks to school we would not refuse to admit her. However, the fact still remained that

I was obliged to say that she could not wear her slacks to her regular classes as long as the existing policy was in effect. I said that I hated to see the girl missing out on her studies and would arrange individual instruction for her if she cared to remain.

It was at this point that newspapermen from publications big and small began to write about the "Slacks Girl." At first, they reported the incident as a news story, but, soon, they were writing editorials and featuring the story in the Sunday supplements. Cartoons showed the principal as an ogre and as a St. George. Pictures of the "Slacks Girl" accompanied the written articles. One newspaperman published a picture of a group of Central School girls wearing slacks and snowsuits and reported that the girls of Central School were in sympathy with the Henderson girl and that they meant to force the principal to change his rule about slacks. Actually, according to Mr. Black, the girls in the picture came a long distance by bus, and, on cold winter days, they usually wore slacks or snowsuits but changed to dresses before reporting for classes. The girls acted no differently on the day the picture was taken.

One New York City fashion magazine sent a lady reporter to interview Mr. Black to find out what interest he had in changing the fashions of the time. Some newspapers charged Mr. Black and the board of education with fascism; others deplored Mr. Black's "attempt to hold back progress"; others accused the school administration of having lost touch with the "progressive" methods of education.

Not all newspapers, however, were against Mr. Black's decision in the matter of slacks. Some editors commended Mr. Black's stand as a "step toward curbing juvenile delinquency"; others blessed him for upholding the Bible; and still others cheered him for "striking a blow against indecent dress."

Prominent people were quoted on the matter of "girls-in-slacks-in-schools." Young people in colleges were asked to give their arguments on the question, "Should girls wear slacks in school?" The best of these arguments for and against were printed side by side in the newspapers.

Authorities of the leading girls' colleges in the east reported that in their schools "girls were not sent home for wearing slacks." School administrators were quoted by the press as saying that the problem did not exist in their school or that they had more important things to do than make rules about slacks.

As a result of all this publicity, the public took sides and deluged Mr. Black and the board of education with hundreds of letters and cards The letters came from all parts of the country. One came from as far away as Guam, in the middle of the Pacific.

Like the newspapers, the letters were divided in praising and condemning Mr. Black's action in regard to "girls wearing slacks in school." From Kent, Ohio, came this note, "I want you to know I am for you on your 'no slacks' rule for female students." From Salem, Virginia, "I hope you will win out, the Bible is very clear on the subject of one sex wearing the clothes of the opposite sex." From the Ohio Soldiers' and Sailors' Home, "Don't you know we just fought a long and bloody war to rid the world of dictators?" From a well-known Hollywood star, "There is nothing wrong with girls wearing slacks if they have the figure for it."

In the midst of all this verbal bombardment, a board meeting was called, and the general public was invited to attend to discuss the principal's action. After much discussion by parents, students, board members, and teachers, the people of the community attending the meeting voted 200 to 1 approving the principal's action.

All the teachers of the system signed a resolution asking for the "continued enforcement of the rule against wearing slacks or similar attire in class until it is amended or rescinded by the board of education."

The district superintendent, Mr. Otto, wrote an open letter to Mr. Black in which he said, "I endorse the stand you are taking."

To friends Mr. Black pointed out, "The frustrating thing in this matter is that regardless of whether they are for me or against me, the newspapers and the letter writers are missing the real issue. They praise or condemn me on the false issue, 'Should girls (anywhere) be permitted to wear slacks in school (any school).' The real issue is 'should the principal of a particular school enforce the regulations of that school which were adopted by that school's board of education and approved by the people of that community.'"

However, Mr. Black could not reach the reading public to explain the issue and to plead, "I have no desire or intention of trying to dictate what our students must wear. It is certainly not a question of what is decent or indecent in dress. I am merely enforcing the school regulations."

Mr. Henderson was threatening legal action, the girl was losing valuable school time, an atmosphere was developing in which good work by teachers and students was impossible. Mr. Black and the board of education pondered what to do to settle the problem.

Administrative Relations with the Community

HAROLD ANDERSON

Harold Anderson came to the Haroldville Central School as supervising principal in 1944. He succeeded Alfred Curtis who left the position to enter the O.S.S. Harold went through the usual trials and tribulations of an administrator during wartime. Most of his men teachers left to enter the armed services. In fact, he had only one man left, Francis Osterhoudt, the vice-principal.

Harold, who was not very athletic himself, took over coaching the basketball team and was quite successful; his team won the championship of the Poconic League.

In 1945, the tenure law went into effect, and the Haroldville board adopted a three-year probationary period for their beginning teachers. At this time, all of the teachers in the system were put on probation; however, Harold requested the board to put him on tenure. The board agreed and approved his tenure appointment.

The next year, with the war over, it was again possible to hire men teachers. Harold hired Jack Banks as physical director for the school. Jack had formerly taught in private schools near Metropolis, had a very pleasant disposition, and seemed to fit into the community very easily. When Jack arrived in Haroldville living quarters were hard to find, so he rented a small place at Queens Lake, which was about five miles from the village, and drove back and forth to school. Although he had been brought up in a city, he took an interest in country living, had a garden, raised a few chickens, and kept a couple of hogs.

In the summertime, Jack and his family stayed in the cottage near Queens Lake. The lake had a good beach, and Jack voluntarily took over the lifeguard duties and swimming classes for the children. He taught swimming each morning and served as a lifeguard each afternoon.

His basketball team, the first year, was not an outstanding one, since most of Harold's championship team had been graduated. However, his team did manage to make a good showing in league games. His teams did improve, and his third year of coaching was a marked success when his team won the league championship.

Meanwhile, Harold Anderson had been taking a prominent part in school and community affairs. Teachers' salaries were a big issue at the time. At a meeting of the District Teachers Association of Middlesex County, Harold made the motion that the association go on record as favoring the retirement of Arthur Norton from the post of executive secretary of the State Teachers Association and that the association seek a high-pressure lawyer to take his place to get some legislation favoring an increase in teachers' salaries through the assembly. This resolution went through, although there was opposition from some members.

In the spring of the same year, Jack Banks came up for tenure. Three other teachers were also eligible. At the board meeting called for the purpose of considering tenure appointments, Harold Anderson recommended the three teachers be placed on tenure, but that Jack Banks not be placed on tenure. Under board rules, this meant that Jack would not be rehired. The board accepted Anderson's recommendation. The following morning Anderson informed Banks of his recommendation and the board's action. Jack left the office downcast and indignant.

By the next day the whole district had heard the news, and board members began to hear complaints from a number of townspeople. The outcry became so loud and insistent the board president, Fred Baker, after talking matters over with other members of the board and with the principal, decided it would be best to hold a public meeting and let the voters, parents, and townspeople, have a say in the discussion.

The meeting was held in the school auditorium on the following Tuesday. The board sat at a big table facing the audience. Harold Anderson did not sit at the table but off to one side of the hall. It was a large crowd; not only the village but the outlying districts were well represented. A big delegation from Queens Lake was present and had with it Alexander Smith, a young lawyer from Terryville. Smith had the reputation of being an agitator and had unsuccessfully opposed the building of a new school building at Terryville a number of years back.

President Baker called the meeting to order and stated the business of the meeting was to discuss the case of Jack Banks who had not been put on tenure. Immediately a parent jumped to his feet and was recognized by the President. He stated, "Before I came to this meeting my little boy, who is in the fourth grade, said to me, 'Daddy don't let them fire Mr. Banks. He is the only one who can put bandages on our cuts when we get hurt at school. Don't let them send him away.'" The speech was greeted with a roar of approval.

Art Tomlinson next took the floor. Art was a member of the Veterans of Foreign Wars and manager of the local baseball team. Art said, "I wish to say something for Mr. Banks. I have always found him to be co-operative. Whenever I was stuck for a shortstop on the town team, I would call Jack Banks. He always said, 'Sure, Art, I'll be there,' and he always was! We need people like Jack Banks in this community. He is a good man!"

Alexander Smith, the lawyer from Terryville, then took the floor and made quite a long speech, telling how Jack had acted as lifeguard and had given swimming lessons at Queens Lake during the summer without pay. At the end of his speech, he turned to the president and asked, "Just what are the reasons that Jack Banks is not being rehired?"

Mr. Baker then rose and, using notes from the previous board meeting, made a few statements as to why Jack had not been put on permanent tenure. He told of an occasion when the principal was away and Jack did not show up for his physical education class. Mr. Osterhoudt sent the class to study hall. Jack appeared near the end of the period dressed in old clothes and with his hands covered with blood. Osterhoudt asked where he had been and Jack answered, "Been killing a hog." This remark was greeted with uproarious laughter by the crowd, and one person sitting in the back of the room yelled, "How much did the hog weigh?" This brought down the house.

When order had been restored, President Baker then gave a few more instances showing Jack's delinquencies. He told how he was continually late for classes, how he had not handed in reports, how he had not come back with the basketball team after a game at a nearby town, but had left them unsupervised on the trip home. Most of these remarks were greeted with laughter and wisecracks from the crowd.

At the end of this recital of the evidence which had been collected on Jack Banks over a period of three years, Bill Taylor, a farmer from the outskirts of the town, rose and cried, "I know why he wasn't rehired! It was because that man sitting in the corner doesn't like him and that is the only reason!" He pointed directly at Mr. Anderson. Harold jumped to his feet to reply, but the crowd booed and hissed, so his words were not heard. Seeing this was so, he sat down.

When the crowd finally had quieted down, Art Tomlinson stood up and said, "No one has heard what Jack Banks has had to say. I think we should hear his side of the story." Jack, who was sitting halfway back in the hall, sprang to his feet and rushed to the front:

"Sure I want to be heard. This is the first time that I have had a chance to speak. No one had told me that I hadn't been doing all right until the principal told me the other day after the meeting that I wasn't coming back. Why wasn't I told of these things before?" He returned to his seat, receiving a thunderous ovation.

Mr. Baker then stated the public meeting was over and the board would go into executive session. He asked Anderson and Banks to remain for the session. The crowd filed out, laughing and joking.

RIVERDALE[1]

In the 1940's, a sociological study was made of Riverdale, a midwestern city of 100,000 population, to determine the nature of the social structure in such a community. The primary, though not the only method of study, was that of the interview, of which the one in this case is a typical example.

Riverdale is an old established community first settled in the 1830's. It derives its wealth from a long history of industrial development, from its function as a trade and financial center for a rich agricultural region, and from a large foreign-born population which, through three fourths of a century, provided the workers necessary for Riverdale's industrial expansion.

To the casual observer these ethnic groups in the community are the outstandingly unique feature of Riverdale. Over half of the population calls itself Swedish, about a tenth Italian, and smaller numbers identify themselves with other national and geographic origins. In many respects, Riverdale is split by these differential identifications: geographically into the "American" and "Swedish" sides of the river; economically with "Americans," "Swedish," and "Italian" banks, stores, and occupations; socially and politically with "Swedish," "American," and "Italian" clubs, churches, societies, political tickets, and, to a certain extent, schools.

The Swedes have the highest prestige of any foreign-born group, with those from Belgium, Poland, and Italy following in that order. Below these groups, in the eyes of the members of the community, are the southern white migrants and the Negroes. The position in the community of each of these groups is closely related to the recency of their immigration and the degree to which their native cultural patterns differ from those of the middle-class culture of the community.

These ethnic differentiations, the high division of labor, the stability of the population, the concentration of wealth in a relatively few families, and the idealization of New England ancestry have been important factors in the development and elaboration of a system of social classes in Riverdale. Seven such classes are recognized in the community—in local terminology these are: "the fine old families," the "nouveau riche" (in Riverdale this is a symbolic not a descriptive term—not everyone with wealth is as high as *nouveau riche*), the "well-to-do professional class," and so on, down through the "poor, but respectable," to the "no goods" or the "lowest of the low."

The people of Riverdale have been proud of the fact that in the past, movement up this class ladder has been possible; but there have always

[1] Prepared at the University of Kansas by Charles K. Warriner. Copyright, 1949, by the University of Kansas. Reprinted by permission.

been limitations on this vertical mobility. It has, for example, always been difficult to rise to the level of the "fine old families" because of the emphasis on New England ancestry for membership in that class.

Mrs. Robert Wilson was one of those people who had attempted to climb the ladder. She had grown up in a smaller nearby community as the daughter of a public school teacher. Mrs. Wilson's parents had sent her to Smith, a woman's college in Massachusetts, and later she had taught French in a small midwestern girls' school.

Mr. Wilson was employed as an official in one of the larger Riverdale industries. The Wilsons were considered by the community to be "fairly well-to-do." They lived on the edge of the "Gold Coast" and were members of the First Congregational Church, the University Club, the Riverdale Country Club, the Junior League, the Music and Art Association, the Civic Symphony, and several smaller associations.

The interviewer had been introduced to the Wilsons by Miss Melton, the principal of Winfield Public School, which was located in the "Gold Coast" district. In talking about the family she had said, "The mother is very active in the PTA. She's a social climber but has had difficulty because everyone knows about her background. The husband is an amateur musician and very good. They have a fine home in one of the better areas of town. Although they live outside of this school district, they pay tuition to send their child here. They are very generous, but I question their motives sometimes. They are very showy people."

When the interviewer called on them, Mr. Wilson met him at the door:

Mr. W.: "Come in, my wife said she was expecting you. We are just in the process of putting our ten-year-old to bed. Mrs. Wilson will be down in a minute. You know when I first heard your name, I thought it was my mother's family name; it is quite similar. There are a lot of them in New England you know."

When Mrs. Wilson came in, Mr. Wilson excused himself, saying that he was an officer in the Civic Symphony and had to do some telephoning.

Mrs. Wilson asked what we were doing and how she could help. I explained that we were making a study of youth in the community and that in order to do that we wanted to know what the community was like. Mrs. Wilson referred to some work we had done in the schools with the children and asked me if I had noticed the big difference between schools in the character of the children. She went on:

Mrs. W.: "You know it is quite apparent to me. I notice it when I go over to the school. The children of my friends in the Junior League stand out from the rest. You can pick them out every time. They have an assurance that the rest of them lack. I don't know just how to describe it. They stand out, they are very self-assured, and . . . Oh, I don't think my Bob is that way. I think he is just a normal boy. He makes friends at all levels. Maybe it is just because he is my son, but I don't think so.

"There is quite a difference in the children over there. You can tell it very easily. Because Bob is an only child I have told him to bring his friends home with him. I tell him I am lonely and like to see people around. The boys from the fine homes are altogether different from the others. He joined the Cub Scouts and brought them here one day. I never heard so much swearing and a lot of obscene words appeared on my blackboard. I was very glad several weeks later when he asked me if he could quit. Are the Scouts like that everywhere? I always thought the Scouts were the boys from the nice homes . . ."

We talked about the Scouts for a while; then Mrs. Wilson started talking about herself.

Mrs. W.: "Since I have reached forty, I have retired. I'm not as active in anything as I was. I've cut out a lot of things. I've decided that now I can afford to be selfish. I was active on a lot of committees and associations, but I feel now that I don't have to take the responsibility of being chairman of committees anymore. I've done my duty to the community and I feel I can afford to be selfish. I think too I should be home looking after Bob. At my insistence, Mr. Wilson has dropped a lot of his activities too. He's still got the Civic Symphony, but he's cut out the rest like the Boy's Club. It's really surprising how much time I have on my hands now to enjoy myself. I was so busy on things like the Junior League and the board of the Settlement House, and Mr. Wilson had the Sunday School, and I had a class and all the other things that we never had time to enjoy ourselves. . ."

Interv.: "You were talking about the things you used to do. Are your friends active in the same things as you were?"

Mrs. W.: "Well, yes and no. There are several groups. Mr. Wilson is employed by Morton's, and there are three or four other families on this street who are officials there also. We get together with them, the men know each other from their work. But then we have friends in the Junior League and in the church groups too. We've been in all groups, but they tend to revolve around the church and the industries and the Junior League. But this town is really a small town for its size. It is a very provincial town. When my mother came to visit us, she commented on how provincial it was. She said, 'Why everybody knows everybody else's business here.' Now, just like my knowing about Mrs. Reece. I knew she had lost a baby last year and one this year. Mother asked me, 'How do you know?' I sat down and thought about it and I really didn't know. I suppose I was talking with someone in the Junior League who went to their church and was in their church circle."

Interv.: "I'm very interested in this city being provincial."

Mrs. W.: "It is provincial. It is not like a New England city, that is a city of 100,000, and nobody except the small groups knows anyone else. You know your friends in your small group, but you don't know anyone else. Here, I know all about everybody else—if I'm interested in finding out. People I never see, probably wouldn't know to speak to, yet I know a lot about them."

Interv.: "This interests me very much. What do you mean by the 'small groups'? Do you have such small groups here?"

Mrs. W.: "Well, I would like to say something about that. There's a group here who are the core of the social life of the community. Everything in the community revolves around them. They are primarily the old families who founded the community and who are wealthy. They form the backbone of the community and community leadership. The social life revolves around them."

Interv.: "Descendants of the people who founded the community?"

Mrs. W.: "Yes, they are the descendants of the pioneer families who came here from New England in covered wagons and founded the community. One of the families is the Stones of the Stone Manufacturing Company. Ernest Stone started the company and was an important man in the community. His children are the leaders now. His son, Stanley, has the company now.

"Then there are the Hawthornes and the Emersons. They are old important families in the community. And the Barretts. The Barrett daughters started the Junior League. These families are the leaders in the community. Most of them are wealthy, though wealth isn't absolutely necessary it helps, but they represent character, wealth, and stability—they are the fine old families in the community, the heart of the social life."

Interv.: "This is the small group that makes up the heart of the social life."

Mrs. W.: "That's right. Most of them belong to the Junior League, though this town is really too small for a Junior League. There were only a few when it started, so each year they had to let in a few unwashed ones in order to have a going organization. Now there are about 140 members.

"Don't misunderstand me. They are a fine group, and you don't have to be old family. They let in some each year who are very active in civic affairs, even though they aren't old family or wealthy.

"Many of my very best friends are in the league. I didn't join until the third year after I was married. I wasn't from an old family, but my husband's family was an old family in a nearby city, so that he was practically old family here."

Interv.: "Are there other small groups like that?"

Mrs. W.: "Well, the next . . . ah . . . strata shall we call it, is the pan-Hellenic group. They are very active, always having something. You'll see them mentioned in the papers almost every day. The tri Delts are doing this, or another sorority is doing that. The women in these sorority groups really go all out for it. But they still can't quite make it. None of the old families belongs to the sororities; many of them don't even know what a sorority is. They send their children East to schools where they don't have them. It is really amusing, all of this fuss and rushing and all that sort of thing. They like to feel they really are something, but they can't quite make it because none of the old families are in those groups."

Mrs. Wilson went on to comment that she had gone to Smith College where there were no sororities; that her husband belonged to a fraternity but never wears his pin. "I'm glad he doesn't. I think all of this show of pins is all very foolish. It really doesn't mean very much." She then went on to say that "Even very nice people don't get invited to join sororities and fraternities sometimes," and that she didn't think it was a good thing to have on small campuses where the Greek-letter people are in the majority. "I'm going to tell Bob when he's ready for college not to feel too badly if he doesn't get invited to join a fraternity, because there are always groups one wants to be in and doesn't get invited to."

Interv.: "There are always some groups one wants to be in but can't."

Mrs. W.: "Yes. (She paused for several seconds, then went on.) Let's see. There's the Country Club set, they are more or less Junior League, though there are more in it than that because it is quite a large group. Then there is the University Club, which is mostly the younger crowd. They are quite active. We belong to the University Club and were very active in it for awhile. Mr. Wilson was president one year, but we haven't attended a University Club party for two years. We are in our forty's and retiring now.

"Oh, yes. And then there are the very earnest women. The ones that go in for the League of Women Voters, the A.A.U.W., and that sort of thing. They are the ones who would like to be in something else but aren't. And the Woman's Club, they don't belong to anything else so use their vitality up in that. They are very active."

Interv.: "You mentioned the Country Club set, what club did you mean?"

Mrs. W.: "Oh that! The Riverdale Country Club, of course. They are the socially important ones. There's the Green Hills Club, but that's mostly Swedish. Then there's the Potowatomie Club. They are mostly workers, the laboring class of people."

Interv.: "The Riverdale club is the important one?"

Mrs. W.: "Yes, that's right. Of course, there are a lot of people in it, and so there are lots of kinds, but they have a big waiting list and it is the club that people want to belong to if they can get in."

Interv.: "We were talking about the League of Women Voters, the A.A.U.W., and the Woman's Club. What about the women that don't belong to those or any of the others? What are they active in?"

Mrs. W.: "Oh, then they are active in church circles. No don't misunderstand me. I've belonged to all of these and have been active in church circles, too, and they are all fine women; but it's just that they can't get into these other organizations. They aren't interested in the same things."

Interv.: "What about the churches themselves? Are there any churches that are primarily made up of any of these groups we have been speaking about?"

Mrs. W.: "Well, the First Congregational Church is the society church in this city. I always thought that the Episcopalian Church was the society church, but it isn't here. I imagine it would come next. It is a smaller church, of course. The Methodist church is a large church and draws a lot of people. I would say that it was primarily a middle-class church. That's about all of the churches that are important."

Interv.: "What about those who aren't in the church circles?"

Mrs. W.: "Well, the next level would be the PTAers. The women who form the backbone of the mothers' study groups. The ones who don't belong to churches and have nothing else to take up their energies. They are usually the ones with the poorest behaved children too. I've never seen it to fail, the women who are the most active in mother study groups are the ones whose children are the worst. I've never in my life belonged to a PTA—oh, I'm a room mother at Winfield School, but it is just because I taught for so long I thought I'd like to be on the other end of it. As I said, I could never see much sense in PTA's."

Interv.: "What is next then?"

Mrs. W.: "Well, now we are getting down to the group that my maid is in. They are the kind that go and see the Brownies play, and who go drinking in taverns."

Interv.: "The Brownies? I've never heard of them, what are they?"

Mrs. W.: "You haven't heard of the Brownies? That's the woman's baseball team. Oh, they are quite an organization. They have a real following. But that's the kind of thing they do, go see the Brownies, go drinking in taverns, and go bowling. They don't necessarily get drunk, but they just go see their friends there and sit around drinking. They don't go to movies much, and I don't think they have much of a social life. That's about the bottom of the heap, except for those that don't count at all."

Interv.: "You were speaking a little while ago about the old families sending their children east to school. Is that characteristic of any other group? Do many other families send their children east?"

Mrs. W.: "No, that's just the old families, the rest of them send their children closer to home. But the old families send their children east, primarily to Princeton and Dartmouth, and the girls go to Vassar. This is quite a Vassar colony. We are gradually building up a large Smith colony here, but there are very few from the other girls' schools.

"Would you like to have someone else to interview? I imagine that you would like to get a number of different opinions. You might go and see Mary Barton. She was president of the Junior League several years ago.

Her parents are old settlers. Her husband is manager of the Barton Company and his is an old family, too. I would like to know what she would have to say about the community. I imagine it might be much the same as what I have told you, but it also might be different. She's active in much the same sort of things that we are.

"Mrs. Wright is another one you might see. They are in the University Club crowd, but not fraternal or Junior League. She is active in the Woman's Club. I don't know how they stand it—they are at the University Club, but everybody snubs them and looks right through them. Don't misunderstand me, my husband and I aren't that kind, but everybody else does. They are always by themselves, nobody pays any attention to them. The old families don't even know they exist. They look right past or through them. They are always in the same places as the old families, but never a part of the group, always by themselves. I couldn't stand it a bit. When I see them, I am always glad I married the man I did because it sure would be hard in this town if I hadn't. I'd probably hate it here."

Mrs. Wilson called to her husband and asked him if there was anything he wanted to tell me. "Do you think of anything else I should tell him? This is a frivolous town in a way and quite set. And it is also a snobbish and cruel town. It would be a hard town to live in if you didn't have the right connections and the wealth to go with it. I said wealth wasn't important but it is. Wealth is one of the primary considerations. You can get by without it, but it is very difficult."

GUIDANCE DIRECTOR

Robert Thorpe, superintendent of schools in the small city of Wachusetts, John Turrell, principal of the Wachusetts High School, Edward Ray, guidance director of the Wachusetts Schools, and Henry Walters, executive director of the Chamber of Commerce were seated around the conference table in the superintendent's office.

Henry Walters of the chamber was talking. "Let me brief you all up-to-date. Two months ago, the chamber sponsored a Senior Industry Visitation Day, during which all seniors in the high school visited the local industries. Before that day, a committee of industrialists arranged to feed these two hundred seniors and twenty teachers after the visits to industries. It was agreed that an evaluation would be made of the visits."

"May I interrupt," Edward Ray said. "I would like to point out that at no time was I invited to participate in this Senior Visitation Day, although I am director of guidance and vocational placement is part of my job as well as directing young people into jobs in local industry. I just want that in the record."

"All right," Walters admitted. "Then just yesterday, there appeared in the paper an article headlined as follows: 'Seniors Don't Want to Work in

Local Industries.' The article originated from the guidance office. This morning, Ronald Jones of the Jones Shoe Company came to see me. He was raging. He claimed the article was a terrible blow to local industry. He blamed me for the article."

"Let me interrupt again," Edward Ray said. "I had all seniors answer a questionnaire, which included such questions as 'Would you like to work in local industries?' 'If so, which ones?' Now, no senior said he wanted to work in Jones' Shoe Company. It's a well-known fact that Jones is a labor baiter and pays below the prevailing wage and has threatened to close his shop if the union organizes in his factory. When the questionnaire was completed, I mimeographed it and sent it to each industry which had seniors in their plants. How this information got to the newspapers, I don't know."

"Well, Jones, after accusing me of sending it to the papers, has accused you, Mr. Ray. Now this morning, he has resigned from the Chamber of Commerce, the Rotary, and as chairman of the new school building committee and permanent scholarship committee. Isn't that right, Mr. Thorpe?"

The superintendent sighed and said, "That's right. As you know, Ray, Jones is highly influential in town. He can block the construction of a new school. He can prevent more seniors from getting scholarship aid. He's a heavy contributor to the Chamber of Commerce. Now, Mr. Turrell and I have talked this thing over and we have decided you've got to go down there and apologize to Jones and tell him the article was a mistake and that your students misunderstood the questionnaire and that they really want to work in his factory."

Edward Ray jumped up. "I won't apologize because there is something else about this you haven't heard. Jones called me up on the phone and told me he was going to get me fired; that I was ruining the city of Wachusetts; that there were a lot of educators he didn't like, and I was one of them; and that I'd better get wise to myself or I'd be looking for a new vocation as he had power throughout the state."

John Turrell spoke up then, "But he also told us that you insulted him over the phone."

"I didn't insult him," Ray said, "I just told him the truth. That I was never invited to participate in the preliminary planning, but that you and Mr. Thorpe had. I also told him it wasn't my fault the boys didn't wear ties. I told him I had suggested that they should but Mr. Turrell overruled me. I told him I hadn't sent that material to the newspaper and that I was not his servant and he had no right to threaten me, especially when he doesn't even live in our city and sends his children to private schools."

Henry Walters of the chamber spoke up, "But he feels he's been insulted and he's badly hurt. Something's got to be done, or else he'll sabotage the Chamber of Commerce, at least the industrial division."

Edward Ray spoke up again. "I'm going to say something else while it's necessary for me to defend myself. It is this. Ronald Jones is sore because the Babbitt brothers, who run the Babbitt Electronic Company, are taking his help away from him, his prestige, his power in the city; and another thing, when Jones' daughter wanted a job teaching here last year, the school committee turned her down. He's just taking his venom out on me. Isn't that right, Mr. Walters?"

The Chamber of Commerce man reluctantly nodded his head. "Yes. All is not sweetness in the chamber. Jones and the Babbitts have been fighting now for some time. That was going on long before we had this visitation day. They don't get along at all. Understand, I'm not blaming anybody. I just want to know what can be done to make Jones change his mind, rejoin the chamber, get back on the scholarships committee and the new school committee?"

Mr. Thorpe, the superintendent, said, "I can't see anything else but for Mr. Ray to visit him and apologize."

"If I go visit him," Ray said, "I'll only tell him a few more things, like what he did to my uncle one time, and it'll be worse than before."

Mr. Turrell, the principal said, "Write him a letter explaining why the students don't want to work there, or rather why they didn't say they wanted to work there."

"They don't want to work there," Ray said, "simply because it's a sweat shop, the pay is low, and conditions are poor all around. Besides that old man Jones is always losing his temper, throwing things around, and acting like a baby, like he did over this."

"But the point is," Mr. Thorpe repeated, "he'll block construction of the school. I know him. He's that type. He's got a lot of people who'll follow him, not because they like him, but because he's important. He'll be a focal point around which the opposition can gather in enough strength to ruin our plans."

"But I'm not going to get down on my knees and humble myself in front of a great, big overgrown b____, when I did nothing wrong, except reveal some of the truth. What you're asking me to do is sacrifice a principle of mine just to kow-tow to him. And if I do what will happen? He'll be expecting the school system like everybody in town to give in to him every time his desires go against somebody else's. I can't see that."

Mr. Turrell said, "I'll go see him and apologize."

Henry Walters said, "It won't do. He's got to have an apology from Edward Ray or nobody. I spoke with him before I came over here and that's what he told me."

"But I've got nothing to apologize about," Ray said.

"And he wants a statement in the local newspaper that the questions were misunderstood and no reflection on the Jones business was intended."

"I refuse," Ray said.

"I'll have to bring this matter up before the school committee," Mr. Thorpe warned.

"Bring it," Ray snapped. "I'll tell them what happened."

Mr. Walters said, "I know exactly how you feel, Mr. Ray. But there's more involved than your feelings toward some abstract principles. You better think it over. But he's got to have an apology before tomorrow night or he'll never return to any of his positions. I'm going now."

SPRINGVALE JUNIOR PROM

Mr. Philip Jensen, superintendent of schools in the city of Springvale, sat in his office pondering over the annual junior prom to be held in the high school gym in three weeks. Each year for the past five years the same problem arose, and each year it grew to greater proportions. Last year the citizens of the city became so angered they wrote letters to the editor of the local newspaper condemning the school system, complained to the police, and had a signed petition sent to the school committee to abolish the dance. All complaints were aimed at the school, and Mr. Jensen knew these were unfair and unreasonable. He decided that this year some definite action must be taken. But what course of action should he take?

Mr. Jensen took out his folder with information accumulated through the years on the prom and reviewed the problem.

The Springvale high school prom itself, held in the gym, posed no problem. It was a dignified, pleasant affair with the faculty and students having an enjoyable time. The problem arose after the dance. The prom was from 8 to 12 P.M.; then after twelve o'clock, when the students had left, the trouble started. The young people visited all eating places and clubs but found them closed because in this Yankee New England city everything closed at midnight except the city diner. The students therefore drove off to New York State, fifty miles beyond, where they found numerous clubs, taverns, cafes, and roadhouses open to them. These trips had many sad results.

In 1952, Bob O'Brien, a senior, was killed driving home on a rainsoaked highway from a small New York town. The rest of the occupants of the car, two girls and another boy, were gravely injured. That same night, four other students returned to their homes during the wee hours of dawn, and Mr. Jensen was at wits' end between police calls and those of frantic parents. Several other incidents happened that year, and the superintendent began thinking of it as an "off-year," and that such disturbances would not happen again. But the following year proved even more disastrous.

Records for 1953 showed two accidents which involved junior prom students returning from New York State. Those who had remained in the city visited the only place available, the Springvale diner. They occupied all the seats available, others stood on foot yelling for service, workers off the night shift who ordinarily came in for a meal were pushed out. Mr. Trova and his helper, Joe, were unable to cope with the situation and, in speaking roughly to the students, aroused their anger to such a degree that they not only made a greater confusion but left the place in a terrible condition. Other groups of youngsters created alarming disturbances in the hotel lobbies and were routed out by the police. Several other smaller incidents occurred.

Mr. Jensen realized that all this made for poor public relations because of the actual connection with the school dance which thereby made the school responsible. He repeatedly pointed out that the school was not liable for incidents occurring after the prom and off school property.

After repeated student conferences and faculty meetings, the problem seemed no nearer a solution. The faculty was of many and various opinions, none of which, it was agreed, would solve the problem satisfactorily, and so voted to leave it entirely in the hands of the superintendent for judgment to be passed on.

The students, on the other hand, had no constructive suggestions except to state, at a student council meeting, that they would have to continue going over to New York State because of the lack of conveniences in Springvale after midnight. The suggestion was made by the principal, Mr. Sheed, that they go home and conclude their merriment there. A few agreed they usually did and had house parties there, but the majority said that there was no fun going home to a party all dressed up. The majority of the girls remarked it was seldom they went to a formal and so would rather conclude the affair at some public place where they could show their gowns to advantage.

With the prom only three weeks off Mr. Jensen thought seriously about the problem and wondered what decision he should make.

THE NEW PRINCIPAL

Harry Mayfield, teacher at the Tule Central High School, was talking to his friend William Johnson. Harry had just been appointed high school principal, his appointment to become effective the following September. He was young, just turned thirty, a graduate of Provo College, a liberal arts institution, where he had majored in political science. He was within a few hours of completing the requirements for the master's degree in school administration at the state university. Harry had taught American history at Tule for six years. Will Johnson and he had been classmates at Provo, and Will was now a junior executive with a nationally known petroleum company. He had stopped in to see Harry as he drove across the state.

Harry was very happy to see Will and, after the pleasantries were over, said, "I'm very happy you dropped in. I'd like to talk with you. I don't have anyone I can confide in here in Tule and I'd like to talk over my appointment as principal and tell you about the situation."

Will: "Go right ahead. I just read 'Pity the Poor Superintendent,' and I guess you fellows do have your problems."

Harry: "Let me tell you something about Tule and then about what is happening here. Tule is a small town of about 3000 people. We are a middle-income community—I believe the census indicates our average income per family is slightly less than $4000. Both farming and business are well represented. Like many central school districts, the town is the shopping center so that we cater to about 30,000 people. With our population of 3000, you would expect about five hundred students; yet we have 1000, as we have the outlying rural areas in our school district. We have been centralized for five years, and last year the district voted to build a new elementary school. With our increasing population and our old and crowded buildings, we certainly needed it. It wasn't easy to get a vote through for either centralization or the new school."

Will: "Why was that? It sounds as though you could afford it and also that you needed to do both."

Harry: "I think it's necessary to understand our community a little more and to see how it is divided into several groups."

Will: "Oh yes, all communities are divided into various groups depending upon the way in which people live, make their money, the churches they attend, together with many other factors."

Harry: "That's right. Tule has three major groups. I suppose each has a division; but, in general, we think of three major groups. Let me describe them to you.

"The first, and the most influential, is comprised of professional and some business men and, of course, their families. It's the smallest in terms of numbers, but in terms of influence it is the greatest. The members of this group are the most active in the community. They are on committees, belong to clubs, study groups, and service organizations. They belong to the exclusive groups, of course, but they also belong to churches and to many other organizations of a philanthropic nature as well. The members of the uppers don't seem to be very active in the Parent Teacher Association, although they attend some of the meetings. The Daughters of the American Revolution is one of the organizations to which many of these people belong. As you know, the DAR is very active in trying to get the schools to teach more history and they have contests which they encourage school children to enter. The children of the uppers do well in school. They are generally our top students and are preparing for college. The parents are very anxious to have their children do well, and they keep the pressure on."

Will: "Sounds like the typical upper class with a few local adaptations.

They seem to be the power group in most all communities. As I travel around, I see much of this same pattern."

Harry: "The second group is the middle-class group. They are very strong in the Parent Teacher Association. They are interested in better schools and have helped out with many services, such as providing glasses for needy students, buying a bicycle rack for one of our elementary schools, and things like that. This middle group also has many members in a club called the Citizens for Better Schools Club. Mr. Van, a business executive, has control of this group, and most of the members are store-keepers and salesmen. It's difficult to know how much this group is interested in helping public education. Some of their actions make it very difficult for the schools to carry on what we believe to be a good program. On the other hand, they are sincere and honest."

Will: "That's very interesting. Now what about the other group?"

Harry: "Our third major group is composed of farmers and laborers. In general, they are not well educated. Most of them did not finish high school. They are not at all active in the community. Oh, some belong to the PTA and a few other groups; but you would not be able to say that they are pillars of strength in any group. We have found that they are quite apathetic about education. Their attitude seems to be reflected in their children, since they get the lowest marks and have the largest drop-out rate. As a group they have opposed anything which would raise their taxes. They are easily persuaded to put their names on petitions and we have found the same names on petitions on both sides of the same question!"

Will: "Well, that's a rather complete analysis of the community. You seem to have given this a great deal of thought."

Harry: "Yes, but the way things have gone, it would be difficult to ignore these factions. We have had rumblings of discontent with the schools for several years. People from each group would come in with complaints. The uppers want a more classical program, the middlers want more technical and diversified education, and the lowers feel their children are being discriminated against by the faculty. Actually, many of the faculty believe they need to help the children of the lowers more than any other group. I suppose we could say that there has been a great deal of argument over the philosophy of education which the school should adopt."

Will: "Did something happen to bring all this out into the open?"

Harry: "Yes, and with a vengeance! Early this year the State Education Department issued a bulletin on revising the secondary school program. It had to do with changing the curriculum to meet the needs of youth. Nothing very exciting; but Mr. Crunch, the editor of the local paper and a leader of the uppers, got a-hold of it. After reading it he called the president of our teachers association and asked that the association prepare a letter on the publication which would appear in the paper. Mr. Skip, the president, agreed, and he asked three teachers to go to work on it.

"Well, a first draft was prepared and was given to a student to type up. She did, and then, by some mistake, the letter was forwarded to Mr. Crunch. It was in the usual condition that most first drafts are in, and the student was not our best typist! Mr. Crunch printed the letter as he received it and then the excitement started. Crunch called Skip and let loose a blast: 'Is this an example of what the teachers can do? No wonder our children can't learn from them. Look at this, eight words spelled wrong, ten errors in grammar! Is that why you teachers have these fancy, foolish courses? What happened to the 3 R's?'"

Will: "I suppose a lot of other people wondered the same."

Harry: "Yes, letters came in from everyone. They all asked, 'What is the matter with our schools?' Then, to continue, the PTA scheduled a meeting, and the word got out that it was going to be a real hot session. Even the kids wanted to go to it. As soon as the meeting was opened, Mr. Crunch took over. He talked for forty-five minutes on what he called 'the solution of some serious problems present in this school now.' He covered the gamut: social promotion, discipline, competitive marking, progressive education, and college preparation. He is a fine public speaker and he was received with great enthusiasm.

"Mr. Van and his Citizens for Better Schools and Mr. Crunch and his group went to work and decided the best thing to do was to elect some new members to the board of education. Our annual meeting is in April, and we had three openings on our seven-man board. Mr. Crunch ran, together with two others who had the full backing of both groups. Mr. Van acted as campaign manager, and all three won. So we had a board with three members pledged to change things. The three were outspoken in their opposition to the administration. Shortly after this, the high school principal resigned to take a better job, and Mr. Quigly, the supervising principal, recommended me. The board approved, and next September I take over."

Will: "I don't know whether to congratulate you or not. It seems as though you will have a rocky path."

Harry: "It will be good experience, and I did want to get into administration."

Will: "Did anything come of this change?"

Harry: "Several things. There is constant pressure in board meetings now for a change in policy, so that more attention will be given to the brighter children and much less to the slower. The PTA elected Mr. Van as chairman of a committee to meet with seven teachers, the principal, and supervising principal to talk over social promotion and report cards. Our two administrators met with the teachers and, after long discussion, arrived at a conclusion that the school should meet the needs of *all* children and that present policies were aimed at doing just that. The two groups then got together and tried to talk things out. No consensus was arrived at. Mr. Van represented his group when he said, 'The philosophy of the school should be opportunity for all—if the poorer students are not equipped mentally to take that opportunity, forget them.' Mr. Peck, the elementary supervisor replied, 'We are not teaching just those children who will go to college. We are teaching all of the children. We must meet the needs of the individual child.'

"Well, that's where we are now. What should I do to get ready to take over my job in September? I'm right smack in the middle of a controversy that has the town split wide open. Things have quieted down this summer, but they will start all over in September. Do you have any ideas?"

GRANDVIEW CENTRAL

In the fall of 1945, the pupils and teachers of Grandview Central moved into their new million-dollar school building. The school was designed to house approximately 1000 pupils. In keeping with the policy of other central districts, the school board also allowed nonresident elementary and secondary pupils to attend the central school on payment of non-resident tuition and transportation charges. About seventy-five nonresidents from ten districts outside of the centralization attended Grandview Central from 1945 to 1947. As the advantages of the central school became apparent, more parents from the nonresident districts expressed the desire to send their children to the central school. Some nonresident districts petitioned the central school board to be taken into the central district; others closed their schools and became "contract districts." A few non-resident districts resisted the general change and made a determined effort to keep their schools open.

Resistance to the central school policy of accepting nonresident pupils first appeared on November 3, 1947, when Trustee Reed of Meridale district No. 11 made a formal protest in behalf of his school district by requesting that the Grandview Central School board refuse to take elementary pupils from the M-11 district without the written permission of the M-11 trustees. The district had no objection to secondary pupils attending Grandview Central and agreed to the payment of $30.00 transportation for each high school pupil attending the central school. The M-11 district did not maintain a high school in its district but did sponsor a three-teacher school in a small town about six miles from Grandview Central. Trustee Reed informed the Central School board that the loss of "state aid" on seven elementary pupils now attending Grandview was seriously hampering the educational program of his home district, which now had a good school building and an adequate staff.

Trustee Reed also made the same request of Valley Central School, another nearby school which had two elementary pupils from the M-11 district.

On October 23, 1948, the Grandview Central School board passed a resolution by unanimous decision "that elementary pupils from the M-11 school district will not be allowed to attend Grandview Central after July 1, 1949, without the written permission of the three trustees of the M-11 common school district." The board of Valley Central School voted to drop the two elementary pupils attending its school within one week and continued to abide by the decision.

Mr. Aitkens, the principal of Grandview Central, notified the parents of the children involved and immediately received protests regarding the action of the board. The parents also wrote letters of protest to the legal department of the State Education Department questioning the legality of refusing entrance to pupils in a school supported by the public.

On December 18, 1949, the legal division of the State Education Department quoted section 401 of the education law: "Nonresidents of a district may be admitted into a school of a district, upon the consent of the board of education, on terms prescribed by the board."

On February 10, 1950, the board of Grandview Central studied the ruling of the State Education Department and then voted to continue their policy regarding the elementary pupils from the M-11 district. They also directed Principal Aitkens to act as intermediary between the M-11 trustees and the parents of the children concerned and try to work out an agreement suitable to both parents and trustees. Following considerable correspondence and conversation between interested parties, an agreement was reached whereby the elementary children would be allowed to attend Grandview Central if the parents paid the M-11 district $90.00 per pupil to reimburse the district for its loss of "state aid" on the seven elementary pupils. A written contract was drawn up and signed by both parents and trustees. This arrangement was made with full consent and knowledge of board members, trustees, superintendents, and the principal. Three families were involved in the contract. The children attended Grandview Central without opposition for the 1950-1951 school year.

During the summer of 1951, Mr. and Mrs. Robinson, with their two children of elementary school age, moved into the M-11 district and expressed a desire to send their children to Grandview Central. They received permission to attend the Central School by signing the agreement to pay the M-11 district $90.00 per child. When payment was due, they refused to pay and sent a letter to Mr. Monroe, the assistant commissioner of education. Mr. Monroe made a complete investigation of the case. He was very much disturbed to find that the parents of the M-11 district were being required to pay in order to send their children to a school outside their district. His investigation showed that the case was new to the history of the State Education Department and that it was also illegal. He also informed both school boards from Grandview Central and Valley Central that they had the right to accept or refuse nonresidents with or without the permission of the nonresident trustees.

Nine elementary pupils from the M-11 district continued to attend Grandview Central without making payment to the M-11 school district until Trustee Reed made another protest to the school board of Grandview Central.

In the fall of 1951, Principal Aitkens accepted a position in the State Education Department and was replaced by the vice-principal, Mr. Townsend.

Principal Townsend brought Trustee Reed's protest before his board. On March 15, 1952, the board passed the resolution not to accept nonresident elementary pupils without the permission of their trustees. Mrs. Robinson immediately informed the assistant commissioner of education of the action and pleaded for his help.

Many letters were written within the next month to the various divisions of the State Education Department. Each writer appeared to have a different interpretation for the letters. Former principal Aitkens who was now in the State Education Department assisted in trying to clear up the misunderstandings.

The assistant commissioner of education issued a notice to all parties involved that a meeting of all persons interested in the controversy would be held in his office on April 29, 1952. The meeting cleared all misunderstandings. The assistant commissioner spoke very frankly to those present. He stated that in his opinion, the parents of children had the right to send their children to the school of their choice and that it was a moral obligation of all state-supported schools to accept nonresident pupils if transportation and classroom facilities were available. He also stated that school boards had a right to refuse nonresident pupils for legitimate reasons, but none seemed to exist in the case before him.

On May 17, 1952, the school board of the Grandview Central school rescinded its resolution of March 15, 1952, and passed a resolution to accept all nonresident pupils as far as facilities and transportation would permit.

Preschool registration in the late summer of 1952 showed that a total of nineteen elementary and twelve secondary pupils would attend Grandview Central from the M-11 district for the school year 1952-1953. The trustees of the M-11 district refused to sign contracts for the payment of nonresident tuition for the thirty-one pupils attending the Central School. The school board of Grandview voted to accept the pupils without a contract and without charge.

Trustee Reed of the M-11 district again wrote to the legal division of the State Education Department protesting the action of the Grandview Central school board. He stated that the Grandview school bus was picking up M-11 pupils in the M-11 district without a contract and without the consent of the trustees of the district.

On October 30, 1952, Mr. Clarkson, senior attorney for the State Education Department, ruled that Grandview Central had no legal right to pick up the pupils in the M-11 district without a contract.

The trustees of the M-11 district refused to enter into a contract for the education of the pupils.

HOMETOWN CENTRAL SCHOOL [2]

In May, 1952, the entire board of education of Hometown resigned. This action was the culmination of nearly two years of stormy sessions centering about a proposed new building program for the Hometown Central School. The school board felt that its resignation might wake up the people of the community to the pressing need for a building program that had been defeated by an overwhelming majority the day before. It was a move of protest, a move determined by the school board because, as one farmer-member said, he was willing "to toggle and use makeshift equipment on his farm, but he just couldn't accept the responsibility of toggling and pursuing a makeshift course with youngsters."

To understand and appreciate the situation in Hometown and the revolutionary move of the school board it is necessary to look back over the two years that preceded the action and to perhaps examine a bit of the social structure of the community and the part it played in the events.

Hometown is a community of many advantages. Situated near a scenic lake, it enjoys the comforts of rural life with the convenience of being close to the city of Metropolis. There is an adequate and modern shopping district in Hometown, plus an up-to-date hotel. An added cultural advantage may be noted in the fact that Hometown has a private girls' junior college located within its community.

The 2000 inhabitants of Hometown are generally divided into two categories ... the station-wagon set and the horse-and-buggy group. The horse-and-buggy group is made up of the old-time residents, some of whom are descended directly from the early Boston-New York summer residents of Hometown. Farmers, local businessmen, and families that have been in residence for twenty or twenty-five years are generally classed in this group. The station-wagon set comprises not more than one hundred families, most of whom are newcomers, having arrived within the last ten years or so. The group is generally considered to be smart, aggressive, and progressive, bringing with them some new ideas that, at times, are rather opposed by the horse-and-buggy group. They noted the

[2] This case was prepared at Colgate University and is reprinted by permission of Colgate University.

inadequacy of the present water and sewage systems, but met opposition from the old-timers, who said it was good enough to do. Most of the station-wagon set work in Metropolis, where they are generally either salesmen or junior executives of the newer industries that have cropped up in the past few years. Some of them send their children to private schools, thinking that the schools in Hometown are not adequate enough.

The school district of Hometown Central School covers an area of 600 square miles. In the early days of centralization, the outlying small towns noted the advantages of being connected with such a community as Hometown, and though there were in some cases communities closer with which they could have centralized, they chose to belong to the Hometown system. This presented many transportation problems. The twelve school busses have to travel hilly and, in many places, unimproved roads every day to bring in the school children. The extent of the district means that in some cases, a bus has to travel twenty miles one way and that some children spend two hours each day riding the bus. Located in the heart of the snow-belt region, Hometown faces especially difficult transportation problems during the winter.

Hometown Central School was built in 1930 at a cost of $350,000. It was designed to house 600 students. At present, the school population totals 1050. In 1951, the school board attempted to alleviate the crowded conditions by purchasing a large summer house near the school to house the 300 students in the kindergarten and first grades. There are, at present, 250 students in the high school, using eight academic classrooms. The remaining 500 students are contained in the other sixteen rooms of the main building. Some of the lower-grade sections contain as many as forty-five, while some of the upper grades have twenty-five students per section.

Among the recognized needs for the school are increased facilities for physical education, the cafeteria, the industrial arts, and the agriculture programs. The space used for physical education is divided between a gym and the auditorium. The auditorium seats 650, and the gym is a junior-size basketball court 65 by 45 feet. There are enough locker-room and shower facilities for the high school, but none available for the junior high school and other grades.

It is necessary that the use of the cafeteria be limited to only those students who live out of town. The cafeteria seats 120, which necessitates three shifts for eating. It is located on the third floor, which means that supplies and garbage must be carried up and down, as there are no elevator facilities available.

The agriculture and industrial arts departments are housed in regular-sized academic classrooms, prohibiting the use of much desired and necessary equipment.

The summer house, purchased as a temporary measure, cost $20,000 in

1951. It is a frame structure, inadequately heated by a hot air furnace plus several small kerosene stoves. In spite of the fact that the State Department of Education recommends that kindergarten and first-grade students attend for a full session, it is necessary that the group be divided into a half-day program. This means that Hometown loses out in its state aid in view of that fact that state aid is computed on full days' attendance. There is a combination steel and wood fire escape, plus two narrow wooden stairs that may be utilized in case of emergency. It was noted that there was a kerosene drum located on the top landing of the fire escape. Quite a number of the parents of the children housed in this building have complained to the school board about the fire hazard present in such a structure.

Before the purchase of the summer house, during the 1950-1951 school year, two sections of the fifth grade were housed in the municipal building, above where the community stored its fire engines.

Prior to the 1952 resignation, the school board was composed of a farmer from the outskirts of Hometown, another farmer from one of the neighboring villages, a well-to-do chicken farmer from Hometown, the president of the local bank, and a wealthy member of the community noted for his various civic activities who was also president of the board of trustees for the junior college. All of the group, except the latter, were considered to be members of the horse-and-buggy set. The last-named member had affiliations with both groups and could be defined specifically as a member of neither set.

In the spring of 1950, the school board found that it had to locate a new place to house the twelve busses that it maintained. Formerly they had rented space in the garage of a local automobile dealer. The automobile dealer had need for the room himself and had been raising the rent successively over a period of years. The school board decided to build a structure that could be used to house the busses and also be used for the much-needed expansion of the agriculture and industrial arts programs.

As a result of their investigations, they presented to the community plans for a $170,000, two-story, concrete-block, brick-faced building that would contain the twelve busses and two station wagons on the ground floor and have additional room on the second floor for agriculture and industrial arts.

Before the May vote, there appeared in the local paper five letters in opposition to this plan. Most of the argument centered about the objections to placing classrooms above what was to be used for bus storage on the grounds that it would be a fire hazard, in spite of the fact that the State Department of Education had approved the plans for such a structure. One of the dormitories in the junior college had burned down recently with a loss of several lives, which left the community rather fire hazard conscious. Although the incident occurred at night, and in a dormitory, it was difficult for the townspeople to see the difference between the two situations. Other objections were that it was only a stopgap measure and that $170,000 was entirely too much to pay for a garage.

However, at the time of the vote, the issue was approved by a margin of 256 to 238, and the school board accepted this narrow margin as a mandate from the public to get the project underway.

Of the thirteen bids that were submitted, it was found that the lowest was $30,000 over the estimate the school board had made. Two weeks after the bids were made public, there was a movement in town to postpone such a project and to re-open the consideration of the whole school need.

In November, 1950, the leaders of the movement, mostly members of the station-wagon set, presented to the school board a petition signed by 891 qualified voters, which noted the inadequacy of the $170,000 project and asked that it be resubmitted to the voters so it could be turned down in favor of a survey that would estimate the over-all needs of the school for a five-year period. The school board, by a unanimous decision, decided to follow this suggestion.

It was as a result of this meeting that a Parent Teacher organization was organized in Hometown. Led by the members of the station-wagon group, the decision was reached that such an organization was sorely needed. As a further indication of the activities of the station-wagon set, there was begun in Hometown a chapter of the League of Women Voters. This body was very much in favor of getting a woman elected to the school board, to which there arose considerable opposition from the horse-and-buggy group.

In December, 1950, the school board held a public meeting, to which were invited several speakers, representing the board of education, the State Department of Education, and the P.T.A. There was much discussion of the $170,000 proposal, and an informal poll was taken of the group present. The results of the poll showed that thirty-two still favored the garage project and that 177 were against it. A further poll was taken as to the scope of the building program that should be initiated in Hometown. There were three different levels considered. A proposal for a $750,-000 project received fifty votes; a $500,000 suggestion got thirty-nine votes; and seventeen people favored spending $300,000.

As a result of this meeting, the school board went ahead and procured a five-year contract with another garage in town to house the school busses.

By January, 1951, the recommendations of the State Department of Education were received concerning suggestions and recommendations for the proposed change in the school building. The department suggested enlargement to a forty-six-room building. The cost of this suggestion would go over the $750,000 figure that had been presented to the voters at the December meeting.

Between January and May of 1951, seven alternate expansion plans were presented to fifteen groups of interested people within the school district. In all, these plans were presented to some three hundred people. The majority of these people, plus the school board, favored the adoption of Plan E, which included expansion to the east and the purchase of the summer house which was located on this easterly property.

Before the June vote on the adoption of such a building plan by the community, a special meeting was held at which time Plan E was outlined to the public. The cost of such a project was set at $850,000, which would include fourteen extra rooms plus facilities for a gymnasium, cafeteria, industrial arts, and agriculture. It would cost $2.00 per cubic-foot (later computations set this figure at $1.30 per cubic foot) and where the tax rate per thousand dollars of taxable real estate had been $15.33, it would now probably be $23.00 with the purchase of the summer house, and would probably go up to $33.00 with the adoption of Plan E.

In June, it was voted 228 to 98 to buy the summer house for $20,000, and to spend an additional $10,000 to adapt it for school use. The school board met later that evening and passed a resolution asking the architect to draw up detailed plans for Plan E.

At the regular July meeting, there were only sixty-nine people present. The $170,000 that had been approved for the garage building was officially canceled, and the $30,000 for the summer house was approved. The new tax rate was set at $21.89, which meant an increase of almost $6.50.

By September, 1951, the school board found that there was an increase in enrollment of seventy-five students and that the State Department of Education recommended that two additional rooms be added to the $850,000 proposal.

In November, 1951, the school board approached the executive committee of the P.T.A. and requested that they take over the function of selling the idea of the $850,000 proposal to the community. The P.T.A. group said that they felt that they did not represent the 891 voters who had signed the petition and that they had no authority to endorse or promote the plan, though they promised to co-operate with the school board in any other way they could.

Following the suggestion made by one of the station-wagon group, the school board organized a Volunteer Citizens Committee, composed of some forty representative people of the school district, and placed the plan before them. The group organized under an executive committee of seven members, three of which were station-wagoners, and invited any citizens of the school district to participate on any one of five or six study groups which were set up. One group was to study state aid, another financing the school, another taxation, another building costs, a fifth the general problems which created the need. They were going to prepare a pamphlet for distribution and to demonstrate the new plan with slides to any groups in the community which were interested.

Several articles about the Volunteer Citizens Committee appeared in the paper during the following weeks, and in February, a picture of the new addition appeared on the front page, together with a detailed account of what the plan called for. The figure was now set at $865,000, a quotation of November prices. As it turned out, prices took a distinct downward trend in the next few months.

The school board was going to bond itself for thirty years at 2½ per cent. It would mean an increase of about $6.50 in the school tax rate, in addition to which was to be added a $3.70 rate for operating the additional unit. The actual tax rate would then be about $28.00. (Of twenty-eight surrounding school districts, the tax rate ranged from a little under $14.00 to over $31.00.)

After the pamphlet of explanation put out by the Volunteer Citizens Committee had been published, the school board received $43,000 additional from the state, which would have the tax rate reduced to $21.00. The supervising principal published a letter to this effect in the local paper, but unfortunately it was thought that few people saw it.

It was difficult for the townspeople to see how a new addition could be built and financed without any additional rise in the tax rate. The people seemed to be confused by the contradictory pamphlet they had received.

The school board tried to reach the public through special meetings held throughout the district. There was an average turnout of less than thirty at these meetings.

In May, 1952, a vote was to be taken on the $865,000 proposal. During the weeks preceding the vote, there was quite a bit of stir created in Hometown concerning the issue. Prices had fallen off considerably, and several townspeople thought that the school board should offer a new estimate.

The local paper gave space to two letters on its front page. One of these letters was in opposition to the proposal and the other favored the project. The grounds of opposition were that it was unnecessarily extravagant by a quarter of a million dollars; that it would not provide enough space because it only met current needs and did not take into account the larger elementary classes which would continue to enter for the next few years; that reconstruction of the old building would interfere with class work; that an entirely separate elementary school building was what was needed; and that the site should be north of the original building instead of to the east, so that the summer house would not have to be torn down. It criticized the state experts for not taking into account the continued growth of the community. The writer also thought the gymnasium and the shops should wait until a later time.

The letter which favored the proposal stressed the fact that the need for the school was desperate; that the extra state aid which had recently been voted would help finance the project; that the plan was adequate and reasonable; that the people had petitioned for such a plan; that the Volunteer Citizens Committee had studied the plan carefully; that the state had approved the plan; and that the youth of the community were not getting the best education possible under the overcrowded conditions.

Both of the letters had been written by station-wagoners who had opposed the original $170,000 project because it did not offer enough.

When the vote was taken in May, the proposition failed to be accepted by a vote of 716 against and 453 in favor. In order to pass, a two-thirds majority was needed. It was noted at the time of the vote that a great number of the voters were people from the fixed-income group, such as retired people, who feared that the increase in the tax rate would be too much for them. In addition, it was felt that a lot of the people in the district didn't live close enough to Hometown to feel much pride in the new school program. They were more attached to their local communities, and a good many of them couldn't see paying taxes to erect a building in another community when they would actually rather have their own schools at home enlarged. Most of the rural communities in the district had local grade schools, all of which were filled to capacity.

It was also felt that the paper's position of neutrality helped to defeat the vote inasmuch as neutrality where a two-thirds majority was required amounted to opposition. Also the school administration had remained neutral throughout the debate, pointing out that it was a servant of the school board and of the people and would abide by their wishes.

Some of the people who were in favor of the defeated motion had criticized the school board for not taking a more active role in the campaign. Several of the board members did not like to make speeches and did not play an active role in selling the proposition.

Most of the favorable 453 votes had come from the station-wagon set and a group that voted more or less in response to their personal friendships with school board members.

The night after the election, the school board met in a rather heated session, at which time one member appeared with a letter of resignation for all the other members to sign. After some debate, the letter was signed by the whole board as a move of protest against the action of the community.

It was then necessary for the community to elect an interim board to hold office until the July meeting. After a lengthy meeting which lasted from 8:30 until 1:00 A.M., and after much debate, the new board was selected. As president of the new school board, the voters selected a college professor who taught in the university in Metropolis and lived in Hometown. The remainder of the board was made up of one of the biggest farmers in the district, a former member of the Volunteer Citizens Committee who was an advocate of the $865,000 proposal, a local business-man, and a young salesman from Metropolis who was also a member of the Volunteer Citizens Committee and pro $865,000. The two men who were members of the Volunteer Citizens Committee were station-wagon-ers, while the others were considered members of the horse-and-buggy group. At this meeting, there was a strong unsuccessful attempt made by the League of Women Voters to have a woman elected to the school board.

At the regular July meeting, the new school board was re-elected with-out opposition. The new budget was passed which increased the expendi-tures by $73,000. The tax rate was lowered to $15.50, and $6,000 was allotted to put in an adequate heating plant for the summer house.

The over-all attitude of the new school board is that they are interested in maintaining better public relations than the old school board did. They feel that they will have to develop confidence in themselves in the minds of the townspeople. Some of them feel that the townspeople had lost con-fidence in the old school board, that the people had not been properly informed about school problems, and that the old school board had not taken its problems to the people.

Administrative Relations with Other Administrators

EDMUND WATTS

James Hall, guidance director and vice-principal at Sycamore Heights Central School, sat in his office and pondered his position. He wished that there was wiser counsel available upon which he could call. One thing seemed certain—something had to be done!

Hall had been in the system for several years, starting as a classroom teacher and eventually becoming guidance teacher and vice-principal. His work in the community and in the school had given him a good deal of leadership opportunity, and both faculty and townsfolk regarded Hall favorably. He had recently married one of the teachers, and people assumed that he would stay in Sycamore Heights as vice-principal until the supervising principal, Edmund Watts, changed jobs. Although Watts had been in the community longer than Hall, few expected him to remain permanently; but practically everyone expected Hall to stay. Watts just didn't seem to "fit in" with the community. Not that there was much open antagonism, but rather, a lack of open acceptance.

The present problem facing Hall arose from the nature of Watts's philosophy. Watts had strong *laissez-faire* tendencies in his makeup and evidenced great reluctance to enforce school regulations among either faculty or students. Consequently, both groups were taking advantage of Watts, and morale was rapidly deteriorating. Watts seemed unaware of the situation, spending almost every day in his office and little time about the building.

Because Hall had "risen from the ranks," he enjoyed closer relations with the faculty than Watts and, as a result of teacher confidences, was constantly aware of the increasing difficulties. Just this morning a teacher had come into his office.

Teacher: "Can I see you for a minute, Jim?"

Hall: "Sure, have a chair!"

Teacher: "Do you know if Wattsie spoke to the night janitors about leaving the aquarium in my room alone?"

431

Hall: "I don't know. In fact, I didn't even know you had trouble with them."

Teacher: "Trouble! I should say so. This is the fourth time this year that I complained about it. They fool with the water inlet and the temperature controls. Each time they do, I lose some valuable fish."

Hall: "Maybe he hasn't had a chance to see them yet."

Teacher: "I think he's afraid to speak to them about it, just the same as he's afraid to speak to them about taking milk from the cafeteria for their lunches. The cafeteria is short each month because of them and the board has had the manager on the carpet about it. Who knows what else they've been taking."

Hall: "I'll speak to him about it and maybe we'll get this thing straightened out."

Teacher: "You know better than that, Jim. He won't do anything about it. I guess I just came in to blow off steam. I wish he'd get a better job so that you would take over. Maybe, he'll drop dead! Wouldn't be a bad idea, if you ask me. Well, I'll see you later."

Hall: "Be good now."

After the teacher had gone, Hall reviewed the conversation. It was the sixth such complaint from a teacher that week. All of them had shown impatience with Watts's failure to take action. Hall knew from his own experience that the complaints were usually justified. He had had similarly unsatisfying encounters. However, he doubted that the principal was afraid. He believed that by nature Watts was infinitely more philosophical than executive and shied away from unpleasant personal contacts. Hall felt that Watts's behavior was putting him in an awkward position.

That night at supper Hall and his wife had the following conversation:

Mrs. H.: "You missed a coffee party third period today."

Hall: "I was pretty busy all morning. What happened?"

Mrs. H.: "The four new teachers from Taylor Teachers College got together and appointed student monitors for their classes and came down to the faculty room for a coffee 'Klatch.' They stayed almost all period."

Hall: "I wonder if they are aware of the school rule against leaving classes without faculty supervision."

Mrs. H.: "They know all right, but figured that since Mr. Watts has only been on the top floor for scheduled observations, he probably wouldn't even know."

Hall: "I thought they were going to be real good teachers, too."

Mrs. H.: "They probably would if things weren't so lax. It's so bad now that the math teacher who has first period free isn't even going to come to school until 9:45. You ought to do something about it."

Hall: "That's just too much. I will do something about it."

But next morning Jim Hall could not determine what to do about it. If only there was some way to get Watts to exercise his authority without seeming to be undermining him, criticizing him, or "squealing" on the faculty. What to do?

MR. JOHNS

A new elementary school building had just been built in the South Burgh Central School District. It was a beautiful structure, and the district was extremely proud that it should have this fine building. Great care was taken to choose the principal of the school, and, after considering several candidates, Mr. Johns was selected. He was a graduate of a state teachers college, where he had majored in elementary education, and had taught for nine years in a sixth grade. Mr. Johns had also received his master's degree in elementary school administration from Metropolis University. He was a mild-mannered, quiet, rather reserved person, about thirty-seven years old. He was married and the father of three children.

South Burgh Central School District was a rather typical district in that it was composed of one village and a large surrounding rural area. About half of the district's 1500 students came from the village. There were two elementary schools and a junior-senior high school in the district. The new elementary school had 400 children and twenty teachers.

Mr. Johns and his family arrived in South Burgh in the middle of the summer, purchased a house, and got down to the job of learning about the school and community. The teachers in Mr. Johns's school were all women and most of the teachers were on tenure. There were only three new teachers on the staff. Mr. Johns reported directly to Mr. Spicer, the supervising principal. Mr. Spicer had been in South Burgh for ten years and during that time had developed a good rapport with both the faculty and the community.

Things went well during the first year of Mr. Johns's principalship. Only occasionally did a teacher comment that Mr. Johns did not have enough drive or the personality needed for the job. It was also remarked that he often forgot little things which affected the smooth operation of the school. This caused irritation to some teachers.

Soon after school started in the fall of Mr. Johns' second year, he notified all teachers that there was to be a faculty meeting each Wednesday afternoon from 3.30 to 5.00 o'clock. Mr. Johns took full responsibility for the agendas of these meetings and did not consult with the teachers. The teachers began to grumble about the meetings, and soon there was considerable discontent. However, none of the teachers ever approached Mr. Johns to tell him of their feelings. Some of the teachers did air their discontent to the teachers in other buildings and to the townsfolk. The townsfolk began to talk, and soon there were many stories circulating.

In the middle of the school year, there occurred an event which added to the talk about Mr. Johns. He had taken an obscene picture from one of the older boys in the school. Some of the teachers heard of this and two of the unmarried women teachers persuaded Mr. Johns to show it to them. One of these teachers was a local girl, and she told her parents that Mr. Johns had showed her an obscene picture. Her parents then told several people in the community about the incident, and the story soon spread quickly.

As this story was spreading through the community, several of the teachers who were on tenure started to circulate a petition calling for the resignation of Mr. Johns. Mr. Spicer heard of the petition before it reached the board of education. He decided that he must act and act fast.

THE VICE-PRINCIPAL

As James Murphy, former teacher and present vice-principal at Hugenot Central School, entered the office of the physical education director at Hugenot, he noticed his close friend, the director, studying a long official-looking sheet of paper and muttering to himself. He thought this strange, for John Hopkins, the physical education director, was a man not easily disturbed. Hopkins saw Murphy and handed him the paper, exclaiming in a highly emotional tone: "Look what that lousy _____ did. We never have seen quite eye to eye on everything, but he has been so friendly lately that I never suspected he has been storing up ammunition to use against me. I ought to punch him one in the mouth."

Looking at the paper, Murphy saw that it was a careful enumeration of complaints against the physical education director, his methods, and his educational philosophy. It further stated that the note's author, District Principal Adam Lawrence, intended to recommend that Hopkins not be permitted to coach varsity athletics or serve as director of physical education, but merely to serve as instructor of gym classes. Copies had been sent to the county superintendent and the board of education.

During Murphy's perusal of the letter, Hopkins kept up a constant stream of vituperative comment concerning the principal's ancestry, racial origin, and probable ultimate destination.

Murphy asked, "What brought all this on, Hoppy? I didn't know you and the old man were on the 'outs.' "

"Well, you know that he and I have had differences from time to time over his failure to back me up. We decide on regulations; I enforce them; parents complain; and he gives in to them. It's tough to conduct a sports program with that kind of discipline. About this letter, I don't know. Last week he requested by note that I give Mr. Small, the senior advisor, a pass to admit him free to all basketball games since the seniors were selling refreshments. On an interoffice memo I observed that he was already getting in free, that he spent all the time watching the game instead of the seniors, and that the only school events Small went to were ones where he could chisel in free. I further pointed out that in my ten years in the system, I had never sought to get in free to any school event. Instead of an answer, I get this bill of particulars dating back, in some instances, for six years. I guess he has been after my scalp all this time and has decided that now he can get board support in the light of our poor football showing."

"Have you been in to see him about it?" Murphy asked.

"I wouldn't give him the satisfaction! If I didn't just build our new home and owe the bank for most of it, I'd just beat hell out of him and quit. But he knows he's got me over a barrel. With this new home over my head, I can't quit, and with him watching every move, I can't stay! What would you do?"

James Murphy thought a moment. He realized fully his position. As a faculty member for five years, he was well aware that there was an area of disharmony between the administrator and Hopkins. He was also aware that the charges against Hopkins were not without foundation; that he had, over the past several years, been involved in controversy with the principal. Murphy knew that Hopkins had exercised more than customary jurisdiction over his department, but thought that he had been given the free hand officially. Principal Lawrence claimed in the latter that authority had arbitrarily been assumed. Murphy and Lawrence had never discussed the physical education department, perhaps because of the known personal friendship between Murphy and Hopkins.

Because of the complexity of the situation, Murphy was very glad that a student entered the office to see Hopkins. Murphy realized that this was a grave matter and that he was in the peculiar position of owing personal loyalty to Hopkins, and professional loyalty to Lawrence. He was glad to leave Hopkins for the time being, but knew that he must take some position by lunchtime, when he customarily ate with Hopkins. He felt torn between duty and desire and wished that he had some means of getting "off the hook," since he was not personally or directly concerned.

APPENDIX

Notes on Teaching by
the Case Method

Every time someone states that he is working on a "new" method of teaching someone else brings him back to earth by indicating that Professor So-and-so did that sort of thing fifty years ago. This is what has happened with the case discussion method. Although it is a new method of teaching as far as average practice in this country is concerned, it has been used by certain people for many years. Teaching by the case method, however, means many things to many people. In the following pages, one approach to the case method will be offered, together with some information on teaching by the case method which has proved to be helpful.

ORIGINS OF THE CASE METHOD

It is interesting to note that the case method of teaching began some time in the nineteenth century, primarily in such fields as medicine, where both diagnosis and treatment have since been taught as being related to specific symptoms or reactions that may be observed in either real or hypothetical persons. You and I, for example, have been "cases" to our medical friends on more than one occasion!

The case method, according to Alan Ross, was introduced at the Harvard Law School in the academic year 1869-1870 by Christopher C. Langdell.[1] The legal case is essentially a decision which must be learned by the student. He develops his background and his understanding of the law as he learns how that decision may be applied to more and more problems. In this way he develops an understanding of precedents. This can and does lead many individuals to a concept of the law which is "past" oriented and sterile. Scholars in the field of law deplore this situation, pointing out that the law is a constantly changing, evolving thing; it is alive and growing. Educators say the same thing about the nature of education but, like the lawyers, they develop methods of teaching which are diametrically

[1] Alan Ross, "Introduction To Case Method," *Human Relations in School Administration* (Bellingham, Western Washington College of Education, 1954), p. 19.

436

opposed to the goal they seek. Needless to say, human relations cases are *not* like legal cases.

The case method in human relations to which we refer here originated with the late Wallace Donham, who was dean of the Harvard School of Business. In an effort to construct a more effective method for the preparation of business executives, Donham and his associates hit upon the case method. Later, following World War II, he moved into the field of human relations in general education and taught classes by the case method to undergraduates at both Harvard and Radcliffe. Since that time, the case method in both business and human relations has spread from coast to coast. There is at present, for example, the Human Relations Conference, which meets annually and rotates its meetings among Harvard University, Ohio University, University of Kansas, Colgate University, and the University of Michigan.

In the field of education the progress has not been so swift. William Burris, late dean of the College of Education, University of Cincinnati, is considered to be the first to use the case method in the study of teaching. Dean Harry Benz of Ohio University has written and used cases in his preparatory courses for school administrators. Four of his cases appear in this text. Sargent and Belisle have used the method extensively at Harvard and have recently published an outstanding book of cases, together with some discussion of the basis for the case method.[2] Cases have also been used elsewhere throughout the country. They have been tried at Texas University, Western Washington College of Education, Colgate University, State University of New York, State College for Teachers at Albany, and Teachers College, Columbia University among others. All in all, it can be said that there is considerable interest in the method which can be expected to grow in the coming days.

DEFINITION OF A CASE

Lawrence has given a terse and accurate description of a case. He states: [3]

A good case is the vehicle by which a chunk of reality is brought into the classroom to be worked over by the class and the instructor. A good case keeps the class discussion grounded upon some of the stubborn facts that must be faced up to in real life situations . . . It is the record of complex situations that must be literally pulled apart and put together again before the situations can be understood.

[2] Cyril G. Sargent and Eugene L. Belisle, *Educational Administration: Cases and Concepts* (Boston, Houghton Mifflin, 1955).

[3] Paul R. Lawrence, "The Preparation of Case Material" in *The Case Method of Teaching Human Relations and Administration*, ed. Kenneth R. Andrews (Cambridge, Mass., Harvard University Press, 1953), p. 215. Copyright, 1953, by the President and Fellows of Harvard College.

What Lawrence is saying is that a case is a report of an actual experience or situation. It is a description of a situation as viewed by an observer. It probably has been noted by now that the cases used in this text have not been complete in every sense of the word. Since these are human relations cases, it has not been necessary for them to be complete. No one has *all* of the evidence when he makes a human relations decision. One should have as much as appears to be available and as much as seems relevant; however, all human relations decisions are made from the point of view of a particular person. The case, then, is the reporting of the actions, deeds, words, places, and situations that will help the student to know and feel the problem at hand.

The question of length is often raised. A good case can be most any length. Length is not a criterion in and of itself. It should always be considered in view of other criteria. Length is dependent upon the type of situation being considered. It is possible to have a very short case, as, for example:

Superintendent *A* was walking down the corridor and he met Teacher *M*, two of whose students had just won scholarships with her aid. The superintendent said, "Good morning Miss *M*. I'd like to congratulate you on your success this year."

This is certainly a *short* case; yet it can give rise to the discussion of a large number of very important issues. The case is complete in the sense that it describes precisely a human relations incident. It gives all the pertinent facts. It does not give the background history of the relationships between the superintendent and teacher; nor does it delve into the many ramifications of the incident. The criterion which it does meet is that of getting a considerable amount of discussion underway. This criterion we call *discussability*.

Although a case as short as the above is not the best type of case, it does have many advantages. As Berrien points out, "in our everyday contacts we cannot expect to get a complete case history on the people we meet and to whom we react." [4] The challenge is to get as much as possible out of the sketchy information that we ordinarily receive in our everyday contacts with individuals. The class could also be asked what other information they would like to have and then how they might go about getting that information. They will find the second question difficult to answer.

A longer case, such as "A Principal for the Montgomery School," is a more complete one and, in general, a better case inasmuch as it meets more of the criteria for a good case. First of all it meets the criterion of discussability, of which we have just spoken. It also meets the criterion of *adequacy*. The case describes, in an adequate fashion, the individuals who

[4] F. K. Berrien, *Comments and Cases on Human Relations* (New York, Harper, 1951), p. 466.

have roles to play in the case, and it also gives an adequate description of the school system and the community. It also provides some indication of the values which the people in the community hold; the basic attitudes of all of the individuals are at least alluded to. It presents a much more adequate report of the situation than the brief case quoted above. It also meets the criterion of *objectivity*. In this criterion, we look for exact statements and for precise descriptions or reports of what people say or do. These reports are made without interpretation by the writer. As an example, we have the discussion concerning Hamilton, a candidate for the new principalship:

"He's a great conference hound, even though he never contributes anything to a conference or takes any new ideas away from it either! He's a Kiwanian, and an official in the Congregational church. He comes of one of the older families in this area; he has a brother-in-law on the board, an older brother is the district court judge, and his best friend is the editor of the *Examiner*. He's been principal of Central Junior High for fifteen years or so . . . A.B. degree in 1911, due for retirement in four years. He looks to Montgomery School as a just reward for thirty-eight years of service: a sort of comfortable, well-paid, 'prestigeful' post from which to retire."

These are the words of the superintendent of schools who must make a recommendation. The case writer quoted him exactly and did not interpret his remarks. We can see the attitude of the superintendent as it is reflected in his choice of words and in his choice of those facts concerning Hamilton which he deems important. This constitutes raw data for a discussion of Hamilton's qualifications; but it also provides raw data for a discussion of the superintendent of schools. Although the case writer does not interpret his data he presents them in such a form that they can be interpreted. This is the criterion of *interpretability*.

We can say that a case is a report of an actual experience which is written for use in the classroom. There are at least four criteria which a case should meet in order to be a satisfactory one. These are discussability, adequacy, objectivity, and interpretability. It should be stated here, however, that even though these criteria are met, they will not guarantee that the case is a good one. Much will depend upon the instructor and the class and the mood they are in at the time of discussion. A case which is good for one class at a given time could very well be inadequate for another class at another time.

PURPOSE OF THE CASE METHOD

Once we have agreed upon the definition of a case, it should occur to us to inquire about the purpose of the case method, the value of using this particular approach. The answers to such questions are not simple. They are concerned with the central purposes of education itself, and although the philosophy of education is not our primary concern, we must consider those elements which are relevant to this problem.

Our world is marked by relentless change. This has been said often and understood little. The established society of the past, which gave its men a sense of internal security, is gone. Lacking the security of an established system, we run the risk of making decisions which could lead to planless, pointless living. Viewing the task of education amid this lack of social stability, Donham says what many others have said, but in addition, he clearly states one of the chief values of the case method in human relations today: [5]

The major problem of education seems to me to give men a sense of internal security, assurance in their capacity to get on with people collaboratively, and to deal successfully with the unpredictable future, which will take the place of the type of security provided by the established society of our ancestors. Without going into the part of this task which must be done by philosophy and religion, I emphasize the fact that a great deal can be done by teaching methods and by training in social science which simulates the active life men will enter when they leave college with its unforeseeable variety of experience and the necessity of making constant responsible interpretations of new concrete situations. Such interpretations will, of course, be influenced by the past and by the traditions of the old established order but they will generally be dominated by unpredictable change. Without such a sense of security in the midst of change, the task of philosophy and religion becomes almost impossible.

Another great objective of education is to pass the wisdom of the ages on to the new generation, because, in so doing, we hope to facilitate the long and tortuous road over which man travels. The educational goal of helping students to arrive at answers in less time than they would take if they had not been educated is one that man has always been aware of and continually strives to accomplish. Even young children attempt to achieve this purpose. I once followed two little girls up the stairs to a second-floor birthday party. Each had her present clutched tightly, and the five-year-old said to the three-year-old, "Now don't forget to say 'Happy Birthday' when you give Priscilla Ann her present." The wisdom of the ages was being transmitted!

Now, the big temptation in passing on this wisdom is to tell others all we know. So many teachers are convinced they are not *teaching* unless they are *telling*. If we have learned anything from the educational psychologist, it is this: *wisdom can't be told*. This is usually the case, for *"can't"* is not an absolute. What is meant by the statement is that the mere telling almost invariably fails to communicate wisdom to the great bulk of the people. In instances where the individual is highly motivated, he

[5] Wallace Brett Donham, "Why Experiment? The Case System in College Teaching of Social Science," *Journal of General Education*, Vol. 3, No. 2 (January, 1949), pp. 145-146.

can learn by being told, but most of the time, teaching by telling is a fiction.

This conclusion that "we cannot effectively use the insight and knowledge of others; it must be our own knowledge and insight that we use," [6] immediately gives rise to the question: If teachers can't tell, how can they teach? The obvious answer is that as teachers, we must use a method which will make the students active participants in the process of learning. Students must be taken out of the role of passive absorbers and put into the role of reactors. The teacher should be the catalyst. To complete the chemical analogy we would have the following formula:

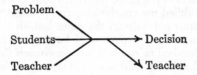

This indicates that although the students react with a problem and the teacher aids the reaction to go to completion, the teacher does not become a *permanent* part of the decision; that is, when another similar problem is raised, the student can reach a decision *unaided by the teacher*.

The case method effects what might loosely be called a democratic approach to the solution of a common problem. The instructor and students have all the material in hand and all are somewhat equal in seeking the solution. This is contrasted with the autocratic approach which occurs when the teacher *tells* the students the answers. It must be pointed out that education is not an exact science, and probably never will be. Our problems do not have exact answers. Most of them have many answers— all of which are right in that they resolve the conflict in a manner satisfactory to all parties concerned. This is not to say that any answer is acceptable, but that answers arrived at through the use of group intelligence usually will be satisfactory.

We will attempt to have the group deal with many cases and to arrive at decisions which are wise and productive. These solutions will be the solutions of the *class* and will not be dictated by the instructor. This may be frustrating at first, but in the long run it will be more profitable. It has been said that not all students can bear the strain of thinking actively! This is especially true if they must defend their decisions in discussions with their peers. We will work toward the goal of independent thinking, clear and decisive decisions, and a clear picture of the consequences.

The following limerick appropriately illustrates the dilemma of many administrators in their first job—provided, of course, that they have not had case training!

---

[6] Charles I. Gragg, "Because Wisdom Can't Be Told," in Andrews, *op. cit.*, p. 7.

A student of Education with tact
Absorbed many answers he lacked.
But acquiring a job,
He said with a sob,
"How does one fit answers to fact?"

One last illustration of this point. Donham tells the story of being approached by a former student: [7]

"You didn't teach us anything in the Business School." I said, "I will accept that but in which sense do you mean it?" "Well," he said, "I studied a great number of cases with care, sought my own interpretations of them, discussed them with other members of the class, went into class where we discussed them with the instructor, modified my conclusions, and reached what I thought were good working conclusions not only on the cases but on the subject matter we were discussing. In ten years of experience I have never met a problem on all fours with any case I studied or reached any conclusion that was controlled by the class discussion." I said I would accept that but, "What did the school do for you?" "That," he said, "is simple. It gave me a sense of assurance that I could tackle any problem either because I had the requisite experience or because I knew in what direction to turn where my experience was inadequate."

The case method is used for the purpose of helping future executives in this changing world make decisions which reflect the individual's sense of internal security. This is done by having the future executive face a large number of cases, think them through for himself, and come up with solutions which he must defend in class. Another value, which is not obvious at first, is that which is gained from the procedures used in the case method. Since the student always discusses the case with the whole class, he is quickly conscious of the fact that many others have as good or better solutions than he has. This forces him to see that in working with others, better decisions can be made. Through this type of training the future administrator gets into the habit of consulting with others and sharing the decision-making process. The case student learns at an early stage what others learn only after long years of experience.

TEACHING BY THE CASE METHOD

We do not intend, in this section, to go into any step by step discussion of teaching by the case method. All teaching is an art and, as such, is tied directly to the personality and abilities of the teacher. In teaching with cases this is particularly true, since the relationship between the teacher and the student is crucial. If a good relationship is not established, the student will not feel free to discuss the case. Failure to free the students so that they can think creatively together marks failure for the method.

[7] Donham, *loc. cit.*, p. 154.

Permissive Atmosphere

The atmosphere of the class is probably the most important factor for the instructor to achieve in teaching by the case method. He must be patient and allow each student to express his point of view. There are times when the instructor becomes most exasperated by the seeming stupidity of the student; but the instructor should remember that if he cuts a student short or interrupts him, the student will feel that he is really not expected to express himself.

Most case instructors start their classes merely by mentioning the name of the case to be discussed and then by asking, "What do you have to say about this case?" He then sits back and waits for discussion from the class. There may be a long wait, but he should resist the idea of giving a speech to start things rolling. The students always do start, even though at first they may be a little slow. As the discussion proceeds, the instructor restricts himself to comments which draw the students out. He seeks to have them express themselves fully and completely, and he does what he can to aid them in this process.

It is difficult for us to emphasize sufficiently the importance of the permissive atmosphere. The author has had classes whose members did not seem to be as competent as he thought they should be, and so he talked too much. As he did this the classes got worse and worse. Upon coming back to a more permissive role and with a real effort to build better relations, the class seemed to improve! It would seem that the burden for success rests heavily on the shoulders of the instructor.

The class needs to be encouraged to help build this permissive atmosphere with the instructor. Each member needs to develop a listening and appreciative attitude toward other members of the class. If the instructor develops a permissive attitude but the class members do not, there will still be serious obstacles to a good discussion.

The Major Pitfall

As the discussion of the first case of the course proceeds, the students seem to get the idea of free discussion; but as the end of the period approaches, some student always says, "Well, what is the answer?" If, at this point, the instructor gives the solution as he sees it, he has destroyed the whole purpose of the case method. The students will realize that the instructor doesn't mean them to be responsible participants in the class. They will realize that the instructor is merely letting them "play" at discussing, because when they are finished, the instructor will tell them the answer. The instructor should resist with all of his reserves giving the students his version of the case solution. The students, of course, will not like this and will protest a noncommittal position at first. They have been so conditioned by sixteen or more years of formal education that they are very frustrated by the instructor's refusal to give them the answer. They use all sorts of entreaties to get the instructor to give them "the benefit of your experience," "the results of your greater insight," and so on. After several cases, this feeling of reliance on the instructor will pass, and the students do become adjusted to the process.

Common Obstacles

There have been several common and recurring blocks to the progress of a class as it seeks solutions to the cases. Probably the first thing that is noticeable is the tendency of the students to "solve" the case by categorizing the characters. This occurs almost universally with the first cases that a class handles, and then it slowly disappears. At a recent conference the case method was being demonstrated. The group was made up of professors. We were discussing the case of "The Guidance Director," and the opening comment was, "Here is a bunch of asses!" Other cases have been opened even more vigorously. This habit of categorizing can be overcome, if the instructor overlooks the tendency and guides the class to a discussion based upon analysis. The person who stereotypes and categorizes soon sees that his efforts do not help in the final solution. This is one type of behavior which definitely is improved by the case procedure, for students can be observed to change from stereotyping to precise analysis.

Many students attempt to solve cases by erecting dichotomies. They set up two extreme solutions, play one off against the other, and then choose one as superior to the other. This is a result of the "either-or" orientation which is so common to most of us. The difficulty with this approach is that many solutions lie between the extremes. The desire of many "to hear both sides" is an extension of this orientation. It is felt that if both sides of a question are heard, the proper solution will be found. This is erroneous in that "both sides" exclude the middle. We should include all sides of a question in our considerations.

Students who have had training in philosophy or mathematics are prone to respond in another manner which blocks a class in its search for solutions. These students want to seek solutions by the process of *reductio ad absurdum*. They heed the advice of John Stuart Mill who believed that any argument, to be valid, must remain valid when carried to an extreme. In other words, if an argument looks ridiculous in its extreme statement, then it cannot be valid. Such students should be reminded that one pound of steak makes for a delicious dinner but five pounds make for indigestion! This does not in any way deny the validity of the conclusion that steak is a good entree.

Other students are prone to use simple cause-to-effect reasoning. They say, for example, if a school is having a teachers' strike, "Fire the superintendent!" The use of this kind of reasoning prevents us from getting at the real causes for the behavior of the characters we are studying.

The instructor will soon find his students using many other methods of short-cutting the long and tortuous path to truth. He needs to "play by ear" and determine the weaknesses of each of his students as he works with them. By knowing them as individuals, he can help them to solve their own problems.

The Lecture in the Case Method

Lectures are used in two ways: to discuss the content of human relations (as represented by Parts 1 and 2 of this text) and to discuss cases. Although lectures are usually much more a part of the content study, they should sometimes be given during case discussions. Fuller has indicated how they should be used in teaching by the case method: [8]

> Neither the timing of lectures nor their content can be determined apart from the individual class. The general rule of thumb, however, might be roughly stated as "put nothing into the lecture that hasn't come out of the class." Or . . . the lecture should reflect what has been said in class discussion, what has been implied but not specifically stated in class discussion, and what the students have not been able to say without help. The instructor's help should *not* take the form of giving a definite answer to each case or a specific statement of the concepts useful in each instance.

The lecture is used in the case method when a need arises in the classroom. The instructor should be able to sense that the class could progress much more profitably if it had some help on a particular part of its work. The lecture would then be constructed around the observed needs of the group. It would *not* take the form of telling the student the answer he has been unable to reach on his own. Neither would it give him a set of principles which he could apply, one by one, to the case at hand and thereby achieve a secondhand answer.

The instructor does try to put into the lecture the kind of results that he wishes to stimulate in his class. He wants independent but careful assumptions and well-reasoned solutions based upon the evidence on hand. More than that, he wants recognition of the human factors in the case.

The lecture should be considered as a useful tool to be put into action as the needs of the class are recognized.

The Instructor as a Resource Person

Although the instructor functions chiefly as the creator of a permissive atmosphere and as a skilled discussion leader, he is also the class's resource

---

[8] Frances Mulhern Fuller, "The Use of the Lecture in a Case-Method Course," in Andrews, *op. cit.*, p. 76.

person. Not only does he draw on a broader range of experience than do the members of his class but he also has information on readings and materials which should be used by students. As the class comes to certain problems, he should be able to refer them to readings which would be helpful. He should also be able to bring in other resource persons who can help the class in particular situations.

CASE WRITING

Sources

We must start this section with the very general statement that case materials are to be found wherever there are people. We are sometimes confused by the thought that we must have major crises or arguments as the basis for human relations cases; this, however, is not so. As a matter of fact, a good case is more apt to be one which deals with what appears to be a minor problem. Human relations education for school administrators is not intended to make specialists of them. Human relations cases are not of the order of the case studies made by social agencies or mental health clinics. A case of the type which we are using is intended to give guided experience in the usual type of human relations problems with which administrators must cope. Berrien has a very useful analogy which he uses to illustrate this point: [9]

The relation between the situations presented here and the specialized agencies is perhaps analogous to the relations that exist between the doctor and the first-aider. Both deal with the same general order of things. The first-aider can bandage a cut, take care of a headache, take proper measures of a temporary kind in more serious situations. He does not need the same kind of specialized rigorous training which a doctor has, but he does need some training, and he does need to know the limits of his skills. The situations dealt with in this course are of the first aid variety. If properly handled, they will not need professional care. If bungled through ineptitude, they may fester into serious problems.

Look then, for case studies in the everyday world of education. Cases can be written around any of the interpersonal relationships that exist at all times.

As part of the course in human relations for school administrators, students should be required to write up cases from their own experiences. In addition, each student should be asked to write an analysis of his case after it has been completed. This allows him to demonstrate his skill in both observation and analysis. The analysis should include recommendations for the action together with the reasons for such action. From the student point of view, case writing provides very valuable practice. Moreover, it has been found that cases written by students can form the basis

[9] Berrien, *op. cit.*, p. 467.

for an excellent file of raw material for future use by the professor, although usually they need to be rewritten to some extent.

There are two other sources of case materials which may be used by either the professor or the student. Neither is so satisfactory as is writing from firsthand observation, but occasionally they do provide good cases. They are the newspapers and reports or novels of sociological and psychological import. In the first of these, the newspapers, the case writer needs to know the theme of the case on which he desires information. He can then refer to the newspapers for specific portions of case information. Particular kinds of information which may be derived from the newspapers include public reaction to the event being discussed; relevant data concerning time, place, etc.; biographical data on the main characters; the point of view of a disinterested third person. It would probably be best if the case were not based entirely on the newspapers. A case written entirely from the news reports is apt to miss the human relationships present in the situation. On the other hand, if one knows of the human relationships, the papers may serve as an excellent supplementary source.

Novels, reports, and other literary sources are rich in their materials for use in human relations studies. Reports such as *Elmtown's Youth* [10] are excellent sources of materials for cases concerning the educational system and its interrelationships with the community. Many novels offer a clear presentation of interpersonal problems. An example of this type of novel is *Knock on Any Door*.[11] In using such materials, one might select portions which can stand alone or possibly condense a large section of the book. In either instance, however, it is necessary to obtain permission from the publishers before the material is reproduced.

There should never be any shortage of case materials. As long as there are people, there will be human relations problems. The case writer needs the ability to make accurate observations and the will to observe. His production of cases is limited only by his industry.

Format and Style

There should be no stock style or format for case writers to follow. The art of case writing is still in its infancy, and it would be disastrous to set up any rules or regulations at the present time. Cases have been written in many forms and styles. The few suggestions that can be given concern the details of writing, not the gross pattern, and at best these suggestions have had only limited testing.

The first deals with a very important point, which was discussed in a different form above. How explicit should the writer be in his presenta-

[10] A. B. Hollingshead, *Elmtown's Youth* (New York, John Wiley, 1949).
[11] Willard Motley, *Knock on Any Door* (New York, Appleton-Century-Crofts, 1947).

tion of the facts of the case? The concepts of objectivity and subjectivity are the relevant concepts at issue. Let us use an illustration and then discuss it. Suppose our case writer states, "Mary was a good teacher." This statement carries with it an illusion of objectivity, yet we know that a judgment has been made by the writer, this judgment is a very subjective one. The writer is not one who should be making judgments concerning the characters in the case. His job is to *report*. Actually, he would be reporting more objectively if he stated, "Mary's principal thought her to be a good teacher." But even though this is a more accurate way of presenting the matter, there is still a vagueness which might be remedied. The case writer could report how he knew that Mary's principal thought her to be a good teacher. He might say, "Mary's principal was heard to tell the superintendent, 'Mary is a good teacher.'" From this we gain the facts of who thought what and how this thought was expressed. Thus, although the principal's statement concerning Mary was subjective, it was reported objectively.

The second suggestion concerns selection. The case writer probably always collects more material than he will ever use. A good case contains only *selected* materials. Much of what is collected on a case will be irrelevant to the decision that must be made. The case writer should cull out all the irrevelant materials and present that which bears upon the actual problem. As a general guide, it is suggested that he minimize background and play up the present. The case writer should present enough background information to enable the student to understand the situation. In most cases, this will include some information concerning the location of the case action, the mores of the community, and a description of the school in human terms, that is, the type of faculty, administration, and the like. It is important that the student gain insight into the ways of thinking of the participants in the case. Background information should be detailed enough to give this insight. Lawrence indicates one rule of thumb which might be used in selecting background information for the case: "The case writer has to decide how much background material is needed to give setting and context without giving so much as to block the students from ever coming to grips with the problem posed by present events." [12] Too much background might well obscure the problem to be solved. It might be worthwhile to use such a case on rare occasions, so that the student can learn to perceive the problem.

The immediate problem in the case, as contrasted with background, needs to be presented with an eye to the criteria that were specified earlier. The writer should be certain that the observed facts are presented clearly.

How do you end a case? Well, you could write until you run out of

[12] Lawrence, *loc. cit.,* p. 223.

material, but this would probably not make a good case. It would violate the criterion of discussability. If all of the information were presented, it would probably include the "real life" solution. This would cut off other possible decisions, and the student would then be restricted to a discussion of whether or not this was the best decision for the participant to have made. In terms of the value of discussion, it has been observed that classes work better on cases which have been concluded before the actual decision is revealed. Several things have been noted. First of all, students are very hesitant to make a decision. They are willing to discuss the case in general and to evaluate the behavior of the participants but not to offer a solution. This hesitancy is to be expected, since it is most difficult to make a good decision and to defend it. Decision-making, however, is one of the functions of administration; the embryo administrator must start it sometime, and it is much better to start as a student than as a responsible individual on the job.

Another value can be attained by discussing cases in which a decision has been reached but has not yet been put into effect. The question for the students to consider then becomes, "How can this decision be made effective?"

As with all other activities, skill as a case writer can be achieved only through practice. The student should observe, write, then subject his cases to the test of the classroom. In this way only will he learn to write good cases.

SUMMARY

This appendix does not pretend to be an exhaustive treatment of the subject of teaching by the case method. It attempts merely to point out some of the procedures and attitudes which will help a person who hesitates to use the case method. Since the case method is such a highly personal way of teaching, there is no single set of procedures. As each instructor uses cases, he adapts them to his own abilities and class requirements.

The case method has proved to be a most stimulating way of teaching. We have little evidence that it is superior to other methods of teaching, but student response to it has been not only favorable but enthusiastic. Behavior has been changed to an observable degree, and many administrators now in the field give considerable credit for their success to the case method.

This author believes the case method to be a sound way to teach human relations, but he does not feel that it is the only way. The embryo school administrator should be taught by a variety of methods, and the best use of the case method is to incorporate it into the total curriculum of the student.

SELECTED BIBLIOGRAPHY

ANDREWS, Kenneth R., "Executive Training by the Case Method," *Harvard Business Review*, Vol. 29 (September, 1951), pp. 58-70.

————, ed., *The Case Method of Teaching Human Relations and Administration* (Cambridge, Mass., Harvard University Press, 1953).

BAUER, Ronald C., *Cases in College Administration* (New York, Teachers College Bureau of Publications, 1955).

BERRIEN, F. K., *Comments and Cases on Human Relations* (New York, Harper, 1951), Instructor's Appendix, pp. 461-495.

CABOT, Hugh, and KAHL, Joseph A., *Human Relations: Concepts in Concrete Social Science* (Cambridge, Mass., Harvard University Press, 1953), Vol. 1.

CASTORE, G. F., "Attitudes of Students toward the Case Method of Instruction in a Human Relations Course," *Journal of Educational Research*, Vol. 45 (November, 1951), pp. 201-213.

CREEGAN, R. F., "Case Methods Unlimited?" *School and Society*, Vol. 74 (October, 1951), pp. 214-216.

DONHAM, W. B., "Why Experiment? The Case System in College Teaching of Social Science," *Journal of General Education*, Vol. 3, No. 2 (January, 1949), pp. 1-11.

GRIFFITHS, D. E., and HOBDAY, A. E., "New Kind of Case Study," *Educational Research Bulletin*, Vol. 31 (January, 1952), pp. 19-21.

HUNT, Pearson, "The Case Method of Instruction," *Harvard Educational Review*, Vol. 21 (Summer, 1951), pp. 175-192.

MARZOLF, S. S., "Case Studies and Teacher Training," *Educational Administration and Supervision*, Vol. 27 (May, 1941), pp. 383-388.

SARGENT, Cyril G., and BELISLE, Eugene L., *Educational Administration: Cases and Concepts* (Boston, Houghton Mifflin, 1955).

SPERLE, D. H., *The Case Method Technique in Professional Training* (New York, Teachers College Bureau of Publications, 1933), 92 pp.

WELKER, R. P., "Case Method in Preparing Superintendents," *Kadelpian Review*, Vol. 8 (March, 1929), pp. 304-311.

INDEX